THE ESSENTIAL
KITCHEN
DESIGN GUIDE

THE ESSENTIAL
KITCHEN
DESIGN GUIDE

NATIONAL KITCHEN & BATH ASSOCIATION

JOHN WILEY & SONS, INC.

New York / Chichester / Brisbane / Toronto / Singapore

Copyright © 1996 by The National Kitchen & Bath Association.
Published by John Wiley & Sons, Inc.

Library of Congress Cataloging-in-Publication Data:
National Kitchen and Bath Association (U.S.)
  The essential kitchen design guide / National Kitchen & Bath
 Association.
    p. cm.
  Includes index.
  ISBN 0-471-12672-1 (alk. paper)
  1. Kitchens—Design and construction. I. Title.
 TX653.N37 1996
 643'.3—dc20   96-33745

Printed in United States of America

10 9 8 7 6 5 4 3 2 1

Preface

The kitchen/bath industry has grown significantly since its genesis, and today is a well regarded design specialty. It is also a lucrative business. Remodeling and new construction projects of kitchens and bathrooms total over $40 billion annually and continue to grow each year. Kitchens are the most frequently remodeled rooms in the home. They are the heart of the home, a gathering place, and, today, a room for much more than cooking and eating.

The evolution of the kitchen, however, has been a long and slow process. It changed along with mankind beginning with the discovery of fire, changing with the building of crude homes and hearths, expanding with the craft of carpentry, developing further with the invention of electricity and appliances, and progressing further with improvements and innovations in manufacturing and materials.

When you consider the inadequacies of the colonial kitchen, with the open flame from the fireplace as the only source of heat; or the cast iron, coal burning ranges of the early 19th century which cooked the cook along with the food; when you remember the homemaker who had to tote water in and garbage out, it becomes obvious that *no designer planned these kitchens of yesteryear*. They were shaped by circumstance and by custom, not by choice.

By the early 20th century, home economists and instructors at major universities recognized that the plan of a kitchen needed to follow an organized set of standards; and that the standards should be designed to minimize both the human energy needed to complete a task and the time required to prepare a meal or clean up afterward.

The 1930s and '40s were a time of research in the kitchen planning arena. Leading researchers of the time were Mary Koll Heiner and Helen McCullough who, in 1948, published a booklet titled *Functional Kitchen Storage*. It identified average food stuff and equipment used by typical U.S. families, and identified the amount of space the equipment needed. In the 1950s and '60s, appliance and cabinet manufacturers also took up the quest for better arranged kitchens.

By 1964, the kitchen planning profession was established as a significant specialty within the remodeling and design fields. Kitchen design professionals and firms, and other significant industry players joined forces to establish the **AMERICAN INSTITUTE OF KITCHEN DEALERS**, which later changed its name to the **NATIONAL KITCHEN & BATH ASSOCIATION (NKBA)**.

The new association aggressively pursued the issue of well planned kitchens. In 1965, NKBA, in conjunction with the University of Illinois, produced the first **Kitchen Industry Technical Manuals**. The publication series formally addressed and presented the knowledge required to design, remodel and build kitchens; and it established a set of kitchen planning guidelines which became the accepted norm for the industry.

Those guidelines have twice been updated by NKBA. In 1989, guidelines were revised and added to reflect the results of new research (conducted by the association) regarding equipment and foodstuffs used by modern U.S. families and the space required to store such things; as well as research conducted on NKBA's behalf by the University of Minnesota to establish the appropriate relationships, sizes and requirements for various workstations within the contemporary kitchen.

In 1995, the association again revised its kitchen planning guidelines -- this time to incorporate Universal Design features and requirements. Key changes in this most recent update centered on planning spaces accessible to all users, present and future, regardless of any physical limitations currently in place or developed/encountered at a later date.

This book covers the foundations of the kitchen design business as outlined by NKBA. Kitchen planning guidelines and safety criteria, equipment and materials, mechanical systems and accepted drawing and presentation standards are all incorporated in this one of a kind, all encompassing text.

Today, NKBA is the leading organization for the kitchen and bathroom industry, known for its quality education programs and materials and its exceptional promotion of the kitchen profession to consumers. We applaud your entrance into the kitchen design field, and congratulate you for beginning or expanding your education with the widely recognized and respected information included herein.

Nick Geragi, CKD, CBD, NCIDQ
Director of Education and Product Development
National Kitchen & Bath Association

About NKBA Membership

NKBA membership is the first step toward building close, powerful working relationships with other NKBA members as well as with clients. You'll benefit from:

- **Networking with the best and brightest.** Exchange ideas, insights and strategies you can use immediately to build business.

- **Consumer advertising and publicity programs.** NKBA consumer marketing programs are designed to link you with qualified prospects pursing kitchen and bathroom projects. Advertising, publicity, our own quarterly consumer magazine, and our exclusive consumer referral program, Direct to Your Door™ make NKBA a powerful enhancement to your existing marketing program.

- **Business management tools.** Supplies that streamline your day-to-day operation, reduce costs, and enhance your professionalism.

- **Certification.** Certified Kitchen Designer (CKD) and Certified Bathroom Designer (CBD) designations bring you added professional recognition, prestige and credibility.

- **Nationally acclaimed trade shows.** Where you can be among the first to see the latest in design and technology.

- **Prestigious design competitions.** Creating valuable publicity for NKBA members only.

Consumer research confirms that NKBA membership creates credibility and confidence among homeowners who plan to remodel their kitchens or bathrooms. It evokes a powerful image of stability and security. A feeling of confidence that delivers business!

Take advantage of the opportunities NKBA affiliation can create! **Call 1-800-THE-NKBA** for a free brochure and membership application, or write to:

NKBA
687 Willow Grove Street,
Hackettstown, New Jersey 07840.

Contents

CHAPTER **1**

Kitchen Mechanical Systems

In addition to being familiar with typical methods of home construction, as an aspiring kitchen designer, you should be familiar with the mechanical systems found in residential kitchens.

The success of your kitchen designs will be based on how well you can plan the electrical, the heating/ventilating/cooling, the lighting and the plumbing systems. This in-depth technical knowledge is required because of the sophisticated engineering of kitchen appliances and lighting systems.

You won't be able to excel in creative kitchen design unless you are as much at ease with the details of the mechanical systems as you are with the planning guidelines.

We'll begin this chapter by reviewing the electrical system, the heart of a well-planned kitchen. It is the electrical power that drives the appliances and lighting system.

We'll then turn our attention to the lighting system. Inadequate lighting is one of the biggest complaints consumers have about their existing kitchens. It is one of

the most interesting challenges before you as a kitchen specialist. This manual does not attempt to teach you to become a lighting expert. Rather, it introduces you to the basic planning elements of a well-organized lighting system.

In Section 3, you'll learn about available equipment and planning concerns for a kitchen ventilation system. Because the kitchen is so often an open space which adjoins other living areas, an effective ventilation system that removes all airborne cooking contaminants and is quiet during its operation is a critical element of good design.

Next, we'll tackle the plumbing system. Approximately one-fourth of all remodeled kitchens today has a second sink. Therefore, you will often be asked to add this second water appliance to a kitchen you're planning. Understanding the plumbing system will help you determine the feasibility and cost of such an addition to a kitchen space, as well as prepare you to handle other plumbing modifications.

In Section 5, we will talk about natural gas as a fuel source. We will conclude this chapter by highlighting heating and cooling systems and dual purpose heat pumps in Sections 6, 7 and 8.

SECTION **1**

Electrical

ELECTRICAL CODE CONSIDERATIONS

Electricity is a mystery to many kitchen planners. It's easy to understand why. Nearly everything is behind walls. However, in an increasingly technological age, electrical know-how is becoming critical.

The wave of new kitchen appliances means that you must have a firm grasp of the basics of home wiring. Home automation and "integrated systems", such as the **Smart House**™, use electricity for every function from security to heat controls. This new technology presents an extra challenge for the designer.

Because of the danger of fatal shock when water and electricity mix, safety is also an important considerations in designing electrical layouts. Safety is the goal of the **National Electrical Code**. While most local codes are based on this national model code, local units of government may have added their own additions to the code.

The details of an electrical installation, such as grounding requirements and the type of outlet boxes, will be handled by the electrical contractor. Electrical contractors are well aware of local code provisions and can tell you whether code requirements will have an impact on the project's budget.

Even though you can rely on your contractor to know the day-to-day code provisions, it's still a good idea to discuss anything out of the ordinary. Go over potential trouble spots, such as unusual locations for appliances, with the general contractor or electrical subcontractor before work begins. You should also make a special note of nonstandard dimensions or locations on your plans. The task of communicating switch and outlet locations is not difficult if your drawings are clear.

THE ELEMENTS OF THE ELECTRICAL SYSTEM

Part of the reason that electricity seems so complex is the extensive terminology. The basic concept, however, is straight forward. Many compare it to the flow of water. **(Electric current is, after all, a flow of electrons.)**

Think of it this way:

- Water pressure is measured in pounds per square inch (psi).

  Electrical pressure is measured in "volts".

- The rate of flow of water is measured in gallons per minute (gpm).

  The rate of flow of electricity is measured in amperes, abbreviated as **"amps"**.

- Power is measured in **"watts"**. The wattage tells you the amount of power available.

  The electrical bill from the utility company is based on the total watts consumed within a given time frame.

  Power [watts] x Time Used = Energy Consumed

  The power (wattage) level of a particular fixture or appliance dictates the required capacity of the electrical circuit.

  The more wattage present, the bigger the electrical wire required.

If you understand how the system works, you will be able to find the service panel on the house and decide whether additional wiring will be needed.

- To find the service panel, stand outside and look to see where the wires from the utility poles connect to the house.

- Standing outside, you will also see the electric meter.

- After passing through the meter, which measures energy in watt-hours, wires feed into a service box.

- The service box is located on the inside of the house near the electric meter or may be in the basement directly below the electric meter. This is the control center for the home's electrical service.

- Inside the service box is an electrical service panel. The service panel is where the circuit breakers or fuses are located.

- Most homes have what is called "three wire service" that feeds into the service panel. **Three wires - two "hot" (which means they have voltage) and one "ground" (zero voltage) - connect to the box from outside.**

- The service panel channels the electrical power into branch circuits.

- Branch circuits run to lights, switches, receptacles, and permanently wired equipment, such as a dishwasher or microwave oven. Branch circuits use smaller wires than main service wires because electrical appliances and devices don't need the full power that's available.

Let's back up for a moment and look at each part of the electrical system in greater detail.

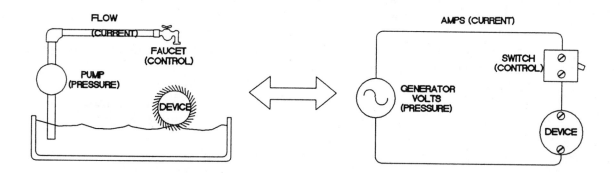

POWER FORMULA

$$V \times A = W \qquad W/V = A$$

V= VOLTAGE   A= AMPERAGE   W= WATTAGE

Figure 1 Electricity is easy to understand if you compare it to water. The power formula allows you to convert watts to amps. Either wattage or amperage ratings are found on all household appliances.

Service Entrance

Electricity is brought into the house via cable that is dropped into a mast. This mast looks a bit like the periscope of a submarine. The wiring may also enter the house underground. (If you are thinking of changing the location of the service entrance, you should talk with the power company first. They determine where this drop line can enter the house.)

As mentioned previously, the cable is brought to a service panel. In remodeling, the service panel may need to be upgraded. The panel may not have enough room for additional circuits. Or, the number of electrical appliances being added might overload the capacity of the main cable.

The minimum service entrance permitted by most local codes is a 100 amp, 240-volt service. A service with only two wires - one hot and one neutral - is inadequate for modern household demand. Generally speaking, homes that do not have 240-volt service should be upgraded to it because electric built-in ovens, cooktops, grill units and clothes dryers each require a separate 240 volt circuit.

In houses over 1400 square feet, a 200-amp service is recommended. A 200-amp service is adequate for most needs, but may not be adequate for very large homes or homes with a large number of major electrical appliances.

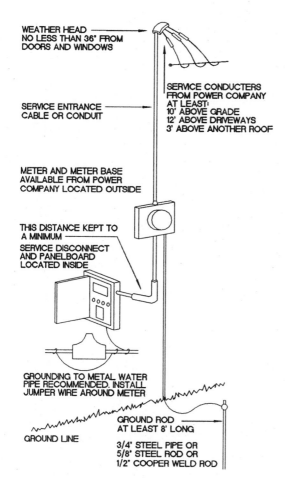

WEATHER HEAD
NO LESS THAN 36" FROM
DOORS AND WINDOWS

SERVICE CONDUCTORS
FROM POWER COMPANY
AT LEAST:
10' ABOVE GRADE
12' ABOVE DRIVEWAYS
3' ABOVE ANOTHER ROOF

SERVICE ENTRANCE
CABLE OR CONDUIT

METER AND METER BASE
AVAILABLE FROM POWER
COMPANY LOCATED OUTSIDE

THIS DISTANCE KEPT TO
A MINIMUM
SERVICE DISCONNECT
AND PANELBOARD
LOCATED INSIDE

GROUNDING TO METAL WATER
PIPE RECOMMENDED. INSTALL
JUMPER WIRE AROUND METER

GROUND LINE

GROUND ROD
AT LEAST 8' LONG
3/4" STEEL PIPE OR
5/8" STEEL ROD OR
1/2" COOPER WELD ROD

Figure 2 Electricity enters the house through the service mast. It passes through an electrical meter into a service box. Inside the service box, a service panel with circuit breakers or fuses distributes power to the branch circuits. The system is grounded to a cold water pipe.

Branch Circuits

The electric current in the service panel is distributed through branch circuits. Each circuit can only carry a limited amount of current. If it is overloaded, the wiring will overheat.

Each circuit is protected by a fuse or circuit breaker. These are the weak points of each circuit, the safety devices that keep the branch circuits and anything connected to them from overheating and catching fire. If there is an overload or a short circuit, a fuse will blow or a circuit breaker will trip, shutting off the flow of current.

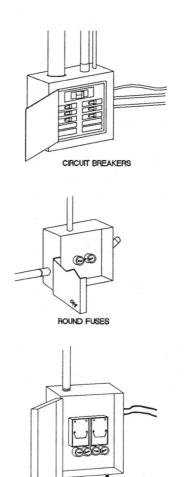

CIRCUIT BREAKERS

ROUND FUSES

CARTRIDGE FUSES

Figure 3 Three types of service panels might be found on a home. The service panel will contain circuit breakers, cartridge fuses or round fuses.

Fuses have a thin metal strip through which current passes into a circuit. If too much current starts to flow, the metal melts and cuts off the current.

Circuit breakers are heavy-duty switches that serve the same purpose as fuses. When a circuit is carrying more current than is safe, the breaker switches to RESET. On most breakers, the switch must be manually pushed to OFF and then back to ON after the circuit trips.

Although most people think of fuses as old-fashioned, they are actually more reliable than circuit breakers. Circuit breakers sometimes malfunction. When a fuse burns out, it must be replaced by a new fuse. This provides absolute protection against overheating. Unfortunately, this absolute protection created a problem. If the fuse kept burning out, the occupants of the house became irritated. They were tempted to put in a larger fuse, substituting a 20-amp fuse for a 15-amp fuse. Or, they might have been tempted to put a penny in the fuse holder. This also delayed fuse burnout.

When homeowners substituted larger fuses, the old knob and tube wiring in their home could overheat. Insulation on the wire would become crisp, or even burn off completely. Thus, if you are doing a jobsite inspection at a house, and you see that the service panel contains fuses, you should investigate the condition of knob and tube wiring. Knob and tube wiring used separate wires spaced a few inches apart. Wherever the wires pass through framing members, they are threaded through porcelain tubes or supported by porcelain knobs. Look in the attic or in the basement where the wiring is exposed. The system could be in good condition if it has not been abused. But if it is not in good condition and the electrical inspector finds unsafe wiring, he or she will require that it be upgraded, whether the cost is included in the original budget or not. Knob and tube wiring was most

often used with fuses, but you could find it even in houses with circuit breakers if the homes have been partially rewired.

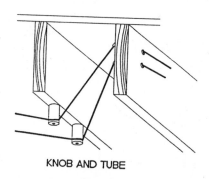

KNOB AND TUBE

Figure 4 Knob and tube wiring used porcelain knobs and tubes to protect framing members from wiring.

Circuit breakers are generally more convenient because they can be reset quickly. If the circuit overloads, the switch on the circuit breaker trips. If a circuit breaker trips continuously, that is an indication the circuit breaker is overloaded or defective. Like fuses, all circuit breakers are rated for a specific amperage. Circuits today typically are rated for 20 amps.

Wiring Options

Wire size depends on how many amps the circuit is carrying. The wire size is expressed as a gauge number; the smaller the number, the larger the wire. The wire size for a 20-amp circuit is #12 wire. Houses with older wiring (and 15 amp circuits) typically used #14 wire. If you are remodeling a kitchen with knob and tube wiring, you must update the wiring for receptacles to the #12 wiring used today. However the lighting could remain as the original knob and tube. Otherwise, the electrician might have to cut out portions of the wall or ceiling surface to run new wiring. If the new kitchen will include built-in equipment that requires a dedicated 120 volt circuit, such as a microwave oven or computer, new wires will be required. If new 240 volt equipment is also part of the plan, extensive additions to the wiring system may be necessary. An entire new electrical service may be a neccessity.

In most parts of the country, the electrical contractor will use non-metallic-sheathed cable (Type NM) for lighting and most appliance circuits. This is the least expensive kind of wiring and the simplest to install. The wiring part of the project will be less expensive if NM cable can be used.

NM cable, popularly known as Romex, contains three wires.

- One is the current carrying wire, or hot wire. It carries current to the receptacle. (The hot wire is black or red.)

- A second current carrying wire is the neutral wire, which completes the loop back to the service panel. (The neutral wire is white.)

- The third wire, which does not carry current, is the ground wire. It can either be bare copper wire or a coated green wire.

The individual wires in NM cable are protected by a tough, thermoplastic covering. In new construction, the electrician drills holes in the framing members and pulls the cable through the holes.

Armored cable (Type AC) is similar to non-metallic-sheathed cable except it has a flexible steel cover replacing the plastic covering. (It is also called BX cable.) Armored cable is installed in the same way as nonmetallic-sheathed cable. Because it is flexible, it is easier to install than conduit, which is rigid.

Conduit is used where additional protection from mechanical damage is needed and where required by building codes. (Chicago's code, for instance, requires conduit as a result of sensitivity to the Chicago fire.) Conduit is a special grade of aluminum or steel pipe, either galvanized or enameled, or nonmetallic pipe, usually polyvinyl chloride (PVC) or polyethylene (PE).

A final alternative to consider in remodeling is surface-mounted raceway. This is similar to conduit, in that it has its own connectors and boxes. However, the boxes and raceway are mounted to the surface of walls, not inside them. Some raceway is low-profile and relatively inconspicuous. Other products are purposefully large and designed to duplicate the profile of baseboards. This type of raceway is large enough to carry television cable or phone wiring as well as non-metallic sheathed cable.

If you design kitchens in an area where the code requires conduit, ask the electrician if armored cable is an acceptable substitute. You will usually save money with armored cable rather than conduit if just a small amount of additional wiring is needed. In new work, using conduit may be just as cost-effective. Electricians find it easy to pull wire through conduit once the conduit has been installed.

Working with armored cable and connecting it to boxes is, comparatively, time consuming. Armored cable must be carefully cut with a hacksaw each time it enters a junction, switch, or receptacle box.

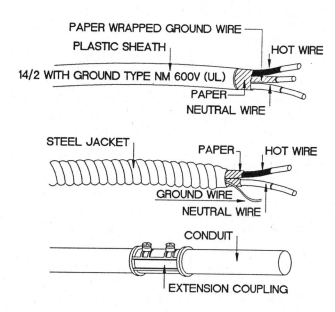

Figure 5 *Non-metallic-sheathed cable (NM) contains three wires surrounded by a tough, thermoplastic sleeve. Armored cable, known as AC or BX cable, surrounds its current carrying wires with a flexible steel covering. Conduit is rigid, hollow tubing made of metal or plastic. Individual wires are pulled through the conduit after it is installed.*

Junction Boxes

Connections between wires are made inside plastic or metal **boxes**. Switches, receptacles, and wall or ceiling-mounted light fixtures must each have their own box. The boxes are rectangular, octagonal or circular, and are made of plastic or metal. The boxes are nailed or screwed to the studs, but if the nearest stud is not where you want the box to be, the installer can also attach the box to a mounting bar.

After snaking wiring through the framing, the electrician may ask to go over the location of the switch and receptacle boxes before he or she installs them. Switch boxes normally are installed with the box bottom exactly 48" below the finished ceiling surface (for a ceiling height of 8'). If the ceiling is to be 5/8" drywall, the bottom of the box would be 48 5/8" from the ceiling joists. As you recall from a previous section, drywall can be hung horizontally. Drywall is 48" wide. Putting the switch at a 48" height makes it easier for drywallers to do a good job. They merely have to cut a notch around the box and slide the drywall over it.

The next best location for the switch is with the **top** of the box at a 48" height. The drywall contractor can then notch the bottom sheet of drywall. For universal considerations, NKBA recommends that all outlets and switches be placed within 15" - 48" above the finished floor.

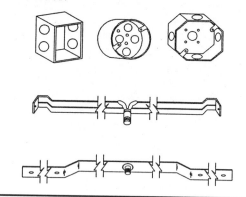

Figure 6 *Boxes can be rectangular, octagonal or circular. Bar hangers can be used to position boxes between studs.*

If the box is installed near the edge of the drywall, the drywaller could have difficulty making an accurate cut. The edges of the drywall are fragile. A 3/4" or 1" strip is likely to break off. This causes problems because the drywall taper must fill this large gap with joint compound. The joint compound may take a long time to dry. Or, it might not be as smooth as the surrounding wall. A standard switch or receptacle plate might not completely cover the patched hole. This problem is so common in construction that many contractors use over-sized cover plates around their switches as a matter of course. Gaps around receptacles are not as much of a problem because receptacles are not placed near the edges of drywall panels.

The electrician may ask that you check the location of receptacle boxes. Make sure you compare your plans with the actual locations proposed. An electrician sometimes overlooks a receptacle or puts it some place other than where you have specified.

If you have a higher than average backsplash, the electrical box might end up behind the backsplash and have to be raised. Also be sure to tell the electrician if you want the receptacle turned horizontally rather than vertically. If your design includes a decorative detail along the backsplash, such as a hand painted tile mural, make sure the electrical plan calls out the exact location for the outlets so that the electrical component does not conflict with the decorative details.

Another problem area can develop if the plan includes a cabinet which extends to the countertop, such as an appliance garage or a microwave cabinet. The outlets must be clearly located on the plan so that they are installed inside these special purpose cabinets.

You should also mark the thickness of the backsplash solid surfacing material, tile, or laminate in your specifications and list the height locations on the plans and elevation drawings. This tells the electrical contractor where to set the boxes. The face of the electrical box must always be flush with the finished wall surface. This is a code requirement.

Boxes are also important in remodeling, especially if knob and tube wiring is to be joined to new wiring. Connections between existing wiring and new wiring must always be made inside electrical boxes. The box protects the flammable parts of the building from sparks in the event of an electrical fire or overheating. The box must always be accessible. This may require a junction box with a blank cover plate in the middle of a wall. Be sure to ask the electrician if he or she plans to include any junction boxes that are not shown on your plans. Make sure the box is moved out of sight or new wiring is used if the location of the junction box will interfere with your design.

PLANNING FOR ELECTRICAL NEEDS

An easy way to organize your electrical layout is to use the four kinds of circuits the **National Electrical Code requires in a residence:**

- Lighting and general purpose;

- Small appliance;

- Individual appliance;

- And ground fault circuit interrupter (GFCI).

Circuits

General purpose circuits supply energy to light fixtures and outlets throughout the house and receptacles everywhere except in the kitchen, dining area, and laundry. Small appliance circuits provide power for equipment in the kitchen and laundry. Typically, the following appliances will require a dedicated 120 volt small appliance circuit:

- Refrigerator

- Freezer

- Microwave Oven

- Dishwasher

- Food Waste Disposer

- Computer

- Large Toaster Oven

- Washing Machine

- Vent hood

- Gas Dryer, Gas Range, Gas Cooktop and Gas Ovens

NOTE: Some communities will allow you to combine the dishwasher and the food waste disposer on the same circuit. Check your local codes.

Other kitchen and laundry room appliances require a 240-volt circuit, such as:

- Electric Dryer, Electric Range, Electric Cooktop and Electric Ovens

The anticipated rate of electrical flow required for the appliance is listed in its amperage, and will determine the size of wire used for these larger appliances.

Amperage

Each circuit in a house, as mentioned previously, also has an amperage rating. The normal household circuit

used for receptacles and lighting is a 20-amp circuit. The **National Electrical Code** contains a chart that will tell you how many receptacles or lights can go on a given circuit. A 20-amp circuit cannot have more than 16 amps loaded onto it. Appliances that require a 240-volt circuit vary in their amperage requirements. *For example,* a single electric oven takes less electrical power to operate than does a double oven. Therefore, the first appliance may require a 30-amp circuit, whereas the second double appliance may require a 40-amp circuit. Again, as the wire number gets smaller, the more amps available.

- A number 14 wire is 15 amps (120v).

- A number 12 wire is 20 amps (120v).

- A number 10 wire is 30 amps (240v).

- A number 8 wire is 40 amps (240v).

- A number 6 wire is 55 amps (240v).

Generally, a 240-volt circuit will be wired with 30, 40 or 55 amperes or with a #10, #8 or #6 wire. As a kitchen planner, you do not have to know how to lay out circuits. However, you should be aware that the electrical contractor may need to do additional work to add enough circuits for the fixtures or appliances you specify.

Surge Protection

Many appliances have motors which require a surge of electricity when they are first turned on. This is the case for the refrigerator's compressor or for the trash compactor's ram. Once the motor is running, the electrical energy requirement drops back. The first energy drain is called an electrical surge.

If you are planning a computer installation in the kitchen or near the kitchen, the outlets serving the computer should include a surge protector and a battery backup. These accessories are available from most computer vendors. They provide an uninterrupted continuous flow of electrical current to the computer.

Video Equipment Considerations

As a kitchen specialist, you may find yourself planning video equipment or stereo systems as part of the kitchen plan. The majority of video and stereo component parts operate on a 120-volt circuit and require very little power. Typically, one circuit will be ample for the television, VCR, video disc player and video game components. The outlet used for this equipment should be polarized. In that the clock display and memory capacity of the various components require continuous power, the outlet cannot be controlled by a wall switch.

When wiring for a television, don't forget to include a cable jack for the television as well. When planning any stereo system, make sure that you protect against sound interference, by only specifying incandescent rheostat switches which are designed to eliminate or reduce static in radio reception. Some dimmer switches use a filter to screen out radio frequency interference. Others include special circuitry that supresses the generation of radio frequency interference. The second type is far superior, it is also far more expensive.

Safeguards

Another requirement of the National Electrical Code is that every circuit have a grounding system. Grounding ensures that in the event of a stray current, all metal parts of the wiring system or of lamps or appliances connected to it, will be maintained at zero volts. The ground wire for each circuit is connected to the distribution center (service panel) and then is run with the hot and neutral wires in the branch circuits. A special type of circuit breaker - the **Ground Fault Circuit Interrupter (GFCI)** - is installed in kitchens adjacent to the water source and in all exterior locations. The GFCI monitors the balance of electrical current moving through the circuit. If an imbalance occurs because of stray current, the GFCI circuit opens the circuit, instantly, cutting off the electricity.

An electrical shock as short as 2/100 of a second can be fatal. The GFCI receptacle is designed to respond to stray current within 5/1000 of a second. Although this will not prevent a shock, it can prevent a fatality. NKBA recommends that all outlets in a kitchen be protected with ground fault circuit interrupters. GFCIs are extremely "user-friendly". When a GFCI has tripped, it is reset like a regular circuit breaker. For a receptacle GFCI, a reset button is pushed.

As a final note on safety, check the electrician's work to make sure he/she is protecting wiring from possible nail penetration. The N.E.C. requires all wiring to be placed 1 1/4" from the edge of framing members. Cables run in notches in the studs or joists must be protected by metal plates 3" long.

These rules are designed to prevent drywall nails from penetrating the cable. Drywall installers are not going to pay attention to the location of wiring. If a nail happens to strike wire embedded in the wall, it could create a short circuit. Tracking down the problem would be a nightmare.

Switches

There are dozens of switch types available. In many cases, selection is based on style, but function is just as important. In addition to choosing switches that accent your design, consider using specialty switches to improve convenience. Most switches in a home are called "single-pole" or "two-way". Single-pole switches control a light or receptacle from one location only. Another type, a three-way switch, operates in pairs to control a light or receptacle from two locations. They are used for rooms with two entrances. Some switches operate with a touch on a plate or button. Others have lighted handles which glow when the switch is off to serve as locators.

Another switch to remember for pantry closets is the **contact switch**. These switches are installed on the door frame. They turn on automatically when the door opens. Because they are installed out of sight, they give the room a less cluttered look. A bank of six or eight switches not only looks cluttered: it's not functional. Clients cannot remember which switch to flip.

LOW-VOLTAGE SWITCH SYSTEMS

Low-voltage lighting is becoming more common in residential work. New low-voltage lighting systems and an increasing selection of attractive fixtures

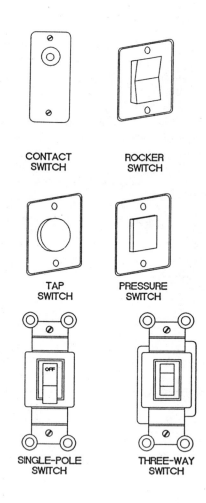

Figure 7 A variety of switches are available. They may be rocked, tapped or raised to activate the light fixture. Switches can also be planned so that one fixture can be turned on from several locations.

are used to provide task lighting along the kitchen countertop. Low-voltage fixtures generate less heat, which makes them ideal for this type of task lighting.

In **low-voltage** switching systems, the wall switches control a special low-voltage circuit. This circuit connects to a relay that operates the line voltage switch. This allows the use of inexpensive switches and doorbell-type wire on the switching circuit. This system can be expanded so that all the lights in the house can be controlled from one or more master panels, usually located in the master bedroom and/or at the main entrance.

RHEOSTAT

Placing your lighting on a **rheostat switch** will also give the kitchen extra personality. Dimmer switches allow the client to vary the light level with the activity. Rapid start fluorescent fixtures can be dimmed if you ask the electrical supplier to install a special dimming ballast in the fixture. This is easiest to do before installation.

Some switches are linked to receptacles, such as a wall switch used to turn on the receptacle for a floor lamp. Never use a dimmer on a switch connected to a receptacle. Turning down the dimmer could ruin an appliance plugged into the outlet. Some switches are designed to save space. *For example,* two switches can fit in the space of one standard-sized box.

If your plan calls for a special lighting system or unusual switch arrangements, you should consult your local lighting store or electrical contractor to see if any special switches would enhance the project.

Receptacles

Most receptacles are "duplex receptacles" because they have two outlets. Duplex receptacles are rated for 15 or 20 amps, and they carry 120-volt current. One or both outlets may be electrically live at all times, or one or both may be controlled by a wall switch. *For example,* a switch near the room entrance could turn on a floor lamp.

On remodeling projects, you'll find receptacles that are both grounded and non-grounded. Grounded receptacles accept three-prong plugs. The third prong connects the frame or housing of the appliance to the grounding system. Electrical codes require that all new residential receptacles must be grounded. Your electrical contractor will be required to bring all receptacles in the kitchen up-to-code at the time of remodeling. The code may require additional ground wires, and it will mean the installation of GFCI receptacles or circuit breakers. This is an added expense you should include in your estimates.

Other special forms of outlets are available. These include receptacle and switch combinations, clock outlets, and radio and television outlets which also supply antenna and ground connection. Among the most useful receptacles are child-proof models that require an adult's grip to uncover them.

LOCATION

Provide sufficient electrical outlets in the kitchen to accommodate all the small hand appliances the family uses such as the coffee maker, toaster, food processor, etc. For minimum quality electrical service, no point along a wall should be more than 6 feet from a receptacle. Every wall space more than 2' wide must have a receptacle. If an open entry door (not a closet door or cabinet door) makes a wall space inaccessible, it does not have to have a receptacle.

Thus, it may be important for you to plan your door swings before planning the receptacle locations.

For convenience, receptacles should be spaced 6' to 8' apart. Greater accessibility is provided when the receptacles are located considering appliance or furniture placement. *For example*, a wall section 12' long can be served by one receptacle in the center. However, a better solution is to locate receptacles near each end of the wall. This is because furniture is more likely to be placed in the center of a wall. Furniture will block access to the receptacle. If you are working on a family room and the client has already selected furniture, you should consider probable furniture location when planning receptacle placement.

Plan where your clients will need receptacles. In a typical kitchen, outlets will be placed on each side of the sink and then along the backsplash every 18" - 30". Outlets should also be planned at each end of an island as well.

RENOVATION CONSIDERATIONS

In remodeling jobs, electricians refer to "new work" and "old work". "New work" refers not so much to new construction as to jobsites where the framing is exposed and running wire is relatively easy. Wiring a renovation with gutted walls, for example, is new work.

"Old work" refers to locations where small holes are cut in the walls and wiring is fished through the covered wall cavities. Boxes are then mounted flush to finished surfaces. You will be in good graces with electrical contractors if you think through the location of outlets. When designing, ask yourself:

- *What is the closest live outlet with power?*

- *What studs, joists, or other framing might be in the way en route?*

To locate the nearest live outlet, think spatially. The outlet may be on the other side of a partition wall. You may find an electrical circuit just above the ceiling. Discussing circuit locations with the electrical contractor before drawing your wiring plan may save you money. The electrical contractor may be able to draw power from a nearby, pre-existing source. To bring new wiring to a remodeled room without doing major demolition, your carpentry contractor may be able to remove baseboard so that wiring can be run in a notch behind the baseboard.

In some cases the electrical contractor may need to cut small holes at the tops and bottoms of walls. The electrical contractor will use **fish tape** to pull new wiring from hole to hole. Fish tape is a stiff wire used to probe wall cavities. Electrical wiring can then be tied to one end and pulled through the wall to the other hole.

Because switches, receptacles and junction boxes must be flush with the finished surface, the electrician may need to add a **box extension** to an existing box to make it the correct depth. Also, if additional wires need to be brought into the box, the box may have to be changed to a larger one. This may require more demolition to the finished surface around the box.

If the local code requires conduit, the electrical contractor will have to open up a channel. The electrician may cut out such a channel in the course of his or her work. However, it is better to have the person responsible for repairing the channel make the cuts.

A crew member of the general contractor's should cut back lath and plaster (or drywall) along a straight line at the center of adjoining studs or joist spaces, or wherever boxes are needed. When the electrician is finished, the area will be easier to patch. If demolition is done carefully, holes can be patched with drywall or they can be replastered.

To avoid demolition, you could also consider using a surface-mounted raceway. Wiring can be run inside the raceway. This solution might be suitable for an inexpensive remodel job or a commercial job where design is not the main consideration. By working with the electrical contractor you can plan how to provide needed wiring without opening large holes in walls.

One other problem that is rare, but can occur, is to find that a house has been wired with aluminum wiring. Aluminum wiring requires one larger wire size than copper wire. If the electrician finds aluminum wiring, expect added expense.

As a quick reminder, remember to check for the following problem areas:

- *Is there knob and tube wiring?*

- *Are there open splices in the wiring in the attic?*

- *Is the insulation on the wiring still in good condition?*

- *Is the location of the service box or service mast in conflict with your plan?*

- *Is the service box in a wall that is*

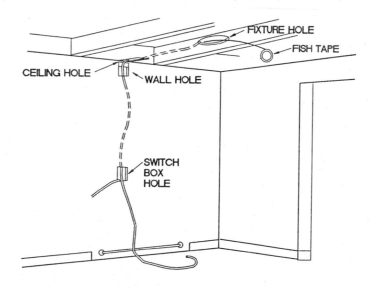

Figure 8 Wiring in remodeling can be fished through wall cavities. Only small holes are needed. Fish tape is used to pull the wire through to the new location.

going to be removed?

- *Is the service box in a wall that will have a door or window placed in it?*

- *Will the service box still be accessible after the remodel?*

- *Is there an undersized service panel (100 amps or less)?*

- *Do you see fuses rather than breakers?*

- *Are there subpanels spun off the main panel or scattered throughout the house?*

These are just a few of the problems you can encounter in remodeling. Wiring and electrical work in new construction is infinitely easier than in existing buildings. Team up with a good electrical contractor - one who is experienced in sorting out existing wiring - and your job will be a lot easier.

Figure 9 (Adapted from Architectural Graphics Standards) Electrical Symbols.

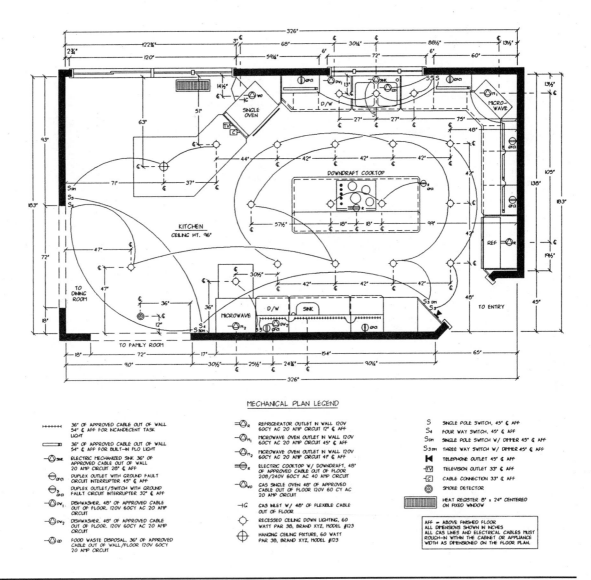

Figure 10 A kitchen mechanical plan.

ELECTRICAL TIPS FROM THE PROS

• The electrician must have access to the wires. His/her path will be obstructed by fire blocks within the walls. His/her path will be blocked without adequate clearance under the house or in the attic. Designers should take a close look at the structure on the initial visit. Needless to say, if the house is a flat-top, cement blockhouse with a slab foundation, electrical changes will be limited.

• Relocating or eliminating outlets, switches and lights is not always an easy matter. All joints or splices in wires or cables must occur inside junction boxes. Many existing boxes will be one of several on a circuit. The box cannot be covered completely. If the plan calls for eliminating an outlet, a blank coverplate may be required.

- Whenever major construction and wall removal is planned, remember to add adequate costs for electrical removal.

- After selecting the decorative surfaces, specify the color requested for the switches and outlets. *For example,* Ivory outlets on a Corian Glacier White backsplash will be unsightly.

- Don't try to place switches or outlets in a wall which houses a sliding pocket door.

- Don't specify an exact outlet or switch placement along a plumbing wall unless you know exactly where the vent pipe is located.

- Although it sounds like a good idea, don't conceal outlets inside cabinet doors for hand appliances, unless you can add a timer and have checked local codes.

SECTION **2**

Lighting

Professional kitchen specialists know that an effective lighting system is more than a light over the sink and one in the center of the room. In this section, we will explain the basics of lighting to you. A more in-depth course in lighting techniques would be required for you to become a true expert. However, the information contained in this section will give you the technical basis you need to plan effective lighting systems.

To assist us in gathering and presenting this information we have incorporated materials from the **American Lighting Association** and from the **General Electric Lighting Lab** for your review.

LIGHTING TERMINOLOGY

Basics Kinds of Lighting

- **General or Ambient Lighting:** Lighting that radiates a comfortable level of brightness, enabling one to see and walk about safely. A basic form of lighting that replaces sunlight, it can be achieved with chandeliers, ceiling or wall-mounted fixtures, recessed or track lights, and with lanterns outside the home.

- **Task Lighting:** Lighting that is focused on a specific task such as reading, sewing, grooming or cooking. Task lighting should be bright enough to prevent eyestrain and can be accomplished with track and recessed lighting, pendant lighting and portable lamps.

- **Accent Lighting:** A decorative form of lighting that spotlights objects such as paintings and houseplants or highlights the texture of a wall, drapery or outdoor garden. This type of lighting is usually provided by track, recessed or wall-mounted fixtures.

General Lighting Terms

- **Ballast:** A device that limits the electric current flowing into a fluorescent or high intensity discharge lamp.

- **Compact Fluorescent Tube:** A smaller type of fluorescent lamp which is being used in place of incandescent lamps. These tubes are becoming more and more flexible so that they are appropriate for a variety of residential applications.

- **Dimmer Control:** A device which is used to vary the light output of an electric lamp. Also known as rheostat switch

- **Fluorescent Light:** Light emitted by the electrical stimulation of mercury vapor molecules inside a tubular lamp with an interior coating of phosphors. Saves energy by using one-fifth to one-third of electricity as incandescents.

- **High-Intensity Discharge Light:** Light emitted by a high-intensity electric lamp containing either mercury vapor, high-pressure sodium or metal halide. Generally used in outdoor street lighting and for other industrial and commercial purposes.

- **Incandescent Light:** Light emitted by an electric lamp in which a metallic (tungsten) filament is burned to incandescence by an electric current.

- **Lamp:** An artificial light source, such as an incandescent bulb or fluorescent tube.

- **Low Voltage Lighting:** The lighting system that utilizes 12-volt current instead of regular 120-volt household current. Requires transformer to reduce current. Produces superior accent lighting when used with tungsten-halogen lamp with built-in reflector.

- **Luminaire:** Correct term for a light fixture.

- **Parabolic Reflector Lamp:** Projector type lamp with maximum light output for use in floodlighting and long light throws. Light output is about four times that of a regular incandescent lamp.

- **Reflector Lamp:** Lamp with built-in reflector that either floods or concentrates spotlight on a subject, giving it twice the light output of a regular incandescent lamp.

- **Transformer:** A device which is used to reduce standard 120-volt household current to the 12-volts needed for low-voltage lighting systems.

- **Tungsten-Halogen Lamp:** An incandescent lamp containing a halogen gas that burns bright white when ignited by a tungsten filament.

Lighting Design Terms

- **Cross Lighting:** Lighting objects such as a statue from two or more sides to soften shadows and reveal more detail.

- **Downlighting or Area Lighting:** Lights mounted high up to cast broad illumination over wide areas.

- **Grazing:** Lighting objects such as tile or masonry walls up close to throw light across their surface and highlight their texture.

- **Lightscaping:** The effective, creative use of outdoor lighting for security, recreation, convenience and decorative purposes.

- **Shadowing:** Lighting an object from the front and below to create intriguing shadows on a wall or other vertical rear surface.

- **Moonlighting:** Lights are aimed downward among tree branches to recreate moonlight filtering through branches, casting attractive shadow.

- **Silhouetting:** Lighting an object from behind and below to create a striking silhouette of the object against a solid backdrop.

- **Spread or Diffused Lighting:** Circular pattern of light cast downward to illuminate a focal point.

- **Spotlighting:** Lights focus a controlled intense beam to highlight art work or family collectibles.

THE DETAILS OF LIGHTING

Measuring Light

Light is measured by illuminating engineers in several ways. They measure the light produced by the source, the light that reaches the work surface and the light that is reflected to the viewer's eye. Let's define the units of measurement used.

- **Wattage**, the rate at which electrical energy is changed into light.

Wattage listings measure input required by the lamp.

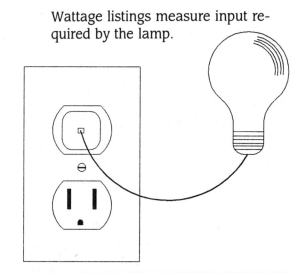

Figure 11 Wattage equals the electrical input required by the source.

- **Lumens** measure the output of a light source. The term "candela" is sometimes used as the unit of measurement. One candela of light equals 12.57 lumens.

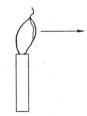

CANDELA-LIGHT PRODUCED FROM
ONE CANDLE IN ONE DIRECTION

LUMEN-LIGHT OUTPUT IN ALL
DIRECTIONS OF SOURCE

Figure 12 Lumen light measurements.

- **Footcandles** measure the illumination that falls on a surface, all parts of which are at a distance of one foot from the candle. Hence, footcandles measure the amount light that reaches a surface. Many lighting recommendations prepared by illumination specialists are given in footcandles. The number of footcandles generated per lumen of light output is affected by the distance from the source to the surface, the equipment that surrounds the source and the pollutants in the air. Because so many variables must be taken into consideration to properly calculate this relationship, most designers normally rely on lumen recommendations during the planning process. For the most accurate guide, refer to lumen recommendations whenever possible.

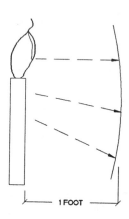

Figure 13 A footcandle measures the light thrown on a surface.

- **Footlamberts** measure the amount of light that is reflected. Illuminating engineers define one footlambert as the uniform lumi-

nance of a perfectly diffusing surface that transmits or reflects light at the rate of one lumen per square foot. In simpler language, the number of footlamberts is determined by multiplying the number of footcandles reaching the surface by the reflectance level or transmittance level (both given in the form of percentages) of the surface.

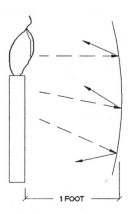

Figure 14 A footlambert measures the light reflected from a surface.

Reflectance Levels

Designers must recognize the importance of surface reflectance levels when specifying finishing materials. Kitchen lighting recommendations usually assume that the following reflectance levels are present in a residential kitchen:

- Ceilings   60%-90% Reflectance

- Walls   35%-60% Reflectance

- Floors   15%-35% Reflectance

- Countertops 30%-50% Reflectance

- Cabinets   35%-60% Reflectance

The lighting plan for a kitchen featuring very dark colors which have reflectance levels below those listed above must include more lighting than that normally recommended. Conversely, an all-white kitchen can be illuminated properly with less lighting than is usually recommended. Following, are typical reflectance values:

Reflectance Levels of Paints

Paint Color	Light Reflected
Black	10%
White	80-90%
Warm Colors	
Pale Yellow, Rose	80%
Pale Pastels	70%
Mustard	35%
Cool Colors	
Blue, Green Pastels	70-85%
Blue, Green	20-30%

Universal design planning standards call for you to be particularly sensitive to the issue of reflectance levels and contrasts between surface finishes when planning a space for a mature client.

Research has proven that as we age, we need higher levels of light to work under. Additionally, the aging eye can distinguish better between various surfaces or materials if there is a high color contrast level between them.

Reflectance levels typically quoted are for individuals with good, clear eyesight. Keep all the surfaces light, colors increase contrast, and increase light levels for elderly clients. If the space will be used by people of varying ages, rheostat or dimmer controls on the lights may be an excellent way to give all users flexibility over the lighting system so that they can tailor it to their preference when using the space.

Familiarity with how light is measured is the first step toward designing a successful lighting plan. Second, you must understand the various light sources available.

LIGHT SOURCES

There are four light sources generally used in residential homes: natural sunlight, incandescent electric light, halogen electric light and fluorescent electric light.

Natural Light Source: Natural light from the sun is an excellent source of illumination. However, it must be combined with electric light because it is not a stable light source. Its efficiency is altered by the weather, local terrain, time of day, landscaping and other exterior conditions. The very placement of the kitchen windows will affect the natural daylight available.

Incandescent Light Source: Incandescent lamps are a popular form of electric light. An incandescent lamp is designed with a wire sealed in a glass enclosure. Electric current passes through the wire, heating it to a white-hot state and the wire then emits light.

Lamp life is directly related to the temperature of the tungsten wire. The brighter lamps have both higher temperatures and shorter life. They generally offer 750 - 1,000 hours of lamp life. These are the general service lamps available in all stores. Conversely, extended life lamps (2,500 hours of lamp life) have lower light outputs (about 20% less). Incandescent lamps are available in a wide variety of shapes and sizes. They can be easily dimmed to provide maximum control over the amount of light emitted.

Incandescent light also has a warm, reddish cast that is flattering to people.

The correct lamp is an important part of the incandescent lighting plan.

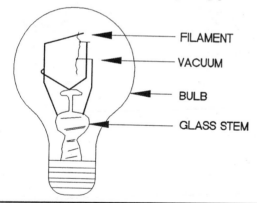

FILAMENT

VACUUM

BULB

GLASS STEM

Figure 15 How an incandescent light fixture produces light.

A Lamp: The "general service" or "A-lamp" is a common household bulb that has been used for years. Because of its multiple directional distribution of light, it is used in surface mounted or suspended fixtures only.

R Lamp: Recessed and enclosed fixtures use the "R-lamp" (short for reflector), which provides a beam of light that is directed outward and downward by a mirror-like reflective surface inside. Thus, the throw of light can be controlled. There is a choice between spotlights and floodlights within the R-lamps available. The difference is in the width of the light beam, which depends on the density of the frosting on the face inside the lamp. For a narrow concentration of light, the designer should select an R-spot which will be lightly frosted. For a wide spread of light, an R-flood would be used.

Halogen Light Source: Halogen lamps have been used for decades in car headlights and slide projectors. They are now speeding into the home as a major new light source alternative. About the size of a fountain-pen cap, the halogen bulb can produce as much light as an incandescent bulb ten times its size. It also consumes about half the power and lasts up to seven times longer than a standard light bulb. The light quality from this source is whiter and richer in blue, lacking the typically yellowish color produced by ordinary incandescent bulbs.

The halogen bulb, like its forerunner, has tungsten wire filaments that are heated until they give off light. In a standard incandescent fixture, the burning tungsten particles are gradually deposited on the inside of the glass bulb, which wears away the elements, darkens the glass and eventually reduces the light. In the new bulb, halogen gas surrounds the filament, offering a regenerative life by redepositing the burning tungsten particles on the filament. That is why the bulb lasts longer (about 2,000 hours) and provides a consistently higher light output.

Halogen lighting systems require only 12 volts of electrical power and are called "*low-voltage*". The system requires a transformer to convert the normal household current to the lower voltage requirement. Low voltage systems also require special rheostat dimming controls.

Fluorescent Light Source: Fluorescent lamps are another efficient form of electric light. A fluorescent lamp is tubular with a small electrode sealed into each end. A small amount of mercury is present in the tube. The tube is also filled with an inert gas kept at a low pressure. When the electrical power is turned on, the electricity heats the electrodes, vaporizes the mercury and then arcs from one electrode to the other. Electrons given off from the arc collide with the mercury atoms, which produce ultraviolet rays. The phosphors which coat the inside of the tube absorb most of the ultraviolet energy and then radiate the remaining energy as visible light.

Fluorescent lamps provide from 7,500 to 20,000 hours of light. Fluorescent rheostats and special dimmer ballasts are now available and the buzzing sound of bad ballasts has been eliminated. The color of the light produced by fluorescent lights depends on the composition of the phosphors coating the tube. To duplicate the color of daylight, special color-corrected fluorescent lamps can be selected. When accurate color rendition is important, deluxe cool white tubes should be used. If fluorescent and incandescent fixtures are to be used together, deluxe warm white or soft white lamps should be specified.

A fluorescent lamp requires a ballast as auxiliary equipment. The ballast limits the amount of current used by the lamp and provides the proper starting voltage. If the electrical current is not limited at an optimum point, the arc would eventually pass so much current that it would destroy the lamp.

New electronic ballasts have been introduced in fluorescent fixtures to replace the old "*wire windings*" ballast. Essentially a transformer, the new electronic ballast uses electronic components to produce the amount of current necessary to excite the lamp. These new ballasts use less wattage, are more energy efficient, produce less heat and will last longer than the old windings ballast.

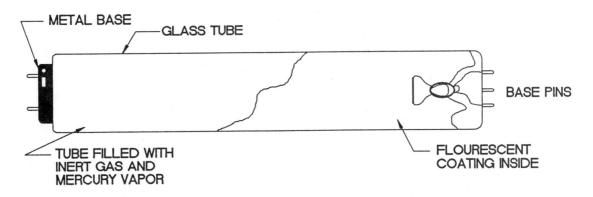

Figure 16 A fluorescent tube cross section.

LIGHT SOURCE EFFICACY

As we compare these light sources, we turn our attention to their energy efficiency. Needless to say, sunlight should be used in place of electric light whenever it is available. When we compare the energy efficiency of incandescent, halogen and fluorescent light sources, we refer to their "efficacy". **Efficacy** is defined as the power to produce an effect. To determine the efficacy of a lighting system, we evaluate the lamp's wattage input and lumen output. The efficacy of an electric light source is determined by comparing the lumens produced per watt of electrical energy used. Incandescent lighting produces from 12 to 21 lumens of light per watt. Fluorescent lamps produce from 40 to 100 lumens of light per watt. For all light sources, higher wattage lamps will produce more lumens per watt. *For example,* a 100 watt lamp will produce more light than two 60 watt lamps.

INCANDESCENT WATTAGE	REPLACE WITH FLUORESCENT	SAVINGS ON ELECTRICITY (1)
2-60W	2-20W Tubes	$ 84.00
1-100W	2-20W Tubes	60.00
2-75W	4-20W Tubes	60.00
1-60W	1-32W Circline	28.00
3-60W	1-32/40W Circline	120.00
1-75W	1-18W "U" Bulb	31.20 (2)
1-75W	2-PL-7W Compact	51.00 (3)
2-75W	2-PL-13W Compact	114.00 (3)

(1) Includes allowance for ballast wattage. Calculated at 10 cents per KWH for rated lamp life of 12,000 hours.

(2) Calculated on 6,000 hour rated lamp life.

(3) Calculated on 10,000 hour rated lamp life.

Energy Savings/Efficiency

Lighting takes only 12% to 15% of the electricity used in a home. Still there are ways to economize on electricity bills with lighting.

- Use dimmers to save energy.

- Use photo-electric cells or timers to turn outdoor lights on and off automatically.

- Use the more efficient reflector bulbs, especially for task and accent lighting. *For example,* a 50W "R" bulb can put as much light on an object as a 100W "A" bulb.

- Use energy-saving fluorescent where practical. Below are some examples:

Artificial Light and Human Health

One of the major questions being asked today is *"are artificial light sources safe?"*

The news media occasionally reports on suspected harmful health effects of various types of artificial lighting. These health concerns generally revolve around the photobiological elements of these light sources rather than the visual light produced by the fixtures. Understandably, this type of publicity raises questions in the minds of our clients concerning the safety of light systems planned for their new kitchens.

Solid answers to these safety questions continue to elude the lighting industry. Thus, there are no indisputable answers to our clients' questions. However, if we understand the basis for the concerns we will be better able to guide our clientele in this difficult area.

Identifying light sources

INCANDESCENT	TYPE	DESCRIPTION AND USE
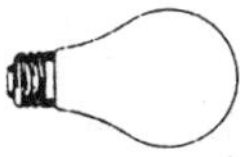	**A-Bulb**	Familiar pear-shaped bulb for everyday household use; available in regular, three-way, and long-life versions.
	**Globe (G)**	Ball-shaped bulb; used in pendant fixtures and theatrical lighting strips.
	**Decorative (D)**	Flame, tear-drop and other shapes; used in chandeliers and sconces.
	**Reflector (R)**	Funnel-shaped bulb with built-in reflector; directs light forward through frosted face; available in flood (FL) and spot (SP) versions; used in recessed downlights.
	**PAR-Parabolic Reflector**	Similar to "R" bulb, but with clear face that provides better beam control; weatherproof casing; used in outdoor spot and flood fixtures, recessed downlights and track fixtures; available in both standard and low-voltage current.

FLUORESCENT		
	**Tube**	Straight tube available in variety of lengths; excellent for general lighting over wide areas; more energy-efficient than incandescents.
	PL-Compact Tube	Twin tube allows fluorescent light to be used in smaller, trimmer fixtures such as recessed downlights; special adapter allows use in standard lamp sockets.
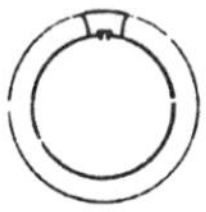	**Circle**	Circular tube used for general lighting in circular fixtures; special adapter allows use in standard lamp sockets.

TUNGSTEN-HALOGEN		
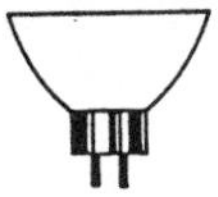	**Low-voltage MR-16**	Tiny bulb with built-in reflector that delivers a controlled beam of bright white light; available in numerous beam spreads; used in track fixtures and recessed downlights for accent lighting; requires transformer.
	**Low-voltage PAR-36**	Parabolic-shaped bulb with built-in reflector; delivers a larger beam of white light than MR-16; comes in three different beam spreads; used in track fixtures and recessed downlights for accent lighting; requires transformer.

Source: American Lighting Association ⊗

Figure 17 Identifying light sources.

There seems to be two very different opinions regarding the photobiological impact of artificial lighting systems.

One side suggests that in creating artificially illuminated environments we have been concerned with only a narrow aspect of light-seeing by brightness contrast. This group of lighting specialists feel our physical well-being would be better served if man-made lighting systems closely simulated natural light. They argue that, historically, man has been exposed to daylight in the daytime and firelight in the nighttime. Thus, we have adapted biologically and psychologically to this type of light. They contend scientific research indicates natural light affects circulating compounds within the body, directly affects skin, affects intestinal calcium absorption, and may affect the teeth, as well as the individual's resistance to respiratory disease. They conclude that these photobiological reactions common to man warn us of the unhealthy long term affects of exposure to artificial light which doesn't duplicate the properties of natural light.

The opposing side responds that recent studies have not been based on sound experimentation and have been reported with sensational generalizations. They feel that present knowledge is based primarily on anecdotal observations, rather than scientific research. They question the ability of anyone to pinpoint the properties of daylight because natural light is constantly changing. Thus, they argue that it is wrong to label one type of daylight as essential to protect the general public's health. They contend that many health problems associated with artificial light sources are in reality caused by improperly designed lighting systems.

The **General Electric Company** sums up this view as it states:

"With over 108 years of experience in the electrical lighting of homes, offices, factories, and institutions of all kinds, we are not aware of any serious, adverse effect upon the health of people. To the contrary, most results from good general lighting, well applied, tend to suggest that people are happier, more productive and better off under good lighting."

Frank Parker, MD, Professor and Chairman, Department of Dermatology at the Oregon Health Sciences University in Portland, Oregon, comments as follows:

"The only report in the medical literature that attempts to relate fluorescent lighting to human skin cancer has stimulated a great deal of scientific disagreement. Further studies are under way to determine its validity. At this time, the Study's findings may be considered as speculative correlation and certainly not proven. It appears that although fluorescent lamps may emit small amounts of UV light, they are not likely to play a significant roll in skin carcenogenesis, especially if the lamps are enclosed within glass and plastic covers."

Comparing Light Sources

To determine our individual position in this debate, we should be familiar with the differences in natural and artificial light.

NATURAL LIGHT

Philip C. Hughes, PH.D., Vice-President of Commercial Engineer, for the

Duro-test Corporation, defines natural light as follows:

- "Natural light color temperature ranges between 5,500°Kelvin and 6,800° Kelvin". When the sun is 90° from the horizon in a clear sky the color temperature is 5,500° Kelvin. The color temperature affects the warmth (toward red) or coolness (towards blue) of the light source. The lower the color temperature of a light source, the warmer, that is, redder, the apparent color. A color temperature of 5,000°Kelvin to 5,500°Kelvin is considered neutral white. Lower temperatures produce a warm light, higher temperatures produce a cool light.

- Natural light has a color rendering index rating of 100 (C.R.I. 100). The C.R.I. is a rating of the light sources ability to reflect colors without distortion. The energy from a light source in each color band is termed the spectral power.

- Natural light includes both the visible regions of the spectrum and invisible solar radiation in ultraviolet wave length. The near ultraviolet radiation is stable, while the middle ultraviolet radiation varies with the suns angle. Global radiation is measured in nanometers, then the ratio between near and middle ultraviolet radiation is compared. In natural light, normally there will be 8 times more near ultraviolet radiation than middle ultraviolet radiation."

Within this definition of natural light, let's compare typical artificial light sources.

ARTIFICIAL LIGHT

Most of the visible energy from the incandescent lamp is in the red end of the spectrum with virtually no ultraviolet emission. This reddish color tint is comparable to the light from a camp fire or candle with a low color temperature of 2,850°Kelvin. Although we generally perceive incandescent light as comfortable and relaxing, it does not duplicate natural light.

HALOGEN LIGHT

Halogen light sources have a color temperature higher than standard incandescent and therefore produce a whiter light which is closer to natural light.

FLUORESCENT LIGHT

The color temperature of a fluorescent light source is determined by the type of light emitted by the lamp. The warm white lamps have lower color temperatures, which make them compatible with incandescent light sources. The higher color temperatures of cool white tubes account for their bluish cast.

While most fluorescent lights do not accurately simulate natural daylight, some manufacturers have developed "*full spectrum*" fluorescent lamps. One produced under the name "*Vita-Lite*" has a color temperature of 5,500°Kelvin, a CRI of 91 and duplicates the ratio of 1 to 8 in near and mid ultraviolet radiation.

To produce a lamp closer to natural light, the lumen to wattage relationship drops, and so the lamp is less efficient than other tubes. However, the manufacturer cites studies completed in England which suggest lower levels of light with good color rendering are as satisfying as high efficiency lamps. Therefore, for people very concerned about duplicating natural light, the *"full spectrum"* fluorescent tubes can be specified.

For those who feel artificial light need not duplicate natural daylight all of the choices are available and should be specified to suit each area's major function. *For example,* warm fluorescent tubes in the work area combined with incandescent lighting in the entertainment center might be an ideal combination.

Whatever the final selection, the designer's familiarity with the nature of artificial light sources and his or hers ability to council the client as they make their decision is one more indication of professionalism.

COLOR RENDITION

Color rendition, which is measured by a **Color Rendition Index (CRI)** is just as important in lighting aesthetics, particularly with fluorescent lamps. Color rendition is difficult to evaluate objectively.

The color that our eyes *"see"* is the effect of light waves bouncing off, or passing through, various objects. The color of a given object, therefore, is determined in part by the characteristics of the light source under which it is viewed.

Color rendition, then, is a relative term; it refers to the extent to which the perceived color of an object under a light source matches the perceived color of that object under another source (such as daylight or incandescent lighting).

On a scale of 1 to 100, with 100 being the color rendition closest to daylight, incandescent light typically has a CRI of about 95.

Formerly, fluorescent lamps made clients look pale in the bathroom mirror. However, in response to criticism of poor color rendition, most manufacturers of fluorescents have introduced lamps that use color-correcting phosphors. The newer compact fluorescents (PL lamps) also contain special phosphors needed to light skin well. The 13-watt version provides excellent color reddening and enough illumination to equal a 60-watt incandescent lamp.

If your clients are hesitant about choosing a fluorescent fixture, you may want to suggest trying out several different lamps in a lighting store or your showroom to find a lamp that gives acceptable skin color. Samples of wallpaper, countertop material, tile and paint should also be checked so they can see if the colors are acceptable under the light source. **Nick Geragi**, CKD, CBD, NCIDQ, (NKBA - Director of Education and Product Development) recommends setting up an area of the showroom to preview different fixture and lamp combinations. Different options in switches and dimmers can also be part of the preview package.

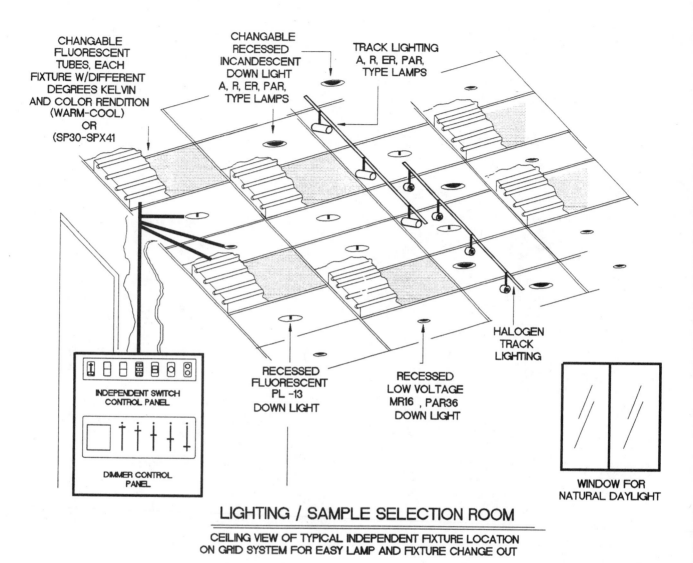

CHANGABLE
FLUORESCENT
TUBES, EACH
FIXTURE W/DIFFERENT
DEGREES KELVIN
AND COLOR RENDITION
(WARM-COOL)
OR
(SP30-SPX41

CHANGABLE
RECESSED
INCANDESCENT
DOWN LIGHT
A, R, ER, PAR,
TYPE LAMPS

TRACK LIGHTING
A, R, ER, PAR,
TYPE LAMPS

HALOGEN
TRACK
LIGHTING

INDEPENDENT SWITCH
CONTROL PANEL

DIMMER CONTROL
PANEL

RECESSED
FLUORESCENT
PL -13
DOWN LIGHT

RECESSED
LOW VOLTAGE
MR16 , PAR36
DOWN LIGHT

WINDOW FOR
NATURAL DAYLIGHT

LIGHTING / SAMPLE SELECTION ROOM

**CEILING VIEW OF TYPICAL INDEPENDENT FIXTURE LOCATION
ON GRID SYSTEM FOR EASY LAMP AND FIXTURE CHANGE OUT**

Figure 18   Preparing a multi-light area in the showroom.

COLOR TEMPERATURE

Color temperature describes whether a light source has warm or cool tones. Color temperature is different from color rendition. The latter describes how accurately a light source represents an object's color. Color temperature, on the other hand, is related to aesthetics rather than accuracy. Low color temperatures emit warm or redder tones, while high color temperatures emit cool or blue tones. The low color temperatures (warm tones) generally are preferred for residential use as they are more flattering.

Some labels describe the color temperatures by numerical degrees. Cool color temperatures range between 3,800°- 5,000° Kelvin, while warm color temperatures generally are less than 3,500°Kelvin. For the best color rendition, pick lamps with a color temperature between 3,000° and 4,000° Kelvin.

CHOOSING THE CORRECT LAMP

Lamps with the same color temperature may have different CRIs and different efficiencies. The CRI of the fluorescent lamp is determined by the bulb's phosphor coating. Do not confuse color temperature with the CRI. Most package labels provide the color temperature but do not provide the lamp's CRI, and yet the CRI is the number you need to know to fine tune color rendition. The manufacturer or electrical supply outlet usually will have this information.

The following chart shows the variation in lamp temperature, color rendition and light output.

CHARACTERISTICS OF COMMON LAMPS (Sylvania)

Color Type	Lamp	Color Temp °K	CRI	Lumens	Watts	Lumens per Watt
Incandescent	A19, frosted, 25-watt	2,900		357	25	14
	A19, frosted, 40-watt	2,900		460	40	12
	A19, frosted, 60-watt	2,950		890	60	15
	A19, frosted, 75-watt	3,000		1,210	75	16
	A19, frosted, 100-watt	3,050		2,850	150	18
	12v quartz-halogen, 20-watt			300	19.4	15
	12v quartz-halogen, 45-watt	3,100		980	44.5	22
Fluorescent	Twin tube 27K	2,700	81	600	9	67
	Incandescent/ fluorescent	2,750	89	1,110	30	37
	Deluxe warm white	2,950	74	1,550	30	52
	Warm white	3,000	52	2,360	30	79
	Designer 3000K	3,000	67	3,300	40	83
	Royal white	3,000	80	2,400	30	80
	Octron 3100K	3,100	75	3,650	40	91
	White	3,450	57	1,900	30	63
	Octron 3500K	3,500	75	3,650	40	91
	Natural white	3,600	86	3,050	55	55
	Designer 4100K	4,100	67	8,800	95	93
	Octron 4100K	4,100	75	3,650	40	91
	Deluxe cool white	4,100	89	2,100	40	53
	Lite white	4,150	48	4,300	60	72
	Cool white	4,200	62	3,150	40	79
	Design 50	5,000	90	1,610	30	54
	Daylight	6,300	76	1,900	30	63

Source: Large Lamp Ordering Guide (Danvers, Mass: Sylvania Lighting Center, 1986)

REFLECTION AND COLOR

Reflection from walls and ceilings affects the overall lighting scheme in a bath. Choose paints carefully.

Semigloss paint reflects more light than flat paint and should be used sparingly because its reflectance will highlight imperfections in the surface of the wall. You can check the reflectance level of paint by obtaining a fan-deck sample from the paint company. The fan deck contains a chart that lists reflectance levels.

Kitchen task lighting recommendations usually assume that certain reflectance levels are present in a residential kitchen as discussed previously. Ceiling reflectance levels are higher than counters and cabinets because ceilings are frequently painted white.

If you are using dark, non-reflective surfaces, such as black matte counters, you should raise the light level to compensate for reduced reflectance.

Light colors, because of reflection, spread light throughout the room. Colors with shorter wave lengths (green, blue, and violet) create an impression of cold. In comparison, colors with longer wave lengths (yellow, orange and red) appear warm. A lighting source should render the color scheme at its best.

KITCHEN LIGHTING

Task Lighting

Our first concern in kitchen lighting is for specific tasks. The chart below lists task lighting recommendations made by the American Home Lighting Institute.

Incandescent, low-voltage strip lighting is also available for decorative accent or under cabinet task lighting. This light source produces a rich amber glow reminiscent of natural light from the sky just before sundown.

General Lighting

General room lighting can incorporate a single fluorescent or incandescent fixture, several recessed incandescent lights, or a fluorescent luminous ceiling. General lighting can be indirect, aimed to bounce off pale walls or ceiling and then into the room. Bouncing diffuses the light for even illumination over the entire area.

To ensure an even spread of light, carefully locate all fixtures based on light beam spread information available from the lamp and luminaire manufacturers. *For example*, use several two lamp fluorescent recessed fixtures spread through the room rather than one four lamp fixture.

KITCHEN LIGHTING GUIDELINES

Kitchen Areas	Fixture Placement	Incandescent Lamping	Fluorescent Lamping
Counter Lighting	Mount fluorescent fixtures under cabinets, as close to the front of the cabinet as possible. to the front of the cabinet as possible.		Tubes long enough to extend 2/3 length of counter; e.g., 36" 30"W or 48" 40"W
	Counters with no overhead cabinets: hang pendant 24" - 27" above the counter.	60-75W for every 20" of counter.	Same as above.
	OR		
	Recessed or surface mounted units: 16"- 24" apart, centered over the counter.	75W reflector lamp.	
At The Range	Built-in hood light.	60W bulb	
	With no hood, place recessed or surface mounted units 15" - 18" apart over the center of the range.	Minimum of two 75W reflector floods.	Two 36" 30W or three 24" 20W.
At The Sink	Same as for range.	Same as for range.	Same as for range.
Eating Area	Pendant centered 30" above table or counter; multiple pendants over counters 4' or longer.	One 100W, or two 60W or three 40W or 50/100/150W	

Accent Lighting

The last lighting concern for the kitchen designer is decorative lighting. It normally revolves around an eating area in the kitchen or a display area.

Kitchen Eating Area: The exact table location should be determined at the time of planning. It may not be in the center of a room, due to traffic patterns or to the presence of a buffet or hutch. When the designer is planning on reusing an existing light fixture location, it should be dimensioned quite clearly on the plan.

Moving a ceiling fixture may become extremely difficult in a two-story house where limited ceiling access prevails.

Dining area fixtures normally distribute light fairly evenly in all directions.

If your client needs task lighting at the table, as well as decorative lighting, a fixture featuring a down light might be ideal. Or consider adding a recessed light in the ceiling above the table. In a room with 8' ceilings, table lights are generally placed 25"-30" off the table surface. This dimension is increased by 3" for each additional foot in finished ceiling height. The fixture should be smaller than the table below it so that a seated diner will not hit their head as they raise from the table. To size the fixture according to the overall room dimensions, select a fixture which equals the horizontal length of the room in inches. *For example*, in a 15' long room, use a fixture with a 15" diameter.

Display Area: Accent lighting can also be installed to focus attention on a display area within the kitchen. Treasured objects can be dramatized by well designed lighting. Paintings, posters, and photographs, especially those under glass, are best lighted with adjustable units mounted 24"-30" from the wall (in a standard 8' ceiling) to minimize ceiling reflections.

Framing projectors allow the beam to be shuttered so that it can be the same size and shape as a painting, eliminating distracting light spill. Low- voltage units can deliver intense beams of light as small as 6" in width from a ceiling-mounted fixture.

Fixtures with adjustable lenses allow the beam to be made larger or smaller, a plus when artwork is changed frequently. Track lights with "barndoors" (derived from theater lighting), control spill light to enhance the dramatic effect of a lighted object and eliminate direct glare.

A general rule to remember is that light from straight in front of an object makes it appear flat. Light striking the object from one or both sides enhances its modeling and dimensionality.

Using different wattages or beam distributions on either side creates darker shadows on one side than the other, which may add to visual interest.

TRACK LIGHTING

ACCENT LIGHTING

For lighting objects on a wall, the wall itself, or any vertical surface, position the track and the fixtures as shown at right.

1. Generally, fixtures should be aimed at a 30° angle from the vertical to prevent light from shining in anyone's eyes and to avoid disturbing reflections on the surface of the object. Usually, one fixture is required for each object being accented.
2. Measure the distance ("B" to "C") from the ceiling to the center of the object. This is "distance" on chart as shown in the table.
3. Mount track at "location" ("A" to "B") from wall, on ceiling, as shown in the table.

(Example: The distance from the ceiling to the center of the painting is 4 ft. Mount the track on the ceiling 27" away from the wall.)

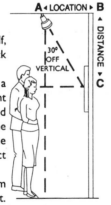

A to B	B to C
LOCATION	DISTANCE
IN INCHES	IN FEET
13"	2 Feet
20"	3 Feet
27"	4 Feet
34"	5 Feet
41"	6 Feet

ACCENT LIGHTING

Use the chart to select a bulb for the size of beam desired to accent the subject. Light levels range from 20 to 60 foot-candles at the center of the beam. Example: At 2 ft. mounting distance, a 50W "MR-16FL" bulb will cast an 8 ft. x 3 ft. beam.

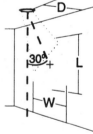

Distance fromWall(D)	Lamp Selection	Beam Length (L)	Beam Width (W)
2 Feet from Wall (8 ft. Ceiling)	50W PAR-36 WFL(12V)	5 ft.	2.5 ft.
	50W MR-16 FL (12V)	8 ft.	3 ft.
	75W R-30 SP	4.5 ft.	2 ft.
	75W R-30 FL	Wall Bottom	7 ft.
3 Feet from Wall (10 ft. Ceiling)	75W PAR-38 FL	5.5 ft.	2 ft.
	25W PAR-36 NSP(12V)	2 ft.	1 ft.
	50W MR-16 NSP (12V)	2 ft.	1.5 ft.
	50W MR-16 NFL (12V)	5.5 ft.	3 ft.
	75W PAR-38 SP	3 ft.	1.5 ft.

Lamps aimed 30° from vertical.
(L) & (W) indicate where candlepower drops 50% of maximum.

Figure 19 (Courtesy of American Lighting Association) Accent lighting details.

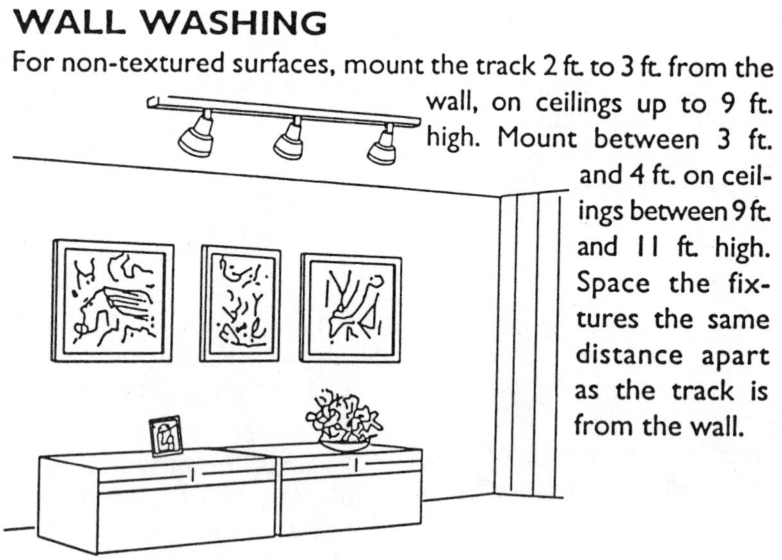

WALL WASHING

For non-textured surfaces, mount the track 2 ft. to 3 ft. from the wall, on ceilings up to 9 ft. high. Mount between 3 ft. and 4 ft. on ceilings between 9 ft. and 11 ft. high. Space the fixtures the same distance apart as the track is from the wall.

Figure 20 (Courtesy of American Lighting Association) How to wash a wall with light.

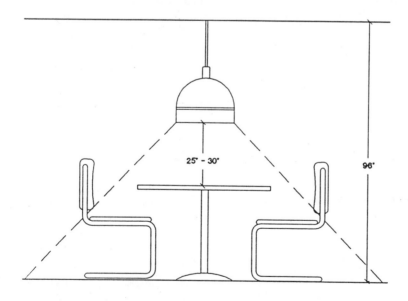

Figure 21 Table area accent lighting.

BRIGHTNESS RELATIONSHIPS

Understanding the types of light sources available, considering reflectance levels and following established lighting guides will still not guarantee a successful plan. The brightness relationship between these various light sources form the pattern of the system, and must be considered as well.

The human eye responds to the reflected light it receives. Extreme contrast between high and low areas of brightness can strain the eyes and slow the seeing process. *For example,* a kitchen with black fixtures and a white decorative laminate countertop would be a difficult kitchen to light effectively.

However, some contrast is essential if seeing is to be comfortable. While a soft diffused light minimizes shadows, it can be dull and unpleasant. The artful use of hard light will provide highlights that emphasize texture and shape. The challenge is to control reflected light for optimum effect.

When evaluating the brightness relationships in a kitchen design, consider the primary nature of the space and any secondary "modes" requested in the finished room. According to **Fran Kellogg Smith**, ASID, IALD, there are four types of modes associated with residential spaces:

- intellectual
- sensual
- escape
- productivity

Intellectual and productivity areas require high levels of "no-nonsense" lighting to make a hard job easier to accomplish. The working area of the kitchen and the home office/study area of a great room would fall into this category.

The dining area and gathering centers of the space may be more pleasant if a lighting contrast design creates a sensual environment that encourages the user to escape from the trivia of everyday life.

We should be familiar with the following terms used by lighting experts to describe brightness relationships:

- **Brightness** is the intensity of light from an object or surface that directly reaches the eye of the viewer.

- **Contrast** is the brightness difference between surfaces in the field of view. When little contrast exists, the light plan provides shadowless illumination. *For example,* indirect lighting plans which provide light through reflection (ambient illumination) eliminate any shadows within the space.

- **Glare** is the unwanted brightness that annoys, distracts or reduces visibility.

- **Sparkle or glitter** are the small areas of high brightness which are desirable to provide sensory stimulation. The interplay of light attracts the eye, alerts the mind and sparks life into the room. Often called a focal glow, the highlighted area can be an effective part of any plan.

To provide the proper brightness relationships in a residential kitchen, each different area should be divided into three zones.

- The **first zone** is the task area itself, such as the sink area.

- The **second zone** is the area immediately surrounding the task area.

- The **third zone** is the general surrounding space.

The light level relationship between these three areas is critical to prevent a brightness contrast that can be tiring.

For kitchen activities that require close attention, the lighting level in the **second zone** (the area adjacent to the counter) should be no greater than that in the **first zone** and no less than one-third of the level in the **first zone**. The **third zone** (the general surrounding space) should not exceed five times that in the **first zone** and be no less than one-fifth of the levels in the **first zone**.

SELECTING LIGHT FIXTURES

There are three major classifications of light fixtures available to the kitchen designer:

- Display fixtures

- Architectural fixtures

- Decorative fixtures

Display Fixtures

Track lighting is a popular type of display fixture. It was originally designed to illuminate and feature products in retail stores and works of art in museums. Today, this light source is used in contemporary and modern residential interiors. When track lighting is used, the selection of a fixture which throws light in all directions will overcome the undesirable down light pattern often associated with the system.

There are two types of tracks:

- Continuous open channel track

- Closed channel track.

Continuous channel track offers the most flexibility. Fixtures twist in anywhere along the track and can be readily changed if needed.

When lighting requirements are not apt to change and flexibility is not a prime concern, closed channel tracks offer a cleaning advantage. Grease and dirt cannot become trapped inside the track.

Both types of track are sold in various lengths and finishes. Track sections plug together easily, and can be cut to fit. With flexible connectors, they can be hooked together to form any shape or length. If track lighting will be used to illuminate a specific work surface, mount it directly above that surface. If track lighting will be used to feature objects on a wall, or to wash a wall with light, the track should be mounted two to three feet from the wall. When ceilings are higher than 9', move the track one foot further from the wall for every two additional feet of ceiling height. If track lighting will be used to illuminate an entire area, the fixtures must utilize open exposed lamps which will throw the light in all directions.

Architectural Fixtures

Architectural fixtures are unobtrusive systems which are built into the structure. The fixtures follow the architectural concept of *"form follows function"*. They are not used as a decorative touch, nor are they graced with applied ornamentation. They simply do their job of giving off light. This approach to lighting is an excellent one for the kitchen specialist.

Recessed lighting is a primary form of architectural lighting growing in popularity in homes across the country. It can provide general or ambient light, task light, or be used to accent objects.

Installed in the ceiling with only the trim showing, recessed lighting combines reflectors, baffles, diffusers, lenses and apertures to direct light downward, shield the light source, and avoid glare. It is unobtrusive and does not conflict with any other decorative element.

Besides recessed lighting, architectural lighting includes lighted cornices, valances, coves, canopies, soffits and wall brackets. It also includes luminous ceilings (for kitchens and baths) and lighted wall panels in other areas.

- **Lighted Valances:** A lighted valance above a window provides both up-light, which reflects off the ceiling for overall lighting in a room, and down-light which accents the window treatment and

vividly highlights their color and texture. Lighted valances should not be mounted closer to the ceiling than 10" to avoid annoying ceiling brightness.

- **Lighted Cornices:** Lighted cornices direct all light downward and give dramatic emphasis to wall coverings, especially those with textured surfaces. They may also be used over windows where space above the window doesn't accommodate valance lighting. Cornice lighting is especially good in rooms with low ceilings.

- **Lighted Soffit/Fascia:** A lighted soffit can provide both effective light and add a decorative touch to a room. Recessed fixtures in the soffit are often used over a sink in the kitchen. They provide a high level of light for performing tasks. Polished reflectors can double the light output. Install louvers or light diffusing glass or plastic in the bottom opening for softer light.

- **Wall Brackets:** Lighted wall brackets, mounted either high or low on a wall, can supply general room lighting. The mounting height is generally determined by window or door height.

Lighted, low wall brackets can be used for special wall emphasis. A low fluorescent wall bracket can also be used to light a kitchen desk for studying, freeing the top surface for books and other paraphernalia. The wall bracket should be fitted with a 30-watt or 40-watt tube, mounted 15 to 18 inches above the desk's surface, on a side wall, and positioned 12" back from the front edge of the desk.

- **Cove Lighting:** Cove lighting is indirect; it flows upward and bounces off the ceiling. Both the cove and the ceiling should be painted flat white or a near-white, natural color. Cove lighting is best used when combined with additional light sources in the room.

- **Recessed Lighting:** Many kitchen designers are partial to recessed incandescent fixtures. Their flush installation allows the light source to become almost invisible. An excellent effect when one considers that light was made to see by, not to look at.

Yet, incandescent recessed fixtures have a serious energy consumption drawback. Because light from one is only directed downward, the wattage and number of fixtures needed per square foot of floor space will be more than the number of surface mounted or suspended fixtures. General illumination in a kitchen using recessed incandescent fixtures calls for three watts per square foot, rather than the normal two. A secondary requirement calls for a floor with a reflectance value of 25% or higher.

When utilizing recessed incandescent fixtures for task lighting, a spacing of 15" to 24" on center is recommended to insure an adequate light spread on the counter surface 48" to 60" away. To determine the exact distance between the fixtures, the designer must consult the illumination data supplied by manufacturers of recessed incandescent fixtures.

Recessed lights also produce a great deal of heat in the attic. The **National Electrical Code** requires that other than the points of support (such as a joist) the sides of the fixture must be at least 1/2" from all combustible materials, and that all insulation must be kept at least 3" away from the fixture.

Additionally, the plan must allow for a constant flow of air around the fixture enclosure. Because of the heat generated (5.31 BTU's per watt), downlight fixtures should never be placed directly above the heads of seated persons. They should be placed 24" away from the table or countertop edge.

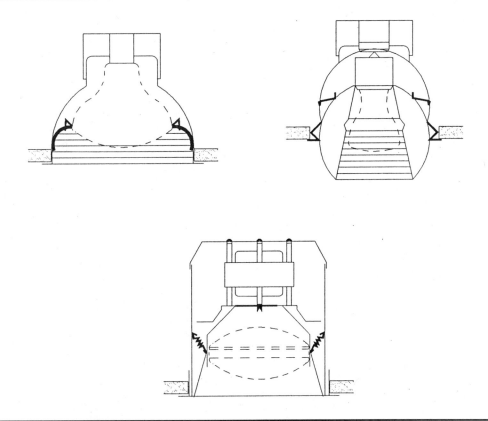

Figure 22 In the upper left-hand corner a step-baffle. In the upper right-hand corner, an eyeball with baffle. Next, a cut-away wall-wash with Alzak column with clear finish trim.

Figure 23 A small L-shaped kitchen is enhanced by a hanging pendant over the island.

LIGHTING TIPS FROM THE PROS

- Tell your client not to worry if a halogen lamp "smokes" at first: it's only the protective coating burning off. Remind the client never to touch the halogen bulb with bare fingers; their skin's oil will weaken the lamp, and it will burn a finger badly.

- Older eyes need more light to see by than young eyes. Mature people also see more amber light than blue light, and slight contrasts in color are harder to distinguish. Increasing the lumen output of the lighting system, and providing rheostat dimming controls will allow users of various ages to be comfortable in the space. Using sharp, strong color contrasts rather than subtle ones to define areas to help the elderly person use the space.

- Don't use under cabinet fluorescent or incandescent task lighting systems with highly polished countertop surfaces or mirrored backsplash designs, unless the client understands that the lighting hardware will be reflected in the splash or countertop material.

- Don't place under-cabinet task lighting system that have plastic diffusers above built-in backsplash appliances that produce heat. *For example,* the heat generated from the built-in toaster will warp a plastic diffuser.

- Jobsite installed under-cabinet lighting systems are not attractive enough to be fully exposed under short peninsula type wall cabinets. Plan on creating a totally concealed light panel in this type of installation. And, get the cost for such custom work in your project estimate.

- Make sure the client understands that fluorescent and incandescent under-cabinet task lighting systems do generate heat. Therefore, the wall cabinet bottom shelf will be warm to the hand if the lighting system is left on for extended periods of time.

- A pot rack above an island may look perfect in your perspective drawing, but can play havoc with an illumination system installed above the rack. Shadows created on the work surface by pots, pans and other paraphernalia hanging below the lights will be annoying.

- Don't try to combine a recessed light fixture which features a diffuser design which extends below the fixture ceiling cover edge and a frameless, full-overlay cabinet system which extends to the ceiling. The cabinet doors may hit the lamp or diffuser. If such a combination is selected, specify a trim molding to separate the wall cabinet from the ceiling fixture profile.

Just as air conditioning gives us physical comfort regardless of the season, light conditioning makes a home a satisfying environment to live in, irrespective of the sun. The kitchen specialist's responsibility for planning a functional lighting system is as impor-

tant as planning time saving storage and easy to maintain surfaces.

Following are some fine examples of kitchens featuring well-planned lighting systems.

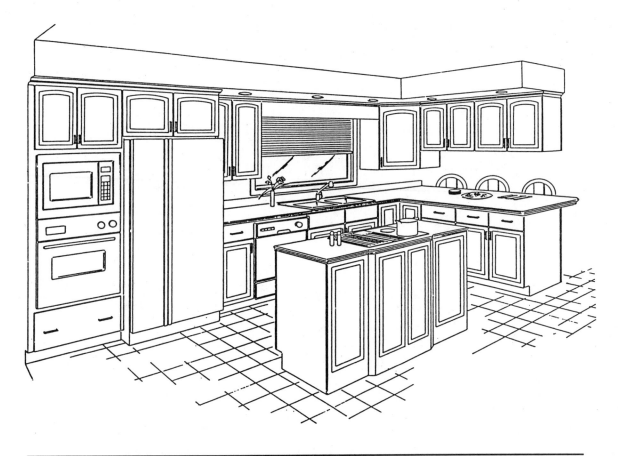

Figure 24 An extended soffit features recessed incandescent light fixtures to provide task lighting in the space.

Figure 25 In this small kitchen, a surface-mounted 2x4 fluorescent fixture provides general illumination.

Figure 26 *In this kitchen track lights are mounted on the beam to provide general illumination.*

Figure 27 Recessed incandescent fixtures are strategically placed in the ceiling, above cabinets that extend to full height wall cabinets, to provide illumination.

Figure 28 In this traditional kitchen, a coffered ceiling incorporates a fluorescent indirect lighting system. The circular room is then further accented by recessed fixtures in the ceiling. Task lighting is included in the form of under-cabinet lighting.

Figure 29 Recessed lighting provides general lighting, while under-cabinet task lighting highlights the decorative backsplash.

Figure 30 A track light provides light above the sink.

SECTION **3**

Ventilation

The kitchen is the major source of pollution in the home today. Grease, smoke, undesirable odors, moisture and some toxic emissions from gas ranges can linger in a room that is poorly ventilated.

Most homeowners wouldn't think of lighting a fireplace without first opening the flue, however they aren't nearly as concerned about planning a kitchen with an ineffective ventilation system. Professional designers must help the consumer understand how important ventilation is.

A well-planned, correctly installed mechanical ventilation system can remove odors, smoke, excess heat and moisture.

MECHANICAL VENTILATION OPTIONS

The **Cold Climate House Center**, part of the Minnesota Extension Service, completed a research project on residential kitchen ventilation. This project was spearheaded by **Wanda Olson**, a leading researcher in residential kitchen design. In her findings, Professor Olson classified mechanical kitchen ventilation options as follows.

- **Kitchen Ceiling Exhaust:** In this type of exhaust system, cooking contaminants are removed after they have mixed with the air in the kitchen. Ceiling exhaust systems were common in the 1950s and 1960s. However, in many of these houses, the duct extended only to the attic area rather than to the outdoors. This is not recommended because of moisture and grease brought to and then left in the attic.

- **Whole-House Mechanical Ventilation:** Typically, in many exhaust systems, cooking contaminants are allowed to mix with the air in the rest of the house before the contaminants are removed. An example of this would be a furnace with exhaust and outdoor makeup air features. If the whole-house system has an exhaust register in the ceiling or soffit area of the kitchen, it should be located away from the range to eliminate excessive grease accumulation. The cooking contaminants are mixed with the air in the kitchen area before being removed. This is true of many heat recovery ventilator (HRV) installations.

- **Kitchen Range Ventilation:** In this type of system, cooking contaminants are captured near the source. Both recirculating and exhaust systems are commonly referred to as "*range ventilation systems*".

A recirculating system is a filtration system and not a ventilation system; the air captured by the unit is forced through filters that remove smoke, odors and grease. Typically, these units are range hoods; a few models are an integral part of a range or cooktop. The air still containing contaminants, such as water vapor, is recirculated into the kitchen space. Maintenance of the filters is critical to the effectiveness of this type of system; typically, a metal mesh screen collects grease particles, a glass fiber filter removes smoke, and a charcoal filter is used to remove odors. Recirculating systems are less effective in removing grease, smoke and odors than exhaust systems. Recirculating systems should not be used with a gas range because they do not remove combustion gases.

In an **exhaust system**, the air captured by the ventilation unit is exhausted to the outdoors (not an attic space). The air containing water vapor, grease, smoke, odors, and also combustion gases when cooking with gas is also exhausted and prevented from mixing with the air in the rest of the house. This results in cleaner surfaces and an improved air quality in the entire home.

Type of Kitchen Range Exhaust Systems: Kitchen range exhaust systems are either hoods located directly over the cooking surface or grill openings located at the cooking surface of downdraft units. Hoods are installed over ranges or cooktops and are wall-mounted, installed over an island, or are an integral part of a microwave appliance.

A few two-oven ranges have a ventilation hood mounted on top of the upper oven. Downdraft systems are usually an integral part of a range or cooktop and may have a center vent, side vent(s) or a rear vent.

A few downdraft systems are separate units and are installed adjacent (either to the side or to the rear) to a range or cooktop. Most downdraft systems are flush with the cooking surface, while some models with rear vents are in a raised position during use.

Some typical airflow rates of range exhaust systems are listed below. The rates shown are from a manufacturer's specification sheet. The actual airflow when installed may be lower because of losses that occur in ducting.

TYPICAL AIRFLOW RATES OF RANGE EXHAUST SYSTEMS	
Range Hood	150-600CFM
Island Hood	400-600CFM
Microwave Hood	200-400CFM
Downdraft Unit	300-500CFM

PHYSICAL PROPERTIES OF AIR MOVEMENT

To design an efficient system, designers must first understand the physical principles behind air movement:

- Air naturally circulates in currents within a given area.

- Hot air is lighter than cold air. It will rise within a room, pushing cold air down.

- Water vaporizes into steam when heated. As it cools, the water will condense back into a liquid form.

- Grease particles become airborne under extreme heat. They condense into solid droplets as they cool.

SURVEYING AN EXISTING VENTILATION SYSTEM

For proper remodeling project estimating you must determine the following:

- *Is there an existing hood or fan?*

- *Is it vented through the roof or wall?* (Go outside and look for the roof-jack or wall cap near the kitchen window area.)

- *What course will the new duct run follow? How long? How many turns?*

- *What type of cooking equipment will be used?*

REPLACEMENT AIR CONSIDERATIONS FOR A HOME UNDER CONSTRUCTION

Recent improvements in building methods have led to air-tight houses. This type of structure adds new areas of concern for the residential ventilation planner.

Exhausting air from the house lowers the air pressure inside the home. This depressurization depends on the tightness of the house and the total flow rate of the exhausted air. A relatively small amount of house depressurization may be large enough to overcome the natural draft of a furnace and/or water heater chimney and reverse the flow of combustion gases in the chimney. This condition is called back drafting and can lead to a potentially hazardous situation when toxic gases, such as carbon monoxide, are not exhausted to the outdoors.

Another potential problem caused by house depressurization is soil gas infiltration. The soil gas which has recently received the most attention is radon. If radon is present in the soil around the house, the lower pressure inside the house may cause the radon gas to migrate into the house.

If depressurization is a concern because of the air tightness of the house, the user should open a window whenever the kitchen range exhaust system is used. Preferably, a supply fan should be installed to force air into the house in order to prevent depressurization when the kitchen range exhaust system is used.

Changing the space and water heating appliances to sealed combustion, powered draft, or to electric, would eliminate the potential for back drafting of naturally vented furnaces and water heaters as well.

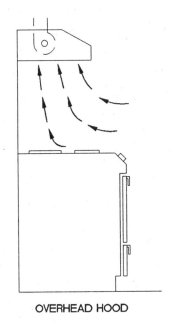

OVERHEAD HOOD

PROXIMITY VENTILATION

Figure 31 (Courtesy of University of Minnesota) Recommended Methods of Kitchen Ventilation: Air velocity below a range exhaust hood. The arrow length is proportional to the velocity magnitude. Air velocity over a range exhaust downdraft unit. The arrow length is proportional to the velocity magnitude.

MECHANICAL VENTILATION SYSTEM DESIGN

Canopy Design

The hood is designed to catch and hold the contaminants while the fan removes them.

Many consumers question the interior openness of a hood from a cleaning stand-point. Yet, this very aspect of the design is the key to successful air removal. As cooking by-products rise naturally from the surface, they will be caught in the hood and remain there. Note the words rise naturally.

The old story about the fan pulling from the cooking surface is incorrect. These vapors must rise naturally and get close to the fan, before it can go to work.

- **Depth:** The depth of the hood's holding area determines its distance from the cooking surface. A hood 16" to 21" deep should be 24" off the surface (60" off the floor). A 24" deep hood can be 30" off the surface (66" off the floor). 30" is the maximum distance between hood and cooking surface in any installation.

The hood's width also affects the holding capacity. Many codes allow a 30" hood above a 30" range. It is much more desirable to have the hood extend 3" past the range on each side. A 30" range should be paired with a 36" hood.

CFM Ratings

The air movement capacity from a ventilation system is measured either in the cubic feet of air per minute that is moved through a mechanical exhaust system, or the number of air changes that occur in the entire room per hour.

ASHRE (**American Society of Heating, Refrigerating and Air Conditioning Engineers**) recommends that a kitchen area be serviced by windows or by a kitchen exhaust system with a minimum air flow capacity of 100 cubic feet per minute (CFM) or by a continuous low flow exhaust system of 25 CFM. The recommendation for the entire house is 0.35 air changes per hour (ACH), but not less than 15 CFM per occupant, whichever is less.

The NKBA recommends the following air flow ratings for ventilation systems:

- **Hood against a wall installation:** 50 to 70 CFM x the area of the hood in square feet (300 CFM minimum).

- **Hood with no back wall:** 100 CFM x the area of the hood in square feet (600 CFM minimum).

- **Open grill or barbecue area with or without wall:** 100 to 150 CFM x the area of the hood in square feet (600 CFM minimum).

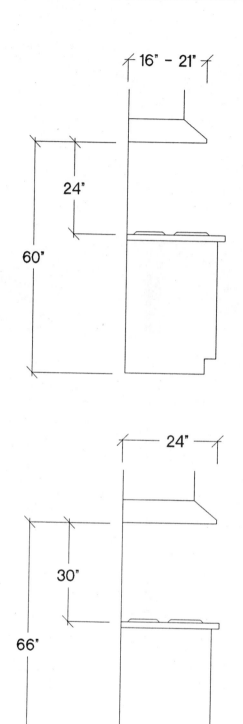

Figure 32 Recommended hood backsplash height.

Figure 33 (Courtesy of Allmilmo) A custom hood is placed above a cooking surface. The overall size of the hood and its distance from the cooktop affects its efficiency.

Figure 34 (Courtesy of Jenn-Air Corporation) A downdraft proximity system is ideal for grill type cooking.

Figure 35 (Courtesy of KitchenAid, Inc.) Downdraft ventilation systems allow the primary cooktop or a secondary unit to be placed within the kitchen without the obstruction of an overhead hood.

Figure 36 (Courtesy of Jenn-Air Corporation) A microwave oven and hood may be combined. This saves a great deal of space in a small kitchen. However, it does not provide the most efficient ventilation system.

Figure 37 (Courtesy of Wood-Mode Cabinetry) Some "slim line" hoods are available today. They are attractive in contemporary kitchens. The efficiency of the ventilation system must be verified.

Hood Motor Choices

In either a hood fan assembly or a simple fan unit, several different types of motors are available. A propeller fan has a stamped disk with three or more blades moving the air. This system has limited air capacity and a high vibration rate. Axial fan and improved air flow fans allow air to flow through an impeller mounted within a close fitting tube. Better air movement is present, but the noise factor is still a problem. The centrifugal blower offers the most effective exhaust system with a minimum noise level. A revolving wheel forces air to flow radially through the impeller mounted within squirrel cage housing.

CONSIDERATIONS FOR SELECTING AND INSTALLING EXHAUST SYSTEMS

In the same previously mentioned **University of Minnesota** survey, Professor Olson suggested the following considerations when selecting and installing an exhaust system.

The choice of a kitchen range exhaust system is often based on kitchen arrangement and fan noise. Consideration should also be given to the type of cooking load and the need for outdoor air to replace the air exhausted by the appliance.

Kitchen Arrangement

Capturing contaminants at their source is critical when the cooking area opens directly onto the general living space. A cooking area in an island uses an island hood or a downdraft unit, with a high CFM rating higher than specified for a cooking area along a wall. The latter can be either a standard hood or one

integrated into a microwave appliance.

Sound Level of the System

Noise is a common objection to operating kitchen exhaust systems. Some manufacturers list the sound level (in sones) on their specification sheets. Many people use the low settings on the better engineered exhaust systems because they are quieter or they select a model that allows for a remote installation of the fan. The **Home Ventilating Institute** has set a limit of 9.0 sones for kitchen fans up to a 500 CFM capacity. When comparing ratings, a fan with a sone rating of 4.0 is twice as loud as a fan with a rating of 2.0. Refrigerators commonly operate at about 1.0 sone; a few range hoods operate as low as 2.5 sones.

Type of Food Load

To capture the contaminants from extensive grilling, frying or cooking of uncovered liquids, the following requirements must be met.

* Select a hood that extends over most of the cooking area or select a downdraft system. If tall pans are used extensively, such as in large quantity cooking or canning, select a downdraft with a raised vent. A hood is the recommended option for this type of specialty cooking.

* Select a range exhaust system with an airflow rate of 250 CFM or above. In general, the higher the flow rate, the better the capture of contaminants. However, adequate outdoor air must be pro-

vided to assure proper operation of the exhaust system.

ENGINEERING THE DUCT WORK

A good hood, properly installed, is only half of an effective system. Our concern with cubic feet of air moved per minute centers on the air movement at the exit termination point of the system (static air pressure), not at the hood canopy on the inside (free air pressure). Generally, designers can deduct 1/3 of the canopy's CFM rating for a 21' duct run to the exterior with one elbow turn.

The resistance created by long, angled ductwork can render the system inoperable. The shortest, straightest route is best. Never restrict the ductwork in any way. Always terminate the system at the house exterior with the proper cap or jack. Make sure that all connections are tight and correctly taped with pressure sensitive tape that will last after the walls are enclosed.

When computing the overall length of the ductwork, individual fittings used in the system must be counted as a specific length. When planning vents in the ductwork, avoid any curves. An "*eddy*" will be created and the air will bounce back and forth. For the same reason, avoid 90° angles in ductwork, 45° angles will provide the best air movement.

General code requirements for proper system ducting are as follows:

- **All ducts** shall be galvanized steel of not less than 28 gauge.

- **Flexible dryer duct** is not an acceptable ducting material.

- All the **seams** in the duct system shall be tight. Pressure-sensitive tape or other methods approved by the administrative code authority can be used to seal seams.

- **Backdraft dampers** shall be provided near the outlet of the duct. These shall be in the closed position when the fan is not operating.

- A 1/2-inch **mesh screen** shall be installed at each exhaust outlet.

- **Fans and duct systems** shall be designed to permit cleaning and servicing.

- Whenever a **duct or fan scroll** lies within 6 inches of a combustible material, it shall be insulated with 1/2-inch glass fiber insulation or the equivalent.

- When a kitchen range hood faces a **combustible material** less than 30 inches above the cooking surface, the hood shall be separated from the combustible material by the appropriate thermal insulation.

- Ducts passing through **unheated spaces** shall be insulated with a minimum of 1 inch of glass fiber insulation or equivalent.

- Ducts located in a **heated space** shall be insulated with 1 inch of glass fiber insulation or equivalent for a distance of 3 feet from the duct outlet.

Duct work run length and configurations vary greatly depending on the manufacturer. An example of one manufacturers' recommendations for duct lengths are as follows.

- Duct runs should be kept as short and straight as possible to maintain a high volume of air movement. Maximum equivalent lengths of duct for vent systems are:

Interior Power: 6" round or 3 1/4" x 10" rectangular, 25' maximum run.

Exterior Power: 9" round or 3 1/4" x 14" rectangular, 55' maximum run.

To insure your installation falls within the maximum length, add the equivalent length in feet of each fitting used in the system to the length in feet of straight duct used. If your total is equal to or less than the maximum shown for your duct size, your installation is proper.

Index of Recommended Standard Fittings

6″ Systems: Equivalent length of 6″ Duct

3¼″ × 10″ Systems: Equivalent length of 3¼″ × 10″ Duct

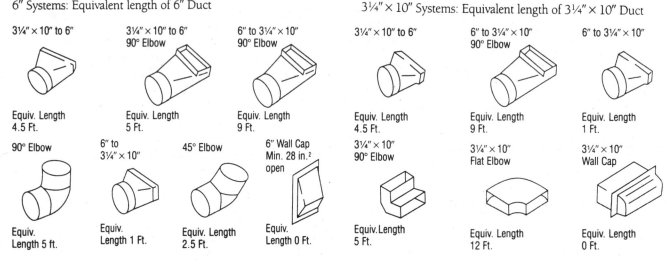

Use 6″ or 3¼″ × 10″ duct on island or peninsula installations.
For best performance, it is suggested that no more than three 90° elbows with 6″ or 3¼″ × 10″ duct be used.

Figure 38 (Courtesy of Kitchen Aide)   Ductwork calculations.

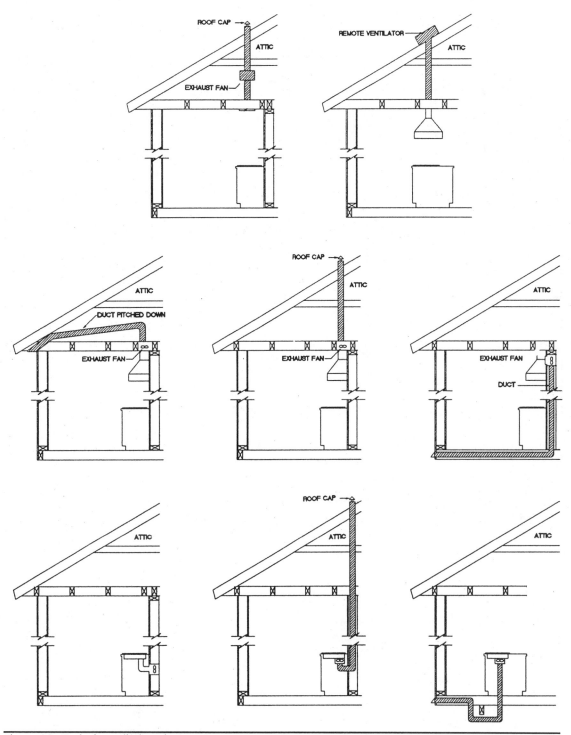

Figure 39 Typical ventilation duct routes.

TYPICAL DUCTWORK PARTS

Duct usually is galvanized steel or aluminum in various sizes and shapes. Popular round sizes are 3" (7cm), 4" (10cm), 6" (15cm), 7" (18cm) and 10" (25cm); rectangular, 3 1/4" x 10" or 12" (8cm x 25cm or 30cm).

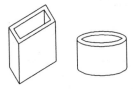

Roof cap or jack is an outside fitting for vertical duct. Pressure-activated damper opens when fan is operating, closes when it stops. Wall cap is an outside fitting for horizontal duct, in slanted shield or flush-mount versions.

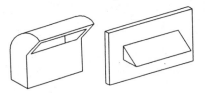

Elbows change the direction of air.

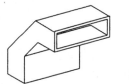

Transition duct is for connecting round to rectangular duct, such as when duct must travel inside wall between studs.

TIPS FROM THE PROS

Match the Product to the Job

- **Good:** Hood with approximately 150 CFM (cubic feet per minute of air removal rating), on/off switch and light. Some are designed to be vented to the house exterior, some are considered "recirculating" models.

- **Better:** Overhead hoods with 300 to 600 CFM ratings. Quiet blower systems, light and multiple speed (or switch) control. If vented to the exterior of the house properly, an effective ventilation system.

- **Best:** Overhead fan systems with remote mounted motors on an exterior wall or roof. Noise level is low, efficiency is high. Separate proximity ventilation (downdraft) ventilation systems that are part of or can be added to cooking surfaces. Some units have an open grill that separates burners, others are designed to stretch along the back of the cooktop. To ensure the effectiveness of this system, the duct work should be as short and straight as possible.

Installation Score Sheet

- Length of duct path from ventilation system to exterior termination point._____

- Number of elbow turns along duct path._____

- Ventilating unit's (free air pressure) CFM rating._____

- Exit (static air pressure) CFM rating estimate._____

- Hood depth in relation to adjacent cabinetry. _____

- Hood distance from cooking surface. _____

- Hood width in relationship to cooking surface width below.

  _____

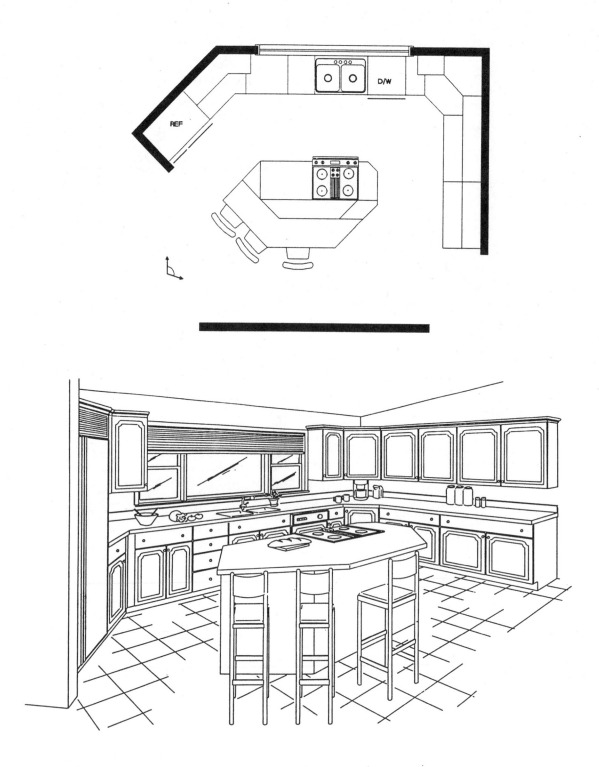

Figure 40 The downdraft cooktop is located on the center angled island in this plan. The proximity ventilation system eliminates the overhead hood.

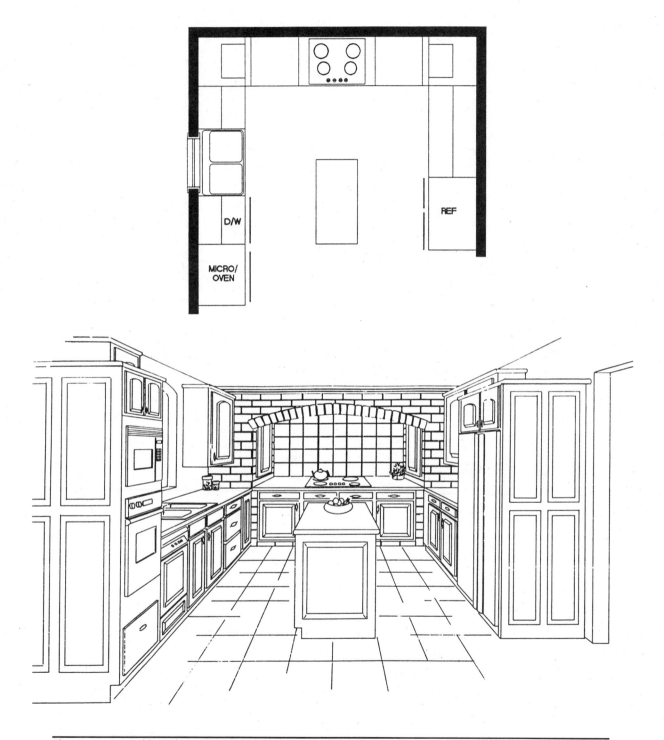

Figure 41 A cooking alcove is created at the end of this country kitchen. An overhead ceiling fan is installed above the cooking surface and is concealed behind the brick work.

SECTION **4**

Plumbing

Successful kitchen designers understand how important it is to be familar with the plumbing system.

Knowing what parts of the plumbing system are buried beneath the floor, hidden in the attic or within the walls will help you design and price your job competitively.

Today, almost one-quarter of all kitchens have two sinks. Many refrigerators feature an icemaker that requires a water line connection. Dishwashers are standard and many sinks have a water purification or water treatment attachment connected to them.

This information is important because today's kitchen is much more than a simple sink and a wall-mounted faucet.

To be able to plan functional spaces that work well for the busy cook, familiarity with the plumbing system is a must.

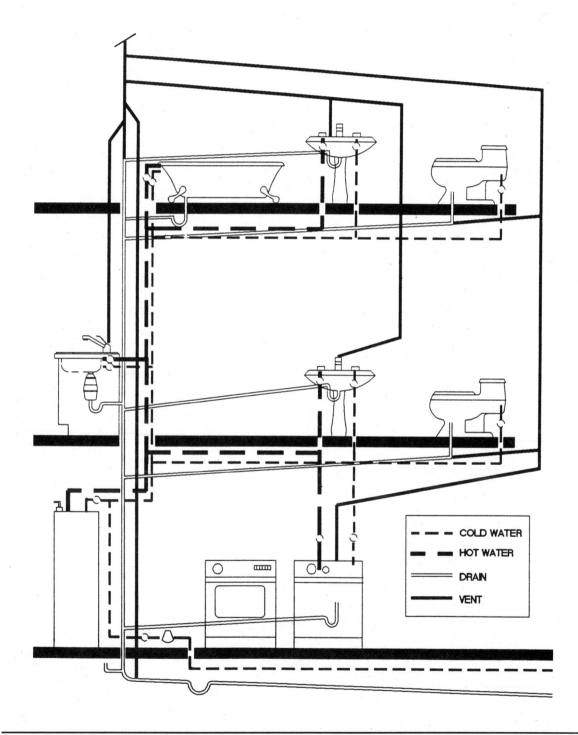

Figure 42 Typical Residential Plumbing System - The home's plumbing system is made up of plumbing lines to deliver water and drain/waste/vent lines that take wastewater away.

CODES AND REGULATIONS

As mentioned in the first volume of these Technical Manuals, building codes vary from community to community. The most widely used plumbing code is the **Uniform Plumbing Code**, a model code written by IAPMO (International Association of Plumbing and Mechanical Officials). However, model codes are also produced by ASME (the American Society of Mechanical Engineers), BOCA (Building Official and Code Administrators), whose code is called the **Basic Plumbing Code**, the SBCCI (Southern Building Code Congress International), producers of the **Southern Standard Plumbing**

Code, and the PHCC (National Association of Plumbing Heating Cooling Contractors), the **National Plumbing Code**.

Major cities such as Chicagohave their own plumbing codes. The CABO (Council of American Building Officials), **One and Two Family Dwelling Code** bases its plumbing code provisions on three other model codes - BOCA, SBCCI and ICBO (International Conference of Building Officials), but IAPMO does not participate in the CABO code. A local government could use parts of the CABO code having to do with structures, but use the IAPMO code for plumbing.

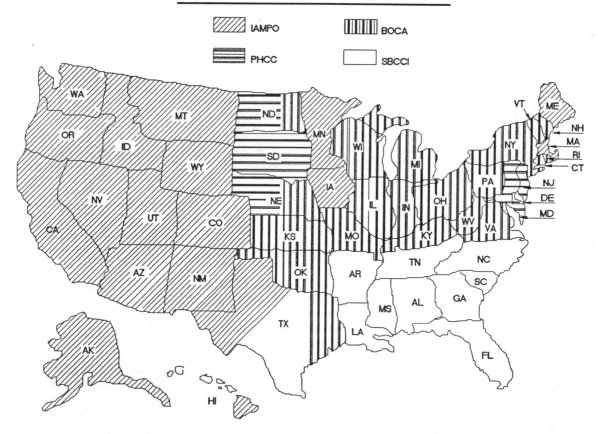

Figure 43 Plumbing codes have been created by many model code bodies. Here are the general geographic regions covered by four of the major codes.

Typical Areas of Difference

Plumbing codes are more similar than they are different. All are designed to ensure a safe and functional plumbing system. Each provides regulations to make sure that plumbing odors will be vented to the outdoors and that the fixtures will have an adequate water pressure. The codes can be very different in the details, however.

The plumbing inspector will be knowledgeable about local code requirements, such as those that might limit the use of plastic pipe or that might require water supply lines of a certain size.

Understanding the plumbing system will help you avoid unnecessary costs. Installing plumbing in new construction or changing fixtures in existing construction can be done economically - if you understand how the pieces of the plumbing system go together. The easiest way to think of the plumbing system is to visualize two different parts:

- The water **supply system**, which carries water from the municipal water system or well into the house and around to fixtures and appliances;

- The **drain/waste/vent system**, (DWV), which carries wastewater and sewer gases out of the house.

To understand the function of each part of the plumbing network, it is easiest to separate each part by its function.

WATER SUPPLY SYSTEM

Water enters the house through a main supply pipe connected to a water utility main or to a well. If the house is served by a utility, the water arrives through a main pipe which will vary according to demand. If the water comes from a private well, it is also carried to the house via a pipe, which is connected to a pump that moves the water through the system. Where the water supply enters the house, you will find a shutoff valve. This main shutoff valve cuts off the water supply to the whole house.

The supply main delivers the water into two sets of pipes called **supply branches**. One branch goes to the water heater. The other is a cold water branch.

The supply branches run horizontally through the floor joists or concrete slab. Where the supply branches run vertically in the wall to an upper story, they are called **supply risers**. In a two- story house, more branch lines could be found in the second-floor joists. In some houses, branch lines are found in the attic.

At the termination of each hot and cold water line, a **tee** (a T-shaped pipe) sticks out of the wall. A shutoff valve is attached to the tee and allows water to be cut off from just one fixture. Repairs can be made without cutting off the water supply to the entire house. Every fixture should have shutoff valves. Supply tubing is used to connect the shutoff valve to the fixture.

Water Pressure

Water coming into the house is under pressure. On municipal water systems, pressures of 50 to 60 pounds per square inch (psi) are common. The pressure should not be lower than 30 psi or higher than 80 psi. Pressure can be affected by the number of outlets being served (and how often they are used at the same time), the distance the piping must travel to those outlets, the number of turns in the piping and other variables.

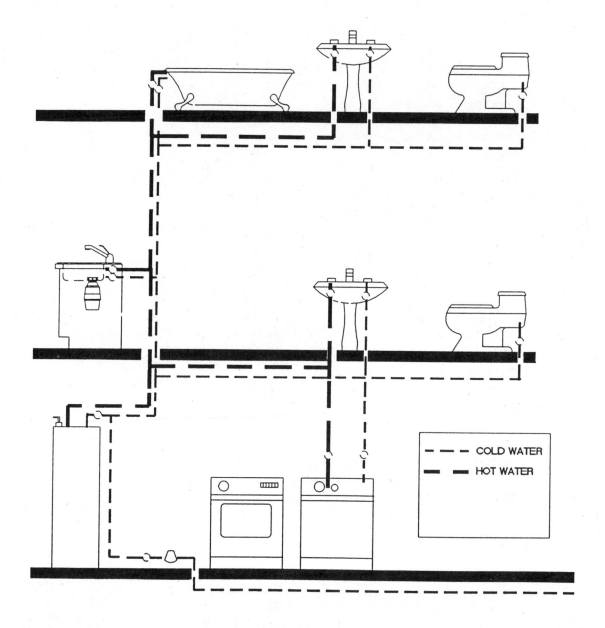

Figure 44 A schematic diagram shows a simplified version of the water supply side of the plumbing system.

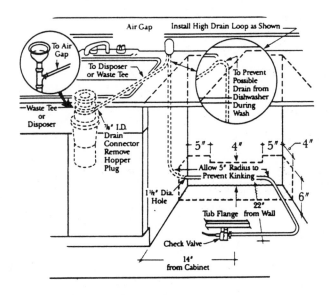

Figure 45 A dishwasher is plumbed through the food waste disposer with an air gap overflow protection.

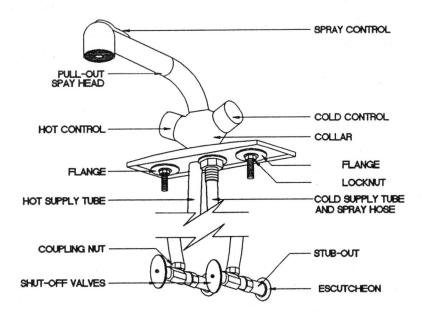

Figure 46 A close-up view of the kitchen sink plumbing.

EXTERNAL USAGE DEMANDS

A drop in pressure can be created by low pressure of the water entering the house. For instance, if a community waters its lawns at 5:00 p.m. every night, the pressure drop would be felt by anyone taking a shower. Cities in drought areas might also have inadequate water pressure.

FIXTURE DISTANCE FROM THE MAIN

Pressure drop can also occur when a fixture is too far from the water main and when the fixture requires a high volume of water.

PIPING CONFIGURATION

A pipe run with many turns and bends will reduce the available water pressure.

Water Velocity

CORROSION IN THE PIPES

Corrosion or scale that builds up on the inside of water supply lines will decrease water velocity. This is most common in hot water lines of galvanized pipe. The problem can be severe in hard water areas.

PIPE SIZE

Pipe size also limits velocity. The normal size of pipe from the city water lines to the house is 1" in diameter. However, in older houses you might find a pipe size of only 5/8" to 3/4". The plumbing lines in a house become smaller the closer they are to the fixture. The 1" main drops to 3/4" branch lines. The lines supplying individual fixtures are smaller yet - 1/2".

Supply Pipe Materials

The plumbing code in your area will spell out which materials can be used for supply pipe. The plumbing contractor will normally decide which type of supply pipe to use. Copper is generally considered to be the most durable supply pipe. However, in agricultural areas where nitrate levels in the drinking water are relatively high, copper can corrode. Galvanized pipe gives better performance in these cases.

The following chart shows the most common types of pipe materials as well as their advantages and disadvantages.

SUPPLY PIPE MATERIALS

MATERIAL	PROS	CONS
Copper Pipe	Lightweight	Not good with very hard or very soft water
	Easy to assemble	Joints can be damaged by water hammer
	Corrosion resistant with most water supplies	Damaged if frozen
Copper Tubing (flexible)	Easy to use in cramped spaces	Pipe walls become thinner if frozen
	Bends easily around corners	Same cautions as above
	Can use flare fittings which can be disassembled	Only used in concrete slabs
	Can withstand a few freeze/thaw cycles	
Galvanized Pipe	Strong & resistant to water hammer	Time consuming to install
	Good for alkaline water	Corroded by soft water
		Scale can reduce inside pipe diameter
CPVC (Chlorinated Polyvinyl Chloride)	Lightweight	Must have support clamps 3' on center
	Can be used for hot or cold	Keep away from heat ducts & flues
	Resists damage from freezing	
Polyethylene (PE)	Can be used for supply main from well to house	Cannot be used for hot water lines
	Low working temperature (-67°F to 112°F)	
	Used in ground; even at low temperatures	
	Will not corrode	

Protecting Pipes from Freezing: In parts of the country with severe winter temperatures, protecting pipes from freezing is a major concern. Because pipes will be enclosed in walls, they will get colder than room temperature. Here are some things you can do to keep pipes from freezing:

- Place fixtures so that supply pipes are placed in inside walls.

- Make sure the walls of the crawl space or basement are insulated and foundation vents blocked during winter.

- Place insulation on top of any supply lines in attics.

Preventing Water Hammer: A washing machine or kitchen sink valve that turns the water supply off quickly can send a shock wave through the supply system. This shock wave is called water hammer because it sounds like a hammer banging on the pipes.

Water hammer is easy to prevent. Coiled air chambers can be attached to the supply pipes at each fixture. The air chamber allows room for the initial surge of water when the fixture closes down.

The plumbing contractor can also provide water hammer protection by extending the supply line 24" above the tee. The extension will normally be filled with air, except when the valve sends a surge of water through the pipe.

Supply Pipe Compatibility: If a plumbing system has already been remodeled, you may see two different kinds of supply pipe used. Copper pipe may be joined to galvanized pipe. These two pipe materials react chemically with each other and cause corrosion.

A **dielectric union** should be used to join these two pipe materials. A dielectric union does not react with either of the metals and will prevent corrosive buildup on the inside of the pipes around the transition.

Recommended Pipe Sizes

House Main	1"
House Service	3/4"
Supply Riser	3/4"
Kitchen Sink	1/2"
Ice Maker	1/4"
Dishwasher	3/8"
Clothes Washer	1/2"

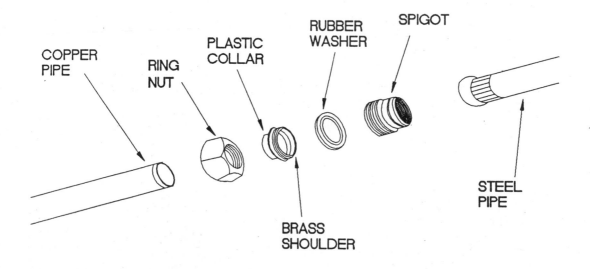

Figure 47 Dielectric unions should always be used when joining galvanized steel to copper pipe. The plastic collar and rubber washer separate the two metals and prevent corrosion.

Access for Repair: If a home is built on a crawl space, it may be difficult for the plumber to reach the work area without crawling the length of the house. To make future repair easier, find a nearby closet and ask the general contractor to prepare an access hatch. The contractor may have to add headers to any joists that need to be cut. The floor will also have to be repaired. But the added convenience for current and future work will save money in the long run.

Alternatively, the craftsmen might open up the floor in the kitchen being remodeled. This works particularly well in a home that has limited crawl space. By stripping the walls of old plaster or drywall and completely opening the floor, the workmen have access to the chaseways between floor joists or wall studs. This makes the retrofit of existing piping much easier, and therefore less costly.

WATER QUALITY

Your clients may be concerned about water quality in their homes. Municipal systems are responsible for testing the condition of the water and treating it as necessary to insure its purity. The condition of the water in a private system is the responsibility of the owner. Regardless of the source, designing a kitchen or upgrading one is the right time to discuss the water quality issue. Water quality is a problem because of contaminants in the water supply.

There are two types of water contamination: one affects the water's purity for drinking (lead, nitrates, bacteria) and the other affects the water's function (hardness, iron).

Protecting the clients' health by providing safe drinking water is always an is-

sue that a design professional must consider when planning a kitchen project. You should also find out if there are any function contaminants because this will limit the products and surfaces you specify.

Contaminants

LEAD

Lead is a plumbing line problem that becomes a dangerous contaminant. The **National Sanitation Foundation** estimates that 16% of the nation's households have unacceptably high drinking water lead levels. A person's health can be affected by even low lead levels. If the clients' drinking water contains more than 10 micrograms of lead per liter of water, they should consider changing the piping in the plumbing system, flushing the lines on a regular basis, or installing a treatment system that removes the lead or neutralizes the water.

TRIHALOMETHANES (THM)

A second contaminant is **trihalomethanes (THM)**. These are a group of chemicals that cause cancer in laboratory animals. The group includes chlorine when found in excessive amounts. Most communities add chlorine to their drinking water. This keeps down the growth of taste- and odor-producing organisms in water. But chlorine, in addition to making water taste like a swimming pool, can also be a contaminant.

Because of this, the **Environmental Protection Agency** will be requiring local water companies to reduce the amount of chlorine in their water. Utilities may soon turn to other ways of treating their water.

Current regulations require a THM concentration of 100 micrograms per liter. If your clients' water supply exceeds this level, or if chloroform is a concern, they should consider water treatment equipment.

In agricultural areas, private systems face two additional contaminants.

NITRATES

Nitrates are by-products of fertilizer that can leach into ground water. If the water company draws water from an underground aquifer or from a river or lake with agricultural runoff, nitrate levels may be seasonally high. However, water companies test for nitrate levels and keep it within safe levels (10 micrograms per liter). If your clients' water supply comes from a well, they should have their water tested regularly, and they might want to consider water treating equipment.

PESTICIDES

Pesticides are also of concern in rural areas. Those who obtain water from their own well should have their wells tested regularly. Or a local utility will provide information about which contaminants are present in the groundwater near the well.

Monitoring/Testing Water Quality

If you or your client have questions, you can request additional information from the **EPA's water quality hotline - 800/426-4791**.

The **Cooperative Extension Service** in your local or state government is a valuable source of information on water quality problems and water treatment equipment as well. Testing laboratories can be used to obtain information about tap water. The following labs send instructions and a mail order kit:

- **National Testing Laboratories**; 6555 Wilson Mills Rd., Cleveland, OH 44143

- **Suburban Water Testing**; 4600 Kutztown Rd., Temple, PA 19560

- **Beland Water Lab**; 548 Donald St., Bedford, NH 03110

Water Treatment

If you discover that your client's water quality exceeds the EPA standards, you can obtain test data on water treatment equipment from the **National Sanitation Foundation**, 3475 Plymouth Rd., Ann Arbor, MI 48105. Ask for the "*listing book*" of drinking water treatment units. **Consumers Union** also tests water treatment devices. Reference **Consumer Reports** at your local library.

CARBON FILTER SYSTEM

The best way to remove excess chlorine (one of the THMs) is to install a whole house **carbon filter** system. This removes the chlorine from all the fixtures in the house. And it is large enough to have sufficient flow of water through the system. It also removes some pesticides, **VOCs (VOCs are chemicals such as paint thinner, dry cleaning fluid and spot remover)** and radon. This treatment system removes contaminants by passing the water through a filter containing particles of carbon. The carbon **absorbs** the contaminants. **(This means the contaminants attach to the surface of the carbon.)** After a time, the surface area of the carbon particles fills up. The filter needs to be changed every couple of months.

REVERSE OSMOSIS

To remove other contaminants, your client will need a different type of treatment equipment. Lead and nitrate, for example, are best removed with a **reverse-osmosis** unit. These units are not a good choice for water conserving areas because about 75% of the incoming water goes down the drain. They are best used beneath a kitchen sink or bathroom lavatory to filter drinking water; they are compact enough to fit in a cabinet. Lead and nitrate are not a problem for bathing - only for drinking.

DISTILLER

Another option for removing lead and nitrate is a **distiller. (A distiller is like a still used to make alcohol.)** A heating element boils the water and, as the steam condenses, most impurities are removed. A distiller is not effective against THMs.

Lead in Plumbing

Not all houses and apartment buildings have lead problems. It depends on when they were built, what kind of plumbing pipes they have and what types of water mains connect the building to the water supply system. The significant doses of lead do not come from water in underground aquifers and reservoirs, but from pipes - both lead pipes and lead solder used to connect copper pipes to carry water.

Contamination can start with a corrosive reaction between lead and water in large lead pipes of municipal water-delivery systems and in smaller lead pipes, called service connections, that link large mains to the pipes in buildings. The service connections in Brooklyn, New York, for example, are still lead. Through the early 1900s, it was common practice to use lead pipes for interior plumbing as well.

You are most likely to find lead pipes in systems installed prior to 1930. Only the water supply pipes are of concern because they deliver drinking water. Many homes also had lead waste pipes, but these are not a cause for concern. Lead water supply pipes should always be removed when remodeling a kitchen. However, this causes us to ask other questions such as; *how far back should the pipes be removed? Will it be necessary to replace the pipes all the way back to the street?* It may be costly to change the whole supply system in the home, but this should be brought to the attention of the homeowner. Replace the pipes with copper, galvanized pipe or plastic. Additions or repairs to copper pipes should not be made with lead solder. The plumber will be familiar with alternatives.

If changes to the system cannot be made, tell your client to run the water for half a minute before drinking, this will flush lead-containing water out of the supply pipes.

Softening Water

In addition to making water safe to drink, the water may need further treatment to prevent it from damaging household surfaces. **Hard water is water that contains scale-forming minerals, such as calcium and magnesium**. Hard water is a major problem in rural areas. When hard water mixes with soap, nonsoluble fatty acids are formed. These coat kitchen fixtures and are difficult to remove.

Water softening equipment will reduce these problems. The softener removes calcium and magnesium and replaces it with sodium. Unfortunately, added sodium is a health concern for many, and it leaves drinking water tasteless.

To avoid these problems in drinking water, many homes only soften hot water. The softening system is attached to the water line leading to the water heater. Because heat intensifies scale buildup, treatment to prevent this buildup in hot water pipes is a critical first step. Untreated cold water lines then are used throughout the rest of the system. However, the ideal installation has both hot and cold lines softened. A special second (cold water only) line is then run to sinks and lavatories for drinking water only.

Two primary tanks comprise a softening system. In the exchange tank incoming water passes over a granular substance to remove calcium and magnesium. A salty solution is kept in the brine tank for the periodic process of regenerating the exchange tank.

THE DRAIN/WASTE/VENT (DWV) SYSTEM

The drain/waste/vent (DWV) system carries water and waste to the city sewer or septic tank. Unlike the water lines, the drain/waste lines are not pressurized. Water and waste drain by gravity. Fixtures should be grouped around a central core where the main soil stack is located.

To keep waste flowing through the lines, drain/waste lines slope downhill. The slope must be 1/4 inch per foot. This means that the pipe must slope 1/4 inch downhill for every horizontal foot.

All of the drain/waste lines in the house eventually end up in a single large sewer line that carries waste to a city sewer system or a septic tank. The city sewer system carries waste away from the property. A septic tank treats waste in an enclosed tank right on the property.

Septic tanks are watertight receptacles that receive the discharge of the drainage system. The solids in the waste biodegrade in the septic tank and sink to the bottom of the tank. The liquids are discharged into the soil outside the tank.

If you are adding fixtures to the home, you should check the size of the septic system. Tanks are sized according to the family's water consumption. Adding large, water-using fixtures may mean the septic system should be made larger.

Additionally, many plumbers counsel against adding a food waste disposer on a system that terminates in a septic tank. Others do not share in this concern.

The general consensus seems to be if you are going to install a food waste disposer on a septic system, the system should be 50 percent larger than without the appliance, or should be cleaned out twice as often. Therefore, if the typical clean-out schedule is once every 6 years, it should be cleaned once every 3 years if a food waste disposer is added to the line.

You'll find it easier to remember what the various parts of the DWV system do if you can remember three key concepts.

- The drain system relies on a **trap** to prevent sewer gas from backing up into the house.

- The system needs **drain lines** to carry waste away.

- And, finally, the **DWV system** needs air circulation to keep the waste flowing downstream.

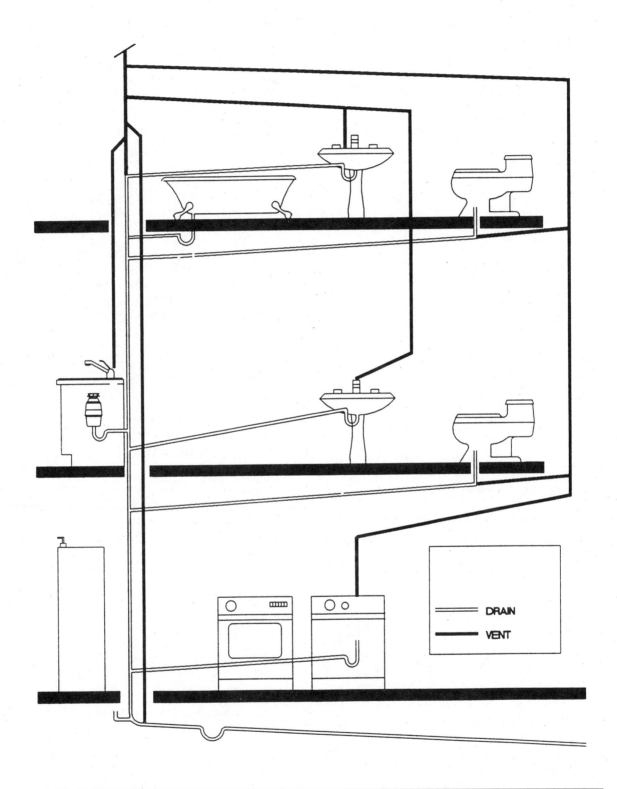

Figure 48 Details of the DWV System. Waste and vent lines are grouped around the central soil stack.

The Trap

The trap is a P-shaped pipe connecting the fixture and the drain pipe. It provides a water seal against sewer gases which could otherwise enter the house through the fixture. When the fixture drains, water flows through the trap and into the drain pipe. However the trap never empties completely. It holds enough water to maintain the seal.

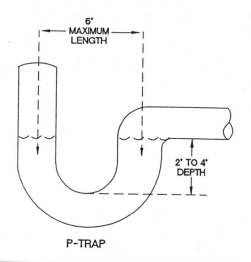

Figure 49 A trap provides the water seal against sewer gases entering the house.

The primary kitchen sink (which is generally a double sink) has one trap leading to one drain. Both sinks drain into the trap. It is because of this extensive amount of plumbing pipe inside the cabinetry that the sink cabinet is generally not counted as an effective storage system in the kitchen. Pull-out towel bars, door-mounted cleaning supply racks, or a roll-out at the bottom of the cabinet can increase the function of the cabinet.

Another type of trap still found in existing construction is the S-trap, which is no longer permitted by building codes.

Most often found under sinks, the S-trap was rarely connected to a vent. It goes straight through the floor. When the sink full of water suddenly empties, the suction from the moving slug of water can clear the trap. Sewer gas would then back up into the room. These traps should be changed during a remodel. A new vent will be required, and a P-trap should be used.

The Waste Lines

The waste lines are identified by function and configuration. The toilet discharge pipe is known as a **soil line** or stack. **Lines** are the horizontal runs. **Stacks** are the vertical components of the system. The size of the soil or waste pipe is determined by the intended use of the fixture. Because pipe sizes vary, interchanging or substituting fixtures may require changes in the waste lines.

Pipe measurements always refer to the inside diameter. The outside dimensions of pipe materials vary tremendously. Cast iron, for example, is much thicker than plastic pipe.

Vent Lines

The vent lines admit air into the system to allow a free flow of liquid waste. The vent pipe also provides an exit for sewer gases which would otherwise build up in the system and force their way through the fixture trap into the house.

Each trap installed must be vented. Common vents can be shared between fixtures, as long as the lowest fixture is the one with the highest flow. The vent extends from the fixture to the house exterior through the roof. The designer can often determine the concealed vent pipe location by observing the roof line from the house exterior or by inspecting the attic.

If you're thinking about enlarging or lowering the kitchen window - watch out! Typically, the sink plumbing vent is directly behind the kitchen sink and faucet. It then makes a right angle turn to the right or left, and then one other turn as it extends along side the window to the roof. If you're changing the window, this vent will need modification as well.

Special attention should be paid to the existing vent path, or a new vent pipe location under consideration if the kitchen will feature an operable skylight.

Figure 50 A typical vent stack and its relationship to the kitchen window.

Vent Pipes and Skylights: Kitchen vent ducts (both from the plumbing waste vent and the fan duct) must be far enough from the skylight to avoid odors or moist air from being drawn indoors - which would occur if the skylight were open. **CABO** code has specific requirements for the distance between plumbing vents and skylights. This code states that a vent must be 5 feet (measured horizontally) from an operable skylight. It must also be at least 2 feet above the top of the opening. Remember, local codes may differ from the **CABO** model code - so check any local requirements before specifying an operable skylight in a kitchen project.

Waste Line Distance from Vent: Limits established for the distance between trap and vent in continuous waste and vent systems include the following for residential applications:

When the distance from the trap to the vent is extended, larger drain lines are needed. The plumbing contractor should be consulted before plans are finalized.

Venting an Island Sink: One of the biggest concerns for you as a kitchen designer regarding the vent lines will be how to vent a second island sink. In some communities you may be allowed to use a special vent substitute that precludes the normal pipe terminating above the roof line.

However, in many municipalities you must connect the island trap with a traditional vent. Therefore, the distance you place the island sink from the vent pipe may limit your design.

Alternatively, many creative designers have planned columns or posts at the end of an island which artistically conceal the vent pipe that runs through this artificial chaseway.

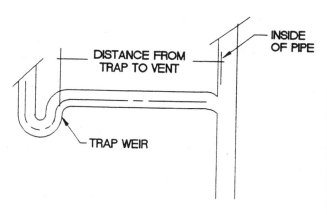

Figure 2.51 The vent must be located so that the length from the fixture trap to the vent does not exceed the distance given.

Pipe Size	Distance to Vent
1 1/4" (3cm)	42" (107cm)
1 1/2" (4cm)	60" (152cm)
2" (5cm)	96" (244cm)
3" (7.6cm)	120" (305cm)
4" (10cm)	144" (366cm)

NOTE: Local codes may specify different requirements. Always check local codes.

DWV Materials

Several pipe materials are used for Drain/Waste/Vent systems.

Plastic pipe is noisier than cast iron. If plumbing waste lines are placed above a room where sound transmission could be distracting (e.g. a dining room), be sure to have the plumbing contractor insulate the waste line.

The following chart lists typical materials.

PLUMBING TIPS FROM THE PROS

Successful kitchen specialists share these helpful hints about planning the supply side of the kitchen plumbing system.

- Is the drain pipe diameter correct for the new fixture?

DWV PIPE MATERIALS		
MATERIAL	**PROS**	**CONS**
Cast Iron (Hubless)	Durable Easy to assemble Resistant to chemicals	Heavy Expensive Must be supported at joints
Cast Iron (Bell & Spigot)	Durable Resistant to chemicals Joints rigid	Requires skill to assemble Workers exposed to lead vapor Expensive Time consuming to install
ABS (Acrylonitrile-butadiene styrene)	High range of temperatures (-40°F to 180°F) Easy to assemble with solvent welding or threaded fittings Lightweight Inexpensive	May not be approved by some codes Not resistant to industrial chemicals
PVC (Polyvinyl Chloride)	Lightweight Easy to assemble Inexpensive	May not be approved by some codes Not resistant to industrial chemicals

- Can the drain pipe be placed with the correct slope to provide adequate water velocity?

- If you're installing a new vent, what is the roof material and have you included the cost necessary to repair it?

- Is there adequate working space below the house or in the attic?

- What will the cost be for repair work necessary to close walls, floors or ceiling which are opened during the plumbing work?

- Make sure you check the distance from the floor to the center of the drain underneath the kitchen sink. If a food waste disposer is being added, the drain should be between 17" and 19" off the finished floor.

- In old houses you may be replacing a wall-hung faucet. Plan on changing the water supply lines from the floor level all the way up inside the wall. There is no reason to work with the old piping when it is very easy to cut open the wall, expose the pipes and replace them before the new sink is installed.

- If your client has an old dishwasher that is plumbed independently of the kitchen sink, make sure they understand the new plumbing connection will be through the food waste disposer. Make the client aware of the noise that will result as the dishwasher drains through the food waste disposer. Alert them that you will be checking for water damage once the old appliance is removed.

- When adding a sink on an island, think through exactly where the plumbing lines are going to be located: *will they come up through the floor, or through a pony wall at the end or behind the island?* If they will come through a wall, make sure that they are out of the way of any venting, wiring or framing. If they enter through the bottom of a cabinet, don't order any interior storage system components that require floor space.

- When you place a sink on an island, think about where you want the faucet. You may want to place it at either end of the sink, as opposed to directly behind it so that the faucet is more accessible.

- When planning a second sink, stay away from small 12x12 stainless steel units. They don't have a drain big enough to receive a food waste disposal - an important part of any sink.

SECTION 5

Natural and Bottled Gas

Gas was first utilized in residential communities for lighting. Today it is one of the preferred fuel sources for gourmet cooking. Gas is also extensively used for house heating, air conditioning and water heating. Gas jets to the fireplace and the outdoor gas-fueled barbeque are other uses of natural gas in residential planning.

TYPES OF GAS

There are two major types of gas available in North America: natural gas and liquified petroleum commonly called "LP" or "bottled gas". The vast majority of gas needs are fulfilled with natural gas. Liquified petroleum gas is supplied in those sections of the country that are beyond the reach of utility company mains.

Natural gas, which is largely methane, is found underground filling the interstices of porous rocks, known as sands. Gas is transported from natural gas fields to the utility company by pipelines operating at pressures between 300 and 800 pounds per square inch.

Liquified petroleum gas (of either butane or propane, or of a mixture of the two) is derived from oil refinery and wet natural gas sources, or from the fractional distillation of natural gasolines. It can be liquified under moderate pressure and is then shipped to distributing centers in special tank cars.

Natural gas is distributed from a central system to the consumer by the utility company and requires no home storage facilities. LP gas is stored in a tank on the premises.

PHYSICS OF GAS

Gas is composed of molecules continually in motion. Since gas tends to expand and diffuse, the molecules completely fill the containing vessel and their motion is limited only by the size of the enclosed space; therefore, they exert equal pressure in all directions. The tendency of gas to diffuse is the fundamental essential for gas flow. Just as water flows from a higher to a lower level and heat flows from a hotter to a cooler body, so gas flows from a place of higher pressure to one of lower pressure.

HEATING VALUE

The heating value of gas is the amount of heat produced when a unit quantity is burned. It is measured in BTUs (British Thermal Units) per cubic foot of gas. The standard cubic foot of gas, as defined by the **American Gas Association**, is the quantity contained in one cubic foot of volume at a barometric pressure of 30 inches of mercury and at a temperature of 60°F . A BTU is a unit of heat energy, the amount of heat required to raise the temperature of one pound of water by one degree Fahrenheit. The amount of heat is equal to that produced by burning an ordinary wooden match.

GAS METER

Gas piped into the home is measured by a meter, which may be in a case of steel, aluminum or cast iron.

The basic principle on which the meter works, is "displacement". Gas entering one chamber of the meter displaces (or pushes out) an equal volume of gas from the other chamber. The meter records the total volume of gas passing through it by counting the number of displacements.

Heating Systems

The activity level of the person using the room, the amount of clothing they are wearing, and the heat produced by fixtures and appliances will all affect how much heat is required.

Today's kitchens are larger than in the past. Keeping the room at a comfortable temperature can be difficult. You need to know how much heat to provide and where to place the registers.

If the kitchen is part of a room addition, you should know what effect distance from the central heating unit will have on comfort. The farther from the furnace, the less heat will be available for the room.

Heating equipment has changed a great deal in the last few years. You need to know when a particular system might be troublesome. Heat pumps, for instance, deliver heated air at lower temperatures (90°F) and higher velocities than forced air furnaces.

THE COMFORT ZONE

Many years ago, when mechanical engineers and physiologists began studying the human response to heat and cold, they coined a phrase that has been a cornerstone of **HVAC (Heating, Ventilating, Air Conditioning)** design ever since - *"the comfort zone"*. Research has shown that humans are comfortable over a rather narrow range of temperatures and humidities.

The activity level and age of the person also affect comfort. For instance, as people age, their metabolic rate slows down. Temperatures that are comfortable for active young adults feel cold to the elderly.

People also feel chilled when an air current, or a draft, blows air past their body. Air currents, even when the air is warm, blow heat away from the body.

Heating systems are designed to keep the human body in the comfort zone. The heating system must be able to provide enough heat so that the indoor temperature remains in this narrow band that we experience as *"comfortable"*.

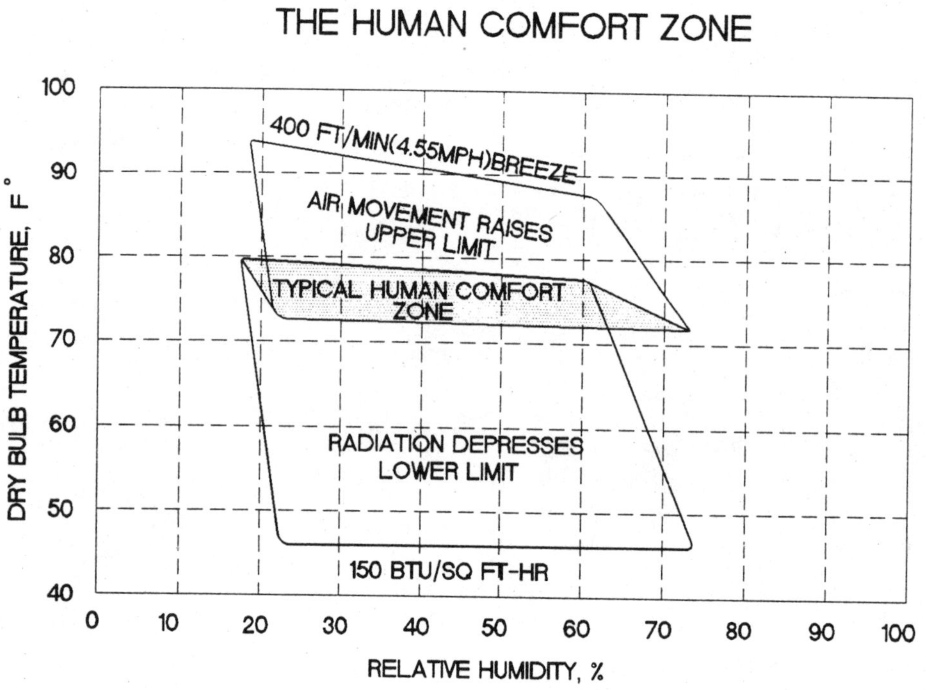

THE HUMAN COMFORT ZONE

Figure 52 The human comfort zone.

HEAT LOSS

A heating system replaces heat that is lost through the shell of the house. How much energy the heating system requires to replace that lost heat depends on four factors:

- Where the house is located;

- How large the house is;

- The energy-efficiency of the house;

- The energy-efficiency of the heating system.

The efficiency of the existing furnace may play a role in whether to extend ducts or buy a larger furnace. Any time you add space to a house, you add more volume. *Will the existing furnace be able to heat the added volume? Is this the right time to replace an inefficient old furnace?*

The only way to accurately answer these questions is to do a heat loss analysis. An energy auditor or HVAC contractor can do a heat loss analysis of the house. The analysis will include measurements of wall, ceiling, floor and window areas. The auditor will also measure insulation levels and infiltration around doors and windows.

You may find that the existing furnace will be large enough if you make the kitchen extremely energy efficient. This might mean using less glass than you would like. Glass areas are the biggest sources of heat loss in a building. Or you might find that adding insulation to the attic would give you a little more leeway in using glass.

In California, kitchen designers working under the constraints of the state's energy code make these trade-offs all the time.

The practical requirements of heating systems and the home's energy requirements may seem like the least glamorous part of kitchen design. But remember that you are designing for comfort. If you know your way around heating systems, your knowledge becomes one more design tool you can use to insure satisfied customers.

HEAT DISTRIBUTION

Central Heat

In most climates, central heating systems are necessary to keep a house warm. Steam, hot water, forced warm air and electric heating systems all function in the same basic way with the same basic set of components to provide heat.

Each central heating system is equipped with a control, a heat producer, a heat exchanger and a heat distributor. The control, called a thermostat, signals a need for heat. The signal turns on the heat producer, an oil or gas burner or an electric heating element. The heat produced warms the transfer medium (air, water, or steam) in a heat exchanger.

The transfer medium moves by gravity or is forced through ducts (warm air) or pipes (water or steam) to the heat distributors (convectors, registers, or radiators) located in living areas. Return ducts (or pipes) carry the medium back to the heat exchanger. When the temperature of the living area reaches the level set on the thermostat, the thermostat automatically shuts down the system.

In addition, heating systems that use gas or oil as a fuel must be vented. When heat is provided by electricity, there are no venting requirements.

Zoned Heat

Central heat refers to a heat source that heats the whole house. *But what if the house is long and sprawling? What if people only live in half their house and want temperatures in the other half to remain cooler except on special occasions?* Another kind of distribution method called **zoning**, divides the house into two or more parts.

Typically associated with hot water and steam, (hydronic heating systems), zoned heat provides the client with greater control of temperatures in large homes or living spaces. Essentially, heat is produced from a single source and distributed through separate loops (pipes), which are each controlled by their own thermostats located in separate sections of the home or space. However, the concept of zoning can apply to the addition of a second heat source designed to heat a separate area or "**zone**" of the home. Zoned heat is an especially useful concept for kitchen designers to remember. It can be used to keep a room addition comfortable, and it can be less expensive than completely reworking the original heating system.

Consult an HVAC contractor early in the planning process whenever you are adding space. Consider zoned heat if the added space is far from the heat source. For instance, if the central heating unit, such as a forced air furnace, is more than 40 feet from a new room addition, the furnace may not be able to adequately heat the new addition. Because the addition is far from the central heating source, it makes more sense to add a second furnace to provide heat. The need for a second source of heat may affect your plans.

Perhaps the HVAC contractor sees space you have designated as a linen closet as a potential spot for a furnace closet. You must understand the space needs of central heating systems in order to incorporate this mechanical equipment into your space planning. It is best to discuss space needs before you finalize your plans.

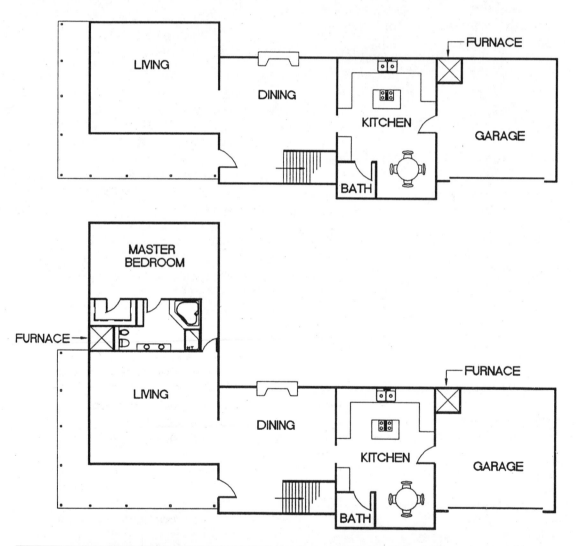

Figure 53 A secondary heat source is added for a room addition that is far from the original furnace.

FORCED AIR FURNACES

Low installation cost, rapid heat delivery and reliability make forced air systems a popular heating choice. Forced air furnaces can use either gas or oil as a fuel. Electric forced air furnaces also exist, but are less common because the cost of electricity is high.

All forced air systems use heating ducts to distribute heat from the furnace to the rooms. In a forced air system, a blower pulls air from the rooms into the return air intake and return duct, through a filter, and into the furnace. There the air is heated. It then flows back to the rooms through the warm-air supply ducts and supply registers or diffusers.

Efficiency

Furnaces and boilers are rated for their Annual Fuel Utilization Efficiency (AFUE). The AFUE number allows you to compare furnaces. A furnace's efficiency has to do with how much heat escapes up the chimney. In a 100% efficient furnace, 100% of the fuel is available to heat the home. In a 78% efficient furnace, 78% of the fuel burned would theoretically be available to heat the home. These are laboratory test values, however. When a furnace is installed, the installed efficiency can be quite a bit lower than the advertised efficiency. Installing a more efficient heating system does not always yield the savings people expect.

New standards for energy efficiency in furnaces went into effect in 1992. These standards require furnaces to be at least 78% efficient. Furnaces and heat pumps must now meet requirements of the National Appliance Energy Conservation Act.

Forced air furnaces that burn oil are also more efficient today than in the past. They use high speed, flame retention heads. This technology ensures a better mix of air (which is needed for combustion) and oil.

Federal Energy Efficiency Standards		
PRODUCT	**NAECA MINIMUM**	**MANUFACTURED AFTER DATE**
Gas Furnaces	78% AFUE	1/1/1992
Gas Furnaces (Mobile home use)	75% AFUE	1/1/1990 - 9/1/1990
Heat Pumps and Air Conditioners (Split Systems)	10.0 SEER 6.8 HSPF	1/1/1992
Heat Pumps and Air Conditioners (Single Package)	9.7 SEER 6.6 HSPF	1/1/1993

Venting

Any heat-producing appliance that uses a fossil fuel must be vented to the outdoors. Combustion of fossil fuels (such as oil, gas, or propane) produces toxic gas. This gas is called **flue gas** because it was vented into flues, or chimneys.

Furnaces that are already installed are probably vented into a flue - either a masonry chimney or a double-walled flue pipe. Furnaces with high AFUE ratings may not need a flue pipe. It is possible to vent them through a side wall.

This knowledge may help you advise your clients about furnace selection. Perhaps they want to choose a new furnace anyway. Choosing one that can be vented through a sidewall might give you greater freedom in siting the furnace closet.

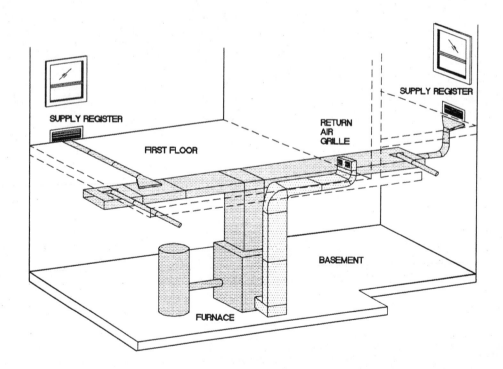

Figure 54 (Courtesy of University of Illinois) A forced-air system has a plenum and branch ducts that deliver heated air to registers or diffusers. Cool air is returned to the furnace through the return air intakes.

Heating Ducts

Up to this point, this section has focused on the workings of the central heating source, its efficiency and venting. *But once heat is created, how does it get distributed?*

The air that is heated by the furnace goes to a plenum. The **plenum** is a large, sheet-metal enclosure, either above or below the furnace. The plenum is designed to distribute heated air coming from the furnace. A second plenum may be located in the attic. Rectangular **trunk ducts** take off from the plenum.

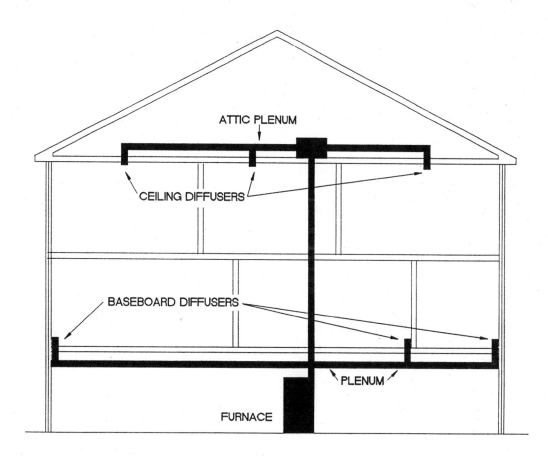

Figure 55 (Courtesy of University of Illinois) In two-story houses, ductwork is often hidden in interior or exterior walls. It may even be in the attic.

Branch ducts, which are smaller, branch out from the trunk duct. In homes built on crawl spaces or over basements, these branch ducts lead to registers or baseboard diffusers. Registers or diffusers are placed along outside walls, usually below windows. Warm air currents rising from the registers counteract cold air currents that cascade down the windows.

Slab houses usually have a different forced warm air duct layout. In slab homes, a duct system may be embedded in the concrete slab. Warm air in the ducts is discharged into rooms through registers placed near outside walls, usually below windows. However, the registers are fed by a perimeter loop that goes around the perimeter of the slab.

Perimeter heating systems are designed to eliminate cold floors.

Most forced, warm-air heating systems can support another register or two if the furnace is centrally located. However, if the furnace is in an attached garage of a ranch house and a new master suite is being added to the opposite end of the house, the long duct runs will make adequate heating difficult.

Also, it is not easy to add new registers to a slab house. Adding registers means jack hammering holes in sections of the floor. Even then, the central heating unit may be too small to heat the added space. If the central heating unit is not large enough, you may need to add a separate furnace to the new space.

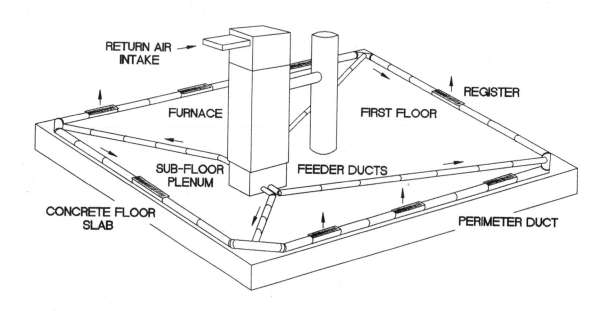

Figure 56 (Courtesy of University of Illinois) Crawl space houses can have forced air systems. The ducts are buried in concrete. Registers are located along the outside walls of the house.

Where to Place Supply Registers

Supply registers (or outlets) or diffusers in a forced air system should be placed so that the air does not blow directly on the occupants.

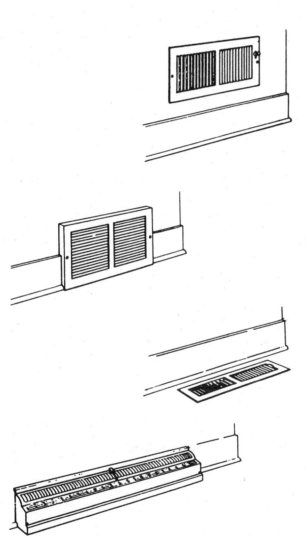

Figure 57 (Courtesy of University of Illinois) Registers and diffusers distribute heat. They have directional vanes to project heat into the room. Return air grilles collect air and do not have adjustable vanes.

Supply registers can be placed high or low on the wall. Low wall outlets are better in cold climates because heated air rises, and if registers are low on the wall, the heat has a chance to spread across the floor before it rises to the ceiling. This keeps the floor at a comfortable temperature.

In the warmer climates, however, high wall locations might be better. This is because heat is required for only short periods. Most of the year, the air conditioner is turned on. In such situations, high wall outlets are best because cool air falls. If registers are close to the floor, a band of cool air hovers above the floor, while the ceiling level temperature remains warm.

Unfortunately, high wall outlets are more visible. Plan their location with the HVAC contractor to avoid conflicts with the design. In climates with equally long heating and cooling seasons, the low wall location is better.

Return-Air Grilles

Placement of the return-air grille is not as critical as placement of the supply registers. Return-air grilles only have detectable air movement 6" from the face of the grille. If the kitchen has a return-air grille, it can be placed high or low on the wall.

COMBINATION SPACE/WATER HEATERS

Combination heaters work on the same principle as an automobile heater, but instead of an engine, the heat source is a gas- or oil-fired water heater.

The theory behind the system is simple: since the water already is using energy to stay warm, heat can be drawn off and circulated to the living area. By capturing the heat that ordinarily would be lost, the efficiency of the system is increased.

When heat is needed, a wall thermostat triggers a small pump, which circulates hot water from the water heater to a coil in an air handler. Air is blown over the coil to absorb the heat and then is distributed through ducts by fans. Meanwhile, slightly cooled water is circulated back to the water tank for reheating.

These combination heaters are best used where heating demands are low. Space must be planned for the storage tank and air handler.

HYDRONIC HEAT

Hydronic heat is another form of central heat. It uses no ducts, but carries its heat in water, which circulates in pipes. (**Hydronic** comes from **hydro**, - meaning water.) One pipe supplies heated water to the room heating units through

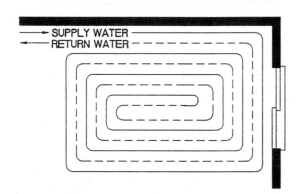

Figure 58 With hydronic heat, one pipe supplies heated water and the other returns cool water to the boiler.

a supply main. The other pipe returns the cooled water to the boiler through a separate return main (or pipe).

Hot Water Panels: Houses with concrete slab floors may have hydronic hot-water heat in the floor. A boiler heats water and circulates it through water lines embedded in the slab. You cannot add on to this kind of heating system. Any demolition that requires cutting holes in the concrete should be done very carefully to avoid cutting into water lines.

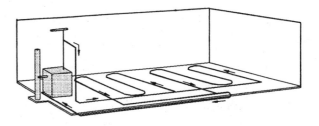

Figure 59 (Courtesy of University of Illinois) Hot water panel heat can be used in slab houses.

Forced Hot Water: In a forced hot water system, a boiler heats water that circulates through pipes. The pipes lead to radiators, fan-coil units, or convectors. These units radiate heat to the room air.

Convectors consist of a core and *"fins"*. Hot water heats the core and the fins, which, in turn, warm the air passing over them. The core and fins are enclosed in a cabinet, causing a more effective air flow over the heating surfaces than if they were exposed. Fan-coil units are similar, but they use small fans to push the heated air out into the room. Fan-coil units can also be used for cooling.

The HVAC contractor is most knowledgeable about what can and cannot be done to move or rearrange parts of the heating system. It can be difficult to move radiators, convectors or fan-coil units to a different location because that involves changing piping. If you are working in a kitchen with this type of heating system, work closely with the HVAC contractor during the planning stage. Also, on your first walk-through, carefully trace the path of pipes. Check any walls to be removed to make sure no pipes are embedded in them.

From a heating standpoint, the best location for these devices is below a window. An alternate location is the toe-kick area beneath a cabinet. Temperatures are not hot enough to burn peoples' toes.

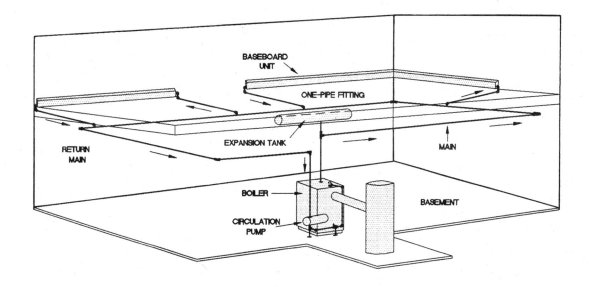

Figure 60 (Courtesy of University of Illinois) In a forced hot water system, the water is heated in a boiler and pumped through pipes to radiators, fan-coils or convectors.

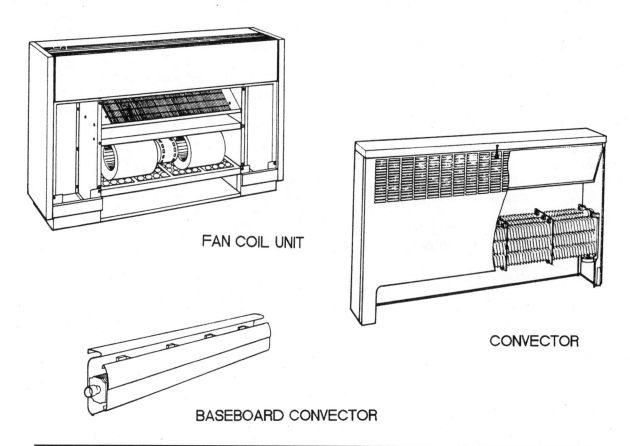

FAN COIL UNIT

CONVECTOR

BASEBOARD CONVECTOR

Figure 61 (Courtesy of University of Illinois) In hot water systems, room air is heated as it circulates around fan-coil units or convectors. Baseboard convectors are the most common in homes.

Steam Heat: Old-fashioned steam-heat systems circulated steam instead of hot water. Steam systems also used radiators. Both one-pipe and two-pipe systems were once common. If you are remodeling a home with steam heat, it is best to leave the radiator in its current location.

These systems should not be rearranged. Because of their age, they can also be difficult to disassemble. Fittings may be partially rusted, and trying to remove a radiator may loosen connections elsewhere in the system.

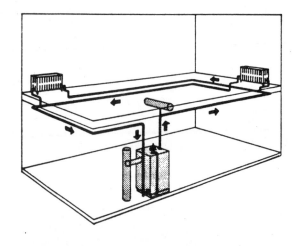

Figure 62 Steam systems circulate steam, produced by a boiler, to radiators.

ELECTRIC HEAT

There are two common types of electric heat: electric resistance heat and electric heat pumps. Electric heat is not as common as it was in the days of cheap electricity. But heat pumps, which also use electricity, are becoming more popular because they can be used for heating and cooling. Because heat pumps are also used for cooling, we will discuss them as a separate system after we finish heating and cooling.

Electric Forced Air

Electric forced air systems are not common today, the cost of electricity has risen and made this heat more expensive. In an electric furnace, heat is provided by air moving across heating elements. The heated air circulates through supply ducts and is returned to the furnace through return intakes. No vents are necessary because no combustion takes place in the furnace.

Electric Resistance Heat

Electric resistance heat works by directly converting electric current into heat. Almost all of the energy in the electric current ends up as usable heat. Electric resistance heat usually is the most expensive form of heat, but it is the least expensive to install and allows the user to control the temperature of each room separately.

Electric resistance heat can be provided by baseboard units. The baseboards look much like hot water baseboards. Instead of having hot water passing through them, however, they are manufactured with an electric heating element similar to that used in an electric range. Units installed in each room or area are controlled by a separate thermostat mounted on the wall or installed as part of the baseboard unit.

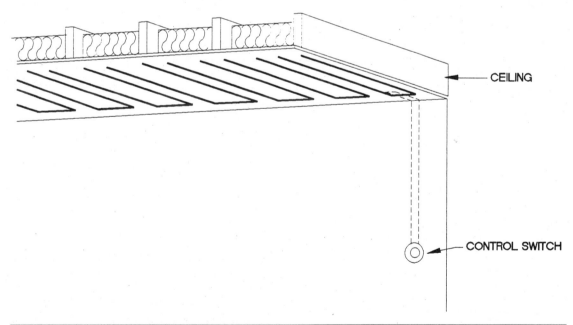

Figure 63 (Courtesy of University of Illinois) Electric radiant heat can be provided by wiring that is embedded in drywall.

Electric resistance heat can also be provided by heating panels. These heating panels are a special kind of drywall, with wiring embedded in them. This eliminates expensive duct work. And, electric resistance heat requires no furnace. You might think of using this heating system in a small kitchen or room addition to provide supplementary heat. Your drywall contractor will need to order special drywall with wiring embedded in it. The electrical contractor will also have to add a circuit to handle the heating load. A disadvantage is that resistance heat takes time to warm up.

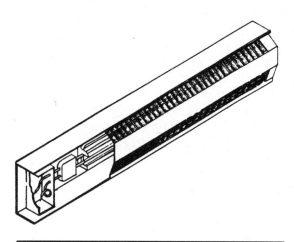

Figure 64 *An electric resistance baseboard heater has a heating element much like the element in an electric range.*

Other Types of Electric Heating

Electric radiant heating installed in flooring is popular in Europe and beginning to make headway in the United States. In this system, electric coils are attached to the subfloor and covered with a lightweight concrete or installed with built-up subflooring. A thermostat connected to a heat sensor inside the flooring regulates the temperature of the system.

Because these systems heat the floor itself instead of warming air, the heat is more evenly distributed and comfortable for cold feet. Although expensive, these systems are an alternative worth considering for "cold" flooring such as tile, wood, marble and granite. (Radiant flooring systems also work with hydronic heating and can be connected to a boiler, water heater, heat pump or solar heating system.)

Another newcomer to the market is thermal mass heat storage. Unlike most conventional heaters, mass heat storage systems can store heat and have controls to regulate when and how much heat is released. This feature allows the homeowner to take advantage of lower electric rates during off-peak hours.

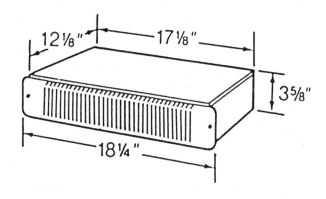

Figure 65 *Heating unit by Beacon Morris delivers hot air through the cabinet kick space.*

THERMOSTATS

Thermostats are like switches, except they control the operation of a boiler, furnace or electric heater. In most houses, one thermostat is used to control the temperature in several rooms. However, the thermostat can only sense the temperature in the room where it is located. For this reason, it is important that the thermostat be located either where the temperature is representative of the whole house or where temperature control is most important.

Locate the top of the thermostat at a height of 48" above the floor. Avoid placing the thermostat on outside walls or near outside doors. Likewise, do not place it near heat outlets, behind doors, or on walls that receive heat from the sun, a fireplace, or lamp.

SOLAR HEATING

Homeowners frequently ask kitchen designers to bring natural light into their homes. Most homeowners have experienced how comfortable a warm sunlit room can become, even on a cold winter day. If your clients have seen pictures of glass atriums, they may ask about this option for their kitchen.

Passive solar heating principles are the easiest to incorporate into a kitchen design. **Passive solar** means that the building itself is designed to capture the sun's heat. In **active solar**, collectors and pumps that distribute heat are needed. A kitchen designer must learn about solar design to use the sun's heat effectively. Make sure the solar option is right for your climate and the building's orientation.

Rooms must be oriented so that window areas face south. To prevent summer overheating, windows must have a shading overhang to exclude the high arc of the summer sun, which would overheat the room. In the winter, the sun's arc is lower and closer to the hori-

zon, so its rays come in below the overhang. If you do decide to incorporate some aspects of passive solar design, provide auxiliary heat for sunless periods and nightime. (A publication that gives details of passive solar design is **Solar Orientation**; also see **Sunspaces & Greenhouses**. Both are available from the **Building Research Council**, 1 East St. Mary's Road, Champaign, IL 61820.)

RENOVATION CONSIDERATIONS

Most heating systems can be revamped to fit your design. Warm-air and heat pump duct work can often be extended. If a new kitchen is located in an addition, it is often possible to extend the duct work to provide for heating and cooling. Before this is done, however, the existing furnace should be checked to be sure there is sufficient heating and/or cooling capacity. The fan on the unit should be checked to see that it is capable of delivering additional air. It may be necessary to replace the fan motor or fan assembly to increase the air-handling capacity of the system, even though the furnace burner has sufficient heating capacity.

When you are working on existing buildings, always check the following items:

- The location of floor registers, diffusers, radiators, etc.

- The location of duct work or pipes.

- The location of the central heating system.

SECTION **7**

Cooling

Nearly 58 million American households (60%) use some type of air conditioning system. In regions where air conditioning is common, you should be familiar with how the equipment works and how any changes you make affect it.

Instead of using energy to create heat, air conditioners use energy to remove heat, or more correctly, humidity. The energy source for air conditioning is electricity.

There are four types of air conditioners:

- room air conditioners

- central air conditioners

- ductless air conditioning

- electric heat pumps

Evaporative coolers and fans can also be used to provide summer comfort. But neither one removes heat, which is the real cause of discomfort. Because heat pumps are also used for heating, we will discuss this system separately in Section 8.

ROOM AIR CONDITIONERS

As the name implies, room air conditioners are sized to cool just one room. Therefore, a number of them are required for a whole house. Standard room air conditioners are noisy and can produce uncomfortably wide fluctuations in temperature from room to room.

CENTRAL AIR CONDITIONERS

Central air conditioners are designed to cool the entire home and they have a number of advantages. They are out of the way, quiet and convenient. If the home already has a forced air heating system, a central air system can easily be tied into the existing duct work. Adding an air conditioner to an existing forced air system is the least expensive way to provide summer cooling.

electricity use and decreases overall energy efficiency of the unit.

Most air conditioners are rated in BTUs per hour. Central air conditioners and heat pumps may also list cooling capacity by tons. One ton is equivalent to 12,000 BTUs. Capacity ratings of most air conditioners are certified under a program administered by the **Air Conditioning and Refrigeration Institute**. With air conditioning systems, equipment cost is more proportional to size than it is with heating equipment. Therefore, doubling the cooling output nearly doubles the cost of the cooling unit.

EFFICIENCY

Efficiency is just as important in an air conditioning system as it is in a heating system. Efficiency of room air conditioners is measured by the energy efficiency rating (EER). This is the ratio of the cooling output in BTUs divided by the power consumption (in wattage). The EER does not factor in performance over the cooling season. A room air conditioner with an EER over 9.5 is considered efficient. Room air conditioners come with energy guide labels to help in selecting the best unit for the application.

Central air conditioners and heat pumps operating in the cooling mode are rated according to their Seasonal Energy Efficiency Rating (SEER). This rating is the seasonal cooling output in BTUs divided by the seasonal energy input in watt hours for an average U.S. climate. The national appliance efficiency standard for central air conditioners, which was first effective in 1992, required a minimum SEER of 10.

Central air conditioners are almost always more efficient than room air condi-

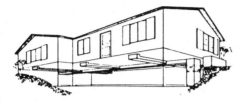

UPFLOW FURNACE-MOUNTED SYSTEM

DOWNFLOW FURNACE-MOUNTED SYSTEM

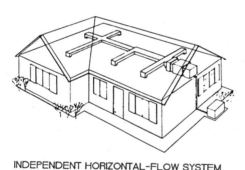

INDEPENDENT HORIZONTAL-FLOW SYSTEM

Figure 66 (Courtesy of University of Illinois) Central air conditioning systems have ductwork, installed below the floor or in the attic. The ductwork may limit changes you are considering for the new room.

SIZING THE COOLING SYSTEM

Bigger is not better when it comes to cooling systems. Proper sizing is critical to efficient operation. Oversized systems not only cost more initially but will cycle on and off frequently. This increases

tioners. Energy-saving features to look for include:

- A fan-only switch (which allows the unit to operate for ventilation and can substantially reduce air conditioning costs);

- A filter check light that acts as a reminder to check the filter after a predetermined number of operating hours;

- An automatic delay fan switch to turn the fan off a few minutes after the compressor turns off.

Central air conditioners are purchased from local HVAC contractors. Your clients can gather product and energy information before making their final choice.

DUCT SYSTEMS

Since warm air rises to the ceiling and cool air falls towards the floor, it is preferable to introduce heated air into a room at a low level and cooled air at a high level. In a combined system, the best compromise is a floor or baseboard outlet that directs the air flow upward with sufficient velocity to reach the ceiling. Otherwise cool air may pool at the floor level.

In small kitchens where wall space is limited, the HVAC contractor may wish to install the supply outlet in the toe-kick area of the cabinets. While this location works well for heating, it does not work well for cooling.

The air does not project into the room. In this case it's better to place the supply outlet high on the wall, be sure

the register does not blow directly on the occupants. The vanes in registers are adjustable for different angles, one of the final items you should check as you walk through the job.

OTHER COOLING SYSTEMS

Evaporative Coolers

Evaporative coolers are most practical in dry climates, such as the Southwest. Sometimes called "*swamp coolers*", they work by blowing house air over a damp pad or by spraying a fine mist of water into the household air supply. The dry air evaporates the moisture and cools off. These cooling systems cannot be used in humid areas because they do not dehumidify the air.

Window Fans

Window fans for cooling and ventilation are a reasonable option for cooling in temperate climates if they are used properly. They should be located on the leeward (downwind) side of the house facing out. A window should be open in each room. Interior doors must remain open to allow air flow. Window fans will not work as well in houses with long, narrow hallways or those with small rooms and many interior partitions. Window fans can be noisy, especially on high settings, but they are inexpensive.

Whole-House Fans

Whole-house fans are more convenient than window fans. Mounted in a hallway ceiling on the top floor, the fan pulls air from the house and blows it into the attic. The fan usually is covered on the bottom by a louver vent. Installing a whole-house fan in the hallway during a kitchen remodeling project might be part of the work you specify.

The fan should have at least two speeds, with the highest one capable of changing the entire volume of air in the house every 3 minutes. *For example,* a 1,500 sq. ft. house with 8-foot ceilings contains 12,000 cubic feet. The fan thus should be rated at 4,000 cubic feet per minute (cfm). Because the fan blows air into the attic, the attic must have sufficient outlet vents. The free vent area, including soffit vents, ridge vents and gable-end vents, should be twice the free vent area of the fan opening. (Free vent area is a measure of the area of the vent opening minus the area blocked by screening and louvers.) For safety reasons, the fan should have manual controls. It should also have a fusible link, which automatically shuts the fan down in case of fire.

Attic Fans

Attic fans, also called roof fans, can substantially reduce the temperature of attic air. Although most attics have openings for ventilation, the vents are usually not large enough to prevent the attic temperature from reaching 140°F or higher on a hot day. This heat is transferred into the living areas below. Mounted as high as possible in a gable or roof surface, an attic fan exhausts hot attic air and pulls in cooler outside air through vents in the eaves or soffits. These fans can reduce the attic temperature 20°F or more.

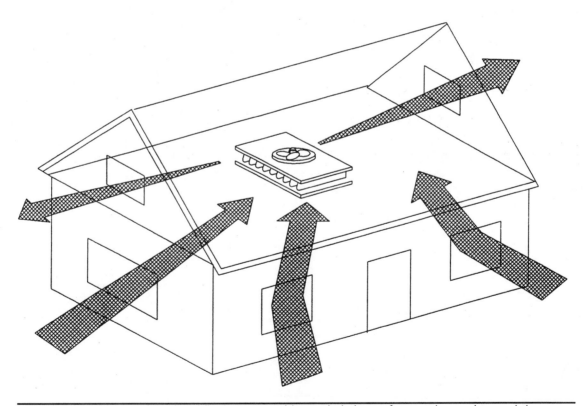

Figure 67 In climates where humidity is not a problem, whole-house fans can be used to cool the house at night.

Ceiling Fans

Ceiling fans can make a room seem cooler by mixing the air and creating a breeze. The air movement across your skin has a cooling effect. Ceiling fans can be used in homes with or without air conditioning. Variable speed fans are desirable to allow adjustment for maximum comfort. A ceiling fan can weigh 30 to 50 pounds. A typical installation is on a special cross brace between ceiling joists. For effective operation, the fan blades should be at least one foot below the ceiling. For safety, a seven foot clearance beneath the blades is required. Also consider if the fan has lights or other projections below the blades, and maintain adequate clearance.

Ceiling fans can operate from a pull chain switch, a wall switch or a remote control. Consult your electrician when planning the location of a ceiling fan to be sure the wiring can be installed as needed.

RENOVATION CONSIDERATIONS

When conducting your jobsite inspection, look for registers in floors and walls. Be especially alert for ducts that might be hidden in walls you plan to remove. If the house has a second story, check rooms above to be sure there are no registers in these rooms. If you are in doubt, check the attic, basement or crawl space to see where ducts turn down or up into the wall cavities.

In existing buildings, you may need to pre-plan new duct and register locations with your subcontractor. The old register may not be in the right place for a new kitchen. Your contractor may need to split ductwork and bring in an additional register.

Find out how much additional demolition will be required. Perhaps you can find a different location that suits the design and requirements for the duct.

If you are adding a kitchen to a house, find out whether the existing air conditioner system can handle the added volume. You may need to add a small room unit.

Adding duct work to cool new space is easier if the ducts are not embedded in a concrete slab. Duct work located in an attic, crawl space or basement generally can be extended if the new space is not too distant from the cooling equipment. Jackhammering out a concrete slab to add duct work might not be cost effective. Again, discuss the options with the HVAC contractor.

SECTION **8**

Heat Pumps

HOW THE SYSTEM WORKS

Used for Both Heating & Cooling

Electric heat pumps operate on a different principle. Instead of directly producing heat from the electric current, they use electricity to move heat from one place to another. They work in the same way as a refrigerator, using a special refrigerant fluid (HCFC) that changes back and forth between liquid and vapor. In the heating mode, the heat pump extracts heat from outside the house and delivers it to the house. In the cooling mode, it extracts heat from the house and takes it outside.

Ideal for Temperate Climates

Air-source heat pumps work most efficiently when there is a small difference between inside and outside temperature. For instance, when the outdoor temperature is 55°F, it is relatively easy for the heat pump to capture heat from the air. But when the outside temperature drops below 40°F, there is relatively little heat left.

At freezing, which is 32°F, the air contains no excess heat. Therefore, air-source heat pumps are not widely used in climates where winter temperatures are below 32°F more than 20% of the heating season. For the colder days, air-source heat pumps have electric coils (like the heating coils on a range) that provide supplementary heat when the temperature outside drops below 32°F.

Air Temperature Concerns

One complaint that has been lodged against heat pumps is that the heated air coming from the register is not as warm as heat from warm air furnaces. A heat pump may deliver air only at about 90°F. To compensate, the heat pump delivers the air at a higher velocity.

Sizing the System

Sizing can be difficult because the same unit is used for both cooling and heating. A heat pump sized for heating loads in a cold climate will be considerably oversized when it comes to cooling. A heat pump sized for cooling loads in a warm climate will tend to be oversized when it comes to heating.

A good heat pump technician should be able to help your clients choose the best compromise between cooling and heating capacity.

Locating the System

Heat pumps are among the most flexible home cooling or heating equipment because they can be mounted almost anywhere. This may be helpful if space is tight, and you have no place to put a utility closet for mechanical equipment. However, these units are again somewhat noisy, so don't plan an exterior location just below the master bedroom window.

Air Cleaners

Clients who are sensitive to indoor pollutants should consider installing an air cleaner in their heating/cooling system. Air cleaners can be used with most brands and styles of forced-air furnaces, heat pumps, and central air conditioners.

According to the Air Conditioning and Refrigeration Institute (ARI) electronic air cleaners are 10 to 20 times more efficient than standard air filters. Electronic air cleaners trap large particles with a screen pre-filter and smaller particles with a form of static electricity.

Another form of air cleaner is the self-charging mechanical filter. This filter is made of polypropylene or polystyrene. These materials are able to hold a static charge across their surface to trap particles. Self-charging mechanical filters are less efficient than electronic air cleaners. Consult an HVAC contractor before specifying an air cleaner. The air cleaner must be compatible with the main heating/cooling system.

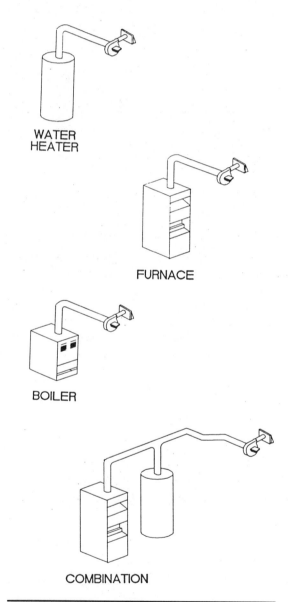

WATER HEATER

FURNACE

BOILER

COMBINATION

Figure 68 Add-on power venters can be used to provide induced draft venting for furnaces and water heaters.

CHAPTER **2**

Kitchen Equipment and Materials

Once you have a clear understanding of typical North American building practices and the mechanical systems that are generally found in domestic homes, it's time to devote your attention to learning about the equipment and materials you'll be specifying for the kitchen project.

The range of choices is extensive. As a professional kitchen designer you must familiarize yourself with the advantages and disadvantages of different categories of materials and equipment. Then, evaluate individual appliances, cabinet systems, fittings

and fixtures by reviewing the products available to you.

In this chapter of The Essential Kitchen Design Guide, we'll study cabinet systems and appliances. We'll also discuss surfacing materials and the fixtures and fittings typically specified for residential kitchens.

A clear understanding of the engineering behind these products will help you specify the right mix of products for each project.

Cabinets

At one time, virtually all kitchen cabinets were custom built by local fabricators for each house. Today, a great majority of kitchen cabinet systems are produced in highly sophisticated manufacturing facilities, both here in North America and internationally in Europe. As a kitchen specialist, you may represent a specific cabinet manufacturer directly, you may work for a manufacturer or distributor, or you may actually fabricate the cabinets within your own manufacturing facility.

CABINET TYPES

Regardless of the type of business you operate, as a cabinet specifier there are three broad categories of cabinets that you will choose from. Within each of these sources the resulting quality levels, production costs, delivery schedules and reliability factors vary.

Stock

Stock cabinet manufacturers offer a full range of cabinets in specified sizes. These cabinets are made in quantity and are then shipped to a distributor or manufacturer's warehouse so that they are available for quick delivery. Because the cabinets are produced in quantity,

the assembly lines cannot be stopped for special units. Therefore, the cabinet manufacturer's catalog generally reflects the entire product offering. Stock manufacturers take advantage of market research and also offer only the most popular finishes and door styles.

This type of manufacturing method offers the specifier good value because of the economies of manufacturing. The biggest advantages of stock cabinetry are its availability, consistency of quality and consistency of service from these very large, stable manufacturers. Stock cabinets offer an excellent product for a project limited by budget constraint, but not by design creativity. Because styles and special sizes are limited, you should investigate the breadth of the line before designing with the product.

With stock cabinets you "get what you pay for". Some of the cheaper lines use doors of mismatched or lower quality woods. They may use thin laminates or actual paper products that simulate wood on finished sides. The parts of the case may be glued together with no mechanical fasteners to ensure durability over the life expectancy of the piece. Make sure that you carefully evaluate the construction of the stock cabinets that you represent.

Semi-Custom

Semi-custom cabinets are produced by both stock and custom manufacturers. This type of product is produced on an assembly line basis, but the offerings include more interior fittings in the form of accessories and some custom size possibilities.

This product combines the advantage of an assembly line process with the ability to create some limited specials with some attention toward the importance of style.

Semi-custom cabinets come in a wide variety of quality and price levels. Because they may be high on style but limited in their size offering, review the manufacturer's catalog carefully.

Custom

Custom cabinet manufacturers make one kitchen at a time. The cabinets are not produced until the kitchen has been designed and all details are finalized. Custom cabinets may be made by a local fabricator, or in a large manufacturing facility. Generally, they are made on the same 3" (7.62cm) modular increments as the other types of cabinets, but special sizes are also available for a perfect fit.

These totally custom "built-to-order" kitchens are considered premier "furniture grade" cabinet systems. These manufacturers generally offer the latest technology, construction methods and case materials, the most extensive array of accessories available, and a long history of excellence in service as well as in product. It is these companies that offer new, trendsetting styles and finishes to the market. These cabinets also are generally the most expensive and take the longest to get. Much like custom furniture, an 8 to 20 week delivery time is to be expected.

CABINET SIZES

Because the cabinet industry is an international one, there are two common methods of sizing cabinets: the English imperial system, based on inches, and the international metric standard. Because both dimensions are used throughout our industry, all the information in these *Kitchen Industry Technical Manuals* is listed in both imperial and metric dimensions.

As you consider representing a cabinet line make sure you find out how the cabinet is sized: *are the cabinets sized on an imperial system; are they sized in a metric system; or are they a hybrid of the two?* This is important as there may be slight differences in cabinet case sizing that will affect the cabinet's fit with adjacent appliances and other pieces of equipment. To introduce you to typical cabinet sizing, *Figure 69* lists elevation dimensions.

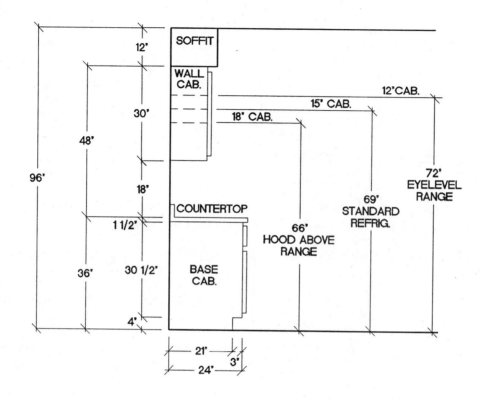

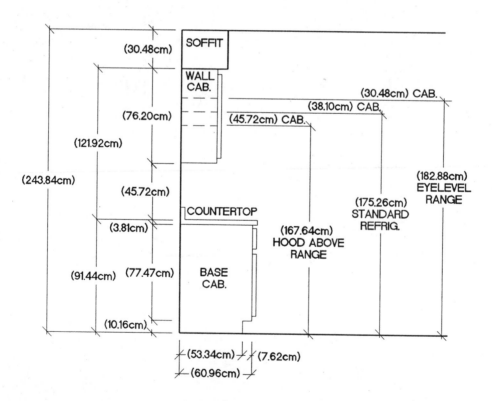

Figure 69 Typical Imperial and Metric Cabinet Sizes.

Base Units

Base cabinets, which are set on the floor, are 24" (60.96cm) deep, front to back, and 34-1/2" (87.63cm) high including the subbase (which is also called the toekick or plinth). This raised portion underneath the cabinets is generally 4" (10.16cm) high. The common base cabinet has a single drawer over a single door which has either a half shelf or a full shelf in the middle, and a full shelf at the bottom of the cabinet.

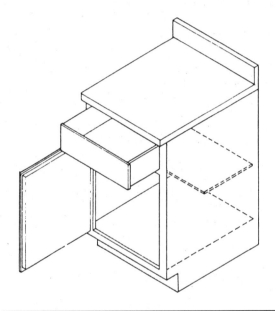

Figure 70 Standard base cabinet with half shelf.

Single door base cabinets are generally available in widths of 9" (22.86cm), 12" (30.48cm), 15" (38.1cm), 18" (45.72cm), 21" (53.34cm) and 24" (60.96cm). The 9" (22.86cm) wide cabinet generally will not have a drawer and may not be available in heavily detailed door styles. Double door cabinets are usually available in widths from 24" to 48" (60.96cm to 121.92cm); however some manufacturers do not provide 39" (99.06cm) wide or 45" (114.3cm) wide units. Others stop the line at 42" (106.68) wide.

SPECIAL PURPOSE BASE CABINETS

In addition to the standard base cabinet, special purpose base cabinets are available for specific needs. At the end of this section, you'll find a listing of typical cabinets is included which will discuss each one of these types of cabinets.

Generally, the categories of base cabinets you can choose from are:

- **Drawer Cabinets:** A cabinet that features two, three, four or five drawers. Two-drawer units are used frequently today to create a recycling unit. Three- and four-drawer units are typically seen near the primary sink for flatware and kitchen linen storage. Wide, three-drawer units are often used below a cooking surface to conveniently store pots, pans, lids and utensils used at the cooking surface. Try to avoid drawer units smaller than 15" (38.1cm) wide because the interior drawer space will be too small to be functional. Many manufacturers offer special-

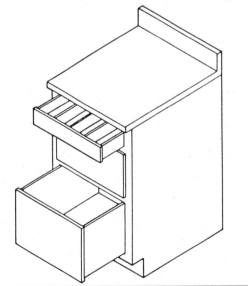

Figure 71 Standard base drawer cabinet.

ized drawer inserts. Drawer interiors may be divided to house flatware, knives, spices or cooking utensils with various combinations of lengthwise and crosswise dividers. Such dividers may be made out of the same material as the case or they may be a drop-in, molded plastic unit. Manufacturers also offer ironing boards that pop out of drawers and meat slicers that fold into a drawer.

- **Corner Cabinets:** A variety of corner cabinets are available:

"Lazy Susan" Cabinet: Generally requires between 33" (83.82cm) and 36" (91.44cm) of wall space. A round shelf swings out into the room and past the door opening. The door may be bifold or may actually swing through the cabinet interior. The wider the door, the more functional the circular shelf.

"Blind" Cabinet: A cabinet that has a shelf, pull-out or swing- out apparatus to provide accessibility into the corner. They generally require 42" to 48" (106.68 to 121.92cm) of wall space. Avoid any unit less than 42" (106.68cm) wide. Always specify a 45" (114.3cm) or a 48" (121.92cm) wide unit to provide the widest opening for clear accessibility to stored items within.

"Pie-Cut" Cabinet: A corner cabinet that requires 36" (91.44cm) on each wall (much like a lazy susan) and features stationary shelving as opposed to a rotating shelf. Maximum shelf space is provided. This type of pie-cut unit may have a curved door.

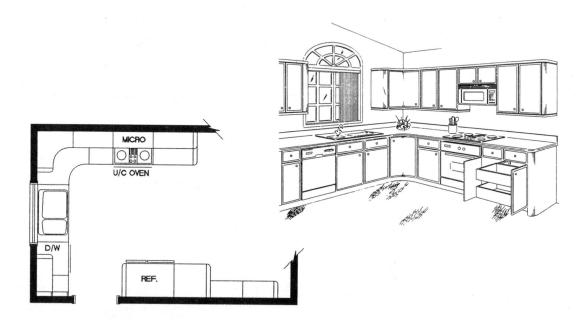

Figure 72 A pie-cut corner base cabinet has a concave curved door on it in this kitchen. Note the repetition of the curved line at the window and end panel.

- **Roll-Out Shelf Cabinet:** A base cabinet with roll-outs. Rather than full or half shelves, a base cabinet may have one roll-out in the middle, one roll-out at the bottom, two roll-outs equally spaced, or stacked roll-outs to fill the entire cavity.

- **Pull-out Trash Can or Recycling Center:** Specialized cabinets which are designed to hold bins to facilitate the separation of refuse.

- **Swing-up Mix Shelf:** A mechanical shelf which lifts up so that hand appliances can be conveniently stored.

- **Pull-out Table:** A section of the cabinet which houses a pull-out surface and is supported so that it can function similar to a table.

- **Sink/Cooktop Cabinet:** Base cabinets with shallow top drawers, or a tilt-down front which houses a plastic or stainless steel container. Designed to utilize the top drawer space that would otherwise be lost once the cooktop or sink is installed.

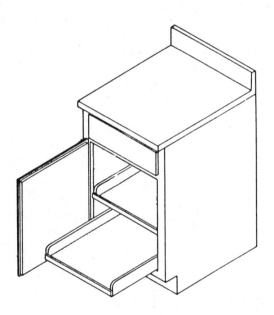

Figure 73 Standard base cabinet with roll-out shelves.

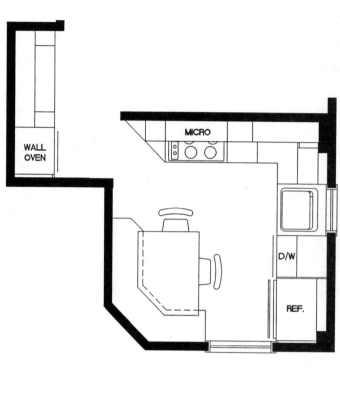

Figure 74 *This kitchen utilizes many standard base cabinet types: a cabinet with full height doors has been used on an angle to the far left. This angled cabinet extends the counter space, while maintaining clear walkway access to the doorway. Wide drawers are below the cooktop, with typical sized units adjacent. A Lazy Susan in the corner features two doors that rotate into the opening.*

Figure 75 This design solution introduces curved base cabinets to soften the lines of the space and maximize the countertop area. Curved doors are available in limited sizes and configurations. The curved line is repeated at the open shelf wall unit in the corner near the range, and the radius end panel to the right of the refrigerator.

Wall Units

Wall cabinets, which are fixed to the walls with screws, are generally 12" (30.48cm) deep. They come in a variety of heights ranging from 30" (76.2cm) to 36" (91.44cm) to 48" (121.92cm). 30" (76.2cm) high wall units are designed to be installed in a room with 96" (243.84cm) high ceilings. They will feature an extended, flush or recessed soffit above them.

"Soffit" is an industry word identifying a boxed-in area above the cabinets. The proper construction term would be a "bulk head", made up of fascia (the front panel) and the soffit (the underside). However, it is typical in the industry to call the entire structure a soffit.

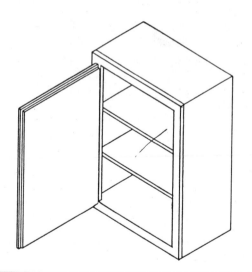

Figure 76 A typical wall cabinet.

36" (91.44cm) high units are designed to be installed in a 96" (243.84cm) high room with a 6" (15.24cm) trim connecting the cabinets to the ceiling. 36" (91.44cm) high units are also used in a 108" (274.32cm) high ceiling to provide better balance between the cabinet spacing and the architectural envelope of the room. 42" (106.68cm) high wall units are designed to extend all the way up to a ceiling in a 96" (243.84cm) high room, or to be used with an extended, flush or recessed soffit in 108" (274.32.cm) or 120" (304.8cm) high ceilings.

For use above microwave ovens, hoods, refrigerators or other tall obstructions, wall cabinets are also available in 12" (30.48cm), 15" (38.1cm), 18"(45.72cm) and 24" (60.96cm) high. Some of these sizes are often available 24" (60.96cm) deep to provide an accessible wall cabinet above a refrigerator. Wall cabinets are generally installed from 15" to 18" (38.1cm to 45.72cm) off the finished counter surface. This clearance is typically required so small hand appliances can fit under the wall cabinet.

As a standard, wall cabinets feature two adjustable interior shelves in a 30" high unit. The 36" (91.44cm) and 42" (106.68cm) high units will generally include three shelves. To maximize the accessibility of wall cabinets, always specify wall units without a center stile. Many manufacturers install this vertical support member in wall cabinets wider than 30", which blocks access. If at all possible, specify a manufacturer that provides an open space the entire width of the cabinet.

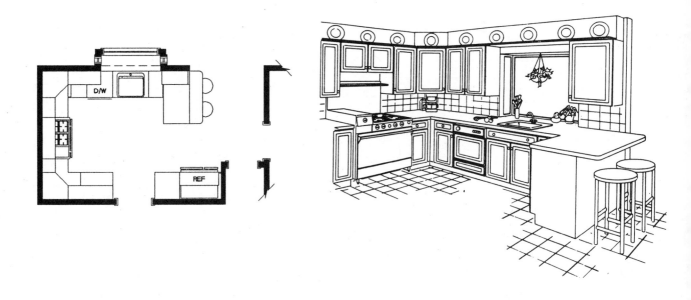

Figure 77 30" (76.2cm) high wall units are combined with a recessed soffit that extends 6" (15.2cm) from the wall to create a plate rail. The corner features a diagonal corner unit and a short 15" (38.1cm) cabinet is placed above the range.

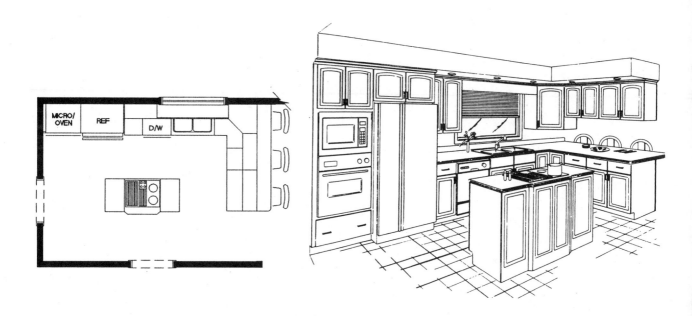

Figure 78 30" (76.2cm) high wall units are installed under an extended soffit. The soffit provides space to recess the incandescent lights. Note the molding that separates the wall cabinets from the soffit. A diagonal corner unit is installed adjacent to shallow peninsula cabinets, which are accessible from both sides. A 24" (60.96cm) deep cabinet is above the refrigerator. Note the door height difference between the cabinet above the refrigerator and the one above the oven. If possible, try to align all doors used above tall units.

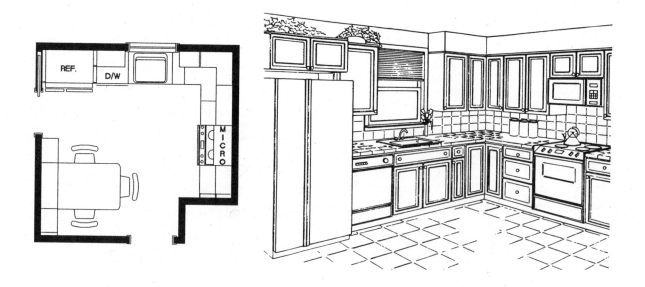

Figure 79 A flush soffit can also be installed against standard 30" (76.2cm) high units. In this solution, the soffit is installed on only one side of the room. In the other area, it is left open for display.

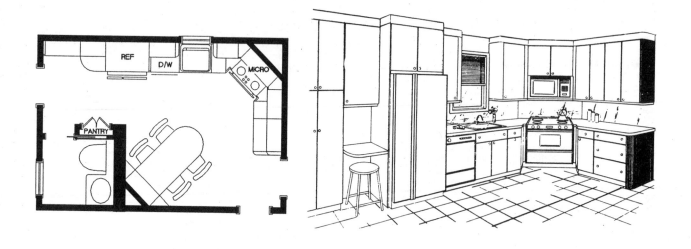

Figure 80 90" (228.6cm) high cabinets are designed to be installed with a 6" (15.24cm) molding to enclose the space between the top of the cabinets and the ceiling. This molding may be held down from 1/2" to 2" (1.27cm to 5.08cm) from the ceiling to create a shadow line. Make sure that curved molding is available for this type of an application if you are planning to use radius end panels as shown here.

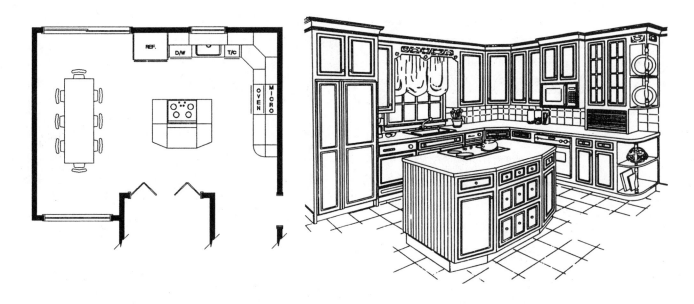

Figure 81 42" (106.68cm) high wall cabinets can extend to the ceiling in a 96" (243.84cm) high room. They can be used with moldings if the backsplash height is lowered to 15" (38.1cm). Note the attractive tambour cabinet extending down to the countertop at the right. Glass inset panels are installed above this unit. Open shelf units are featured at the end of the run to support the English Country theme.

Figure 82 In a room with a 108" to 120" (274.32cm to 304.8cm) high ceiling, the 42" (106.68cm) wall cabinets may be used with the molding or soffit to finish the space between the cabinets and the ceiling. The proportional relationship between the doors and the height of the soffit is critical. In this room with 9' (274.32cm) ceilings, the massive hood area balances the long, slender doors.

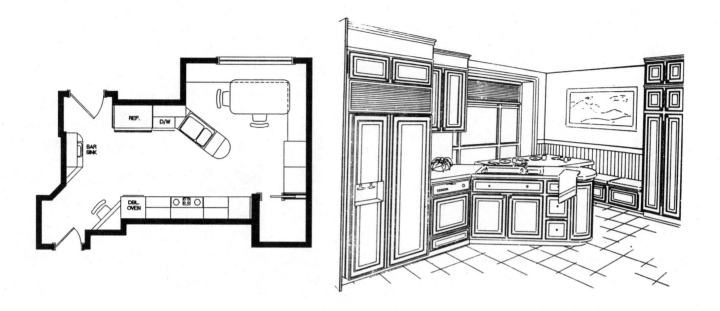

Figure 83 Another approach to installing cabinets is to "stack" them on top of one another. The 84" (213.36cm) tall units on the right side of this kitchen feature a second set of 18" (45.72cm) high cabinets placed above them. This balances with the enclosed soffit on the left hand side of the perspective.

Figure 84 Cabinet heights can be combined. In this example, 42" (106.68cm) high units are featured in the working portion of the kitchen. A custom tall cabinet in the breakfast nook finishes off at 84" (213.36cm), leaving an open soffit above for display.

SPECIAL PURPOSE WALL CABINETS

- **Corner Cabinet:** Much like base units, blind corner units and pie-cut cabinets are available. An angled, diagonal corner wall unit is also frequently specified.

- **Special Interior Accessories:** Include door-mounted spice racks, interior step shelving, swing-out can goods or spice shelf units. Some manufacturers also offer wall cabinets that have built-in integral fluorescent or low-voltage halogen lighting systems, which provide optimum task lighting above the work surface.

- **Open Shelf Unit:** Open shelf units can be attractively mixed with enclosed cabinets to provide design relief to the overall room by introducing a display of the client's collectibles.

- **Glass Door Cabinet:** Full glass panels, or glass sheets that are framed in the door material are popular. The cabinet interior should be finished to match the exterior. Glass may be clear, frosted, etched. They may also feature decorative, stained, or leaded glass patterns.

- **Peninsula Cabinet:** A wall cabinet that is accessible from two sides and is installed above a cabinet that juts out into the center of the room.

- **Tambour Unit:** A cabinet with a roll-up door, called a "tambour" unit, that extends to the countertop. Sometimes referred to as a small appliance garage. Appliance garages can also be created with regular cabinet doors.

Tall Units

Tall cabinets are used for a variety of purposes in kitchen planning: as a tall closet with no shelves to house cleaning equipment, as a food storage cabinet with specialized swing-out shelves, and as a replacement for standard base or wall units with adjustable shelves and/or roll-outs.

Tall units are generally available in 84" (213.36cm) or 96" (243.84cm) heights, and are typically specified in 12" (30.48cm) or 24" (60.96cm) depths for kitchen use. These units are often available in 18" (45.72cm) and 24" (60.96cm) widths. Some manufacturers also provide them in 15" (38.1cm), 30" (76.2cm) and 36" (91.44cm) widths as well.

A typical configuration includes a tall door that is approximately 65" (165.1cm) high below a smaller door. This door size is specified to minimize warpage problems. Because of this concern about warpage, tall cabinets do not have a single full-height door.

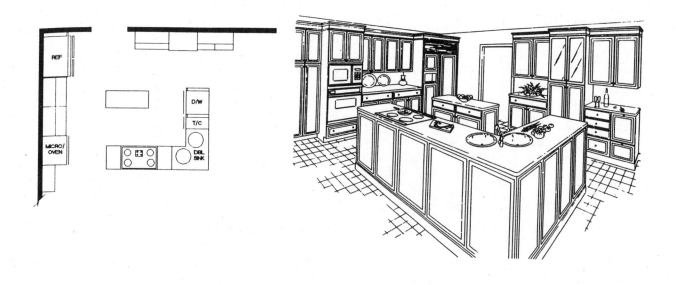

Figure 85 Tall units are generally best located at the end of a run of cabinets. Oftentimes, an oven cabinet will be placed at the end of a counter, with a refrigerator at the oppostie end. We see this in the left hand view of this kitchen. Tall units may be a bit awkward if placed in the center of a run unless perfectly balanced on each side, as we see in this same example to the far right.

Figure 86 If space is limited, consider placing a tall cabinet along the side of either a refrigerator end panel, or an oven cabinet as seen in this plan. A 12" (30.48cm) deep pantry that is 24" (60.96cm) wide is much easier to access than a 12" (30.48cm) wide one which is 24" (60.96cm) deep.

SPECIAL PURPOSE TALL CABINETS

- **Built-in Oven Unit:** Cabinets that house double ovens generally have one drawer below the oven. Single oven cabinets have two or three drawers below the appliances. Many manufacturers provide a "universal" oven case, which has three drawers that are designed to be eliminated at the jobsite if necessary, to accommodate a double oven.

- **Built-in Refrigerator Unit:** Some manufacturers offer a 3-sided tall enclosure with a 24" (60.96cm) deep upper cabinet to surround a refrigerator.

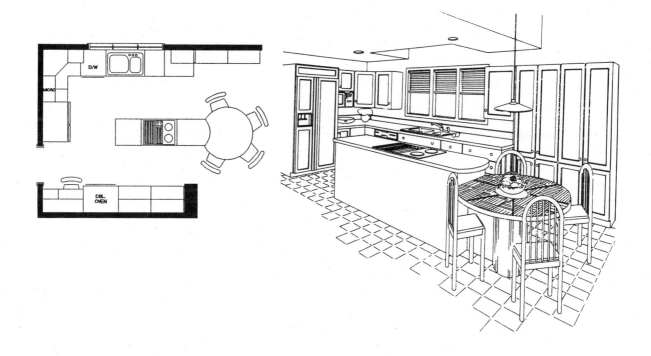

Figure 87 12" (30.48cm) deep tall units can take the place of normal wall cabinets or base cabinets. Here is an excellent example of using tall cabinets once all countertop requirements have been met.

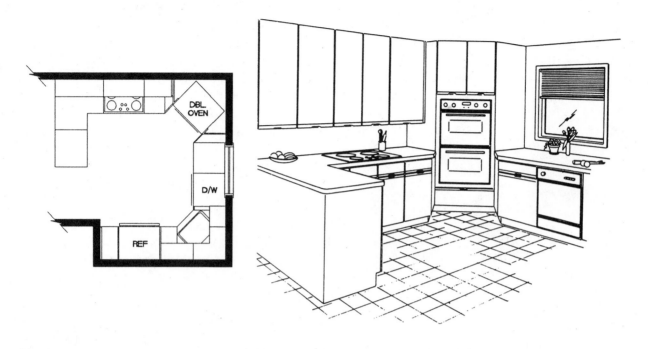

Figure 88 Oven cabinets are oftentimes placed at an angle in the corner. If recessed into the corner, this type of an installation meets planning guidelines because the countertop is still accessible on each side. For wheelchair accessibility, the base cabinet between the oven and dishwasher must be removed to create kneespace.

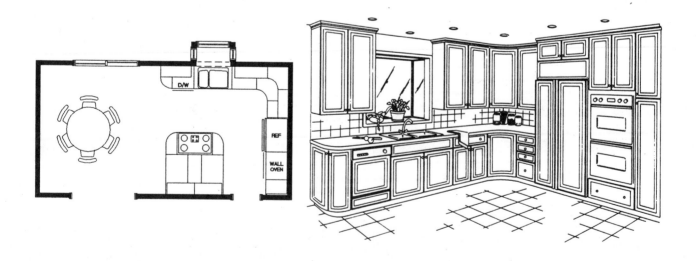

Figure 89 Elevation drawings are important when placing tall elements adjacent to one another. In this de-sign, the small doors above the refrigerator, the doors above the oven and the upper pantry doors are not sized to match one another and are therefore, visually distracting.

CABINET CONSTRUCTION

As you consider cabinet options, one of the first decisions you must make is whether you will represent a cabinet featuring frame construction or one featuring a frameless.

Frame Construction

In frame cabinet construction thin component parts make up the sides, back, top and bottom of the cabinet. These parts are then joined together and attached to a frame that is the primary support for the cabinet. Doors and drawers are then fit in one of three ways: flush with the frame (called "inset"), partially inlaying the frame or completely overlaying the frame.

Frame cabinets are easy to install, because they do not have the minimal clearance tolerances found in the frameless method of cabinet construction. However, this method of construction has less interior storage space. Consequently, the interior size of drawers or roll-out accessories is significantly smaller than the overall width of the cabinet. 1 1/4" to 1 1/2" (3.18cm to 3.81cm) front frames are usually made of hardwood, 1/2" to 3/4" (1.27cm to 1.91cm) thick. Rails, stiles and mullions are doweled (or mortise and tenon) as well as glued and stapled for rigidity. Lap joints and screw joints are also used.

End panels typically consist of 1/4" to 3/4" (.64cm to 1.91cm) plywood or particleboard which is dadoed into the back of the stiles and then glued, stapled or nailed in place. They are secured square in each corner with a plastic, metal or fall-off scrap material gusset.

Backs are generally 1/8" (.32cm) hardboard or 3/4" (1.91cm) plywood. Bottoms and tops are 3- or 5-ply hardwood plywood. These cabinet parts are 1/4" to 1/2" (.64cm to 1.27cm), and are dadoed into the sides of the cabinet.

Shelves are lumber, plywood or particleboard, 1/2" to 3/4" (1.27cm to 1.91cm) in specification, with square or rounded front edges. Plywood and particleboard shelves are generally banded with hardwood or with a PVC plastic front edging.

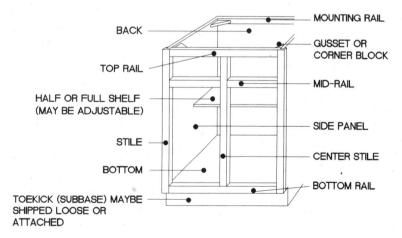

FRAMED CABINET CONSTRUCTION

Figure 90 Typical Cabinet Construction - Framed.

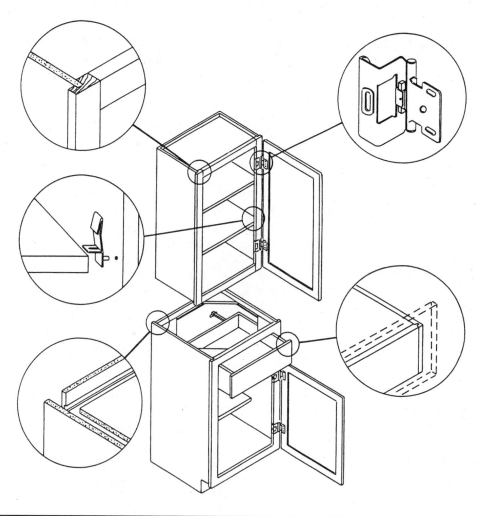

Figure 91
Framed cabinets are fitted together with various forms of wood joinery and without special hardware fitings.
Door hinges attach to face frame and generally do not have multiple adjustments.

Frameless Construction

This second major category of case construction is called "frameless". With this method of construction, 5/8" to 3/4" (1.59cm to 1.91cm) core material sides are connected, with either a mechanical fastening system or a dowel method of construction. Because of their thickness, these case parts form a box that does not need a front frame for stability or squareness. Doors and drawers cover the entire face of the cabinet.

The top, bottom and sides are routed to receive the back panel and hanging rails. The sides are drilled for adjustable shelf clip holes or dadoed for fixed shelves. The doors are bored top and bottom for adjustable, fully-concealed, self-closing hinges. All exposed edges are generally banded.

You will hear these cabinets sometimes referred to as "32mm" or "System 32" cabinets. The term 32 refers to the basic matrix of all these cabinets: all the holes, hinge fittings, cabinet joints and mountings are set 32mm apart. This spacing is based on the boring equipment that is used in the manufacturing process.

The major advantages of frameless construction are total accessibility to the case interior, and the clean, simple design statement made by the finished product. Some concerns exist regarding the stability of this type of construction: the tendency for frameless cases to "rack" and the additional planning exper-

tise required to insure proper clearance between these full overlay doors and between the cabinets and other elements of the plan.

When evaluating frame or frameless cabinet lines, design professionals should consider the method of wood joints employed, the thickness of the cabinet component parts, the type and quality of hardware offered, the core material specifications and the depth of the line's cabinet size offering.

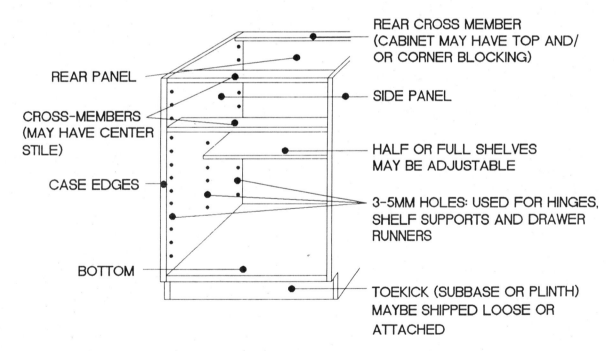

FRAMELESS CABINET CONSTRUCTION

Figure 92 Typical Cabinet Construction - Frameless.

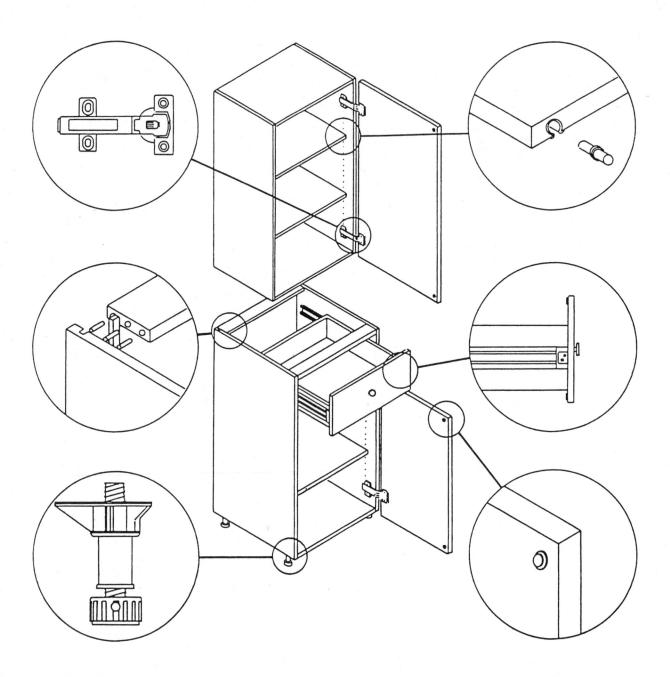

Figure 93 Typical frameless cabinet construction is oriented to hardware and production. Pins and dowels, which might be wood or metal, are made to fit specific holes, all of which are drilled when the cabinet is manufactured. Hinges are completely concealed. Leveling legs may be used instead of an attached subbase.

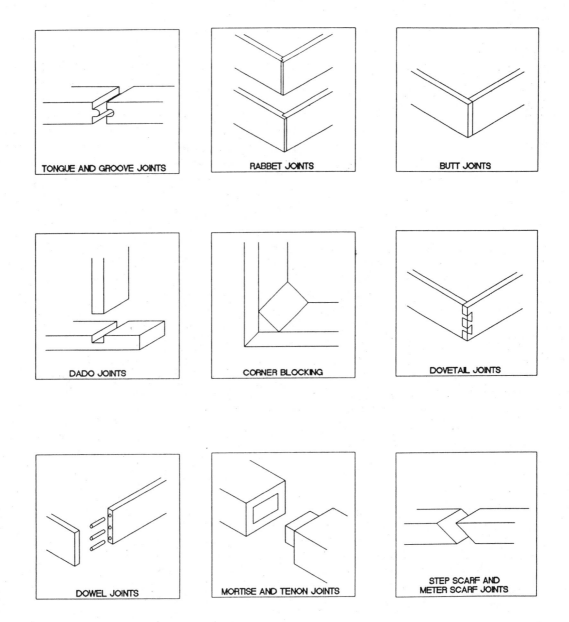

Figure 94 Cabinet joinery methods can include all of the details above. In nearly all cases, the joints are held together with staples or brads to allow glue time to cure. It is glue that locks the joints. Rabbet and dado cuts are used in case construciton. Dovetail joints and dowels provide more drawer strength.

CABINET CORE MATERIALS

In both frameless and frame construction, the cabinet core material determines the cabinet stability. In frameless built products the core material is extremely important because there is no frame surrounding the box. In a recent article in *Cabinet Manufacturing and Finishing*, **Harry C. Osvold**, owner of H.C. Osvold Company (a Minneapolis- based firm that manufactures custom laminated and wood architectural products), gave an overview of core materials used today.

Particleboard

Mr. Osvold began by pointing out that particleboard is the most widely used core material for cabinet construction today. Particleboard was originally a by-product of the western lumber and plywood mills which utilized sawdust, shavings and other off-fall from the industry. Today its usage is so great that it is made from trees harvested specifically for particleboard production.

In broad terms, particleboards fall into three general categories: Western board, Midwest aspen board and Southern pine board. For all-around quality, Western board is generally considered the best. It is easy to cut and shape, and does not tend to fuzz up when machined for radius edges. **Particleboard obtained its name based on its composition of particles of wood off-fall bonded together with resin under pressure.** The size of the particles in these man-made boards generally is used to identify the stability and screw holding capacity of different levels of core material.

For example, underlayment is a form of particleboard that has a low density and low resin content. Therefore, it is not recommended for a laminate substrate because it has lower dimensional stability, structural strength and moisture resistance.

Better particleboard materials are rated as "45 pound commercial grade". This board is highly recommended for normal laminating. It has smaller particles of wood by-products, which then increase the surface space available for the resin to bond to. It therefore has good dimensional stability and provides a smooth surface for laminate bonding. The "45 lb." rating refers to the pounds per square inch of pressure applied during the fabrication process.

One of the most frequently used types of substrate material is medium density fiber board identified as MDF. This board is made of even finer fibers than normal particleboard. Its density adds superior screw holding power, a very tight clean edge, and an extremely smooth surface. The MDF edge can be shaped to a profile and painted, resulting in an acceptable finished edge for many surfaces.

A limited number of manufacturers offer a fire-rated particleboard for use in commercial applications requiring fire resistant capability. This board is a 45 pound density produced under a similar process as the normal core materials. The primary difference is that salts are added in the manufacturing process. This board is more difficult to cut and machine than normal particleboards, is limited in sizes available, and few distributors stock the item. Additionally, the salts in the board make it susceptible to moisture. Storage conditions are therefore a prime consideration, as well as a balanced glue system that will be compatible with the board during fabrication.

Today, with the advent of new technology and improved resin and glue methods, the best interior surface for many cabinet applications is some type of man-made board that has been covered with either a laminate solid colored surface or a laminated wood grain surface.

Plywood

Some designers and consumers consider a "solid wood" cabinet to be better than one made from man-made materials. Therefore, plywood is often still used as a core material in cabinet construction. It provides good strength and superior screw holding ability. Fire-rated plywoods are also available in limited sizes. The addition of salts is again employed, so that the same concerns exist for fire-rated plywood as those listed for fire-rated particleboards. When considering a plywood interior, designers should specify that the face veneers on the plywood not produce a grain rise, that a high grade of solid core plywood be used to avoid the presence of voids in the built-up layers of veneer and that the finish surface of the plywood have only a limited number of "plugs". **Plugs are the "football" shaped plywood sections that are used to replace knots in the veneer.**

CABINET FINISH MATERIALS

Cabinet manufacturers use a variety of materials for construction of cabinets. Four major classifications are predominantly used in the kitchen industry: furniture grade steel, decorative laminates, solid woods and wood products.

Furniture Grade Steel

With proper finishing, furniture grade steel is a durable cabinet material. The major benefits of steel are durability, strength without bulk and maintenance-free service. Although limited to one major American manufacturer today, furniture grade steel kitchens are still popular in the United States.

Laminate Surfaces

The use of laminated panels in the manufacture of cabinets and furniture has grown enormously in recent years.

This is attributable to the market factor of the growing popularity of European-style cabinets and the material factor of the increasing scarcity of solid wood. Fueling this growth are higher-quality substrates, better glues and resins, and more sophisticated processes for applying the laminates to substrates. The laminates themselves are now available in a dazzling and often bewildering, variety of colors, patterns, thicknesses, performance characteristics and prices.

There are six major laminate categories available today. In descending order of performance and price, they are:

- high-pressure laminates

- continuous high-performance laminates

- low-pressure laminates

- resin-impregnated foils

- vinyl films

- hot-stamped transfer foils.

HIGH-PRESSURE LAMINATES (HPL)

High-pressure laminates (HPL) are produced in sheets in many decorative colors and in thicknesses from 0.030" to 0.050". These products have been around a long time. In fact, they were, for years, the only laminates available. The most common uses of HPLs are for kitchen countertops, desk tops, dining room and dinette tables, and restaurant countertops and work stations.

- **Advantages:** Best performance of any laminate for most purposes; available in a multitude of colors; readily available from several manufacturers in the United States, Canada and Europe.

- **Disadvantages:** Relatively expensive; performance features may be excessive for most applications.

CONTINUOUS HIGH-PERFORMANCE LAMINATES (CHPL)

Continuous high-performance laminates (CHPL) are the newest laminating materials to come on the scene. Made of the same raw materials as HPLs, they have the same basic characteristics, but are thinner and slightly softer. This means that durability and impact resistance are proportionately lower.

- **Advantages:** Lower cost than HPLs, but the product has many of the same performance characteristics; can buy panels prelaminated.

- **Disadvantages:** Not yet widely available; colors are limited.

LOW-PRESSURE LAMINATES (LPLS)

Low-pressure laminates (LPLs), also known as Premalam, low-pressure melamine, just melamine, or MCP, are melamine-impregnated papers or polyester materials that can be fused to a substrate by heat and pressure.

- **Advantages:** Good performance for most applications; availability of colors; lack of environmental concerns sometimes related to use of glues.

- **Disadvantages:** Tendency to chip and crack, which can be mitigated through the use of better substrates and proper cutting tools. Is not as impact resistant as HPLs.

RESIN-IMPREGNATED FOIL

Resin-impregnated foil is an alpha-cellulose paper impregnated with either urea, acrylic or melamine resins. It is sometimes called paper, or melamine paper, and in Europe it is called foil.

Generally, impregnated papers are offered in wood grains and some solid colors. The paper can be used for profiling and can be embossed to simulate real wood veneer graining. Some manufacturers consider their product to be a synthetic veneer.

Impregnated papers have a cost advantage over high-pressure laminate and composite panels. It is about equivalent to the cost of vinyl, but has a better look than vinyl.

There's a big difference between the durability of heavier and lighter weights of paper. The paper is measured in weight per square meter. Weights range from eighteen gram to thirty gram papers (most imported from Japan), also known as low-basis-eight-papers, through intermediate weights (forty grams to seventy grams). Heavy weight paper has an internal impregnation that gives it some surface integrity. The heavier the weight, the more scratch and scuff resistant the paper will be. Lighter weight papers use waxes or silicon coatings to protect the surface and these will wear off under use.

A simple test to judge the quality of the paper is to attach a small piece of ordinary scotch tape for a few hours to an unobtrusive spot. When removed, the surface should be unharmed on a high quality, heavy weight paper.

- **Advantages:** Lower cost than LPLs because they are laminated on roll-laminating equipment, which is less expensive than thermo-fusing equipment; lower chipout rate than LPLs.

- **Disadvantages:** Most paper suppliers are foreign, which means prices fluctuate sharply with the value of the dollar.

VINYL FILMS

Vinyl films of 2-4 mils are used on many low-end cabinets and furniture items. Vinyl films are heat-laminated using adhesives. The surface of a panel laminated with vinyl film is not very durable unless it is top-coated.

- **Advantages:** Low cost; material is more impervious to water than other materials.

- **Disadvantages:** Inferior quality of print and design.

HOT-STAMPED TRANSFER FOILS (HSTF)

Hot-stamped transfer foils (HSTF) are laminated by the continuous hot-roll method. They produce good printing quality and fidelity. HSTF is basically paint or ink reverse printed on a mylar carrier foil, with an adhesive top-coat. Heat and pressure activate the top-coat and deposit the ink or paint and the mylar is peeled away. It is offered in wood grains and solid colors, and used most often on edges and profiles.

It is self-seaming or self-trimming, since it only leaves the mylar backing where heat and pressure is applied. It can be used on medium density fiberboard or wood, but not on particleboard.

- **Advantages:** The product offers cost savings over most other methods of surfacing. It can be applied to curves and profiles with contour rollers, with virtually no evidence of a seam. A wide range of colors and patterns is offered.

- **Disadvantages:** Hot-stamped foils have very little stain, scuff or wear resistance due to the extreme thinness of the material. It cannot fill a gap or defect, since it is almost without mass. It does not give as good an appearance on flat panels as papers or even vinyls.

EDGEBANDING CHOICES

There are six major edgebanding choices available.

- Laminated Vinyl

- PVC

- Polyester Laminates

- Melamine

- Wood Veneers

- Reconstructed Wood Strips

When considering laminate cabinetry, the edgebanding material must also be evaluated.

- **Laminated Vinyl:** A lamination of two materials, generally vinyl to vinyl, although ABS and paper backers may be used.

  The carrier is generally a rigid PVC 0.101" to 0.030" thick and may be clear or in color. The surface is a printed or solid color lamination grade vinyl, usually reverse printed, and 0.002" to 0.008" thick.

- **PVC:** A thermoplastic edgebanding made of polyvinyl chloride, used to match vinyl, paper, paint or high-pressure laminates. PVC offers unlimited color and pattern availability, a wide range of widths (to 3.5"), thicknesses (0.016" to 0.187"), surface textures and gloss levels. The printed surfaces as well as the solid colors are generally top-coated with a

UV-cured resin for protection.

PVC is mainly used for straight line and contour automatic edgebanding applications. Thicker versions are available preglued for hot air applications. PVC is not recommended for softform applications.

- **Polyester Laminates:** Decorative papers, often matching popular high-pressure laminates, are impregnated with polyester resin and laminated to a variety of backers. Typically produced in light and heavy weight versions, either can be preglued for heat bar or hot air application. The heavy weight version is excellent for straight line, contour and softform automatic edgebanding applications.

- **Melamine:** The term melamine edgebanding covers a broad range of paper edgebanding materials, including single layer printed products, laminated foils and continuous melamine laminates. Largely produced in Europe, melamine is an economical, preglued, automatic edgebanding product, suitable for straight line, contour and softform edgebanding applications.

- **Wood Veneers:** Wood veneers that are either rotary cut or sliced from a variety of domestic and imported hardwood species. The veneers are sliced from 1/25" to 1/15" thick and are available plain, paper or fleece-backed in varying degrees of flexibility. The backers provide stability and strength to the veneer, and minimize splintering, cracking and checking. The veneers may be finger- or butt-jointed to produce continuous coil edgebanding. Veneer edging products are suitable for straight line, contour and softform applications.

- **Reconstructed Wood Strips:** A man-made veneer generally manufactured in Europe. Light colored woods are cut, dyed and reformed into logs before being resliced into sheets that approximate flat cut or quartered veneer. This produces a consistent, custom colored and grained wood veneer. These veneers can be processed into fleece or paper-backed strips or coils for straight line, contour or softform automatic edgebanding applications.

Natural Wood

Woods are universally popular and generally readily available to the cabinet industry in the United States. They are used in both local custom cabinet fabrication and in large national and international cabinet manufacturing facilities.

HARDWOOD VS. SOFTWOOD

Hardwood lumber is produced from deciduous trees that drop their broad leaves each year. Softwood lumber is produced from coniferous or evergreen species that have needles or scale-like leaves and remain green throughout the year.

Because of the differing inherent qualities and growth characteristics, the end uses of hardwoods are considerably different than softwoods. Softwoods are normally used in construction, while hardwoods are reserved for flooring, furniture and cabinets.

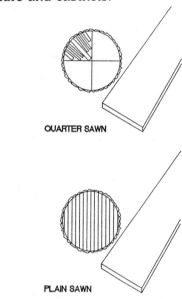

Figure 95 Quarter sawn wood, shown at top, has better grain pattern and is usually used on doors in more expensive cabinetry. Plain sawn is used for less expensive cabinet doors and produces a much more random, wild grain effect. It is also typically used on cabinet finished ends and paneling, which may be undesirable if combined with quarter sawn doors.

WOOD WARPAGE

Warping is a common worry in the kitchen cabinet industry. The relationship between the relative humidity of the atmosphere at the place of installation, and the moisture content of the wood causes changes in wood structure. If the moisture content of the wood is higher than the relative humidity, the wood will give off moisture and shrink in volume. If the wood is dryer than the relative humidity, it will take on moisture and swell.

The shrinking and swelling tendency of wood varies with the species and the direction of the grain. For minimal problems, the moisture content of the wood at the time of manufacture and finishing should be approximately the average moisture content that it will eventually attain in use, or slightly less. The possibility of warpage is considerably reduced when the cabinet is finished at the manufacturing facility. A cabinet which must be shipped to an area of different relative humidity should be finished, with all exposed surfaces covered, before it begins the journey. Unfinished casework installed in a new home and then left unfinished for some time is an invitation to disaster.

In conjunction with the inherent warpage problem in woods, the door style construction will affect its stability. A stile-and-rail door with a fixed-in-place flat panel will not be stable. A similar door, with a floating center panel, will withstand humidity changes much better. A solid lumber door is susceptible to a great deal of movement, while a veneered plywood will overcome the wood's natural shrinkage and swelling tendencies. Alternative products also solve the warpage problems; steel, particleboards, hardboards and laminates all relieve the cabinet of movement problems.

POPULAR SPECIES

Ash (Fraximus)

- **Range:** Of the 65 species of trees and shrubs called ash, six-white, pumpkin, blue, black, green and Oregon ash - are commercially important for lumber and other wood products. White ash grows throughout almost the entire wooded area of the U.S. east of the Great Plains, except the Gulf and South Atlantic coasts, and in southern Ontario and Quebec. Green ash has practically the same geographic distribution except that it also grows along the coast, follows the tributaries of the Mississippi River westward across the prairies, and extends farther northward in Canada. Black ash grows along the Great Lakes and St. Lawrence River from New England westward to Minnesota and northeastern Iowa.

- **Uses:** The principal use of ash is in furniture, interior parts of upholstered furniture, kitchen cabinets and architectural trim and cabinetry. Ash is straight-grained, still, strong and hard. White ash is superior to other ash species in these qualities. Ash also has good bending properties, high shock resistance and it wears smooth in use.

- **Characteristics:** White ash shrinks moderately but can be kiln dried rapidly and satisfactorily. Ash commonly is dried from the green condition in the kiln and requires 10-15 days for 1-inch lumber. It machines well, is better than average in nail and screw holding strength, and is intermediate for gluing. Other ash species have lower strength properties than white ash but still compare favorably with other native hardwoods. These species also split easier, shrink more, are average in workability and perform somewhat less favorably than white ash when exposed to extreme cycles of moisture content.

Birch (Betual)

- **Range:** Yellow birch grows in the Lake states, New England, New York, New Jersey, Pennsylvania and along the Appalachian Mountains into southern Georgia. It reaches its best development near the Canadian border. Sweet birch grows in New England, New York, New Jersey and Pennsylvania, and extends southward along the Appalachian Mountains to northern Georgia and Alabama. Paper birch has a transcontinental range extending throughout Canada to Alaska. In the U.S., it occurs eastward from the Lake states to New York and New England.

- **Uses:** Yellow birch is one of the principal furniture woods in the U.S. because of its good machining and finishing properties, hardness, pleasing figure and attractive color. Sweet birch lumber and veneer also are used in furniture. Both species are also used in kitchen cabinets and architectural trim, paneling and cabinetry. Much paper birch is used for specialty veneer products, such as toothpicks and tongue depressors.

- **Characteristics:** The wood of yellow and sweet birch is relatively heavy, hard and strong, and has high shock resistance. Although the wood is difficult to work with hand tools, it can be readily shaped by machine and ranks

high in nail-withdrawal resistance. Sweet birch ranks slightly above yellow birch in most strength properties. The wood of paper birch is considerably lighter than the other two birches and ranks below them in hardness, strength and stiffness.

All birches shrink considerably during drying. Yellow birch must be seasoned carefully to prevent checking and warping. Eleven to fifteen days are required to dry 1-inch lumber from the green condition to 6% moisture content. Because yellow and sweet birch are difficult to glue, special veneer and adhesive treatments are usually required to obtain the best results. They're glued more easily with synthetic-resin glues than with natural glues.

Cherry (Prunus Serotina)

- **Range:** Black cherry is found principally throughout the eastern half of the U.S. but grows in significant commercial quantities only in the northern Allegheny Mountains.

- **Uses:** Cherry wood is reddish and takes a lustrous finish. It's a prized furniture wood and brings high prices in veneer log form. It's increasingly popular in kitchen cabinets and is often used in architectural trim, paneling and cabinetry.

- **Characteristics:** Black cherry is relatively easy to dry, requiring 10-14 days to kiln dry 1-inch lumber from green to 6% moisture content. It stays in place well after seasoning and is comparatively free from checking and warping. It's easily machined, can be sawed cleanly, turns well and planes excellently with standard cutting angles. Screw-holding ability is good. Gluing also is good except when gum streaks are present. The wood has sufficient hardness to allow it to take hard use and withstand knocks without marring.

Maple (Acer)

- **Range:** Commercial maples grow throughout the eastern U.S. and southeastern U.S. and southeastern Canada, with the exception of bigleaf maple, which grows on the West Coast. The wood of maples is often divided into two classes - hard maple and soft maple. Hard maple includes sugar maple and black maple. Soft maple is made up largely of silver maple and red maple with a very small proportion of boxelder.

- **Uses:** Maple is a consistently popular wood for furniture and cabinetry. As much as 90% of the maple lumber produced is further manufactured into a variety of products such as furniture, kitchen cabinets, architectural woodwork and flooring.

- **Characteristics:** Maple is heavy, strong, stiff and hard; has a high resistance to shock; and ranks high in nail-holding ability. The wood turns well on a lathe and is

markedly resistant to abrasive wear. It takes stain satisfactorily and is capable of a high polish. In ease of gluing, it has an intermediate rank. The wood of soft maples is not as heavy, as hard or as strong as that of the hard maples. Kiln drying 1-inch soft maple lumber from green to 6% moisture content requires 7-13 days and 11-15 days for hard maple.

Oak (Quercus)

- **Range:** Oak species are found throughout the U.S. Commercial stands generally grow east of the Great Plains. Oaks are grouped as white oaks or red oaks.

- **Uses:** Both red and white oak are used extensively for furniture and flooring. Oak is the most popular wood for kitchen cabinets and is widely used in architectural trim, paneling and cabinetry.

- **Ponderosa Pine (Pinus Ponderosa)**

- **Range:** Ponderosa pine is the most widely distributed pine in North America, extending from British Columbia into Mexico and from the Pacific coast to Nebraska.

- **Uses:** Ponderosa pine is the principal millwork species and is used for window framing, sashes, doors, molding, shelving and paneling. It's well suited for furniture, kitchen cabinets and architectural woodwork if hardness or high strength are not required.

- **Characteristics:** The wood is comparatively light in weight, soft, moderately weak in bending and moderately low in shock resistance. The grain is generally straight, but frequently shows dimpling on the tangential surface. It resists splitting when nailed but is only average in nail-holding ability. Ponderosa pine dries easily, either in dry kilns or by air seasoning, and is moderately low in shrinkage.

White Pine (Pinus)

- **Range:** Western white pine (Pinus monticola) grows on western mountain ranges from southern British Columbia and southwestern Alberta to northern Idaho, northwestern Montana, and eastern Oregon to the southern end of the Sierra Nevada Mountains in California. Eastern white pine (Pinus strobus) grows from Newfoundland to Lake Winnipeg in Canada and southward through the Lake states and New England and in the Appalachians as far south as northern Georgia.

- **Uses:** Eastern white pine is more commonly used for furniture, although some western white pine is used. Western white pine is often used for colonial period furniture reproductions.

- **Characteristics:** The wood of eastern and western white pine have similar characteristics. Both are moderately soft, straight-grained, light woods that are mod-

erately low in shock resistance. They work easily with tools, are easy to glue and hold paint very well. They don't split readily when nailed, but have only medium nail holding ability. They're fairly easy to dry, shrink moderately and stay in place well when properly dried. The occurrence of "wet pockets" or "wetwood" in some lumber may require special attention during drying.

FINISHING SYSTEMS

Although most kitchen cabinet manufacturers supply prefinished casework, designers should have a working knowledge of wood coloring and wood finishing.

Variations in Color: The designer should be aware that many finishing problems are directly attributable to the type of wood used for the cabinet exteriors.

For example, a common finish fault (that is related to physical features of wood instead of chemical causes) is the different absorption rates present within one piece of wood. This defect is associated with random variation in porosity. The variation can be natural, as for example the tissue around knots in pine; or it can be induced artificially as in pond logging. (Long periods of pond logging can lead to leaching out by water of cell contents, which increases porosity through removal of matter from between the fibers.)

The natural variation in the wood is due to the various porosity levels caused by a bundle of fibers growing in a wavy fashion within the tree and at angles to the vertical access. When the log is sawn, some bundles of fiber are cut parallel to the main direction of growth and some are cut at an angle, exposing the fiber end and the open water conducting channels or pores. Such open surface inevitably will assume darker hues than surfaces composed of near parallel bundles of fiber.

Similarly, the natural pigments to which wood owes its color can affect the color stability of the wood once the finishing process is completed. Some natural wood colors, in the presence of oxygen and light, will change to darker finishes. *For example*, cherry will become much redder during the life of the furniture piece. When this darkening occurs in lacquered veneers it is often viewed - erroneously - as the fault of the finish.

For a client who wishes the finish on a wood cabinet to be perfectly even and consistent throughout all the elevations in the entire room, designers are encouraged to suggest a "wood-looking" man-made substitute.

A similar recommendation should be given to a client considering a heavily detailed or stylized special cabinet finish that they have seen on living furniture or bedroom pieces. Designers must help the client understand that bedroom, living room and dining room furniture pieces are "stand-alone" design statements. These beautifully detailed furniture sections rarely touch one another. Slight variations in finish color, or finish detailing are therefore certainly acceptable. In kitchen casework, the individual units are attached to one another with as little as 2 millimeters of space between adjacent doors on different cases. Therefore, the finishing differences acceptable on two nightstands on each

side of a bed will not be acceptable in a kitchen.

Enhancing Natural Wood Tones:
The natural color of the wood can be enhanced by oiling it. The approximate color which will result from such an application of a transparent finish can be determined with a "wet test". Simply moisten an area of the unfinished wood with clean water. The more porous woods will show a greater change in color than woods with closed grains.

Pure linseed oil, applied in an equal mixture with pure turpentine to a wood surface that has been freshly sanded, smoothed and cleaned, will produce rich colors. These colors may range from various shades of yellow to reddish-brown, depending upon whether raw or boiled linseed oil is used, the number of applications, the condition of the wood and whether the wood is open-grained or close-grained.

Raw linseed oil is lighter in body than boiled oil, penetrates deeper and usually results in a lighter color.

Staining Woods: Stains are employed to bring out the full beauty of the grain, or to emphasize the color of the woods.

Woods with no color that must be stained are: basswood, poplar, gum-wood and white pine.

Light-colored woods that may be finished in their natural color or stained include: ash, beech, birch, elm, oak, maple, chestnut and Philippine mahogany.

Stain is not usually used on veneers or wood with natural beauty and rich color, such as butternut, cherry, mahogany, rosewood, teak and walnut. These woods, which have a natural beauty of pattern and color, should receive a clear finish which will magnify their beauty.

It must be remembered that a stain is not a finish, and that a finishing coat must be applied over it, except in the case of varnish stains, penetrating wood-sealer finishes and lacquer containing stain.

Types of stain are:

- **Water Stain:** Powder. Best applied with spray equipment. Will raise grain of wood. No preliminary sealer coat required.

- **NGR Stain (non-grain-raising):** Stains in which powders are dissolved in a solvent other than water to minimize the problem of grain raising. Best applied with spray equipment, which carries

mixture into the pores of the wood and later evaporates.

- **Oil Stain:** Easy to apply. Oil stains should be protected with a paste-wax top coat. There are two types of oil stains used.

  Pigment oil stain: Best on close-grained woods, such as bass-wood, birch, cherry, gumwood, maple, pine and poplar.

  Penetrating oil stain: Best on course-grained woods, such as ash, beech, chestnut, elm, hickory, mahogany, oak, rosewood, sycamore and walnut. Since these woods have large pores and a coarse texture they will often clog up too much with a pigment stain. The greatest drawback to this type of stain is that when used on an extremely porous surface, it penetrates deeply and is difficult to remove.

- **Spirit Stain:** Powders soluble in alcohol. Very quick drying. Best applied with spray equipment. Stain will stick through almost any type of finishing coat, which will cause a slight muddiness in the finish.

- **Pigmented Wiping Stain:** Pigments are in suspension in a penetrating resin vehicle. Effective in staining a cabinet made from different woods. Must be stirred frequently. While all stains are wiped, wiping is the most important step in the application of this type of stain.

Color charts show the various stains available. The most commonly found are oak, maple, mahogany and walnut.

Oak:	light oak - yellowish dark oak - brownish-yellow golden oak - reddish dark
Maple:	maple - brownish-yellow honey - reddish-brown Vermont - brownish red
Mahogany:	mahogany - reddish-brown dark mahogany - brownish-red
Walnut:	variation of brown to blackish brown

- **Varnish Stain:** Not often used for fine wood finishes, these stains fill, color and add a gloss to the surface, all in one coat. When a product is made from less expensive grades of lumber, varnish stains may be successful because they give a uniform coloring to woods streaked with very soft and porous parts. If varnish stains are made too dark in color, they completely hide the wood grain and give the appearance of an enameled surface.

Coloring Woods: Paint, colored lacquer and varnish will provide a painted appearance on cabinetry. Painting will conceal the wood grain. During painting, an undercoat with no gloss is applied, then followed by a finish coat of high gloss, semi-gloss or satin. The lacquer will give a colored finish, yet retain the beauty of the wood grain.

Antiquing or highlighting with a contrasting or complementary color can be appealing. A popular finish today reflects the 19th century appeal of an enameled white finish on a stile-and-rail raised or flat paneled door. Manufacturers today offer this finish on doors with a wood substrate, molded plastic substrate finishes and MDF substrates. An inherent problem exists when this type of finish is applied to a wood stile-and-rail door - the joints between the stiles and rails will typically open.

If the client is not aware of this before they purchase the kitchen they may find it unacceptable. If this happens, you can be assured they will call their kitchen specialist and complain! Manufacturers that offer this "olde world" cabinet look on alternative substrates are far more successful in presenting an easy to maintain and continually beautiful material.

Pickled finishes (white pigment rubbed into woods to enhance the grain) give wood cabinets the look of an antique scrubbed surface. Pickling is most dramatic on woods with large pores such as oak, although it works well on others too.

Additionally, paint dragging - white or off-white paint left in cabinet joints and within distressed sections - heightens this "olde world" antique look. This appealing vintage effect works beautifully in country and contemporary kitchens.

Sealing Woods: A sealer coat should be applied to a wood surface after a stain has been used, unless otherwise directed. The sealer coat is normally a thin coat of the material used for the coloring. The purpose of the sealer is to keep the stain from bleeding into succeeding coats, by sealing the pores and to smooth it for the final finish.

Top Coating (Finishing) Wood: The finish coat will give a high gloss, satin-rubbed or polish-rubbed finish. The most common clear finishes are lacquer, oil, penetrating wood sealer, shellac and varnish.

- **Lacquer Finish:** A finish which has generally replaced varnish and shellac. Spray equipment is required for proper application. The lacquer offers a hard, durable, water-resistant surface. It is mirror-smooth and transparent, enhances the colors over which it is laid, and brings out the beauty of the wood grain.

- **Oil Finish:** A most satisfactory finish on hard or close-grained woods.

  When this finish is properly applied, the wood is impervious to water, heat, scratches and most stains. The original method of application consisted of a mixture of two-thirds commercially boiled linseed oil and one-third pure turpentine. From five to twenty coats of the oil mixture is applied. An endless amount of time, patience and rubbing was required. Today, a quick-method oil finish requiring four coats is available, as well as premixed commercial oil finishes needing three coats.

- **Penetrating Wood Sealer Finish and Penetrating Resin-oil Finish:** The finish withstands stains, water marks, minor burns and scratches. These sealer finishes are of two general types: one which contains wax and one which contains varnish. The finish containing wax will give a soft sheen rather than a high gloss. Thin, medium and heavy consistencies are available.

- **Polyurethane Finish:** In addition to the conventional varnishes, there are several other synthetic clear coatings which make excellent finishes for furniture. Of these finishes, the clear, oil-modified urethanes are the most popular. They are highly resistant to abrasion, scratching, water, chemicals, grease, solvents, food stains, alcohol and oils. They form a coating on the surface without penetrating. They can be applied over bare wood, or sealer, or a varnish finish. Do not apply a polyurethane finish over shellac or lacquer finish, unless it has been specifically formulated for polyurethane finishes.

- **Shellac Finish:** Not recommended for cabinets. Shellac stains easily, and is easily removed with everyday cleaning products.

- **Varnish:** Available in all gloss finishes. Will provide a finish that is resistant to water, alcohol and other liquids. A good finish requires at least two, and preferably three coats, with a light sanding between each. Most varnishes today are made of synthetic resins which dry fairly rapidly to form a hard surface coating that is exceptionally resistant to rough wear.

- **Wax Finish:** A simple, effective way of finishing wood. Brown waxes are better than yellow waxes. Only paste waxes are recommended. Generally, the wax is applied over a dried and sanded sealer coat of shellac, varnish or oil.

TYPICAL DOOR STYLES

The door and drawer fronts are the most visible part of the cabinets, so they determine the style of the cabinets and usually set the design theme for the entire kitchen. While a single cabinet maker might have dozens of door styles, they generally fall into several broad categories:

Flat or Slab Doors

These are flat pieces of lumber or plywood. They may be routed with a design. If a veneer is used, you should verify how consistent the graining will be. For some slab doors, there will be no attempt to match grains or to feature repetitive grain patterns. You and your client need to know this before you select this type of door. Details about wood grading are covered in Volume 1 of these manuals.

Panel Doors

Doors that have a frame made up of two horizontal rails and two vertical stiles, with a panel floating in between. The center panel is machined down at the four edges so that the panel is raised. When this look is created by routing a one-piece door, it is a false raised panel door. If the panel is flat, it is a recessed panel door. If the center section is raised, it is called a raised panel door. A raised or recessed panel door with an arch that is formed into the top and/or bottom rail is called a cathedral door. These doors are typically seen in traditional settings.

Framed Doors

Laminate or wood doors may be of a slab configuration, with a wood, thick

PVC edging or metal frame around the doors and drawers. This can provide a very high-tech, contemporary look, or can have a transitional sense if laminate and wood is combined.

Continuous Pull Door

A wood or laminate slab door can have a metal or wood continuous strip of routed or shaped hardware that acts as the pull on the cabinet. This hardware may be placed at both the top of drawers and the top of doors to create two horizontal lines through the space.

Alternatively, the hardware may be at the top of the doors and the bottom of the drawers so that one wider strip is featured.

HOW TO CARE FOR CABINETS

Woods and veneers with natural looking, penetrating finishes can be waxed to provide added protection against stains. These cabinets should be polished periodically to renew their luster. Wax should be applied once or twice a year.

Scratches can be repaired with an oil base stain that matches the original finish on the cabinets. Your clients should be advised never to use abrasive cleaners on any wood cabinets.

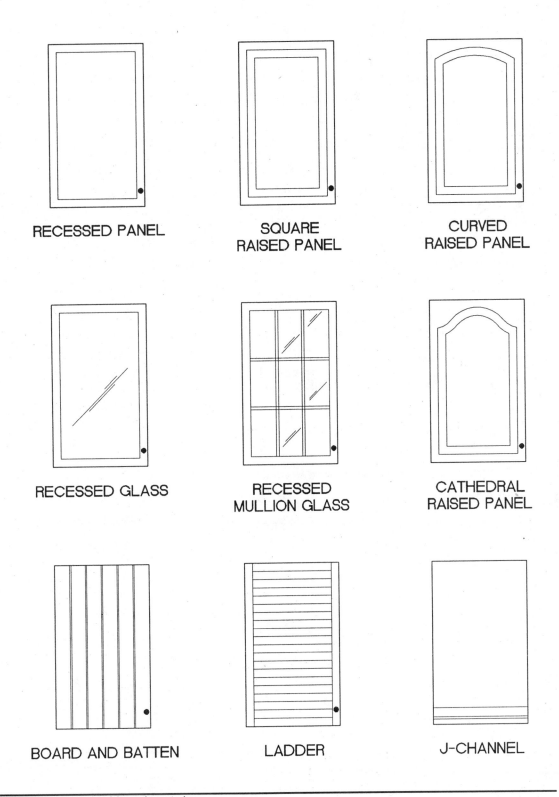

RECESSED PANEL

SQUARE
RAISED PANEL

CURVED
RAISED PANEL

RECESSED GLASS

RECESSED
MULLION GLASS

CATHEDRAL
RAISED PANEL

BOARD AND BATTEN

LADDER

J-CHANNEL

Figure 96 Typical cabinet door styles.

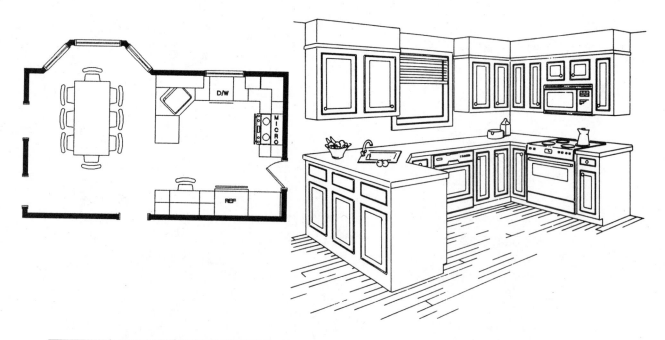

Figure 97 Note the cabinets to the right of the dishwasher: in both the base and the wall, the doors are hinged right. This maximizes the accessibility of the space. The wall cabinet to the left hinges in the center so that inside the wall cabinet is accessible on either side of the peninsula.

Figure 98 Make sure that door sizes are the same. The two base cabinets to the left of the cooking surface would have been more attractive had they been evenly sized. This size change might have affected the cabinet to the right of the cooking surface as well. Elevation drawings will help you lay out cabinet door size continuity.

Non-penetrating finishes on wood, such as polyurethane, can be wiped clean with a damp cloth. Wax is not used on this finish. Spot repair can be done with fine steel wool, but this should be reserved for very small areas only.

Enamel and polyester finishes can be wiped clean with water and, if needed, a mild, non-abrasive cleaner. However, make sure your client tests any abrasive cleaner on a small area before completing a major repair. You should advise your client to add a little vinegar to the cleaning water to prevent streaks on high- gloss surfaces.

Decorative laminates and melamine cabinet finishes can be wiped with a wet cloth or a sponge. These finishes stand up well to most non-abrasive cleaning products without any damage to their surface. However, be careful not to let water sit on the edges of cabinets and never near a seam where water could penetrate down into the substrate and cause the laminate to lift as the core material expands. Needless to say, wax or oil-based polishes are not used.

CABINET HARDWARE CONSIDERATIONS

Once you have selected the cabinet manufacturer and the door style, the cabinet hardware should be chosen. The hardware will enhance or detract from the kitchen's design statement.

You should first decide if the cabinet pull will blend with the cabinet or be an accent in the overall design. *For example*, a white pull on a white laminate door will disappear. The cook or kitchen visitor will really concentrate on other surfaces in the room: a decorative ceramic tile along the backsplash or an at-

tractively patterned floor. Alternatively, you may select a pull that becomes a major part of the design statement. Remember that white kitchen? If you added a bright red pull, it would certainly catch everyone's attention.

In addition to aesthetic considerations, the pulls must be selected with functionality in mind. **Sarah Reep**, CKD, ASID, Director of Design and Training for Fieldstone Cabinetry, has these following helpful hints for you:

- Match the hardware size to the cabinet door size. A 7-1/2" (19.05cm) wire pull won't fit on a 9" (22.86cm) wide drawer with most standard drillings. That same 7-1/2" (22.86cm) long pull will look off-balance on a 12" (30.48cm) wide drawer as well.

- Position hardware vertically for swinging type doors. Horizontal positioning is ideal for drawers and roll-outs.

- If you're selecting a continuous pull, think about the clients' physical ability. Will they be able to get their fingers comfortably in the groove to open the door?

- Avoid these continuous pulls in difficult to reach locations as well: above a hood for example, or along a tambour door that sits on the countertop.

- Make sure the hardware will stay in place. *For example*, a flat, square pull with a single hole for mounting will tend to flop, as will an oval knob.

- Make sure the hardware on one cabinet doesn't block access to another. This type of problem can generally be solved by incorporating scribes or fillers in the overall design plan.

Selecting the right hardware - both from a functional and an aesthetic standpoint - is a key ingredient in a successful kitchen plan. Make sure you pay attention to this element of the plan, so that the cabinets you specify are easy for all members of the client's family to open and close.

GENERIC NOMENCLATURE

The **National Kitchen and Bath Association** has established a generic cabinet coding system. This nomenclature provides standardized definitions for sizes and types of cabinets in this manual.

The system is based on an 11-character code which explains each cabinet category, type of cabinet, width of cabinet, and height (if variable). This system also identifies non-standard cabinet configuration details. The code includes both alpha and numeric symbols.

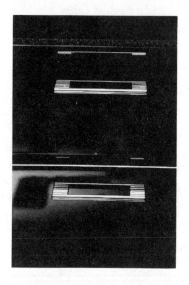

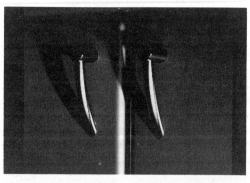

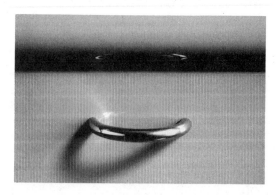

Figure 99 A sampling of available cabinet hardware.

The code is divided as follows:

- **The first character defines the general type of cabinet.**
  Molding and trim pieces are identified by a separate code that describes each piece. There is no major category that sets them apart from the other groupings.

- **The second set of characters identifies the type of cabinet.**

  For example, a "BB" is a base blind corner cabinet.

  A "BC" is a base corner cabinet. It may have fixed, adjustable or rotary shelving, which is designated by a letter.

  A "BD" is a base cabinet that features a stack of drawers. A standard "B" is assumed to have a drawer above the door.

There are six general cabinet categories, one accessory category and one molding/trim category. The six general cabinet categories are:

"W" defines all wall cabinets.

"T" defines all tall cabinets.

"B" defines all base cabinets.

"V" defines all vanity cabinets.

"D" defines all desk cabinets.

"F" defines all furniture cabinets.

(For some manufacturers vanity and desk cabinets are interchangeable. Therefore, the "V" designation is used in both applications. A "D" designation is applied only if sizing between the two casework systems differs.)

A "WO" is a wall cabinet that has no doors, therefore it is called an open cabinet.

- **The next two numeric symbols identify the width of the cabinet.**

  This dimension is always listed because case widths are variable. For most manufacturers these are on 3" (7 cm) modules, from 9" (23 cm) to 48" (122 cm).

- **The next two numeric symbols identify the height of the cabinet.**

  These two digits are used only if there are varying heights to choose from.

  For example, in wall cabinets you can choose from heights of 12" (30.48cm), 15" (38.1cm), 18" (45.72 cm), 24" (60.96cm) and 30" (76.2cm). Some manufacturers also offer heights of 36" (91.44cm) and 42" (106.68cm).

  This is not the case in base cabinets where one standard height is used throughout the kitchen, so no height dimension is part of that code.

- **The last two characters in the nomenclature system identify any non-standard configurations within that specific cabinet unit.**

  For example, a "D" would identify a diagonal corner unit; a "GD" would identify glass doors; "D3" would mean three drawers; "TO" would mean tilt-out drawer head, and so forth.

Accessories to be added to the cabinet are designated following the cabinet code.

Examples are "BB" for bread box; "CB" for cutting board; "HU" for hamper unit; "MU" for mixer unit, etc.

Heights assumed for the general categories are as follows (all plus 1-1/2", or 4 cm, for countertop):

Kitchen Base Cabinets, 34 1/2" (87cm)

Furniture and Vanities, 28 1/2"-31" (72-79 cm)

Tall Cabinets, 84"(213 cm) except as specified

- **Miscellaneous trim and finish pieces with no specific category heading have individual codes.**

Thus, "VP" is a valance panel, "VP-C" is one in contemporary styling, "VP-T" is traditional.

A corbel bracket is "CB". "OCM" is outside corner molding. "CM" is crown molding.

It is important for you as a designer to be aware of the certification requirements for cabinet construction and durability. Cabinets bearing this certification have met or exceeded the necessary requirements and are recommended by KCMA.

You should also be aware of the KCMA certification requirements so that you may recommend cabinets that meet or exceed these standards of manufacturing to your clients.

Cabinet Description		Nomenclature	Tips from the Pros
WALL CABINETS			
12" high (30 cm) Double Door		W3012 W3612	
15" High (38 cm) Double Door	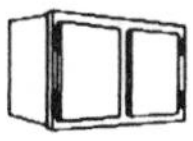	W3015 W3315 W3615 W3915	
15" High (38 cm) 24" Deep (61 cm) Double Door	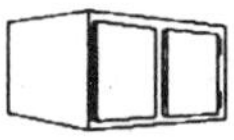	W301524D W331524D W361524D W391524D	
18" High (46 cm) Single Door		W1818 W2418	
18" High (46 cm) Double Door	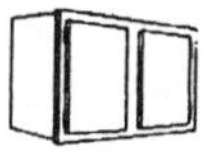	W2718 to W4818 in 3" increments	
18" High (46 cm) Peninsula Double Door		WP3018 WP3618 WP4218 WP4815	
24" High (61 cm) Single Door		W1824 W2424	
24" High (61cm), 24" Deep (61 cm) Single Door * One shelf		W182424D W242424D	
24" High Double Door * One shelf	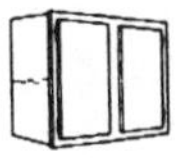	W2724 to W4824 in 3" increments	
24" High (61 cm) 24" Deep (61 cm) Double Door * One shelf	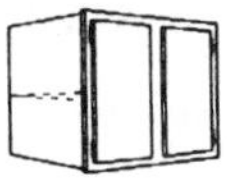	W272424D W302424D W362424D	
24" High (61 cm) Peninsula Single Door *One shelf *One door both sides, usually hinged same side of cabinet	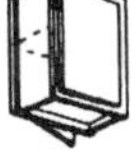	WP1224 WP1524 WP1824 WP2424	
24" High (61 cm) Peninsula Double Door		WP3024 WP3624 WP4224 WP4824	

Figure 100 Typical kitchen cabinet sizes.

Cabinet Description

30" High (76 cm)
Single Door
*2 shelves

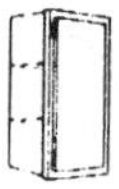

30" High (76 cm)
Double Door
*2 shelves

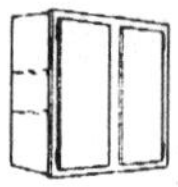

30" High (76 cm)
Peninsula
Single Door
* 2 shelves
*1 door each side,
usually hinged same
side of cabinet.

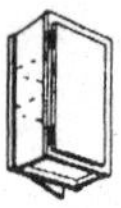

30" High (76 cm)
Peninsula
Double Door
* 2 shelves
* 2 doors each side

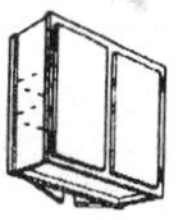

30" High (76 cm)
Peninsula
Blind Corner
* 2 shelves. * 3 doors;
1 front, 2 back. *Blind
corner with 1" (2.5
cm) filler is typical.

30" High
Blind Corner
Single Door
* 2 shelves. * blind
panel with 1" (2.5 cm)
filler is typical.

30" High (76 cm)
Diagonal
45° Corner
Single Door
* 2 shelves

30" High (76 cm)
90° Corner
Pie-Cut Cabinet
* 2 shelves
*2-piece bifold door
typical; may have
curved door

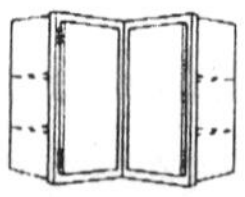

Nomenclature

W930
W1230
W1530
W1830
W2130
W2430

W2730
W3030
W3330
W3630
W3930
W4230
W4530
W4830

WP1230
WP1530
WP1830
WP2430

WP3030
WP3630
WP4230
WP4830

WPC24/2730
WPC36/3930

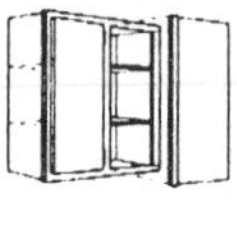

WB24/2730
WB27/3030
WB30/3330
WB33/3630
WB36/3930

WC2430D

WC2430PC

Tips from the Pros

• For some makers, you specify hinging L
or R. For others it's reversible so not
detailed with cabinet order. Plan must
specify R or L so installer will know how to
place cabinet.

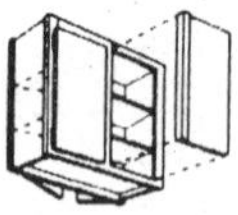

• In framed cabinets, single door splits into
two usually at 27" wide, with center stile.
Can be ordered without center stile in
some lines for easier access. In frameless, double doors usually begin at 24"
wide, no center stile up to 36".

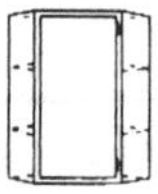

• Blinds may have to be specified L or R.
Determine, for your line, if R or L specifies
blind side or door side.

Figure 100 Typical kitchen cabinet sizes.

Cabinet Description		Nomenclature	Tips from the Pros

36" High (91 cm)
Blind Corner
Single Door
*2 shelves
*blind panel with 1"
filler (2.5 cm) is typical

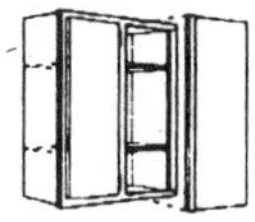

WBC27/3036
WBD36/3936

36" High 45°
Diagonal Corner
Single Door
* 2 shelves

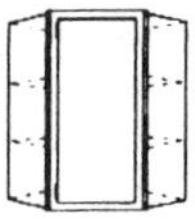

WC2436D

36" High (91 cm)
90° Corner Pie-cut
* 2 shelves
* 2-piece bifold door is
typical. May have
concave curved door

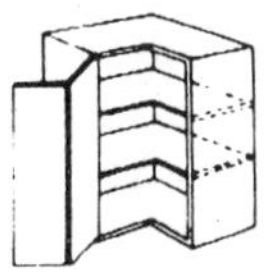

WC2436PC

Wall Cabinet for
Microwave Oven
* trim kit may be avlbl
from cabinet or appli-
ance manufacturer.
* for use with built-in
front-vented micro-
wave units

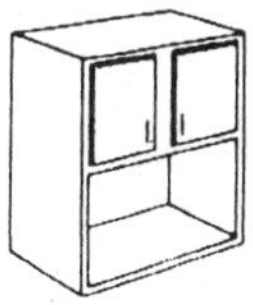

WM303618D

Wall Cabinet for
microwave oven
* standard cabinet
depth
* fits all free-standing
microwaves

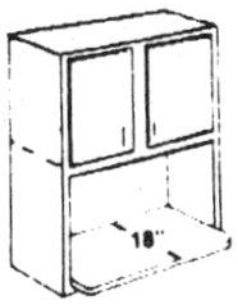

WM3036

* interior back, sides and top veneered and finished to match shelf and frame is typical.

42" High (107 cm)
Single Door
* 3 shelves

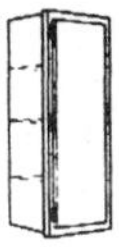

W1242
W1542
W1842
W2142
W2442

42" High (107 cm)
Double Door
* 3 shelves

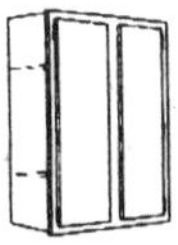

W2742
W3042
W3342
W3642

- When a wall cabinet is planned that is continuous from countertop to soffit or ceiling, (a 48"-
60"-high unit) (122-152 cm), consider special
clearance. Reduce overall cabinet height
slightly. A countertop platform should be
planned beneath the wall cabinet, finished
either to match the cabinet with molding, or the
counter material, so doors willl not rest on the
countertop. Scribing room is built in. A
platform 3/4"-1 1/2" (2-4 cm) is recommended.

- When installing wall cabinets to the ceiling,
make sure there are not recessed lights
designed with the lamp below the edge of the
diffuser (which is flush with the ceiling)., nor
any surface-mounted light closer than the
dimension of the cabinet door when open.
Ideally, the cabinet should be down from the
ceiling an inch or so and trimmed out with
molding to let doors open and close.

Figure 100 Typical kitchen cabinet sizes.

Cabinet Description		Nomenclature	Tips from the Pros

Cabinet Description

42" High (107 cm)
Blind Corner
Single Door
* 3 shelves
* blind panel w/1" filler
(2.5 cm) is typical

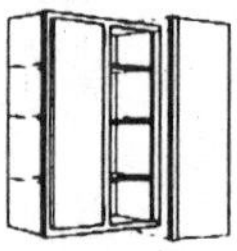

Nomenclature

WB27/3042
WB36/3942

42" High (107 cm) 45°
Diagonal Corner
Single Door
* 3 shelves

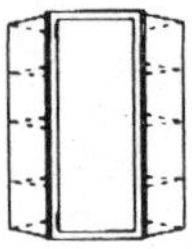

WC2442D

42" High (107 cm) 90°
Corner
* 3 shelves
* 2-piece bifold door is
typical
* may have concave
curved doors

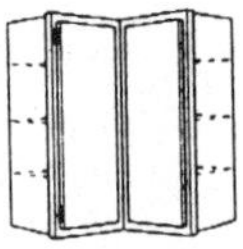

WC2442PC

Wall Cabinet
for Microwave
* trim kit may be avlbl
from cabinet or
appliance manufac-
turer.
* for use with built-in
front-vented micro-
wave units

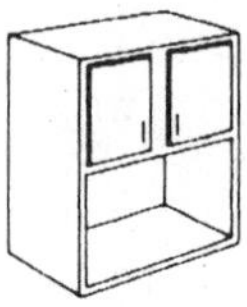

WM304218D

Wall Cabinet
for Microwave
* standard cabinet
depth
* fits all free-standing
units

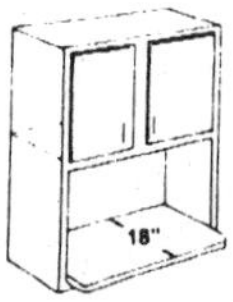

WM3042

---

* interior back, sides and top veneered and
finished to match shelf and frame is typical.

BASE CABINETS

Tray divider cabinet
* full height door
* 2 vertical tray divid-
ers is typical

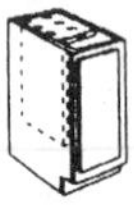

B9T

• Some cabinet styles (particularly with
heavy molding) can't be built in 9" (23 cm)
width. Check lines you represent.

Single Door
*1 door
* may have full or
half-depth shelf

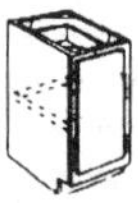

B12FD
B15FD
B18FD
B21FD

Single Door
* 1 door
* 1 drawer
* may have full- or
half-depth shelf

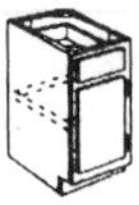

B12
B15
B18
B21
B24

Double Door
* 2 doors
* 2 drawers
* may have full- or
half-depth shelf

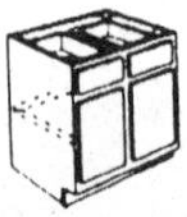

B27 to B48
in 3" (7.6 cm) incre-
ments

• In many lines, shallow drawers are
available for B30, B33 and B36 so storage
can be provided directly below a conventional cooktop.

Figure 100 Typical kitchen cabinet sizes.

Cabinet Description		Nomenclature	Tips from the Pros

**Peninsula
Single Door**
* drawer operates from one side
* door on each side hinged at same end is typical

BP18
BP24

**Peninsula
Double Door**
* 2 doors both sides
* 2 drawers operate from one side

BP30
BP36
BP42
BP48

Single Drawer
* 2 doors
* 1 wide drawer with reinforced bottom
* 2 wide roll-out trays w/ reinforced bottoms
* no center stile for more efficiency

B36/2ROS

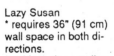

Blind Corner
* blind panel w/3" filler (8 cm) is typical
* may be reversible for L or R blind
* cabinet size is smaller than wall space required.. End panel needed for any exposed end.

BB36/39
BB39/42
BB42/45
BB45/48
BB48/51

• Blind bases of 36", 39" or 42" (91, 99 or 107 cm) have very small doors. For example, a 36" BB will have only a 9" (23 cm) door opening. It is better to specify 45" or 48" (114 or 122 cm) because door size will be 18" or 21" (46 or 53 cm) wide.

Lazy Susan
* requires 36" (91 cm) wall space in both directions.
* cabinet size smaller than wall space. End panel needed for exposed end.
* 2 28" (71 cm) diameter pie-cut revolving plastic shelves typical.

BC36LS

• When specifying a lazy susan, corner sink cabinet or pie-cut corner base with a bifold door that is hinged right or left, always bifold the door away from adjacent appliances. If cabinet hinging is on the same side as appliance, and the appliance extends beyond the face of the cabinet, the door will not open completely, limiting access.

Base Corner
* bifold hinged door
* 1 shelf is typical
* requires 36" (91 cm) wall space both directions
* cabinet size smaller than wall space. End panel needed for exposed end.
* may have concave curved door

BC36

• None of these is 24" deep (61 cm). If they were you could not fit one through a standard interior door. They usually are 18"-20" (46-51 cm) deep. Make sure installer knows that he pulls it to 24" (61 cm) deep and doesn't push it back to the wall.

• When specifying any corner unit with a half-moon swing-out shelf system, make sure you know how much of the interior shelf space is used by the swing-out apparatus. Sometimes much space is wasted.

Four Drawer
* 1 deep bottom drawer
* 3 standard drawers

BD12D4
BD15D4
BD18D4
BD21D4
BD24D4

• If placing a drawer unit against a wall with a window or door opening, use a 1"-1 1/2" (2.5-4 cm) filler between cabinet and wall so drawer will miss casing. Do the same with a drawer unit in a corner so drawers at right angles will miss each other.

Figure 100 Typical kitchen cabinet sizes.

Cabinet Description	Nomenclature	Tips from the Pros

Three Drawer
* 2 extra deep lower drawers
* 1 standard drawer

BD12D3
BD15D3
BD18D3
BD21D3
BD24D3
BD30D3
BD36D3

• Designers disagree whether it is better to line up base with wall cabinets or to keep upper cabinet doors even in size. Since base runs are interrupted by drawer banks and appliances, aligning upper doors so all sizes are consistent provides a more uniform design statement.

Base Sink
* double door
* false drawer heads

BS24 to BS48 in 3" (8 cm) increments

Base Sink
90° corner
* requires 36"-40" (91-102 cm) wall space both directions.
* cabinet size smaller than wall space.
* need end panel for any exposed end
* bottom must be ordered

BSC36
BSC39
BSC42

*BSCF36 (for front only)

Base Sink
Diagonal
* single door
* can design to fit flush with adjacent cabinets or be recessed between two cabinets

BSC36D
BSC39D
BSC42D

*BSCF36D (for front only)

Base Sink Front
Straight
* double door
* toekick included and shipped is typical

BSF24
BSF30
BSF33
BSF36

TALL CABINETS

Oven Cabinet
Universal
* 4 drawer. Remove as needed to accommodate oven.
* in 84", 90", 96" (213, 229. 244 cm) heights.

TOV2784/90/96
TOV3084/90/96
TOV3384/90/96

• "Universal" oven cabinets take either single or double ovens by removing drawers. But in some lines you specify single or double. Generally you make the cutout at the jobsite. Standard tall cabinets are generally the same depth as base cabinets. An oven cabinet at the end of a run will be flush, but the counertop will extend out beyond the face of the tall cabinet. The counter edge should be beveled or finished on this slight return, or the tall unit can be pulled out to align with the counter.

Utility Cabinet
* Avlbl in 12" or 24" (30 or 61 cm) depths.
* for use with shelf kits w/single or double doors depending on width

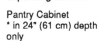

TU24/84/90/96
TU27/84/90/96
TU30/84/90/96
TU36/84/90/96

• When specifying any tall cabinet, prod clients on how they will use it. You may want to order added shelving when cabinet is ordered.

Pantry Cabinet
* in 24" (61 cm) depth only

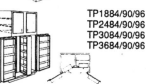

TP1884/90/96
TP2484/90/96
TP3084/90/96
TP3684/90/96

• Some tall pantry cabinets have swing-out units that require the door to open more than 90°. For these, you might need a filler.
Tall cabinets are usable for more than canned goods and cleaning supplies. Best storage space is 22"-56" (56-142 cm) above floor, so pantry cabinet space can be used for china, silver or serving pieces, small hand appliances and many other things.

Linen Cabinet
* Available in 12", 18", 21" depths
* For use with shelf kits w/single or double doors depending on width

TL12/84/90/96
TL18/84/90/96
TL24/84/90/96
TL36/84/90/96

Figure 100 Typical kitchen cabinet sizes.

Cabinet Description	Nomenclature	Tips from the Pros

VANITY CABINETS

Single Door
* full height door
* 1 shelf

V12FD
V15FD
V18FD
V21FD

• When specifying, find out if the standard shelf is included or if a second one is available. A second shelf is often usable in this cabinet.

Single Door
* 1 door
* 1 drawer
* 1 shelf

V12
V15
V18
V21

Double Door
* full height doors
* 1 shelf

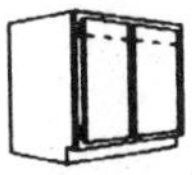

V24FD
V27FD
V33FD
V36FD

Double Door
* 2 doors
* 1 drawer
* 1 shelf

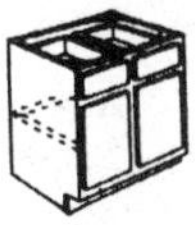

V24
V27
V33
V36
V38

Vanity Bowl Unit
* 3 full height doors

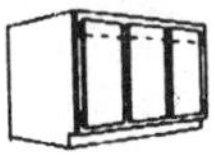

VS42FD
VS48FD

Vanity Bowl
Drawer Unit
* 1 full height door
* 2 deep drawers L or R, top drawer false

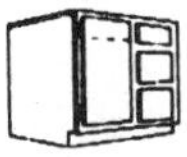

VSD24
VSD30
VSD36

Vanity Bowl
Double Drawer Unit
* full height door
* 6 drawers

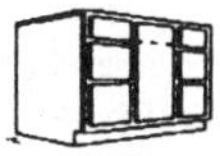

VSDD42
VSDD48

Vanity Drawer
* 3 drawers

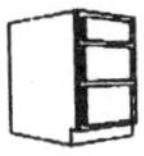

VD12D3
VD15D3
VD18D3

Suspended Drawer
* full width shallow drawer
* optional desk leg recesses may be avlbl

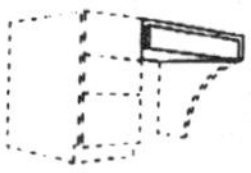

VD24SD
VD30SD
VD36SD

Vanity Hamper
* full height door
* detachable wire basket tilts out w/door or separate

V18HA

Vanity Storage
48" (122 cm) height
* 2 adjustable shelves

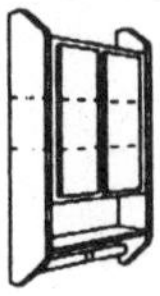

VS2648

Figure 100 Typical kitchen cabinet sizes.

Cabinet Description	Nomenclature	Tips from the Pros

INTERIOR FITTINGS

Roll-Out Shelves
* for all base and tall cabinets in place of standard shelves.

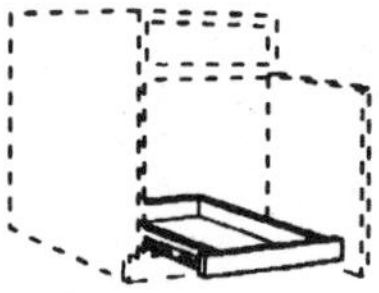

ROS

- Make sure the door opens past 90° to allow the shelves to roll out.
- In a large pull-out system for multiple waste containers, alert client not to push waste down too strongly. Drawer guide system can be bent.

Swing-Out Pantry Rack
* For tall cabinet, swings out for access.
* Double-sided, oak with oak adjustable shelves is typical

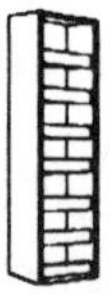

SPR

Door Shelf Kit
* Mounts on back of door
* plastic or wood

PR

Square Shelf Kit
* for tall utility cabinets
* 5 shelves is typical

SK

Revolving Shelf Kit
* for tall utility cabinets
* revolving plastic shelves w/center rod & brackets typical

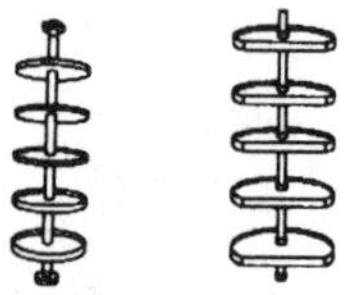

RP

Tilt-Out Sink Tray
* fits in sink cabinet
* white, almond or stainless steel avlbl

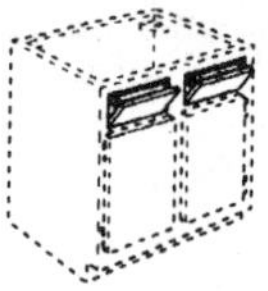

TO

- Some are stainless steel, some plastic. Some go length of sink cabinet. Know your product before presenting it to client.
- When specifying, make sure sink cutout is far enough back for space. Some integral sinks don't allow space.

Spice Tray Insert
* fits top drawer of base cabinet.
* molded plastic, white or almost typical

ST

Bread Box
* fits in lower drawer of BD cabinets
* plastic or stainless

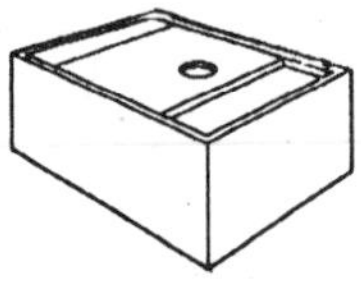

BB

Wine Rack
* may be insert for standard cabinet, for bottles to lay in square compartments
* may be lattice for special cabinet

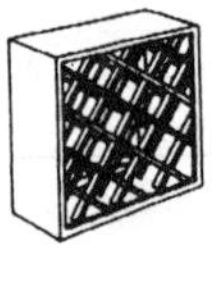

WR

- Check length of bottles if installing behind closed doors. Reds will probably fit, some whites. German bottles are longer.
- When specifying an inverted glass holder, check size of wine glasses. Some won't fit. Be sure rack won't conceal backsplash outlets.

Cutting Board
* pull-out wood above top drawer in BD typical.
* may be concealed behind fold-down top drawer front

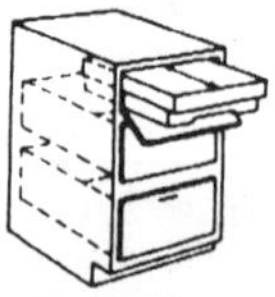

CB

Figure 100 Typical kitchen cabinet sizes.

Cabinet Description		Nomenclature	Tips from the Pros

Drawer Organizer
* plastic storage unit fits in drawer

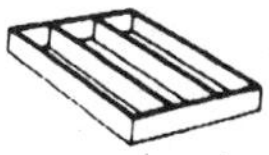

DO

* Generally put near dishwasher and sink for immediate access as we load or unload dishwasher or set table. Also useful in desk units.

Mixer Unit
* pull-up hardware for mixer storage

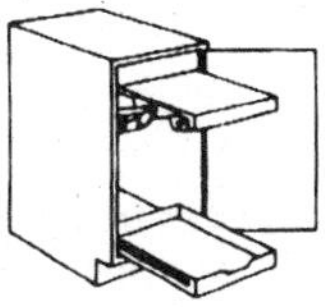

MU

Towel Bar
* pull-out 2-prong or 3-prong is typical

TB

* Don't specify sliding bar under sink if client plans on waste basket directly under it. Know what cleaning supplies will be kept there so you can place everything properly.

Waste Paper Basket
* attached to sink door is typical
* pull-out recycling bin also avaible

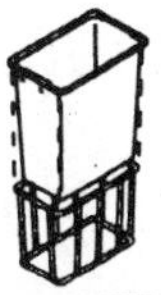

WP

Range Hood
* metal liner is typical

RH

Glass Doors

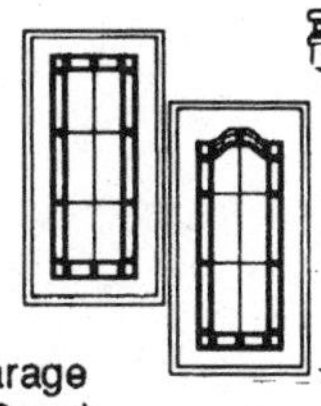

GD

* Glass doors may have mullion, munton designations. This can mean wood strips that divide glass panes, or an applied molding framework that might be fixed or removable. The latter makes cleaning easier.

Appliance Garage
* 15" High (38 cm)
* 18" High (46 cm)
* features roll-up tambour or bifold doors

AG1818
AG2418

* Don't use a continuous wood pull on a tambour door. Fingers won't go under it. Make sure client and electrical contractor understand what it is and install outlets so they won't block tambour door.

Appliance Garage--Diagonal
* 15" High (38 cm)
* 18" High (46 cm)
* features roll-up tambour or bifold doors
* fits to the backsplash height

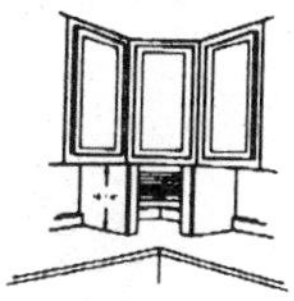

AGC2418D

Fillers

WF3
TF3
VF3
BF3

* Be sure to specify whether fillers should flush out with the case, or whether they have an attached flange so they can flush out with the door with the flange continuing back past the case edge.
* For corner wall fillers, don't forget a lower panel that will extend back to the wall. If there is an open soffit you also will need a top return.
* Scribing fillers are used to separate cabinets in corners, provide a surface for a flange to fit against, or to finish a cabinet against a wall and provide clearance for drawer hardware and for interior shelving to work.

Countertop Bracket
* has integral mounting kit
* use for shelf or counter support

CB

* Corbel brackets support extended counters. Generally, an overhang more than 12" (30 cm) needs a support bracket every 36" (91 cm).

Pigeon Hole

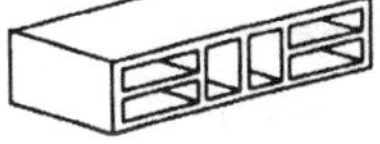

PH30
PG36

* May be used vertically or horizontally. Heights will vary according to manufacturer.

Figure 100 Typical kitchen cabinet sizes.

Cabinet Description		Nomenclature	Tips from the Pros
Valance, Contemporary * 4 1/4" High (11 cm)	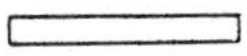	VP-C	
Valance, Traditional * 4 1/4" High (11 cm)		VP-T	
Appliance End Panel	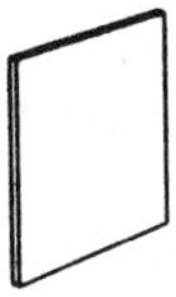	AEP	• With frameless cabinets, include a panel adjacent to any appliances that have a flange that should rest against the cabinet component. In framed cabinets, the frame provides a place for the appliance flange to fit against.
Decorative Appliance Front Panel * may match door detail * generally avlbl for dishwasher, compactor and refrigerator		DWP RP TCP	
Wall Finished Sides	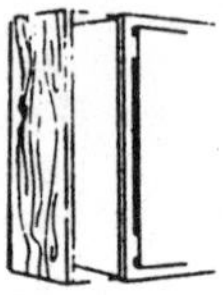	FS	
Decorative Finished Sides * panels with overlay for furniture look		FS-D	• In ordering door style panels for a cabinet side, do you want the panel to finish at the case dimension (12", 30 cm) or the dimension of the case and door (12 3/4" , 32 cm). Consider this for a crown molding above, as well.
Outside Corner Molding		OCM	• Outside corner molding is used to seal a joint between two panels at right angles.
Inside Corner Molding		ICM	
Scribe Molding		SM	• Scribe molding is used to finish along an uneven ceiling.
Batten Molding		BM	• Batten molding is used to cover joints between adjacent cabinets.
Crown Molding		CM	• Crown molding is a decorative piece used on top of cabinets.
Galley Rail	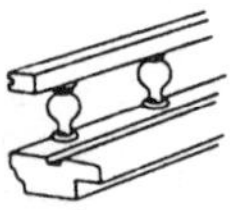	GR	• Galley rails are used on top of cabinets to create a display area.
Countertop Molding	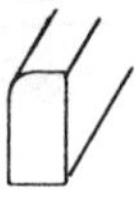	TCM	• Countertop edge moldings and backsplash moldings are used to finish the top with solid surface, ceramic tile and laminates. These surfaces should be finished all the way around if used with tile. With solid surface, moldings may be installed unfinished so they can be sanded flush with the top, then finished. Or finished moldings can be installed slightly offset from the solid surface edging.

Figure 100 Typical kitchen cabinet sizes.

About The KCMA Certification Program

The Kitchen Cabinet Manufacturers Association Certification Program assures the specifier or user of kitchen cabinets and bath vanities that the cabinet bearing the blue and white seal complies with the rigorous standards set by the American National Standards Institute (ANSI) and sponsored by the Kitchen Cabinet Manufacturers Association (KCMA). Further, the cabinet is an exact duplicate of samples that have been independently tested. The KCMA Certification Program is open to all cabinet manufacturers. Manufacturers may certify one, several, or all of their cabinet lines. Because of this option, only those lines certified are listed.

Compliance with ANSI/KCMA standards is assured by initial cabinet testing, periodic unannounced plant pick-up and testing, and additional testing resulting from complaints. All testing is performed by an experienced independent laboratory.

The kitchen and bath cabinets of certified manufacturers comply with ANSI/KCMA A 161.1-1990, "Recommended Performance and construction Standards for Kitchen Cabinets." The cabinets also comply with the provision of paragraph 611-1.1, "HUD Minimum Property Standards - Housing 4910.1," 9/8/86.

Companies not licensed with the KCMA Program may not claim or imply conformance with these standards for their products. KCMA, as the proprietary sponsor, reserves the right to question any claims of conformance and to test the products of any manufacturer making such claims. Should KCMA discover that a manufacturer is falsely representing that his products meet these standards, KCMA will take appropriate legal action.

Requirements Cabinets Must Meet To Earn The KCMA Certification Seal

GENERAL CONSTRUCTION REQUIREMENTS

- All cabinets must be fully enclosed with backs, bottoms, sides, and tops on wall cabinets; and backs, bottoms, and sides on base cabinets, with certain specified exceptions on kitchen sink fronts, sink bases, oven cabinets, and refrigerator cabinets.
- All cabinets designed to rest on the floor must be provided with a toe space at least two inches deep and three inches high.
- All utility cabinets must meet the same construction requirements as base and wall cabinets.
- Doors must be properly aligned, have means of closure, and close without excessive binding or looseness.
- All materials must ensure rigidity in compliance with performance standards.

- Face frames, when used, must provide rigid construction.
- For frameless cabinets, the ends, tops/bottoms, and back shall be of thickness necessary to provide rigid construction.

A 10-pound sand bag strikes a cabinet door to measure the ability of the door and connections to withstand impacts.

- Corner or lineal bracing must be provided at points where necessary to ensure rigidity and proper joining of various components.
- All wood parts must be dried to a moisture content of 10 percent or less at time of fabrication.

- All materials used in cabinets must be suitable for use in the kitchen and bath environment where they may be exposed to grease, solvents, water, detergent, steam and other substances usually found in these rooms.
- All exposed plywood and composition board edges must be filled and sanded, edge-banded, or otherwise finished to ensure compliance with the performance standards.
- All exterior exposed parts of cabinets must have nails and staples set and holes filled.
- All exposed construction joints must be fitted in a workmanlike manner consistent with specifications.
- Exposed cabinet hardware must comply with the finishing standards of ANSI/BHMA A 156.9-1988.

Figure 101 The KCMA certification program.

Requirements Cabinets Must Meet
To Earn The KCMA Certification Seal

A door is opened and closed 25,000 times to test its ability to operate under the stress of normal use.

FOUR STRUCTURAL TESTS MEASURE CABINET'S STRUCTURAL INTEGRITY, INSTALLATION

- All shelves and bottoms are loaded at 15 pounds per square foot, and loading is maintained for seven days to ensure that there is no excessive deflection and no visible sign of joint separation or failure of any part of the cabinets or the mounting system.
- Mounted wall cabinets are loaded to ensure that the cabinet will accept a net loading of 500 pounds without any visible sign of failure in the cabinet or the mounting system.
- To test the strength of base-front joints, a load of 250 pounds is applied against the inside of cabinet-front stiles for cabinets with drawer rail, or 200 pounds is applied for cabinets without drawer rail, to ensure reliable front joints that will not open during stress in service or during installation.

- To test the ability of shelves, bottoms, and drawer bottoms to withstand the dropping of cans and other items, a three-pound steel ball is dropped from six inches above the surface. After the test the drawer must not be damaged and must operate as before the test with no visible sign of joint separation or failure of any part of the cabinet or mounting system.
- To test the ability of cabinet doors and connections to withstand impacts, a 10-pound sandbag is used to strike the center of a closed cabinet door and repeated with the door opened to a 45-degree angle. The door must operate as before the test and show no damage or sign of separation or failure in the system.

TWO DOOR OPERATION TESTS MEASURE DURABILITY

- To test the ability of doors, hinges, and means of attachment to withstand loading, 65 pounds of weight is applied on

the door. The weighted door is slowly operated for 10 cycles from 90 degrees open to 20 degrees open and returned to the 90 degree position. The door must remain weighted for 10 minutes, after which the door and hinges must show no visible signs of damage, and connections between cabinet-and-hinge and door-and-hinge must show no sign of looseness.
- To test the ability of doors, door-holding devices, hinges, and attachment devices to operate under the stress of normal use, doors are opened and closed through a full 90-degree swing for 25,000 cycles. At the test's conclusion the door must be operable, the door-holding device must hold the door in closed position, hinges must show no visible signs of damage, connections between

cabinet and hinge and door and hinge must show no sign of looseness, and other specifications must be met.

TWO DRAWER TESTS REQUIRED

- To test the ability of drawers and drawer mechanisms to operate with loading during normal use, drawers are loaded at 15 pounds per square foot and operated through 25,000 cycles. The drawers must then remain operable with no failure in any part of the drawer assembly or operating system, and drawer bottoms must not be deflected to interfere with drawer operation.
- To test the ability of the drawer-front assembly to withstand the impact of closing the drawer under normal use, a three-pound weight is dropped 8 inches against loading bars 10 times, after which

A cabinet door is weighted with 65 pounds, then operated 10 times to test the ability of the door and hinges to withstand loading.

Figure 101 The KCMA certification program.

Requirements Cabinets Must Meet
To Earn The KCMA Certification Seal

looseness or structural damage to the drawer-front assembly that impairs operation must not be evident.

FIVE FINISH TESTS CONDUCTED

These tests create, in accelerated form, the cumulative effects of years of normal kitchen conditions on pre-finished cabinets. Cabinet finishes are inspected to ensure that stringent standards of appearance are also met.

- To test the ability of the finish to withstand high heat, a cabinet door is placed in a hotbox at 120 degrees Fahrenheit (plus or minus 2 degrees) and 70 percent relative humidity (plus or minus 2 percent) for 24 hours. After this test the finish must show no appreciable discoloration and no evidence of blistering, checks, or other film failures.
- To test the ability of the finish to withstand hot and cold cycles for prolonged periods, a cabinet door is placed in a hotbox at 120 degrees Fahrenheit (plus or minus 2 degrees) for 1 hour, removed for 1/2 hour, and allowed to return to room temperature and humidity conditions, and then placed in a coldbox for 1 hour at -5 degrees Fahrenheit (plus or minus 2 degrees). The cycle is repeated five times. The finish must then show no appreciable discoloration and no evidence of blistering, cold checking, or other film failure.
- To test the ability of the finish to withstand substances typically found in the kitchen and bath, exterior exposed surfaces of doors, front frames, and drawer fronts are subjected to vinegar, lemon, orange and grape juices, tomato catsup, coffee, olive oil, and 100-proof alcohol for 24 hours and to mustard for 1 hour. After this test, the finish must show no appreciable discoloration, stain, or whitening that will not disperse with ordinary polishing and no indication of blistering, checks, or other film failure.
- To test the ability of the finish to withstand long periods of exposure to a detergent and water solution, a cabinet door edge is subjected to exposure to a standardized detergent formula for 24 hours. The door edge must then show no delamination or swelling and no appreciable discoloration or evidence of blistering, checking, whitening, or other film failure.

A steel ball drop tests the ability of drawers and shelves to withstand the dropping of cans or other items.

A 24-hour detergent and water solution test checks the door's finish.

Figure 101 The KCMA certification program.

Figure 102 (Courtesy of Quaker Maid) Combining square panel doors and arched is a popular approach. This traditional space is enhanced by such a combination.

Figure 103 (Courtesy of Quaker Maid) The popular English Country look is often accomplished using a "beaded" inset door.

Figure 104 (Courtesy of Quaker Maid) Sleek, contemporary doors can be softened by the addition of a wood handle, and by combining laminate and wood in different cabinetry sections.

Figure105   (Courtesy of Quaker Maid) Laminate doors can also be trimmed in wood to create a transitional look. Note how effectively wood and laminate are combined in this example.

Figure 106 (Courtesy of Quaker Maid) Gloss laminates, polyesters and other materials are typically seen in sleek, contemporary rooms.

Figure 107 (Courtesy of Quaker Maid) The use of laminates is also seen extensively in kitchens where curved cabinets are used.

SECTION **2**

Appliances

Responsible designers and homeowners know that the phrase "think globally, act locally" applys as much to the planning and usage of the kitchen as it does to other facts of our life. The kitchen design, the family's purchasing habits and the use of the kitchen and its equipment must all be considered.

The international need to understand and employ conservation tactics and waste management techniques is so important, that we have decided to begin this section on appliances by tackling these two key topics.

SELECTING MORE EFFICIENT APPLIANCES

Families today realize that they must minimize the mechanical energy necessary to operate their new time-saving appliances. To save money on the monthly utility bill and to protect our environment, energy conservation is an important consideration when planning appliances for any new kitchen.

One of the problems with conservation efforts is that it is difficult for the homeowner to see any results. The cook can see wasted food, but he or she can't see wasted energy. There is no tell-tale mess left behind - only a few numbers on a utility bill that could have been lower.

However, energy conservation must become a way of life in the future. Although conservation is not a total solution, it is a means to provide time to develop new technologies for using and converting the world's available fuel sources into working energy.

When it comes to residential conservation, just how can you, as a kitchen designer and the homeowners you work with help limit our world energy needs? **The National Energy Watch Program**, developed by the **Edison Electric Institute**, several years ago, outlined three basic approaches which provide an excellent foundation for residential energy conservation.

- Install more efficient appliances and equipment.

- Adapt better everyday energy usage habits.

- Improve the thermal integrity of the building.

Your job is to help your client select the most energy efficient appliances, and then urge them to adopt better daily energy use habits as they begin using their new kitchen.

Federal regulations continuously challenge appliance manufacturers to develop new energy efficient and environmentally safe equipment. The first milestone was the introduction of the energy guide label in 1972.

Energy Guide Labels

To help your client select the best appliances, you need to become familiar with energy labels that appear on refrigerators, freezers, dishwashers, ice makers, clothes washers, room air conditioners and water heaters. These energy guides tell you the following:

- How much it will cost in a year's time to operate the appliance based on an average charge per kilowatt hour of electricity, or an average charge per therm gas.

- What the yearly operating costs are of the least energy-efficient comparable appliance.

- What the yearly operating costs are of the most energy-efficient model in the same category.

- A table showing the yearly operational cost of the model being considered based on different utility rates.

More recent federal regulations include the following:

- Dishwashers manufactured after May 1994 must not consume more than 2.7KWH of energy in a normal cycle.

- Energy requirements for clothes dryers became effective in mid-1994 based on the determination that automatic temperature controls use 12% less energy than dryers with only timed cycles.

- Global agreement was reached in 1994 to revise the 1990 Montreal Protocol to reduce the production and consumption of chlorofluorocarbons (CFC's) used in refrigerators and air conditioners annually, with a complete phase out of CFC's by the end of 1995. The use of CFC's depletes the earths ozone layer faster than it can repair itself. As a result, most refrigerators manufactured today utilize hydrochlorofluorocarbons (HCFC's) which are 90% better for the environment than CFC's. The ultimate goal is to find a substitute chemical that will have zero effect on the earths ozone by the year 2030 when HCFC's are banned.

KitchenAid
Model KTR*18KX**0*

Refrigerator-Freezer
Capacity: 18.1 Cubic Feet

Type of Defrost: Automatic

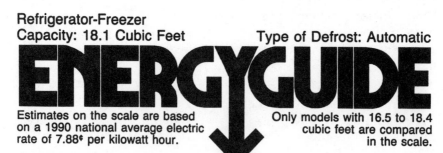

Estimates on the scale are based
on a 1990 national average electric
rate of 7.88¢ per kilowatt hour.

Only models with 16.5 to 18.4
cubic feet are compared
in the scale.

Model with
lowest
energy cost
$60
▼▼THIS MODEL

$61

Model with
highest
energy cost
$88
▼

Estimated yearly energy cost

**Your cost will vary depending on your local energy rate and how
you use the product.** This energy cost is based on U.S. Government standard tests.

How much will this model cost you to run yearly?

Yearly cost

Estimated yearly $ cost shown below

Cost per kilowatt hour		
	2¢	$15
	4¢	$31
	6¢	$46
	8¢	$62
	10¢	$77
	12¢	$93

Ask your salesperson or local utility for the energy rate (cost per
kilowatt hour) in your area.

Important: Removal of this label before consumer purchase is a violation
of federal law (42 U.S.C. 6302).

1126246

Figure 108   The Energy Guide Label.

Adopting Better Everyday Usage Habits

However, your assistance in helping the client select the most energy-efficient appliance is not enough. All family members must adopt new ways of using the equipment to minimize the energy consumption of each appliance.

The following is a list of information that appears in the *NKBA Beyond The Basics...Advanced Kitchen Design Textbook* that has been gathered from major utility companies across the United States.

DISHWASHER

- Wash full loads.

- Do not pre-rinse dishes under a steady stream of water. A study, conducted at Ohio State University, concluded that a dishwasher required 9.9 gallons (37.47liters) of water (without pre-rinsing), while washing by hand used 15.7 gallons (59.42liters) with rinsing under a running stream of water. Use the energy-saving drying cycle.

- Don't use the dishwasher to warm plates.

- Pots and pans with charred-on soils from delayed meals or fast cooking should be scraped or soaked before placing in the dishwasher.

FOOD WASTE DISPOSER

- Use a strong flow of cold water and keep it running at least 30 seconds after the noise of grinding has stopped.

- Always use cold water when operating the disposer to solidify fatty and greasy wastes.

- When washing dishes in a sink with a disposer, check to be sure all small objects are removed from the sudsy water before draining the sink.

- Run the disposer each time food waste is put in it.

- Before leaving home for several days, check to be sure all wastes have been flushed out of the disposer to avoid odors developing. If odors do occur, they can be removed by running orange or lemon peels or ice cubes through the disposer.

- Periodically (and always after disposing of fibrous food wastes) purge the drain line by filling the sink with two or three inches of cold water. Turn on the disposer and allow this water to run through with no wastes added.

- If the home uses a septic tank, plan on cleaning the tank about twice more than the normal schedule.

REFRIGERATOR/FREEZERS

- Open the door only when necessary and for a minimum amount of time.

- Cover all liquids and most foods before placing in the refrigerator.

- Set the refrigerator temperature at no higher than 38°F (3.33°C). Set the freezer at 0°F (-17.78°C).

- Make sure the doors seal tightly. To check the gasket, close the door on a dollar bill. Pull the dollar bill straight out. There should be some resistance. If not, replace gaskets or tighten the hinges.

- Vacuum/clean the condenser coils on the back or the bottom of the refrigerator at least twice a year.

- Organize the storage of items in the refrigerator. Label all frozen food packages.

- Do not overload the food storage compartment, especially with items that do not require refrigeration.

- Keep the freezer compartment as full as possible. This will reduce cold air lost when the door is opened.

- Locate the refrigerator-freezer away from other heat-producing equipment, such as the range, and out of direct sunlight.

- **NOTE:** Prior to disposal of any old refrigerator/freezer, the consumer must call a service representative to drain and recapture the coolant.

GAS AND ELECTRIC RANGES

- Small electrical appliances often require less energy for the cooking job than the oven or the surface cooktop of a range because they have an enclosed heating element and after a thermostatic control. Select small appliances for some cooking jobs.

- Defrost frozen foods before cooking to cut down on the cooking time. A defrosted roast requires 33% less cooking time than one still frozen.

- For more efficient range top cooking, use pots and pans with flat bottoms. Cook on a surface unit no larger than the pan. Use tight fitting covers on pots. Turn off the surface units as soon as you have finished, or shortly before and allow foods to finish cooking on retained heat.

- Preheat the oven only as long as necessary, usually for no longer than 10 minutes.

- If the range has two ovens, use the smaller one whenever possible.

- Bake several food items at once and then freeze for future dinners.

- Don't peek! The temperature may drop every time the door is opened.

- Never use the oven to heat the kitchen.

- Keep the oven clean. Make sure the gaskets on the oven door provide a good, tight seal. Maintain the drip bowls on the cooking surface so that they can efficiently reflect the heat upward.

- When using the broiler, put the food under the broiler before turning it on. Turn it off before removing food.

- When cooking with gas, use a low or medium flame. Cooking seldom requires a high flame and then only for a short while. Tailor the size of the flame to the size of the pan. A high flame licking up the sides of a pan wastes gas.

KITCHEN WASTE MANAGEMENT

Kitchen waste management is an important part of residential energy conservation. The importance of effective waste management was detailed by **Edmund J. Skernolis, Manager of Regulatory Affairs** for **Waste Management, Inc.,** in a presentation made at the **American Home Appliance Manufacturers** membership meeting.

Mr. Skernolis started out by telling the audience that garbage was not a business for the uneducated or the uninformed. The speaker reminded the audience that solid waste management was likely to become one of a handful of environmental issues that may have a profound impact on how we live and how we conduct our business.

America has been called the "throw away society". It appears we richly deserve the name. Studies show that each day Americans throw away about 160 million tons of municipal refuse - or about 4 pounds per day for every person in the United States. By the end of the decade, this number will probably be about 200 million tons a year. This huge river of waste is certainly diverse in its composition. However, upon close inspection two materials stand out: paper and yard waste account for nearly 60% of the total waste stream. Plastics represent 7%. Durable goods (major and small appliances, furniture/furnishings, rubber tires) comprise about 12%. The same type of packaging pollution is occurring in Canada. **John Hanse, Executive Director** of the **Recycling Council of Ontario**, recently stated that, by volume, 50% of Canadian garbage is packing - paper, aluminum, steel, glass and plastic.

The solution to our management problem seems to be centered in three areas: reduction, recycling and control. We can produce less waste, we can reuse more of what we would otherwise throw away, or we can allow the consumer product itself to be controlled by virtue of its disposability.

To produce less waste, we need to reduce packaging. *For example,* overpackaged goods can be avoided:

- Blister packs which combine a clear plastic case sealed to a sheet of cardboard.

- Individual snack and beverage containers.

- Luxury items that contain more packaging than product.

- Anything polystyrene: egg cartons, meat and product trays, cups and fast food containers.

- Disposable food containers, plastic grocery store bags.

Consumers should also be informed about the environmental implications of all sorts of packaging so that they can help bring these important issues into the open by talking about their choices.

A chart follows which details the most common packaging materials.

Needless to say, the entire concept of recycling means that we can reuse products and materials. Well-planned kitchens must include multiple recycling bins in or near the primary cleanup area. Collection areas should be designed away from the primary cook's working space.

Regulatory approaches are also being considered. Some individuals support the outright banning of certain packaging types. Others suggest sales tax or deposit incentives that would allow packaging costs to reflect the cost of pollution cleanup, resource usage, energy consumption and landfill use. Industry clearly is interested in regulating itself to improve the environment. Such voluntary and regulatory efforts are critical because it is this area - control leading to reduction - that will have the biggest impact on the environment in the long run.

Dramatically reducing the waste products we create means massive savings in initial production costs and transportation costs, as well as disposal costs.

BE PACKAGE-SMART WHEN YOU SHOP

MATERIAL	RESOURCES USED IN PRODUCTION	ENERGY USED IN PRODUCTION	REUSABLE?	RECYCLABLE?	BIODEGRADABLE?	REMARKS
glass	sand, limestone, soda ash	high (heat energy)	yes	yes - 30% energy savings over glass from new material	no	weight and shape make it energy-expensive to transport
paperboard cardboard	trees (a renewable but dwindling resource) and chemicals	high for new paper low for recycled paper	not usually	yes, but limited - must be mixed with new material	yes	not necessarily benign in environment may contain dyes, bleaches and other hazardous chemicals
aluminum cans	aluminum (scarce, expensive to mine)	very high	no	yes - 95% energy savings over new materials	no	smelting operations are a source of air pollution, acid rain
steel (tin) cans	iron and tin ores	high	some home reuse only	yes - 74% energy savings over new materials	eventually (10 - 20 years or more)	smelting operations create pollution lead seam sealer can contaminate food
polystyrene foam - egg cartons, meat trays	petrochemicals and additives (CFC's or substitute)	low	no	no	no	may contain ozone-destroying CFC's maior source of litter high volume in landfill sites
hard plastic (PET, HDPE, PP or PVC) bottles, tubs, jars	petrochemicals and additives	low	some home reuse only	yes - once (very little currently recycled	no	may emit toxic chemicals during production and disposal
plastic (usually LDPE) shopping and garbage bags	petrochemicals and additives	low	home reuse only	in theory only	no	may emit toxic chenmicals during production and disposal
plastic-coated card - board milk cartons	trees, chemicals and petrochemicals	high	no	no	eventually (longer than uncoated paper)	studies show trace amounts of dioxins and furans in milk cartons
laminates - "tetra pak" juice cartons, micro- waveable containers	variety of resources - paper, plastic and aluminum	high	no	no	no	not recyclable due to mixed materials
blister packaging	petrochemicals (plastic) and trees (paper)	medium to high	no	no	no	not recyclable due to mixed materials often used for overpackaging
aerosol containers	steel and plastic	high	no	no	no	may contain ozone-destroying CFC's usually a prime example of overpackaging

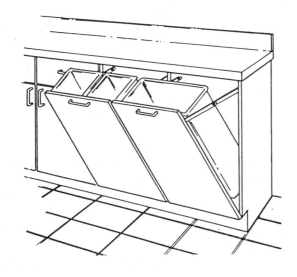

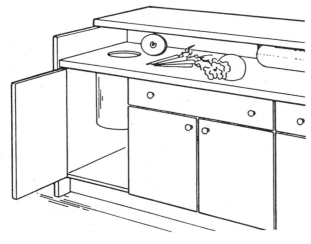

Figure 109 Recycling centers can include tilt-out or pull-out bins that assist in sorting. Or, may actually include a countertop opening into which

Globally, we must realize that the *"Where-to-put-it?"* question is only a small part of this issue. World citizens must start to look at our environment as a whole, and question each step in the consumption process which has led to the huge toll taken on our natural resources to produce (trees for paper, petrochemicals for plastics, metals for cans) our energy (for production, transportation, disposing) and our land (where landfill sites are overflowing and our environment threatened by unsightly litter).

SELECTING APPLIANCES

Once you understand the importance of conservation and begin selecting equipment based on this knowledge, as well as advising your client on how to use the equipment, it is appropriate for you to study the major appliances that are an integral part of any kitchen.

When the original research was done concerning kitchen design, the typical home had a sink, free-standing range and a refrigerator. Ventilation hoods were new on the horizon, and dishwashers were owned by only a lucky few.

NKBA research conducted by the University of Minnesota indicates that more appliances are being specified in kitchens today. A well-designed range with an effective ventilation hood system above it is the basis of the simplest of cooking centers.

More typically, this area will have a cooking surface with ventilation above, and then a separate conventional oven and microwave oven located elsewhere in the plan. In 26% of the kitchens, two sinks are planned. The primary sink generally featured a double-bowl compartment, with a single sink reserved for the secondary location.

A food waste disposer is included to facilitate waste cleanup and, dishwashers are almost standard today. The refrigerator remains an important, integral part of the plan and is now available in many different models.

Refrigerator Center

The first home delivery of ice in America occurred in 1802. This necessitated the inclusion of an ice chest (a heavy wooden box, large enough to hold both ice and food together in a single compartment) in the kitchen.

METHOD OF COOLING

The most important concept to grasp is that refrigeration is the removal of heat. It is heat that causes food to deteriorate. Tests have shown that bacteria multiply rapidly at high temperatures; therefore, all modern refrigerators are constructed to maintain temperatures at not more than 40°F (4.45°C). Lower temperatures are usually recommended for specific foods: between 32°F (13.33°C) and 35°F (1.67°C) for milk and 25°F to 31°F (-3.89°C to -.56°C) for fresh meat, for example. It is because of these different temperature requirements that many refrigerator models include different compartments for meats and vegetables so that currents of extra cold air can be circulated around the specific compartment.

Refrigerator cabinets are made of various materials designed to create an inner and outer shell with insulation between. Experiments have proven that 80% to 90% of the heat that gets into the refrigerator comes through the walls of the appliance. Consequently, a great deal of engineering and design time is spent perfecting the insulation and making sure that the door gaskets prove a tight seal.

Ellen Rand and **Florence Perchuk** in their book, "*Complete Book of Kitchen Design*", published in conjunction with the editors of Consumer Reports, explained the refrigerator operations as follows:

"*Refrigerator design has evolved dramatically over the years to include better energy efficiency, more convenience features, better-organized storage and ever-increasing capacity.*

The major components of a refrigerator are the following:

The compressor consists of a motor and pump sealed inside a steel case concealed within the refrigerator structure. The pump compresses refrigerant vapor and sends it to the condenser.

The condenser is a long folded tube that receives hot, high-pressure refrigerant vapor pumped by the compressor. As the heat leaves, the vapor inside it cools and condenses back to liquid. Condensers in many built-in refrigerators are located at the top of the appliance. Free-standing refrigerators are engineered with the condenser on the back or underneath the appliance.

The capillary tube connects the condenser to the evaporator, metering the flow of liquid refrigerant to the evaporator.

The evaporator, also a long tube, receives liquid refrigerant from the condenser. The liquid boils and vaporizes as it picks up heat from inside the cabinet. In a side-by-side refrigerator, it may be found behind the rear wall of the freezer, whereas in a top-or bottom-mount, it is usually found between the refrigerator and freezer."

SELECTION CRITERIA

Before selecting a specific piece of equipment for a project, you should consider all of your options from the sizing, configuration and installation stand-points.

Wanda W. Olson, a household equipment specialist in the Department of Design, Housing and Apparel at the University of Minnesota, recently published a paper guiding consumers in the selection of a new refrigerator. Ms. Olson identified the following types of refrigerators available for purchase:

"There are three basic types of refrigerators to choose from. The most common unit is the combination refrigerator/freezer where 1/4 to 1/2 of the unit is a separate freezer section that maintains 8°F. (-13.33°C), or below and that can be adjusted to 0°F (-17.78°C). Another choice is the refrigerator with a freezer storage compartment with temperatures at or about 15°F (-9.45°C). This temperature is not low enough to keep ice cream frozen or to keep frozen food at its best quality for the maximum recommended storage time. A third choice is the 'all refrigerator' with no freezer compartment or only a very small one (0.50 cubic feet or less).

All types of refrigerators should maintain 33°F to 38°F (.56°C to 3.33°C) in a fresh food section. A few refrigerators/freezers have special compartments with temperatures a few degrees cooler or warmer than the rest of the fresh food section. An example of a cooler area is a meat keeper compartment that is connected to the air circulating around the freezer section. A refrigerator has a single temperature control while the refrigerator/freezer model has either single or multi controls for the fresh food and freezer sections. In most models with multiple controls the primary sensor is in the fresh food section. In these models the refrigerator may not run enough to keep the freezer temperature low enough if the room temperature around the refrigerator is lower than 60°F (15.56°C), or if the fresh food section has large amounts of very cold food in it (such as frozen food defrosting). A few multiple-control models have dual compressors and the sections are cooled independently.

Refrigerators/freezers may have the freezer mounted on the bottom, the top (with either a right or left handed door), or side-by-side. In a side-by-side model, the fresh food section is on the right and has some fresh food space and freezer space accessible to persons of any height. Refrigerator/freezers with top-mounted freezers tend to have a lower energy consumption than units with side-by-side or bottom-mounted freezers because the freezer section is farther away from the warm compressor and condenser. The side-by-side models usually have a large freezer section and there is more door seal for the freezer than top or bottom mounted freezer models."

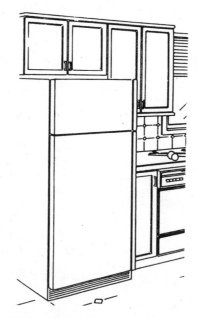

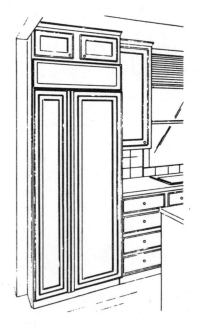

FREE-STANDING SIDE BY SIDE:
THESE OFFER LARGE CAPACITY (UP TO 25 CUBIC FT.) WITH A RELATIVELY LARGE SECTION OF FREEZER SPACE.

FREE-STANDING TOP MOUNT:
AVAILABLE IN MANY SIZES, THESE HAVE MORE REFRIGERATOR SPACE PROPORTIONALLY THAN SIDE-BY-SIDE UNITS.

BUILT-IN SIDE BY SIDE:
TALLER (84") THAN STANDARDS, THEY ARE SHALLOW (24") SO THEY LINE UP WITH CABINETS.

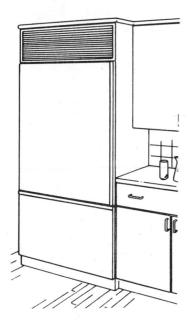

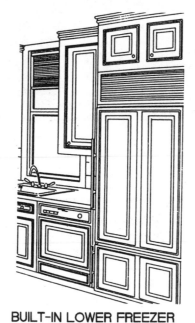

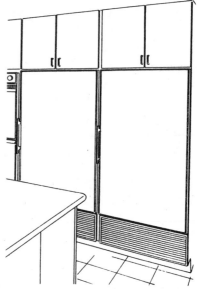

BUILT-IN LOWER FREEZER DRAWER:
FEATURES A HINGED DOOR; TRIM KITS ALLOW UNIT TO BLEND IN WITH CABINETRY.

BUILT-IN LOWER FREEZER DRAWER:
THIS BUILT-IN UNIT HAS A 24-INCH DEEP DRAWER, MAKING IT EASY TO REACH IN FOR FROZEN FOOD.

SEPARATE UNITS:
WHILE AN INDIVIDUAL REFRIGERATOR AND FREEZER TAKE UP A LOT OF SPACE, THEY ARE IDEAL FOR FOOD STORAGE.

Figure 110 Refrigerators/Freezer Choices.

Experienced designers also suggest the following considerations when selecting a new refrigerator.

PLANNING TIPS FROM KITCHEN PROS

- **Separate Units:** The all-refrigerator and all-freezer residential units that are available are ideal for large kitchens where the appliances are heavily used. However, they require extensive wall space (36" (91.44cm) each, a total of 72" (182.88cm) of wall and floor space) and are expensive.

- **Commercial Equipment:** High tech commercial refrigerators are available. Some offer glass door units. They require the inclusion of a separate freezer close by for the cook's convenience. Additionally, once the kitchen is in use, the see-through glass doors necessitate keeping things in perfect order within the refrigerator, or the room looks cluttered.

- **Freezer Location:** Because the most accessible shelf space is located between 22" (55.88cm) and 56" (142.24cm) off the floor, appliances that are designed with a lower freezer are more desirable than top freezer models. Ideally, the lower freezer should be a bin that pulls out to the user.

- **Accessibility:** In side-by-side models, the vertical door split minimizes the door projection into walkway spaces. Unfortunately though, the left and right hinging configuration blocks adjacent countertops on either side of

the appliances. Additionally, in smaller models the freezer may be so narrow that a frozen pie package will not fit into the space, let alone the 25 pound Thanksgiving turkey.

New modular type refrigerators/freezers have recently shown up in the marketplace. These models can be used in a number of locations throughout the kitchen to provide accessibility and convenience to all family members.

- **Storage Above:** Ideally, a 24" (60.96cm) deep cabinet should be placed above the refrigerator so that this cabinet is accessible.

- **Boxed-in vs. Built-in:** If the appliance is framed with panels that extend to the floor, it is called a "boxed-in" look. Experience pros caution, "Do not call this a 'built-in' look." The necessary air space on each side and above the refrigerator, as well as the oversized depth of this type of free-standing unit prohibits it from being a true "built-in" look.

- **Door Swing:** If you are planning to reuse an existing refrigerator verify if there are any door swing engineering problems which limit access to the crisper bins within. Some of the old models require that doors open far beyond 90° to allow bins to be pulled out from the interior. This will severely limit where that appliance can be placed in the kitchen.

- **Appliance Placement:** If a client is going to reuse an existing refrigerator that only has a few more years of service, do not plan the entire kitchen around this outdated appliance. New models today have reversible doors, so there is no longer a left hinge or right hinge limitation. However, many older refrigerators are permanently hinged in one direction.

  If the refrigerator will be replaced in a short time, design the best kitchen first. Then suggest to your clients that they work with the old appliance until it is replaced with a new one with the proper hinging to support the overall design concept.

- **Decorative Panel:** If you are selecting a decorative wood panel for the refrigerator, be cautious about specifying a 1/4" (.64cm) sheet of paneling in a kitchen that features solid wood raised panel doors. The graining difference between the veneer panel and the solid wood panel might be unacceptable. If you have a heavily styled raised panel door on the cabinetry, suggest to the client that an equally intricate styled panel be ordered for the refrigerator.

Figure 111 (Courtesy of Sub-Zero Refrigeration) A built-in refrigerator with an icemaker.

Figure 112 (Courtesy of Sub-Zero Refrigeration) Multiple refrigerator and/or freezer combinations may be installed to improve accessiblility for users and efficiency of work centers.

Clean-up Center

SINKS

Sinks are made out of many materials today. We will be addressing sink construction and configuration as it relates to sizes and mounting methods.

Configuration: Sinks come in a variety of sizes. The **National Kitchen and Bath Association** has surveyed its members and cataloged entries in the Annual Design Competition to determine the most popular sink configurations specified by kitchen designers.

In small kitchens (less than 150 square feet in size), it is not uncommon to have one, single-bowl sink specified in the kitchen. This sink is generally 24" x 21" (60.96cm x 53.34cm) in size. This sink can fit in a 27" (68.58cm) wide cabinet. A 36" (91.44cm) wide cabinet is required for a double-sink. Double- or triple-bowl sinks are more often specified in kitchens larger than 150 square feet.

Second sinks in kitchens are often single sinks. Round or other shaped configurations are popular today.

SINGLE SINKS

DOUBLE SINKS

TRIPLE SINKS

Figure 113 Typical sink configurations.

MOUNTING METHODS

There are several ways to mount a sink:

- **Self-rimming:** The sink sits on top of the countertop. A hole is cut in the surface and the fixture is dropped in by the installers. A bead of caulking is applied between the sink and countertop forming a seal.

- **Under-Mounted:** The sink is installed underneath the countertop. This works particularly well with solid surface countertops. A sink can be under-mounted in a laminate top if extra precautions are taken to make sure the underside of the laminate top is sealed against water. Even with the best seal, it is better to top-mount a sink in a laminate top.

  If you are under-mounting a cast iron sink, always order it with a glazed rim. Make sure your client understands that there will be a joint where the sink and the countertop meet for sinks that are of dissimilar materials.

  A traditional under-mount sink has a square countertop lip extending down to the curved top edge of the sink. A second type of installation can be specified if the sink has a square edge so that the joint contour is minimized. With solid surfacing, a seamed undermount can create a flush joint between the bowl with the square top edge and the similar countertop material.

- **Flush-Mounted:** The sink is recessed into the countertop substrate material so that it is even with the counter material. This is particularly effective in a ceramic tile top. Special sinks are designed which have square ledges so that the sink sits in the countertop and can flush-out with the ceramic tile on the deck.

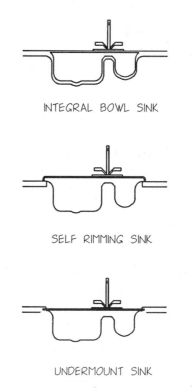

INTEGRAL BOWL SINK

SELF RIMMING SINK

UNDERMOUNT SINK

Figure 114 Sink mounting methods.

- **Rimmed:** The sink sits slightly above the countertop with the joint between the sink and the countertop concealed by a metal rim.

- **Integral:** As the name implies, the sink and countertop are all made out of one piece. This can be done with stainless steel or solid surface materials. The opportunity to create a uniquely arranged sink configuration, the ability to specify an attached drain board and the ease of maintenance are all advantages to this type of installation.

MATERIALS

You have the following materials to choose from:

- **Enameled Steel:** This is an inexpensive sink that is prone to chipping. Steel is stamped or pressed into a shape and then an enamel coating is applied and fired in a furnace. Because of the smooth nature of the steel and its tendency to flex, this sink is easily chipped. It is generally installed with a stainless steel rim that is cinched to the countertop with clamps from below.

- **Cast Iron:** You may have heard the term cast iron, but have never known what the term really means. "Cast iron" actually describes a manufacturing process used for more than a century to produce bathtubs.

The difference between the mechanical operations used to form sheet metal fixtures and the cast iron manufacturing process is that the metal in this second process is formed by molding it when it is so hot it is a liquid.

Sand is used to create the shape of the mold. The molten iron, a 2,700°F (1482°C), is poured into a channel, filling the cavity. After the molten iron has cooled and solidified, the sand cast is removed (the sand is recycled) and the exposed product is ready for finishing. The exterior surface must be smoothed to a uniform finish. Once this is done, the final enamel finish coat is added. This finish is a combination of clay, frit, color oxides and opacifiers. It's applied to the exposed surfaces of the fixture in powder form, and then fired at 1,250°F (695°C) which melts the powder uniformly into a smooth coating which fuses to the cast iron base material.

Figure 115 (Courtesy of Kohler Co.) Single cast iron sinks are available today with inserts and accessories that provide more flexibility.

The enamel coating on iron is much thicker, and the cast iron more resistant to movement that is the case with an enameled steel fixture. Therefore, a cast iron product is more chip-resistant.

The higher the gauge number, the thinner the steel. A 22-gauge, mirror-like stainless steel sink is the least expensive and the least desirable stainless steel product. Because of its thinness it will dent easily and its mirror finish will show scratches.

A 20-gauge brush finished stainless steel sink that has a high nickel content, will resist water spotting, conceal fine scratches within the brush finish, and is thick enough to resist dents.

The most durable stainless steel sink is an 18- gauge, brushed finish, high nickel content sink that has an undercoating on the back side to control noise transmission. This sink is also much more costly than the other two gauge thickness fixtures.

Figure 116 (Courtesy of Kohler Co.) Many kitchens feature self-rimming double cast iron sinks.

- **Stainless Steel:** The quality of the stainless steel sink is judged by the thickness of the steel, the finish on the sink, and the depth and configuration of the bowl.

Figure 117 (Courtesy of Kohler Co.) Triple compartment sinks are also available.

Figure 118 (Courtesy of Elkay Manufacturing Co.) Double stainless steel sinks are extremely popular in kitchen planning. A basket attachment is seen here that increases the functional use of the sink.

Figure 119 (Courtesy of Elkay Manufacturing Co.)
A stainless steel sink can have a drain board attached to it. Sinks that are integrated into the
countertop can also offer this option.

Figure 120 (Courtesy of Kohler Co.) A small
stainless sink is used as the second water source.

- **Solid Surface:** Solid surface
  sinks are designed to be both an
  integral part of the countertop, as
  well as mounted underneath a
  solid surface countertop. Solid surface sinks come in a variety of
  sizes and shapes, and are available with various attached drain
  boards. Because the sink is an extension of the countertop, maintenance requirements are minimal.

These sinks withstand heavy use,
can be scrubbed with an abrasive
cleaner and are not affected by
hot water used during the cooking
processed.

Figure 121 (Courtesy of Elkay Manufacturing Co.)
A popular approach to sink design today is to under-mount the sink in a solid surface countertop.

Figure 122 (Courtesy of Wood-Mode Cabinetry
and Dupont Corian) The sink is part of the Corian countertop and is totally integrated into the
surface.

Another product on the market is called **"Asterite"**. This quartz and acrylic man-made material is non-porous and scratch/chip resistant. It is available in a variety of shapes and more than 100 colors in both gloss and matte finishes. It is even available in a finish that looks like granite.

Figure 123   (Courtesy of Wood-Mode Cabinetry and Dupont Corian) This integrated Corian sink also features a custom- designed drain board built-in to the countertop.

- **Proprietary Materials:** New sink materials are continually being introduced.

Another manufacturer has a product called **"Silacron 2000"**. This composite material unites the benefits of a number of different materials. It consists of 70% silicate quartz which gives it the hard-wearing properties needed to withstand the wear a kitchen sink receives from utensils and food products. Acrylic resins insure that the silicate quartz is firmly bonded to an elastic resin matrix. This results in a resilient material that allows the sink to withstand knocks or dents expected in day to day use. The color goes all the way through, therefore it is not susceptible to chipping.

Figure 124 (Courtesy of Elkay Manufacturing Co.) New man-made materials are also available for self-rimming sinks.

PLANNING TIPS FROM KITCHEN PROS

- **Small Sinks:** Avoid small, 12" x 12" (30.48cm x 30.48cm) sinks. They have a drain that does not accept a food waste disposer and are so small that there will be a water-splash problem when the cook uses the sink for food preparation.

- **Round Shapes:** If you are going to specify two round sinks as the primary sink arrangement, make sure your client understands that the interior space of these sinks is less than a comparable square model. Also realize that these sinks require deck-mounted faucet locations; therefore, you must specify the faucet location on your plan.

- **Under-Mounted Sinks:** If you use separate under-mounted sinks in place of a sink manufactured in a double configuration, warn your client that if water is running and the faucet is swung from one sink to the other, water will splash on the countertop. Consider routing down the countertop section that separates the two sinks, or recessing the entire configuration into the counter surface 1/4" (.64cm) or so in order to eliminate the potential for water to run across the countertop and down to the floor as the spout is moved from sink to sink while water is running.

- **Food Waste Disposer Compartment:** Some sink configurations are a single size (24" x 21") (60.96cm x 53.34cm) but have a small, round compartment for the food waste disposer in one back corner. Because the compartment for the food waste disposer is almost too small to use, this is not the most desirable sink configuration.

- **Strainer:** If you're not ordering a food waste disposer to be mounted on the sink, make sure you order a good quality strainer.

- **Bowl Arrangement:** Unless your client is going to wash and rinse dishes in a double sink configuration, demonstrate how a sink with one large compartment and one small compartment functions. This configuration gives you the largest sink for everyday use, and then a smaller - yet usable - compartment for other uses.

- **Drain Boards:** A sink with an attached drain board is an excellent accessory to specify for a client who does a lot of fresh food preparation.

- **Recycle Center:** Some sinks today on the market that have an opening within the sink which allows access to a chute for a compost container or a waste receptacle below.

- **The Real Size:** When specifying a solid surface integral sink, verify what the actual overall dimensions of the sink are. The sink literature may list the interior dimension of the sink, not the overall. This overall dimension will determine your spacing in a standard side-by-side double configuration. You may find it necessary to increase the cabinet size if you're planning to create a "butterfly" corner arrangement with such sinks.

- **Damage:** Make sure your client realizes that cast iron self-rimming sinks are susceptible to damaged edges or to warpage. This is particularly a problem with larger sinks. Make sure that you inspect the sink before it goes to the jobsite. Look for chips along the lead edge. The client must accept the possibility of a wide caulking joint connecting the sink to the countertop for large sink configurations. If this won't be acceptable, specify another type of sink. With these self-rimming sinks, also make sure that you specify caulking that will either match the countertop or the sink so that the joint compound does not become a focal point in the sink area.

- **Corner Sinks:** When placing a sink in a corner, don't push it back more than 2" or 3" (5.08cm or 7.62cm) away from the front edge of the countertop. That's the normal installation location and it should be maintained (even in a custom design) so that the client has comfortable access to the water source.

- **The Holes:** Make sure that you know how many holes are on the back ledge of the sink and how many holes you need for the faucet and water attachments. If a hot water dispenser, a faucet, a dishwasher air gap, other dispensers and/or water treatment spouts are planned, you may run out of predrilled holes. Typically, cast iron sinks have four holes. A fifth hole can be drilled, but it's expensive and the sink may be damaged. Adding extra holes is much easier in a stainless steel sink. In solid surface sinks, the holes are drilled in the countertop deck so the number and placement is flexible.

- **How Deep:** The deeper the sink, the straighter the sides of the

sink, the tighter the angle where the sink side and bottom meet and the flatter the sink bottom are the bigger the interior space is.

- **Accessories:** A variety of sink accessories are also available. You may consider specifying plastic covered wire or stainless steel baskets that are useful for washing and peeling fresh vegetables. They take the place of a colander. Plate racks that fit inside the sink are also available. Specialized chopping surfaces that completely or partially cover the sink, are also available. These accessories may match the sink color, contrast with the sink color, or be a combination of the sink's color and stainless steel. They enhance the sink's function as well as its appearance. Don't overlook them.

Disposer

FOOD WASTE DISPOSER

A food waste disposer is a popular means of disposing of food waste products. The food waste disposer is an appliance much like the compactor: some clients will not live without it, others have one and don't want one in their new kitchen. Find out what your client thinks is important before you specify this or any other appliance.

There is a great deal of difference of opinion about whether a disposer can be installed in a home on a septic tank system. Plumbers generally recommend that if you have a home that is on a septic system, and you are adding a dishwasher and a food waste disposal, the septic system should be 40% to 50%

larger than one for a house without these appliances. In a renovation situation, the tank should be cleaned out 50% more often if these appliances are added. Therefore, instead of every 6 years, it should be cleaned out every 3 years.

In addition to the concerns about a food waste disposer installed in a home using a septic system, verify if local codes will allow the use of this appliance. In some high-rise condominium developments you cannot install a food waste disposer. In some municipalities they're simply not allowed; in others they're required.

Operation Choices: Once you've determined whether or not you'll include a disposer, there are two choices you will select from:

- **Continuous Feed:** This appliance operates from a toggle switch on the wall or an air switch on the sink. It operates continuously as it is fed refuse; consequently the name. It allows the most flexibility in use, but it is also the most dangerous because a person's hand or utensil can unexpectedly be caught in the disposal when it is turned on.

- **Batch Feed:** This appliance is activated when the lid is turned. This is a safer appliance because it cannot be in operation unless the lid is in place. However, it can be more complicated to use: to activate the disposal, the lid must be in a halfway position; to use it as a stopper for the sink, it must be pushed to a full close position. This action can be confusing and

require dexterity difficult for a child or an elderly family member.

Regardless of the method of activation, the disposer actually disposes food waste in the same manner.

Basically, six types of action are employed in the waste disposal process:

- hammering

- shredding

- cutting

- grinding

- rubbing

- pulverizing

As waste reaches the bottom of the shredding compartment, the whirling impeller comes in contact with the food. Therefore, centrifugal force in action presses the waste against the impeller arms, the fibrous waste cutting blades and the grind positioner. As the action continues, waste is finally divided into particles small enough to pass through into a lower evacuation chamber. From this point, the particles enter the drain and flow to the stack of the drain system to exit the house. Because of the movement of food waste particles to the drain system, it is imperative that the drain line enter the wall low enough so that the food waste is not forced to "flow up hill". Generally, the centerline to the drain pipe at the wall should be between 17" and 19" (43.18cm to 48.26cm) high.

Many people don't realize that the effectiveness of the operation of the disposer is directly related to the rate of flow of cold water. Cold water should be flowing during the entire process of disposing of food and several minutes afterwards to clear the waste line. Cold water is used, not hot, so that fat or grease can be hardened so that it will be cut and flushed away with other types of waste. If warm water is used, grease will be melted and as it comes in contact with lower waste pipes in the system it may harden and cause a stoppage. Many specialists recommend periodically flushing the drain lines through the disposal by filling the sink with 3" to 4" (7.62cm to 10.16cm) of cold water and then activating the disposal.

Disposals come with different sized motors and require different amounts of insulation. The larger motors provide extra thrust for tough-to-grind loads. The increased sound insulation makes it much more pleasant for the cook to use the disposal because noise levels are kept low.

All disposals have some type of an anti-jam feature: it may simply be a reset button at the bottom of the disposal, or it may be an automatic reversing action. In this latter case, if the disposal jams, the unit will pause for a brief time and then automatically reverse the direction of the impeller blades.

In addition to a larger motor and more insulation, better disposals also use better interior materials to improve the durability of the appliance.

If you're working on a renovation project and the client wants to reuse their food waste disposer, be cautious. Typically, when you remove an existing disposer and dishwasher and leave them inoperable for several weeks during the renovation, these appliances will not function properly when reinstalled.

If the disposal is older than three or four years, recommend that the client purchase a new one or add a clause in your contract stipulating that you'll not be responsible for the operation of this appliance once reinstalled. The same concern exists for a dishwasher if it is ten years or older.

TRASH COMPACTOR

Environmentalists do not recommend trash compactors because the compacted mixed refuse slows down the decomposition process. However, you may have a client who has had a compactor in the past and wishes to have a new version of the appliance.

On the other side of the argument, trash compactor manufacturers feel that the concern for the environment is one of the rallying cries for purchasing a trash compactor. Their argument is that when you have compacted refuse that is one-quarter the volume of that found in a loose trash can, you minimize the burden on garbage company landfills. A discussion worth continuing.

Under-countertop trash compactors are available in 12" (30.48cm), 15" (38.1cm) and 18" (45.72cm) wide units. They may have a charcoal filtering system built-in or use a deodorizer to minimize the odors associated with refuge that is left at room temperature for an extended period of time in the compactor. Even with this deodorizing mechanism, the appliance's use and care manual will instruct the user to carefully rinse all containers before placing them in the compactor.

You must consider the weight of the bag of compacted trash in relationship to your client's physical capabilities.

The larger 18" wide units can have a bag that weighs as much as 40 pounds (18.16kilograms) - you're client may not be able to handle this heavy trash bag.

Some units have pull-out bin doors, others have doors that swing to the left or right and then include a pull-out bin within the opening. Several models have a small tilt-out door at the top to facilitate disposing of one small container or such.

The compactor plugs into a standard household circuit, much like the dishwasher and disposer. They are operated by motors that vary in size. The motor drives a single ram down that compacts the trash. Some of the appliances on the market can be operated by a foot peddle and most have a key lock to prevent children from playing with the appliance.

Figure 125   In this small kitchen, a compactor is placed on the left-hand cabinet run, with the dishwasher to the right of the sink. Good placement in this small space because it allows both to be used simultaneously.

DISHWASHERS

Dishwashers are typically installed as a built-in appliance adjacent to the sink. Although there are some special purpose units on the market, this installation is the preferred choice.

The type of dishwashing action varies to some degree with each manufacturer. Rotating arms, fan jets and other enhancements are used to maximize the effectiveness of the washing actions. In most machines, the water is filtered and recirculated during the washing process, thereby reducing the amount of water required. In fact, a recent research study demonstrated that dishwasher wash cycles used less energy, less time and less water than handwashing.

According to the Ohio State University Study, dishwashers used 5.8 fewer gallons (21.95liters) of water a day than handwashing the same dishes. The comparison was between a load of dishes washed in a dishwasher versus that washed in soapy water and rinsed under a running stream of water - the typical way North Americans wash dishes by hand. Also, in a study completed by the American Home Appliance Manufacturers, homemakers estimated that approximately 3.8 hours per week were saved by using the dishwasher instead of handwashing. This translates into nearly 200 hours per year, or about the equivalent of a two- week vacation.

When evaluating a dishwasher, first look at the racks. Better units offer some flexibility in racking arrangements and provide various rack height options. Most manufacturers have two racks that accommodate glasses in the top, plates and larger pieces at the bottom rack. One manufacturer reverses this rack design. Another has three racks rather than two.

One of the most important things to understand about well-designed dishwashers is that, because of the improved washing action and better filters, prerinsing is a thing of the past. Filters built in to the dishwasher trap food particles and prevent them from being redeposited on the dishes. To overcome the necessity of cleaning filters, some models feature a small disposer that chops food particles and discharges them into the drain.

The best water temperature for dishwashing is between 140°F and 160°F . (60°C and 71.11°C). This is important both from the standpoint of sanitation and from the requirement for hot water of at least 140°F (60°C) to dissolve typical dishwasher detergents. While many families do set their hot water tanks at 140°F (60°C), many people today are turning down their domestic hot water heaters to conserve energy. Therefore, newer dishwashers have thermostatically controlled delay features to allow the built-in heating element to raise the water temperature to 140°F (60°C) before beginning the washing cycle. All dishwashers have one or more washing cycles and one or more rinsing cycles, as well as a drying cycle. Drying is generally done by warm air blowing across the dishes, heated by an internal heating element. Many models today have an "energy saver" switch which turns off the heating element during the drying cycle and simply relies on heat within the dishwasher, and room air for drying.

Appliance Usage Statistics: The way that people use their dishwashers today was highlighted in a *Better Homes and Gardens* magazine survey report.

The following information is included for your review:

DISHWASHERS

What they own now:

Own a dishwasher	73.6%
Dishwasher is built-in	87%
Median age	5 years old

How they use it:

Scrape, rinse, load	70.8%

What they still wash by hand:

Wooden utensils	43%
Pots and Pans	43%
Fine china	42%
Plastic utensils	28%
Knives	25%

Use per week:

Once	9%
Twice	12%

Cooking Center

Cooking: that's what most people think about when they hear the word "kitchen". A kitchen specialist needs to carefully select the equipment that will help the cook roast, bake, broil and saute delectable meals for family and friends. The quandary of determining which appliance (or a combination of appliances) will best suit the work space available and the homeowner's cooking style can only be resolved by adapting a systematic approach to the selection process. Surprisingly, the old "gas vs. electric" issue should not be your first decision.

- Step one is choosing the appliance style - built-in, drop-in, slide-in.

- Step two is the ventilation system.

- Step three involves the heat source.

- Step four is based on the method of heat transference selected: convection, conduction, radiation.

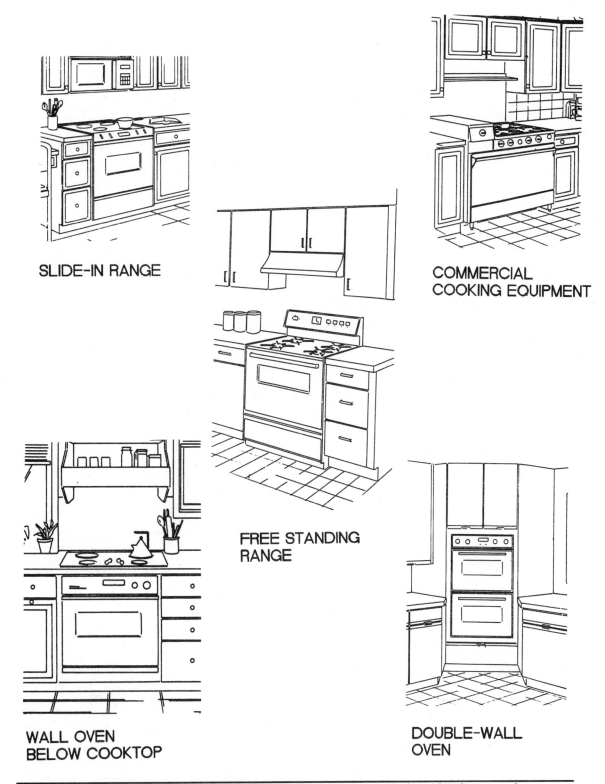

SLIDE-IN RANGE

COMMERCIAL
COOKING EQUIPMENT

FREE STANDING
RANGE

WALL OVEN
BELOW COOKTOP

DOUBLE-WALL
OVEN

Figure 126   Cooking equipment comes in many configurations. You need to select between these options before continuing the design process.

SELECTING THE APPLIANCE TYPE

If, as in the case of most kitchens, residential appliances are recommended, the next decision lies in determining which style unit or units will suit the space and cooking needs of the client.

Built-in Equipment: Built-in appliances offer the convenience of an oven at waist height, or one at eye-level and one below in the case of double ovens. One oven may be placed in the base cabinet so that counter space is not eliminated. A separate built-in cooktop allows handy storage space below for cookware and utensils.

One of the biggest advantages of built-in units is that the designer and client have complete freedom and flexibility in placement. The two appliances can be placed side by side or separated to create distinct work cells.

The major disadvantage of built-in appliances is found in their high cost. On an average, a built-in oven and cooktop will cost about 10 to 20% more than a one-piece appliance. Additionally, installation fees will be greater than those for other type units. Built-in units also require a minimum of 60" to 66" (152.4cm to 167.64cm) of wall space, which might cramp countertops in a compact kitchen.

Lastly, note that the interior dimension of most built-in ovens is smaller than that of a 30" (76.2cm) wide freestanding range oven.

Figure 127 Many contemporary kitchens feature an oven built-in below a cooktop.

Figure 128 (Courtesy of Jenn Air) In kitchen designs today, the area where the cooktop is housed oftentimes features a deeper cabinet than the adjacent cabinet units.

Figure 129 (Courtesy of Jenn Air) Built-in ovens are available in single or double configurations and bottom or side hinged doors. Typically they are installed in a tall cabinet.

Slide-In, Free-Standing Equipment: Slide-in, free-standing ranges feature an oven below the cooking surface. This type of appliance may suit the cook's cooking needs, space limitations and budget. However, it won't add the sleek look that distinguishes the other choices, and the narrow spaces between the range and the adjacent cabinet will prove difficult to keep clean. Also worth noting is that many models place the controls along the range's backsplash - an awkward and potentially dangerous location.

One style of slide-in range is called an eye-level or bi-level stove. This appliance features one large oven below the cooking surface and a second smaller oven - either conventional or microwave

Figure 130 (Courtesy of KitchenAid, Inc.) A free-standing range.

- above it. The eye-level range is extremely space efficient: all of these cooking options fit within a 30" (76.2cm) wide space. However, be sure to check the distance from the cooking surface to the underside of the upper oven - it may be too low to accommodate the cook's favorite stock pot. This is not a good type of range for a client who does a lot of quantity cooking. The second major drawback of this type of range is that the efficiency of the ventilation system installed as part of this appliance is generally not as effective as a separate one. Additionally, the front of the upper oven tends to get quite dirty from airborne cooking grease and particles.

Commercial Equipment: When it comes to free-standing equipment, in years past, many cooks were attracted by the high-tech styling of commercial ranges. Designers had to carefully explain to the consumer the advantages and disadvantages of this type of cooking equipment when used residentially. In many cases, commercial restaurant ranges could not be legally used in residential installations because of code restrictions. Even if it was allowed, the extra ventilation, bigger gas lines and the oversized nature of the appliance caused many concerns.

Today commercially-styled cooking equipment is available in a free-standing configuration designed for residential applications. The big difference between residential and commercial equipment is the burner BTU (British Thermal Units) ratings. Many cooks feel that higher BTU ratings are an important criterion for suc-

Figure 131 (Courtesy of Viking) Commercial type ranges are now engineered to be suitable and safe for residential use.

cessful gourmet cooking. The BTU rating per hour of the burner must be high enough to generate intense heat for some types of cooking.

For example, stir fry cooking requires a great deal of heat to initially preheat the frying pan or wok and then to provide the correct temperature for quick searing of meats and vegetables. Typical residential equipment provides a burner at 9,000 to 12,000 BTUs per burner. Commercial-sized burners or residential equipment offer about 15,000 BTUs.

The most important thing to remember is that these pieces are engineered for home use and they therefore generally meet building codes. However, they are oversized appliances that may require bigger gas lines and more extensive ventilation. They are also bigger and heavier than standard appliances.

Do not specify one of these ranges until you have reviewed the manufacturer's literature.

Drop-in Equipment: Your third option is a drop-in range. Although similar in looks and price to the slide-in, this appliance is installed between base cabinets and supported by cabinetry of appropriate height. There is a rim to pro-

Figure 132 (Courtesy of Jenn Air) This kitchen features a drop-in range suspended from the countertop.

vide the transition from range to counter-top which helps avoid cleaning problems. Generally the controls are placed along the front so that they are simple to reach and safe to use.

Appliance Usage Statistics: With all of these choices, designers may wonder just how cooking appliances are used by chefs today. The results of the *Better Homes and Gardens Magazine* survey follow for your review.

COOKTOPS	
How they use their cooktops:	
Weekday dinners	79%
Weekend breakfasts	78.5%
Monday - Friday	7.4 minutes per day
Weekends	46.5 minutes per day

They use their cooktop for everyday dinners and weekend breakfasts for 30-60 minutes for each use.

OVENS	
How they use their ovens:	
Weekend dinners	79.5%
Weekday dinners	71.6%
Monday - Friday	49.7 minutes per day
Weekends	77.0 minutes per day

They use their ovens for roasting or baking on weekends and for everyday dinners, about one hour each use.

VENTILATION

Once you have considered the categories of equipment available, you should evaluate whether the model you are considering has the type of ventilation system available that will enhance your design as well.

Proximity or down-draft ventilation systems allow total design freedom and creativity above and around the cooking surface. When an overhead ventilation system is planned, it can be concealed within the cabinets, be a low-profile, pull-out hood, focus on an appliance that is a combination microwave and hood, or be a ventilator that is housed in a custom enclosure and acts as a focal point in the space. *Figures 133 and 134* give you design ideas for these two approaches.

Please review the material in Chapter 1 "Mechanical Systems", to refamiliarize yourself with the basic engineering and mechanical concerns of a well-designed ventilation system.

Figure 133 *When a down-draft ventilation system is used, an open, airy feeling can be maintained in the kitchen.*

Figure 134 *If an overhead ventilation system is included, it may become part of the cabinets or it may be featured as a focal point.*

HEAT SOURCES

The designer now has finally arrived at the factor foremost in most consumers minds as they talk about a cooking appliance: the decision between a gas or electric heat source.

Gas: Gourmet cooks usually prefer gas because it permits precise control of heat and offers an instant "on/off" feature. Gas appliances feature pilotless ignition systems which eliminate continuously burning pilot lights and save about 30% of the gas used by the range when compared with older equipment.

Designers should understand how gas cooking works. Gas is composed of molecules continually in motion. Since a gas tends to expand and diffuse, the molecules completely fill the containing vessel and their motion is limited only by the size of the enclosed space. They exert equal pressure in all directions. The tendency of gas to diffuse is the fundamental essential for gas flow.

Just as water flows from a higher to a lower level, and heat flows from a hotter to a cooler body, so gas flows from a place of higher pressure to one of lower pressure.

The heating value of a gas is the amount of heat produced when a unit quantity is burned. It is measured in **BTU (British Thermal Units)** per cubic foot. The standard cubic foot of gas, as defined by the **American Gas Association**, is the quantity contained in one cubic foot of volume at a barometric pressure of 30° of mercury, and at a temperature of 60°F.

A BTU is a unit of heat energy; the amount of heat required to raise the temperature of one pound of water by one degree Fahrenheit. This amount of heat is equal to that produced by burning an ordinary wooden match.

Gas is regulated by a meter on the house exterior. Gas travels through a copper line from the meter to the appliance. The BTU rating of the appliance determines the diameter of the copper supply line. The flow of gas is directed by the turning of a valve handle. Gas cooking appliances incorporate a grate over the flame to allow for the necessary oxygen for correct combustion of the gas.

Gas burners are designed to give a circular flame pattern, the size of which can be controlled to some degree by the amount of gas delivered to the burner. The burners are usually controlled by a throttling valve which resembles a rotary switch in appearance. The intensity of the flame can be controlled on a graduated basis from low to high. Some burners are equipped with special simmer units which are, in effect, a very small burner located in the center of the main burner.

Although gas burners differ somewhat in form, the principle parts are the same and the way that the gas is ignited is the same. A horizontal pipe through which gas flows from the fuel line to the different orifices is called the manifold. Attached to the manifold are burner valve handles which direct the gas through the orifice and mixer head into the burner.

Forced through the orifice at velocities of 100 to 160 feet per section, the gas develops sufficient suction to draw air through the partly open shutter. This air, called the primary air, mixes with the gas before it is ignited in a porcelain lined mixing tube, the smooth finish of which increases the injection of primary air and gives a clean, sharp flame.

The gas/air mixture now flows through the ignition port on the side of the burner head. This port is connected to the solid state ignition. The spark that ignites the gas when the burner is turned on is caused by the electric ignition. It is also the electric system that turns the gas off.

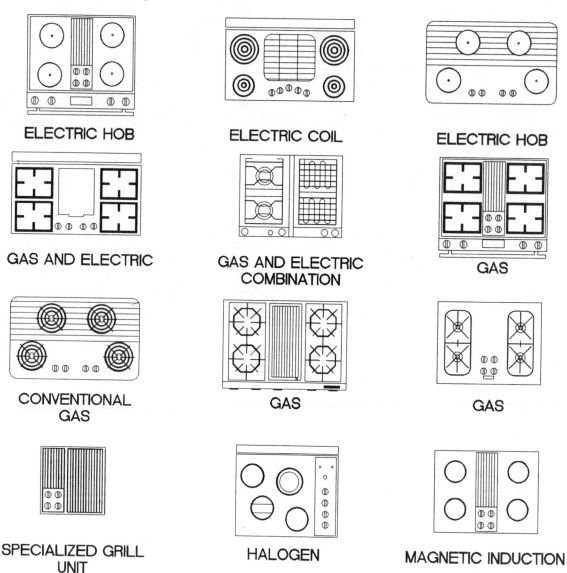

ELECTRIC HOB   ELECTRIC COIL   ELECTRIC HOB

GAS AND ELECTRIC   GAS AND ELECTRIC COMBINATION   GAS

CONVENTIONAL GAS   GAS   GAS

SPECIALIZED GRILL UNIT   HALOGEN   MAGNETIC INDUCTION

Figure 135 Today's cooktops and ranges are better than ever. Gas and electric have been augmented by magnetic induction heating and halogen light bulbs - both offering performance characteristics similar to gas. Sealed glass surface units ease cleaning, and integral or countertop vents make range hoods unnecessary.

Electricity: Alternatively, an electric heat source can be specified. There are three types of electric cooktops generally available for home kitchens today.

- **Conventional Coil Elements:** The cooktops we all grew up with have maintained their popularity for a good reason. This is the most inexpensive of all available electric cooktops and has a good heating speed. Coil elements are versatile as well. If equipped with a special raised canning element or a contoured wok element, they will accept large canners or woks. With conventional coils, electrical resistance is used to create heat. Wire is encased in a metallic tube filled with an insulation material. The tube is shaped into a coil and flattened for maximum contact with cooking utensils. Heat travels from the hot coils to the cookware both by conduction (where there is contact) and radiation.

- **Solid Disk Elements:** Originally from Europe, the solid disk elements are popular today because of their sleek lines and cleanability. The cast iron surface, which contains electric resistance wires below, has a non-corrosive coating and is grooved for traction. It is surrounded by a stainless steel spill ring and sealed to the cooktop. With the solid elements the entire disk becomes hot and conducts heat to the cookware. Since the solid element disk is cast iron, it shares many of the positive qualities of cast iron: gradual heat up and heat retention so that the cook can finish cooking after the

power has been turned off.

There are **two types** of solid disk elements available: the **thermostatically controlled** version has a central thermostat that senses the temperature of the pan bottom. Controls can be set for a range of temperatures. The second version has a **thermal protector or limiter** that assures the long life of the element by preventing overheating in situations in which heat is not properly conducted away from the element surface. Regardless of the type of control, solid elements do not glow red, an indication that the temperature of the element does not become high enough to be a fire hazard.

Because the element is a thick plate of metal, the problem of warping is eliminated. Sealing the element into the cooktop eliminates the need for cleaning drip pans or the area underneath. Periodic treatment may be needed to prevent rusting, but generally is not necessary if the manufacturer's directions for care are followed. Heavy guage, flat bottom metal cookware of the same diameter as the element is recommended.

- **Glass Ceramic Cooktops:** These cooktops have been available for nearly twenty years. Electric resistance coils under the attractive smooth glass ceramic top are the source of heat. The heat radiates to the glass surface where it is transferred to the pot by conduction and some radiation. In order to efficiently conduct heat, contact between the pan bottom and the cooktop must be good. Designs on the cooktop indicate heating areas. Early glass tops weren't as quick or as cleanable as promised, but glass ceramics are again hot news - especially in white and black. Withstanding temperatures to 1300°F (704.44°C). without expanding or contracting, the new glass ceramics won't warp and are very hard to break. Yellowing has been eliminated, and elements have been redesigned to achieve faster heating.

In addition to conventional radiant heat, two other technologies are used with glass ceramic cooking surfaces. The first is induction, the second halogen.

- **Induction:** In induction cooking, solid state power causes induction coils, located beneath the glass ceramic surface, to generate a magnetic field that induces current within ferromagnetic cookware. Ferromagnetic cookware is as a material, such as iron, which reacts to a magnetic field. Magnetic utensils are made of materials such as cast iron, porcelain enamel on steel, porcelain enamel on cast iron, triple stainless steel and magnetic stainless steel.

In simple terms the way this works is as follows: below the cooking area of the smooth glass cooktop is an induction coil. Each coil has a solid state power supply. When the control is turned on, electric current to the coils is converted into a high frequency alternating current which flows through the coil and creates an alternating magnetic field. When a utensil made of magnetic material is introduced into this field, the current from the coil is induced into the utensil which sets the molecules in the pot into motion. When molecules move fast, they generate heat. The intensity of the alternating magnetic field can be varied by the cooktop's control and that regulates the amount of heat being produced by the pot.

Because the entire vessel is heated, induction cooking is cooler, faster and cleaner than conventional cooktop methods. Little heat is generated in the room, and total control is possible over the cooking source. Much like gas, it's instant on and off and easily controlled down to very low temperatures. It is also a safe method of cooking because the cooking surface is only heated by bounced back heat from the cooking vessel, so it is always safe to the touch.

- **Halogen:** The newest in cooking technology is halogen range burners which combine the elegance of smooth glass ceramic cooktops without giving up cooking performance. Whereas a conventional electric burner gets hot because of electrical resistance as electricity flows through a nichrome wire, a halogen burner works like an incandescent light bulb. Electricity passes through a tungsten filament inside a quartz-glass tube. Resistance causes the filament to heat up, and in the process, tungsten particles boil off. Therefore, conventional electric energy is converted into light and heat beneath the glass ceramic surface.

In conventional light bulbs the tungsten particles settle inside the glass which darkens it. In a halogen bulb, halogen gas combines with the evaporated tungsten to form tungsten halide. When this compound nears the filament, the heat breaks down and redeposits the tungsten on the filament, so the lamp does not darken and the filament lasts longer. The energy emitted is mostly infrared and wavelength. Therefore, the waves pass readily through the glass ceramic cooktop. About 10% of the output is visible light. Consequently, the burner's red glow instantly shines through the translucent cooktop. This allows the cook to know immediately if the burner is on, overcoming a problem with traditional glass top cooktops.

A halogen burner heats up quickly. Most tests show that a halogen cooktop will heat up faster than any other smooth top except the induction type. Halogen burners are not quite as fast to heat as the best electric surface coils though.

- **Thermostatically Controlled Surface Units:** Some cooking surfaces on the market have one or more surface units that are thermostatically controlled. This type of element has a central sensitive disk backed by a spring that holds the disk in contact with the bottom of the utensil. The control is connected to the switch or valve handle and operates to maintain the temperature for which the dial is set. Such a controlled burner is equivalent to using a small electric appliance and helps to eliminate scorching of food. Since the action of the thermostat is regulated by the temperature of the center of the pan in contact with the disk, it is good practice to have the food cover the center of the pan. Additionally, utensils used with these thermostatically controlled burners should be made of heavy guage material that is a good conductor of heat. The pan must also have a flat bottom.

METHODS OF HEAT TRANSFERENCE

When it comes to oven cooking, we need to turn our attention away from heat sources and consider methods of heat transference. Whatever form of energy is used to create heat, the transference of it is what cooks the food.

There are three general ways by which heat is transferred.

Conduction: Conduction is a process by which heat is transferred through a substance, or from one substance to another that is in direct contact with it, by molecular activity. In conventional cooking, the source of heat starts the molecules at the bottom of a pan into rapid vibration. They strike other molecules in the metal, putting them in motion. The molecules on the inside of the pan put the layer of water molecules next to them in motion and they, in turn, start other water molecules moving. The motion of molecules, called heat, has been given to the water in the pan. Heat has been transferred by conduction from the heat source to the pan and from the pan to the water touching it.

In microwave and magnetic cooking, the energy is placed in direct contact with the food substance, bypassing the cooking vessel. Normal conduction activity then takes place.

Convection: Convection is a more rapid process of heat transfer involving the motion of heated matter itself from one place to another. This transference of heat appears in both liquid currents and in air currents. On the range surface, water is kept in motion by convection while it heats. The layer of water at the bottom of the pan is heated first by conduction. Because of the rise in temperature, the water expands and becomes lighter. The lighter water is then displaced by the heavier cold water. In the oven, air is heated by the electric element or gas burner at the bottom of the oven. It expands and rises to the top of the oven, allowing the cooler, heavier air to come to the bottom to be heated.

Radiation: Radiation of heat takes place at the speed of light (186,300 miles per second) in electromagnetic waves. No material medium is required for its transmission. Heat transfers by conduction and convection are involved in cookery on top of the range. Radiation and convection are of primary concern in oven cookery. All bodies, warmer than their surroundings, radiate heat. If a cold object is brought into a warm room, the walls of the room radiate heat to the cold object and the cold object when heated, radiates heat to the walls of the room. Since the walls are at a higher temperature, they give more heat per second to the cold object than the cold object gives up. The temperature of the cold object, therefore, rises until it comes to the same temperature as the room. When an oven is heated, the bottom and sides of the oven become hot and radiate heat directly to utensils and foods in the oven. In a conventional oven, 60% to 70% of the heat is radiant heat.

METHODS OF HEATING

Gas Ovens: The gas oven is heated by a burner which is beneath the oven floor. The floor plate has openings at the corners or along the sides through which the convection currents rise to circulate throughout the oven. The food in the oven is heated partly by these convection currents and partly by the radiation that occurs once the lining of the oven becomes heated. Because oxygen must be available for the combustion of gas, gas ovens are generally not as tightly constructed as electric ovens.

Gas ovens offer pilotless ignition systems which have eliminated the need for a constantly burning pilot flame. It is estimated that this innovation has saved up to 30% of the gas used in residential cooking.

Most gas ovens have broiler drawers below the oven, some appliances have a waist-high broiling element which allows oven broiling.

Electric Ovens: Because electric heat is flameless, the electric heating units are placed within the oven itself, which is of a tight construction. Generally, there is a heating element at the top and another at the bottom of the oven. There may be tubular enclosed or open wiring. The lower unit is usually a single coil and the top unit will be either a single coil or several loops or it may be two coils. The oven vents through the center of the reflector pan beneath one of the back surface units.

Temperature in both gas and electric ovens is controlled by a thermostat. However, the thermostatic action is different in gas and electric ovens. *For example,* if the thermostat in an electric oven has been set for 325°F (162.77°C) and the switch is turned on, the unit will operate until a temperature of about 400°F (204.44°C) is reached.

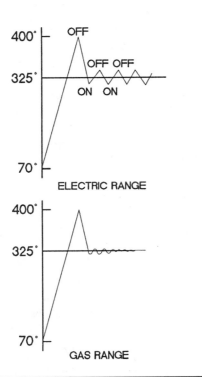

Figure 136 *Heating cycles differ between electric and gas ranges.*

This temperature is known as the preheat overshoot - it allows the door to be opened and cool food to be placed within the oven without losing too much heat. At the end of this preheat period the electricity cycles off automatically and the temperature drops somewhat lower than the 325°F (162.77°C) setting. The current then turns on again and continues to cycle on and off usually 10° above and below the 325°F (162.77°C) setting.

In a gas oven, there is also a preheat overshoot. However, the gas does not shutoff completely, rather the valve partially closes, reducing the flame size to maintain a fairly constant preset temperature. Ranges that feature the low 140°F to 250°F (60°C to 121.11°C) temperature may use the cycling method, but the curves have smaller aptitudes than the electric range. Temperature in the food does not cycle but continues to rise until the food is cooked.

TYPES OF OVENS

Convection Ovens: Convected hot air for baking was introduced to the baking industry as a commercial advantage in the '50s. It was an immediate success, creating considerable savings in energy and time, offering greater flexibility in baking with a more even bake. Virtually all bakeries and restaurants now use convection ovens and the convection cooking principle is now widely available for home use in several brands of ovens.

A convection oven simply means that an element heats the air and a fan then circulates this air evenly throughout the oven cavity. The circulating hot air penetrates food faster than the motionless air in a conventional oven. Therefore, several cooking advantages are offered to the consumer.

The circulating hot air cooks foods evenly and in a shorter period of time. Eggs and cheese dishes bake higher and lighter. Meats and poultry remain juicy, tender and brown beautifully. Any dish normally baked in a standard oven can be cooked in a convection oven with no special bakeware required. Additionally, several items can be baked at the same time or the oven can be filled with several trays of the same item because air circulation space need not be so generous around all the foods as in a conventional oven.

On the down side, baking pans and casseroles must have low sides and be uncovered to take advantage of the circulating air. For cooking covered foods, convection ovens offer no time or energy savings. Additionally, converting recipes to convection ovens can be tricky. The cook needs to take the time to experiment to find the best combination of time and temperature for favorite recipes.

Microwave Ovens: The last cooking appliance that will be considered is the microwave oven. After debuting in American kitchens about 25 years ago, the countertop microwave oven is now a household staple. Estimates claim that from 75% to 90% of all U.S. homes own at least one microwave oven. It's an appliance that many ten-year-olds have grown up knowing as the major cooking unit. Surveys have shown that the microwave oven is the kitchen appliance most used by those under the age of 18.

To insure user satisfaction, designers must be able to provide information about how microwave energy provides a

heat source, and then carefully question the family to find the right place in the plan for the oven.

Microwave energy is a form of non-ionizing radiation. Ionizing radiation, (X-rays, gamma, cosmic rays) can cause chemical changes to take place with little or no temperature rise. Non-ionizing radiation, (infrared, microwaves, broadcasting waves) in sufficient intensity, will cause a rise in temperature, but will not cause cell changes. Radiant waves are characterized by their wavelength and their frequency of vibration.

Microwaves vibrate millions of times per second, and are therefore very short waves, hence the term microwave. There is one microwave frequency in general use for microwave ovens, 2450 MHZ (wave length 5" (12.7cm) long). The term MHZ stand for megahertz and means a million cycles. The 2450 MHZ stand for 2450 million cycles per second. The 2450 MHZ is considered the most successful wavelength, because it cooks faster. This wave has a vibration amplitude about the thickness of a pencil. This thickness prevents the waves from passing through the small metal mesh installed in the oven doors.

The microwave oven cooks food within the oven by activating the dipolar (water) molecules so that they rotate in a rapidly alternating electrical field. Thus, the amount of moisture in food has a direct bearing on its heating rate in the oven. The molecular rotation occurs as the molecules behave like microscopic magnets and attempt to line up within the field. However, when the electrical field is changing millions of times each second, these tiny magnets are unable to keep up because of other forces acting to slow them down. Such forces which restrict their movement may be mechanical, such as ice, or viscous, such as syrup. The energy of the microwave in trying to overcome these forces is converted into heat. Thus, the heat is restricted to within the food product and the cool oven interior is explained.

Microwave energy penetrates deeply into the food materials and produces heat instantaneously as it penetrates. This is a sharp contrast to conventional heating, which depends on the conduction of heat from the food surface to the inside.

Because of this energy penetration, the highest temperature occurs one inch in from the surface. The remaining interior is cooking by conduction. The cooking by conduction takes place during the recommended standing time. Because the heat is generated within the food substance, the heat conduction process should occur without the continuing input of microwave energies. Disregard for this principle will result in overcooking of the outer surface. Because of the penetration limitation, the ideal food configuration is that of a doughnut. This allows a maximum of surface area for maximum penetration.

The exterior surface of an item cooked in a microwave oven will be lower in temperature than the interior. This is caused by radiation of heat from the food surface to the cooler surroundings of cooking vessel or oven interior. Thus, the homemaker cannot judge the doneness of a food product by the outer temperature. Nor should he or she be told that the cooking vessel will always be cool. Some utensils will require the use of a potholder for removal.

The magnetron is the device that creates the waves. It is a little broadcasting station with an antenna. It has a central cathode from which electrons escape, pressured by high voltage, and as they move outward circularly, they pass by many little charged cavities in the surrounding anode. This sets up a vibration which creates the electro-magnetic microwaves. These are discharged by the antennae into the wave guide. The waves enter the cavity through the wave guide, and are circulated by the stirrer. It diffuses the waves in order for them to enter the food material from all directions. A transformer within the oven converts the ordinary 120 or 240 volts to a voltage between 3,000 to 6,000 volts. This high voltage is needed for the magnetron to operate.

To properly develop a sense of timing in microwave cooking, it is first necessary to know how much power is available in the oven. Research has shown that it is not uncommon for the actual available power to be 10% to 15% less than that specified by the manufacturers.

The cooking wattage is a major factor in cooking times. Other factors include the food density, arrangement, quantity, temperature, moisture content and bone conformation. A local manufacturer's demonstrator or utility home economist can elaborate on these items for your staff or client.

Popularity of residential microwave ovens has created new demands on the kitchen planner. When attempting to locate the microwave, careful client questioning must come first. The same Better Homes and Gardens Magazine research report identified what features consumers use on their microwave today and what they use their microwaves for.

FEATURES	OWN	USE THESE FEATURES
Built-in Clock	67.5%	61%
Defrost	93.7%	87%
Turntable/Carousel	46%	33%
Auto-Setting	42%	1.9 to 12%
Temperature Probe	61%	22% Sometimes Use
Browning Element	29%	10.4%
Multistage Cooking	57%	19%
Keep Warm	43%	15%

USE MICROWAVE FOR:	OFTEN	SOMETIMES	NEVER
Preparing food designed for MWO	47%	43%	
Heating take-out food	39%	43%	
Try microwave recipes	17%	62%	
Adapt conventional recipes	11%	45%	
Heating or drying non-food items			81%

When selecting the proper location for the microwave oven, kitchen specialists must consider the following:

- **Who Will Use It?** If the unit will be used by the homemaker during normal food preparation activities, it should be placed within the work triangle. If the unit will be used mainly by other family members, or by a second cook, it can be located away from the homemaker's traffic pattern. Additionally, it must be easily accessible by all users in regard to their physical stature and ability.

- **What Will It Be Used For?** If the unit will be used for defrost-

ing, vegetable cooking, snacks, baking and some general cooking, it should be placed between the refrigerator and the sink (mix center and cleanup center). When the main function of the oven will be for auxiliary cooking and warmups, it is best located near the cooktop (food preparation area).

- **Where Will Microwave Center Counter Space Be Placed?** If the oven has a bottom-hinged door, space should be provided on the left for left-handed cooks and on the right for right-handed clients. If the door is hinged on the left, counter space should be planned to the right or below the unit. 15" (38.1cm) of counter space is recommended. For microwaves placed in base cabinets, counter landing space above the unit is also an option.

- **How Tall Is The Principal User Of The Oven?** The cook should look into the oven and down upon the product. He or she should be able to comfortably reach into the oven for placing and removing food items. A recent study conducted at the University of Minnesota by Professors **Wanda W. Olson** and **Becky L. Yust** explains these two criteria:

A) The safety criteria: The microwave oven should be located so that the oven shelf or rack(s) is no higher than the user's shoulder height for safe use. In order to achieve this, the height of the surface on which the oven is placed should be no higher than approximately 3" (7.62cm) below the shoulder. The oven used by persons aged 55 years and over should be located so that the oven shelf or rack(s) is at least 6" (15.24cm) below the user's shoulder.

B) The convenience criteria:
The microwave oven should be located so that the interior shelf or rack(s) is between 2" (5.08cm) below the elbow and 10" (25.4cm) above the elbow of the user for most convenient use. This places the height of the surface at which the oven is placed at approximately the elbow plus or minus 6" (15.24cm).

NOTE: Microwave placement based on the users physical abilities may require placement outside the preferred 24" - 48" (60.96cm - 121.92cm) AFF recommendation.

- **What Types Of Cooking Does The Family Enjoy?** This information will be a guide in microwave center storage recommendations. Drawer space should be allocated for stirring, puncturing and separating utensils. Vertical storage for trays, platters and shallow casseroles is very helpful. The main type of vessel used will be bowls. Shelf space or roll-outs will be appropriate for these items. Potholders should be within easy reach for utensil removal. Paper goods storage is also needed. The homemakers should be encouraged to utilize their serving pieces for cooking vessels. A simple test will tell them if they are safe--place a measuring cup of room-temperature water next to the empty serving bowl in the microwave oven. Heat for one minute and fifteen seconds. If the water is hot and the bowl is cool, all is safe. If the water is cool while the bowl is warm, do not use it for microwave cooking.

When these questions have been answered, the designer can select one of several built-in oven installations.

- **Placing it in a corner:** One approach is to install the oven under a corner angled wall cabinet. The oven can sit in a cabinet on the countertop, or be suspended under the cabinet. The counter space lost in its installation is usually not primary work space. This installation <u>cannot</u> be accomplished with a standard corner wall cabinet. The angled door width must line up with the microwave overall dimensions, plus trim kit, plus wood enclosure sides.

- **Caution**--avoid installing an oven with a fold-down door until the door handle clearance has been checked in relationship to countertop bullnose or coved front edge. Also, avoid installations of side-hinged door models if access to the sink, appliances or counter space will be blocked.

- **Combining it with a built-in oven:** Another installation combines the microwave oven and the conventional oven into one appliance. Versions are available which separate the microwave unit from the conventional one or combine the two. Such a combination allows the cook to enjoy an expanded range of cooking methods. Although expensive, these units are excellent considerations for better kitchens. One word of caution: if the microwave is used by the primary cook, the combination oven must be part of the work triangle. Although past kitchen planning guidelines allow the planner to separate the oven from the three primary work centers, the introduction of the microwave changes the design criteria.

- **Installing it above a built-in oven:** Installing a microwave separately above a single conventional oven is practical. The oven and microwave placement must be determined before cabinet construction and rough electrical wiring. The designer must verify the manufacturer's recommended distances between the two appliances.

For left-hinge models, provide counter space to the right of the oven case. If this is impossible, consider installing a pull-out bread board or chopping block designed to be used in the pull-out position between the two appliances. This will provide an acceptable transfer location as foodstuffs enter and leave the oven. Fold down door models can use counter space located at the left or right of the oven case. The

bread board approach is not practical for this type of unit.

- **Combining it with the ventilation hood:** Combining the ventilation hood and microwave oven is a great way to save space--if the cook is tall and the best of ventilation systems is not a high priority on the client's kitchen shopping list. The elimination of the hood's holding area (the open interior of the hood) omits the room needed for cooking contaminants to be caught and held until the motor can push them through the duct. A petite cook will not be able to look into and down on the food if the oven is installed in a normal hood position 57" to 60" (144.78cm to 152.4cm) off the floor.

- **Placing it in a wall cabinet:** Custom wall cabinets can be manufactured to receive the weight and size of microwave ovens. The cabinet must be deep enough to receive the oven. The cabinet opening must be built according to the trim kit cut-out dimensions of the manufacturer. Specify the electrical outlet location for the unit on the electrical plan. The homemaker's height will determine the available counter space under the microwave oven enclosure.

- **Installing it with a trim kit:** The need for adequate ventilation must also be considered. All microwave ovens are vented. Vents are located on top, side or back of the unit. The required air circulation is the basis for the trim kit design. Whenever a unit is "built-in", the manufacturer's trim kit, or another system allowing air movement, is required. The kit assembly must be removable so that the unit can be taken out for servicing.

The microwave oven places an exciting challenge before the kitchen specialist. With careful questioning and thoughtful planning, this new appliance can be designed creatively into any custom kitchen.

OVEN CLEANING SYSTEMS

Pyrolytic Systems (Self-cleaning): Pyrolysis is a chemical change brought about by the action of heat. "Heat" is the key word in describing this self-cleaning or pyrolytic oven. In this system, the oven is heated at temperatures ranging from 850°F (454.44°C) to 1,000°F (537.78°C). At the end of the completed cycle, after the cool down period, all that remains of the food soil is a powdery ash that is easily removed with a damp cloth.

To activate the cleaning system a lever is moved to lock the oven door and two controls are set. An inner lock is provided so that the oven door cannot be unlocked when the oven temperature is too high for safety. An electrostatic precipitator is usually included to remove the smoke that would otherwise come from the oven vent. However, do warn the clients that they'll probably smell an odd odor during the cleaning process. Supporters of the pyrolysis system claim that with this method all six sides of the oven interior are cleaned completely and no special care is required to prevent scratching or damage

to the oven surface. Additionally, the extra insulation provided in these ovens to protect against heat transference from the oven to the adjacent living spaces means cooler cooking throughout the year.

Catalytic System (Continuous Cleaning): The catalytic system is designed to eliminate the need for cleaning an oven. A catalytic material is mixed into the porcelain enamel coating on the oven liner panels. This material causes a chemical reaction at normal cooking temperatures that oxidizes food soils continuously as they occur during the cooking operation. This method, then, does not require a separate cleaning cycle at high temperatures because the cleaning takes place simultaneously as the food is cooked. Manufacturers using this system emphasize three points:

- Heavy spill-overs will not be cleaned without first wiping up the excess with a damp cloth.

- Harsh abrasives, chemical oven cleaners and scouring pads should not be used on excessive soil or stubborn stains.

- Certain types of food stains may not disappear in one operation, but will fade during continuous subsequent use of the oven.

You will find this type of catalytic system is the most commonly specified cooking appliance in Europe. When combined with a true convection oven the continuous cleaning cycle works in an acceptable fashion. However, when it is not a part of a convection oven, many people find the ovens unacceptable for a clean appearance. Advocates of the catalytic approach point out that the oven is always available for cleaning, since the cleaning is continuous during normal usage; that continuous cleaning prevents any built- up of soil; and that very little basic redesign of existing ovens is required since high temperatures are not used. This is another reason why this system is employed in European appliances, which are generally smaller than domestically produced ones. If the interior oven size on a European manufac- turer model was further reduced because of the extra insulation required for the pyrolysis system, it would probably not be a usable appliance.

Use the **Appliance Checklist** on the following pages as you complete the final specifications for each kitchen project you work on. It will help you estimate and specify all the planning details of appliance placement.

APPLIANCE CHECKLIST

Refrigerator Installation Considerations

1. Required door swing dimension verified.   _____

2. Overall appliance depth (including air space and handles listed on plans). _____

3. Overall width, including air space and countertop overhang dimension
    determined before overhead cabinet width size and height specified.   _____

4. Appliance doors drawn in an open position on the plan to verify walkway
    clearances.   _____

5. Ice maker copper water lines specified.   _____

Sink Installation Considerations

1. Number of sink holes and fitting placement has been specified on the plans. _____

2. Dishwasher air gap requirements have been met in design.   _____

3. Method of securing sink to counter surface has been determined: _____

    Flat rim with stainless steel rim and clip installation.   _____

    Self-rimming sink, color of caulking to be used between sink and
    countertop.   _____

    Under-mounted sink   _____

    Integral sink   _____

Dishwasher Installation Considerations

1. Trim kits and/or panels have been ordered. Labor to install has been included
    in estimate.   _____

2. Existing water lines and drain location to be reused.   _____

    New water line to be installed.   _____

3. Existing dishwasher wiring to be reused.   _____

    New dishwasher wiring to be added.   _____

4. Appliance door drawn in an open position on the plan to verify walkway
    clearances.   _____

Trash Compactor Installation Considerations

1. Trim kits and/or panels have been ordered. Labor to install has been included
    in estimate.   _____

2. Existing compactor wiring to be reused.   _____

    New compactor wiring to be added.   _____

3. Appliance door drawn in an opened position on the plan to verify walkway
    clearances.   _____

APPLIANCE CHECKLIST

Food Waste Disposer Installation Considerations

1. Unit to be batch fed _____ or switch operated _____   _____

2. Switch location located after considering primary user's handedness.   _____

3. Waste line no higher than 17" on center off the floor.   _____

Backsplash Convenience Appliance Installation Considerations

1. Backsplash appliance does not interfere with wall stud placement.   _____

2. Recess required for appliance is not obstructed by vents, ducts or pocket doors._____

3. Recessed convenience appliances do not interfere with backsplash design, or use.   _____

4. Convenience outlets along backsplash do not interfere with built-in backsplash appliance location.   _____

5. Heat generating backsplash appliances are not specified below task lighting that features a plastic diffuser.   _____

Drop-In or Free-Standing Range Installation Considerations

1. Gas or electrical requirements:

   Gas   Size of existing gas line.   _____

   Existing gas line to be reused in its existing location.   _____

   Existing gas line to be relocated.   _____

   Diameter of new gas line required.   _____

   Electric Electrical amperage of existing line:

   30 amp _____   40 amp _____   50 amp _____

   Electrical amperage requirement of new appliance:

   30 amp _____   40 amp _____   50 amp _____

   Existing electrical line to be reused in its existing location.   _____

   Existing electrical line to be relocated.   _____

   New electrical line to be added.   _____

2. Ventilation system specified on plans..   _____

3. Drop-in range method of support and distance from floor to bottom of range specified on plans.   _____

4. Countertop cut-out for drop-in units specified on plans.   _____

5. Side clearance for drop-in units which have a flange overlapping adjacent cabinetry has been considered in the planning process.   _____

6. Appliance overall depth, including handles, listed on the plans.   _____

7. Appliance door drawn in an open position to verify walkway clearances.   _____

APPLIANCE CHECKLIST

Built-In Oven Installation Considerations

1. Gas or electrical requirements:

   Gas   Size of existing gas line.   _____

   Existing gas line to be reused in its existing location.   _____

   Existing gas line to be relocated.   _____

   Diameter of new gas line required.   _____

   Electric Electrical amperage of existing line:

   30 amp _____   40 amp _____   50 amp _____

   Electrical amperage requirement of new appliance:

   30 amp _____   40 amp _____   50 amp _____

   Existing electrical line to be reused in its existing location.   _____

   Existing electrical line to be relocated.   _____

   New electrical line to be added.   _____

2. Ventilation requirement for new oven.   Ducted _____   Non-Ducted   _____

3. Countertop overhang treatment against oven cabinet side to be:

   a) Countertop extends past oven case.   _____

   b) Countertop ties into side of special depth oven cabinet.   _____

   Case depth to be _____

   Toe kick to be _____

4. All dimensions are included in specifications and plans:

   a) Overall appliance depth (including handles).   _____

   b) Appliance height placement in relationship to primary cook's height.   _____

   c) Cut-out and overall dimensions.   _____

5. For under counter installation, manufacturer's specifications have been verified
   for minimum cut-out height from the floor.   _____

Cooktop Installation Considerations

1. Gas or electrical requirements:

   Gas   Size of existing gas line.   _____

   Existing gas line to be reused in its present location.   _____

   Existing gas line to be relocated.   _____

   Diameter of new gas line required.   _____

APPLIANCE CHECKLIST

Cooktop Installation Considerations (continued)

1. **Electric** Electrical amperage of existing line:

    30 amp _____   40 amp _____   50 amp _____

    Electrical amperage requirement of new appliance:

    30 amp _____   40 amp _____   50 amp _____

    Existing electrical line to be reused in its present location. _____

    Existing electrical line to be relocated. _____

    New electrical line to be added. _____

2. Ventilation system specified on plans. _____
3. Can cabinet drawers be ordered below the oven? _____
4. Can roll-outs be installed below the cooktop? _____
5. All dimensions (cut-out and overall) are listed on the plan. _____

Microwave Oven Installation Considerations

1. Dedicated electrical circuit specified. _____
2. Trim kit ordered with appliance. _____

    Labor to install trim kit included in estimate. _____

3. Microwave oven placement is away from other heat generating appliances. _____
4. Microwave oven placement is away from television set in the kitchen. _____
5. Appliance height has been determined in relation to the height of the primary cook for both safety and convenience. _____
6. Cut-out and overall dimensions are listed on the plan. _____

Ventilation Hood Installation Considerations

1. Length of duct path from ventilation system to exterior termination point. _____
2. Number of elbow turns along duct path. _____
3. Ventilating unit's (free air pressure) CFM rating. _____

    Exit (static air pressure) CFM rating estimate. _____

4. Hood depth in relation to adjacent cabinetry. _____
5. Hood distance from cooking surface. _____
6. Hood width in relationship to cooktop width below. _____

SECTION **3**

Faucet Materials and Engineering

FAUCET FINISHING OPTIONS

Kitchen faucets have undergone major technical innovations over the last 10 years. While brass is still the main material inside, faucets feature ceramic valve seats, which are more serviceable than in past years. While chrome finishes still predominate, modern faucets be finished in brass, glass, colored plastic, vitreous china, epoxy, gold or silver.

Chrome

POLISHED CHROME

Polished chrome is the most popular finish for kitchen fittings and hardware. It is extremely hard and does not oxidize in the air as do most other metals, thereby eliminating the need for regular polishing. Chrome is electro-chemically deposited over the nickel plated base metal. The nickel provides luster, brilliance and corrosion prevention, while the chrome contributes color and tarnish resistance. It is a bright and durable finish.

BRUSHED OR MATTED CHROME

A brushed finish is created by using a wire wheel to score the surface of the component part. This can result in a surface with sharp peaks and valleys that does not take the chrome finish quite as well during the plating process because the coating shears away from the peaks and accumulates in the valleys.

A matte finish produces similar appearance without producing noticeable brush marks or the sharp peaks that are difficult for plating. This process is similar to sand blasting the components with fine glass beads to create a soft matted surface that plates better, to produce a finish as durable as polished chrome.

Brass

POLISHED BRASS

The fitting may be solid brass or a thin coating of brass applied over a base metal. Polishing a solid brass fitting is an expensive process where the brass components are buffed with a jeweler's rouge to a fine luster.

Alternatively, the look of polished brass can be created by applying a flash coating of brass, or gold formulated to be the color of brass, to a fitting via an electrode chemical bath. In either case, the brass must be protected.

One of two types of protective coating may be used: a **lacquer top coat**, or a **clear epoxy** coating. The latter is considered to be the more durable choice.

- The lacquer coating is sprayed on in a liquid form that quickly dries without baking. It provides protection only if the fixture is seldom, if ever, used. Lacquer is attacked by water, therefore it must be dried quickly after each use.

- The epoxy coating is the second, clear finish used over brass. It is a powder or a liquid which is sprayed on to the components and then baked at approximately 375°F to 425°F (190°C to 218°C) to provide thorough, even coverage and protection. As with lacquer, the epoxy coating can be scratched, even by mild abrasives, which will result in a milky or cloudy appearance. Additionally, strong solvents will attack the coating. However, epoxy-coated brass fixtures are tested to insure durability in a constant moisture environment.

ANTIQUE BRASS

Antique brass is a popular finish for a traditional look. With higher quality products, the finish is electro-plated. With less expensive products, the finish is sprayed over the metal with tinted lacquers.

Durability of an antique brass finish is fair. With its darker coloring, oxidation may not be as noticeable as on polished brass.

Polished and Satin Gold Plate

Gold plate has once again come into fashion for fittings and hardware. Gold plate provides a truly stunning, unique finish, but the consumer should be aware of vast differences in the quality and durability of gold plate available.

The highly polished brass product is first nickel plated and then 24 karat gold is applied. Durability depends on the thickness of the gold layer.

According to industry standards, plating to a thickness of less than 7 millionths of an inch gold is "gold wash" or "gold flash". Between 8 and 12 millionths, is "gold plating" and from 13 to 50 millionths is "heavy gold plating".

All quality gold plated fittings should fall into the latter category. Low quality gold wash or gold flash is not durable and can wear after only 3 to 6 months of normal handling. It is very difficult for the layman to distinguish between high and low quality gold plate. It is important to always purchase fittings from reputable dealers and never hesitate to ask for data on gold plated parts.

Gold plate is available in either a polished or satin finish. Given a quality plating job, both finishes provide good durability.

Quality gold will not tarnish. Maintenance of a satin gold finish is somewhat easier than polished gold because it hides marks better. The secret to long lasting gold plate is to clean it only with a soft, damp cloth. **NEVER** expose gold plate to abrasives or acids as can be found in many commercial cleaners.

Nickel

This hard, silver-white metal is used extensively in alloys and for plating because of its resistance to oxidation. It has a deep, rich luster to the finish.

Pewter

This is a dull, silvery-gray alloy of tin with brass, copper or lead added during the manufacturing process. Faucets are available in polished and brushed pewter finishes.

Colored Coatings

A tinted, epoxy coating is used to create a colored finish. The powder is sprinkled on (or a liquid is sprayed on to the components) and then baked at about 375°F to 425°F (190°C to 218°C) to provide thorough, even coverage and protection. The coating can be scratched by mild abrasives, which results in an unattractive finish. The key is to clean and dry the faucet frequently after use to avoid the need for heavy cleaning and to never use an abrasive cleaner.

FAUCET ENGINEERING

From an engineering standpoint, faucets offer a great variety of choices.

First we will consider how the cook uses the faucet. The standard kitchen faucet has a hot and cold lever on each side of the spout which sits on an escutcheon plate mounted to the back ledge of the sink.

Equally popular today are single handle faucets which operate with a twist and turn or a push and pull action to mix the water. This type of faucet may or may not be mounted on an escutcheon plate. A single handle control faucet frees up other holes along the back ledge for the dishwasher air gap, food waste disposer, lotion/soap dispenser or other water treatment facilities. The configuration of this handle will affect how easy it is to use. Make sure it is easy to grasp and easy to operate.

Alternatively, in place of a single control there may be two separate hot and cold valves that angle off of this single hole faucet. Generally, these valves are harder to use because of their placement.

Spray Attachments

Many faucets today have a built-in, pull-out spray attachment that is part of the spout. This has eliminated the requirement to install a faucet with a separate spray attachment to the side.

Integral sprays offer a conventional spray device at the end of a flexible hose. A separate spray is connected to the water line underneath the sink. You must provide an acceptable backflow preventing device when using such a spray. Some municipalities require that a vacuum breaker be installed if you specify a pull- out, integrated spray faucet. Alternatively, a faucet with check valves should also satisfy the inspector. Either of these protections is required because of the functional differences between the two types of sprays:

- **Conventional Faucet:** With a conventional separate faucet and spray you have both a basic spout and the spray spout, providing two fluid channels. Therefore, if a negative pressure condition developed while someone had left the hose submerged in a lavatory filled with contaminated water, the basic spout would still draw in air which would break the vacuum. This would prevent the contaminated water from entering the clean water supply.

- **Pull-out Spray Faucet:** With the pull-out spray you only have one hose. Therefore, if the city's water supply was reduced in pressure for any reason and a pull-out spray was submerged in a sink full of contaminated water, the water would be pulled into the city pipelines and would contaminate the potable (fresh) water source.

A "vacuum breaker" prevents such contamination by allowing air into the system, which will stop the flow of contaminated water back into the system.

Before the introduction of the double stop protection built into new, well-engineered faucets which feature check valves (a device which only lets water travel in one direction), the specification of a vacuum breaker as the only acceptable method available to protect the potable supply has come under question.

Testing has demonstrated that a faucet designed with a check valve mechanism prevents the backflow situation as well as the typical vacuum breaker and therefore is becoming more acceptable.

Spout Shapes

The shape of the spout also affects the functionality of the sink. A "goose neck" spout has a high arc and is ideally suited for a family that engages in quantity cooking or a lot of canning. One manufacturer offers a faucet spout that raises up and down so that the spout stays in a normal position most of the time and then rises up to a higher position when needed.

Standard spouts are generally available in 10" (25.4cm), 12"(30.48cm) and 14"(35.56cm) lengths. Longer spouts are needed for corner sink, or if you are installing integral sinks in a countertop in a custom arrangement and separating them a bit further than is the norm.

The faucet engineering will affect its performance over its years of use. In addition to the design of the faucet, the professional kitchen design specialist must understand how faucets operate. All faucets feature either a washer or a washerless design. Each manufacturer has detailed training material available to introduce you to your range of choices. The following description is reprinted, courtesy of **American Standard Inc**.

Washer Design

Faucets with washers feature a compression seal mechanism. Water enters the valve area through the "seat" and is controlled by a rubber washer. When the user turns the handle, the stem twists, causing the washer to raise or lower in relation to the seat. This action provides the "on/off" and volume control in the washer design faucet.

There is also a primary seal to shut the water off and a secondary seal on the stem to prevent the mechanism from leaking. If there is no limiting control over the amount of torque applied to the handle, washers can be abused and wear out. These types of faucets are called "compression" faucets and always have two handles.

COMPRESSION VALVING - TWO-HANDLE: RISING STEM COMPRESSION VALVES

Attributes: The one-piece threaded valve stem rises (along with handle) when rotated to open water flow and lowers to close. As the valve stem rises, the washer, O-ring or diaphragm fixed at the bottom of the valve stem is lifted away from the valve seat, allowing water to flow through the valve body.

Advantages: Low manufacturing cost. Easy low-cost repair by replacing washer or O-ring. Simplest valve operation; easiest repair by homeowner. Very unlikely to clog.

Disadvantages: Seat washers and O-rings wear out quickly because of the grinding action caused when rotated and squeezed between valve stem and valve seat - frequent maintenance required. If seat washer or screw loosens, "chatter" or water hammer can occur.

COMPRESSION VALVING - TWO-HANDLE: NON-RISING STEM COMPRESSION VALVES

Attributes: Multiple-piece valve assembly usually consisting of a housing with a tabbed plunger that rises and falls when handle is operated, but without rotating plunger or washer attached to it. Handle does not rise when opened.

Advantages: Longer life because washer does not rotate against seat, eliminating grinding action. Handle does not rise when valve is opened. Easy, low-cost repair by replacing washer. Simple operation, easy repair by homeowner. Less handle wobble than rising stem compression valve.

Disadvantages: Manufacturing cost higher than rising stem compression due to additional parts. Still a compression valve with washer.

Lever handles become out of alignment as washer begins to wear. If seat washer or screw loosens, "chatter" or water hammer can occur.

Handle must be rotated several turns to reach full open.

Changes in water temperature will cause valve stem to expand or contract, causing change in amount of water flowing, as well as output temperature.

If handle is over-tightened when closing, or washer is not replaced in a timely manner, seat can become scored by valve stem, requiring replacement of seat and possibly the valve stem.

Handle rotation tends to become harder over time as valve stem lubricants are washed away.

Tendency to leak where valve stem exits bonnet beneath the handles.

Washerless Design

Other types of faucets are collectively called "washerless". They are named after the particular mechanism they employ to control water flow: a cartridge, a ball or a disc. Although they're collectively known as washerless, they do utilize neoprene rubber seals or O-rings around various parts of the faucet assembly to prevent leaking. A more detailed discussion of how each mechanism controls water flow is available from the manufacturers that you represent.

SHEER-ACTION VALVING - TWO-HANDLE: ROTATING PLASTIC DISC AGAINST SEPARATE SEATS

Attributes: Plastic discs with holes (usually assembled as a cartridge to the valve stem) that rotates against rubber seats (washers or O-rings) which are forced against disc by separate springs. Water flow controlled by rotating holes in disc to align with seats and hole in valve body.

Advantages: Usually quarter-turn action; handles always in alignment. Low manufacturing cost. Easy, relatively low-cost repair. Simple operation - repair by the client. Built-in stops prevent over-tightening. Reversing valve rotation is possible.

Disadvantages: Rubber seats wear out quickly due to grinding action of ro-

tating disc. Soft rubber seats grip to plastic disc to maintain water-tight seal, but this gripping action also causes rapid wear of seats as disc slides across them.

Not recommended for extreme hot water applications.

Prone to quick failure in water with line contaminants (sand, rust, silt, solder) as they will score plastic disc or rubber seat. Problem is aggravated by small openings in disc which tends to catch rather than pass line debris.

SHEER-ACTION VALVING - TWO-HANDLE: ROTATING PLASTIC DISC OR SLEEVE AGAINST SEATS WITHIN A SELF-CONTAINED CARTRIDGE

Attributes: Same as rotating plastic disc against separate seats, but seats or O-rings are in a self-contained cartridge for easy replacement.

Advantages: Quarter- and half-turn action, handles always in alignment. Low manufacturing cost. Fast and easy replacement, relatively low-cost repair. Simple operation, repair by the homeowner.

Disadvantages: Tends to wear quickly as with rotating plastic disc against separate seats, but may have slightly longer life due to cartridge design maintaining better lubrication and tighter fit between components.

Prone to quick failure in water with line contaminants (sand, rust, silt, solder) as they will score plastic disc or rubber seat. Problem is aggravated by small openings in disc which tends to catch rather than pass line debris.

SHEER-ACTION VALVING - TWO-HANDLE: TWO ROTATING CERAMIC DISCS WITHIN A SELF-CONTAINED CARTRIDGE

Attributes: Current state-of-the-art in valving technologies. Ceramic is an extremely hard, durable material that is unaffected by water temperature or line debris. Valve consists of two polished ceramic discs that rotate against each other when the handle is turned and allow water to pass through as holes in each disc become aligned.

Advantages: After being "fired" the ceramic discs are nearly as hard as diamonds. The discs are completely unaffected by water temperature or debris in the line such as sand, silt or solder. There are actual cases where a ceramic disc valve has cut pieces of line solder with absolutely no damage to the valve. A ceramic disc cartridge may easily outlive the finish on the faucet.

When properly polished to an almost perfect smoothness and flatness, there is no room for air or water to seep between the two discs eliminating the possibility of leaks.

A perfectly smooth pair of ceramic discs do not rely on lubricants for easy operation. The two surfaces continue to polish each other through normal use so a lifetime of smooth, easy operation is assured.

Disadvantages: Compared to an all-plastic cartridge, a relatively high cost to produce and replace. But viewed over the life of the fitting, the best investment and lowest "life-cycle" cost.

There are some ceramic disc valves on the market that do not feature the level of polishing required for smoothness and flatness, and instead rely on extensive lubrication for smooth rotation. This lubrication quickly washes out in use (especially on the hot side) causing very stiff rotation. This continues for many thousands of on/off cycles until the discs have been ground sufficiently smooth (through the user's hard efforts). Discuss the different types of ceramic disc valves available with your plumbing fixture and fittings supplier or manufacturer.

SHEER-ACTION VALVING - ONE-HANDLE: ROTATING BALL WITH SEPARATE SEATS

Attributes: A hollow plastic, brass or stainless steel ball attached to the end of the handle stem that rotates in a housing against soft rubber seats pushed towards the ball by separate springs. Ball valve held in body via screwed on bonnet with an O-ring seal. Water flow is controlled by aligning the holes in the ball against the water inlets.

Advantages: Inexpensive, simple design easily understood by installer. Requires frequent maintenance due to leaks.

Disadvantages: Grinding action of ball valve against seats and stem seal causes excessive wear and frequent failure - water will leak out between valve body and ball and deck of lavatory. Remedy is either constant replacement (difficult because of separate seats and springs) or tightening the bonnet nut. Latter results in stiffer handle operation each time bonnet is tightened to eliminate leaking.

Ball system creates awkward operation - the only off position is full-forward in the center. This means a complex "gear shift" motion is required with every use to find both the correct temperature and water flow - a real inconvenience when used frequently. Because the ball design is not a perfect sphere, it has high and low spots which translates to stiff and soft spots in the handle movement. This is further aggravated as the bonnet is tightened to stop leaks.

SHEER-ACTION VALVING - ONE-HANDLE: PLASTIC DISCS OR SLEEVES

Attributes: Either two plastic discs or rotating sleeves that control water flow through a sheering action. Usually a completely self-contained cartridge system. Rubber seals or O-rings provide the seal between plastic parts. Sleeve design requires two-step handle movement: lift to control flow, rotate to control temperature.

Advantages: Relatively inexpensive valving system to manufacture. Cartridge design provides easy replacement. Can provide long dependable life in clean water conditions. Most permit user to rotate handle to desired temperature and then activate water flow through simple lift motion.

Disadvantages: Sleeve system, because of the greater surface areas coming in contact with each other, becomes stiff through use as lubricants are washed away. This is especially difficult with knob handles that must be firmly gripped and pulled to activate - a difficult operation for small children or the elderly. Motion can be so stiff and removal so difficult that a special tool was created for this purpose.

When in use, the push/pull motion of sleeve systems expose an area beneath the handle that traditionally builds up with crud from cleansers and water seepage that is very difficult to keep clean. Lever handles, also because of this push/pull motion, operate as a lever and fulcrum and are notorious for being loose and having excessive handle play.

As with plastic two-handle valving, these are prone to scoring and leaks when sand, scale, rust, silt or line solder pass through the valve.

SHEER-ACTION VALVING - ONE-HANDLE: CERAMIC DISCS

Attributes: Current state-of-the-art in valving technologies. Ceramic is an extremely hard, durable material that is unaffected by water temperature or line debris. Valve consists of two polished ceramic discs that slide rather than rotate against each other when the handle is lifted and turned. Water passes through holes in each disc as they are aligned.

Advantages: After being "fired" the ceramic discs are nearly as hard as diamonds and are impervious to water. The discs are completely unaffected by water temperature or debris in the line such as sand, silt or solder. There are actual cases where a ceramic disc valve has cut pieces of line solder with absolutely no damage to the valve. A ceramic disc cartridge may easily outlive the finish on the faucet.

When properly polished to an almost perfect smoothness and flatness, there is no room for air or water to seep between the two discs, eliminating the possibility of leaks.

A perfectly smooth pair of ceramic discs do not rely on lubricants for easy operation. The two surfaces continue to polish eachother through normal use so a lifetime of smooth, easy operation is assured.

Simple handle movement and "memory" positioning - handle can be rotated to desired water temperature, and then simply lifted to operate. Fast, safe, efficient operation for use when rinsing. Elimination of fulcrum and lever handle attachment (required by push/pull valves) means positive handle attachment with minimal play or looseness.

Disadvantages: Compared to an all-plastic cartridge, a relatively high cost to produce and replace. But viewed over the life of the fitting, the best investment and lowest "life-cycle" cost.

ACCESSORIES

In addition to the sink having a variety of accessories available, there are special attachments and/or enhancements available for the faucet.

Lotion/Soap Dispenser: Installed on the sink ledge or in a countertop, these units have a plastic bottle below the sink and a "pump handle" above the deck. Hand lotion or liquid soap then can be conveniently available at the sink without unsightly bottles or jars sitting on top of the countertop.

Hot Water Dispenser: This accessory has a faucet that is connected to a small storage tank mounted below the sink. The tank is connected to the cold water supply line and a 120 volt household current. The dispenser tank stores enough water hot for instant coffee, soups or tea; therefore eliminating the need to heat water in the microwave or boil water at the range top.

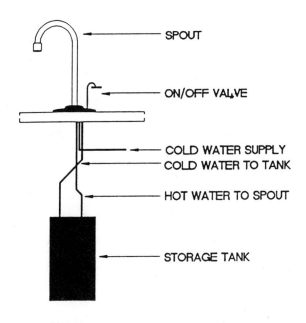

Figure 137
Hot water dispenser.

Air Gap: Many codes require that a dishwasher have an air gap installed at the sink to prevent any back-up of water in the dishwasher. The air gap is a metal or plastic cap that sits on the sink and is connected to a hose that leads to the dishwasher. A second hose leads to the knock-out on the side of the food waste disposer.

The dishwasher drains through the tubing below the air gap. There are small openings on the air gap, so that an overflow will drain into the sink.

Warn the client not to be surprised if there is a "gurgling" sound as the dishwasher drains in their new kitchen with an air gap.

The food waste disposer should be cleared after every use because the dishwasher will drain through the disposer.

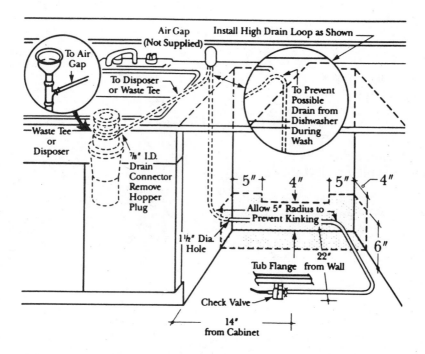

Figure 138
How the typical dishwasher air gap works at the kitchen sink.

Water Treatment System: In some areas of the country it may be important for you to be familiar with water purification systems. The water quality of a home can be improved as it enters the house, or it can be improved at a point of use within the house (one of the faucets).

The issue of water quality has been addressed in Chapter 1, *"Mechanical Systems"*, when we discussed plumbing. Our concern here is what equipment would be necessary at the sink.

There are three broad categories of systems that you should be familiar with. One includes installing a filter on the cold water line that leads to a kitchen faucet. The second focuses on mounting a filter on the faucet itself. The third method mounts a filter on the line that diverts cold water to a separate faucet.

The first two methods do not affect the overall equipment at the sink, but the last option does require a third and separate faucet. Make sure you know what type of equipment may need to be installed inside the sink cabinet - it may affect a tilt-down drawer head front, a pull-out towel bar, or a lower roll-out shelf that you're planning. Also, find out what electrical requirements and/or plumbing connections you need to specify.

Surfacing Materials

In addition to the cabinets and appliances in the kitchen, another key ingredient of a successful project is the surfacing materials that you select.

Surfacing materials run the gamut from hardwood floors to natural stone slabs, to individual ceramic tiles. Decorative laminates and solid surfacing materials are also choices. However, before selecting any of these surfaces, you must first understand the importance of a proper substrate material. Volume 1 of the *Kitchen Industry Technical Manuals* covered the basic construction elements of a well-planned kitchen.

BUTCHER BLOCK

Countertops made from laminated wood products are commonly referred to as butcher block. In addition to full countertops, insert blocks are often installed in the kitchen work surface.

The insert blocks are available in a variety of sizes and finishes. Both edge and end grain laminations are popular. The inserts are designed in two ways. The first requires a stainless steel installation ring which can be used in all countertops except mortar bed cement tile tops. The second provides a lip in the block for a drop-in-place installation, possible in all counter surfaces.

Unique kitchens will often feature the entire countertop in butcher block. When this type of surface is planned, the designer must specify what type of wood will be used, what type of finish the block will have, and what water and heat protection the block will receive.

Several types of woods are available from different manufacturers:

- **Eastern Hard Rock Sugar Maple:** This wood is considered the hardest, thus cutting or scratching damage will be minimized.

- **Western Maple; Western Alder:** This wood is not as hard as Eastern Maple and will be more susceptible to wear through cutting or scratching.

Grain patterns within the laminations will vary according to the fabrication procedure used.

- **Full length edge grain laminations** feature long unbroken strips of the wood laminated together. The edge widths remain constant.

- **Butt-joined edge grain laminations** feature various strips within the overall length of the top. The edge widths remain constant.

- **End grain laminations** feature a checkerboard effect of small squares of wood. This type of fabrication is normally limited to counter inserts.

The wood tops may be finished in several ways. The intended use of the block should determine the finish selection.

Unfinished Wood: The finish will consist of oiling wood throughout the counter surface life span. This method is most desirable if the entire counter surface will be wood and local fabrication of seams or miters is required. The prefinished tops hinder proper adhesion of seams and must be refinished if any sanding will be done. Care and maintenance will consist of protecting the wood from any standing water, scraping with a steel scraper or spatula after use, and oiling the top weekly with mineral oil. To sanitize maple tops:

- Spray or sponge the surface with a solution of hot water (130°F (54.44°C)) and hypochlorite (bleach).

- Scrub with a firm (not wire) brush.

- Pick up residue and rinse with cold water.

- Towel dry immediately.

Prefinished Wood: The factory finish will include a penetrating sealer and a non-toxic lacquer finish. The combination of sealer and varnish prevents moisture penetration. No oiling is necessary and a damp cloth may be used to wipe the board clean. Chopping on the surface may not damage the finish. This type of finish is appropriate for countertop sections, such as island tops or sandwich centers.

Wood Sealed with Varethane: This sealer is used on unfinished wood tops which will not be used as a chopping surface and will not come in contact with food. The finish is very good on tops which will be exposed to moisture and liquids.

CERAMIC TILE

Ceramic tile is a favorite surface product for many kitchen designers. A beautifully natural material, it also offers wide design flexibility. However, without a solid understanding of the product, installation methods and care recommendations, the profitable job and a pleased client may elude you.

Tile is composed of clays, shales, porcelain or baked earth. These raw products are pressed or extruded into shapes and then fired in a kiln, baked in an oven or cured in the sun. The differences between raw materials, manufacturing methods and surface finishes make some types of tile more durable in heavy use areas than others. The firing method will also affect the moisture absorption rate of different types of tile, therefore making some more appropriate for high moisture kitchen countertop areas.

Tile specified by kitchen designers for any surface other than decorative vertical areas should be selected after careful investigation into its appropriateness for the planned installation. As you consider a tile for a specific installation, first refer to the manufacturer's literature for usage recommendations. Secondly, check the porosity of the tile. Thirdly, check the availability of trim (curved shapes for smooth corners, edges and coves). Fourth, think through your grout selection. And lastly, make sure that you have specified the recommended installation method for the tile you have selected.

To help you do that, **American Olean Tile Company** has generously contributed the following information from their program "Start to Finish":

Types of Tile Available

GLAZED TILE

A coating of glass-forming minerals and ceramic stains is called the glaze.

The glaze is sprayed onto the body of the tile (known as the bisque) before firing. The finished surface may have a shiny luster. Some glazed surfaces can be slippery to certain footwear, especially when the footwear or surface is wet.

Glazed tiles are also available in a variety of finishes, some have slip- resistant glazed texture. Various sizes, shapes and thicknesses are available.

Shiny, high-gloss glazed tiles may dull slightly with wear over a period of time with continued use. Black or dark-colored glazed tiles will show wear more rapidly than lighter colors. The type of glaze often determines the recommended end use of the tile, (i.e., walls, floors, counters).

Figure 139 Glazed tiles are used at the backsplash and quarry tile is featured on the floor of this contemporary kitchen.

CERAMIC MOSAICS

Ceramic mosaic tiles are distinguished from other kinds of ceramic tile by their small size which must not exceed 6 sq. in. (2.45 x 2.45 in. if square shape). The most common types are natural clay and porcelain in which the color is throughout the tile rather than having it applied on the surface such as a glaze. However, glazes may be applied as well. Porcelain ceramic mosaic tiles are always vitreous (natural clay) or impervious (porcelain). Therefore, they have a very low water absorption rate, less than 0.5%. They've a harder, denser body than non-vitreous wall tile.

Ceramic mosaics are usually sold face-mounted with paper, back-mounted with a mesh or plastic tab backing, or mesh-backed in 12" x 12" (30.48cm x 30.48cm) or 12" x 24" (30.48cm x 60.96cm) sheets. Mounted sheets facilitate installation and control the evenness of spacing.

Porcelain mosaics are impervious, stain-resistant, dent-proof and frost-proof. They are suitable for interior and exterior walls, floor and countertops. They are also used extensively in the linings of swimming pools. Creative graphics, murals and geometric designs can be planned with ceramic mosaics.

PREGROUTED SHEETS

Glazed and ceramic mosaic tile may be ordered from manufacturers in pregrouted 2 square foot sheets. These sheets come in several size tiles, glazes and colors. These sheets save installation time and produce a uniform installation.

QUARRY TILE

Quarry tile is made from shale, clays or earth extruded to produce an unglazed product which has color throughout the tile body. There is a great variety of quality levels within the broad term, quarry tile. The earthen clay tiles may be very soft and irregular in shape. Other types of quarry tile are so porous that they require a penetrating sealer to protect the surface. Before such a sealer is applied, the tile and grout must be allowed to cure for at least two weeks. During this curing time, this area must be protected and ideally work must stop.

Other so-called quarry tiles must be stained and sealed. If such extra steps in the installation process must be completed, the designer should include the extra costs incurred in the estimate.

Certain manufacturers' quarry tile meet the ANSI standards and are considered stain-resistant, although not stain-proof. Thus, application and renewal of a sealer is optional. To achieve the subtle patina or rich glow of natural quarry clay, seasoning the tile with oil-based cleaners (e.g., Murphy's Oil Soap or Lestoil) is preferred to sealing. Quarry tile is suitable for interior residential and commercial floors, walls and fireplace facings. Quarry tile may be used on exterior surfaces when proper installation methods are followed.

DECORATIVE TILE

Within the glazed family of ceramic tile, there is a sub-category often called "Decos". These attractive accent pieces may include a raised or recessed relief pattern or feature a painted or silkscreened design. Generally the relief designs are planned for vertical use only because the three-dimensional tiles are difficult to clean on a counter surface or floor area. Some of the hand-painted tiles may be so delicate that general countertop or floor cleaning will damage the pattern but they are popular for walls and as inserts in a backsplash.

Some decorative tiles create a design which flows from tile to tile to give designers great flexibility for a unique, one-of-a-kind wall, border or back-splash. Others are one-of-a-kind art pieces that should be showcased within a field of plain tile.

Figure 140 Decorative tile is used in this country kitchen along the backsplash and as a detail at the custom hood. The countertop deck material is a solid surface.

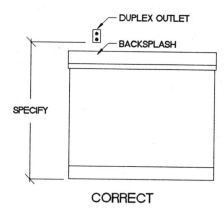

CORRECT

INCORRECT

Figure 141 When considering tiles along the backsplash, make sure that their placement does not interfere with electrical outlets and such.

CERAMIC TILE PLANNING TIPS FROM THE PROS

Ceramic tile specified by kitchen designers for any surface other than decorative vertical areas should be selected after careful investigation into their appropriateness for the planned installation.

- **Manufacturers' Recommendation:** The hardness of a glaze plus tile body determines a tile's end use. Manufacturer's specification sheets or catalogs will suggest approved applications.

As you and your client consider ceramic tile for a specific installation, first refer to the manufacturer's literature for usage recommendations. If recommendations are not available, ask if the tile meets the ANSI standards. If not, find out what is non-standard about the tile. As harmony in color is one of the parts of this standard, the tile may meet all other tests necessary for approval, but rather than a blended color, may offer a lovely variety of hues.

- **Determine Porosity:** The porosity of the tile is also critical for kitchen countertops. Cooking food stuffs can ruin a new counter surface if the wrong tile has been selected. Tiles are considered vitreous if the absorption is 3% or less and impervious if their absorption is 0.5% or less (porcelain ceramic mosaics).

- **Select Glazed or Unglazed Surfaces:** The glaze finish is another criteria to consider. Some tiles come two ways - high-gloss or matte. A glossy finish tile should only be used on walls. The heavy use of a kitchen countertop may cause a glossy surface to become dull over time. With a matte glaze, wear is not nearly as noticeable. Both tiles have the same degree of hardness. For floors, matte or unglazed porcelain are recommended.

Glazed tile, smooth to the touch, can be slip-resistant due to a special manufacturing process. Textured glazes with noticeably rough surface are also slip-resistant. Varying degrees of slip resistance are needed for a variety of end uses. Safe kitchen design demands that slip resistant tiles be specified for floor applications.

- **Select the Correct Surface Trim:** Just as important as the tile shapes is the availability of trim shapes. While the floor can be installed with nothing more than a plain or field tile edge (tile without any finished or shaped edge), the countertop or backsplash calls for specially designed pieces to complete the installation.

Trim shapes are available with 3/4" (1.91cm) radius for conventional mortar installation, and 1/4" (.64cm) radius for thin set installations.

These trim shapes are generally more expensive than the square footage price of the field tile because of the cost of production. The color and texture match is generally good between field tile and trim shapes, but there may be a slight or pronounced texture difference in some selections. When you're using ceramic tile for the first time, visually compare a field tile and trim shapes before the order is placed. If there is any variation, the client should approve the difference before the order is placed.

TILE TRIM

The purpose of tile trim is to give an installation a finished look. And, according to the Tile Council of America, Inc., American manufacturers produce the widest selection of trim for every installation. Note that tiles can be set on thin or thick beds of mortar; the silhouette of trim pieces will reflect the difference. Illustrated below are some examples.

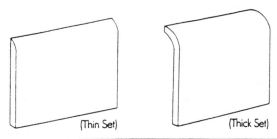

(Thin Set)   (Thick Set)

Bullnose

This trim piece is used to finish a tiled area with a rounded edge, at the top of wainscoting, to give a custom look where the tile meets the wall, or around a kitchen sink, for example.

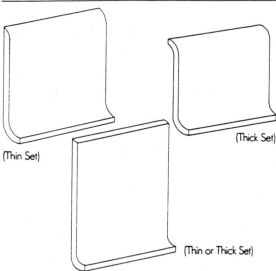

(Thin Set)   (Thick Set)

(Thin or Thick Set)

Cove Base

A combination of bullnose and cove tiles, this trim piece is especially appropriate for a flooring installation where wall tiles will not be used. The round top provides a finished transition between flooring and wall covering as well as the easy-to-clean concave feature of the cove tile.

Cove

Installed at the intersection of wall and floor, the smooth, rounded transition piece makes this 90-degree angle easy to clean.

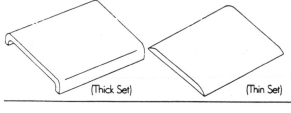

(Thick Set)   (Thin Set)

Curb

This piece is used to cover the curb of the shower stall. It offers the finish of a bullnose tile on either side.

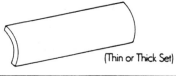

(Thin or Thick Set)

Bead

A rounded piece of tile, usually 4¼ to 6-inches long, similar to a quarter-round piece of wood moulding. The bead can be used horizontally, instead of a bullnose trim piece, to finish a wall installation or vertically as corner trim.

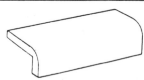

Counter Trim

This piece is used to finish the edge of a ceramic tile counter, vanity or table top.

Figure 142 (Courtesy of American Olean Tile Company) Types of Tile Trim.

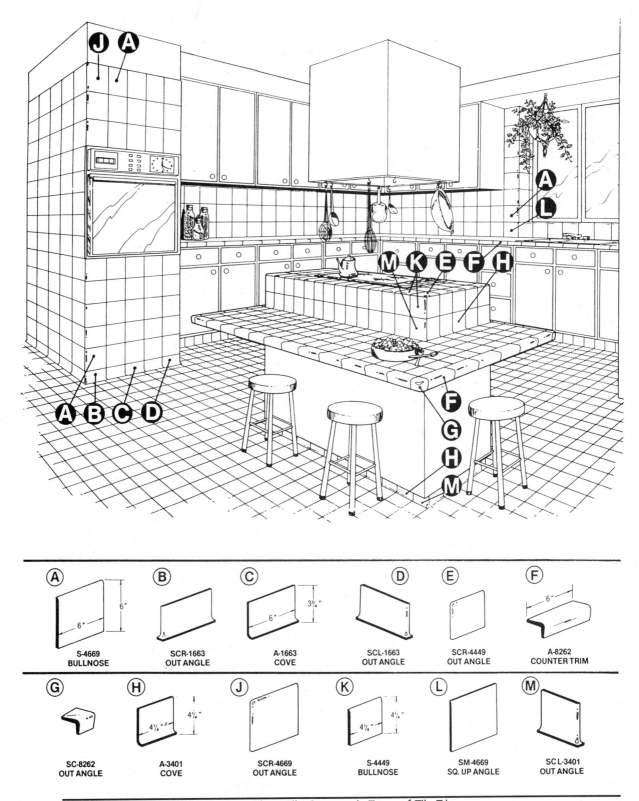

Ⓐ	**Ⓑ**	**Ⓒ**	**Ⓓ**	**Ⓔ**	**Ⓕ**
S-4669 BULLNOSE	SCR-1663 OUT ANGLE	A-1663 COVE	SCL-1663 OUT ANGLE	SCR-4449 OUT ANGLE	A-8262 COUNTER TRIM
Ⓖ	**Ⓗ**	**Ⓙ**	**Ⓚ**	**Ⓛ**	**Ⓜ**
SC-8262 OUT ANGLE	A-3401 COVE	SCR-4669 OUT ANGLE	S-4449 BULLNOSE	SM-4669 SQ. UP ANGLE	SCL-3401 OUT ANGLE

Figure 143 (Courtesy of American Olean Tile Company) Types of Tile Trim.

Grouts

Different types of grout are available, each designed for a particular kind of installation and to be used with specific tile sizes and shapes. Definitions of various grout types may be found in the **Tile Council of American Inc. "Handbook for Ceramic Tile Installation"** (P.O. Box 326, Princeton, NJ 08540).

Generally, four broad categories of grout will be specified by the kitchen designer:

EPOXY

Epoxy grouts, in several colors, are used when superior strength and chemical resistance are desired. New formulas produce nearly flush joints and are effective in vertical joints such as backsplashes and cove base trim. Epoxy grouts are more expensive than other types of grouts.

SILICONE RUBBER

Silicone rubber grouts, in white, are used in areas where great elasticity and moisture resistance are required. These grouts are not recommended for kitchen countertops because their chemical properties make them unsuitable for food areas.

DRY-SET

Dry-set grouts (non-sanded grout), in white or colors, are suited for grout joints not exceeding 1/8" (.32cm) in width.

SANDED

Sanded grouts, in white and colors, are used for grout joints up to 3/8" (.95cm) in width. The sand is added to the grout to insure proper strength of the wider joint. Most often used for floors and ceramic mosaics.

Both dry-set and sanded grout are enhanced by the addition of a latex additive during the installation process. The latex additive increases the bonding strength and provides a better cure. Also, you can expect less water absorption, so use latex for wet areas.

GROUT PLANNING TIPS FROM THE PROS

• **Coordinate the Tile and Grout Color:** A tile surface will offer a more harmonious look if the grout color and the tile color are similar. The pronounced grid pattern, which is created with contrasting grout, can enhance the design potential of large kitchen spaces. Plan a design with contrasting grout as you would one with grid wall covering. Check for proper scale.

• **Test color first:** Follow manufacturer's installation directions precisely to avoid possible staining. If you're unsure about grout and tile relationship, try a test panel first to avoid problems.

• **Make sure clients understand what they're getting:** Talk about grout with your customers every time. Many customers expect white grout; others may have seen tile with colored grout. Find out what they want; help them select the best combination to meet their expectations.

- **Sealing the grout:** Sealers help preserve true grout colors. Epoxy grouts do not require sealers. For cement joints, you must wait until the joint is completely cured. Use in a test area first to be sure the effect is right. Several coats of sealer may be applied in areas of heavy use.

- **Show clients colored grouts:** This selection is as important as the tile. Most manufacturer showrooms feature colored grout in vignettes and sample panels. Invite your customers to browse for ideas.

- **Explain variations in grout color:** Help clients understand that grout color may appear darker when wet immediately after it is installed. After curing it will return to the expected shade. Make sure they understand that the grout around the kitchen sink may always look darker than that on the adjacent countertop because it is always damp.

- **Beware of uneven grout colors caused by jobsite conditions:** Beware of uneven drying when grouting near a heat duct, hot air vent or air conditioner. Peculiar shade variations sometimes occur. This can be prevented by shutting off the source of air or frequently wetting the grout in that area. Uniform drying will produce more uniform color.

- **Stress Proper Maintenance:** Poor maintenance can discolor any grout. Colorful grout in a decorative island top will soon be dull and discolored if poorly maintained. Floors with sanded cement grout are sometimes washed with dirty water and carelessly rinsed. The suspended dirt in wash water can be absorbed by the cement floor grout. This can be avoided by changing water frequently.

Method of Installation

Four methods of installation are used for ceramic tile projects.

MASTIC (ORGANIC ADHESIVE)

In this method, tile is directly applied to the subfloor, countertop, decking or cement surface with troweled-on mastic. When this method is used, the finished floor will only be raised the thickness of the tile. Manufacturers state that a mastic installation may use any of the following base surfaces: existing tile, fiberglass, wood, paneling, brick, masonry, concrete, plywood or vinyl. The surface must be dry, flat and free of dirt and grease.

Any existing structural problems cannot be camouflaged by the tile installation. If there is a bow in the floor before the tile is installed, it will be there after the tile is installed.

CONVENTIONAL MORTAR BED (MUD)

In this method, the tile is installed on a bed of mortar 3/4" to 1-1/4" (1.91cm to 3.18cm) thick. Two systems are popular in the United States. In one, the tile is set on a mortar bed while it is still soft. In the other, tile is set on a cured mortar bed.

THIN SET OVER BACKERBOARD

A glass mesh concrete backerboard may take the place of a conventional mortar bed. It is unaffected by moisture and has one of the lowest coefficients of expansion of all building panels. Additionally, the boards are only one-half the weight of conventional mortar installations.

CONVENTIONAL MORTAR OR BACKERBOARD

With this installation, the floor or cabinet height will be raised the thickness of the tile and the mortar bed or glass mesh concrete board. This height difference may require special floor preparation. In new construction, the subfloor can be recessed to accommodate a tile floor. In renovation projects, a transition method between the new higher tile floor and adjoining floors must be specified. Special toe-kicks must also be detailed so that the industrial standard of 3" (7.62cm) high kick space is maintained.

Most tile setters recommend the mortar installation be used over wood subfloors. The advantage to this type of installation is that the tile (installed with a cleavage membrane) will "float" on top of the wood. Normal wood expansion and contraction will not cause cracks in

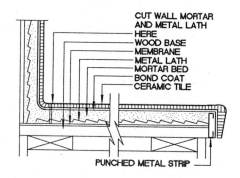

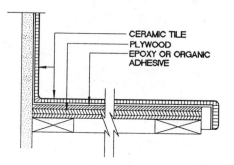

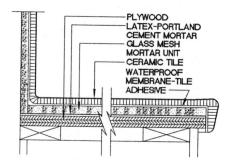

Figure 144
Examples of typical tile installations.

the tile or grout. The mortar installation is also more desirable when there is heavy traffic.

CABINET INSTALLER'S PREPARATION

What should the cabinet installers do to prepare the kitchen cabinet run for the tile setter?

Tile, much like a house, is only as strong as its foundation, and the foundation is made up of what is installed below the tile surface.

	Walls	Floors & Counters
Dry-set Mortar	1/8" in 8' run	1/8" in 10' run
Epoxy Mortar	1/8" in 8' run	1/8" in 10' run
Organic Adhesive	1/8" in 8' run	1/16" in 3' run

The cabinets must be level and plumb. The maximum variations allowable are as follows:

The use of a 4' to 6' (121.92cm to 182.88cm) level and an 8' to 10' (243.84cm to 25.4cm) straight edge is recommended to insure a level surface. When necessary, cabinets should be shimmed underneath the toe kicks. A baseboard, floor covering or toe kick skin is then installed to conceal the shims.

If the backsplash area is to be tiled, it must be patched and solid. The tile installation requires a smooth and even surface.

The type of decking material and the decking installation varies with each type of tile setting method. Detailed methods and standards are listed in the **Handbook for Ceramic Tile Installation**.

TILE PLANNING TIPS FROM THE PROS

Kitchen Countertops:

- The **cabinets** must be level and square so that backsplash grout

lines will be straight. A 4' to 6' (121.92cm to 182.88cm) level should be used. For longer runs, a 4' (121.92cm) level and 8' (243.84cm) straight edge should be used.

- If the **backsplash** area is to be tiled, it must be patched and solid. An organic adhesive installation requires a smooth and even surface.

- In many parts of the country, **plywood decking** is used. In other locales, traditional lumber decking is preferred. Traditional decking is often specified to provide flexibility under the tile. Generally, grade-one or grade-two kiln-dried Douglas fir, 1" x 4" (2.54cm x 10.16cm) or 1" x 6", (2.54cm x 15.24cm) spaced 1/4" (.64cm) apart, is used. It may be installed perpendicular to the backsplash (from the front of the cabinet to the back) or running parallel with the cabinet face. Tile craftspeople and carpenters differ in their opinions as to which is better. The decking should be delivered to the house several days before the installation to allow the wood to reach the relative humidity of the room.

- The **decking** should overhang the cabinets and flush out with the face of the drawers and doors.

- **Fixture cutouts** are made during the tile decking installation. Unbox any fixtures and place them in the cutout to ensure a proper fit before the tile craftspeople arrive at the jobsite. Whenever possible, any cutout should be a minimum of 2" (5.08cm) away from a wall board or plastered backsplash.

- The **elimination of stress** is critical when countertop overhangs

are planned. The tile must have a solid base. If any movement occurs when pressure is placed on the top, the tile and/or grout will crack. The underside of the decking should be finished to match the cabinets or correspond with other products used in the project.

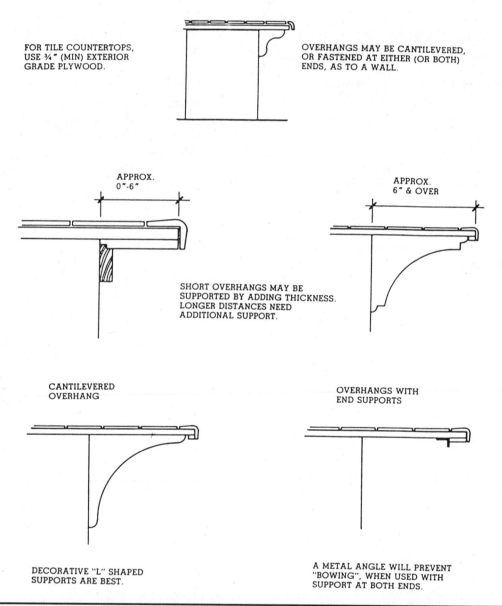

FOR TILE COUNTERTOPS, USE ¾" (MIN) EXTERIOR GRADE PLYWOOD.

OVERHANGS MAY BE CANTILEVERED, OR FASTENED AT EITHER (OR BOTH) ENDS, AS TO A WALL.

APPROX. 0"-6"

APPROX. 6" & OVER

SHORT OVERHANGS MAY BE SUPPORTED BY ADDING THICKNESS. LONGER DISTANCES NEED ADDITIONAL SUPPORT.

CANTILEVERED OVERHANG

OVERHANGS WITH END SUPPORTS

DECORATIVE "L" SHAPED SUPPORTS ARE BEST.

A METAL ANGLE WILL PREVENT "BOWING", WHEN USED WITH SUPPORT AT BOTH ENDS.

Figure 145 (Courtesy of American Olean Tile Co.) The tile overhang must be supported so that the surface does not flex, causing tile or grout to crack.

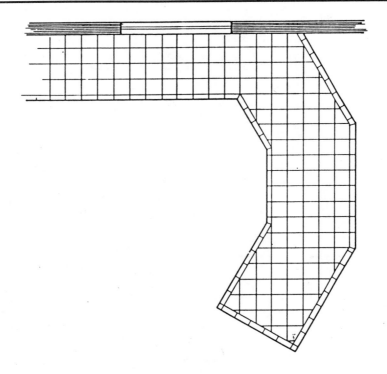

ANGLED COUNTER LAYOUT #1

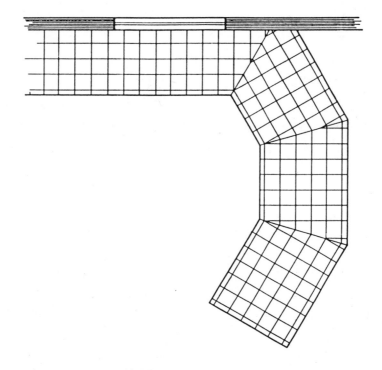

ANGLED COUNTER LAYOUT #2

Figure 146 (Courtesy of American Olean Tile Co.) Carefully lay out tile on a countertop that is part of an angled kitchen design.

TILE AND EXISTING WINDOWS

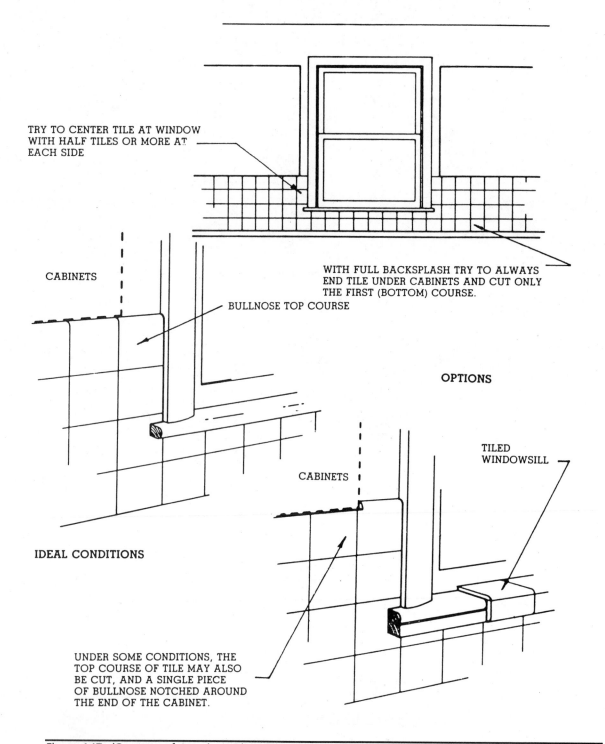

TRY TO CENTER TILE AT WINDOW
WITH HALF TILES OR MORE AT
EACH SIDE

CABINETS

WITH FULL BACKSPLASH TRY TO ALWAYS
END TILE UNDER CABINETS AND CUT ONLY
THE FIRST (BOTTOM) COURSE.

BULLNOSE TOP COURSE

OPTIONS

TILED
WINDOWSILL

CABINETS

IDEAL CONDITIONS

UNDER SOME CONDITIONS, THE
TOP COURSE OF TILE MAY ALSO
BE CUT, AND A SINGLE PIECE
OF BULLNOSE NOTCHED AROUND
THE END OF THE CABINET.

Figure 147 (Courtesy of American Olean Tile Co.) Detail how you want the tile to be finished around the windows in your elevation drawings.

AT WINDOWS WITH SHEETROCK RETURNS

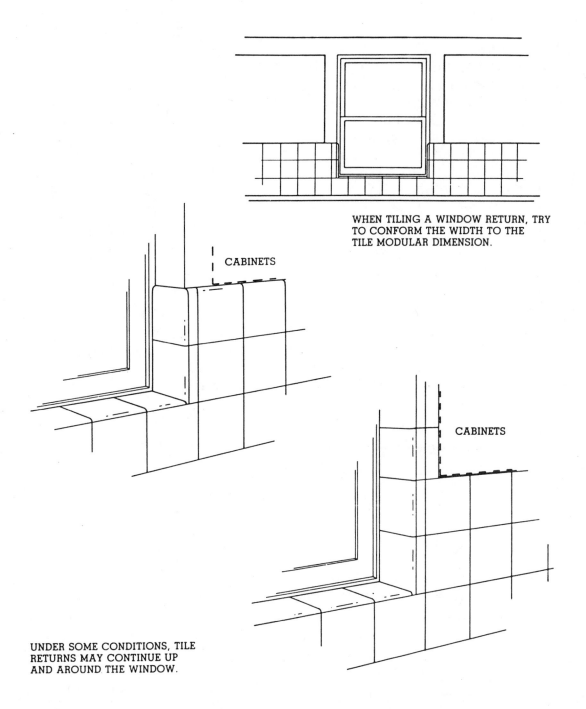

WHEN TILING A WINDOW RETURN, TRY
TO CONFORM THE WIDTH TO THE
TILE MODULAR DIMENSION.

CABINETS

CABINETS

UNDER SOME CONDITIONS, TILE
RETURNS MAY CONTINUE UP
AND AROUND THE WINDOW.

Figure 148 (Courtesy of American Olean Tile Co.) Include details of finished windows in your elevations.

TILE PLANNING TIPS FROM THE PROS

Floors

- **In renovation jobs, removing the existing floor covering is recommended.** Generally, this is necessary if vinyl tiles or cushioned vinyl floors are installed over a slab or wood foundation. In many parts of the country, tile is installed directly over old non-cushioned sheet vinyl.

- **Doors may require modification** to accommodate a tile floor. With a mastic installation, the designer is only concerned with the thickness of the tile. When a conventional mortar installation is planned, the designer must allow clearance for a 3/4" to 1-1/4" thick mortar bed, plus the thickness of the tile. A glass mesh concrete board installation will require a clearance dimension equal to the thickness of the board, plus the tile.

- **Allow enough time for the door modification.** Interior hollow-core or solid-core doors are easy to cut down. Pocket doors must be the type which can be removed from the pocket.

- If the new tile floor will be higher than the finished flooring of an adjacent room, **the tile selected must have trim pieces or a threshold must be planned.** Thresholds are generally marble or wood. Solid surface material can also be used as a threshold.

- Make sure that the distance from the finished tile floor to the underside of the countertop **leaves enough room for a built-in dishwasher.**

IDEAL CONDITION

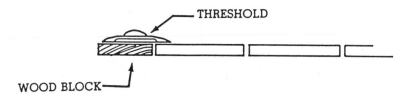

LESS ACCEPTABLE INSTALLATION

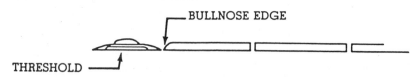

Figure 149 (Courtesy of American Olean Tile Co.) A tile floor must be carefully planned so that it meets the threshold or weather stripping at an exterior door.

TRANSITION METHODS

THIN SET TILE ON WOOD OR SHEET FOUNDATION –

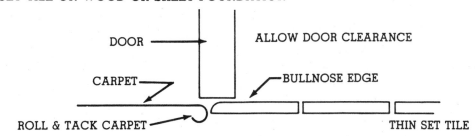

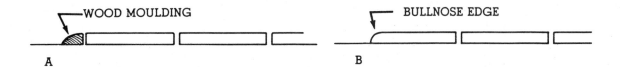

A

B

TRANSITION TRIM

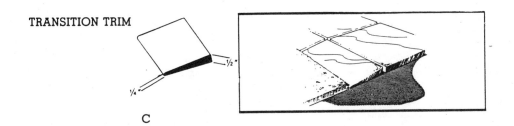

C

For a professional transition of varying floor levels, use one course of Transition Trim as a threshold. Slanted shapes gives smooth reduction from ½" to a ¼" thickness. Edge is modified bullnose on lower edge for finished appearance. May be applied in thin-set or mortar bed installations. Nominal size is 4"x 8".

PS-8484 available in Primitive® Encore® and Ultra Pavers® on special order.

Q-8485U available in Quarry Naturals® on special order. Rated Moderate Duty.

MORTAR INSTALLATION ON WOOD FOUNDATION

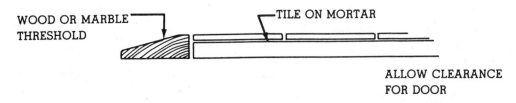

Figure 150 (Courtesy of American Olean Tile Co.) Transition methods from a tile floor to other interior floor surfaces.

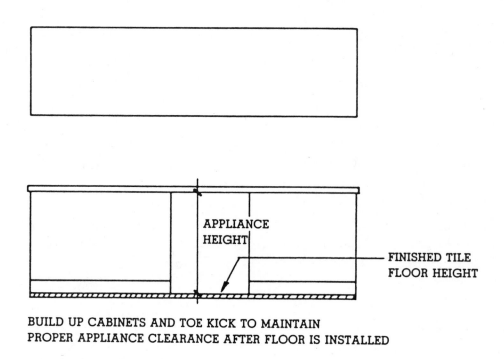

BUILD UP CABINETS AND TOE KICK TO MAINTAIN
PROPER APPLIANCE CLEARANCE AFTER FLOOR IS INSTALLED

Figure 151 (Courtesy of American Olean Tile Co.) Make sure there is enough room from the finished tile floor height to the underside of the countertop for the appliances.

GLASS BLOCK

Glass block is enjoying a rekindled interest among designers. While popular in the 1930s and 1940s, the use of glass block came to a standstill in the 1970s. These translucent hollow blocks of glass are ideal for kitchen use. They transmit light, yet provide privacy. When used in exterior wall installations, they deaden outside noise and offer insulating qualities similar to thermal- pane windows. Available in a variety of shapes, sizes, textures and colors, glass block offers great design flexibility.

However, installation is not easy and should not be attempted by anyone other than a skilled mason. The blocks are non-porous, slick and heavy. During installation, they are slippery and difficult to align.

Alternatives to glass block are decorative glass-looking products that are made out of plastic materials. These substitutes are very strong, as well as being light weight. Assembly is generally quicker with these types of acrylic and proprietary polymer blocks because they have an engineered inner locking system which fastens them together.

Therefore, traditional mortar joints are not required. Some of the manufacturers have available preformed, weather-resistant sealant that looks like a mortar joint to complete the finished product.

LAMINATES

Laminate surfaces are found on kitchen countertops, as well as cabinet interiors and exteriors.

The following information describes the different types of laminates available:

High-Pressure Decorative Laminates

High-pressure decorative laminate is composed of three types of paper fused under heat and pressure into a single surface. The top coat is a melamine resin-saturated overlay. The second sheet is the decorative surface. It is a melamine resin-saturated paper carrying either a surface color or a gravure print. Under these two levels is a core or body made up of three to nine sheets of phenolic resin-saturated kraft paper.

The entire assembly is pressed at between 1,000 to 1,200 pounds (454kilograms to 544.8kilograms) per square inch for about an hour, at temperatures exceeding 280°F (137.78°C).

High-pressure decorative laminates are divided into forming and non-forming grades. Non-forming laminate is rigid, while forming laminate has been adjusted in the curing process to be more flexible so that it can be bent under heat. This process is called "post-forming".

The cabinet industry uses vertical-grade high-pressure decorative laminate which is .030" thick. Countertop fabricators use a horizontal grade of high pressure decorative laminate which is .050" thick. Both thicknesses are offered in forming and non- forming grades. The post forming grade is .042" thick.

High-pressure decorative laminates are used most frequently on countertop surfaces. They are also used by many cabinet manufacturers for door styles. The high-pressure decorative laminate is generally applied to a particle board substrate. Occasionally, codes may call for a plywood substrate for a countertop.

Of all the laminates available, high-pressure decorative laminates offer the greatest impact resistance. They are available in a wide range of colors, patterns, textures and finishes. Some manufacturers offer special fire-resistant, abrasion-resistant, chemical-resistant surfaces. Others fabricate laminate in a grooved tambour form. Generally, all high-pressure decorative laminates have excellent stain, abrasion, scuff and wear resistance. However, because the laminate is applied to a substrate, if a chip occurs, it is not repairable. Shiny surfaces show scratches more easily than dull finishes. Solid colors show scratches to a greater extent than pattern surfaces.

In addition to the wide spectrum of colors and patterns available, several special purpose laminates are also offered for the designer's consideration:

Color-Through Laminates

Color-through laminates are similar to standard, high- pressure, decorative laminates, except that the melamine colorsheets are used throughout the material instead of the phenolic core or body kraft paper layer. Therefore, the laminate contains color throughout and no joint line will be visible after fabrication. These laminates are used for special edge treatments where the surface is engraved or routed to reveal other colors. Or they can be used throughout the room for the total countertop installation. The material is more costly than ordinary high- pressure, decorative laminates and the fabrication takes a bit more attention and care.

Figure 152 The decorative laminate countertop has a coved back edge and full backsplash. The front edge is finished in wood to match the cabinetry.

Figure 153 Decorative laminate top lends itself to angles and curves when a self edge is used. This countertop is attractively combined with a ceramic tile backsplash.

PAINT

Painting is one of the finishing steps in a kitchen project. Often the designer is not responsible for this activity, but is expected to understand the craft and make recommendations to the client.

A basic understanding of paints will aid the designer.

Paint Coverage

Paints is designed to bond itself to either a fresh, new surface or an old, uneven one. It should cover and help to protect the surface against the assaults of weather, airborne chemicals and dirt. It should remain flexible enough to stay intact for years while the walls settle, vibrate, expand and contract.

Paint Material Composition

An astonishing variety of materials have gone into paint mixture over the years, but most commonly used paints today contain certain ingredients, each with a specific function.

Pigments are made from minute particles of earth, metals or chemical compounds and give paint its color.

Resins are binders that give paint the ability to form a thin, tough film. The binders are normally chemicals or plastics such as alkyds, acrylics, polyvinyls or urethanes.

Plasticizers are chemical agents used to keep the paint elastic after it dries. Solvents make the mixture of pigment, resin and plasticizer thin enough to be used with a brush or roller.

Paint Gloss Choices

The two major types of finishing coats - **latex and alkyd paints** - come in versions labeled flat, satin semi-gloss, egg shell and high gloss. High gloss paints are the most wear-resistant and moisture-resistant because of their relatively high proportion of resin. The more resin, the heavier and tougher the film. The high resin film of the glossy paints makes them ideal for areas subject to heavy use and frequent washing. Semi-gloss paints afford moderate durability with a less obtrusive shine for most woodwork. Flat paints provide a desirable low-glare surface for walls and ceilings that do not need frequent washing.

Paint Classifications

Latex Paint: This paint provides simplified cleanup, is odor-free and quick-drying. Water is the solvent for latex paint, which is made of plastic resin and either acrylics or tough polyvinyls. Its water solvency gives latex advantages which have made it the most widely used paint for walls and ceilings in living areas, other than kitchens and bathrooms. Tools, spills and hands can be cleaned with soap and water while the latex is wet. Latex paint is almost free of odor and harmful fumes, and a coat is usually dry in little more than an hour.

Latex adheres to most surfaces painted with flat oil or latex paint; it does not adhere to some alkyds and tends to peel away from any high gloss finish. Latex can be used over unprimed wall board, bare masonry and fresh plaster patches that have set but are not quite dry.

Its water solvency imposes certain limitations on latex paint. Although it can be applied directly over wallpaper, the water in the paint may soak the paper away from the wall. If latex is applied to raw wood, the water swells the fibers and roughens the surface - a disadvantage where smooth finish is desirable. Used on bare steel, it rusts the metal.

Flat latex is less resistant to abrasion and washing than either oil or alkyd paint, and the high gloss latex is less shiny and less durable than comparable alkyds or oils.

Alkyd Paint: This paint has replaced oil-based paints in most cases. It is considered the best type of paint to use in rooms which will receive a great deal of use. Any painted or wallpapered surface, or bare wood, can be covered with paint made from a synthetic resin called alkyd (often combined with other resins). This type of paint will adhere to bare masonry or plaster but should not be used on bare wallboard because it will raise a nap on the wallboard's paper covering.

Alkyd is the most durable of the common finishing paints. It is practically odor-free. Most alkyds are sufficiently dry for a second coat in four to six hours.

Although some latex paints will not bond well to alkyd, most other paints can be applied over it.

SOLID SURFACING

General Introduction

The designer has many solid surfacing materials to choose from. Materials currently available from major manufacturers are Avonite, Du Pont Corian, Fountainhead by Nevamar, Wilsonart Gibralter Solid Surface and Surrell by Formica. Other materials are being continually introduced onto the market.

The designer should compare these new materials against the guidelines detailed in the following review of the major products to ascertain their level of quality and durability. Although the major product offerings vary in composition and breadth of product line, there are some common features:

- All solid surfacing material is stain resistant because it is non-porous, and repairable because the color runs through the material.

- All manufacturers recommend cleaning with a damp cloth or sponge and ordinary household soap or mild cleanser.

- The color-through feature of these materials means that severe stains (including cigarette burns) can be removed with a 320 to 400 grit sandpaper, steel wool and/or a buffing pad.

- While most products have excellent resistance to household chemicals, paint removers and oven cleaners can sometimes cause damage. Further, industrial chemicals, as might be found in a commercial installation may affect various products in different ways. If exposure to industrial chemicals is a concern, check with the manufacturer.

- All of the manufacturers offer solid surfaces with a factory finish which may be sanded to a matte finish or can be buffed or polished to a high gloss. None of the manufacturers recommend high-gloss finishes on dark colors in heavy use areas, such as kitchen countertop surfaces.

- When properly fabricated, the seam between two pieces of all the solid surfacing materials is almost imperceptible. However, you should never promise an invisible seam.

- Solid surfacing is quite "fabricator sensitive" and all manufacturers stress the importance of retaining only qualified and/or certified fabricators.

- Companies offer sheet goods in 1/2" (1.27cm) and 3/4" (1.91cm) thicknesses. Other thicknesses are available and vary by company. The availability of molded lavatories also varies by company.

- Manufacturers recommend that unsupported overhangs should not exceed 12" (30.48cm) with 3/4" (1.91cm) sheets and 6" (15.24cm) with 1/2" (1.27cm) sheets.

- Manufacturers recommend that the material "float" on the substrate; most recommend perimeter frames and a web support system rather than a full substrate.

- Although solid surfacing is considered more durable than laminates, it is not impervious to heat. Because solid surface materials expand when heated, all manufacturers recommend at least 1/8" (.32cm) clearance on wall-to-wall installation.

- Most manufacturers recommend these materials for interior use only. Potential problems with exterior use of some of the materials include shrinkage and expansion as well as color changes with exposure to direct sunlight.

Current Products

Although these similarities exist in the major materials, there are differences in each of the major brands that relate to composition, warranties and applications.

The makers of **Avonite** describe the product as follows:

AVONITE

A patented formulation composed of polyester alloys and fillers not found in standard polyesters. Because of this, it is exceptionally durable. Avonite offers a 10-year warranty to back up that claim. The replacement expense for material and labor are covered by the warranty for projects that were installed properly.

Avonite's textured granite, gemstone or crystelle look, is first created by curing a special liquid polymer into a solid, then pulverizing it into particles. These particles are then used as suspended particulates during the final casting. This process gives Avonite its depth of color and translucency. There is an extensive color pallet. A new material called **"Formstone"** has been formulated with a modified acrylic matrix which provides exceptional post-forming capabilities for creating extremes in curved shapes.

Avonite produces a Class I fire rated material and a Class III designer material ideal for moderate post-forming and high polishing. The Class III coefficient of expansion and contraction is greater than Class I and different fabrication procedures are recommended in extreme heat conditions.

Avonite also warrants that its materials will not fade. A special patch kit provides the ability to repair accidental nicks and a unique inlay kit can create stone in stone or "Intarsia" looks.

Du Pont describes **Corian** as follows:

CORIAN

A solid color, veined or stone look material. Corian is available in 1/4"(.64cm), 1/2" (1.27cm), 3/4" (1.91cm) and 1 -1/2"(3.81cm) thick sheets and in a full range of kitchen sinks and bathroom lavatories for creating custom integrated sink worktops with Du Pont's joint adhesive system. All are of homogeneous, mineral-filled methyl methacrylate polymer, a tough, rigid, high performance, transparent acrylic with a Class 1 fire rating. Corian solid surface material is 100 percent acrylic-based.

Because it is a thermoformable acrylic with a mineral filler, Corian is an excellent product for thermoforming into custom designs such as bathtub and shower surrounds, and for forming sweeping, graceful curves. Corian also is available in a liquid form so color inlay patterns in Corian can be created. Du Pont-certified or approved fabricators should fabricate and install the product.

Corian is not recommended for exterior surfaces, steam room wet walls, below-grade masonry walls, direct application on cinder block or concrete, on flooring or structural applications.

Du Pont has a 10-year limited installed warranty covering the material, fabrication and installation against defects when fabricated by a Du Pont-certified or approved fabricator/installer, effective January, 1992.

Nevamar describes **Fountainhead** as follows:

FOUNTAINHEAD

A solid color and textured surface with a soft stone appearance. Classic color pallet for sheets, kitchen sinks and vanities. The manufacturer also supplies liquid inlay so fabricator can create solid or matrix color designs. The material is a combination of engineered polyester and acrylic with alumina trihydrate as a filler. Fountainhead is a thermal-set plastic that can be thermal-formed to accommodate most common applications.

Nevamar designates "Accredited" fabricators who have demonstrated competent fabrication in actual installations;

accreditation can be verified by the fabricator's ID card, which carries his accreditation number. The product does carry a 10-year limited warranty.

Wilsonart International describes **Gibraltar** as follows:

GIBRALTAR

A solid color and stone look collection, the product is a polyester and acrylic blend with fire-retardant mineral fillers.

In terms of design, Gibraltar solid colors match Wilsonart Internationals plastics laminate colors for increased design versatility - for perfectly matching laminate cabinets and backsplashes with solid surfacing tops. In addition, Gibraltar features a unique computerized color consistency, so that problems with mismatching are eliminated.

The product is warranted for 10-years against failure, based on being installed by a Certified Fabricator.

Formica describes **Surrell** as follows:

SURRELL

A unique, totally homogeneous, densified, mineral-filled polyester. Available in a wide variety of sheets, vanities, lavatory bowls, kitchen sinks, shower bases, bathtubs and wet wall kits. A fully densified casting process is one in which all the air is removed from the mixture before it is cast. This results in a material that is denser and stronger than traditional cast polymer materials.

STONE

Flagstone

Flagging is a process whereby stone is split into thin slabs suitable for paving. Although generally identified as "flagstone", bluestone and slate are the most common types of flagging stones used.

Bluestone is a rough sandstone paver, usually buff, blue, green or gray in color. Slate is a smooth, gray, sedimentary stone. The thicker the stones, the less likely that cracks will occur over the lifetime of the floor. The weight of the floor must be carefully computed when used over wood foundations.

Figure 154 In a solid surface countertop the sink can literally be a part of the surface. Note the attractive rolled front edge on this countertop and backsplash area.

Figure 155 Solid surface countertops and integral sinks are specified for this room that beautifully combines laminate and wood in the cabinetry. The room is further enhanced with the wood trim around the window, the wood beams at the ceiling and the wood floor.

Figure 156 A country kitchen combines many materials.

Figure 157 An attractive example of combining countertop materials.

Both bluestone and slate absorb heat rather than reflect it and can get quite hot. Irregularly cut stones are the least expensive pre-cut patterned stone.

Granite

Polished granite countertops are a popular element of up-scale kitchens. A natural stone countertop conveys a sense of beauty and warmth that is combined with a durable work surface that can withstand the expected high use of the new kitchen.

Granite is an igneous rock (class of rock formed by a change of the molten material to a solid state) with visible coarse grains. It consists of quartz, feldspar, mica, and other colored minerals.

Granite isn't as subject to staining as marble is because of an extremely low absorption rate. The stone is less prone than marble to scratching. Its coarse grain also makes it more slip- resistant than marble.

Coloration: When specifying color variation, include shade, clarity and movement of the granite. There will be slight variations from slab to slab because of mineral content and veining, which adds to the character of the natural stone. Granite is available in three different finishes: a highly polished surface, which is appropriate for most countertop applications; a thermal finish, which has a rough-textured touch; and a honed finish, which provides a matte surface ideal for a kitchen floor application.

Fabrication: Granite countertops differ from solid surfacing tops in that the fabrication is simpler and completed at the factory; therefore, installation costs are generally less for granite surfaces. Consequently, designers should only compare installed prices when attempting to identify a realistic cost difference between a solid surface top and a granite one.

Measuring the countertops for installation has evolved into a precise process that can be completed when the cabinets are ordered. Working from the kitchen design layout and using newly developed measuring techniques to calculate exact dimensions, granite can be prefabricated and delivered to the jobsite ready for installation.

Sizing: For most countertops, the optimum thickness is 1-1/4" (3.18cm). The difference in cost over more fragile 3/4" (1.91cm) slabs is minimal and the added thickness gives more strength for extensions and cutouts, while reducing the risk of breakage during transport and installation. *For example,* a 1-1/4" (3.18cm) granite slab can support 12" (30.48cm) of overhang. Keep in mind the weight of these tops as you schedule the installation crews.

Granite slabs for countertops can measure up to 4-1/2' (131.16cm) wide and up to 9' (274.32cm) long. This allows greater flexibility in countertop design. Should more than one piece be necessary, the slabs can be matched for color and grain consistency and then cut to butt squarely against each other. For this type of installation, locate seams in the most inconspicuous locations possible, around cutouts or back corners.

Figure 158 A polished granite counter surface will require some attention to maintain its luster.

Figure 159 A granite floor is a beautiful foundation for this white-on-white kitchen, which features solid surface countertops and integral sinks.

Figure 160 An attractive pattern is created by combining a textured and a solid color granite on the floor and countertop in this traditional kitchen.

Marble

Marble is naturally occurring, recrystallized limestone. After earthen materials are crystallized into limestone, they are subjected to pressure and heat from the earth's movement.

Italian marble is world renowned. Belgium, Spain, Greece and France are also known for quarry marble. Alabama and Tennessee offer U.S. marble products.

Unless the finish is etched, honed or pummeled, marble is slippery when wet. Therefore, use it as a kitchen flooring only if it features one of these slip-resistant finishing treatments.

Marble is brittle and must be handled like glass during installation. Once installed, edges at doorways must be protected by a sturdy threshold.

Coloration: Numerous minerals are present which account for the markings and color range associated with marble. Marble is available in white, red, green, yellow and black. Some marbles feature directional patterns; others offer a general, overall design.

The more colorful and decorative the marble, the more fragile it is. Each vein in a stone is the result of natural discoloration from water. It is like a tiny fracture which, under pressure, can lead to breakage.

Durability: Marble is rated according to an A-B-C-D classification based on the fragility of the stones. A and B marbles are solid and sound. C and D marbles are the most fragile, but also the most colorful and decorative.

The grade of marble affects pricing: the more fragile and decorative it is, the more expensive. Before specifying marble, advise the client about durability.

Slab vs. Tile: Traditionally, marble is used in large slabs. Suppliers differ on the size and thickness of countertops they stock. Many slabs are available 1-1/4" (3.18cm) thick. Other suppliers, however, stock 3/4" (1.91cm) thick countertops; some carry 1-1/2" (3.81cm) thick slabs. The appearance of a 1-1/2" (3.81cm) thick counter can be achieved by joining the 3/4" (1.91cm) counter to a 3/4" (1.91cm) edge treatment. The pieces can be glued together so that the seam is unnoticeable.

An alternative is 6" x 6" x 1/2" (15.24 x 15.24 x 1.27cm) marble tiles that are installed by a tile setter following specifications developed by the Ceramic Tile Institute.

Maintenance: Marble is soft and porous. This means it stains easily if not initially sealed with at least two coats of a penetrating sealer. And it must be frequently resealed. White marble is softer and less dense then colored marble, so it's more easily stained. Dark marble shows scratches more easily.

Finishing: Marble may be polished so that it has a shiny appearance. Although there are degrees of shine to which marble can be polished, the final polish is achieved by adding a slightly moistened acidic compound to a smooth marble surface.

A heavy brush or felt pad is applied under tremendous pressure. This action produces heat which creates a chemical reaction that changes the surface of the stone itself. The compound is rinsed off and the stone is left polished.

Terrazzo

Terrazzo is a slurry mixture of stone chips consisting of marble and cement. This marble aggregate concrete produces a hard and durable flooring surface. It is also used as a wall treatment. It is available in field tiles of a more solid nature and decorative border tiles in various patterns and colors to match or contrast with the field tiles. Such a combination can provide a dramatic "old world" look.

VINYL RESILIENT FLOORING

Better materials and the manufacturers' ability to improve photographic realism have improved the ability of vinyl to mimic natural materials such as wood, marble, slate, granite and ceramic tile. However, the trend today in vinyl floor patterns is towards graphic simplicity which highlights simple, geometric patterns. Vinyl remains one of the easiest floors to maintain.

Vinyl Sheet

Vinyl sheet flooring is available as "inlaid" (the pattern going throughout the wear layer of vinyl) and as "rotogravure" (the pattern is printed on a sheet). Both are then covered with a layer of wearing surface. The thickness of the wear layer does not affect the durability of the floor or the price. Thick vinyl wear layers resist scuff and stains well, but lose their gloss more quickly than a thinner urethane wear layer which maintains a high-gloss surface better and provides a more scuff-resistant surface.

Vinyl sheet floor coverings range from having no cushion at all to a thick cushion beneath the wear layer. Although the thick cushion increases comfort, the vinyl can be dented by heavy objects.

Vinyl Tile

Solid or pure vinyl tiles are homogeneous vinyl which is unbacked and usually has uniform composition throughout. By far, the biggest seller is vinyl composition tile called "vinyl tile". Both can be installed on suspended wood subfloors or over on-grade and below-grade concrete. They're durable and easily cleaned. Solid vinyl tiles don't have a wear layer top coat. Vinyl tiles do feature this easy maintenance advantage.

WALLPAPER

Within the kitchen industry, a perplexing dilemma continually faces the designer - how to combine style with function. Wallcoverings are often the planner's salvation.

Manufacturing Methods

The patterns in wallcoverings are achieved by using two methods: machine prints and hand prints. In machine printing, all the wallpaper rolls are printed in a continuous "run" and are identical in color. Hand prints are printed by a process called "silk screening" and cannot be matched for color as closely as machine prints because each roll is individually handscreened with slight color or variations occurring from roll to roll. To protect the hand print edges, the rolls are normally manufactured with selvages (untrimmed edges). A color variation will also occur in grass cloths and similar materials. The fibers from which they are made do not respond evenly to dyes; color gradually lightens or darkens from one edge of a strip to the other and varies along the length of the roll.

Determining Quantities

The following procedure is suggested to determine wallpaper quantities for papers from American sources, which are based on Imperial sizes and generally have 50 to 60 square feet of product on each double roll.

- Measure the width of each wall to be prepared. Round the figure up to the next full foot measurement.

- Add the wall dimensions together.

- Multiply this figure by the ceiling height plus 4" (10.16cm). Again, round up the figure to the next full foot measurement.

- Subtract the wall space covered by windows, doors and appliances from the total square footage to be covered.

- Depending on the pattern match, divide the actual wall space to be covered as follows:

    18" Repeat = Divide by 30
    19 to 24" Repeat = Divide by 27
    25" Repeat = Divide by 24

- Always round up to the next full number of rolls.

For papers which are sized metrically, you can assume 28 to 30 square feet. Therefore, you generally need to order twice the amount of product.

Jobsite Considerations

The finished appearance of the wall covering can only be as good as the wall surface under it. The walls must be clean and smooth. Although foils are notorious for allowing imperfections to telescope through the covering, all wall coverings will reveal the surface below them to some extent. The walls must be properly sealed. The correct adhesive must be used.

Always open all rolls and inspect them for color match or defects before any installation begins. Because dye-lots vary, it is important to check the material before installation begins. This same concern prohibits the installation of part of the wall covering before all the material ordered arrives.

The following chart lists typical wallpaper material available for your consideration.

WALL COVERING

TYPE	HOW SOLD	SPECIAL COMMENTS
Common Papers		
Untreated Vinyl-Coated Cloth-Backed	Single, double & triple rolls, 18" - 27" wide; length & width combine to provide 30 sq.ft. per roll after waste allowance.	Susceptible to grease stains and abrasions; pattern inks may run if washed; strippable if cloth-backed
Vinyls		
Laminated to Paper Laminated to Woven Fabric Impregnated Cloth on Paper Backing Laminated to Unwoven Fabric	Same as common papers; heaviest grades also available in widths to 54" and lengths to 30yards.	Most durable type currently available; may be scrubbed; almost always strippable.
Foils		
Metallic Aluminum Laminated to Paper Aluminum Laminated to Cloth	Same as common papers.	Fragile and hard to handle; may cause glare in sunny areas; available in striking super graphics.
Flocks		
On Paper On Vinyl On Foil	Same as common papers.	Vinyl flocks washable; all may be damaged by excessive rubbing.
Pre-Pasted Coverings		
Papers Vinyls/Foils Flocks	Same as common papers.	Ideal for the inexperienced.
Fabrics		
Untreated Laminated to Paper Self Adhesive	Bolts usually 45" wide, but also in widths of 54" & 60"; sold by the yard.	Easy to clean with dry-cleaning fluids or powders.
Felt		
Laminated to Paper	Bolts 54" wide; sold by the yard.	May be vacuumed, but stains are hard to remove; some colors fade.
Textured Coverings		
Grass Cloth Hemp Burlap Overprinted Designs	Double rolls, 36" wide and 24' long except burlap, which is also available in widths to 54"	All available in either natural or synthetic fibers.
Murals		
On Paper OnVinyl On Foil	Strips 10' to 12' long, with matching paper for surrounding areas.	Muslin or unbleached cotton may be substituted for lining paper to create strippable material.
Cork		
Laminated to Paper Laminated to Burlap	Widths up to 36" lengths in 24' or 36'.	Keep well vacuumed; all cork surfaces are washable; cork absorbs and deadens sounds within a room.
Laminated Wood Veneers		
Random Patterns	Strips 10" to 24" wide and up to 12' long; end-matched strips for taller walls available on request from manufacturer.	Fire-resistant; allowed by strictest codes where solid wood paneling is banned.
Gypsum Coated Wall Fabric	Single rolls, 4' wide and 40 yards long.	Dries to plaster-like surface; available only in pastel shades, but may be painted in other colors.
Leather	Single dressed hides; one large cowhide covers from 25 to 40 square feet.	Expensive, handsome and durable; stains are difficult, but can be removed by brushing on rubber cement and peeling it off.

WOOD FLOORING

Throughout the house, wood floors are in great demand today. Wood is also a viable flooring material for some kitchen projects.

Wood floors are graded according to standards that measure color, grain and imperfections. Clear or Select grades are generally specified for a formal look and for lighter finishes. Select and #1 Common grades are used for traditional and light-to-medium stained floors. For rustic and specialty areas specify #2 Common, which features wide color variations and character marks like knots, streaks and worm holes.

Wood used for floors are all cold weather hardwoods. The slow growth in cold temperatures provides the most durable wood possible.

Wood Species

Oak is the most popular wood flooring in residential use because of its beautiful grain and durability. Maple is popular for commercial use because it is the hardiest. Awaiting the homeowner seeking broader horizons are exotic woods in either manufactured or custom floors, starting at roughly twice the price of oak. These woods range from the unusually beautiful rose wood to the exceptionally rugged iron wood, with stops in between for pecan, teak, kumbac, karpa wood and darkest ebony.

Floor Styles

There are several styles of flooring currently being used.

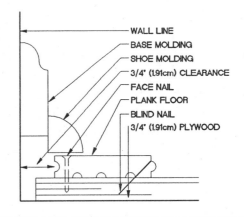

Figure 161 Hardwood floor installation.

- **Plank Flooring:** Interlocking flooring which is blind-nailed. Generally, random lengths of 9" to 96" (22.86cm to 243.84cm) are used, as well as random widths. The width combinations are: 3" and 4" (7.62cm and 10.16cm); 3", 4" and 6" (7.62cm, 10.16cm and 15.24cm); 3", 5" and 7" (7.62cm, 12.7cm and 17.78cm); and 4", 6" and 8" (10.16cm, 15.24cm and 20.32cm). The plank flooring is generally sold in bundles. In this case random lengths and widths cannot be varied. Allow for waste and cutting.

- **Strip Flooring:** Butt flooring which is top-nailed. All boards are the same width (2" (5.08cm) and 2-1/4" (5.72cm)) and random lengths. Both plank and strip flooring is sold by board feet. Provide allowance for waste and cutting.

- **Parquet:** Simulated 12" x 12" (30.48cm x 30.48cm) tiles or actual individual pieces of wood. Interlocking, blind nailed. Sold by square footage. Allow for waste and cutting.

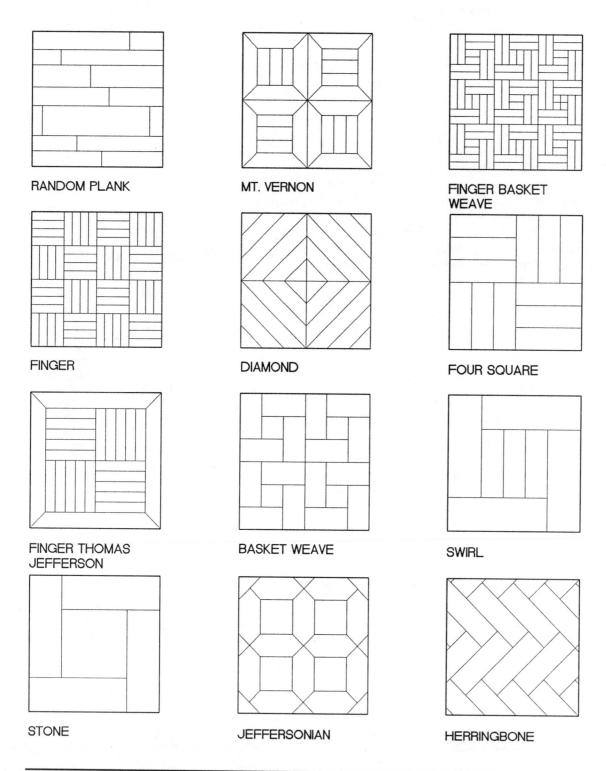

RANDOM PLANK   MT. VERNON   FINGER BASKET
                                          WEAVE

FINGER   DIAMOND   FOUR SQUARE

FINGER THOMAS   BASKET WEAVE   SWIRL
JEFFERSON

STONE   JEFFERSONIAN   HERRINGBONE

Figure 162 Typical hardwood floor patterns.

Finishing

To jobsite finish or to spec prefinish - to wax or not - the great debate between finishing techniques and materials rages on.

Roland Cormier, a veteran hardwood flooring installer talked about both finishing types and methods in a *Home Mechanix* magazine article.

Finish for Dye-Stained or Natural Floors:

"I think tung oil and wax is a nearly forgotten, but beautiful, way to protect new or resurfaced floors. It can be renewed indefinitely by waxing as required. Two coats of a name-brand polyurethane is a great way to protect floors, too-but eventually it will wear and need to be recoated. This requires resanding since cured urethanes are so hard that a new coat does not adhere well to the old one. Patching worn areas that had been protected by polyurethane is rarely successful."

Wax Maintenance:

"When I mention wax, most people go into hysterics. They think they will continually be on their knees with a polishing rag. Actually, a waxed floor might need rewaxing once a year-and it can be done with a small buffing machine that homeowners can buy or rent. It's really a choice between periodic maintenance, or sanding and recoating your floors with polyurethane every five or six years. Penetrating oil and wax is the way it was done for years. The soft look of it is incomparable."

White-wash Flooring:

"The white-gray stain is called a pigmented stain. It creates color by causing finely ground particles to adhere to the floor's surface. Unlike a dye-based stain that penetrates the wood, a pigmented stain floats mostly on the floor's surface like paint. The particles and resins of the pigmented stain limit penetration by the tung oil and, hence, make good adhesion difficult. Besides, tung oil or polyurethane would well give the floors an amber tone. A clear, non-yellowing varnish with an alcohol, toluene, oraliphatic-resin base is best; they're available through suppliers to professional floor finishers."

Prefinished Floors: Modern prefinished floors have a durable penetrating sealer finish applied at the factory. A lovely finish that increases with beauty as one walks on it, yet if it is waxed there are several major disadvantages. First the wax will be affected by water. The factory finish will not accept an additional protective coat of urethane. The installer must completely sand the floor, remove the factory finish and start from scratch if the water resistant properties of a urethane are required. Second, the prefinished floor does not allow the installer the opportunity to sand the entire surface after installation to ensure a perfectly even surface. Lastly, the prefinished tiles or planks do not provide a completely sealed top surface. Therefore, moisture from kitchen spills can get down between and under the wood floor.

Unfinished Floors: Another approach in a kitchen is to install an unfinished floor. The urethane finish, which is impervious to stains and moisture, can then be installed after the unfinished wood has been sanded smooth. The multiple coats provide a sealed top surface for the cook work environment.

Once finished the floors should be inspected from a standing position. Flooring in not furniture; a finish similar to the one on a grand piano should not be expected. Trash in the finish, a wavy look or feel along the strips, deep swirls or sander marks, and splotchy areas are indications of inadequate finishing or cleaning. The quality of the finish may be acceptable and include some of these problems, but they ought not to appear over the entire floor.

Chapter 3

Kitchen Planning Standards and Safety Criteria

*T*hree major research projects were the basis for the new planning standards that are contained within this chapter: The University of Minnesota Study, The NKBA Design Competition Survey, and The NKBA Utensil/Food Stuff Survey.

In the first two chapters you've studied the mechanical systems that will affect your design solutions and the equipment and materials you have to work with. You will now take these tools and creatively arrange the space to suit your client's family lifestyle and ergonomic considerations.

A NOTE ABOUT THESE GUIDELINES

These standards have been established to provide a yardstick by which you can judge the efficiency of a kitchen plan you've created. They should not be interpreted as hard and fast rules that you must never deviate from. The true kitchen planning professional knows that meeting each client's specific requests within the space constraints before you and the budget limitations set is the true standard of excellence. Never break a building or safety code to accommodate a client's request. However, modifying these guidelines is certainly acceptable as long as both you and the client know that you are deviating from an industry standard.

Always remember how hard it is for your client to visualize what a new kitchen space will look like. So don't be too quick to make the walkway smaller or to limit the size of a doorway. But, once you've demonstrated before the client in your showroom display, or in another manner, the space constraints, accept the challenge of defining the space to satisfy their preferences, using these guidelines for information and inspiration.

Section **1**

Early Kitchen Planning Research

The first kitchen planning guidelines were published in the 1920s by home economists and instructors at major universities. These management specialists recognized that the plan of a kitchen needed to follow an organized set of standards designed to minimize the human energy needed to complete a task, and the amount of time required to prepare a meal or clean up afterwards.

The Functional Kitchen Storage Booklet

Throughout the 1930s and '40s, many research projects were conducted and papers published on the same subject at major universities. These activities further developed and refined the guidelines followed by residential kitchen designers.

The leading researchers of the time were **Mary Koll Heiner** and **Helen McCullough**. Their *Functional Kitchen Storage* booklet was published in June of 1948. The basis of this booklet was a study that identified average food stuff and equipment used by typical families in the United States. The researchers then went on to identify the amount of space the equipment needed, which led to recommendations for a functional storage system.

The space allotted in each kitchen center of activity, the type of storage planned, and the recommended cabinet and countertop frontage dimensions that kitchen specialists followed until the early 1990s was predominantly based on this 1948 publication.

Major Manufacturers Set Standards in the 1950s

Activities to inform the consumer and teach the professional how to design better kitchens expanded in the '50s and '60s. The quest for better arranged kitchens was taken up by major manufacturers. First, General Electric had a kitchen design studio which was staffed by several **Certified Kitchen Designers**. During the '60s, major cabinet manufacturers began publishing brochures that talked about proper kitchen planning. Electric and gas utility companies and university extension services taught the consumer how to plan a functional kitchen environment.

The Original Kitchen Industry Technical Manuals

In 1965 a major kitchen planning publication was produced by the **National Kitchen & Bath Association** and the University of Illinois: the first version of the *Kitchen Industry Technical*

Manuals. Developed under the auspices of the **NKBA** and the University, this set of manuals became the basis for the CKD certification. However, even in the '60s this document relied on the recommendations made in the 1948 *Functional Kitchen Storage* publication. Kitchen designers began questioning the wisdom of planning kitchens in the '70s and '80s that were based on a food stuff list created in the '40s. Successful designers realized that the family was changing: the way they cooked, who cooked, and what they cooked. Therefore, they reasoned, the arrangement of the space needed to change as well.

The Changing American Family

Some of the major lifestyle and kitchen equipment changes that emerged and lead to the need for new guidelines were:

THE KITCHEN BECAME PART OF THE SOCIALIZING AREA OF THE HOME

First and most importantly, the home is a weekday retreat, a weekend resort. In our homes, the kitchen has become an important part of the socializing center. It is a place where we cook, as well as enjoy friends and family members.

COOKING IS VIEWED AS A HOBBY

While eating has always been considered an important part of our social life, cooking is a recreational hobby today. The preparation of a meal is considered as important as enjoying the repast. Additionally, who prepares the meal is no longer as critical as enjoying the meal together. Many busy homemakers/hostesses think nothing of stopping by the gourmet deli to pick up an entree for dinner guests who may be arriving shortly.

THE GREAT-ROOM CONCEPT

The shift in the importance of the kitchen within the home dramatically changes the look, feel and integration of all materials, equipment and systems within a combination cooking and living space - oftentimes called a "Great-Room". *For example,* such a "great-room" space requires more emphasis on flexible lighting systems, appliances that minimize noise and maximize odor removal, and cabinetry that blends attractively with furnishings in the adjacent, social segment of the kitchen space.

MORE PEOPLE THAN JUST MOM COOK

In addition to the changes in the way we use our kitchens, another major trend affecting our industry is who uses the kitchen. The dramatic increase in the number of working women in North America over the last 30 years has blurred the formerly clear lines of responsibility for household management.

Today, family members and friends often visit with the cook in the kitchen, and may actually help the cook prepare a meal, or take charge of the clean-up responsibilities after the meal has been eaten.

Planning a kitchen for more than one cook requires changing the basic rules. The work triangle must be stretched and family traffic patterns must be changed as well.

FAMILIES ARE SHRINKING AND CHANGING

We will see multi-generational families living together in the future, as well as more individuals living in non-traditional groupings. The "All-American" family will have fewer children - but more parents in need of elder-care. Therefore, safety within the kitchen, and a space that presents no barriers is a critical part of planning for today and tomorrow.

Time is our most precious commodity. Busy North Americans have more money than they have time. Therefore, the advantage of a more efficient work space remains at the heart of a well-planned kitchen. Time-saving equipment and surfaces that are easy to maintain are critical elements of a well-planned kitchen.

QUALITY IS NO LONGER A LUXURY, IT IS EXPECTED

The consumer of today demands quality: in service, professional skills and product. This emphasis on quality has increased the importance of your services as a comparative shopper and a true design expert.

NEW RESEARCH MODIFIES THE FORMER STANDARDS

In the late 1980s, the **National Kitchen & Bath Association** began a three year research project designed to validate, update or replace existing planning standards with guidelines more appropriate for today's family. This endeavor was guided by a group of dedicated, volunteer industry leaders and recognized academic experts at major universities.

The University of Minnesota Study

The cornerstone of this broad study was a research project conducted by the **University of Minnesota's Design, Housing and Apparel Department** under the direction of Professors **Becky Love-Yust** and **Wanda Olson**. The project, entitled "*Residential Kitchens: Planning Principles for the 1990's*", was compiled in 1991.

The overall objective of this project was to identify the relationships that have emerged as contemporary kitchen technologies integrate with family roles, preferences and management styles. That the results of this project address the effects these factors have on the utilization and organization of space in a kitchen. That recommendations for new planning standards results which are designed to meet the needs of contemporary households.

Professors Yust and Olson began the study by sending a survey form to 171 clients identified by **Certified Kitchen Designers**. 101 clients returned the surveys, a response of 59%. Of those responding, 50% of the information came from the Eastern part of the United States, 27% from the West, and 23% from the Midwest. Therefore, major population centers were fairly represented.

In addition to making sure the survey represented general areas of population, every attempt was made to investigate projects that reflected typical kitchen designs. To further monitor this representative mix of projects submitted, the results were compared against averages compiled from the **NKBA Annual Trend Survey** and the submissions to the **NKBA Annual Design Competi-**

tion. Additionally, where available, the statistics were compared against other published information provided by the **Kitchen Cabinet Manufacturers Association**, the **National Association of Home Builders, Kitchen and Bath Business Magazine, Kitchen and Bath Design News Magazine**, and **Decorating Remodeling Magazine** currently known as **American Homestyles Magazine**.

The kitchen plans studied by the **University of Minnesota** ranged in size from 85 square feet to 319 square feet. The average size was 175.5 square feet. One-third of the kitchens were less than 150 square feet, two-thirds were from 150 to 209 square feet and two kitchens in the sampling were over 300 square feet. These kitchens then do represent typical North American housing stock.

The structure of the families surveyed was also typical of the remodeling public. 93% of those completing the form were females and most were married. The average age was 46.6 years, and the average family size was approximately three people.

Although the University of Minnesota did not identify the value of the house, nor total family income, the educational and employment information indicates an affluent clientele. 60% of both respondents and spouses had completed at least 4 years of college. Many had gone on to further study. Of the respondents, 33% were homemakers, 33% were employed in professions and 25% were employed in services or trades. 50% of the spouses were employed in professions, with 33% employed in services and trade.

The owners of these kitchens were happy with them - 98% were satisfied with the amount and type of storage, and 97% were satisfied with the kitchen arrangement for meal preparation, as well as being satisfied with the amount and location of counter space and meal preparation. However, a full 46% of these kitchens scored poorly in one or more of the scoring criteria published in the first version of the *Kitchen Industry Technical Manuals*, which was based on the 1948 document referenced earlier. Thus, results of this survey proved that planning standards developed in 1948 were not appropriate for today.

Soon after this research project, NKBA teamed up with universal design experts to reexamine the basic assumptions of design for the idealized, able-bodied, non-elderly adult. The result was an increased appreciation for diversity, flexibility and adaptability in design and the basis for the new NKBA 40 Kitchen Planning Guidelines. This research is included for your review in Appendix A.

- **Appendix "A"** includes a chart that compares the old **University of Illinois Small Homes Council** rules, contemporary variables affecting the appropriateness of those rules and the **NKBA** Committee's recommendation for changes to these guidelines.

NKBA Design Competition Survey

The second project was a statistical analysis of 60 kitchens in 3 different size categories from the **NKBA Annual Design Competition**. This project was completed to augment and to validate the information gleaned from the University of Minnesota project.

In this study, each one of the 60 kitchens was measured to determine the average lineal footage of cabinetry, number of drawers and lineal footage of countertop. Each center of activity was then compared regarding the equipment included within the center and the relationship of centers to one another. The researchers also cataloged which kitchen arrangements were most often specified, what percentage of kitchens were open to adjacent living spaces, and what percentage of kitchens had some sort of eating center or other specialized area within the work space. Lastly, the researchers measured the work triangle of each space.

The overall results from this **NKBA** survey paralleled the information reported on within the **University of Minnesota**'s research project.

NKBA Utensil/Food Stuff Survey

GOALS

The third project completed was entitled the "**KITM Utensil Survey Project**". The overall objective was to:

- Develop a new core list of equipment typically found in a North American kitchen.

- To identify the base/wall cabinet shelf space and countertop frontage required to accommodate these utensils/food stuff items.

- To compare these new dimensional requirements with the existing information listed in the Small

Homes Council *Kitchen Industry Technical Manuals,* Volume 5.

- To develop new industry standards for acceptable kitchens in two categories: small kitchens of under 150 square feet and kitchens of over 150 square feet.

METHODOLOGY

To accomplish this task, the original list of equipment and food stuffs developed by **Helen McCullough** and referenced in the *Kitchen Industry Technical Manuals* was augmented by additional items typically found in kitchens today as identified by 10 test families.

Once the master utensil/food stuff list was developed the items were listed alphabetically, and surveys were sent to 40 families. 25 surveys were completed and returned.

Respondents were asked to identify what they kept in their kitchen and how often they used these items (daily, weekly, monthly, or at least once a year). Secondly, they were asked to identify where they used the item and where the item was stored. Lastly, they were asked how many of these specific items were kept in the kitchen.

RESPONDENTS WERE TYPICAL FAMILIES

As in the University of Minnesota survey, the families surveyed reflected typical American families.

HOW THE RECOMMENDATIONS WERE DEVELOPED

Once all of this information was tabulated, examples of all the materials were collected. These individual items were then grouped according to the center of use most often specified by the survey respondents.

Figure 165 The same steps were taken for items typically stored in wall cabinets.

Figure 163 The NKBA Utensil Survey concluded with all items on the kitchen core list being assembled and placed in storage cabinets.

Figure 164 The shelf space required to house items typically stored below countertop level was then measured.

Figure 166 The number of drawers in a normal kitchen were also identified.

The shelf space required for items stored in each center was then identified. It is important that you realize that the Core List reports on the minimum number of items typically maintained in a kitchen. The Core List only included the items that were common to the majority of family types included in our survey.

Virtually all respondents had additional equipment to store; things that pertained to their ethnic cooking (woks, pasta pots, etc.), to the age of their family members (baby food to bags of chips for the teenagers) or equipment for food fads (expresso machines to fondu pots to yogurt makers). Therefore, it is up to you to determine how much, where, and what type of storage will be appropriate for each client.

Each primary center of activity was listed, with secondary centers grouped below.

Required countertop space for each one of these centers was then calculated for kitchens over 150 square feet based on the space needed for all the equipment.

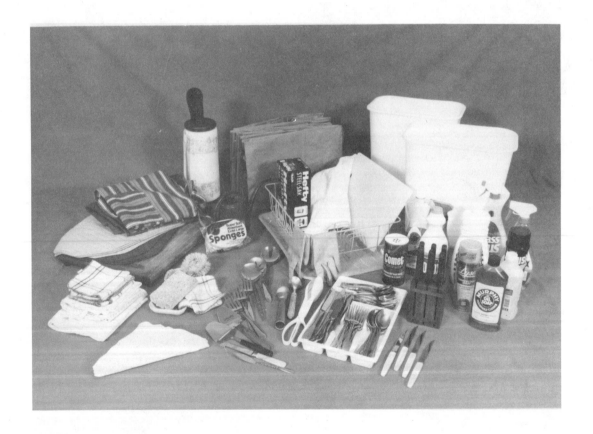

Figure 167 Items found in the sink area.

Figure 168 Everyday dinnerware and glassware found in a kitchen.

Figure 169 These family coffee items need to be stored either next to the sink or near the range.

Figure 170 The mix center contains these items.

Figure 171 These storage containers and wraps are stored either near the sink or by the refrigerator in most kitchens.

Figure 172 Packaged and boxed food stuffs are maintained in either a pantry or in a combination of wall and base cabinets.

Figure 173 Although work simplification principles suggest several sauce pans should be kept by the sink, most families keep all the pots and pans together near the cooking area.

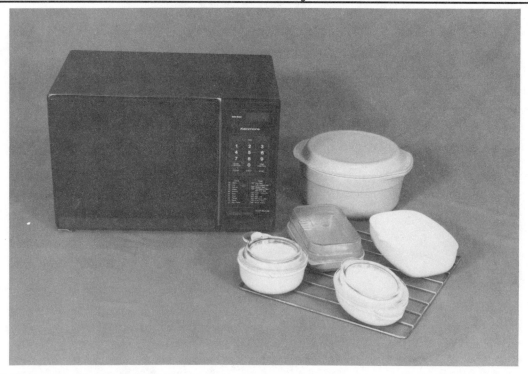

Figure 174 *Few families have large quantities of specialized dishes for the microwave. Most use dishes for multiple purposes.*

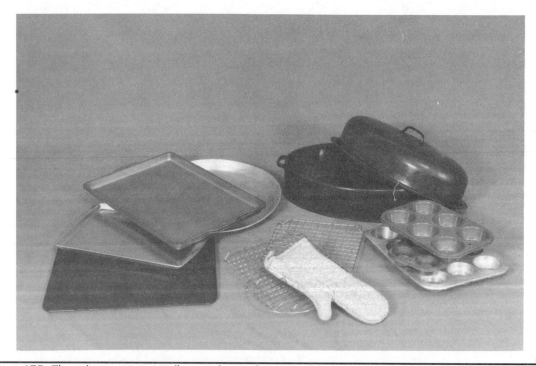

Figure 175 *These items are generally stored near the oven.*

Figure 176 This collection of serving items is generally kept near the table.

Figure 177 Most kitchens include some sort of a desk where numerous cookbooks are stored.

Figure 178 *The information gathered for this research project was used to calculate the necessary amount of base and wall cabinets, the number of drawers, and the countertop frontage recommendations that are the basis of NKBA's kitchen planning guidelines.*

Figure 179 *This information takes into account storage needs for contemporary families, no matter what decorative style they prefer.*

Figure 180 In addition to work areas, specialized areas are equally important, for example, an organized desk area.

THE RESULTS OF THE SURVEY

This tabulation revealed that the new recommendations were anywhere from 50% to 100% larger than the original **McCullough** survey for the average sized kitchen. Such information will not surprise practicing kitchen specialists. This does indeed reflect the type of

spaces that we plan today. Our clients have more equipment in their kitchens today.

The following chart compares the original **McCullough** survey inventory count and those items identified as being a part of the core group in the **NKBA Utensil Survey**.

1992 KITM RESEARCH PROJECT - EQUIPMENT/UTENSIL COMPARISON

Center of Activity	McCullough Survey Total Quantity	NKBA Utensil Survey Total Quantity	Increased # of Items
Sink Area	68	161	+ 93
Mix/Preparation Area	100	103	+ 3
Range/Cooking/Oven Areas 48	65		+ 17
Microwave Area	N/A	11	+ 11
Serving Area	62	63	+ 1
Coffee Area	3	6	+ 3
China & Glassware (occasional)	N/A	N/A	0
Dish/Glassware (daily)	95	182	+ 87
Pantry	N/A	124	+124
Leftover Storage/Wrapping N/A	24		+ 24
Desk/Bookcase Area*	N/A	52	+ 52
TOTAL ITEMS STORED	**376**	**791**	**415**
% Increase			(+110%)

* Did not count coupons separately, weighed as one (1) item.

The cabinet and countertop frontage recommendations were also verified against the 60 kitchens in the NKBA Design Competition referenced earlier. Once again, the results were similar.

Based on these findings, the following recommendations were made for base and wall storage frontage, number of drawers required and countertop frontage for a large kitchen (> 150 Sq. Ft.) and a small kitchen (= or < 150 Sq. Ft.).

RECOMMENDATIONS FOR SMALLER KITCHENS

These lineal footage reductions from the research recommendations were made based on the following observations:

- **No Desk:** Serving space and desk areas can be located in another part of the home. Therefore, the wall cabinet frontage was reduced from 186" to 144" (472.44cm to 365.766cm).

- **Still Need Wall Units:** No change in the 60" (152.4cm) requirement of wall cabinet space for dish storage because there are no acceptable alternative storage areas outside of the primary kitchen area.

- **Less Equipment:** In a small kitchen, a separate cabinet built for a trash receptacle could be eliminated. 36" (91.44cm) of space would be acceptable for a preparation area, and a smaller cooking appliance could be specified. Therefore, the base cabinet frontage was reduced from 192" to 132" (487.68cm to 335.28cm).

- **Fewer Drawers:** The number of drawers was reduced to an average of 8, for a total of 120" (304.8cm) in a small kitchen.

- **Less Countertop:** Because there would generally be less room around the sink, no desk space, and a free-standing range as opposed to a built-in one, the usable counter frontage was reduced from 198" to 132" (502.92cm to 335.28cm) in a small kitchen.

1992 KITM RESEARCH PROJECT - STORAGE/COUNTERTOP FRONTAGE REQUIREMENTS		
	Large Kitchen	Small Kitchen
Base Cabinetry	192" = 16 LF	156" = 13 LF
Wall Cabinetry	186" = 15.5 LF	144" = 12 LF
Drawers	165" = 13'9" LF	120" = 10 LF
	Avg. = 11 Drawers	Avg. = 8 Drawers
Amount of Countertop needed	198" = 16'6" LF	132" = 11 LF
Note: LF = Linear Foot		

SECTION **2**

Universal Design

Before we begin our study of human ergonomic standards, you should become familar with the concept of Universal Design.

A DEFINITION OF UNIVERSAL DESIGN

There has been much written about the aging of America. A full one-third of the North American population today is currently between the ages of 35 and 54. Our life expectancy has been extended far beyond that of our parents or grandparents. People's attitude toward aging has also dramatically changed - they're looking forward to healthy years at home. You, as a conscientious kitchen designer, can make those years at home productive, fun, and safe.

An article appeared in the *Home Economics Research Journal* in December of 1991, Volume 20, Number 2. Written by **Betty S. Guetzko** and **Betty Jo White**, the title is *"Kitchen Designers as Change Agents in Planning for Aging in Place"*.

The authors conducted a study designed to examine how kitchen designers address the special needs of maturing clients, and to assess design-

ers' perceptions about the demand for kitchens that facilitated aging in place.

With the authors' permission, the following discussion of barrier-free kitchen planning has been excerpted from the article.

Kitchen Designers as Change Agents in Planning for Aging In Place

The vast majority of older Americans age in place, i.e., remain in their single family homes for at least the first 10 years of retirement. Most older people inevitably face age-related changes that can affect mobility, reach, hand grip, strength, stamina, vision, hearing, sense of smell and tactile and thermal touch. The ability to function independently may be a major factor in determining whether a person is able to remain at home in spite of temporary or permanent disabilities.

The kitchen is considered by older adults to be the most important room in the house because of its role in independent living. The ability to cook is an instrumental activity of daily living that may help an older person remain independent. Older Americans want, need and are willing to pay for products and services that afford them convenience, dignity and independence.

Kitchen design that facilitates aging in place involves new ideas, as well as long-standing, but underutilized practices and products. Kitchen designers can play a key role as change agents in diffusing those new and old ideas because of their mediator role between (a) developers of innovative features and products, and (b) the consumer.

In planning new homes and remodeled kitchens for mature clients, designers can incorporate and encourage the inclusion of features that respond to the user's decreasing physical capabilities. The resulting environments will therefore compensate for age-related changes and optimize independence and safety.

What are the typical physical limits faced by aging persons? An aging person's surroundings become progressively more important as they become less able to tolerate demands from their environment. Age-related changes that create special needs relevant to kitchen design include normal declines in strength, reaction time, sense of balance and sensory perception. Furthermore, the debilitating affects of specific diseases or chronic conditions affect the functional ability of a large percentage of older people.

Specific conditions that directly affect the use of the kitchen and that are most common among the elderly are arthritis, sensory impairments, heart conditions and orthopedic impairments.

The overall objective in kitchen planning for aging in place includes anthro-

pometrically designed work and rest areas, reduced safety hazard and increased environmental cues.

Kitchen design features can provide a prosthetic or an accommodating environment for mature adults and their potential, perhaps multiple, physical impairments.

RECOMMENDATIONS

Design recommendations for mature clients' kitchens:

Appliances/Fixtures

- Side-by-side refrigerators, or bottom freezer models provide ideal access to both sections of the appliance.

- In-door ice/water dispensers and automatic icemakers simplify tasks.

- Self-cleaning ovens minimize cleaning chores. A separate cooktop and oven accommodate height differences.

- Electric ranges, rather than open flame gas ranges.

- Controls for ranges and cooktops placed at the front of the appliance provide easy access.

- Side hinged oven doors (models are limited to date) facilitate access to oven interior.

- Microwave oven placement at counter level make it easy for the user to look in to the appliance and down on the food, and move products in and out of the oven.

- Double-bowl sinks (equal sized or a large/small configuration) and faucets with lever type handles and scald-guard protection engineering keep the sink center organized and safe.

- A food waste disposer that is a batch feed-type appliance, with an easy-to-handle control lid. (A batch feed disposer is operated when the lid is placed in the drain. However, some models are difficult to manage because of the intricate twist and pull half-stop position required to activate the disposer. This requires great dexterity and a firm grip, that maturing users may not have. Conversely, a disposer operated by a switch on the wall offers no protection against utensils accidentally falling in the disposer while it's in operation.)

- Easy to read numbers on controls.

- Controls that are easy to manipulate during use and easy to remove and replace during cleaning activities are highly recommended.

Shape of the Kitchen

Although research suggests an L-shaped arrangement is ideal, the **Certified Kitchen Designers** polled recommended a U-shape or an L- shape with an island, more than a straight L assembly.

Lowering the countertop to accommodate existing or potential physical requirements of the client was recommended by the professionals surveyed.

Cabinet Arrangement

- A great majority of the **Certified Kitchen Designers** recommended lower than standard wall cabinets for older cooks.

- C-shaped door and handle pulls were recommended on cabinets to maximize flexibility.

- Interior storage systems, such as divider drawers, roll-out shelves and tray dividers are oftentimes suggested for maturing clients to provide clear accessibility and easy retrieval of items stored in cabinets.

- A seated working area at a sink or in the preparation area is also highly recommended for an aging consumer.

Visibility Restrictions

Our eyes begin to change in our mid-40s. The lenses start to thicken and become yellow. The surface becomes less even. The pupil becomes smaller, and the muscles that control its opening and closing become increasingly slow to respond. In addition, the yellow film that forms over the eye with age tends to change color perception - for instance, light blue, pink and salmon, seen as very distinct shades through the eyes of a young client, may be hard to differentiate by the middle-aged and older consumer, just as black, gray, dark blue and brown begin to seem increasingly similar.

- Contrasting colors for countertop edges, electrical outlets and sinks were suggested to compensate for low vision aging traits.

- Include higher general lighting levels.

- Increase task lighting above the work surfaces.

- Matte finishes on surfaces, rather than shiny.

Flooring

- One-third of the **CKDs** suggested non-slip carpeting for older clients. This makes sense to insure comfort and to minimize breakage of items that may be dropped a bit more often than with younger clients.

- Loose area rugs are never recommended on a floor surface where a mature client might accidentally stumble.

Conclusions

In conclusion, the authors of the study noted that this research focused on kitchen design that responded to declining physical abilities. An alternative approach is that of planning kitchens that increase older people's abilities. Future research could investigate design features that both accommodate age re-

lated changes and stimulate older people to greater productivity and enjoyment of the kitchen. More study of innovative products that are both prosthetic and fun to use is also needed.

THE CONCEPT OF UNIVERSAL DESIGN

Additionally, although design to meet the special needs of older people may be an appropriate step, the authors stressed that the best goal ultimately may be universal or adaptable design.

Instead of labeling people as "special" or incorporating non-standard features, universal or life-span design addresses the needs of persons of all ages and functional levels. Thus, no group is stigmatized and the products appeal to a wider market.

Barrier-free or universal design is a planning concept where safety is of paramount importance and no technological or physical barriers are placed in front of the user as they attempt to work in the space. In kitchen planning, this means the room must be safe for children as well as mature adults. The planning considerations suggested by the **CKDs** make sense for all of us.

Controls that are easy to operate, food waste disposers that will not accidentally grind up a spoon, a place to be seated when one works - these are important considerations for the 6-year-old helping mom, or a busy single cooking dinner after a long day, as well as a mature adult.

FURTHER READING SUGGESTIONS

For an indepth examination of universal kitchen planning, refer to **NKBA's**

Universal Kitchen Planning, Design That Adapts To People, written by **Mary Jo Peterson**, CKD, CBD, CHE, and **Enabling Products Sourcebook 2**, written by **ProMature Group** and published by NKBA. Contact NKBA, 687 Willow Grove Street, Hackettstown, NJ. 07840

The authors of the survey quoted are as follows:

- **B. S. Guetzko**
  Charleston School of Art & Design
  University of Charleston
  Charleston, West Virginia 25304

- **Betty Jo White**
  Department of Clothing, Textiles and Interior Design
  Kansas State University
  Manhattan, Kansas 66506

Other published sources on this subject are:

- Whirlpool Information Service, **Designs for Independent Living** and, **Kitchen and Laundry Designs for Disabled Persons**. The Whirlpool Corporation, Benton Harbor, Michigan

- **Wanda Olson**, University of Minnesota Extension Service, University of Minnesota Design, Housing and Apparel, 240 McNeal Hall, 1985 Buford Ave., St. Paul, Minnesota 55108

- **Betty Raschko, Housing Interiors for the Disabled and Elderly**. 115 Fifth Ave., NY, NY 10003 Van Nostrand Reinhold Co., Inc.

- Department of Housing and Urban Development, **Adaptable Housing: A Technical Manual for Implementing Adaptable Dwelling Units Specifications**. Washington, D.C., U.S. Government Printing Office

SECTION **3**

Typical Planning Dimensions

ALLOCATING SPACE FOR APPLIANCES

The space you allot for the sink and appliances is variable. Below is a listing of typical sizes:

- **Double-bowl sinks** may be from 33" to 42" (84cm to 107cm) wide. 33" wide by 22" (84cm x 56cm) deep is fairly typical.

- **Single-bowl sinks** may be 24" to 30" (61cm to 76cm) wide. 24" (61cm) wide by 22" (56cm) deep is standard. Round sinks are typically 18" (46cm) in diameter. Round sinks always have a smaller interior space than square sinks.

- **Dishwashers** are nearly all 24" (61cm) wide. Compact dishwashers are available 18" (46cm) wide. European models range in width between 18" and 24" (46cm and 61cm) and are often available as countertop models.

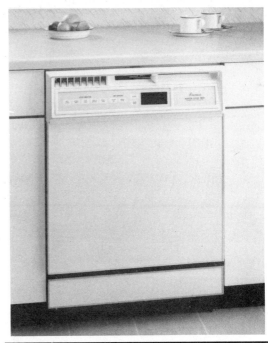

Figure 182 (Courtesy of Amana) Built-in, full-sized dishwashers.

Figure 181 Stainless steel sinks are popular in kitchens.

- **Trash compactors** are typically available in 12", 15" or 18" wide (30cm, 38cm or 46cm).

Figure 183 (Courtesy of KitchenAid Inc.) Trash compactors are available in three sizes.

Figure 184 (Courtesy of General Electric) Refrigerators may be boxed in, as we see in this example, or can be totally built-in.

- **Free-standing refrigerators** typically are 30", 32" or 35-3/4" (76cm, 81cm, 91cm) wide. Always work to the next 3" (7.6cm) incremental size to plan a refrigerator space. Many planners leave a 36" to 39" (91cm to 99cm) wide space, regardless of the size of refrigerator planned, so that a bigger appliance owned by future families can be accommodated in the enclosure.

- **Built-in refrigerators** are typically available in 30", 36", 42" and 48" (76cm, 91cm, 107cm and 122cm) wide. They are often taller - 84" (213cm) high is common. A major difference between built-in and free-standing appliances is the depth: free-standing refrigerators are often as much as 32" (81cm) deep, built-in models are 24" (61cm) deep and are designed

to be totally integrated into the cabinetry.

- **Domestic Cooktops** can take from 30" to 36" (76cm to 91cm) of counter space on an average. There are triple cooktops that require up to 48" (122cm) of space - or more and single units that require only 18" (46cm) of space. Many European models are 24" to 30" (61cm to 76cm) wide.

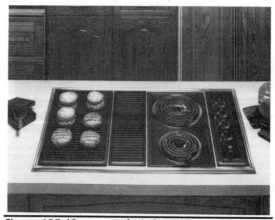

Figure 185 (Courtesy of KitchenAid Inc.) Electric cooktops come in a wide variety of sizes. Proximity ventilation systems change their dimensions as well.

Figure 186 (Courtesy of KitchenAid Inc.) Gas cooktops are also available in different sizes and configurations.

- **Built-in ovens** are from 22" to 30" (56 to 76cm) wide. This can be tricky. The built-in oven's overall size and cutout size must both be considered when planning cabinets for the appliance. Most appliances have a "flange" designed to fit against or "lip over" the frame of the cabinet, which means that the actual dimension that slips into the cabinet is smaller than the overall dimension. Always verify, via the appliance literature, what size cabinet must be ordered to accommodate the oven.

- Most **free-standing or drop-in residential ranges** are 30" (76cm) wide. Residentially approved commercial equipment is also available in free-standing ranges. These appliances are deeper and wider than typical units. Verify the actual size with the manufacturer before designing a kitchen featuring one of these appliances.

Figure 187(Courtesy of Whirlpool Corporation) Built-in ovens are available in single and double units.

Figure 188 (Courtesy of KitchenAid Inc.) Most drop-in or free-standing ranges are 30" (76cm) wide.

Needless to say, appliances require a great deal of attention in the kitchen plan. In the '40s, three appliances were typical in most kitchens. Today, the average kitchen has six. You cannot successfully plan a kitchen unless you know the appliances the client wishes to include. If you don't have this information, always list the space allocation that you're planning for that appliance so your clients will know what overall dimensional limitations they should work within as they make their final selection. *Why is this so important?* Remember, compactors come in three sizes (12", 15" and 18") (30cm, 38cm and 46cm) wide, therefore you need to note on your plan "12" (30cm) wide compactor space allowed" to make sure your client doesn't buy an 18" (46cm) wide unit and then blame you for the miss-fit.

Figure 189 This kitchen features a full appliance compliment: built-in refrigerator, microwave oven, trash compactor, double sink and dishwasher. Note the side-by-side placement of the built-in ovens on the right side of the kitchen.

BUILDING ELEMENTS

When planning kitchen spaces, you should remember the following dimensions:

- Standard doors are 6'-8" (80") (203.2cm) high. You must have at least one 2'-10" (86.36cm) to 3'-0" (91.44cm) door leading to a kitchen that provides a clear 32" (81.28cm) walkway space to meet today's barrier-free planning guidelines. This may not be possible in a renovation plan, but it is a critical design element in a well-planned new kitchen of the future which will accommodate users of varying physical capabilities.

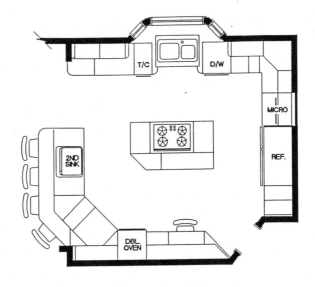

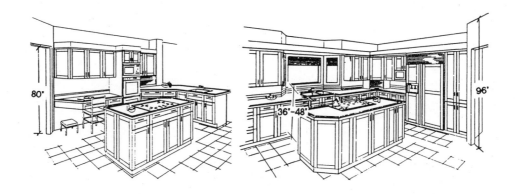

Figure 190   Standard door heights are 6' 8" (80") (203.2cm). The overall casing must be added to that dimension. Typical windows in the kitchen can be anywhere from 36" (91.44cm) to 48" (121.92cm) off the floor. They generally will also finish at 80" (203.2cm) off the floor. The standard kitchen ceiling height is 96" (243.84cm).

- Typical windows in kitchens can be anywhere from 36" (91.44cm) to 48" (121.92cm) off the floor. Their width can vary from 24" (60.96cm) to 84" (213.36cm). They generally also finish 80" (203.2cm) off the floor.

- The standard kitchen ceiling height is 96" (243.84cm). However, you will oftentimes find 109" (276.86cm) or 120" (304.8cm) high ceilings in both renovation work and new construction.

FURNITURE DIMENSIONS

Kitchens today are socializing spaces, which means that the kitchen may include furniture pieces. The following charts are in 1/4" and 1/2" scale and include normal dining and living room furniture dimensions. You may want to photocopy these and have them laminated to create furniture templates.

Alternatively, many drafting, art stores or university bookstores include furniture templates in 1/4" and 1/2" scales to be used for this purpose.

A good kitchen designer never lays out a space that includes furniture without also dimensioning these individual pieces. Don't just concentrate on the corner of the room that features the kitchen. Remember, you're designing a complete living environment, not just a work laboratory. Get those furniture sizes right so that you'll know that the entire room will flow efficiently and attractively.

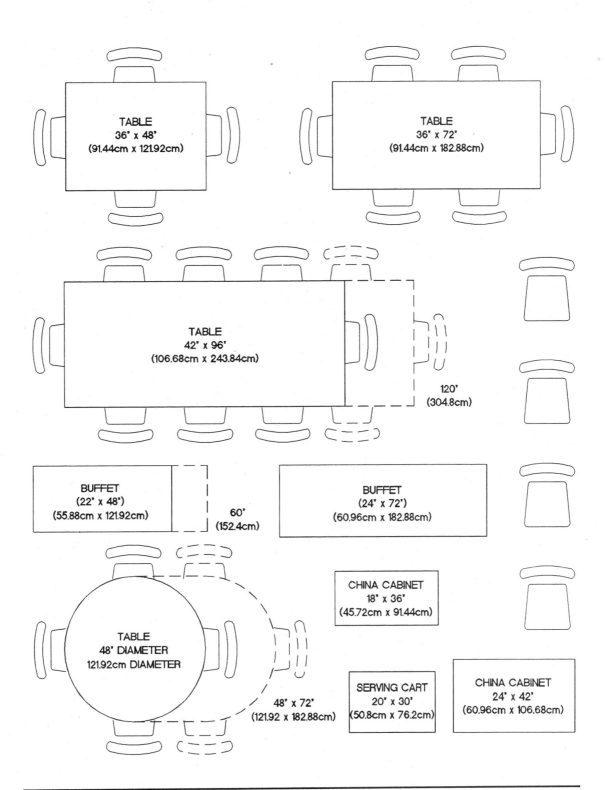

Figure 191 Typical dining room furniture dimensions.

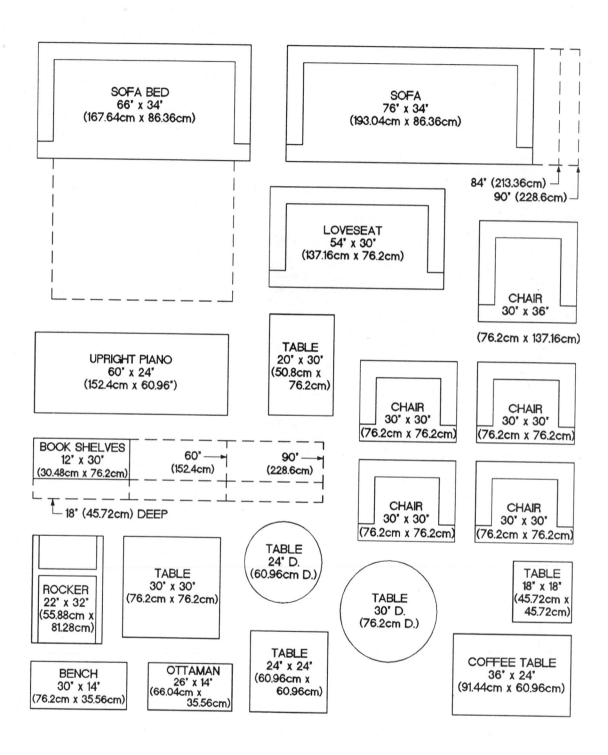

Figure 192 Typical living room furniture dimensions.

SECTION 4

Human Ergonomic Considerations

THE HUMAN FIGURE

You will need to consider human anatomy standards as you begin the kitchen planning process.

Many designers mistakenly assume that carefully calculating spatial limits to accommodate cooks as they work is an easy task to accomplish. In a recent survey conducted by the **University of Minnesota** for the **National Kitchen & Bath Association**, 102 families were asked if they were surprised about the finished room or dissatisfied with any elements of the space. 58% of those surveyed would have changed something about that room, or found that it was different than they anticipated.

An unusually high number of the complaints surrounded simple ergonomic considerations: walkways that weren't wide enough for two people, an eating space that didn't accommodate the grandchildren, cabinet doors that hit one another, or appliances that were not strategically placed.

To make sure that you don't make these types of planning errors, never compromise on these basic clearance dimensions. If your client has a hard time visualizing the dimensions that you are suggesting, use a showroom display and your tape measure to realistically show them the amount of room you are planning. This will help them to more clearly see the layout and sense how it will "feel" when they begin working in their new kitchen.

Reaching Limits

Researchers judge the efficiency of a kitchen plan by measuring how much energy is consumed by the cook when completing tasks in the kitchen, as well as how long it takes to complete a task. When the cook is forced to reach, bend, stoop or twist to the outer limits of recommended maximums, unnecessary body energy is required to complete the activity. These outer limits were determined by a 1951 study entitled *"Oxygen Consumed for Household Tasks"*. The study determined how much energy was required for the following tasks:

- Reaching up with the arms to three heights above the floor: 46", 56" and 72" (116.84cm, 142.24cm, 182.88cm).

- Reaching down by trunk bend to two heights above the floor: 22" and 3" (55.88cm and 7.62cm).

- Reaching down by knee bend to 3" (7.62cm) above the floor.

- Stepping up 7" (17.78cm) above the floor.

- Pivoting the body with arms extended at a height of 36" (91.44cm) above the floor.

The study measured the physiological energy expended for these different tasks. Oxygen intake was used as a yardstick because of its part in the body's energy cycle.

The conclusions of the study were as follows:

- Reaching up with the arms required less energy than bending the body.

- Energy consumption was directly related to the height and stretch required for the reach.

- Reaching down to 3" (7.62cm) above the floor by a trunk bend required less energy than reaching by a knee bend. **Be forewarned** - physicians always recommend stooping down by knee bends to limit body strain.

Ideal Storage Area

This study tells us that the most frequently used items in the kitchen for standing cooks should be stored between 22" (55.88cm) off the floor and 56" (142.24cm) off the floor. The top shelf in a base cabinet, the drawer, the countertop and the lower shelf in a wall cabinet normally fall within this height spectrum. Because of this dimensional recommendation, once all the countertop requirements are met, many designers plan tall, floor-to-ceiling or floor to soffit cabinets that provide adjustable shelving throughout the entire elevation This will maximize the storage potential by keeping this key area easy to access.

PLANNING PRINCIPLES

When planning a kitchen, the designer must consider the homeowner's available time and energy level. To make sure the tasks performed can be completed in the least amount of time, using the least amount of energy, three guiding principles should be followed:

- Build the cabinets to fit the cook.

- Build the shelves to fit the supplies.

- Build the kitchen to fit the family.

Building the Cabinets to Fit the Cook

Before you can "build the cabinet to fit the cook" you need to be familiar with motion and energy data available. Think vertically!

FUNCTIONAL LIMITS

Reaching: To determine the functional limits of storage areas, work curves were drawn for 300 women, ranging in height from 4'-10" to 6'-0", (147.32cm to 182.88cm) at **Cornell University**. The maximum composite, shoulder-to-grasping, fingertip reach of the individuals in the middle group (5'-3" to 5'-7") (160.02cm to 170.18cm) established 79.6" (202.18cm) as the highest comfortable overhead reach, free from obstruction. When the user was forced to reach over a 25" (63.5cm) deep counter surface, the maximum top shelf height was reduced to 69" (175.26cm). 24" (60.96cm) off the floor was identified as the lowest point or fingertip level from the floor.

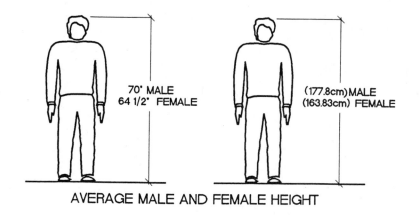

AVERAGE MALE AND FEMALE HEIGHT

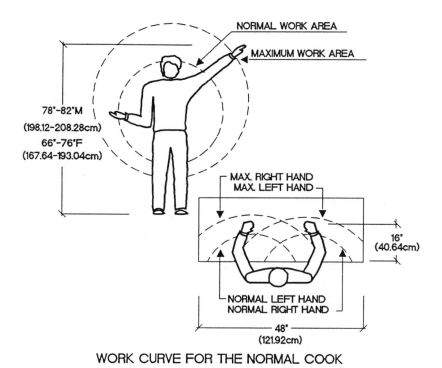

WORK CURVE FOR THE NORMAL COOK

Figure 193 Typical reaching capabilities for a standing person.

According to the Center of Universal Design, the average person that remains seated to work in a kitchen has a forward reach range of 15" to 48" (38.1cm to 121.92cm) off the floor. When the user is forced to reach over a 20" (50.8cm) deep counter surface, the maximum top shelf height is reduced to 44" (111.76cm). For a seat position reaching to the side, the range is 15" - 54" (38.1cm to 137.16cm). If the counter/obstruction is more than 10" (25.4cm) deep the top shelf height is reduced to 46" (116.84cm).

A person using crutches or a walker will have trouble reaching very high or very low. The lower reach range is 15" to 24" (38.1cm to 60.96cm) off the floor and the upper reach range is 69" to 72" (175.26cm to 182.88cm).

Combining the reach range for standing, seated and standing mobility-impaired individuals results in a suggested universal reach range of 15" to 48" (38.1cm to 121.92cm).

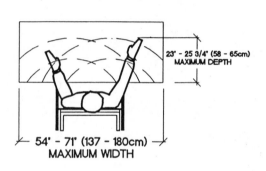

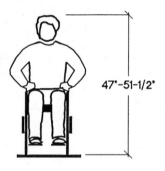

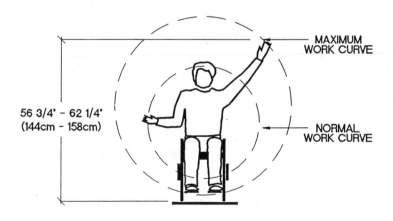

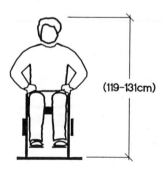

Figure 194 Typical reaching capabilities for a seated person.

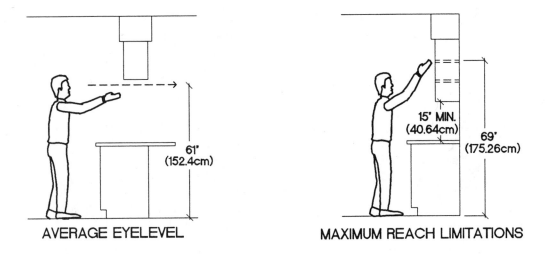

AVERAGE EYELEVEL   MAXIMUM REACH LIMITATIONS

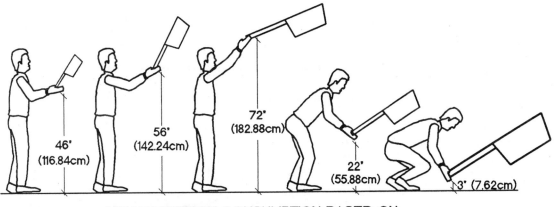

HUMAN ENERGY CONSUMPTION BASED ON
REACHING AND BENDING ACTIVITIES
(SIZE OF PAN INDICATES AMOUNT
OF ENERRGY CONSUMED)

Figure 195 Typical reaching capabilities.

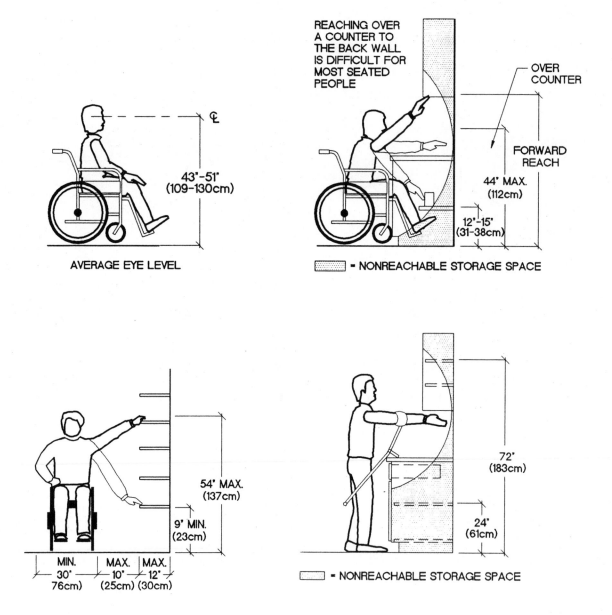

Figure 196 Typical reaching capabilities for mobility-impaired individual.

Eye Level: In another survey, the researchers measured the eye level of 562 standing people. The average eye level for a standing person was 61" (154.94cm) off the floor. The dimensions varied from 54" to 69" (137.16cm to 175.26cm), but 72% of those studied were included in the 59" to 63" (160.02) range. Typically, a person's eye level will be 3" (7.62cm) below their overall height. According to **Architectural Graphic Standards**, the average eye level of a seated person is 43" to 51" (109.22cm to 129.54cm).

Countertop Width: The survey determined that 48" (121.92cm) was the widest side-to-side reach for a typical standing user. For a seated user the side-to-side reach was determined to be 54" to 71" (137.16cm to 180.34cm).

Countertop Depth: The study determined the normal work curve, or elbow circle, had a maximum depth of 16". This means that when the cook sits/stands in front of a standard 24" (60.96cm) deep countertop surface, what he/she uses is the first 16" (40.64cm) of work space to spread out supplies or food stuffs. The balance of the countertop is typically used for storage containers or items that the cook needs that can be out of reach, for example, a cookbook on a rack.

Countertop Height: The industry countertop standard height is 36" to 37" (91.44 to 93.98cm) off the floor. This generally is maintained to accommodate free-standing or under-counter appliances. However, to accommodate universal criteria, you should incorporate a lowered or raised countertop surface for beating, chopping and stirring operations. One counter should be between 28" to 36" (71cm to 91cm) above the finished floor and the other should be between 36" to 45" (91cm to 114cm) above the finished floor. These activities are normally associated with the preparation center. Therefore, it may be ideal to lower one section of the counter surface in the preparation area. Another approach is to lower the counter area where the cooktop is located. This makes it much easier for the cook to reach over the pots and pans, look into the pot and stir the contents.

This special countertop consideration should be planned because of the vital importance good posture plays in avoiding strain, limiting fatigue and minimizing energy expenditure during normal kitchen activities.

A good standing posture is one where the head, neck, chest and abdomen are balanced vertically, one upon the other, so that the body's weight is carried mainly by the bony framework, placing a minimum of effort and strain upon the muscles and ligaments. Good posture is possible only when the height of the working surface is adjusted to fit the physique of the worker.

To determine the proper counter surface height for these processes, ask your client to stand erect with elbows flexed. The ideal countertop height will be 2" to 3" (5.08cm to 7.62cm) below the floor-to-elbow dimension of the user. The correct mixing counter for baking type activities will be 5" (12.7cm) below that dimension. By adjusting the countertop height, you will allow the cook to work without raising his/her arm above the elbow, and without stooping over the counter surface.

For seated users, **American National Standards Institute (ANSI)**, recommends 28" to 34" (71cm to 86cm) high counters. If you start with 27" to 29" (69cm to 74cm) high knee space (as per ANSI), add 1 1/2" (4cm) for an apron panel to hide support for the counter over a knee space, and 1 1/2" (4cm) for the thickness of the counter, this places the counter height at 30" to 32" (76cm to 81cm) which is comfortable and workable for most seated users.

PASSAGEWAY CLEARANCES

Doorway Requirements

Typical North American building practices have led to a standard 3'-0" (91.44cm) by 6'-8" (203.2cm) door being used as an entry door to the house - the front door, the back door, the garage door. Interior doors can be as small as 2'-0" (60.96cm) by 6'-8" (203.2cm) leading into a bathroom, or a 2'-6" (76.2cm) by 6'-8" (203.2cm) leading into a kitchen.

As you will remember, we discussed the concept of universal design in the introduction of this volume. Based on standards established by **ANSI A117.1** (1986), the **Uniform Federal Accessibility Standard (UFAS)** and the **National Institute for Disability and**

Rehabilitation Research Building Codes, specify a minimum 32" (81.28cm) wide door opening leading to the kitchen. This means that there is at least 32" (81.28cm) of space between the face of the door and the door stop when the door is standing open 90 degrees. A 2'-10" (86.36cm) door or 3'-0" (91.44cm) door is required to provide this 32" (81.28cm) opening.

This door opening width will permit a person using a wheelchair, walker or crutches to pass through without striking the door, door frame or door hardware.

Traditionally, the built environment has been designed for an idealized, able-bodied, non-elderly adult. Since that description fits less than 15% of our population, the result is environments, including kitchens, which create handicaps or barriers for the rest of us.

Because of the existing housing inventory in North America, you may not be able to meet this criteria in some cases. However, if the project includes any construction changes, suggest that your client widen the entry door to the kitchen.

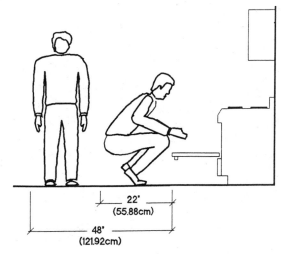

AVERAGE FLOOR SPACE REQUIRED
FOR PERSON TO BEND OVER BY KNEE BEND

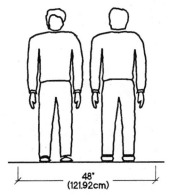

AVERAGE WALKWAY CLEARANCE FOR
TWO PEOPLE PASSING PARALLEL TO
ONE ANOTHER

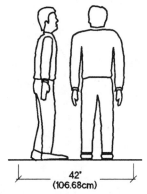

AVERAGE WALKWAY CLEARANCE FOR
TWO PEOPLE PASSING PERPENDICULAR
TO ONE ANOTHER

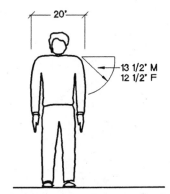

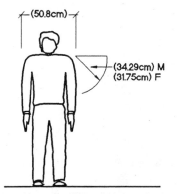

AVERAGE FEMALE AND MALE SHOULDER AND ELBOW DIMENSION

Figure 197   Typical clearance dimensions for a standing person.

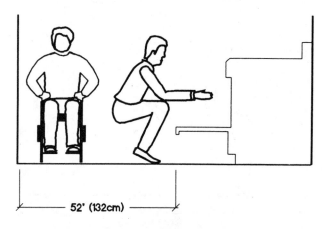

AVERAGE FLOOR SPACE REQUIRED FOR A
WHEELCHAIR USER TO PASS BEHIND A PERSON BENDING

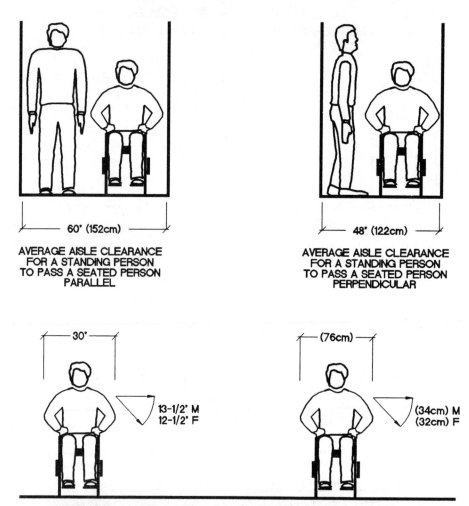

AVERAGE AISLE CLEARANCE
FOR A STANDING PERSON
TO PASS A SEATED PERSON
PARALLEL

AVERAGE AISLE CLEARANCE
FOR A STANDING PERSON
TO PASS A SEATED PERSON
PERPENDICULAR

AVERAGE REQUIREMENT FOR MALE AND FEMALE ELBOW CLEARANCE

Figure 198   Typical clearance dimensions for a seated person.

Corner-to-Corner Cabinet Clearances

This same clearance request applies to cabinets opposite one another as a person enters the kitchen. A minimum clearance of 32" (81.28cm) wide and not more than 24" (60.96cm) deep in the direction of travel must be maintained between any obstacles or barriers within the kitchen.

Work/Walk Aisles

For years, designers have followed a practical, minimum clearance dimension of 42" (106.68cm) between cabinets or appliances to provide adequate work aisle clearance. New research suggests that differentiating between a walkway space and a work aisle makes sense. Additionally, different walkway clearance dimensions are required for a kitchen planned for one cook and one designed for multiple cooks.

Recent research has indicated the following minimum dimensions for walkways and work aisles.

- **Walkway - One Cook:** 36" (91.44cm) between vertical objects from countertop edge to countertop edge required in a walkway which is not an aisle in front of a major kitchen center of activity.

- **Work Aisle - One Cook:** 42" (106.68cm) of clearance between vertical objects in a work aisle that provides passage space immediately in front of a work counter or appliance.

- **Work Aisle - Two Cooks:** The work aisle dimension of 42" (106.68cm) increases to a minimum of 48" (121.92cm) if two people typically pass one another in that space while sharing kitchen responsibilities.

DINING AREAS IN THE KITCHEN

Almost all kitchens today include some type of dining area. Whether it is a cozy area for two, or a large country table for eight, eating often takes place in the kitchen. The family may eat their breakfast on the run or may serve most family dinners in the kitchen. Therefore, before planning any kitchen dining space, you need to determine how many people will be seated and at what meals.

You then can consider many of the different types of seating arrangements that you may suggest.

Seating Arrangements

TABLE HEIGHT COUNTER

A counter may be 28" to 30" (71.12cm to 76.2cm) high. If so, it will require a chair that has an 18" high seat. Allow 19" (48.26cm) of leg room underneath the overhang.

This type of counter is ideal for small children or elderly family members because standard height chairs are used. Therefore, it's easy for everyone to maneuver in and out of the chairs. It also provides a working counter surface which allows a family member to sit while completing a task in a chair. The disadvantage to this type of counter is that it does not provide an extension of standard 36" (91.44cm) high work space. It may also require support underneath the counter because it is generally attached at the back of standard cabinetry.

Various types of counter surfaces require specific support clearances. A general rule of thumb is that a support bracket (corbel) should be spaced every 36" (91.44cm). This bracket may be a decorative, triangular shaped, or simply an L-shaped metal support. Alternatively, this type of counter may be supported with a table base that extends from the underside of the counter to the floor. The disadvantage to this approach is that it interferes with complete flexibility along the counter. You may be able to make this floor support a design feature in the space. Be creative!

STANDARD HEIGHT COUNTER

The standard 36" (91.44cm) high work counter can be extended beyond the last cabinet to provide a casual dining area. This type of counter is used with a stool that has a seat 24" (60.96cm) off the floor. The stool should have a foot rest 6" to 8" from the floor. At least 15" (38.1cm) of knee space must be planned for this type of overhang.

This type of overhang is ideal in a small kitchen where the eating area needs to double as standing work space. A counter can stretch behind an island or be part of an L-shaped return. If a countertop extension is placed behind a cooking surface, make sure that there is 9" to 12" (22.86cm to 30.48cm) between the back of the cooktop and the beginning of this overhang so that people seated behind the appliance will not be in danger of being scalded or burned by spatters.

RAISED HEIGHT COUNTER

A counter 42" (106.68cm) high with a stool seat 30" to 32" (76.2cm to 81.28cm) high is also a typical solution in a kitchen. The stool should have a footrest 18" (45.72cm) from the seat. There should be at least 12" (30.48cm) of knee space. Make sure that you or your clients check the seat height when shopping for stools for this counter. Many are designed for home bars, which are taller than a 42" (106.68cm) high eating counter and will not be comfortable for dining. Avoid this type of eating arrangement if at all possible in a kitchen planned for a family with small children or elderly family members.

The advantage to this type of eating bar is that the stepped-up height can conceal some of the normal kitchen clutter. The disadvantage is that its use is limited to a counter for dining and as a shield.

ATTACHED TABLE

If your client is interested in a seating space that "feels" like a free-standing table, a custom counter may be the answer for a small kitchen. You may create such a table by attaching a round, angled or free-form shape at the end of a counter, back of an island or against a wall. In tight spaces, suggest backless stools which can be stored underneath such a counter.

This type of custom table will allow people to be seated facing one another as opposed to adjacent to one another which is a more desirable arrangement for socializing.

BANQUETTE

Built-in tables with benches in an alcove require less space than free-standing tables and chairs. A banquette can be inconvenient for seating if family members continually leave and return to the table. If planned, use 22" (55.88cm) deep benches and plan space on the table end for a free-standing chair or wheelchair.

FREE-STANDING TABLE AND CHAIRS

Other dimensional requirements must be considered when a free-standing table and chairs are used. The most important thing to remember is that clearance must be provided all the way around the table. That means that a much larger space must be devoted to this area in the kitchen.

Typical table sizes that you will work with are as follows:

- Eight adults can sit comfortably, three on each side and one at each end, around a 40" x 72" (101.6cm x 182.88cm) table.

- The minimum size for six adults with two at each side and one at each end is 36" x 60" (91.44cm x 152.4cm).

- A 48" (121.92cm) round table will accommodate four to six people.

- A 42" (106.68cm) round table is the minimum for four people.

- Two people can be seated facing one another at a 36" x 36"

(91.44cm x 91.44cm) square or round table.

Space for Each Diner

For a kitchen with a seating area, a minimum space of 30" (76.2cm) wide and 19" (48.26cm) deep and at least 19" (48.26cm) of clear knee space is required for each diner.

Circulation Clearances

Regardless of the type of table arrangement selected, circulation clearances must be planned. These clearances are affected by whether the chair or stool has arms on it that prevent the chair from slipping all the way underneath the table. Additionally, whether room is only required for one person to push back his/her chair, stand and leave the table, as opposed to space for one person to pass behind a second seated diner affects the clearances as well.

- To allow room to pull out and return the chair when seating or rising, the recommended clearances are a minimum of 36" (91.44cm) from the counter/table to any wall or obstacle behind it. This dimension can only be used if the area will never serve as a walk space behind a seated diner.

- If space is required for a second person to walk behind the one that is seated, the recommended clearance is 65" (165.1cm) of space from the counter/table to any wall or obstacle behind it.

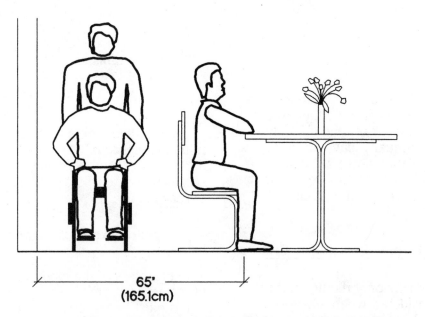

**RECOMMENDED CLEARANCE FOR
PERSON WALKING BEHIND SEATED DINER**

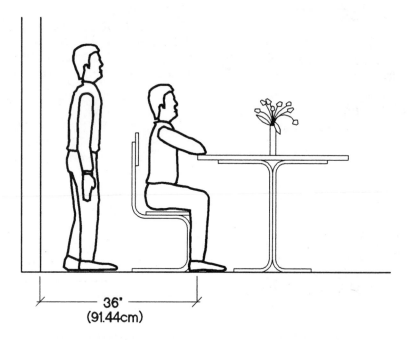

**RECOMMENDED CLEARANCE FROM
TABLE/COUNTER TO A WALL OR OBSTACLE**

*Figure 199   Typical Clearance Dimensions - Recommended clearances for walking behind seated diner
and from table/counter to wall or obstacle.*

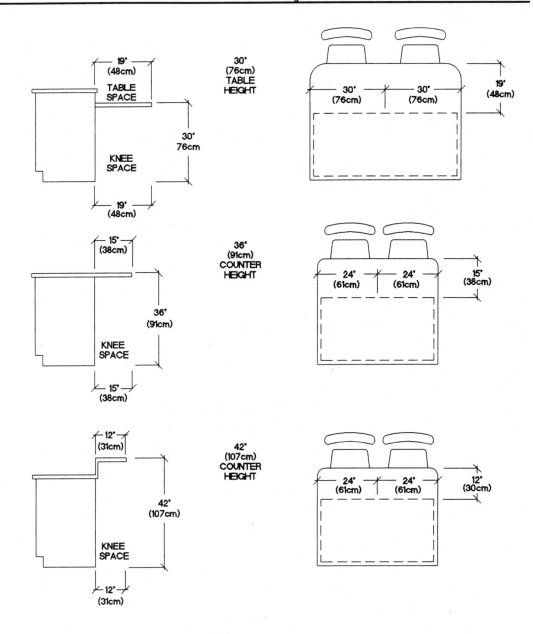

30" (76cm) HIGH TABLES/COUNTERS:
  allow a 30" (76cm) wide x 19" (48cm) deep counter/table space
  for each seated diner, and at least 19" (48cm) of clear knee space

36" (91cm) HIGH COUNTERS:
  allow a 24" (61cm) wide x 15" (38cm) deep counter space for
  each seated diner, and at least 15" (38cm) of clear knee space

42" (107cm) HIGH COUNTERS:
  allow a 24" (61cm) wide x 12" (30cm) deep counter space for
  each seated diner, and at least 12" (30cm) of clear knee space

Figure 200   Typical Clearance Dimensions - Knee space requirements.

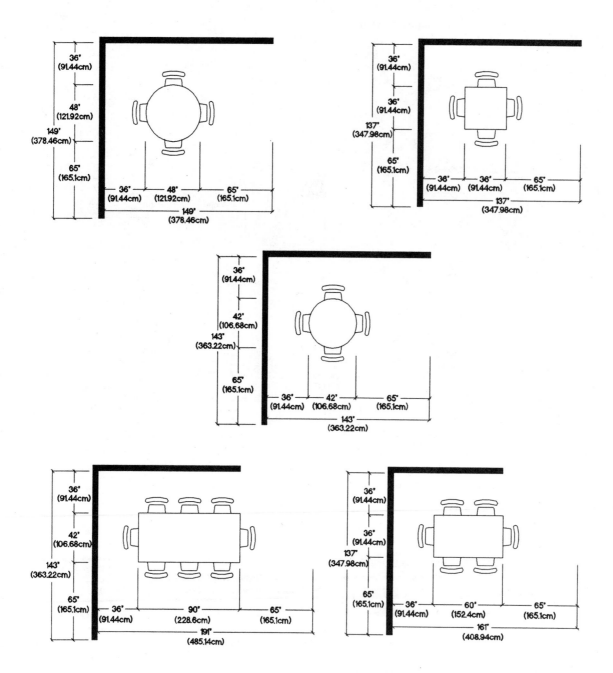

Figure 201   Typical Clearance Dimensions - Clearance dimensions around the table.

Figure 202   This kitchen features a 30" (76.2cm) high counter.

Figure 203 (Courtesy of Wood-Mode Inc.) 30" (76.2cm) high tables can be free-standing, a stretched bar arrangement or placed at the end of an island as we see here.

Figure 204   36" (91.44cm) high eating counters serve as extended working surfaces for standard cabinet arrangements.

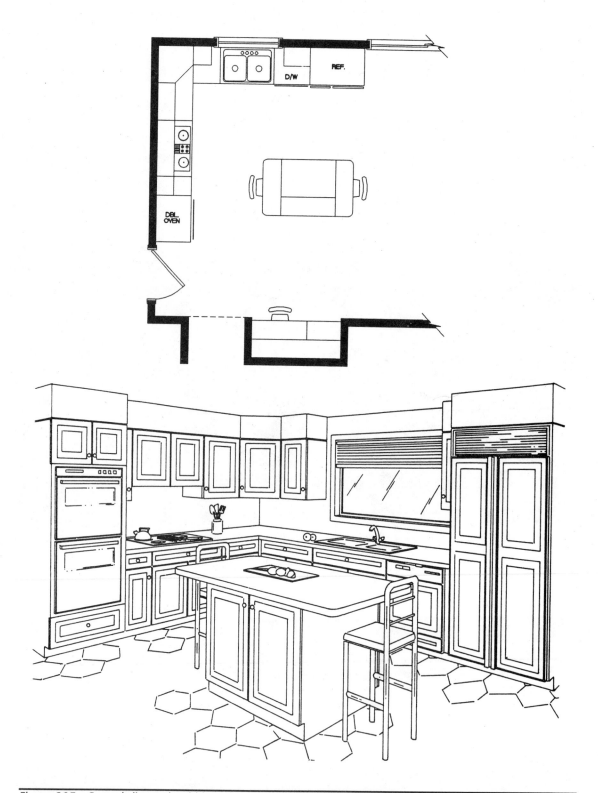

Figure 205   Seated diners should be able to see one another. In a small kitchen, consider placing a diner at each end of a small island.

Figure 206   A 42" (106.68cm) high raised counter conceals the kitchen clutter from view.

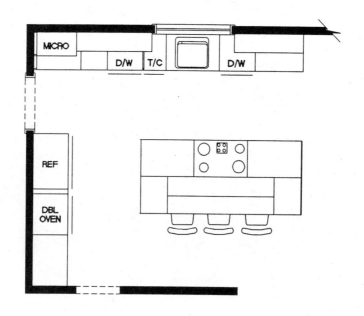

Figure 207 The 42" (106.68cm) high counter can wrap around an island or be located at the back of the island. Here the raised section is in the center of the island. Design continuity is maintained by repeating the door styling detail in this area.

Figure 208 (Courtesy of Heritage Custom Kitchens) A banquette may be an excellent way to accommodate the eating area.

A KITCHEN DESK

Many kitchen designs incorporate some sort of desk. It may be little more than a simple countertop with space for a telephone, or it might be an elaborate center that includes a computer.

Items typically found in a desk area include a substantial collection of cookbooks, recipe cards, coupons, assorted pens and pencils, telephone books, note pads and the telephone. Shelf space, drawer space and files are therefore appropriate to consider for this space.

If a computer is used in the center, special planning considerations should be taken. Although most computer systems contain the same component parts, sizes of equipment vary and must be measured before the work station is planned. When designing the center, in addition to space for the equipment, plan a work surface on at least one side of the computer system.

The CRT terminal (monitor) must be positioned to insure comfortable usage. For use while seated, a standard desk may be too high if the monitor will sit atop the CPU (central processing unit). A surface that is 26" (66.04cm) off the floor is considered ideal for this arrangement. A stand-up pedestal is typically 37" to 39" (93.98cm to 99.06cm) high. If the computer screen and keyboard are separated, the display screen should be placed near eye level so that the user need not go into contortions to see the screen.

Clearance requirements are a very important design consideration when planning a new or remodeling kitchen project.

As a designer you should pay careful attention to the critical ergonomic requirements. Minimum clearance recommendations should be followed in every design project.

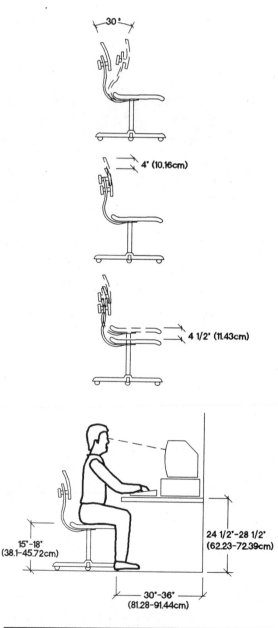

Figure 209 Dimensioning a desk with a computer.

Figure 210   (Courtesy of Wood-Mode Inc.) A shallow drawer below this desk surface stores pens and pencils. A cookbook collection or serving ware can be stored behind the glass doors.

Figure 211 (Courtesy of Wilsonart International) A desk can also serve as a room divider.

*Figure 212   (Courtesy of Heritage Custom Kitchens) Placing a desk in a small alcove and angling
shelves on both sides may increase the functionality of the space.*

SECTION 5

Kitchen Arrangement Considerations

Understanding the amount of space it takes for people to move throughout a kitchen is a good foundation for functional kitchen design. And you need to understand the relationship of the kitchen with the balance of the house. New home designs generally open the kitchen to the adjacent breakfast nook or nearby family room. Many renovation projects restructure a home's interior so that the kitchen is more open to adjacent socializing spaces as well.

As you study a plan for a new home or survey a kitchen to be remodeled, make sure that you ask your clients: *"Would you like the kitchen to remain a completely separate space, or would you enjoy it being open to the adjacent rooms?"*

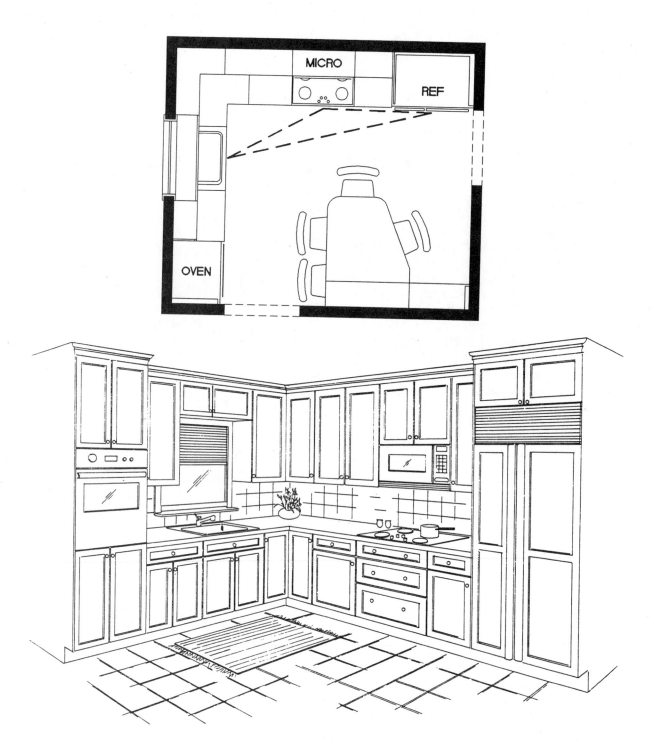

Figure 213 This small kitchen is completely separate from the balance of the house.

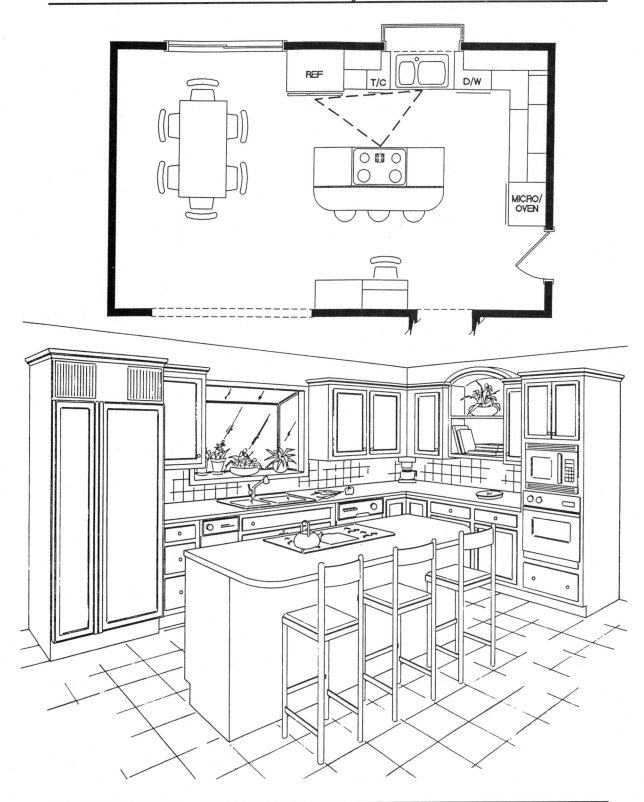

Figure 214 Many kitchens include a breakfast nook in their square footage.

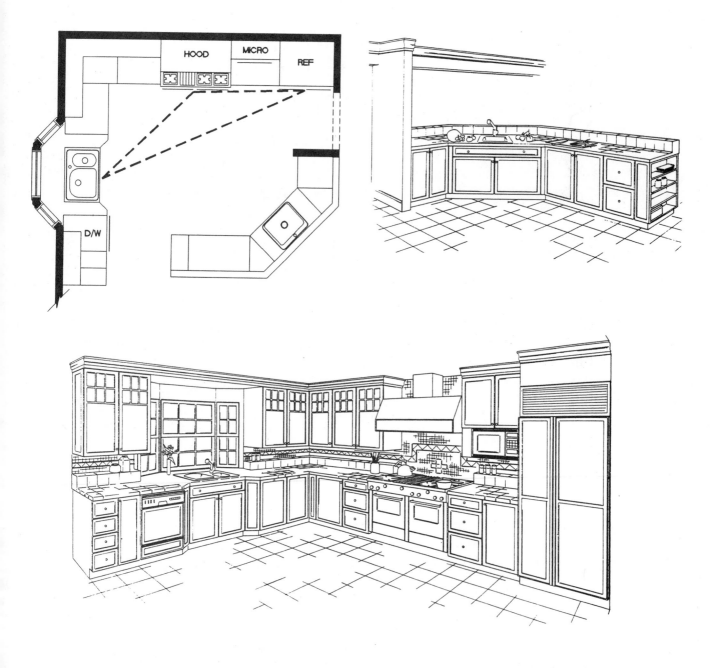

Figure 215 Open floor planning combines the casual family area, dining area and kitchen. Such a combination can be enhanced with a partial wall separating the kitchen work space from the adjacent living area, as we see with this angled peninsula.

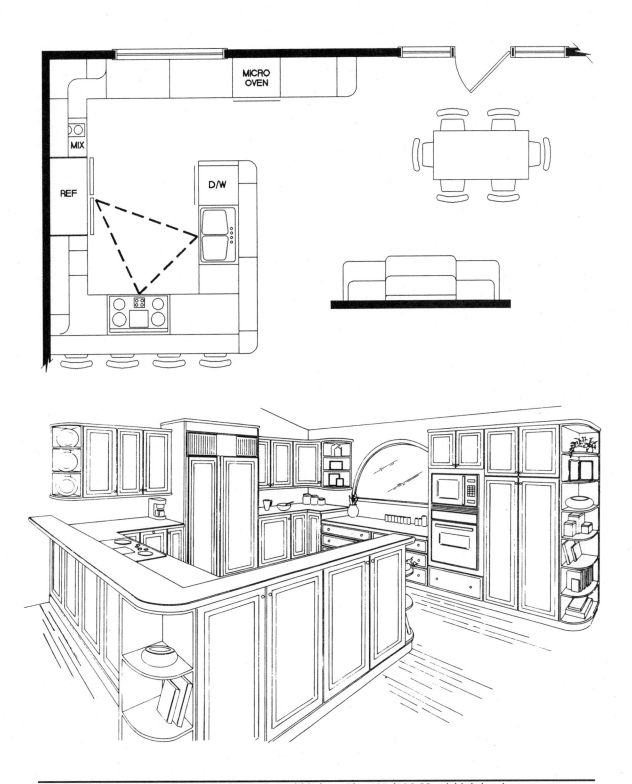

Figure 216 Two walls are open in this G-shaped kitchen. The 42" (106.68cm) high barrier protects seated diners from the cooking surface and shields the sink from full view.

THE WORK TRIANGLE

As you consider how you will arrange a kitchen, one way to judge the efficiency of your idea is to consider the "work triangle". During the 1950s, the **University of Illinois Small Homes Council** developed a method to evaluate the efficiency of a kitchen plan. A line was drawn from the center of the sink to the center of the cooking surface to the center of the refrigerator and then back to the sink. These three lines formed a "balanced triangle". The three points of the triangle identified major centers of activity within the kitchen. Typically, today's kitchens have more appliances and more centers. This has led to some experts questioning the appropriateness of the work triangle.

The research conducted by the **University of Minnesota** demonstrated that the concept of a triangle is still appropriate. However, you need to be prepared to stretch that triangle into a rectangle, or create two triangles in some kitchens.

Flexibility within the triangle shape is required because of the multiple centers that are found in many kitchens today. Today, the work triangle is between the refrigerator, primary food prep sink and primary cooking surface, measured from the center front of each.

The following size recommendations are suggested:

- Each leg of a triangle should be between 4' (121.92cm) and 9' (274.32cm) long.

- The total of all three legs of the triangle should be less than or equal to 26' (792.48cm).

- Family traffic patterns should not interfere with the primary triangle.

- Cabinetry should not intersect any one triangle leg by more than 12" (30.48cm).

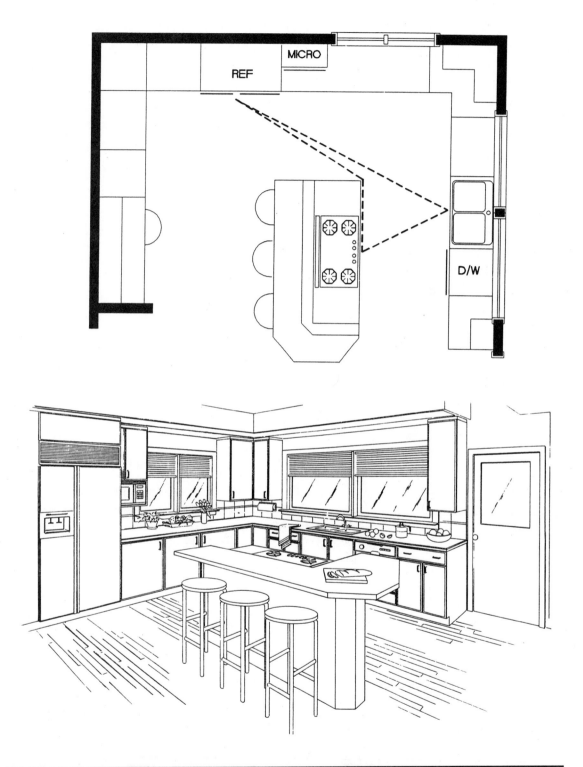

Figure 217 *The work triangle leads from the refrigerator to the sink, to the cooking surface. The micro-*
wave oven should generally be within that area for a one cook kitchen.

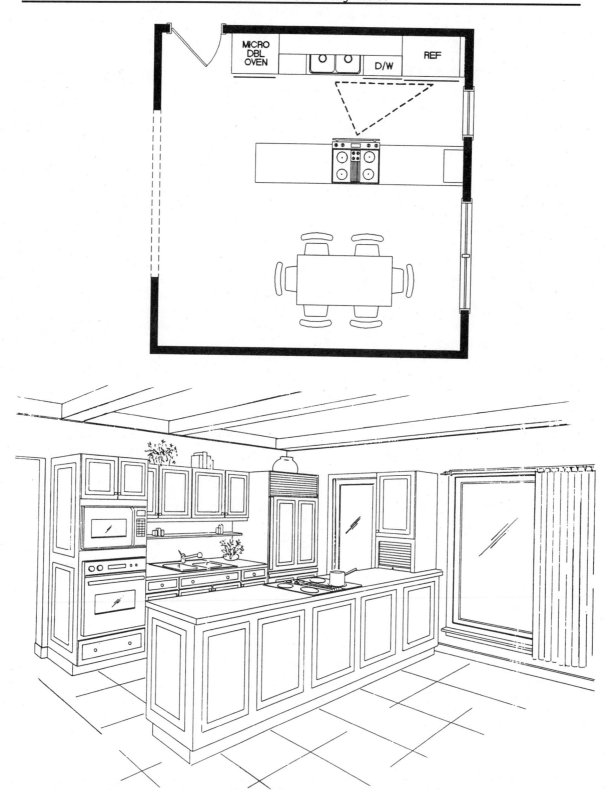

Figure 218 *The triangle is as important in a small kitchen as it is in a large one. In this corridor arrangement, the cook moves from the sink to the refrigerator to the range.*

CENTERS OF ACTIVITY

Types

Although the American kitchen evolved around three basic appliances; the sink, the range and the refrigerator, today's kitchen has many more centers of activity.

In a contemporary kitchen you may find some or all of the following areas:

- **Primary Clean-up Sink Center:** Houses the recycling center, dishwasher and food waste disposer.

- **Secondary Sink Center:** May serve clean-up functions as well. Generally associated with food preparation center.

- **Preparation Center:** Long, uninterrupted counter that may be placed between the sink and the cooking surface, or the sink and the refrigerator. In a kitchen for multiple cooks, there will be more than one preparation area.

- **Cooking Center:** Revolves around the cooking surface. Separate built-in oven need not be a part of this center unless it includes a microwave oven.

- **Microwave Oven Center:** Because of the frequency of use of this appliance, it must be near to the major areas of activity.

- **Pantry Center:** Many kitchen plans include floor-to-soffit or floor-to-ceiling tall storage cabinetry to store the food stuff maintained near the preparation area. This type of a tall cabinet may also be used in the serving or dining area.

- **Serving Center:** This storage area generally houses serving items. It may be in the kitchen or closer to the dining area.

- **Dining Center:** As stated before, typical kitchens include some sort of dining space.

- **Laundry Center:** Although the laundry area is often found in the basement or in the garage, it can also be located in the kitchen as well.

- **Home Office Center:** A space for the telephone, cookbooks and household records is an important part of the kitchen.

- **Media Center:** Many kitchens today include a radio and/or television. Locating this center so that it can be viewed by the cook and other family members in the space is an important consideration.

- **Socializing Center:** In the University of Minnesota survey, a surprising 69% of the time someone was in the kitchen with the cook, but not necessarily cooking. Visiting was as important as clean-up or culinary tasks. A casual furniture setting or an additional seating area so family members and friends can visit with the cook is an important concept.

Locating the Centers of Activity

The exact amount of counter space surrounding each one of these centers of activity will be discussed when we review the 40 Guidelines of Kitchen Planning. However, before you locate countertops, appliances or cabinets in your plan, it is important that you understand the relationship of these centers to one another.

THE COOK FOLLOWS A LOGICAL PATH

When work is being done in a kitchen, a logical path leads the cook from one work center to another. The efficiency of a kitchen plan is closely related to the amount of this travel.

Primary work centers should be arranged so that the amount of travel is reduced as much as possible. This type of space management will result in the least amount of effort or energy being expended by the cook or the cook's helpers.

Three major research projects have been conducted over the years to identify the ideal "food flow" throughout a residential kitchen space. One study, entitled *Motion Study of Kitchen Arrangements*, was conducted at **Cornell University** many years ago. In 1961, **Helen McCullough** and **Mary M. Farnham** continued the study in a research report entitled *Kitchens To Date*. In 1990, both the **National Kitchen & Bath Association** and the **University of Minnesota** again studied the arrangement of centers in kitchens today.

THE SINK IS THE MOST FREQUENTLY USED CENTER

The sink consistently has proven to be the most frequently used center of activity. Therefore, it should be located in the center of the cook's work path. Additionally, when feasible, a second sink should be included to minimize steps back and forth, or to provide a work station for an assistant chef or a clean-up helper. Indeed, in the NKBA research a full 25% of kitchens being planned today include a second sink.

THE PREPARATION CENTER LOCATION HAS SHIFTED

One change that has occurred from the early research to the most recent is the recommended location for the preparation center. Historically, this area was used for raw food assembly and was ideally located between the refrigerator and the sink. In kitchens today, the preparation center may be better located between the sink and the cooktop because less food assembly is being done, and more fresh food preparation and cooking is taking place at the surface unit burners.

To provide the maximum efficiency in a space, try to include more than one long, uninterrupted counter surface in a kitchen. If possible, plan on ample counter space stretching from the refrigerator to the sink, as well as another section leading from the sink to the cooking surface. Such placement of these two centers suits either the cook who is working with fresh foods by the cooking area or preparing baked items between the sink and the refrigerator.

Alternatively, the preparation center can be located on an island opposite the refrigerator, with a sink and cooking surface near by.

Food Flow Sequence

The path that food preparation activities take through the kitchen is generally from the garage entrance to either the food storage cabinet or the refrigerator, to the sink, to the preparation area, to the cooking surface/microwave/oven, to the serving area and then to the table. Ideally, activity centers should be arranged in this order.

Most references recommend a right to left sequence for the arrangement of kitchen centers. This recommendation seems to stem from a 1948 **U.S. Department of Agriculture** publication, entitled *"A Step Saving U-Shaped Kitchen"*, which states: "The production line is from right to left, since most women prefer this."

Needless to say, this recommendation is best suited for right-handed homemakers. Ask your client in which direction they are most comfortable working.

No matter which sequence the client opts for, arrange the kitchen so that the number of trips between any of these work centers is limited.

KITCHEN SHAPES

Once you understand the concept of the work triangle as a way to judge the efficiency of your arrangement of the various centers, you can begin sketching solutions.

Selecting the shape of a kitchen is one of the most important decisions you will make. There is an alphabet soup choice of shapes to choose from that have been a part of kitchen planning guidelines for the past 50 years. Let's review the basic shapes and then some contemporary adaptations featured in award-winning kitchens.

One-Wall Kitchen

A one wall kitchen has all the work centers stretched along a single wall. This is the least efficient kitchen plan, especially for a gourmet cook. However, it is an ideal plan for a small apartment or studio in which little cooking takes place.

A one-wall kitchen can be concealed behind a wall of sliding doors in an efficiency unit.

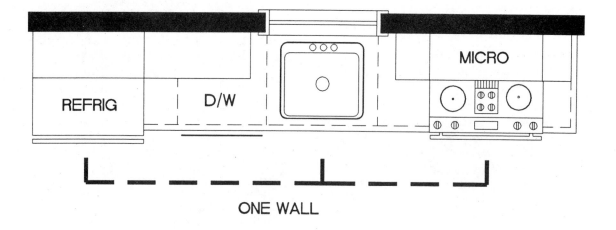

Figure 219 A one wall kitchen is only acceptable in small apartments or efficiency units.

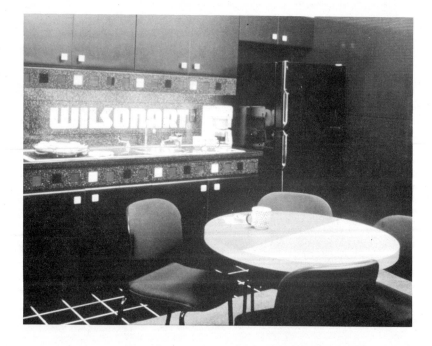

Figure 220 (Courtesy of Wilsonart International) This one wall kitchen is a compact cooking center.

Corridor-Shaped Kitchen

A corridor kitchen offers one cook the advantage of an efficient, close grouping of work centers on parallel walls. However, household traffic may cross back and forth through the area. This shape is typically too small for two cooks as well.

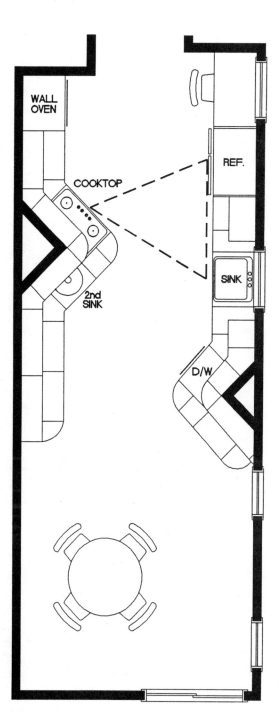

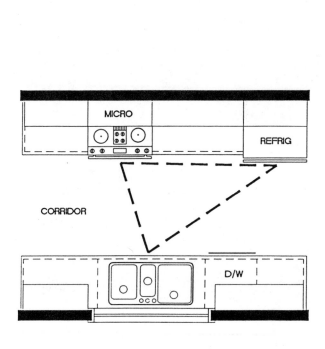

Figure 221 The corridor or pullman kitchen features two sets of cabinets placed opposite one an-

Figure 222 Here is a dramatic example of how to enhance a simple corridor plan.

Figure 223 Traditional cherry cabinets are featured in this corridor kitchen. Note the detailed doors and use of moldings.

L-Shaped Kitchen

An L-shaped kitchen gives the cook a generous amount of continuous counter space, though generally less than that of a U-shaped area or an L-shape with an island. However, with work centers on two adjacent walls, a natural triangle is formed and traffic by passes the work area. This layout is an excellent one if a dining area will be included in the space.

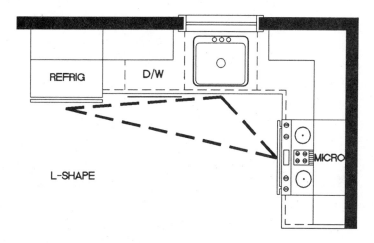

REFRIG   D/W

MICRO

L-SHAPE

Figure 224 An L-shaped arrangement provides a very compact kitchen for one cook.

Figure 225 This contemporary kitchen is well planned for a small space. The refrigerator and sink are relatively close together, allowing an expansive counter surface to be placed between the sink and range.

L-Shaped Kitchen with an Island

If an L-shape is combined with a free-standing center structure all of the benefits of a U-shaped kitchen are available, with a more open free-flowing plan. An L-shaped kitchen with an island is a perfect solution if the kitchen is open to an adjacent area. The island invites interaction between the cook and visitors or helpers, because more than one person can work around this open counter. At the same time, the efficiency of a compact U-shape arrangement is maintained.

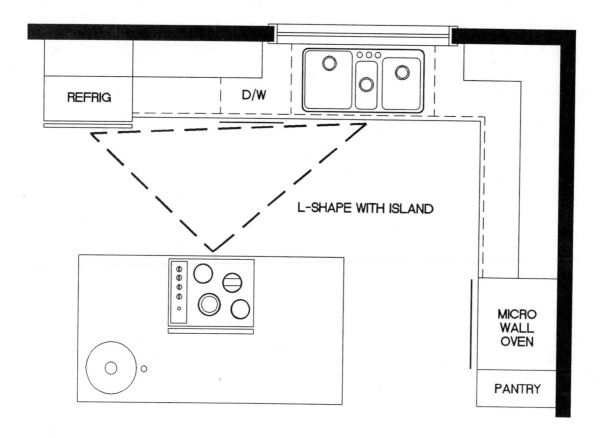

Figure 226 The L-shaped kitchen arrangement is oftentimes enhanced by the addition of an island.

Figure 227 This contemporary kitchen is a well organized L-shaped arrangement with an island. Note the ingenious wine storage that also supports the countertop overhang.

U-Shaped Kitchen

The U-shaped kitchen has always been considered the most efficient plan. Steps are saved because the cook is surrounded on three sides with a continuous countertop and storage system. Additionally, family traffic is directed around the work area.

Studies made at the **Motion and Time Study Laboratory** at **Purdue University**, some years ago, compared the efficiency of three kitchen plans. A meal for four people was prepared in each kitchen. The researchers found that the U-shaped kitchen required 450 steps; the L-shaped kitchen 490 steps; and the one wall kitchen 760 steps.

It was also noted that the cooking process took the least amount of time in the U-shaped kitchen. Therefore, for a cook who wants to handle kitchen chores alone, in the most efficient way, the U-shape is the best choice.

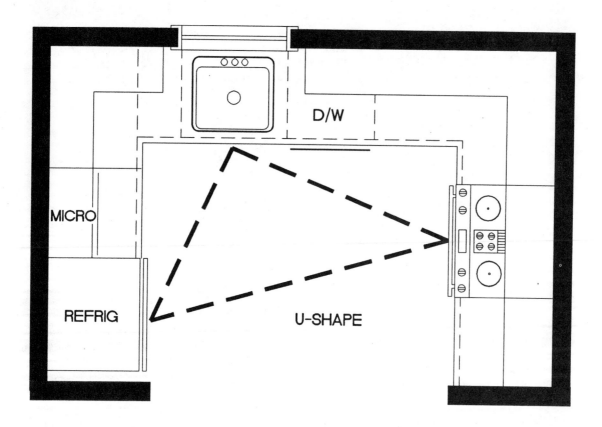

Figure 228 The U-shape kitchen surrounds the cook on three walls with continous storage and counter.

Figure 229 This charming, small kitchen demonstrates an effective way to use a U-shape arrangement.

G-Shaped Kitchen

The G-shaped kitchen is the newest approach to kitchen space layout. It is another extension of the U-shape, with an extra wall of cabinets and appliances as a peninsula leg or fourth wall. It is a very efficient plan; however, it can feel enclosed. It is best employed when one or two of the cabinet sections are open to adjacent spaces.

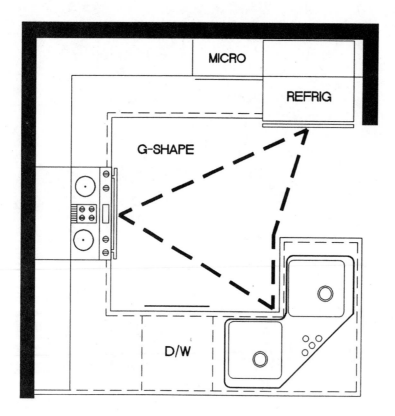

Figure 230 A G-shaped kitchen stretches counter surface and storage along all four walls.

Figure 231 A G-shaped kitchen is the most effective if at least one, if not two, of the cabinet sections are open to adjacent living spaces.

Customizing the Kitchen Shape

Talented designers oftentimes incorporate angles or curves to create custom kitchen shapes. Once you have mastered the basics of kitchen design, this type of advanced planning is your next challenge.

In *Figures 231* through *234* four plans are illustrated for your review, created by talented **Certified Kitchen Designers**. These rooms have been featured in major consumer magazine editorial projects. Such exposure helps lead consumers interested in a new kitchen to the true professional - the **Certified Kitchen Designer**.

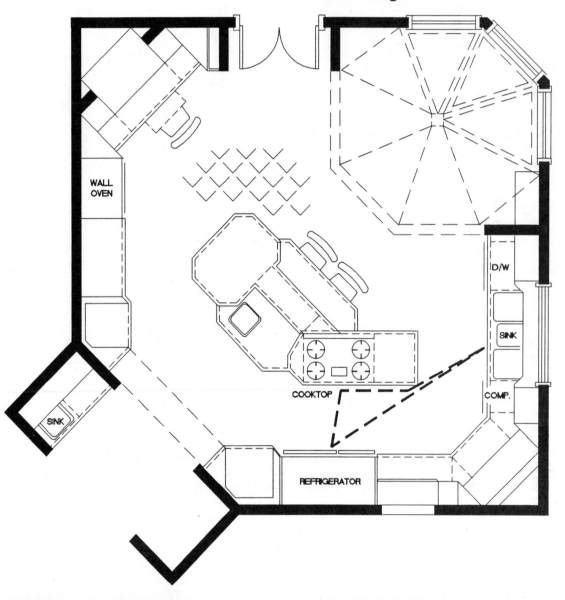

Figure 232 (Courtesy of Heritage Custom Kitchens) In this kitchen, featured in Better Homes & Gardens Kitchens & Baths, three different designers collaborated to create a space that could change as the family grew. Note the use of angles in the corners, as well as the custom shape of the center island. The adjacent dining area echoes these angles. This is a good interpretation of a G-shaped kitchen.

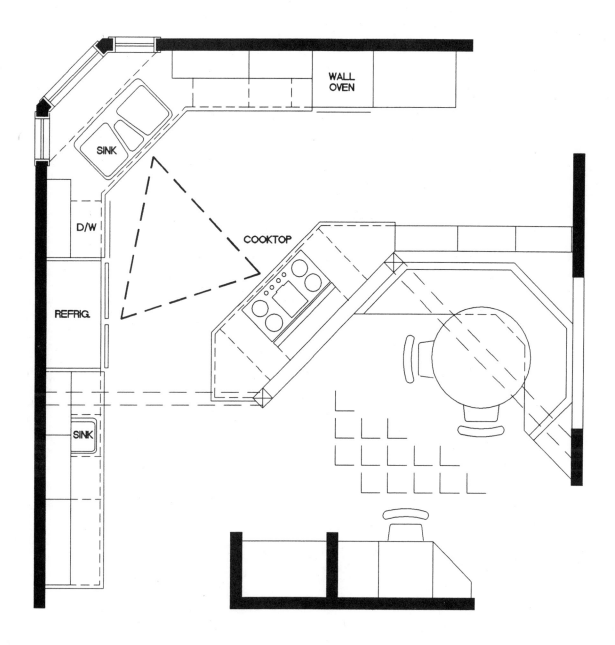

Figure 233 (Courtesy of Fieldstone) In this kitchen, which was featured in 1,001 Home Ideas, a double L-shaped arrangement carved a space for the table area, and created an effective "corridor" arrangement for the primary work centers. Using angles to get out into the floor space is an excellent way to increase the functionality of large rooms.

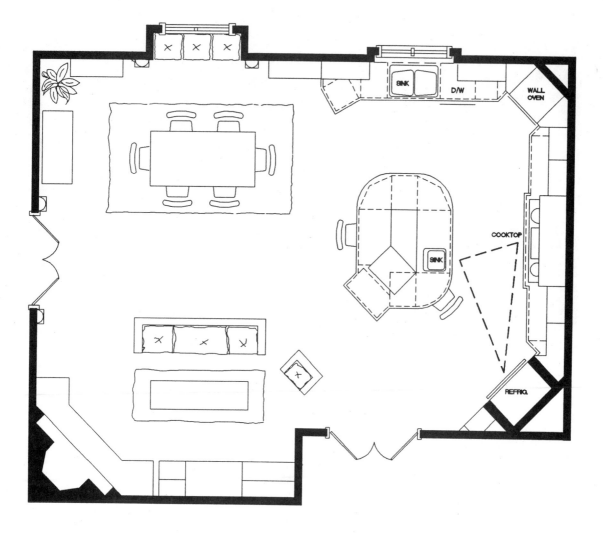

Figure 234 (Courtesy of Merrilat) In this kitchen, featured in Country Home Magazine, angling the tall units in the corner echos the shape of the fireplace in this great room. Note how the designer angled one base cabinet to the left of the sink to add to the counter space. Angled cabinets are also featured under a curved countertop in the custom shaped island.

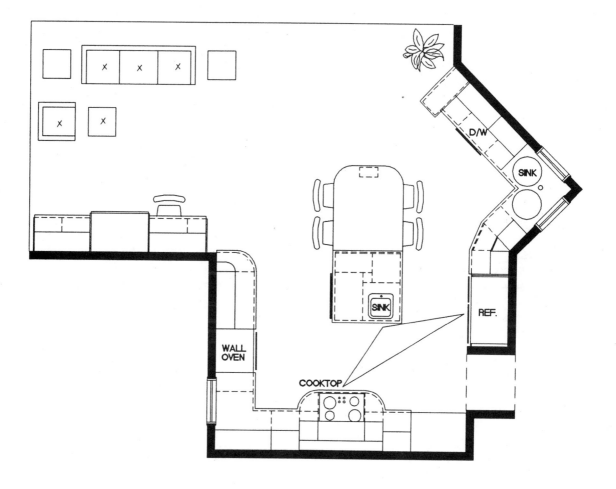

Figure 235 (Courtesy of Kraftmaid) In this kitchen, also featured in Country Home Magazine, the designer was faced with an oddly shaped room. By employing curves throughout the space, as well as zeroing in on a corner sink, the overall room was well used. This is an excellent example of a double L-shape with an island plan.

WORK SIMPLIFICATION PRINCIPLES

Earlier on we identified three things that you must do to minimize the time and energy required to complete any kitchen activity. These guiding principles were:

- Build the cabinets to fit the cook.

- Build the shelves to fit the supplies.

- Build the kitchen to fit the family.

When you studied human ergonomic considerations in Section 3, you were focusing on that first requirement. Now we will talk about building the shelves to fit the supplies.

Build the Shelves to Fit the Supplies

The time and motion studies conducted over the past 50 years have led to the development of storage guidelines. These guidelines help the designer meet this second principle of building the shelves to fit the supplies.

In traditional storage, similar objects are grouped in a given spot. In functional storage, rather than the similarity of form, the means of reducing unnecessary walking, searching and groping is governed by these principles:

- Storage at center of use

- Clear visibility of all supplies

- Easy accessibility of the desired item

There are several basic storage principles that will help during planning.

They are also excellent sales tools for use during a presentation. The storage principles will act as a guide for total space utilization within the cabinetry. The client and designer must agree on the principles, so that the space planned will be used effectively.

- **Store items at first or last place of use.** *For example:* most people store all pans in the cooking area. Yet, during many types of preparation, water is placed in the container first. Thus, it is a step-saving storage principle to provide space for several pans near the sink. Another example is everyday dish storage. Storage at first place of use would be near the table. Storage at last place of use would be near the sink.

- **Storing items in multiple locations if used for different tasks.** *For example:* measuring cups and spoons might be needed at the sink and in the food preparation area. Thus, two sets of tools placed at each point of use will be more efficient.

- **Items used together should be stored together.** *For example:* recipe books, paper and pencil are grouped together. Food stuffs, mixing equipment and hand appliances are stored together in baking center. Paper, foil, tape and marking pen for freezing are placed together.

- **Stored items should be easy to locate at a glance.** *For example:* canned goods stored one deep on narrow shelving are easy to identify and eliminates searching. Contents of drawers should be organized in compartments. This principle directly relates to the many storage aids available for cabinetry. They should be presented as storage aids, not gadgets.

- **Like articles should be stored or grouped together.** *For example:* canned goods, organized in storage units according to likeness of contents are easy to locate. This principle will also provide a visual inventory when the shopping list is made. Keeping all frying pans together allows the homemaker to quickly locate the correct utensil.

- **Frequently used items should be stored within easy reach.** Easy reach is normally defined as between eye-level and hip-level, at the front of the cabinet shelf. *For example,* a roll-out shelf allows complete use of the cabinet and is considered one of the most desirable aids in cabinetry.

- **Items should be easy to grasp at point of storage.** "Nesting" or stacking one item on top of another should be avoided. Tray or vertical storage is a prime example of this rule.

This principle also gives the designer a firm justification for the use of the soffit. The top shelf of a ceiling-height cabinet is very difficult to reach and remove items from. The client will be tempted

to stand on the drawer or the countertop; both are dangerous.

Through proper organization and elimination of unused articles, this 12" (30.48cm) space is not needed for dangerous and awkward storage.

- **Items should be easily removed without removing other items first.** *For example:* stepped-shelving within wall cabinets for easy sight and reach.

- **Heavy equipment should be stored at or near floor level.** *For example:* a heavy or bulky appliance stored on a high shelf could accidentally fall on a person removing it from storage. Heavy items near floor level will be easier to lift because the entire body can be used for leverage.

- **All space should be utilized for utmost efficiency.** This principle should include consideration of what is stored. A "two-year test" is a good rule of thumb. If an item hasn't been used in two years, perhaps it should be discarded or given away, rather than stored in valuable space.

Storage in a kitchen is truly a challenge, since organization of one's equipment and supplies is basic to an orderly life. A professional kitchen designer will carefully study the space allowed, ask important questions, understand the client's individual needs, and design a functional storage system for each client.

Figure 236 In the upper example we see an attractive island. In the second example the interior storage system is exposed. The cook's energy and time will be conserved if the cabinets feature organized interior storage accessories.

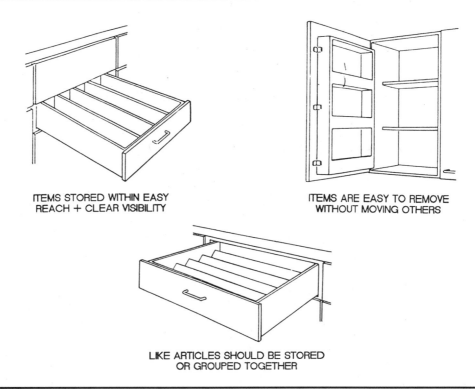

Figure 237 Shallow swing shelves and divided drawers keep equipment easy to locate at a glance.

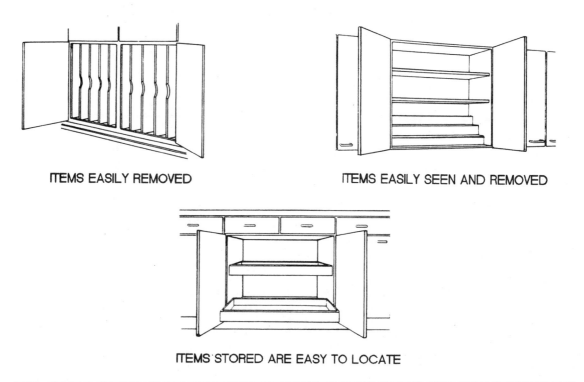

Figure 238 Organized interior storage systems make things easy to remove and replace.

Figure 239 Pull-out cutting surface protects countertop.

Figure 240 Wire racks installed under the cooking surface or sink make use of this space that is often wasted.

Figure 241 An attractive hutch actually contains specially designed drawers and roll-outs.

Figure 242 Tray dividers should be carefully sized: in cabinets above the refrigerator, which are less than 18" high, the openings may be too short. In areas above an oven, an extra shelf may be a good way to divide the space.

Figure 243 The backsplash area separating a worktop and a raised bar could be used for storage.

PLANNING A KITCHEN FOR MORE THAN ONE COOK

There is a major lifestyle change taking place in American families which will challenge you in the 1990s. Busy adults are unraveling the family's jammed calendar by sharing kitchen duties.

Academic Recommendations

Suggestions for kitchen planning adaptations for two workers had been made as early as 1914 in a publication entitled *"Efficiency Kitchens"*, published by *Good Housekeeping Magazine,* Institute Bulletin No. 1, page 5. However, extensive research had not been done to determine the impact of basic planning standards of a second worker in the kitchen until just recently. **Professors Wanda W. Olson** and **Becky L. Yust**, of the Department of Design, Housing and Apparel at the **University of Minnesota**, St. Paul, Minnesota, had a paper published in the *Journal of Consumer Studies in Home Economics* in 1987, entitled *"Shared Meal Preparation in Residential Kitchens: Implications for Kitchen Design"*. Their conclusions and recommendations are as follows:

CONCLUSIONS

The results of this study showed that there was no difference in the use of work centers and tasks performed between two workers when they prepared a meal together.

When more than one worker prepared a meal, the workers tended to divide the work load by menu item rather than sharing the preparation of each item, and only one worker prepared the menu items that required actual cooking. This work allocation may have contributed to workers using separate primary work stations. When workers did share the preparation of a menu item, they also shared work stations.

It is important to note that because the kitchen arrangements were based on existing kitchen planning standards for counter work spaces and for storage of foods, supplies and equipment, the two workers frequented the same major work centers - the sink and preparation area. The worker who did not use the preparation center as the primary work station made trips to the preparation center for supplies or equipment.

RECOMMENDATIONS

For clients choosing kitchen equipment and appliances, and for professionals faced with planning kitchens for two workers at the same time, it is important to first examine the patterns of meal preparation by the workers. The following recommendations will help you plan an efficient and comfortable space for two cooks:

- **For kitchens in which two workers prepare a meal simultaneously**, plan two work stations each no less than 36" (91.44cm) wide, the recommended minimum dimension for a preparation center according to the Small Homes Council/Building Research Council publication on Kitchen Planning Standards. If two separate work stations are not feasible, an extended preparation center, 72" (182.88cm) wide, should be planned to accommodate two workers simultaneously.

This dimension includes two 36" (91.44cm) preparation centers. Providing 1-36" (91.44cm) work center for each person.

- **Storage for frequently used equipment and supplies** should be duplicated in order to reduce trips and conflicts between two workers in the kitchen, or be easily accessible to both workers. If it is not feasible to duplicate storage for equipment and supplies usually used at the preparation center, the storage in the extended work center discussed in the recommendation above should be utilized.

- The **two work stations** should be in close proximity to the sink or a supplementary sink should be installed because of the importance of the sink center to both workers.

- **When only one worker participates in the actual cooking,** one cooking center, which may be a combined microwave/range center, is adequate. Two cooking centers, which may be a separate range center and microwave center, would be desirable for kitchens where two workers participate in the actual cooking of menu items.

PEOPLE SPEND TIME TOGETHER IN THE KITCHEN

The trend towards more people cooking and visiting in the kitchen is well documented. NKBA surveys report that between 30 - 35% of all kitchens being planned today are for more than one cook. In the University of Minnesota's survey, while only about 50% of the existing kitchens could accommodate more than one person, in the new kitchens over 95% of the time more than one person was in the cooking space.

In an actual day's use of the kitchen, 65% of the households surveyed had two or more people in the kitchen space during the time food was prepared in the evening. 61% of the time guests helped in the kitchen during entertaining events. Family members and friends either assisted in preparing one item for dinner or handled the clean up chores. Frequently, this assistant was the cook's spouse.

HOW PEOPLE COOK TOGETHER

Just as no two cooks prepare a meal in the same fashion, no two people cook together in the same way.

As with any successful kitchen design, the secret is found in an in-depth client survey. When the clients tell you that they cook together, identifying their heights and handedness is only the beginning. The planner should also focus attention on identifying the type of communal cooking the family hopes to enjoy. *For example,* let's study four very different types of families who all cook together.

- **Taking Turns:** Both adults in our first family really don't enjoy cooking. The preparation of the meal is simply seen as a home management job. They might delegate the responsibility to whomever arrives home first.

- **Team Cooking:** The second couple both love to cook. They jointly share in the preparation of meals and frequently interchange responsibilities.

- **Specialty Cook:** Our third family followed the path of the medical profession and each adult has his or her particular specialty. One might enjoy barbecuing while the other would be the salad specialist.

- **Assistant Chef:** Our fourth couple has clear lines of leadership drawn. One individual is the primary cook, while the other is assigned the role of "cook's helper".

Each one of these families could easily answer the question, *"Do you both cook?"* by a simple "Yes". The successful designer will identify how they cook together.

Let's study each of our four families and consider design ideas which should be incorporated in these unique kitchens.

When One-Cook Kitchen Planning Guidelines Apply

Although our first couple share in the meal preparation responsibilities, they alternate these chores. Thus, only one person is cooking at any one time. For this type of family, the one-cook kitchen planning rules still apply.

A variation of this first family may occur when one adult enjoys a cooking hobby. *For example,* one of the cooks may specialize in baking. He or she will bake in the evening or over the weekend when general meal preparation is not taking place. Again, the rules established for a one-cook kitchen would certainly suit this family. The special modification for this family would be to plan an extensive and complete baking center.

WHEN NEW GUIDELINES ARE NEEDED

The three other family prototypes require a whole new approach to design.

Avoid Traffic Jams

The major concern is to avoid traffic jams. Traditionally, planners locate the walkways for non-cooking family members so that they do not cross the primary cook's triangle and interfere with his/her activities. A two-cook kitchen needs an expanded triangle or perhaps a double triangle so that the traffic pattern of each cook can be free from interruption. Therefore, two can work together without bumping into one another.

Increase Walkway Clearance

Designers use a practical minimum clearance dimension of 42" (106.68cm) between cabinets or appliances to provide adequate walking space in a kitchen designed for one cook. A different set of minimum spatial requirements must be considered when more than one person is in the kitchen.

Edging space allows one person enough room to pass behind another by turning and passing with bodies parallel. The minimum space required is 48" (121.92cm) from obstacle to obstacle. This is adequate for edging space when two cooks simultaneously occupy the space.

To determine the best walkway clearance for your client, you must consider the size and weight of the individuals, as well as current or future need for mobility aids.

For liberal work space, a clearance of 60" (152.4cm) is suggested. In this more expansive walkway, two individuals can pass one another with bodies parallel.

Separate Center

When space and funds are available, the gourmet cooking family will find two sinks (which separate their activities) a very practical solution. If a kitchen can be planned so the two cooks commonly share the refrigerator and the cooking area then move in different directions to two cleanup centers, the room will be very functional. The 1994 NKBA survey reports that 26% of kitchens designed have more than one sink.

The talented designer will be sure to draw both work triangles on the drawings when such a plan is developed. Such an addition to the space study will demonstrate to the clients how carefully the designer has plotted their paths in the new kitchen.

Expand Countertop Space

Expand the countertop work surfaces to accommodate the needs of both persons when the space simply won't allow two sinks. Rather than excessive duplication of equipment, concentrate on the accessibility of equipment. Place the sink and dishwasher in a central location. Have the spice cabinet, implement storage, cutlery storage and chopping area placed so that both of the cooks can

reach the storage centers easily.

Consider an Island

A large working island may be a solution. The island offers a unique opportunity for two people to share use of one appliance and work facing one another.

The sink may be installed with the faucets at the side rather than at the back, so that it can be reached by a person on either side. The same type of solution can apply to the cooktop.

Create a Special Center

Depending on the specialty of the second cook, one of the work centers may need to be expanded or a fourth center included.

For example, the cook who barbecues could be stationed at an extra countertop area near the cooktop/grill, but away from the primary cook's normal working surface. Or, the barbecue specialist might be centered at a separate counter surface featuring an indoor grill located away from the primary cook's work triangle.

For many specialties, the separate area should be near the refrigerator. Rather than the traditional approach of placing the refrigerator at the end of a cabinet run, consider placing the refrigerator in the middle of the run.

Provide the primary cook with a minimum of 36" (91.44cm) uninterrupted working space on one side of the refrigerator and then plan a second 36" (91.44cm) space on the other side. This area is perhaps the perfect application for a side-by-side refrigerator so both cooks have adequate access to the appliance.

Customize Countertop Heights

When planning a separate center for a specialty cook, it is also critical to be aware of his or her height. The 6'-2" (187.96cm) man who loves to barbecue should not be forced to work at a counter surface designed for a 5'-4" (162.56cm) woman.

Although the countertop standard of 36" (91.44cm) is normally maintained for appliance placement and home resale value, the designer should consider incorporating lowered and/or raised surfaces to accommodate a variety of current and future users.

In each of our four families, the common denominator of more than one adult cook is shared. Yet each lifestyle requires an individual solution to the kitchen plan. When duplication of centers and/or appliances is possible, the sky is the limit.

When such an extravagance is not allowed, the successful designer concentrates on planning adequate countertop frontages, sufficient storage space and workable walkways.

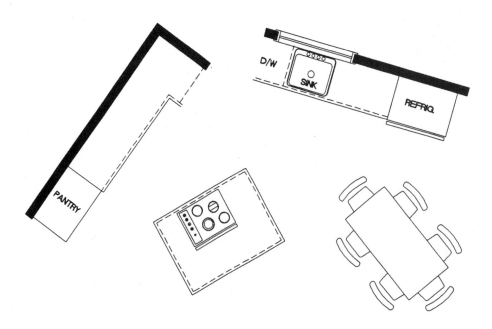

Figure 244 A well-planned kitchen is based on the proper arrangement of individual centers that are designed to accommodate all of the equipment/food stuffs and activities anticipated in each area.

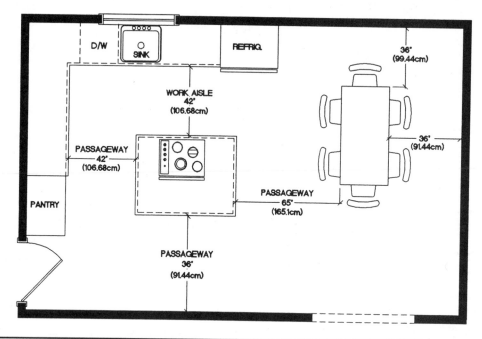

Figure 245 Kitchens in the past were made up of three primary centers: the refrigerator/mix area, a sink/dishwasher area and a range/cooking area. Kitchens today have more appliances and more centers. The arrangement of work centers and the passageway and work aisle clearances around the individual appliances are critical to a well planned kitchen.

Criteria For Kitchen Design

The ideal kitchen design for any home will depend on a number of factors, particularly upon the individual family's possessions and their living habits. Therefore, a design which is considered excellent for one family may be totally unsuitable for another. Nevertheless, you need a set of guidelines as a basis to start the planning process. The following planning guidelines have been developed by the **National Kitchen & Bath Association** in conjunction with the **University of Illinois Small Homes Council** to serve as a basis for acceptable kitchen planning. These standards are based on the research projects that were outlined for you in the introduction of this volume.

Adherence to these recommendations should result in good kitchen design for all but the most unusual cases.

These recommendations are not based on any criteria relating to the size of the home. Kitchen sizes vary regardless of the square footage of the house. The size of the house is not as significant a factor as are the family's cooking and socializing preferences in determining kitchen square footage. Therefore, these recommendations are based on a small kitchen size defined as 150 square feet (13.94 square meters) or less and an average size kitchen greater than 150 square feet (13.94 square meters). These standards are all based on kitchens designed for one cook. Where appropriate, additional information or clarifications are made to expand upon the guideline.

These guidelines also include environmental considerations, safety factors and universal design standards. Although these issues were not addressed in earlier research, the importance of accommodating our environment cannot be overlooked in contemporary planning guidelines.

The 40 Guidelines of Kitchen Planning in Section 6 are presented for five major components of a well-planned kitchen:

- Traffic and Workflow

- Cabinets and Storage

- Appliance Placement and Use/Clearance Space

- Counter Surface and Landing Space

- Room, Appliance and Equipment Controls

AVERAGE KITCHEN SIZES

The size of the kitchen depends greatly on the client's cooking style and preferences. However, designers are sometimes asked what the average square footage of a kitchen is.

The **National Kitchen & Bath Association** defines a small kitchen as one that is 150 square feet (13.94 square meters) or less in size and a large kitchen is greater than 150 square feet (13.94 square meters).

The kitchen space is defined as the work space and walking or aisle area 36" (91.44cm) from any peninsula or island that divides the kitchen from an adjacent socializing space.

DEFINITION OF USABLE FRONTAGE

The counter, base and wall cabinet frontage criterion is expressed in terms of accessible frontage. Frontage is measured in terms of the horizontal dimension across the face of an appliance, base cabinet, counter surface or wall cabinet.

To be credited as frontage, the component must be directly accessible from the area located in front of the component. In accordance with this definition, cabinet base and countertop surface located in corners are not credited in counting accessible frontage.

DIMENSIONING CLEARANCE SPACES

Clearances must be provided in front of cabinets, kitchen equipment and kitchen furniture to allow for access to and use of these facilities. This may require room for such activities as walking, reaching, bending and crouching. Although a cook may want to be uninterrupted while preparing meals, room for aid by others is equally as important.

All walkway clearance dimensions are measured from the front edge of the counter surface to a wall, obstacle, counter edge, appliance or furniture opposite it. The countertop edge, rather than the cabinet face, is used so that varying counter overhangs found throughout the country can be accommodated within these clearance dimensions. Therefore, a clear walkway space is the area in which an individual can move about the room.

APPLICATION OF GUIDELINES

As you use these guidelines, it is important to realize that arranging space so that it suits your client's requests, construction constraints and budget should be your first goal. **You must never deviate from local safety or building codes.** However, these guidelines can be adapted or modified to meet specific project requirements. The important thing is for you to know the guidelines first, and then make an intelligent design decision to follow or to modify that guideline as you customize the space for each client.

The 40 Guidelines Of Kitchen Planning

Accepted industry guidelines for kitchen design are based on planning standards developed by both the **National Kitchen & Bath Association** and the **University of Illinois Small Homes Council**.

In 1992, the **National Kitchen & Bath Association** and the **University of Illinois Small Homes Council**, introduced new standards based on an extensive research project conducted by the Association in conjunction with the **University of Minnesota**.

In 1995, NKBA teamed up with universal design experts to re-examine the basic assumptions of design for the idealized, able-bodied, non-elderly adult. The result was an increased appreciation for diversity, flexibility and adaptability in design, and the basis for the new **40 Guidelines of Kitchen Planning**.

SECTION I: Traffic and Workflow - Guideline 1 to Guideline 5

SECTION I: Traffic and Workflow - Guideline 1 to Guideline 5

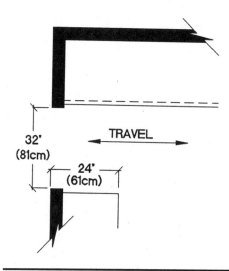

Figure 246 Guideline 1a - Doorways should be at least 32" (81cm) wide and not more than 24" (61cm) deep in the direction of travel.

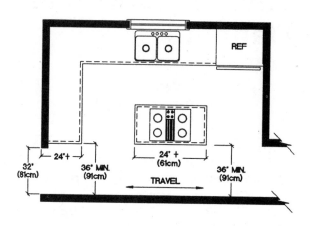

Figure 247 Guideline 1b - Walkways (passages between vertical objects greater than 24" (61cm) deep in the direction of travel, where not more than one is a work counter or appliance) should be at least 36" (91cm) wide.

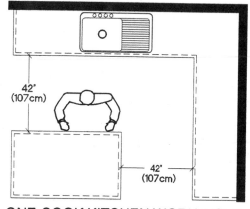

ONE-COOK KITCHEN WORK AISLE

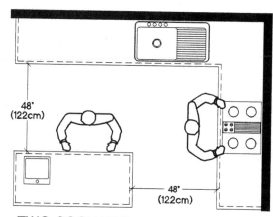

TWO-COOK KITCHEN WORK AISLE

Figure 248 Guideline 1c - Work aisles (passages between vertical objects, both of which are work counters or appliances) should be at least 42" (107cm) wide in one-cook kitchens, at least 48" (122cm) wide in multiple-cook kitchens.

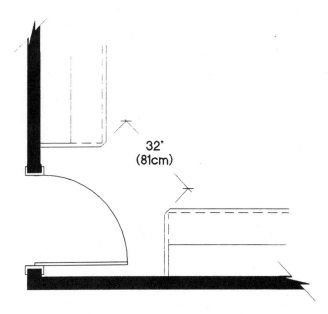

Figure 249 Guideline 1a - Clarification - When two counters flank a doorway entry, the minimum 32" (81cm) wide clearance should be allowed from the point of one counter to the closest point of the opposite counter.

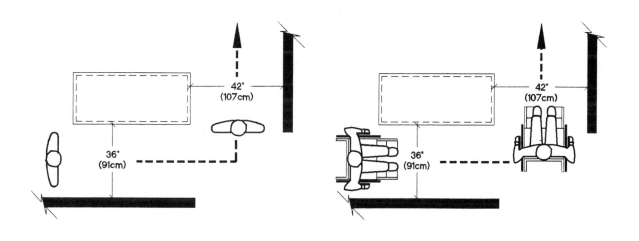

Figure 250 Guideline 1b - Clarification - If there are perpendicular walkways, one should be a minimum of 42" (107cm) wide.

The 36" (91cm) width of a walkway allows a person using a wheelchair to pass. However, in order to turn when two walkways intersect at right angles, one of the walkways must be a minimum of 42" (107cm) wide.

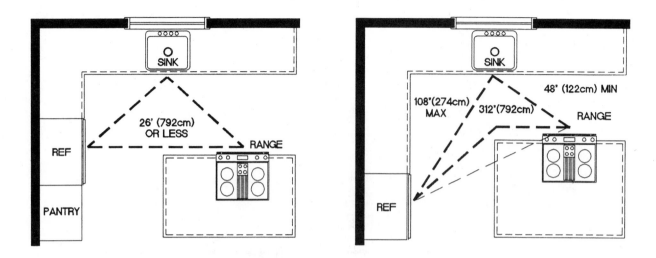

Figure 251 Guideline 2 - The work triangle should total 26' (792cm) or less, with no single leg of the triangle shorter than 4' (122cm) nor longer than 9' (274cm). The work triangle should not intersect an island or peninsula by more than 12" (30cm). (The triangle is the shortest walking distance between the refrigerator, primary food preparation sink and primary cooking surface, measured from the center front of each appliance.)

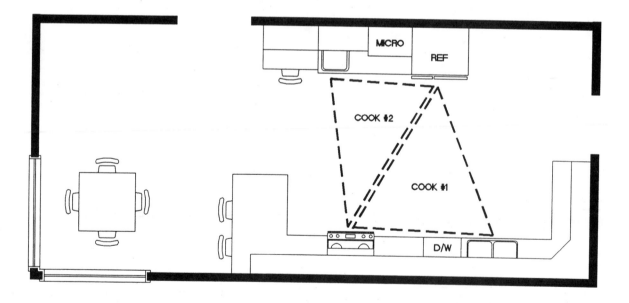

Figure 252 Guideline 2 - Clarification - If two or more people cook simultaneously, a work triangle should be placed for each cook. One leg of the primary and secondary triangles may be shared, but the two should not cross one another. Appliances may be shared or separate.

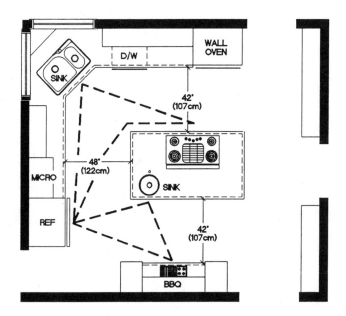

Figure 253 Guideline 2 Example 1 - A square room can work for two people if a sink is added at the back of an island which also features the primary cook's cooktop. One cook moves from the refrigerator to the island sink, to the BBQ center; the second cook, from the refrigerator to the primary sink to the cooking surface.

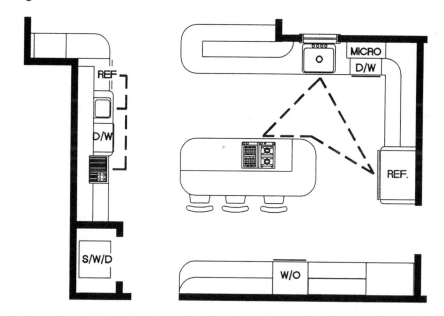

Figure 254 Guideline 2 Example 2 - In a large, expansive kitchen created for two cooks, two very separate cooking areas are created. There is very little interaction between the cooks unless they are both working at the counter to the left of the sink. The primary cook works from the refrigerator to the sink to the cooktop. Note the microwave placement close to the sink. The secondary cook has access to his own grill, second microwave, sink and under cabinet refrigerator. Two dishwashers complete the separate work environment.

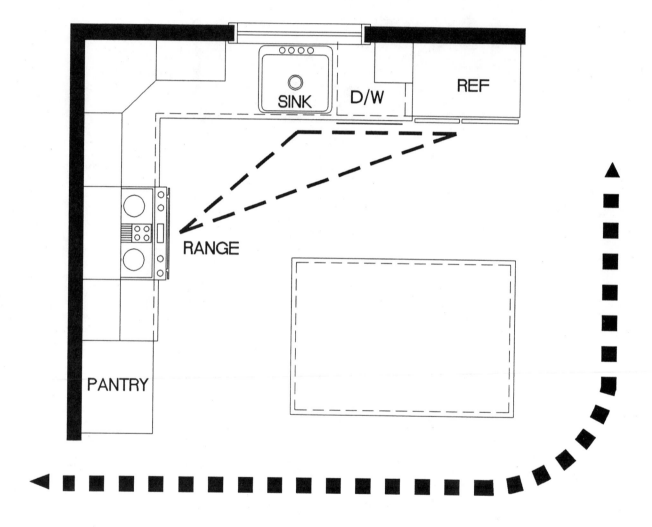

Figure 255 Guideline 3 - No major traffic patterns should cross through the work triangle.

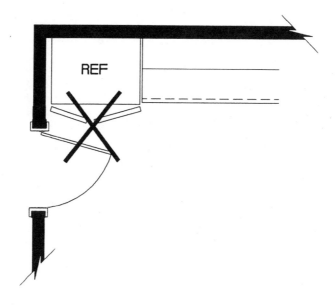

Figure 256 Guideline 4 - No entry, appliance or cabinet doors should interfere with one another.

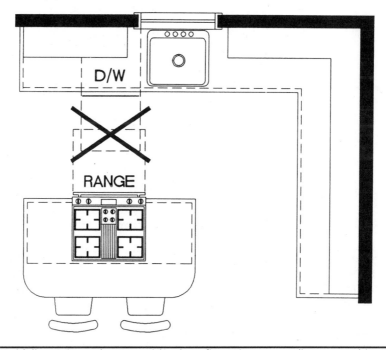

Figure 257 Guideline 4 Example - In an island configuration, an appliance or cabinet door on an island should not conflict with an appliance or cabinet door opposite it.

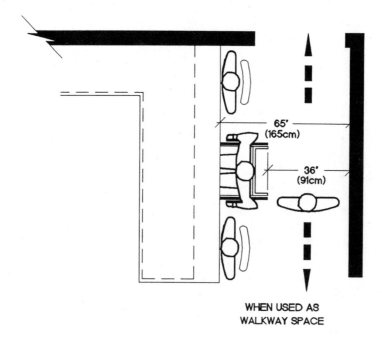

WHEN USED AS
WALKWAY SPACE

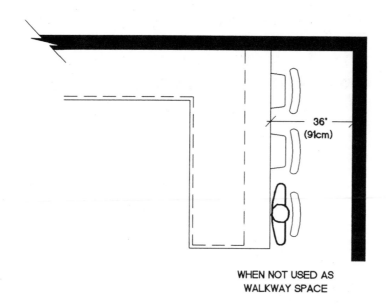

WHEN NOT USED AS
WALKWAY SPACE

Figure 258 Guideline 5 - In a seating area, 36" (91cm) of clearance should be allowed from the counter/table edge to any wall/obstruction behind it if no traffic will pass behind a seated diner. If there is a walkway behind the seating area, 65" (165cm) of clearance, total, including the walkway, should be allowed between the counter/table edge and any wall or obstruction.

The 65" (165cm) walkway clearance required for a seating area allows room for passage by or behind the person using a wheelchair

SECTION II: Cabinets and Storage
Guideline 6 to Guideline 12

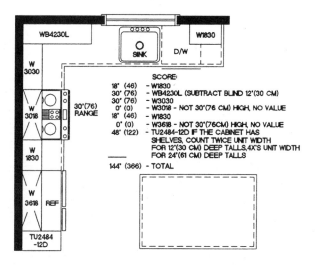

Figure 259 Guideline 6 - Wall Cabinet Frontage, Small Kitchens - = or < 150 sq. ft. (14 sq.m) - allow at least 144" (366cm) of wall cabinet frontage, with cabinets at least 12" (30cm) deep, and a minimum of 30" (76cm) high (or equivalent) which feature adjustable shelving. Difficult to reach cabinets above the hood, oven or refrigerator do not count unless devices are installed within the case to improve accessibility.

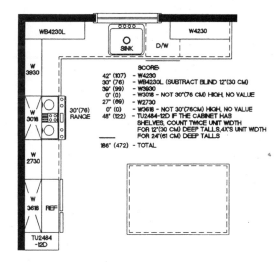

Figure 260 Guideline 6 - Wall Cabinet Frontage, Large Kitchens - over 150 sq. ft. (14 sq.m) - allow at least 186" (472cm) of wall cabinet frontage, with cabinets at least 12" (30cm) deep, and a minimum of 30" (76cm) high (or equivalent) which feature adjustable shelving. Difficult to reach cabinets above the hood, oven or refrigerator do not count unless devices are installed within the case to improve accessibility.

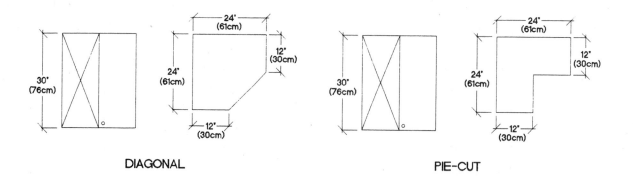

DIAGONAL   PIE-CUT

WALL CABINETS

Figure 261 Guideline 6 - Clarification - In Small and Large Kitchens, diagonal or pie cut wall cabinets count as a total of 24" (61cm).

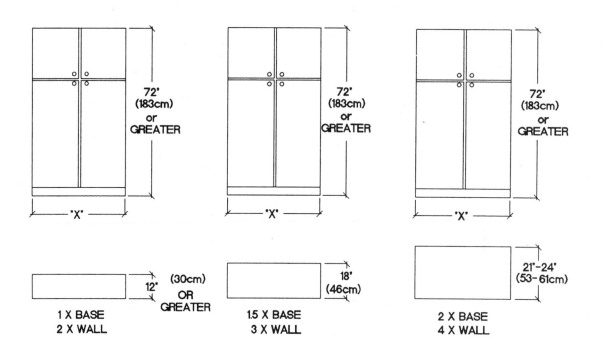

1 X BASE   1.5 X BASE   2 X BASE
2 X WALL   3 X WALL   4 X WALL

Figure 262 Guideline 6 - Clarification - Tall cabinets 72" (183cm) or taller can count as either base or wall cabinet storage, but not both.
The calculation is as follows:
12" (30cm) deep tall units = 1 x the base lineal footage, 2 x the wall lineal footage
18" (46cm) deep tall units = 1.5 x the base lineal footage, 3 x the wall lineal footage
21" to 24" (53cm - 61cm) deep tall units = 2 x the base lineal footage, 4 x the wall lineal footage

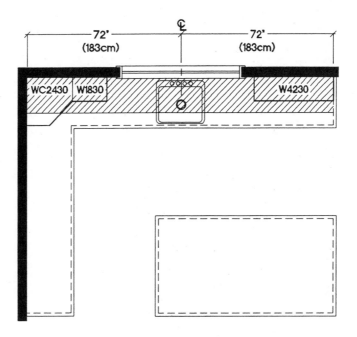

Figure 263 Guideline 7 - At least 60" (152cm) of wall cabinet frontage, with cabinets at least 12" (30cm) deep, a minimum of 30" (76cm) high (or equivalent), should be included within 72" (183cm) of the primary sink centerline.

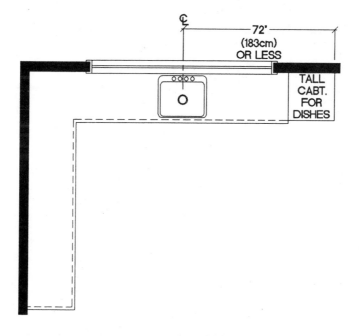

Figure 264 Guideline 7 - Clarification - A tall cabinet can be substituted for the required wall cabinets if it is placed within 72" (183cm) of the sink centerline.

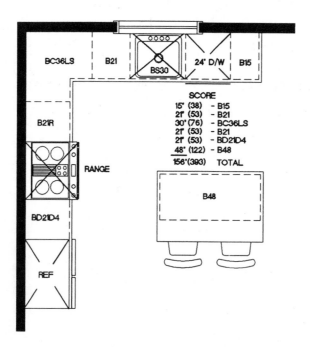

Figure 265 Guideline 8 - Base Cabinet Frontage, Small Kitchens - = or < 150 sq. ft. (14 sq.m) - allow at least 156" (393cm) of base cabinet frontage, with cabinets at least 21" (53cm) deep (or equivalent). The blind portion of a blind corner box does not count.

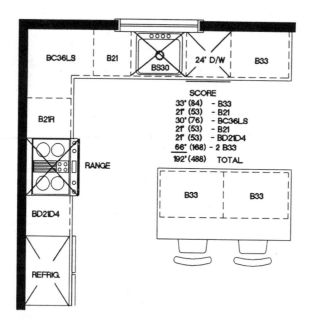

Figure 266 Guideline 8 - Base Cabinet Frontage, Large Kitchens - over 150 sq. ft. (14 sq.m) - require at least 192" (488cm) of base cabinet frontage, with cabinets at least 21" (53cm) deep (or equivalent). The blind portion of a blind corner box does not count.

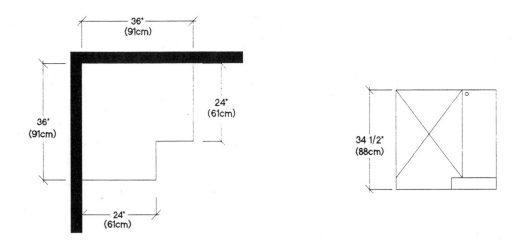

Figure 267 Guideline 8 - Clarification - In both Small and Large kitchens, pie cut lazy susan base cabinets count as a total of 30" (72cm).

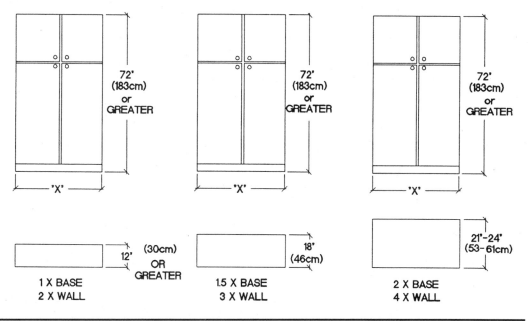

Figure 268 Guideline 8 - Clarification - Tall cabinets 72" (183cm) or taller can count as either base or wall cabinet storage, but not both.
The calculation is as follows:
12" (30cm) deep tall units = 1 x the base lineal footage, 2 x the wall lineal footage
18" (46cm) deep tall units = 1.5 x the base lineal footage, 3 x the wall lineal footage
21" to 24" (53cm to 61cm) deep tall units = 2 x the base lineal footage, 4 x the wall lineal footage

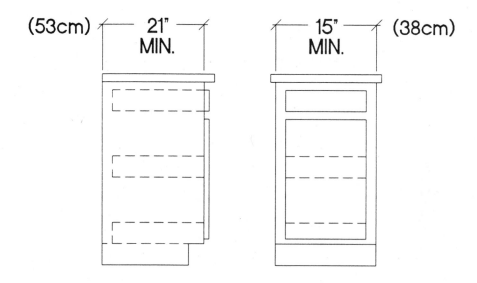

Figure 269 Guideline 9 - Drawer/Roll-out Shelf Frontage - Small Kitchens - = or < 150 sq. ft.(14 sq.m) - allow at least 120" (305cm) of drawer or roll-out shelf frontage. Large Kitchens - over 150 sq. ft. (14 sq.m) - allow at least 165" (419cm) of drawer or roll-out shelf frontage. Multiply cabinet width by number of drawers/roll-outs to determine frontage. Drawer/roll-out cabinets must be at least 15" (38cm) wide and 21" (53cm) deep to be counted.

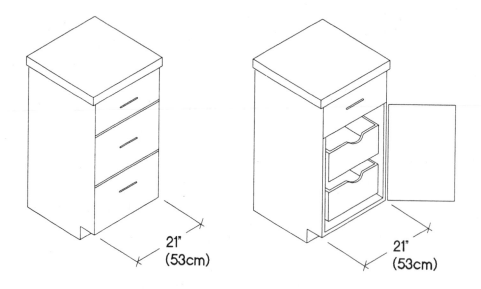

Figure 270 Guideline 9 Example 1 - A 21" (53cm) wide three drawer base would count as 63" (160cm) toward the drawer total. A 21" (53cm) wide single drawer base with one drawer and two sliding shelves would also count as 63" (160cm) towards the total drawer measurement.

Figure 271 Guideline 9 Example 2 - In this example, drawers flank the range.

Figure 272 Guideline 9 Example 3 - Drawers can be placed close to the sink so that items used at the sink or stored near the dishwasher are close at hand.

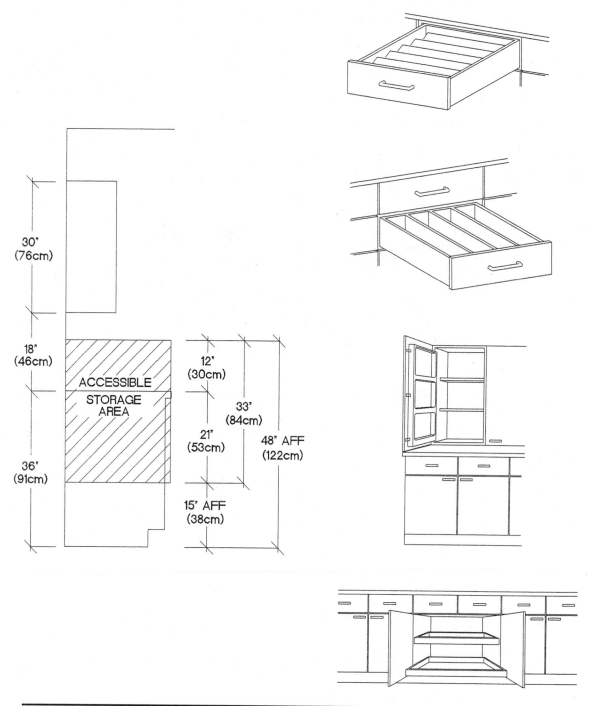

Figure273 Guideline 10 - At least five storage/organizing items, located between 15" - 48" (38cm - 122cm) above the finished floor (or extending into that area), should be included in the kitchen to improve functionality and accessibility. These items may include, but are not limited to: lowered wall cabinets, raised base cabinets, tall cabinets, appliances garages, bins/racks, swing-out pantries, interior vertical dividers, specialized drawers/shelves etc.. Full-extension drawers/roll-out shelves greater than the 120" (305cm) minimum for small kitchens or 165" (419cm) for larger kitchens may also be included.

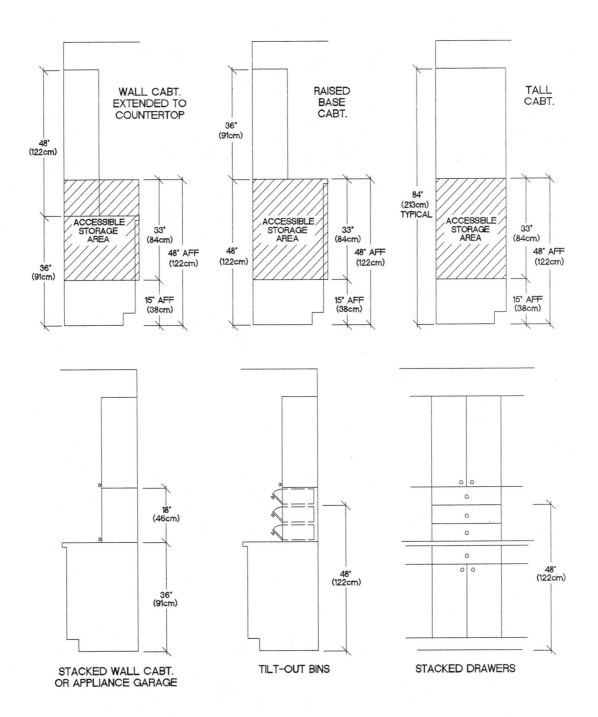

*Figure 274 Guideline 10 Examples - Each of these applications puts storage within the 15" - 48"
(38cm - 122cm) range.*

Figure 275 Guideline 10 Examples - The goal of this guideline is to increase the amount of accessible storage within the universal reach range of 15" - 48" (38cm - 122cm).

Figure 276 Guideline 10 Examples - The goal of this guideline is to increase the amount of accessible storage within the universal reach range of 15" - 48" (38cm - 122cm).

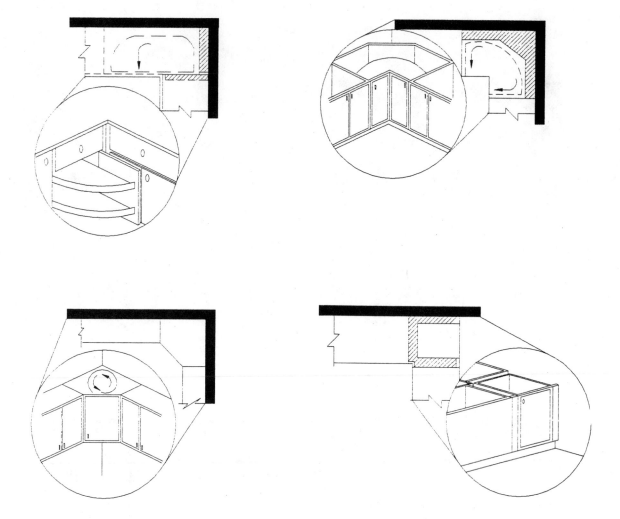

Figure 277 Guideline 11 - For a kitchen with usable corner areas in the plan, at least one functional corner storage unit should be included.

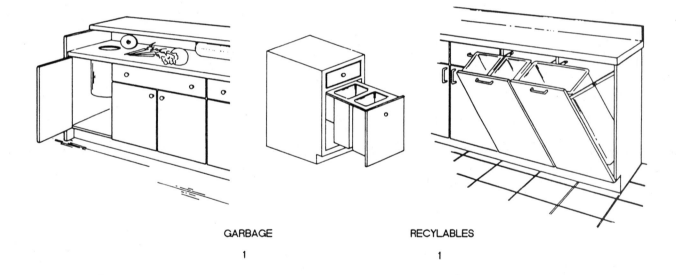

GARBAGE   RECYLABLES

1   1

Figure 278 Guideline 12 - At least two waste receptacles should be included in the plan, one for garbage and one for recyclables; or other recycling facilities should be planned.

Garbage disposer does not count as a waste receptacle.

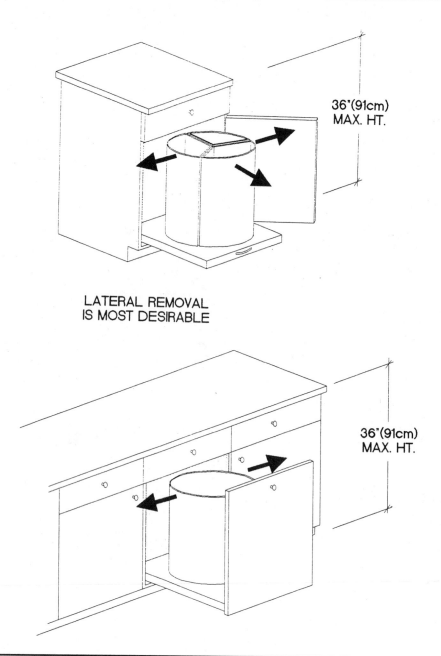

LATERAL REMOVAL
IS MOST DESIRABLE

36"(91cm)
MAX. HT.

36"(91cm)
MAX. HT.

Figure 279 Guideline 12 - Clarification - The top edge of a waste receptacle should be no higher than 36" (91cm). The receptacle should be easily accessible and should be removable without raising the receptacle bottom higher than the unit's physical height. Lateral removal of the receptacle which does not require lifting is most desirable.

Many recycling and waste receptacles, such as those in deep drawers or tilt out cabinets require lifting them above the cabinet to empty them. Because this can be difficult for a person of shorter stature or a person with limited strength or mobility, it is more desirable to choose a receptacle that slides out or requires minimum lifting.

SECTION III Appliance Placement and Use/Clearance Space
Guideline 13 to Guideline 21

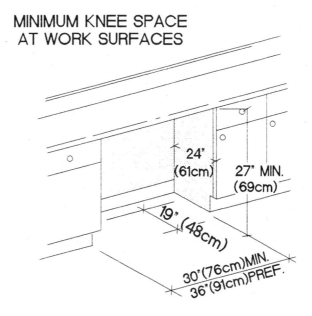

MINIMUM KNEE SPACE
AT WORK SURFACES

24"
(61cm)

27" MIN.
(69cm)

19" (48cm)

30"(76cm)MIN.
36"(91cm)PREF.

Figure 280 Guideline 13 - Knee space (which may be open or adaptable) should be planned below or adjacent to sinks, cooktops, ranges, dishwashers, refrigerators and ovens whenever possible. Knee space should be a minimum of 30" (76cm) wide by 27" (69cm) high by 19" (48cm) deep under the counter. The 27" (69cm) height at the front of the knee space may decrease progressively as depth increases.

The actual counter height at a knee space will vary. For a person in a wheelchair, the preferred height is 30" (76cm), but it may be as high as 34" (86cm). For a person with limited endurance or balance, a 36" (91cm) high counter may be comfortable if a stool is provided that is compatible with that counter height. The height of the armrest on a wheelchair or the depth of an appliance will also influence the counter height required for clearance.

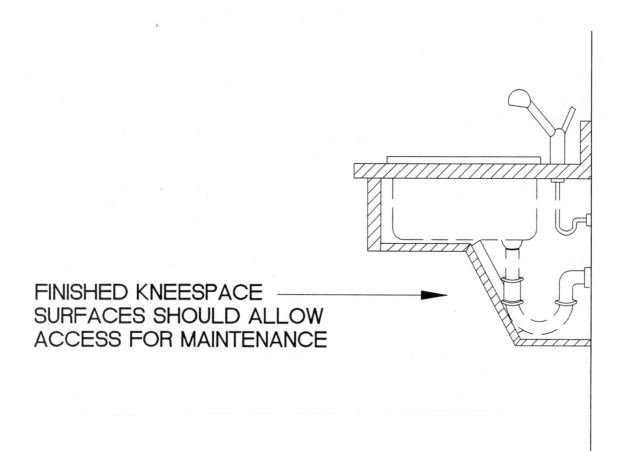

FINISHED KNEESPACE
SURFACES SHOULD ALLOW
ACCESS FOR MAINTENANCE

Figure 281 Guideline 13 - Clarification - Surfaces in the knee space area should be finished for safety and aesthetic purposes.

A protective and decorative panel should be part of the design of a knee space. A seated user should be protected from rough surfaces, hot elements, and the working parts of the appliance or fixture. In addition, the appliance, fixture, or plumbing should be protected from repeated impact. Finally, aesthetics dictate the use of a covering to coordinate with the look of the space.

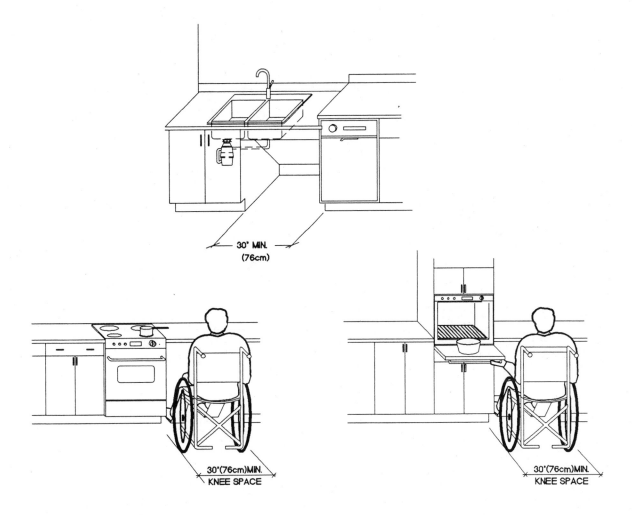

Figure 282 Guideline 13 Examples - Knee space provided at appliances makes them universally ac-cessible. Surfaces in the knee space area should be finished for safety and aesthetic purposes.

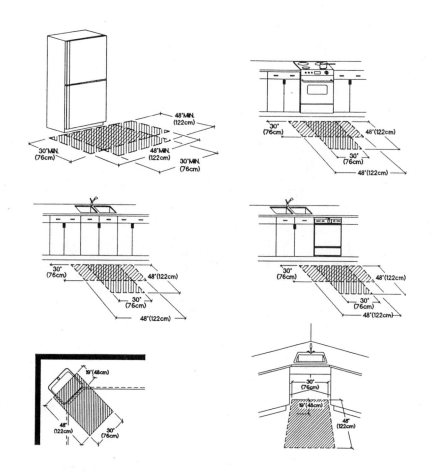

Figure 283 Guideline 14 - A clear floor space of 30" x 48" (76cm x 122cm) should be provided at the sink, dishwasher, cooktop, oven and refrigerator. (Measure from face of cabinet or appliance if toe kick is less than 9" (23cm) high.)

If you are working with a standard height toekick, calculate the clear floor space from the face of the cabinetry. If the toekick is raised to 9" (23cm) or higher, you may include the depth of the toekick when figuring clear floor space. The reason is that a 9" - 12" (23cm - 30cm) toekick allows clearance for the footrest on most wheelchairs.

When a sink or cooktop is designed in an angled corner, there must be the minimum 30" x 48" (76cm x 122cm) clear floor space access. Note the corner sink drawing that incorporates knee space where the actual angled countertop edge is less than 30" (76cm) but the distance between the two cabinets is greater. The 30" x 48" (76cm x 122cm) clear floor space may however include the knee space below, which begins 19" (48cm) in from the front edge of the counter as measured at the floor.

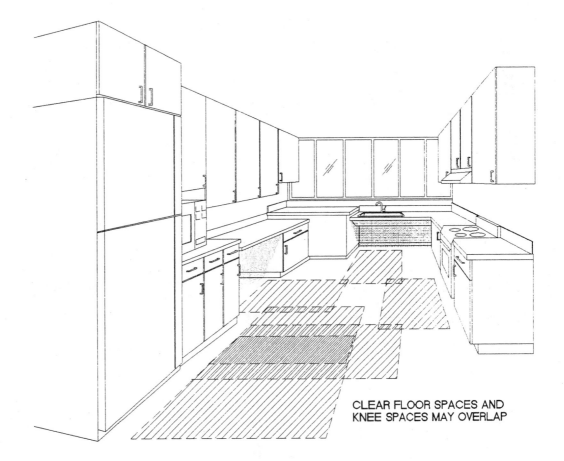

CLEAR FLOOR SPACES AND
KNEE SPACES MAY OVERLAP

Figure 284 Guideline 14 - Clarification - These spaces may overlap and up to 19" (48cm) of knee space (beneath an appliance, counter, cabinet, etc.) may be part of the total 30" (76cm) and/or 48" (122cm) dimension.

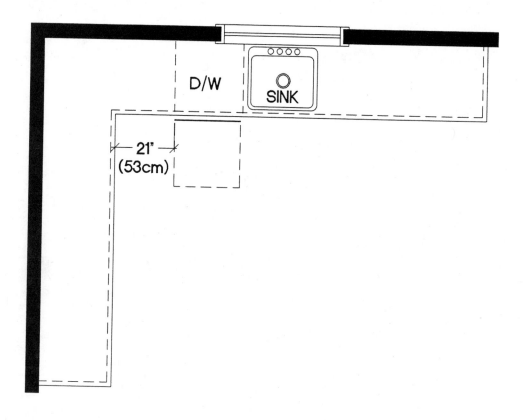

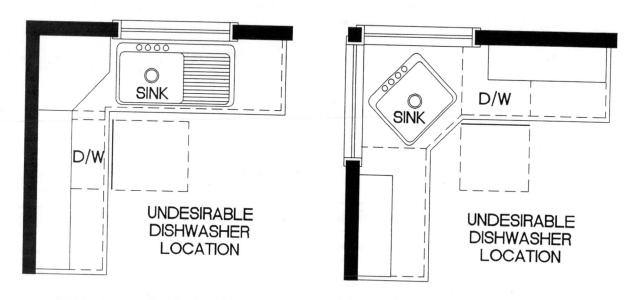

Figure 285 Guideline 15 - A minimum of 21" (53cm) clear floor space should be allowed between the edge of the dishwasher and counters, appliances and/or cabinets which are placed at a right angle to the dishwasher.

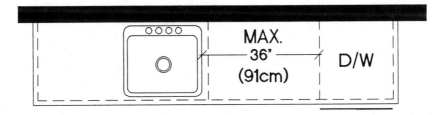

Figure 286 Guideline 16 - The edge of the primary dishwasher should be within 36" (91cm) of the edge of one sink.

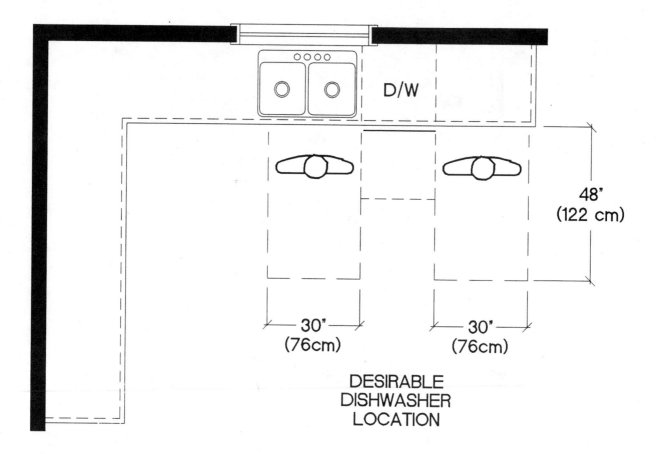

DESIRABLE
DISHWASHER
LOCATION

48"
(122 cm)

30"
(76cm)

30"
(76cm)

D/W

Figure 287 Guideline 16 - Clarification - The dishwasher should be reachable by more than one person at a time to accommodate other cooks, kitchen clean-up helpers and/or other family members.

A 30" x 48" (76cm x 122cm) clear floor space on both sides of the dishwasher will allow a person access to the dishwasher from either side.

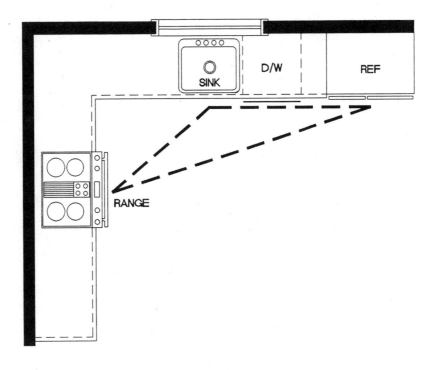

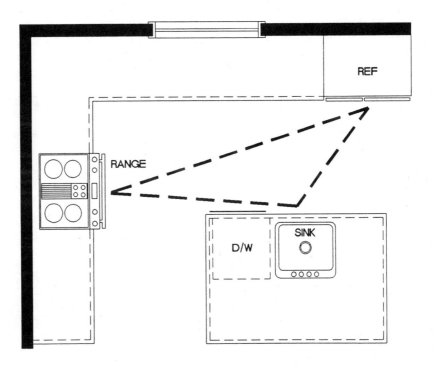

Figure 288 Guideline 17 - If the kitchen has only one sink, it should be located between or across from the cooking surface, preparation area or refrigerator.

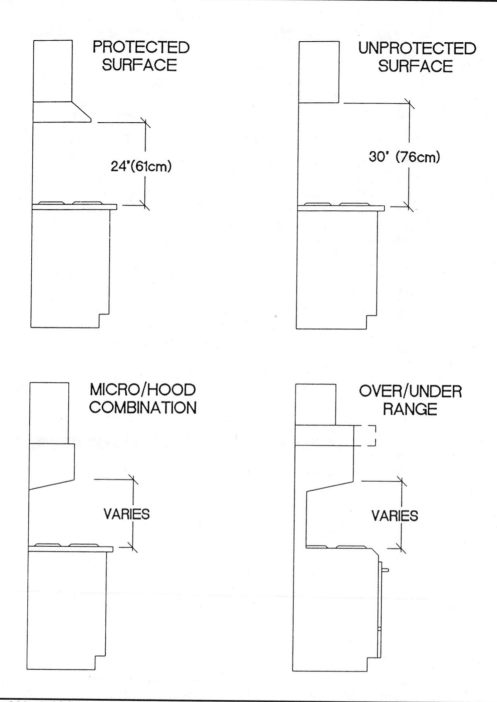

Figure 289 Guideline 18 - There should be at least 24" (61cm) of clearance between the cooking surface and a protected surface above, or at least 30" (76cm) of clearance between the cooking surface and an unprotected surface above. (If the protected surface is a microwave hood combination manufacturer's specifications may dictate a clearance less than 24" (61cm).)

While manufacturer specifications may call for less clearance with a microwave/hood or an oven over a cooking surface, safety and access relating to an upper oven or back burners should be considered.

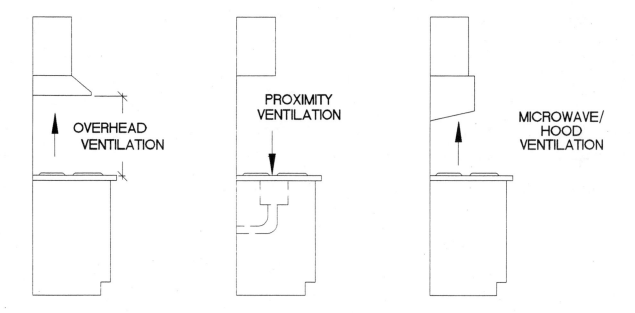

OVERHEAD
VENTILATION

PROXIMITY
VENTILATION

MICROWAVE/
HOOD
VENTILATION

Figure 290 Guideline 19 - All major appliances used for surface cooking should have a ventilation system, with a fan rated at 150 CFM minimum.

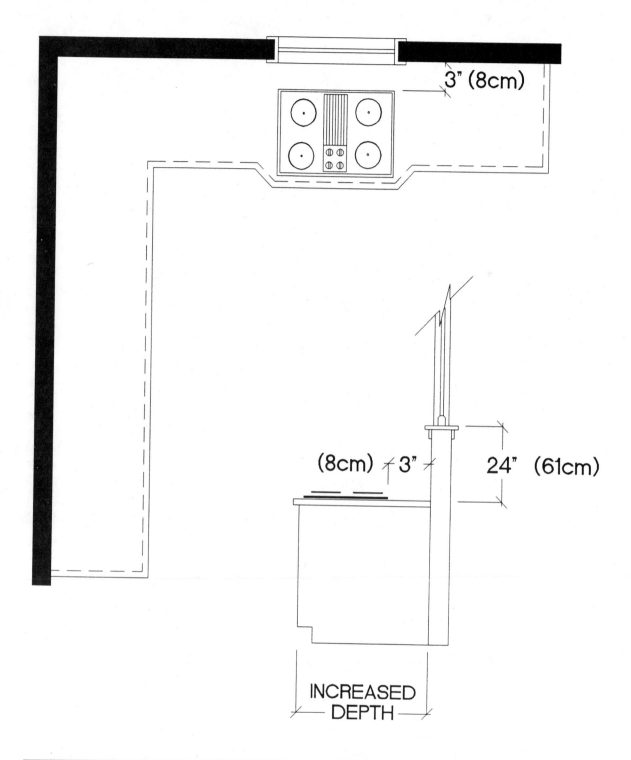

Figure 291 Guideline 20 - The cooking surface should not be placed below an operable window unless the window is 3" (8cm) or more behind the appliance and more than 24" (61cm) above it. Windows, operable or inoperable, above a cooking surface should not be dressed with flammable window treatments.

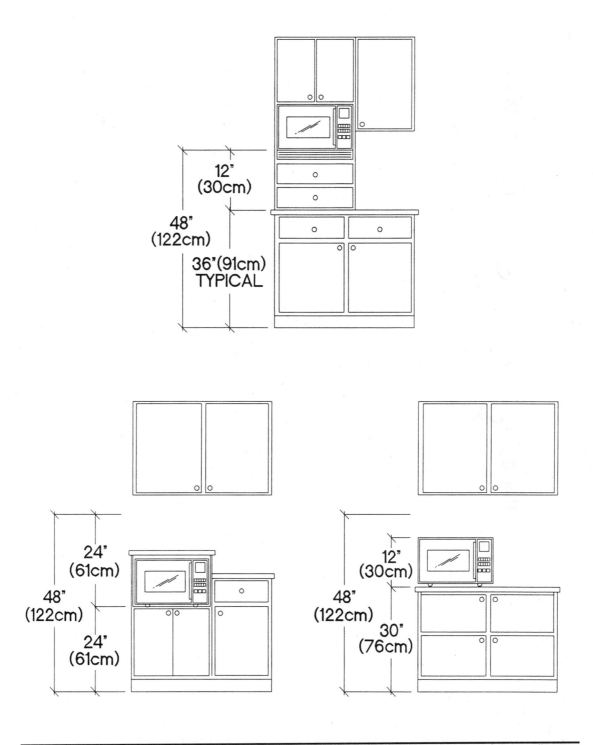

Figure 292 Guideline 21 - Microwave ovens should be placed so that the bottom of the appliance is 24" to 48" (61cm to 122cm) above the floor.

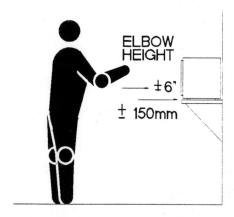
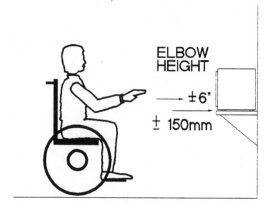

CONVENIENT MICROWAVE
HEIGHT

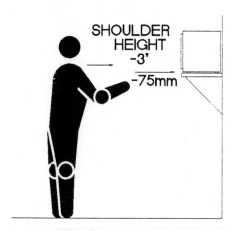
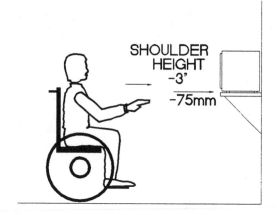

SAFE MICROWAVE
HEIGHT

Figure 293 Guideline 21 - Clarification - The final placement recommendation should be based on the user's physical abilities, which may require placement outside of the preferred 24" to 48" (61cm to 122cm) range.

Appliances designed with a microwave/hood or oven over a range will not meet this guideline but may be a necessary choice. When designing for a seated user, it may be desirable to go below the 24" (61cm) guideline. If this is the case, safety for toddlers becomes an issue and must be addressed.

SECTION IV Counter Surface and Landing Space
Guideline 22 to Guideline 34

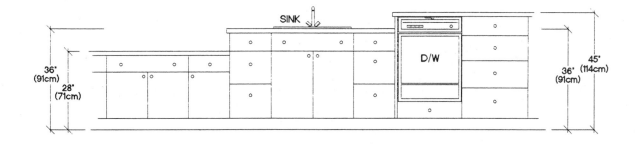

Figure 294 Guideline 22 - At least two work-counter heights should be offered in the kitchen, with one 28" - 36" (71cm - 91cm) above the finished floor and the other 36" - 45" (91cm - 114cm) above the finished floor.

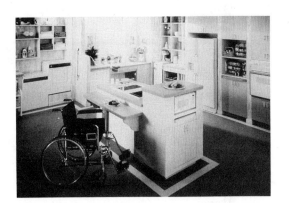

Varying counter heights will create work spaces for various tasks and for cooks of varying stature, including seated cooks.

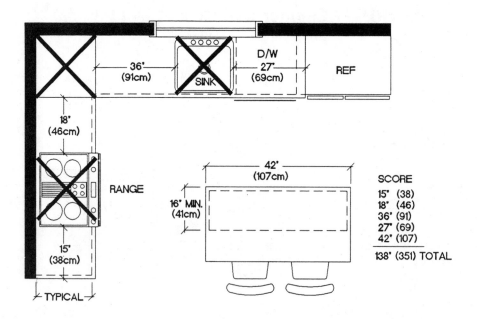

Figure 295 Guideline 23 - Countertop Frontage, Small kitchens - = or < 150 sq.ft. (14 sq.m) - allow at least 132" (335cm) of usable countertop frontage.

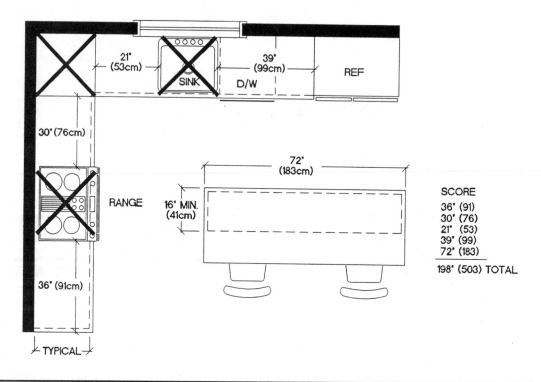

Figure 296 Guideline 23 - Countertop Frontage, Large kitchens - over 150 sq.ft. (14 sq.m) - allow at least 198" (503cm) of usable countertop frontage.

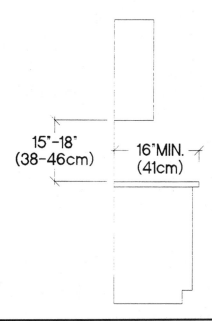

15"-18"
(38-46cm)

16"MIN.
(41cm)

Figure 297 Guideline 23 - Countertop Frontage - Counters must be a minimum of 16" (41cm) deep, and wall cabinets must be at least 15" (38cm) above their surface for counter to be included in total frontage measurement. (Measure only countertop frontage, do not count corner space.)

The minimum 15" (38cm) of clearance between a work surface and a wall cabinet relates to appliance storage and line of sight. However, there are times when dropping the wall cabinets lower, even onto the counter, will provide needed storage in the universal reach range.

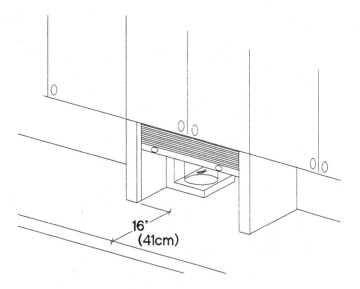

16"
(41cm)

Figure 298 Guideline 23 - Clarification - If an appliance garage/storage cabinet extends to the counter, there must be 16" (41cm) or more of clear space in front of this cabinet for the area to be counted as usable countertop frontage.

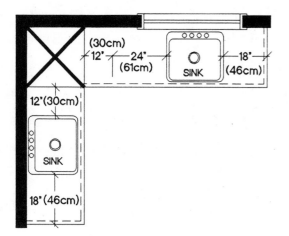

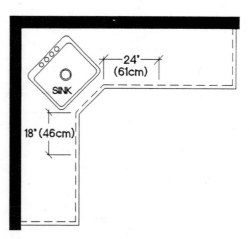

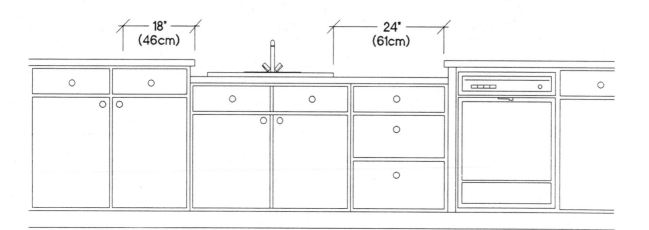

Figure 299 Guideline 24 - There should be at least 24" (61cm) of countertop frontage to one side of the primary sink, and 18" (46cm) on the other side (including corner sink applications) with the 24" (61cm) counter frontage at the same counter height as the sink. The countertop frontage may be a continuous surface, or the total of two angled countertop sections. (Measure only countertop frontage, do not count corner space.) For further instruction on these requirements see Guideline 31.

Whenever possible, the counter space on both sides of the sink should be at the same height.

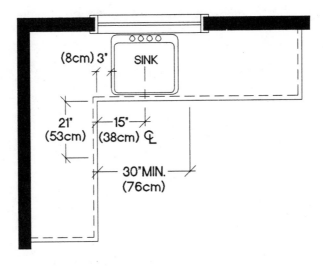

Figure 300 Guideline 24 - Clarification - The minimum allowable space from a corner to the edge of the primary sink is 3" (8cm); it should also be a minimum of 15" (38cm) from that corner to the sink centerline.

The minimum 15" (38cm) to centerline allows 30" x 48" (76cm x 122cm) clear floor space to be planned centered on the sink.

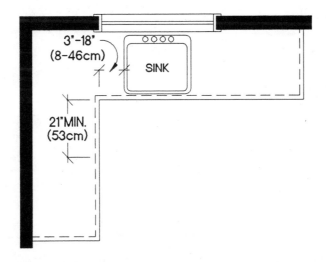

Figure 301 Guideline 24 - Clarification - If there is anything less than 18" (46cm) of frontage from the edge of the primary sink to a corner, 21" (53cm) of clear counter (measure frontage) should be allowed on the return.

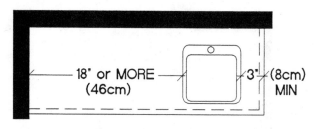

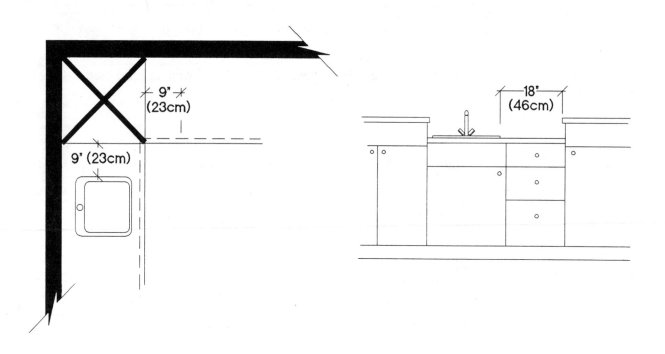

Figure 302 Guideline 25 - At least 3" (8cm) of countertop frontage should be provided on one side of secondary sinks, and 18" (46cm) on the other side (including corner sink applications) with the 18" (46cm) counter frontage at the same counter height as the sink. The countertop frontage may be a continuous surface, or the total of two angled countertop sections. (Measure only countertop frontage, do not count corner space.) For further instruction on these requirements see Guideline 31.

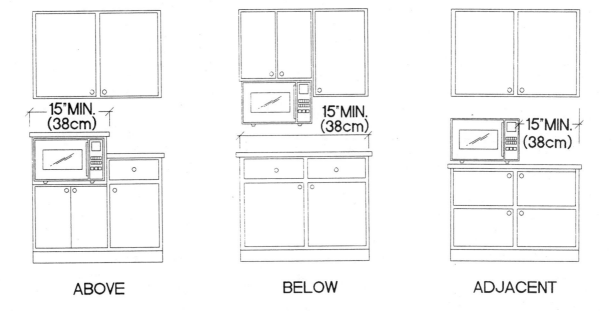

ABOVE   BELOW   ADJACENT

Figure 303 Guideline 26 - At least 15" (38cm) of landing space, a minimum of 16" (41cm) deep, should be planned above, below or adjacent to a microwave oven. For further instruction on these requirements see Guideline 31.

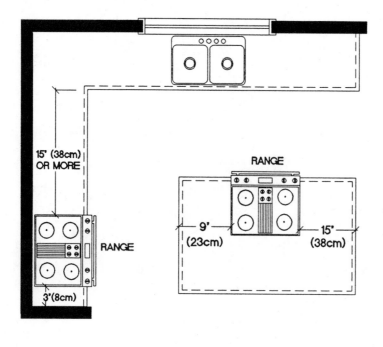

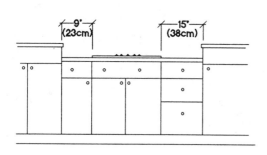

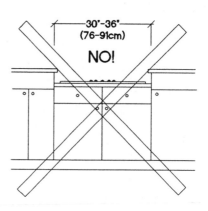

Figure 304 Guideline 27 - In an open-ended kitchen configuration, at least 9" (23cm) of counter space should be allowed on one side of the cooking surface and 15" (38cm) on the other, at the same counter height as the appliance. For an enclosed configuration, at least 3" (8cm) of clearance space should be planned at an end wall protected by flame retardant surfacing material and 15" (38cm) should be allowed on the other side of the appliance, at the same counter height as the appliance. For further instruction on these requirements see Guideline 31.

Maintaining the minimum counter area adjacent to a cooktop at the same height as the cooktop improves safety and accessibility. In case of emergency/fire, the cook should be able to slide a pot right off the burner onto adjacent counter without lifting or lowering. A person with limited strength, grip, or balance will use this technique on a regular basis and in this case, adjacent spaces should be heat resistant.

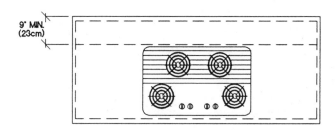

Figure 305 Guideline 27 - Clarification - For safety reasons, countertop should also extend a minimum of 9" (23cm) behind the cooking surface, at the same counter height as the appliance, in any instance where there is not an abutting wall/backsplash.

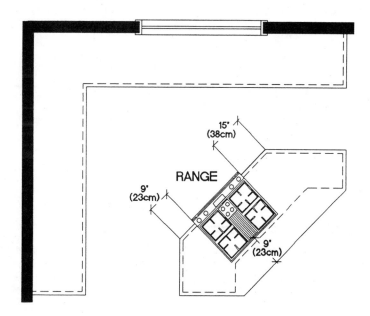

Figure 306 Guideline 27 - Clarification - In an outside angle installation of cooking surfaces, there should be at least 9" (23cm) of straight counter space on one side and 15" (38cm) of straight counter space on the other side, at the same counter height as the appliance.

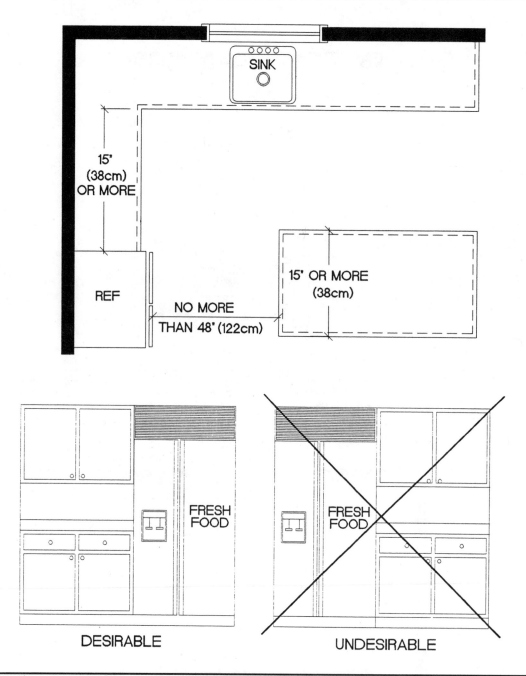

Figure 307 Guideline 28 - The plan should allow at least 15" (38cm) of counter space on the handle side of the refrigerator or on either side of a side-by-side refrigerator or, at least 15" (38cm) of landing space which is no more than 48" (122cm) across from the refrigerator. (Measure the 48" (122cm) distance from the center front of the refrigerator to the countertop opposite it.) For further instruction on these requirements see Guideline 31.

When side-by-side refrigerators are specified, it is preferable to design the space so that the countertop can be easily accessed by a person using the fresh food section.

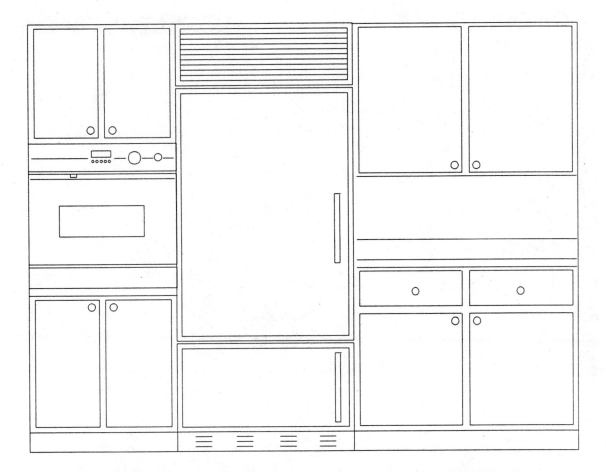

ACCEPTABLE OVEN / REFRIGERATOR PLACEMENT

Figure 308 Guideline 28 - Clarification - Although not ideal, it is acceptable to place an oven adjacent to a refrigerator. For convenience, the refrigerator should be the appliance placed next to available countertop. If there is no safe landing area across from the oven, this arrangement may be reversed.

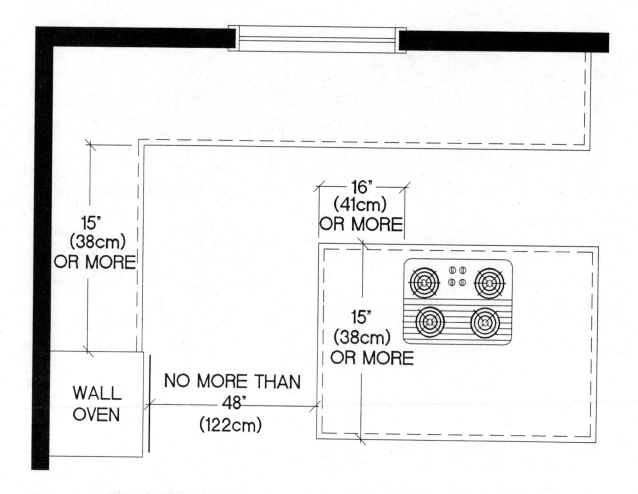

Figure 309 Guideline 29 - There should be at least 15" (38cm) of landing space which is at least 16"(41cm) deep next to or above the oven if the appliance door opens into a primary traffic pattern. At least 15" x 16" (38cm x 41cm) of landing space which is no more than 48" (122cm) across from the oven is acceptable if the appliance does not open into a traffic area. (Measure the 48" (122cm) distance from the center front of the oven to the countertop opposite it.) For further instruction on these requirements see Guideline 31.

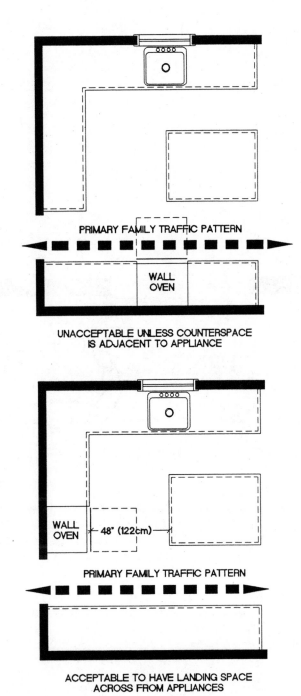

PRIMARY FAMILY TRAFFIC PATTERN

WALL OVEN

UNACCEPTABLE UNLESS COUNTERSPACE
IS ADJACENT TO APPLIANCE

WALL OVEN — 48" (122cm) —

PRIMARY FAMILY TRAFFIC PATTERN

ACCEPTABLE TO HAVE LANDING SPACE
ACROSS FROM APPLIANCES

Figure 310 Guideline 29 Examples - In the top example, the oven opens directly into a major traffic pattern leading from the utility area to the family room. This is a dangerous installation which should be avoided unless there is landing space on either side of the oven. In the bottom example, the oven is located within the cook's primary work space, away from the family traffic pattern. Therefore, a landing area can be directly opposite it.

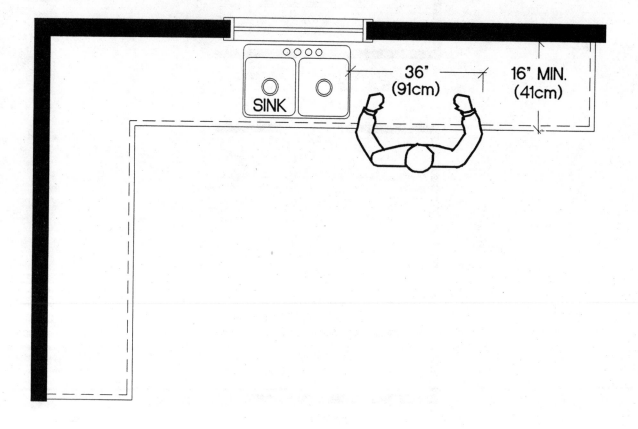

Figure 311 Guideline 30 - At least 36" (91cm) of continuous countertop which is at least 16" (41cm) deep should be planned for the preparation center. The preparation center should be immediately adjacent to a water source. For further instruction on these requirements see Guideline 31.

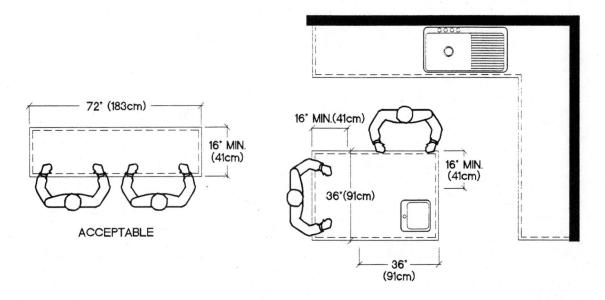

Figure 312 Guideline 30 - Clarification - If two or more people work in the kitchen simultaneously, each will need a minimum 36" (91cm) wide by 16" (41cm) deep preparation center of their own. If two people will stand adjacent to one another, a 72" (183cm) wide by 16" (41cm) deep space should be planned.

Try to orient the two people so that conversation can be continued during cooking and/or clean up process.

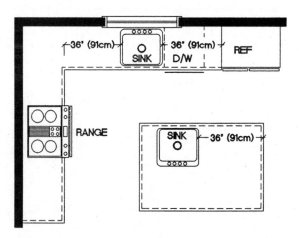

Figure 313 Guideline 30 - Clarification - The preparation center can be placed between the primary sink and the cooking surface, between the refrigerator and the primary sink, or adjacent to a secondary sink on an island or other cabinet section.

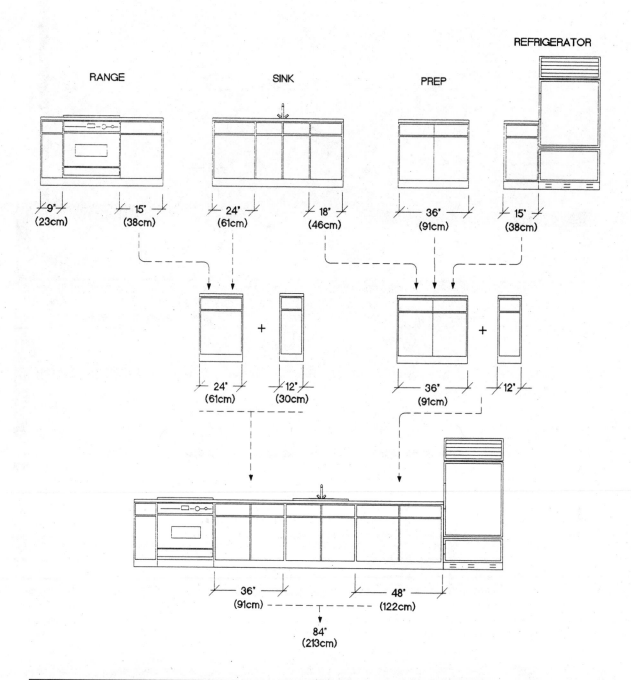

Figure 314 Guideline 31 - If two work centers are adjacent to one another, determine a new minimum counter frontage requirement for the two adjoining spaces by taking the longest of the two required counter lengths and adding 12" (30cm).

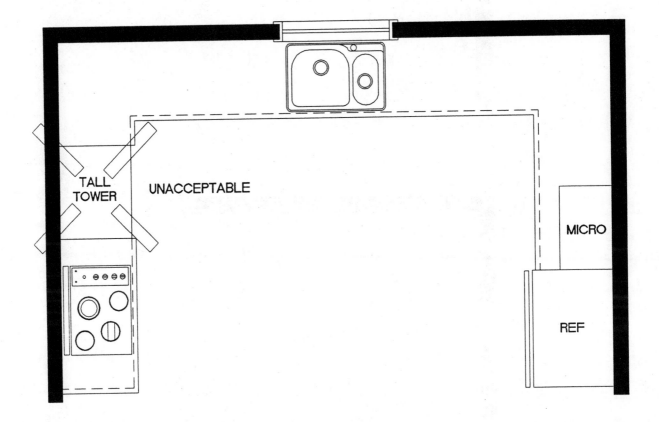

Figure 315 Guideline 32 - No two primary work centers (the primary sink, refrigerator, preparation or cooktop/range center) should be separated by a full-height, full-depth tall tower, such as an oven cabinet, pantry cabinet or refrigerator.

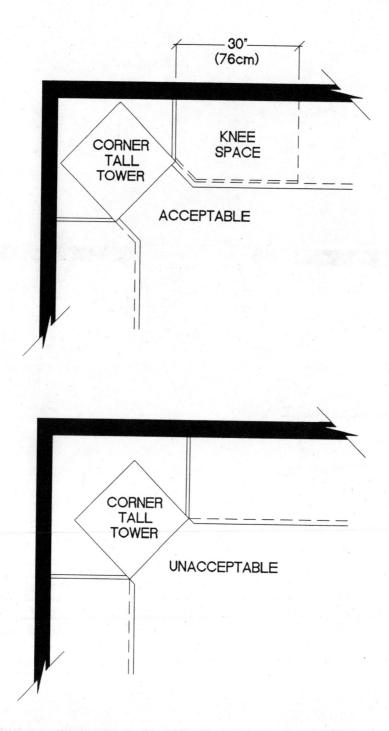

Figure 316 Guideline 32 - Clarification - A corner-recessed tall tower between primary work centers is acceptable if knee space is planned to one side of the tower.

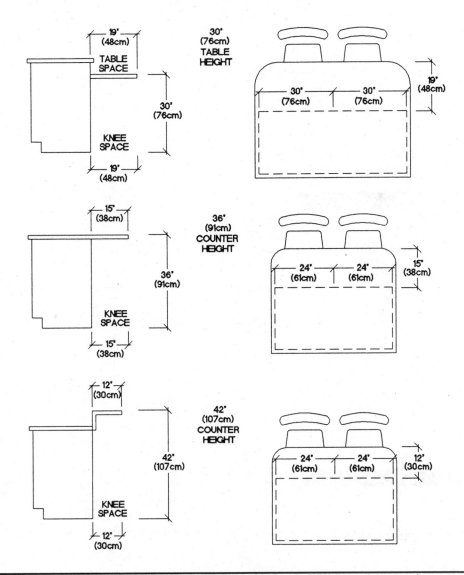

Figure 317 Guideline 33 - Kitchen seating areas require the following minimum clearances:

   30" (76cm) high tables/counters:
      allow a 30" (76cm) wide x 19" (48cm) deep counter/table space
      for each seated diner, and at least 19" (48cm) of clear knee space
   36" (91cm) high counters:
      allow a 24" (61cm) wide by 15" (38cm) deep counter space for
      each seated diner, and at least 15" (38cm) of clear knee space
   42" (107cm) high counters:
      allow a 24" (61cm) wide by 12" (30cm) deep counter space for
      each seated diner, and 12" (30cm) of clear knee space

Given that a 30" (76cm) high table or counter will work for a person in a wheelchair, the width of the allowance for each seated diner has been increased to allow for diners using wheelchairs.

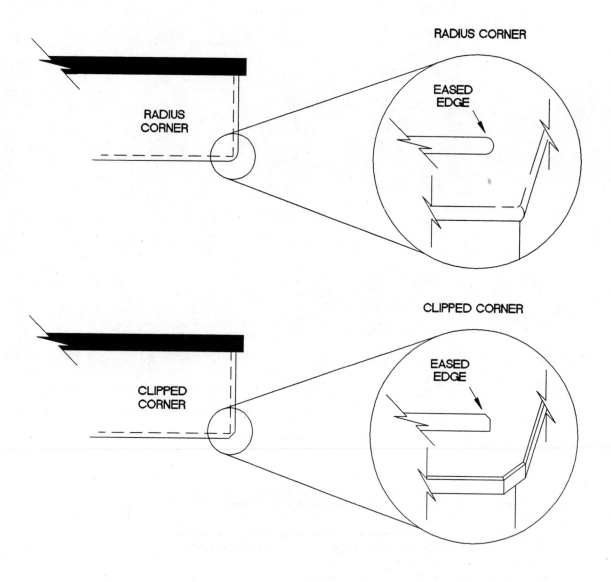

Figure 318 Guideline 34 - (Open) countertop corners should be clipped or radius; countertop edges should be eased to eliminate sharp edges.

SECTION V: Room, Appliance and Equipment Controls
Guideline 35 to Guideline 40

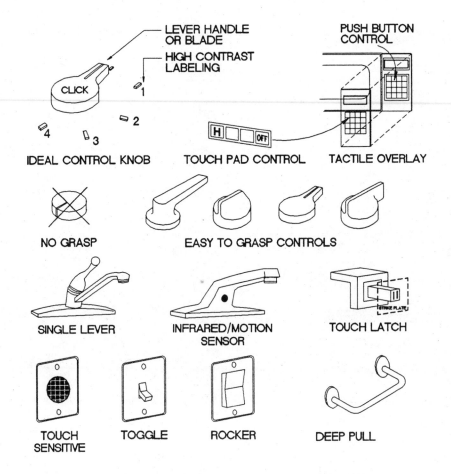

Figure 319 Guideline 35 - Controls, handles and door/drawer pulls should be operable with one hand, require only a minimal amount of strength for operation, and should not require tight grasping, pinching or twisting of the wrist. (Includes handles/knobs/pulls on entry and exit doors, appliances, cabinets, drawers and plumbing fixtures, as well as light and thermostat controls, switches, intercoms, and other room controls.)

Controls that meet this guideline expand their use to include people with limited strength, dexterity and grasping abilities. A simple test is to try operating the controls with a closed fist.

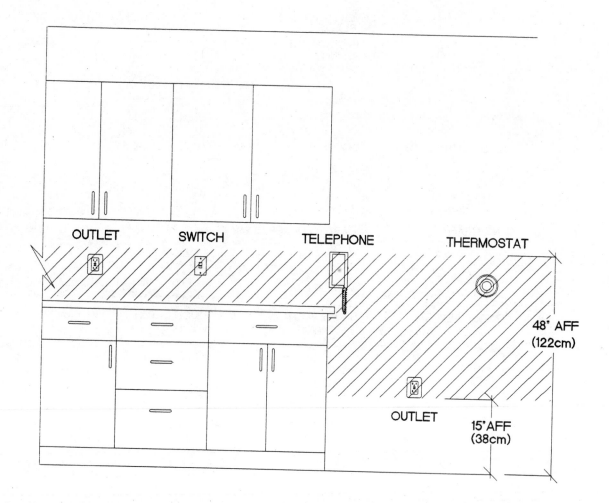

Figure 320 Guideline 36 - Wall-mounted room controls (i.e.: wall receptacles, switches, thermostats, telephones, intercoms etc.) should be 15" to 48"(38cm to 122cm) above the finished floor. The switch plate can extend beyond that dimension, but the control itself should be within it.

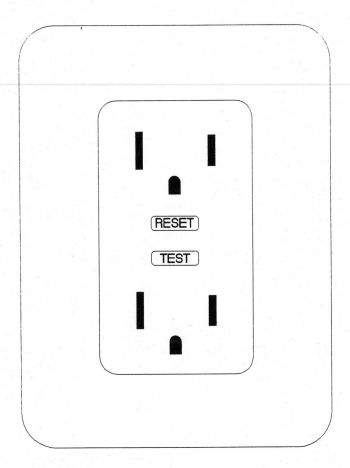

Figure 321 Guideline 37 - Ground fault circuit interrupters should be specified on all receptacles within the kitchen.

GFCI are a safety feature throughout the kitchen, including protection when foreign objects are accidentally inserted in an outlet, as well as, when an outlet is close to water.

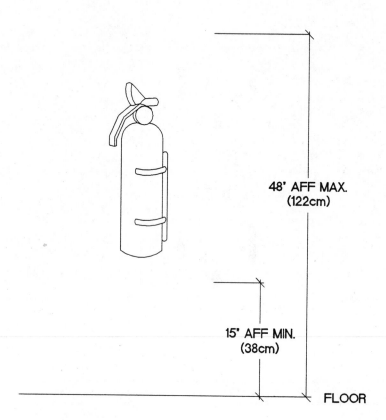

48" AFF MAX.
(122cm)

15" AFF MIN.
(38cm)

FLOOR

Figure 322 Guideline 38 - A fire extinguisher should be visibly located in the kitchen, away from cooking equipment and 15" to 48" (38cm to 122cm) above the floor. Smoke alarms should be included near the kitchen.

A fire extinguisher that can be seen and reached easily expands access to most people.

Figure 323 Guideline 39 - Window/skylight area should equal at least 10% of the total square footage of the separate kitchen, or a total living space which includes a kitchen.

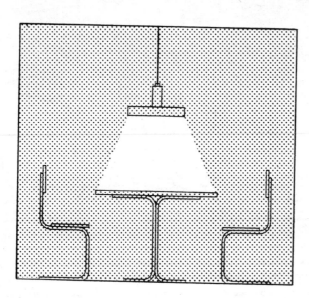

Figure 324 Guideline 40 - Every work surface in the kitchen should be well-illuminated by appropriate task and/or general lighting.

40 Guidelines of Kitchen Planning - Checklist

Yes No

1. **Guideline 1** - Doorways should be at least 32" (81cm) wide and not more than 24" (61cm) deep in the direction of travel.

   Walkways (passages between vertical objects greater than 24" (61cm) deep in the direction of travel, where not more than one is a work counter or appliance) should be at least 36" (91cm) wide.

   Work aisles (passages between vertical objects, both of which are work counters or appliances) should be at least 42" (107cm) wide in one-cook kitchens, at least 48" (122cm) wide in multiple-cook kitchens. ☐ ☐

2. **Guideline 2** - The work triangle should total 26' (792cm) or less, with no single leg of the triangle shorter than 4' (122cm) nor longer than 9' (274cm). The work triangle should not intersect an island or peninsula by more than 12" (30cm). (The triangle is the shortest walking distance between the refrigerator, primary food preparation sink and primary cooking surface, measured from the center front of each appliance.) ☐ ☐

3. **Guideline 3** - No major traffic patterns should cross through the work triangle. ☐ ☐

4. **Guideline 4** - No entry, appliance or cabinet doors should interfere with one another. ☐ ☐

5. **Guideline 5 -** In a seating area, 36" (91cm) of clearance should be allowed from the counter/table edge to any wall/obstruction behind it if no traffic will pass behind a seated diner. If there is a walkway behind the seating area, 65" (165cm) of clearance, total, including the walkway, should be allowed between the counter/table edge and any wall or obstruction. ☐ ☐

6. **Guideline 6** - Wall Cabinet Frontage, Small Kitchens - = or < 150 sq. ft. (14 sq.m) - allow at least 144" (366cm) of wall cabinet frontage, with cabinets at least 12" (30cm) deep, and a minimum of 30" (76cm) high (or equivalent) which feature adjustable shelving. Difficult to reach cabinets above the hood, oven or refrigerator do not count unless devices are installed within the case to improve accessibility.

   Wall Cabinet Frontage, Large Kitchens - over 150 sq. ft. (14 sq.m) - allow at least 186" (472cm) of wall cabinet frontage, with cabinets at least 12" (30cm) deep, and a minimum of 30" (76cm) high (or equivalent) which feature adjustable shelving. Difficult to reach cabinets above the hood, oven or refrigerator do not count unless devices are installed within the case to improve accessibility. ☐ ☐

Yes No

7. **Guideline 7** - At least 60" (152cm) of wall cabinet frontage, with cabinets at least 12" (30cm) deep, a minimum of 30" (76cm) high (or equivalent), should be included within 72" (183cm) of the primary sink centerline.   ☐   ☐

8. **Guideline 8** - Base Cabinet Frontage, Small Kitchens - = or < 150 sq. ft. (14 sq.m) - allow at least 156" (393cm) of base cabinet frontage, with cabinets at least 21" (53cm) deep (or equivalent). The blind portion of a blind corner box does not count.

    Base Cabinet Frontage, Large Kitchens - over 150 sq. ft. (14 sq.m) - require at least 192" (488cm) of base cabinet frontage, with cabinets at least 21" (53cm) deep (or equivalent). The blind portion of a blind corner box does not count.   ☐   ☐

9. **Guideline 9** - Drawer/Roll-out Shelf Frontage - Small Kitchens - = or < 150 sq. ft.(14 sq.m) - allow at least 120" (305cm) of drawer or roll-out shelf frontage. Large Kitchens - over 150 sq. ft. (14 sq.m) - allow at least 165" (419cm) of drawer or roll-out shelf frontage. Multiply cabinet width by number of drawers/roll-outs to determine frontage. Drawer/roll-out cabinets must be at least 15" (38cm) wide and 21" (53cm) deep to be counted.   ☐   ☐

10. **Guideline 10** - At least five storage/organizing items, located between 15" - 48" (38cm - 122cm) above the finished floor (or extending into that area), should be included in the kitchen to improve functionality and accessibility. These items may include, but are not limited to: lowered wall cabinets, raised base cabinets, tall cabinets, appliances garages, bins/racks, swing-out pantries, interior vertical dividers, specialized drawers/shelves etc.. Full-extension drawers/roll-out shelves greater than the 120" (305cm) minimum for small kitchens or 165" (419cm) for larger kitchens may also be included.   ☐   ☐

11. **Guideline 11** - For a kitchen with usable corner areas in the plan, at least one functional corner storage unit should be included.   ☐   ☐

12. **Guideline 12** - At least two waste receptacles should be included in the plan, one for garbage and one for recyclables; or other recycling facilities should be planned.   ☐   ☐

13. **Guideline 13** - Knee space (which may be open or adaptable) should be planned below or adjacent to sinks, cooktops, ranges, dishwashers, refrigerators and ovens whenever possible. Knee space should be a minimum of 30" (76cm) wide by 27" (69cm) high by 19" (48cm) deep under the counter. The 27" (69cm) height at the front of the knee space may decrease progressively as depth increases.   ☐   ☐

14. **Guideline 14** - A clear floor space of 30" x 48" (76cm x 122cm) should be provided at the sink, dishwasher, cooktop, oven and refrigerator. (Measure from face of cabinet or appliance if toe kick is less than 9" (23cm) high.)   ☐   ☐

15. **Guideline 15 -** A minimum of 21" (53cm) clear floor space should be allowed between the edge of the dishwasher and counters, appliances and/or cabinets which are placed at a right angle to the dishwasher.   ☐   ☐

16. **Guideline 16** - The edge of the primary dishwasher should be within 36" (91cm) of the edge of one sink.   ☐   ☐

17. **Guideline 17** - If the kitchen has only one sink, it should be located between or across from the cooking surface, preparation area or refrigerator.   ☐   ☐

18. **Guideline 18** - There should be at least 24" (61cm) of clearance between the cooking surface and a protected surface above, or at least 30" (76cm) of clearance between the cooking surface and an unprotected surface above. (If the protected surface is a microwave hood combination manufacturer's specifications may dictate a clearance less than 24" (61cm).)   ☐   ☐

19. **Guideline 19** - All major appliances used for surface cooking should have a ventilation system, with a fan rated at 150 CFM minimum.   ☐   ☐

20. **Guideline 20** - The cooking surface should not be placed below an operable window unless the window is 3" (8cm) or more behind the appliance and more than 24" (61cm) above it. Windows, operable or inoperable, above a cooking surface should not be dressed with flammable window treatments.   ☐   ☐

21. **Guideline 21** - Microwave ovens should be placed so that the bottom of the appliance is 24" to 48" (61cm to 122cm) above the floor.   ☐   ☐

22. **Guideline 22** - At least two work-counter heights should be offered in the kitchen, with one 28" - 36" (71cm - 91cm) above the finished floor and the other 36" - 45" (91cm - 114cm) above the finished floor.   ☐   ☐

23. Guideline 23 - Countertop Frontage - Small kitchens - under 150 sq.ft. (14 sq.m) - allow at least 132" (335cm) of usable countertop frontage.

Countertop Frontage - Large kitchens - over 150 sq.ft. (14 sq.m) - allow at least 198" (503cm) of usable countertop frontage.

Countertop Frontage - Counters must be a minimum of 16" (41cm) deep, and wall cabinets must be at least 15" (38cm) above their surface for counter to be included in total frontage measurement. (Measure only countertop frontage, do not count corner space.)   ☐   ☐

24. Guideline 24 - There should be at least 24" (61cm) of countertop frontage to one side of the primary sink, and 18" (46cm) on the other side (including corner sink applications) with the 24" (61cm) counter frontage at the same counter height as the sink. The countertop frontage may be a continuous surface, or the total of two angled countertop sections. (Measure only countertop frontage, do not count corner space.) For further instruction on these requirements see Guideline 31.   ☐   ☐

25. Guideline 25 - At least 3" (8cm) of countertop frontage should be provided on one side of secondary sinks, and 18" (46cm) on the other side (including corner sink applications) with the 18" (46cm) counter frontage at the same counter height as the sink. The countertop frontage may be a continuous surface, or the total of two angled counter top sections. (Measure only counter top frontage, do not count corner space.) For further instruction on these requirements see Guideline 31.   ☐   ☐

26. Guideline 26 - At least 15" (38cm) of landing space, a minimum of 16" (41cm) deep, should be planned above, below or adjacent to a microwave oven. For further instruction on these requirements see Guideline 31.   ☐   ☐

27. Guideline 27 - In an open-ended kitchen configuration, at least 9" (23cm) of counter space should be allowed on one side of the cooking surface and 15" (38cm) on the other, at the same counter height as the appliance. For an enclosed configuration, at least 3" (8cm) of clearance space should be planned at an end wall protected by flame retardant surfacing material and 15" (38cm) should be allowed on the other side of the appliance, at the same counter height as the appliance. For further instruction on these requirements see Guideline 31.   ☐   ☐

28. **Guideline 28** - The plan should allow at least 15" (38cm) of counter space on the handle side of the refrigerator or on either side of a side-by-side refrigerator or, at least 15" (38cm) of landing space which is no more than 48" (122cm) across from the refrigerator. (Measure the 48" (122cm) distance from the center front of the refrigerator to the countertop opposite it.) For further instruction on these requirements see Guideline 31.   ☐ ☐

29. **Guideline 29** - There should be at least 15" (38cm) of landing space which is at least 16"(41cm) deep next to or above the oven if the appliance door opens into a primary traffic pattern. At least 15" x 16" (38cm x 41cm) of landing space which is no more than 48" (122cm) across from the oven is acceptable if the appliance does not open into a traffic area. (Measure the 48" (122cm) distance from the center front of the oven to the countertop opposite it.) For further instruction on these requirements see Guideline 31.   ☐ ☐

30. **Guideline 30** - At least 36" (91cm) of continuous countertop which is at least 16" (41cm) deep should be planned for the preparation center. The preparation center should be immediately adjacent to a water source. For further instruction on these requirements see Guideline 31.   ☐ ☐

31. **Guideline 31** - If two work centers are adjacent to one another, determine a new minimum counter frontage requirement for the two adjoining spaces by taking the longest of the two required counter lengths and adding 12" (30cm).   ☐ ☐

32. **Guideline 32** - No two primary work centers (the primary sink, refrigerator, preparation or cooktop/range center) should be separated by a full-height, full-depth tall tower, such as an oven cabinet, pantry cabinet or refrigerator.   ☐ ☐

33. **Guideline 33** - Kitchen seating areas require the following minimum clearances:

        30" (76cm) high tables/counters:
allow a 30" (76cm) wide x 19" (48cm) deep counter/table space for each seated diner, and at least 19" (48cm) of clear knee space   ☐ ☐

        36" (91cm) high counters:
allow a 24" (61cm) wide by 15" (38cm) deep counter space for each seated diner, and at least 15" (38cm) of clear knee space   ☐ ☐

        42" (107cm) high counters:
allow a 24" (61cm) wide by 12" (30cm) deep counter space for each seated diner, and 12" (30cm) of clear knee space   ☐ ☐

Yes No

34. **Guideline 34** - (Open) countertop corners should be clipped or radiused; countertop edges should be eased to eliminate sharp edges. ☐ ☐

35. **Guideline 35** - Controls, handles and door/drawer pulls should be operable with one hand, require only a minimal amount of strength for operation, and should not require tight grasping, pinching or twisting of the wrist. (Includes handles/knobs/pulls on entry and exit doors, appliances, cabinets, drawers and plumbing fixtures, as well as light and thermostat controls, switches, intercoms, and other room controls.) ☐ ☐

36. **Guideline 36** - Wall-mounted room controls (i.e.: wall receptacles, switches, thermostats, telephones, intercoms etc.) should be 15" to 48" (38cm to 122cm) above the finished floor. The switch plate can extend beyond that dimension, but the control itself should be within it. ☐ ☐

37. **Guideline 37** - Ground fault circuit interrupters should be specified on all receptacles within the kitchen. ☐ ☐

38. **Guideline 38** - A fire extinguisher should be visibly located in the kitchen, away from cooking equipment and 15" to 48" (38cm to 122cm) above the floor. Smoke alarms should be included near the kitchen. ☐ ☐

39. **Guideline 39** - Window/skylight area should equal at least 10% of the total square footage of the separate kitchen, or a total living space which includes a kitchen. ☐ ☐

40. **Guideline 40** - Every work surface in the kitchen should be well-illuminated by appropriate task and/or general lighting. ☐ ☐

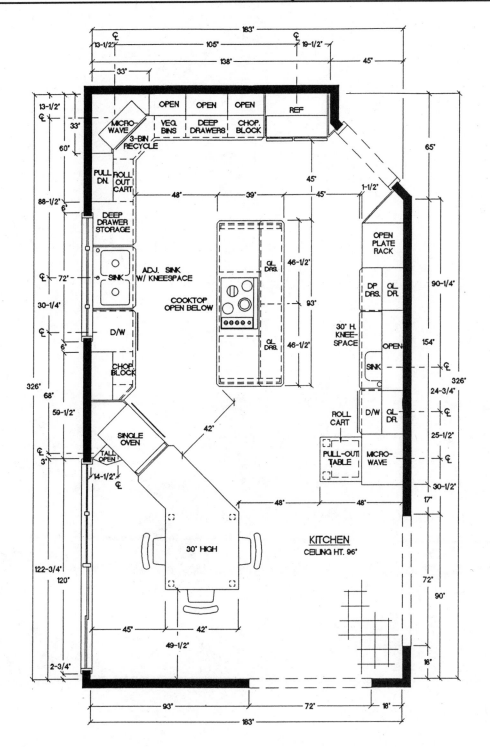

Figure 325 Example - A kitchen that has adapted these new guidelines was recently featured by General Electric in a "real life design" consumer promotion. The floor plan demonstrates spacious aisles and flexible work areas for universal appeal.

Figure 326 (Courtesy of General Electric) The wide aisle and multiple counter heights and work centers encourage all to join in meal preparation.

Figure 327 Storage within universal reach.

Figure 329 Raised toekicks for clearance of mobility aids.

Figure 328 Open knee space below cooktop with pull-out stool behind fold back doors.

Figure 330 Glass smooth top cooktop with high contrast and safety indicator light that stays on until unit is cool.

Figure 331 Adjustable sink with knee space, motorized control and lever faucet. Shown at 30" (76cm) height.

Figure 333 Adjustable sink with knee space, motorized control and lever faucet. Shown at 42" (107cm) height.

Figure 332 Wall cabinet features pull-out and down shelves to optimize accessibility.

Figure 334 Roll-out cart with heat resistant surface and curb on three sides assists in transport of items from cooktop or oven to table.

Figure 335 Side-by-side refrigerator with ice and water dispenser in door.

Figure 337 Fold out step stool and pull-out vegetable bins.

Figure 336 Microwave with touch controls and word prompting feature. Side swing door at counter height allows items to slide out and onto counter with little lifting.

Figure 338 Base corner recycling bin.

How To Lay Out A Kitchen

THE SUBTRACTION METHOD

Once you are familiar with the guidelines of good kitchen planning, you're ready to lay out a kitchen. Drafting techniques will be covered in detail in Volume 6 of this set of manuals. What follows is an organized approach to space management called *"The Subtraction Method."*

We'll do a one-wall kitchen in detail, step by step, and then a U-shaped kitchen. We will use the subtraction method, which is generally known and accepted in the industry.

Before starting you should have any dimensions and information provided by the customer and your own sketch and measurements, plus the cabinet sizes and specifications of the cabinet line you will use. You should familiarize yourself thoroughly with your customer survey.

Step #1 - A One Wall Kitchen - Example - Draw the Room Outline

The first step is to consult your notes and your sketch. Draw the walls of the kitchen and place the window, carefully and accurately, all in inches and not mixing feet and inches. The overall inside dimension is 222 3/4" (565.79cm). There is a window opening that is 40 1/2" wide (102.87cm) including casing. The window C/L (center line) is 120 3/4" (306.71cm) from the right wall and 102" (259.08cm) from the left wall.

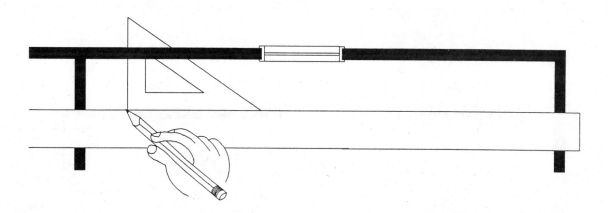

Figure 339 Subtraction Method Step #1 - One wall example - Draw the room outline.

Step #2 - A One Wall Kitchen Example - Dimension the Plan

After drawing the walls and the window, take the dimensions from your sketch and put them on your drawing in accord with the *Graphics and Presentation Standards.* Enter the usable space on either side of the window and the window measurement, including trim. There is 81 3/4" (207.65cm) to the left of the

window, 100 1/2" (255.27cm) to the right of the window. The window with trim is 40 1/2" (102.87cm). Because our client has said she wants the sink centered on the window, enter the center line (C/L) of the window on the next line above that. There is 120 3/4" (306.71cm) from the right wall and 102" (259.08cm) from the left wall. Fill in these figures. Your third line above the drawing will be the total inside length of the wall, 222 3/4" (565.79cm).

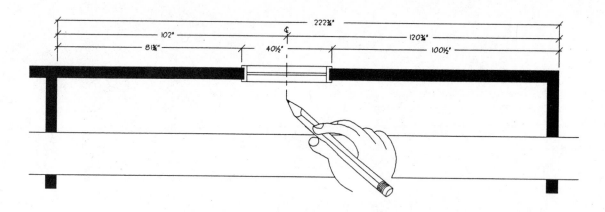

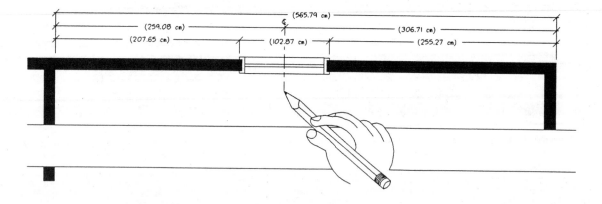

Figure 340 Subtraction Method Step #2 - One wall example - Dimension the plan.

Step #3 - A One Wall Kitchen Example - Lay Out the Kitchen

Now we are ready to lay out the kitchen. First draw two horizontal lines, one 12" (30.48cm) from the wall and 24" (60.96cm) from the wall. The first shows the depth of the wall cabinets; the second, the depth of the base cabinets, the equipment (appliances) and the tall cabinet we intend to include. The next step is to decide where to put the work centers so the amount of travel is reduced as much as possible. Since the sink/clean-up center is most used, it will be near the center. Most people prefer the sink under the window, so here we center it under the window. We are using a refrigerator hinged at the right, we will put it on the right side so the door will open into the work area. The range, then, should be on the left.

Now we will start putting in the base cabinets. Before putting another line on the paper, do your computations using the subtraction line method of planning to make sure everything will fit properly. Start at the right of the C/L and figure base cabinets. We have 120 3/4" (306.71cm) to work with. We will figure a 36" (91.44 cm) sink base under the window. By centering it we have half, or 18" (45.72cm) to deduct from 120 3/4" (306.71cm), leaving us 102 3/4" (260.99cm).

We will place the dishwasher to the right of the sink and deduct 24" (60.96 cm) from 102 3/4" (260.99cm), leaving 78 3/4" (200.03cm). We need 48" (121.92cm) for the food preparation area

between the refrigerator and the sink, so we add a 24" (60.96cm) base cabinet. Since we may want to use a bread box and bulk storage in this area, we will use a drawer base and deduct 24" (60.96cm) from 78 3/4" (200.03 cm), leaving 54 3/4" (139.07cm).

We are using a 35" (88.9cm) refrigerator and will provide an extra inch (2.54cm) for clearance (35" + 1" = 36") (89.9cm + 2.54cm = 91.44cm). Deducting 36" (91.44cm) from 54 3/4" (139.07cm), we have 18 3/4" (47.63cm) left. This is sufficient for a tall storage unit that can be used for staple foods in packages. It would be a unit 18" (45.72cm) wide with door hinged to the right, 24" (60.96cm) deep and 84" (213.36cm) high.

To the left of the C/L we have 222 3/4" (565.79cm) less 120 3/4" (306.71cm), leaving 102" (259.08cm) to work with. Deducting the left side of the sink base, or 18" (45.72cm) from 102" (259.08cm), leaves 84" (213.36cm). We want a work area on each side of the range. The range is 30" (76.2cm) wide and a slide-in. Deducting this from 84" (213.36cm) leaves 54" (137.16cm). We learned previously that we should strive for a desirable 18" (45.72cm) on the far side of the range, so we deduct 18" (45.72cm) from 54" (137.16cm) and we have 36" (91.44cm) left for a 36" (91.44cm) base unit between the range and the sink. (We now have our base section).

REMEMBER, we are doing all of this on scrap paper, and will fill in the drawings later.

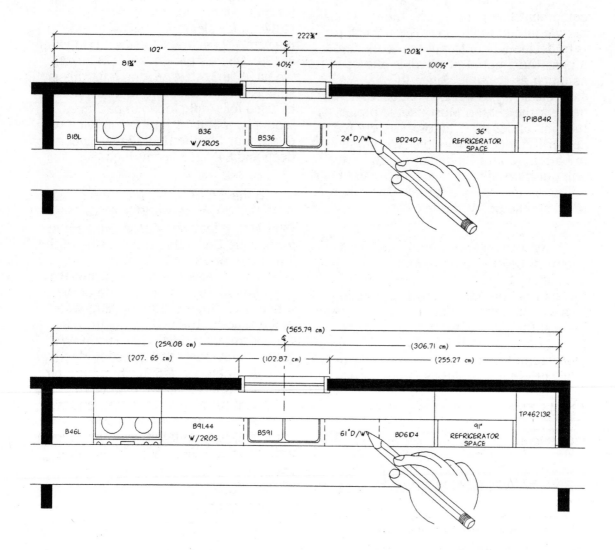

Figure 341 Subtraction Method Step #3 - One wall example - Position work centers and lay out base cabinets.

Step #4 - A One Wall Kitchen Example - Lay Out the Wall Cabinets

We will now plan the wall cabinets. Wall cabinets usually are sized to line up as nearly as possible with base cabinets. The usable wall space on the right side of the window is 100 1/2" (255.27cm). Our tall cabinet and filler on the extreme right takes 18 3/4" (45.63cm) of that space, leaving 81 3/4" (207.65cm). To fit the space over the refrigerator we will use a W3615, which is the designation for a wall cabinet 36" (91.44cm) wide and 15" (38.1cm) high. Deducting this from 81 3/4" (207.65cm) we have 45 3/4" (116.21cm) left. We could use a W4530 here, but most stock cabinet manufacturers do not make a unit this size.

Instead, we will use two cabinets, W2130R next to the window and a W2430R over the 24" (60.96cm) base. The W2130R is a wall cabinet 21" (53.34cm) wide and 30" (76.2cm) high, hinged on the right. The W2430R is a wall cabinet 24" (60.96cm) wide and 30" (76.2cm) high, hinged right. Deducting that total of 45" (114.3cm) from 45 3/4" (116.21cm), we have a 3/4" (1.91cm) reveal between the window casing and the cabinet.

To the left of the window we have 81 3/4" (207.65cm) from the wall to the edge of the casing. We will use a W1830L wall cabinet over the B18L base. Deducting this from 81 3/4" we have 63 3/4" (161.93cm) left. We then use a W3018 cabinet over the range to provide for a ventilating hood under it. Most hoods are about 6" (15.24cm) high, allowing sufficient clearance over the cooktop when used with a W3018. However, when using extra high and deep hoods it will be necessary to use a W3015. Deducting 30" (76.2cm) from 63 3/4" (161.93cm), we have 33 3/4" (85.73cm) left. Using a W3330L in the remaining space will leave a 3/4" (1.91cm) reveal between it and the casing, matching the reveal on the other side.

Should there be need for a greater amount of reveal on each side of the window, such as for drapery stack-up, the two cabinets on either side of the window could be reduced in size by 3" (7.62cm). In a kitchen of this small size it may be preferable to provide as much storage space as possible and keep the reveal to a minimum. The cabinets on each side of the window are tied together by using a valance board between them. The valance board is flush with the front face of the cabinets and under the bulkhead or soffit. A standard width valance is 48" (121.92cm). We need only 42" (106.68cm) of valance, so the board would be cut to fit on the job site.

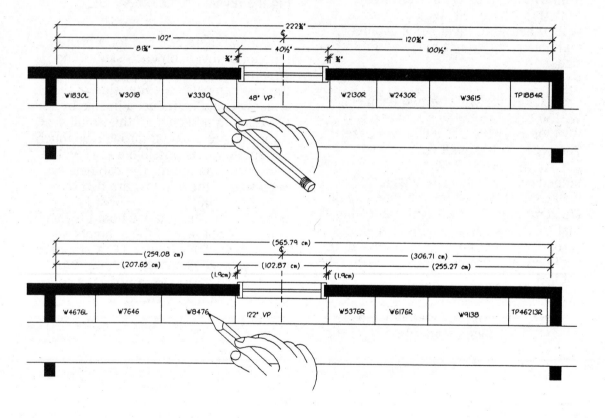

Figure 342 Subtraction Method Step #4 - One wall example - Lay out the wall cabinets.

Step #5 - A One Wall Kitchen Example - Transfer design to final presentation drawing and add centerlines for all appliances

Now that we have worked out the cabinet layout we will put in the lines representing the widths of the various units. The lines for the base units will be dotted and extend only to the front line of the wall units. Then draw a solid counter line in front of all base cabinets to indicate the overhang. When you have completed the layout, go over the lines representing the front edges of the wall and base cabinets to strengthen them. Then letter the nomenclature of the cabinets and appliances, using top and bottom guide lines for the letters and numbers to give them a uniform size. Using your template, draw in a sink bowl, refrigerator, range burners and hood to complete the plan. It's good to have a separate listing of appliances and cabinets with your proposal.

To trim the cabinets where they meet the soffit or bulkhead, it is desirable to use a molding. If the bulkhead is deeper than the cabinets, a cove molding should be used under it and against the face of the cabinets above the doors. If the bulkhead is built flush with the face of the cabinets, a batten molding is used to cover the crack between the top of the cabinet and the face board of the bulkhead.

Most molding comes in 96" (243.84cm) lengths. Specify the number of pieces required. In this kitchen, the overall length is 222 3/4" (565.79cm), so three pieces would be required. The molding would be carried across the valance board as well as the cabinets.

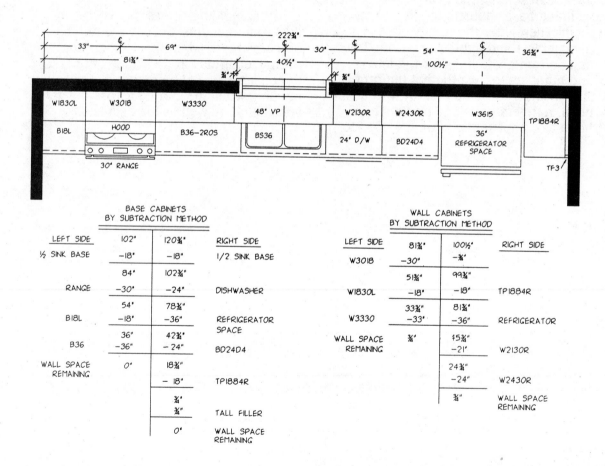

Figure 343 Subtraction Method Step #5 - One wall imperial example - Transfer design to final presentation drawing.

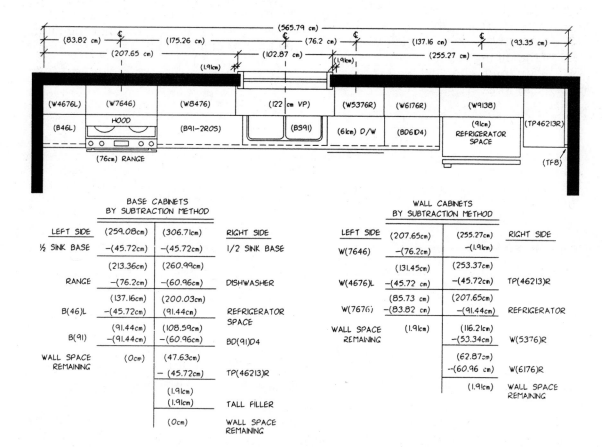

Figure 344 Subtraction Method Step #5 - One wall metric example - Transfer design to final presentation drawing.

Step #1 & 2 - A U-Shape Kitchen Example - Draw the Room Outline and Dimension the Plan

The U-shape kitchen is more complicated in that it has two inside corners. We have a room that is 141" x 208" (358.14 cm x 528.32cm). Since we do not intend to develop any storage space initially in the dining room we have not shown it on the drawing. The window wall is 141" (358.14cm) wide. There is a 42" (106.68cm) window including trim, centered 66" (167.64cm) from the left corner. Usable space to the left of the window is 45" (114.3cm) and 54" (137.16cm) to the right. The left wall next to the dining room is 97" (246.38cm) long. The right wall is 87" (220.98cm) long.

Our first step is to measure out from each wall, 12" (30.48cm) and 24" (60.96cm) respectively, then draw lines around the three sides to indicate the front lines of the wall and base cabinets. You can see that there is sufficient space to develop a U-shaped kitchen. Next we will locate the appliances. We are using a 36" wide (91.44cm) side-by-side refrigerator and will locate it at the bottom right of our plan because this is adjacent to the entrance door. This will be convenient for food brought in from the market. The sink will be centered under the window and the range will be on the dining room wall to the left of the sink for convenience in serving to either the dining area or dining room.

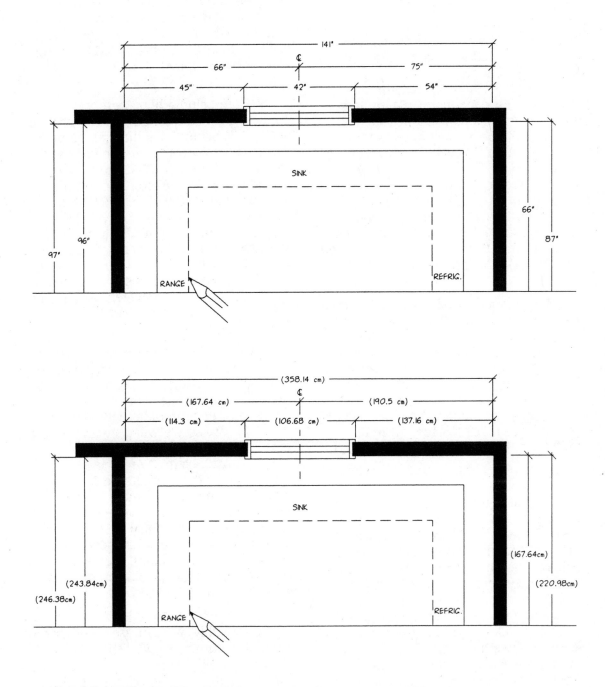

Figure 345 Subtraction Method Step #1 & 2 - U-shape examples - Dimension the plan.

Step #3 - A U-Shape Kitchen Example - Lay Out the Base Cabinets

The next step is to fit in the base units. We will start at the center line of the window and work to the right. We are using a single-bowl sink 24" x 21" (61.44cm x 53.34cm). A self-rimming sink would be one inch (2.54cm) larger in each dimension. We'll provide a 30" (76.2cm) sink base. We have 141" (358.14cm) on this wall. The C/L of the window is 66" (167.64cm) from the left wall, so we deduct this from 141" (358.14cm) to find we have 75" (190.5cm) to the right of the window C/L. Deduct half of the sink cabinet, or 15" (38.1cm), from 75" (190.5cm) and we have 60" (152.4cm) left.

We will place a B24R cabinet to the right of the sink. Deduct 24" (60.96cm) from 60" (152.4cm) and we have 36" (91.44cm) left. This is enough space for a corner rotary on this wall, so temporarily we will figure on this unit. To the left of the window C/L we have 66" (167.64cm). We deduct the other half of the sink base, 15" (38.1cm) from 66" (167.64cm) and we have 51" (129.54cm) left.

We will figure a blind corner unit on the left wall. This takes 24" (60.96cm) on the window wall, so we take that from 51" (129.54cm) and have 27" (68.58cm) left. We should provide a filler here to permit easy opening of doors and drawers. Since we are on the 3" (7.62cm) module on this wall, we will use a BF3, or 3" base filler. Deducting this from 27" (68.58cm), we have 24" (60.96cm) left for a dishwasher. However, being so close to the corner might not allow easy loading from the dishwasher to the wall cabinets above so check with the customer.

On the left hand wall we are placing an eye-level free-standing range, with an oven above and another below. It takes 30" (76.2cm) of space. We deduct that from the 97" (246.38cm) we have to work with and we have 67" (170.18cm) left for base cabinet storage.

We are using a blind corner cabinet to the right of the range and will choose a 42" (106.68cm) base that can be pulled 45" (114.3cm) away from the back wall. Pull it out the full 3" (7.62cm) to correspond to the 3" (7.62cm) filler on the window wall. We deduct 45" (114.3cm) from 67" (170.18cm) and have 22" (55.88cm) remaining to use to the left of the range. There is no standard 22"-wide cabinet in stock units, so we will use a 21" (53.34cm) drawer base, allowing an extra inch (2.54cm) between the cabinet and the casing.

If we wanted to fill the space, which isn't necessary, we might pull the corner unit just 1" (2.54cm) and use a BD24 at the end of the range. However, this would give us a problem with wall cabinets later on, so we will go with the first arrangement. On the right hand wall we have 87" (220.98cm). We need 36" (91.44cm) for the refrigerator. It is on the end, so no special clearance problem arises. We choose to leave a 3" (7.62cm) reveal to widen the entry walkway. We deduct 3" (7.62cm) from 87" (220.98cm) and have 84" (213.36cm). We deduct 36" (91.44cm) from 84" (213.36cm) and have 48" (121.92cm) left.

Conceivably, we can use a corner rotary in the corner, so we deduct 36" (91.44cm) from 48" (121.92cm) and have 12" (30.48cm) left, enough for a B12R base unit next to the refrigerator. Whether we use a L or R cabinet depends on whether we want access to the cabinet from the refrigerator or the sink area.

In this example, the client has requested that all the cabinets should open away from sink area, so those to the left of the sink would be L cabinets and those to the right, R cabinets where they are single door units. (L indicates left-hinged door as you face the cabinet. R indicates right-hinged.)

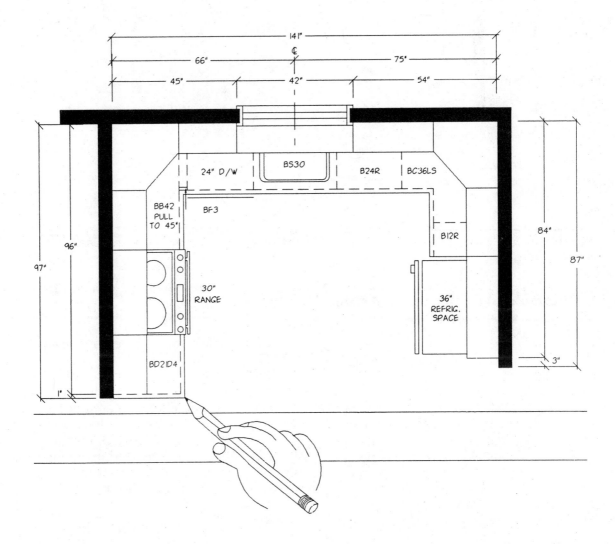

Figure 346 Subtraction Method Step #3 - A U-Shape imperial example - Lay out the base cabinets.

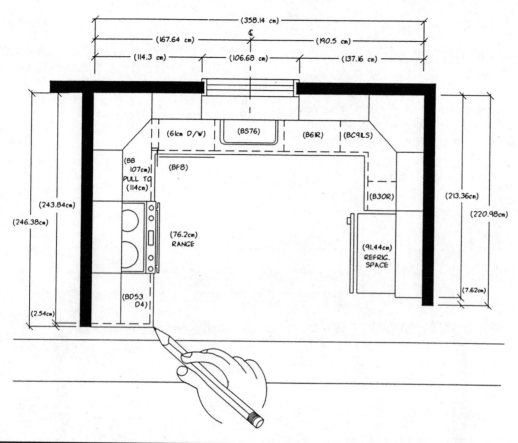

Figure 347 Subtraction Method Step #3 - A U-Shape metric example - Lay out the base cabinets.

Step #4 - A U-Shape Kitchen Example - Lay Out the Wall Cabinets

Our next job is to plan the wall cabinets. To the right of the window we show a distance of 54" (137.16cm) from the casing to the wall to be filled with wall cabinets. We will start in the corner with a diagonal corner wall cabinet. It takes up 24" (60.96cm) of space along the wall, so we deduct 24" (60.96cm) from 54" (137.16cm) and have 30" (76.2cm) left, or enough for a W3030.

To the left of the window we have 45" (114.3cm). Using a diagonal corner wall cabinet in the left corner, we deduct 24" (60.96cm) from 45" (114.3cm)

and have 21" (53.34cm) left, enough for a W2130L.

On the left hand wall we have used 96" (243.84cm) of space for the base units. We have 45" (114.3cm) between the wall and the range. Deducting 24" (60.96cm) for the other wall area of the diagonal corner wall unit, we have 21" (53.34cm) left for a W2130R. Since this cabinet probably will be used in conjunction with the cooking center, we will use an R cabinet, hinged on the right.

Depending on the height of the range unit, we might use a W3015 or W3012 unit over it. If the space is not sufficient for a cabinet, a panel is needed to close the space between the surrounding wall cabinets. A piece cut from plywood shelving or plywood paneling, finished to match, would do the trick if the manufacturer doesn't have a piece to fit. Over the BD21 to the left of the range unit we would use a W2130L.

On the right hand wall we probably would use a W3615 over the refrigerator. The height would depend on the height of the refrigerator. The total space used by base units on this wall was 84" (213.36cm). Deducting 36" (91.44cm), we have 48" (121.92cm) left. We have to deduct 24" (60.96cm) for the corner cabinet, and have 24" (61.44cm) left, enough for a W2430. We would then figure a 48" (121.92cm) valance, cut to size, at the window.

In figuring molding, we would measure out from the wall at the left to the front of the wall cabinet, then along the front edge of the wall cabinets to the corner cabinet. Then on the diagonal face of this cabinet, across the wall cabinets on the window wall, including the valance, to the diagonal corner cabinet on the other wall. Then measure across its face and the face of the adjoining cabinets to the end, and back to the wall at the refrigerator cabinet. This adds up to about 289" (734.06cm).

Dividing by 96" (243.84cm), the length of a piece of molding, we come out with just a fraction of an inch over three pieces. This will leave us with a margin for error in cutting and fitting. In fact, when figuring jobs for ordering it's good to order an extra piece of molding to save time in case a bad cut is made or you measured wrong.

We indicate doors on cabinets hinged so they open away from the sink area. This is generally good practice, but must be modified in line with the customer requirements and location of work centers. This information should be included on your survey form.

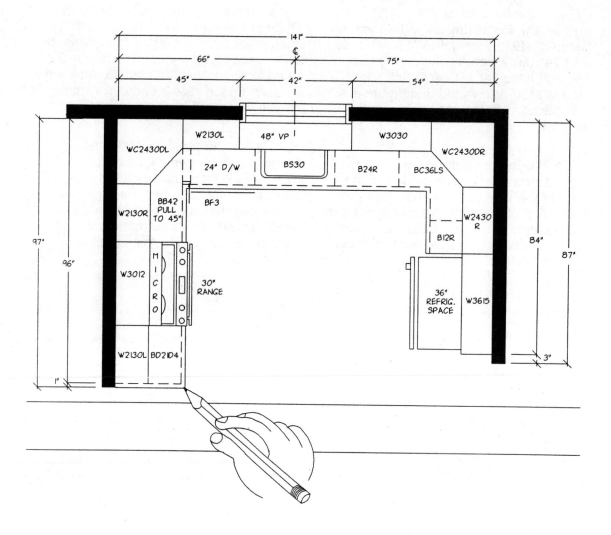

Figure 348 Subtraction Method Step #4 - A U-Shape imperial example - Lay out the wall cabinets.

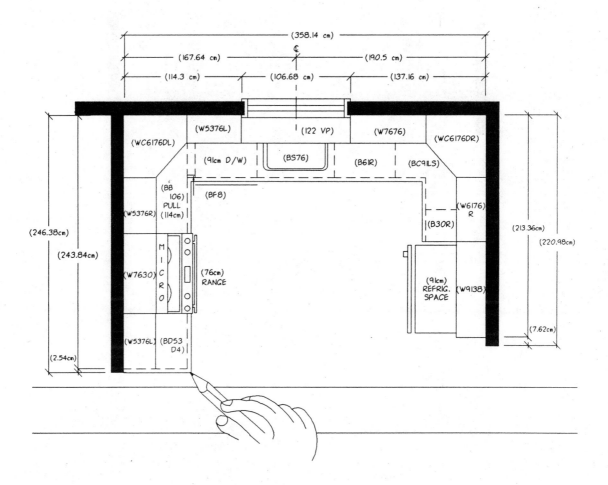

Figure 349 Subtraction Method Step #4 - A U-Shape metric example - Lay out the wall cabinets.

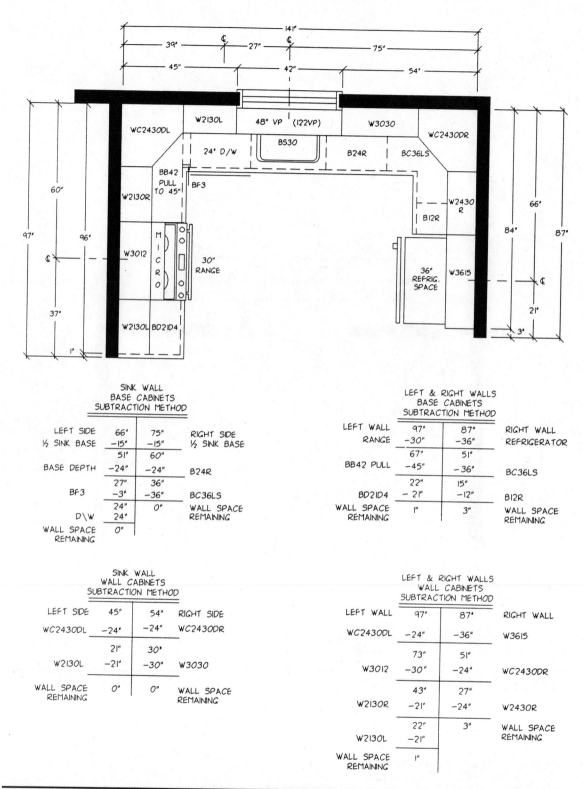

Figure 350 The finished project using imperial measurement.

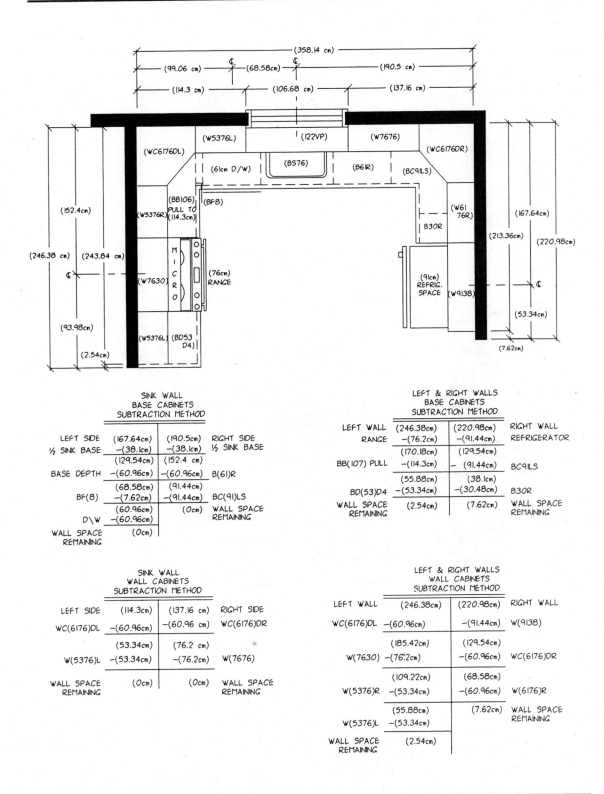

SINK WALL BASE CABINETS SUBTRACTION METHOD

LEFT SIDE ½ SINK BASE	(167.64cm) −(38.1cm)	(190.5cm) −(38.1cm)	RIGHT SIDE ½ SINK BASE
BASE DEPTH	(129.54cm) −(60.96cm)	(152.4 cm) −(60.96cm)	B(61)R
BF(8)	(68.58cm) −(7.62cm)	(91.44cm) −(91.44cm)	BC(91)LS
D\W	(60.96cm) −(60.96cm)	(0cm)	WALL SPACE REMAINING
WALL SPACE REMAINING	(0cm)		

LEFT & RIGHT WALLS BASE CABINETS SUBTRACTION METHOD

LEFT WALL RANGE	(246.38cm) −(76.2cm)	(220.98cm) −(91.44cm)	RIGHT WALL REFRIGERATOR
BB(107) PULL	(170.18cm) −(114.3cm)	(129.54cm) −(91.44cm)	BC9LS
BD(53)D4	(55.88cm) −(53.34cm)	(38.1cm) −(30.48cm)	B30R
WALL SPACE REMAINING	(2.54cm)	(7.62cm)	WALL SPACE REMAINING

SINK WALL WALL CABINETS SUBTRACTION METHOD

LEFT SIDE WC(6176)DL	(114.3cm) −(60.96cm)	(137.16 cm) −(60.96 cm)	RIGHT SIDE WC(6176)DR
W(5376)L	(53.34cm) −(53.34cm)	(76.2 cm) −(76.2cm)	W(7676)
WALL SPACE REMAINING	(0cm)	(0cm)	WALL SPACE REMAINING

LEFT & RIGHT WALLS WALL CABINETS SUBTRACTION METHOD

LEFT WALL WC(6176)DL	(246.38cm) −(60.96cm)	(220.98cm) −(91.44cm)	RIGHT WALL W(9138)
W(7630)	(185.42cm) −(76.2cm)	(129.54cn) −(60.96cm)	WC(6176)DR
W(5376)R	(109.22cm) −(53.34cm)	(68.58cm) −(60.96cm)	W(6176)R
W(5376)L	(55.88cm) −(53.34cm)	(7.62cm)	WALL SPACE REMAINING
WALL SPACE REMAINING	(2.54cm)		

Figure 351 The finished project using metric measurement.

Figure 352 A perspective view.

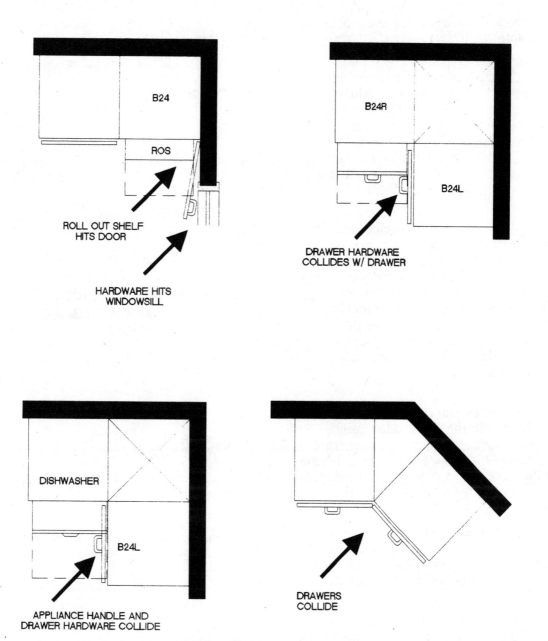

Figure 353 Without the right fillers, in the right places, the kitchen won't fit.

CLEARANCE AND THE USE OF FILLERS

Laying out a kitchen on paper by subtraction is one thing. On the jobsite we run into realities.

Kitchen cabinets are precision-made; walls and houses are not. Cabinets usually are made in 3" (7.62cm) modules, houses are not. To provide clearance for cabinet doors, handles/hinges, oversized appliances, door/window casings or irregularities in walls, we use wood or veneer strips called fillers.

Fillers supplied by cabinet manufacturers can be ordered to match the cabinet finish or they can be unfinished. They can come as separate pieces or they can be in the form of extended stiles. The stile is a vertical member of the cabinet frame, and an extended stile is a piece of the front frame that is made extra wide so it can be trimmed, or scribed, to fit the wall.

In framed cabinets the filler usually is flush with the front of the cabinet frame, not the door and drawer front. The drawing shows this filler as a separate piece, but it could be an extended stile that only has to be cut to fit.

For frameless cabinets where the entire front is flush, overlaying the cabinet case, the filler would have to be flush with the fronts of the doors and drawers.

To hold the filler, a cleat can be attached to the case so the filler can be attached to the cleat. The reveal between the filler and the door should match the reveal between doors throughout the kitchen.

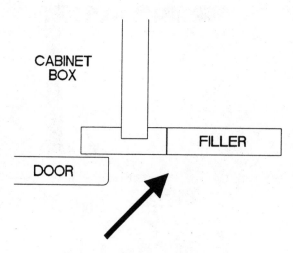

FILLER INSTALLED FLUSH WITH
FRAMED STOCK CABINET
OR EXTENDED STILE

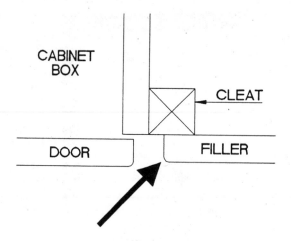

FILLER INSTALLED FLUSH WITH
FRAMELESS CABINET DOOR

Figure 354 Filler designs vary between cabinet lines.

Determining Filler Style and Size

For either framed or frameless cabinets, the filler might be an unfinished construction piece installed flush with the case. Then it requires a decorative overlay, such as a veneer or piece of laminate which will match the cabinets. When the filler repeats door detail, it is installed flush with the doors in either framed or frameless cabinets.

When corners are not turned with corner cabinets, a filler is always needed where the two cabinet runs abut.

When a blind corner cabinet is used, it is pulled out from the corner so its door and/or drawer will have clearance. But the abutting cabinet will have no clearance without the filler. It needs at least 1" (2.54cm). However, clearance must be sufficient to clear any door or appliance handle plus 1/2" (1.27cm). On frameless cabinets or for framed cabinets with flush overlay doors, the filler should be mounted flush with the doors, with a reveal to match the other cabinets. With base cabinets, the filler needs a toekick matching other cabinets.

If the two cabinet fronts join leaving a dead space in the corner, the filler will turn the corner with at least 1" (2.54cm) in each direction.

When a cabinet run abuts directly to a wall, a 1" (2.54cm) filler is needed, but up to 4" (10cm) may be required, if roll-out shelves must be pulled out past the hinge end of the cabinet door. On a framed cabinet, a scribing filler might suffice.

Wall cabinet fillers must be finished back to the wall, as the bottoms are visible.

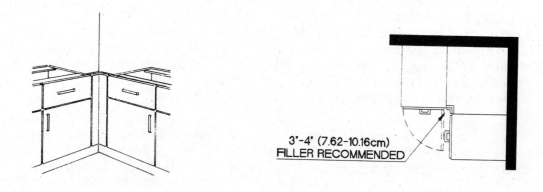

3'-4' (7.62-10.16cm)
FILLER RECOMMENDED

Figure 355 The filler must be enough for clearance for handles of doors, drawers or appliances on either side of a corner.

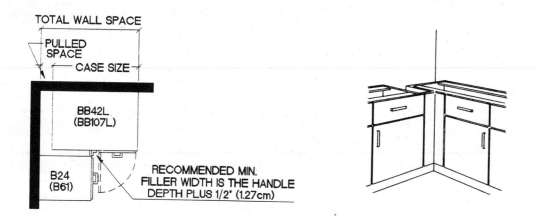

TOTAL WALL SPACE

PULLED
SPACE

CASE SIZE

BB42L
(BB107L)

B24
(B61)

RECOMMENDED MIN.
FILLER WIDTH IS THE HANDLE
DEPTH PLUS 1/2' (1.27cm)

Figure 356 The cabinet run needs 1/2" (1.27cm) filler at wall, but more if clearance is needed for roll-out shelves.

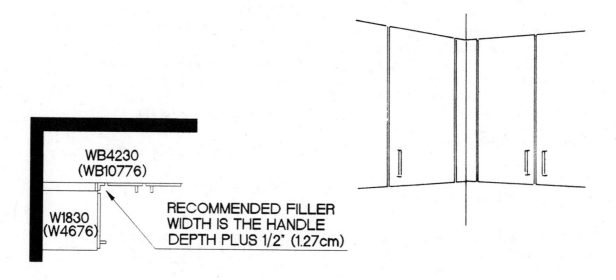

Figure 357 A cabinet run that meets a blind corner wall cabinet needs a filler so door handles don't hit.

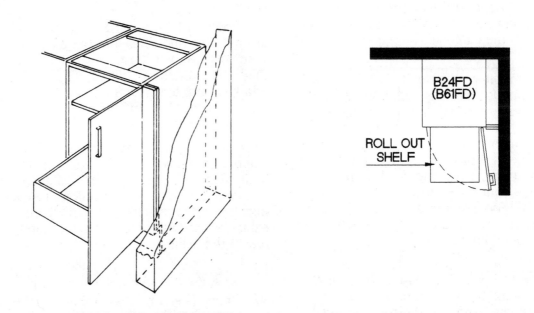

Figure 358 A base cabinet run that meets a wall needs a filler so the door can open more than 90° and a roll-out shelf will not collide with it.

CABINET HARDWARE

Cabinet door and drawer pulls are known collectively as "cabinet hardware." They might be metal, wood, plastic or ceramic. Many mount on the surface, but many are grooved or angled into the doors and drawer fronts. Euro-style cabinets introduced the technique of continuous metal and wood channel pulls.

Selecting Styles

Pulls should have aesthetic as well as functional value. They should fit the cabinet style. *For example,* a continuous channel pull blends with contemporary style, but would be out of place on anything else. Any style might take a round, square or wire pull. The 7 1/2" (19cm) wire pulls that are popular might not look good on doors of various widths in one kitchen, and if used vertically you would have to match them with a shorter length for drawers. Also, you must be aware of standard drillings for pulls in the cabinets.

As indicated in the drawings, some continuous channels might be a bit difficult to some consumers to visualize and should be explained. And these same pulls might not be accessible in a cabinet over a protruding refrigerator or range hood. They also can ruin horizontal line continuity when used on drawers. In this case it might be good to mix styles and use round knobs beneath the horizontal lines.

Round pulls are always good. Or are they? On a tambour door, a knob could repeatedly bang into the counter and might not be accessible by the cook. Small knobs or other small pulls might be inadequate for a large pantry door.

Small squares or rectangles, popular in shiny metals, usually mount with a single screw and easily move out of line.

The important points to remember about cabinet hardware are:

- make sure it works

- make sure it will mount properly

- make sure it looks right.

MOLDINGS, PANELING FINISH THE JOB RIGHT

There are some perfectionists who say moldings are used only to cover up mistakes in craftsmanship. But many others are sure they offer the only way to make a job look truly finished.

Molding Styles

Wood moldings come in many standard patterns and sizes, but there also are many extra-fancy shapes available. They might be painted or stained, vinyl-wrapped, printed with a wood finish, wood-veneered or unfinished.

Many cabinet manufacturers offer standard and special moldings to match their cabinets. Often, kitchen designers will combine two or three different moldings for special effects, such as where cabinets or soffits meet (or don't quite reach) the ceiling.

Ready-made moldings usually are sold in 96" (244cm) lengths. For specifying, remember the thickness always is listed first, then the width, then the length. Both thickness and width always are measured at the widest point.

Sizing Moldings

When designing continuous moldings that wrap around and tie in with the cabinet elevations, you must be sure to calculate the heights and forms of kitchen elements that will be affected. *For example,* baseboard molding should align perfectly with the cabinet toekick. A wainscoating chair rail should tie in with a wood countertop edge, or relate to the top in a way that is visually attractive. It is not unusual for kitchen designers to buy extra cabinet doors to use on walls around a dining area, topped with chair rails or other moldings. All of these, when within the kitchen, should line up with the cabinet doors and countertops.

TURNING CORNERS IN A KITCHEN

The way you turn corners in a kitchen is an important part of the design. Basically, there are four ways to turn a base and a wall corner.

Void the Corner

The simplest, least expensive and least desirable way is to "void" the corner and connect the two cabinet runs, wall or base, with a corner filler. However, this wastes available storage space.

Pie-cut/Lazy Susan Cabinets

A pie-cut wall or base corner cabinet turns a corner. This ordinarily will take reach-in shelving rather than rotary shelves, and a door that will hang from hinges on one side but also will be hinged in the middle so it can turn the square corner. Base corner cabinets 33" and 36" (84 and 91cm) wide are also available with rotating shelves, com-monly called lazy susans. The door may be attached to the susan so it swings inside the cabinet, or it may be hinged so it bifolds away from the user. The wall space requirement is more than the actual cabinet size, therefore the cabinet is pulled away from the wall during installation so that it finishes flush with the adjacent cabinets.

Blind Corner Cabinets

A blind base or wall corner cabinet is designed to pull out from the corner several inches, as specified by the manufacturer. This might have half-moon shelves that fit in the cabinet and are attached to the door. Shelves swing out when the door is opened. The cabinet run on the adjacent wall must have a filler.

Wall blinds generally have simple shelving. Wall space required for these cabinets is more than the actual cabinet size. Make sure both the customer and installer understand this. Always specify how far you want the blind unit pulled, and make sure you match this dimension up with cabinets above.

Reverse Peninsula Cabinets

For a base installation, a reverse peninsula cabinet can be fitted into a peninsula corner, opening into a dining room or other space outside the kitchen. It is useful for occupying dead corner space when there is not enough space in the kitchen for the opening and door of a corner cabinet.

If an eating counter will overhang a reverse peninsula cabinet, plan a full door unit because access to a drawer would be blocked.

The cabinet is always ordered 3" - 6" (8-15cm) smaller than the 24" (61cm) available so fillers can be installed on each side. This prevents the back edge of the cabinet from interfering with the toekick on the kitchen side. It also keeps the cabinet away from the return wall on the dining room side.

Diagonal Wall Cabinets

A popular way to turn a wall corner is with a diagonal unit. It takes 24" (61cm) on each wall and has a diagonal door connecting the two adjacent cabinet runs. It can feature a rotating shelf system or have standard shelving.

Interviewing The Client - Finding Out What The Family Wants

GATHERING YOUR INFORMATION

Before you apply any of the kitchen planning principles, you must interview the client and inspect the jobsite in order to identify the family's wants and needs, the jobsite limitations and the funds available for the project. Even the smallest kitchen can fulfill the client's dreams if you, as the designer, take the time to find out what those dreams are.

Depending on your type of business, you'll either complete this interview in the client's home or in your showroom. In either situation, an organized list helps you to ask all the important questions. The **National Kitchen & Bath Association** offers an interview form to help you gather all pertinent information.

The form covers the following areas:

- General Client Information

- Specific Kitchen Questions

- Design Information

- A Storage Checklist

- Product/Project Specifications

- Existing Construction Details

- Jobsite Dimensions

At first glance, this form might seem too long. Don't be intimidated by its length. Look at the individual segments and identify which are appropriate for your business. Only NKBA members can use this copyrighted form or modify it as they see fit.

REVIEWING THE SURVEY FORM

Cover Sheet

The cover sheet is designed to record all of the specific client information. The residence and the jobsite address (if different) are noted. Space for all appropriate telephone numbers is included. If the family is working with an allied professional, jot the necessary information in the bottom right-hand corner. Presentation dates are highlighted in the lower left-hand corner. These remind you to schedule an appointment to present your ideas during your first meeting, or indicate that you'll call them for an appointment when the design is ready. Use this form to jot down the times that are most convenient for your clients. This will help you schedule your time more efficiently.

NATIONAL KITCHEN NKBA & BATH ASSOCIATION

KITCHEN DESIGN SURVEY FORM

Name: _____

Residence Address: _____

_____

Jobsite Address: _____

_____

Phone: _____

Work: _____

Work: _____

Date: _____

Designer: _____

Appointment:

Scheduled: _____

Call When Ready: _____

Times Available: _____

Directions: _____

Allied Professionals:

Name: _____

Firm: _____

Address: _____

Phone: _____

SAMPLE

General Client Information

If the clients are planning to remodel, start by asking how long they've lived at their present address and when the house was built. This information is important when you begin to consider construction constraints.

Next ask: "*How did you learn about our firm?*" By obtaining this information from each client you'll be able to track where most of your business comes from; referrals, the Yellow Pages, showroom location or another source.

Ask when the homeowners would like to start and to finish the project. The dates could affect the materials you specify. It is also helpful to know if the prospective clients have worked with any other designers in the past. If so, ask what they were dissatisfied with and why they're still looking for the expert they wish to do business with.

The form also helps you find out if an allied professional or a specific builder will be part of the design and/or construction team. You can use the questions to determine if the clients plan to handle any portion of the project on their own.

Next ask: "*What budget range have you established for your kitchen project?*" If your clients hesitate to reveal the budget, impress on them that unless you have an established budget figure from them, you cannot begin the planning process. *Why?* Because the budget will affect the extensiveness of the construction changes and the number and quality of products specified.

Many designers waste a great deal of time designing rooms that don't fall within the budget for the project - because they neglected to find out the financial parameters during the information gathering stage.

Pricing a kitchen is easy if there's little or no design involved. Add up the prices of the products, include set charges for any other services and complete the estimate. Completely redesigning a room requires a different approach.

To prepare yourself to lead the budget discussion you need to understand how the cost of different portions of the project affects the overall price.

The brands, style and quality of the products specified affect the item price. *For example,* you might specify a typical freestanding refrigerator that retails for $699.00, or you might specify a built-in refrigerator for $2699.00. Such cost differences greatly affect the selling price of the kitchen. To easily explain this to your client, try to separate the products that you represent into good, better, best and ultra categories.

The amount of equipment needed will have a major impact on the price of the project. *For example,* 120" (304.8cm) of base cabinetry consisting of 4 - 30" (76.2cm) wide cabinets is more costly than a single 30" (76.2cm) wide cabinet.

Specifying major structural changes to accommodate the new plan can boost the labor cost so that it equals or exceeds the total cost of all the materials combined.

Next, determine the reasons for remodeling. If the home is being remodeled for long-term investment, the owners may be willing to invest more money than if they're simply "fixing up" the house to sell it.

Determine exactly who is going to make the final buying decision.

Once you've gathered the business and family information, it's time to find out about the room itself. *What do the clients dislike about their present kitchen? What do they like about the room?*

General Client Information

1. How long have you lived at, or how much time do you spend at the jobsite residence?_____

2. When was the house built?_____ How old is the present kitchen?_____

3. How did you learn about our firm?_____

4. When would you like to start the project?_____

5. When would you like the project to be completed?_____

_____

6. Has anyone assisted you in preparing a design for the kitchen?_____

_____

7. Do you plan on retaining an interior designer or architect to assist in the kitchen planning?_____

_____

8. Do you have a specific builder/contractor or other subcontractor/specialist with whom you would like to work?_____

_____

9. What portion of the project, if any, will be your responsibility?_____

_____

10. What budget range have you established for your kitchen project?_____

11. How long do you intend to own the jobsite residence?_____

12. What are your plans regarding this home?_____

    a. Is it a long or short-term investment?_____

    b. Is return on investment a primary concern?_____

    c. Do you plan on renting the jobsite residence in the future?_____

13. What family members will share in the final decision-making process?_____

_____

14. Would you like our firm to assist you in securing project financing? _____Yes _____ No

15. What do you dislike most about your present kitchen?_____

_____

_____

16. What do you like about your present kitchen?_____

_____

BMF6

Specific Kitchen Questions

After you know a bit about the family and the reasons for the project, it's time to concentrate on the specifics of the kitchen under discussion.

The next section of the interview form reminds you to find out what type of kitchen it is, who uses it, when they use it and if they use it alone or with other people. Specific activities that take place in the kitchen and specific equipment needs are also identified in this section of the survey.

This information will help personalize the space. *For example,* ask the cook what their preferences are regarding sink configurations so that the appropriate sink design and installation can be specified.

The *"Family Member Characteristics"* chart gives you a spot to jot down any physical limitations the users of the space might have. Special attention should be paid to a room designed for an older client or someone who is physically limited. Be sure to take limited sight, balance problems or grasping difficulties into consideration. Regardless of age, many people suffer from these limitations.

The ability to incorporate solutions to these physical limitations in the kitchen is an important part of successful design. *For example,* include a rear drain shallow bowl sink with an open area below to accommodate the use of a wheelchair.

Specific Kitchen Questions

1. How many household members? (Ask for approximate ages.)

    _____ Adults   _____ Teens   _____ Children   _____ Other

    _____ Pets   What types: _____

2. Are you planning on enlarging your family while living here? _____

    _____

3. Who is the primary cook? _____

    Is the primary cook left-handed _____ or right-handed _____ ?

    How tall is the primary cook? _____

    Does the primary cook have any physical limitations? _____

4. How many other household members cook? _____

    Who are they? _____

    Do they have a cooking hobby _____ , assist the primary cook with a specific task _____ ,

    or share a menu item with the primary cook? _____

    Is the secondary cook(s) right-handed _____ left-handed _____ ?

    How tall is the secondary cook(s)? _____

    Is a specialized cooking center required for the secondary cook(s)? _____

    Do they have physical limitations? _____

5. How does the family use the kitchen? _____

    _____ Daily Heat & Serve Meals   _____ Daily Full-Course, "From Scratch" Meals

    _____ Weekend Quantity Cooking   _____ Weekend Family Meals

    Other _____

6. Is the kitchen a socializing space? _____

7. How would you like the new kitchen to relate to adjacent rooms? _____

    _____

    _____

    _____ Family Room   _____ Dining Room

    _____ Family Home Office   _____ Family TV Viewing

8. What time of day is the kitchen used most frequently? _____

9. What are your kitchen and dining area requests? _____

    _____ Separate Table   _____ 30" Table Height Dining Counter

    _____ New _____ Existing   _____ 36" Counter Height

    _____ Size _____ Leaf Extension _____ 42" Elevated Bar Height Dining Center

    _____ Number of Seated Diners

10. Do you do any specialty cooking? _____ Gourmet   _____ Canning   _____ Ethnic

11. Do you cook in bulk for freezing _____ and/or leftovers _____ ?

Design Information

The "*Design Information*" questions help you create a kitchen that looks as good as it functions. Volume 5 of this series details how you can use this section to collect all the pertinent design information from the client.

Design Information

1. What type of feeling would you like your new kitchen space to have?

    Sleek/Contemporary _____   Warm & Cozy Country   _____

    Traditional   _____   Open & Airy   _____

    Strictly Functional _____   Formal   _____

    Family Retreat   _____   Personal Design Statement _____

2. What colors do you like _____ and dislike _____ ?

3. What colors are you considering for your new kitchen? _____

4. What are color preferences of other family members? _____

5. Have you made a sketch or collected pictures of ideas for your new kitchen? _____

6. Design Notes:

    _____

    _____

    _____

    _____

    _____

    _____

    _____

    _____

    _____

    _____

    _____

    _____

    _____

Storage Checklist

Even the smallest kitchen can be more than a room filled with three primary appliances. You should be a storage specialist as well as a kitchen planner. Therefore, the survey includes a list of specific types of storage needs the client might request in the kitchen.

Take a few moments to find out if any of these specific items are important to the client and you'll do a better job customizing the room for the needs of the user.

Specific Kitchen Questions (continued)

12. Do you entertain frequently?_____ Formally _____ Informally

13. Designing the kitchen so that it supports your entertainment style is part of the planning process. Tell me which statement fits you the best:

_____I like to be the only one in the kitchen with my guests in a separate space that is away from the kitchen

_____I like to be the only cook in the kitchen, with my guests close by in a family room space that opens onto the kitchen.

_____I like my guests to be sitting in the kitchen visiting with me while I cook.

_____I like my guests to help me in the kitchen in meal preparation.

_____I like my guests to help in the cleanup process after the meal.

_____I retain caterers who prepare all meals for entertaining.

    _____ The caterers come to the home to serve and cleanup.

    _____ I stop by the caterers and pick up the food.

    _____ I stop at the deli/take-out restaurant to bring part or all of the meal home before entertaining.

The items that I purchase from outside sources are:

_____ Appetizers	_____ Salads	_____ Soups
_____ Entrees	_____ Desserts	_____ Other

14. What secondary activities will take place in your kitchen?

_____ Computer	_____ Laundry	_____ TV/Radio
_____ Eating	_____ Planning Desk	_____ Wet Bar
_____ Growing Plants	_____ Sewing	_____ Other
_____ Hobbies	_____ Study	_____ Other

15. What is your cycle of shopping for food?

_____ Weekly	_____ Bi-weekly	_____ Daily

16. What types of products/materials do you purchase at the grocery store?

Predominantly fresh food purchased for a specific meal. _____

Predominantly frozen foods purchased for stock. _____

Traditional pantry boxed/packaged/canned goods purchased for stock. _____

    (1) Types of canned goods:

       _____Condiments _____ Fruits _____Soft Drinks _____Vegetables

    (2) Cleaning products stocked in bulk _____

    (3) Paper products stocked in bulk _____

    (4) Other boxed/packaged food items stocked in bulk _____

    (5) Other _____

Specific Kitchen Questions (continued)

17. Where do you presently store:

_____ Baking Equipment

_____ Boxed Goods

_____ Canned Goods

_____ Cleaning Supplies

_____ Dishes

_____ Glassware

_____ Laundry/Iron
Equipment

_____ Non-Refrigerated
Fruits/Vegs.

_____ Paper Products

_____ Pet Food

_____ Pots & Pans

_____ Recycle Containers

_____ Serving Trays

_____ Specialty Cooking
Vessels (Wok, Etc.)

_____ Spices

_____ Table/Appointments

_____ Linens

_____ Wrapping Materials

_____ Leftover Containers

_____ Other

_____ Other

_____ Other

Legend: B = Base Cabinet   C = Countertop   L = Laundry Room
BA = Basement   AG = Appliance Garage   T = Tall Cabinet
BC = Bookcase   D = Desk   W = Wall Cabinet

18. What type of specialized storage is desired?

_____ Bottle

_____ Bread Board

_____ Bread Box

_____ Cookbook

_____ Cutlery

_____ Other

_____ Dishes

_____ Display Items

_____ Glassware

_____ Lids

_____ Linen

_____ Other

_____ Plastic

_____ Soft Drink Cans

_____ Spice

_____ Vegetables

_____ Wine

_____ Other

19. What type of cabinet interior storage are you interested in?

_____ Lazy Susan

_____ Pantry

_____ Vertical Dividers

_____ Recycling/Waste Bins

_____ Roll-outs

_____ Towel Bar

_____ Tilt-out

_____ Drawer Head

_____ Drawer Ironing Board

_____ Toe-Kick Step Stool

_____ Other

_____ Other

20. What small specialty electrical appliances do you use in your kitchen?

_____ Blender

_____ Can Opener

_____ Crock Pot

_____ Coffee Pot

_____ Elec. Fry Pan

_____ Food Processor

_____ Griddle

_____ Toaster

_____ Wok

_____ Other

_____ Other

_____ Other

21. Have you considered relocating or changing windows or doors in the new plan? _____

_____

22. How do you plan on sorting recyclable trash in your new kitchen?

Sorting into: _____ Plastic   _____ Compact refuse

_____ Paper   _____ Trash

_____ Glass

a._____ clear

b._____ brown

c._____ green

23. Would you like a sorting station in the:

_____ kitchen   _____ utility room _____ garage _____ basement _____ outside?

Project Specifications

The interview form then identifies each major product category and gives you an excellent chart to record pertinent information about these key elements of the kitchen.

Part of the chart allows you to note whether you, the kitchen specialist, or the owner, is going to furnish the item and install it. Typical choices, finishes and materials are listed. In many cases, most of this information will be based on the designer's recommendations. In other cases, the client will have specific requests or might have identified preferences when they toured the showroom with you.

Some designers rely heavily on this section of the survey, others rarely use it. It is particularly useful if you work in partnership with other employees of the firm who prepare your drawings or detailed specifications. If you fill out this part of the form out at the jobsite or while you're visiting with the client in the office, you'll do a better job gathering all the information you need to share with your design colleague.

Project Specifications

Is this to be a complete kitchen, including:

Category	Source				Description
		Furn By		Install By	
	Use Exist	KS	O/OA	KS	O/OA	Check Appropriate Space(s)
Cabinetry						_____ Wood Species _____ Decorative Lam. _____ Furn. Steel _____ Polyester Other _____ Style _____ Hardware _____ Exterior Color/Finish _____ Interior Color/Finish _____
Countertops						_____ Wood _____ Decorative Lam. _____ Marble _____ Solid Surface _____ Granite Other _____ _____ Tile Size _____ Grout _____ Inserts Edge Treatment _____ Backsplash: Height _____ Backsplash: Material _____ End Splash Sides _____ Decking: _____ Plywood _____ Loose Other _____
Fascia/Soffit						_____ Open _____ Flush _____ Extended _____ Recessed _____ Wallpaper _____ Paint _____ Wood _____ Lighted _____ Gallery Rail _____ Cornice Other _____
Lighting System						Source: _____ Incandescent _____ Fluorescent _____ Halogen Other _____ Location: _____ Cooking _____ Sink _____ Desk _____ Soffit _____ Gen'l Ceiling _____ Table _____ Island/Penn. _____ Under Wall Cab. _____ Mixing Area _____ Window _____ Pantry Other _____ Type: _____ Cove _____ Suspended _____ Recessed _____ Track _____ Surface Mtd. Other _____

KEY

KS = Kitchen Specialist   O = Owner   OA = Owner's Agent

Category	Source					Description
	Furn. By		Install By			
	Use Exist	KS	O/OA	KS	O/OA	Check appropriate space(s)
Appliances						
Range						_____ Gas _____ Electric _____ Microwave _____ Convection _____ Drop-In _____ Slide-In _____ Free-Standing _____ Eye Level _____ Self Clean _____ Continuous Clean Size If Retaining Existing _____
Cooktop						_____ Gas _____ Electric _____ Enamel Steel _____ Conven. Coil _____ Ceramic _____ Solid Disk _____ Stainless St. _____ Halogen _____ Induction Color _____ Size If Retaining Existing _____ Accessories _____
Oven						_____ Gas _____ Electric _____ Single _____ Double _____ Self Clean _____ Continuous Clean _____ Microwave _____ Micro/Convection _____ Convection _____ Other Size If Retaining Existing _____
Hood						_____ Decorative _____ Standard _____ Wood _____ Metal Other Material _____ _____ Vented _____ Ductless New Ductwork Need _____ Duct Termination _____ Size If Retaining Existing _____ Ability to Run Ductwork _____
Warming Drawer						_____ Single _____ Double
Indoor Grill						_____ Single _____ Double _____ Combo _____ Gas _____ Electric
Microwave						_____ Built-In _____ Free Standing _____ Trim Kit Other _____ Size If Retaining Existing _____
Refrigerator						_____ Side-By-Side _____ Top Freezer _____ Btm Freezer _____ Rt/Lft Side Hinge _____ Reversible _____ Ice Maker _____ Built-In _____ Under Counter _____ Front Panel _____ Trim Kit Size If Retaining Existing _____
Freezer						_____ Upright _____ Size _____ Chest _____ Size _____ Front Panel _____ Trim Kit

Category	Source				Description
		Furn By		Install By	
	Use Exist	KS	O/OA	KS	O/OA	Check Appropriate Space(s)

Category	Use Exist	KS	O/OA	KS	O/OA	Description
Appliances (Continued)						
Dishwasher						_____ Front Panel _____ Trim Kit _____ Conv. Kit Existing Plumbing _____
Food Waste Disposal						_____ Batch Feed _____ Continuous Feed
Compactor						_____ Left/Right/Pullout Hinging _____ Front Panel _____ Trim Kit Width If Retaining Existing _____
Built-in Can Opener						_____ Under Cabinet _____ In Wall
Built-in Toaster						_____ Under Cabinet _____ In Wall
Built-in Mixing Center						_____ Under Cabinet _____ In Counter
Telephone/Intercom						
Television						
Radio						
VCR						
Washer						
Dryer						
Fixtures and Fittings						
Sink #1						_____ Single _____ Double _____ Triple _____ Small/Large Bowl _____ St. Steel _____ Porcelain Steel _____ Cast Iron _____ Solid Surface _____ Quartz/Sila. Other _____ Mounting Method _____ No. of Holes _____ Size If Retaining Existing _____ Drain Board: Right _____ Left _____
Sink #2						_____ Single _____ Double _____ Triple _____ Small/Large Bowl _____ St. Steel _____ Porcelain Steel _____ Cast Iron _____ Solid Surface _____ Quartz/Sila. Other _____ Mounting Method _____ No. of Holes _____ Size If Retaining Existing _____ Drain Board: Right _____ Left _____

Category	Source					Description
		Furn By		Install By		
	Use Exist	KS	O/OA	KS	O/OA	Check Appropriate Space(s)
Fixtures (Continued)						
Faucet(s)						_____ 1 Handle _____ 2 Handle _____ With Spray _____ Lotion Disp. _____ Water Purifier Other _____
Instant Hot Water						_____ In Sink _____ In Counter
Chilled Water						_____ In Sink _____ In Counter
Lotion Dispenser						_____ In Sink _____ In Counter
Water Purifier						Located _____
Windows and Doors						

Windows						Casing: _____ Match Existing _____ Finish
						        _____ Replace All _____ Finish
						        _____ Size _____ Profile
						Size _____ Finish _____
						_____ Slider _____ Bow
						_____ Casement _____ Bay
						_____ Double-Hung _____ Support
						_____ Skylight _____ Roof
						Other _____
						Exterior Wall Patch _____
						Sink Vent Relocation _____
						Pass-Thru Surfacing _____
						New Window Sizes: _____
						#1 _____ Screen _____
						#2 _____ Screen _____
						#3 _____ Screen _____
						#4 _____ Screen _____

Doors						Casing: _____ Match Existing _____ Finish
						        _____ Replace All _____ Finish
						        _____ Size _____ Profile
						New Doors:
						_____ Solid Core Size _____
						    Hinge _____ Screen _____
						_____ Steel Size _____
						    Hinge _____ Screen _____
						_____ Hollow Core Size _____ Hinge _____
						_____ Bifold Size _____ Hinge _____
						_____ Pocket Size _____ Hinge _____
						_____ Accordian Size _____ Hinge _____
						Other _____ Size _____ Hinge _____
						Ext. Wall Patch _____
						Int. Wall /Floor Patch _____
						Hardware: Finish _____
						_____ Passage _____ Knob
						_____ Privacy _____ Lever

Category	Source					Description
	Use Exist	Furn By		Install By		Check Appropriate Space(s)
		KS	O/OA	KS	O/OA	
Flooring						
Floor Preparation						Removal _____ Leveling & Shimming _____ Subfloor Material _____ Underlayment: _____ Plywood _____ Particleboard Baseboard _____ Transition Treatment _____
Floor Covering						_____ Wood _____ Carpet _____ Vinyl _____ Natural Stone _____ Tile Size _____ Grout _____
Decorative Surfaces						
Wall Covering						_____ Tile _____ Wood _____ Wallpaper _____ Mirror _____ Paint Other _____
Wall Preparation						_____ New Plaster/ Drywall _____ Clean _____ Patch Exist. _____ Remove Exist. Covering Other _____ Repairs _____
Ceiling Covering						_____ Paint _____ Wallpaper _____ Suspended _____ Vaulted _____ Skylights Other _____
Ceiling Preparation						_____ New Plaster/ Drywall _____ Clean _____ Plywood _____ Stapled/Glued _____ Patch Exist. _____ Remove Exist. Covering Other _____ Repairs _____
Window Treatment						_____ Blinds _____ Fabric _____ Shutters Other _____
Construction						(Describe Required Work)
Electrical						
Plumbing						
General Carpentry						
Demolition						
Trash Removal						
Structural Changes						
Installation						

Miscellaneous Information: _____

Existing Construction Details

If your business methods include a jobsite inspection for remodeling work, the information that you'll gather under the "*Existing Construction Details*" section is critical.

Creative kitchen plans are firmly grounded in the designer's technical expertise in the mechanical elements of the plan and the designer's knowledge of the construction constraints that exist on the individual jobsites. You learned about typical North American building systems in Volumes 1 and 2 of this series.

The survey form provides you with an organized way to survey the existing conditons on the jobsite. To begin, walk through the house, inspect the basement or attic, and make sure you understand the orientation of the kitchen to the balance of the floor plan.

Next, identify construction limitations: *Where are the water supply pipes located? What kind of condition are the walls, floors and ceilings in? What type of flooring exists and what direction do the floor joists run in? What is the exterior finish of the dwelling?*

Find out what type of windows are used, and if they can be moved. The same two questions need to be answered about doors. These are two very important questions. Oftentimes the overall plan can be dramatically enhanced by a relatively minor interior door change. Or, there may be a spectacular view that the client would like to include in the kitchen. If you don't ask the right questions, you won't gather this information.

Existing Construction Details

Construction:

Construction of House: ☐ Single Story ☐ Multi Story Style of house _____

Room above or below kitchen: _____

Condition and covering of walls: _____

floors: _____

ceilings: _____

soffit/fascia: _____

Squareness of corners _____ Parallel walls to within 3/4" _____

Construction of Floor: ☐ Slab ☐ Frame

Direction of floor joist: ☐ Parallel to longest wall ☐ Perpendicular to longest wall   Joist Height _____

Exterior: ☐ Brick ☐ Aluminum ☐ Stucco ☐ Wood ☐ Other

Interior: ☐ Drywall ☐ Lath & Plaster ☐ Wood ☐ Stone/Brick

Windows can be changed: ☐ Yes ☐ No

Windows: ☐ Sliders ☐ Double-Hung ☐ Skylights ☐ Casement ☐ Greenhouse

Doors can be relocated: ☐ Yes ☐ No

Location of walls can be changed: ☐ Yes ☐ No

Sewage System: ☐ City Service ☐ Septic System Other _____

Type of roof material _____ Age of roof _____

Household heating/cooling system _____ Age of home _____

Access:

Can equipment fit into room? _____

Basement _____ Crawlspace _____ Attic _____

Material Storage _____ Trash Collection Area _____

Plumbing:

Location of existing vent stack _____ Type of trap_____

Electrical:

GFCI existing: ☐ Yes ☐ No

New wiring access: ☐ Hard ☐ Average ☐ Easy

Existing electrical service capacity _____ The following # of 120V circuits available: _____

The following # of 240V circuits available: _____

Miscellaneous Information: _____

_____

_____

_____

_____

The next set of questions will help the installation experts: *Can you get material in the house? Where will you store it? What electrical service is available? What needs to be added?*

The form concludes with charts you can use to note the placement of windows, doors, heating/cooling outlets, and other mechanical elements. Any fixtures/appliances you are retaining or relocating are also dimensioned on the final page. Add a piece of graph paper to the survey to use to take preliminary dimensions.

Existing Wall Elevation Dimensioning

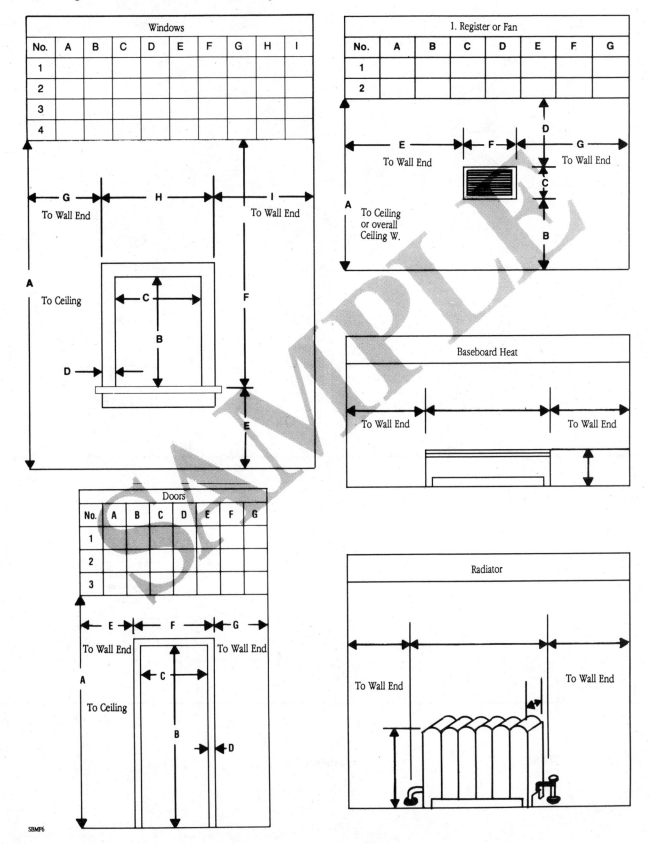

Windows									
No.	A	B	C	D	E	F	G	H	I
1									
2									
3									
4									

1. Register or Fan							
No.	A	B	C	D	E	F	G
1							
2							

Doors							
No.	A	B	C	D	E	F	G
1							
2							
3							

Baseboard Heat

Radiator

SBMF6

Existing Appliance Dimensioning

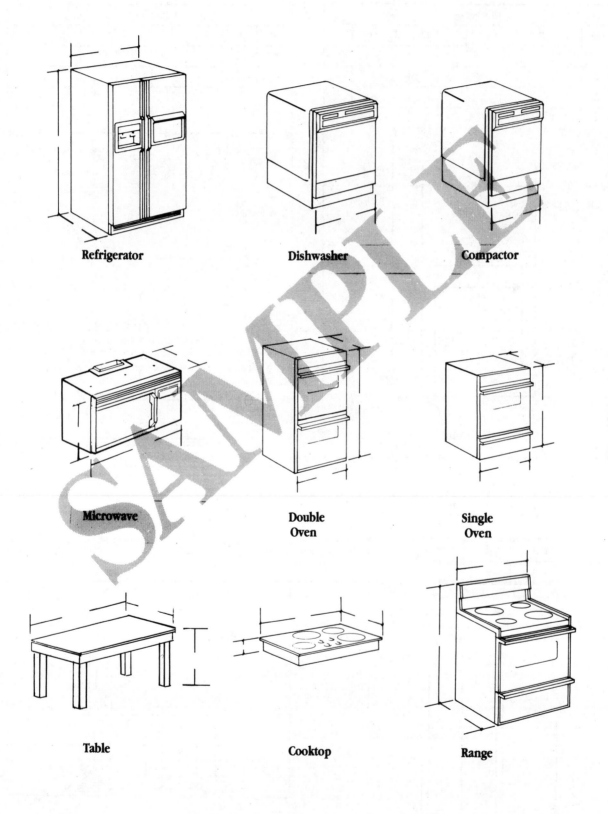

Refrigerator

Dishwasher

Compactor

Microwave

Double
Oven

Single
Oven

Table

Cooktop

Range

Final Considerations

Regardless of the size of the kitchen, planning the room so that it reflects the client's lifestyle, fits within budget, and can be constructed within the construction constraints of the project requires careful questioning and sensitive listening by the designer.

Many novice kitchen specialists make the mistake of thinking everyone uses his/her kitchen just as the designer does. Another misconception is that small spaces are impossible design challenges. Really successful kitchen specialists don't fall into either one of these traps. They begin the planning process with a careful information gathering program. Whether you are sitting down with a client in your showroom reviewing the information necessary to specify products for a new home under construction, or gather around the dining room table on the jobsite as the clients begin to plan a remodeling program, you need to carefully gather this information.

Before we leave the topic of information gathering, let's return to that key issue.

"HOW MUCH DOES A KITCHEN COST?"

That's the tough question, usually the first one, every consumer will ask either in the showroom or when you visit them in their home.

Pricing a kitchen can be fairly easy in a straight product sale when design isn't involved. You add up the prices of the products and add your set charges for any services and that's it.

But when a complete redesign must be accomplished based on a lengthy interview the question becomes as impossible as it is inevitable. A stammer or a furtive look here can raise doubts and send the consumer scurrying off to another source. That's why it is essential that you prepare yourself for the question by mastering the cost factors that affect prices.

The factors involved in pricing a kitchen include the following:

- **The Products Involved:** *For example,* a simple mirror-finish double-compartment sink of 22-gauge stainless steel can go for $75. A deluxe sink with two or three compartments in 18-gauge stainless steel, quartz or other solid material can run $400 to $900. You can buy a simple 2-cycle dishwasher for $250, but the best and quietest runs up to $2,500. A 4-element cooktop can be as low as $150 or, with halogen heat or magnetic induction, up to $1,500. For countertops, not installed, 10 lineal feet (305cm) in decorative laminate can be as low as $250; in ceramic tile $500 to $800, but decorative tiles can be as high as $40 each. In solid surface, the top can be $1,000 to $1,500, in granite or marble it can be $2,000 to $2,750.

For cabinets, the biggest product purchase, see the accompanying box.

As those figures indicate, prices of products alone can skyrocket the price of a kitchen by as much as 1000%. So in answering the client's price question, think "G-B-B-U," for Good, Better, Best and Ultimate. It is important to know these facts for the products your company offers.

- **Design Complications:** The more complex the lay-out and more involved the construction work required to reorganize the floor area, the more costly the project will be. *For example,* moving the back door can cost up to $1,400, plus new door hardware ($70 to $500) and a new screen/storm door ($75-$200).

- **Who Does the Work?** The price of a kitchen can be cut substantially if the customer can do some of the work.
  For example, the client can save $1,000 by doing the painting and papering; $1,000 to $1,200 by doing the trash removal; $300 to $1,000 by removing the old cabinets.

But be very wary of recommending that the customer install cabinets and/or countertops. This calls for skilled labor, for workers who appreciate the importance of plumbing the walls and leveling the floor and who know how to do it right.

If a do-it-yourselfer tries to install and ruins an expensive cabinet, you will be blamed.

If a wall cabinet is dropped on the counter it can ruin both the cabinet and the countertop.

CABINET PRICES AND ASSOCIATED UPCHARGES

The most inexpensive way to fill 48" (122cm) of lower wall space is with a single base cabinet in that width. These figures are for a stock line.

Basic box 48" (121.92cm) wide	**Cost:**	**$400**
Two roll-out shelves:	$100	
Concealed stepstool in toekick area:	$170	
One drawer with cutlery dividers:	$ 75	
One drawer to receive stepped spice insert:	$ 50	
TOTAL UPCHARGE:		**$795**
Door style: Framed, raised-panel, cherry in place of plain wood, add 25%:		**$100**
TOTAL UPGRADED CABINET COST:		**$895**

NOTE: If that same space were broken down to a 15" (38cm) 3-drawer unit ($300), a 9" (23cm) tray storage unit ($200), and a 2-door 24" (61cm) cabinet ($350), it would total $850 plus three freight and installation surcharges. That would come to $450 more.

Barrier-Free Planning

SPECIAL KITCHENS FOR
<u>SPECIAL PEOPLE</u>

Webster defines a "homemaker" as "one who makes a home, as distinguished from one who keeps a house". When a homemaker becomes disabled, the event can be catastrophic.

The professional kitchen designer should be aware of the complex limitations and possibilities of the wheelchair in the kitchen. The space must be planned so that the cook can achieve his or her highest potential of mobility and efficiency.

Physical Characteristics

You must first understand the client's particular physical characteristics.

This goes beyond the fact of immobile legs. The strength and efficiency of the person's grasp, the length of their arm reach, the extent to which they can bend at the waist; all must be determined. If available, the occupational therapist who has worked with the homemaker should be consulted.

NKBA has developed an auxillary client survey that will help you determine the questions to ask and the information to gather. From time to time, this survey may need to be customized to fit the specific requirements of your project.

A sample of this survey form follows and may be obtained by contacting NKBA and requesting Form #4025.

Wheelchair Measurements

Each wheelchair must be measured carefully, especially front-to-back measurement, which determines the turning radius. The following dimensions are based on an average adult-sized wheelchair:

- Usual height at top of arm rests is 30" (76.2cm). This is important for moving under countertops.

- Space for knees is a minimum of 27" (68.58cm) above the floor and 18" wide.

- With foot rests in use, the average toe height is 8" (20.32cm) above the floor.

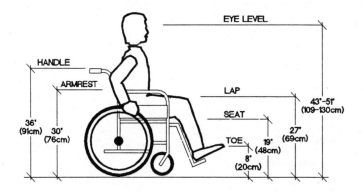 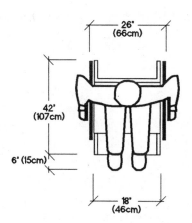

Figure 359 Average Adult-Sized Wheelchair Dimensions

As you begin planning the kitchen, the wheelchair's turning radius will require at least 60" (152.4cm) of floorspace. At 9" - 12" (22.86cm - 30.48cm) above the floor, this dimensional requirement of 60" (152.4cm) will decrease.

Up to 6" (15.24cm) of required 60" (152.4cm) can be provided by a toekick

that is a minimum 6" (15.24cm) deep and 9" (22.86cm) high. Up to 19" (48.26cm) of the required 60" (152.4cm) can be provided by the clear floor of a kneespace if the kneespace is a minimum of 48" (121.92cm) wide.

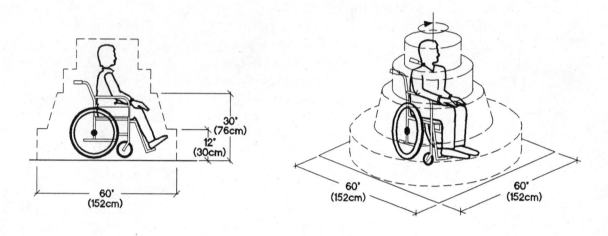

Figure 360 Space requirements decrease as height above the floor increases.

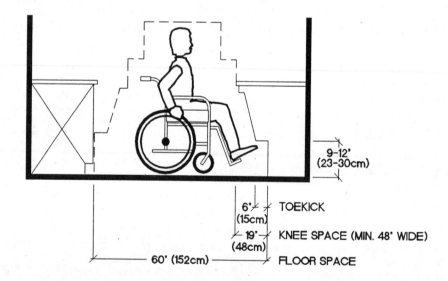

Figure 361 Clear floorspace may include toekick and kneespace if minimum dimensions are met.

When a full radius turn can not be accommodated, provide a floorspace for a T-turn. A T-turn requires a 36" x 60" (91.44cm x 152.4cm) aisle with a 36" x 36" (91.44cm x 91.44cm) leg at its center. Yet another option in a small galley kitchen is to provide space for a turning circle at the end of an aisle.

Beyond turning floorspace requirements, you will also need to consider floor space needs at an appliance. Based on the average wheelchair dimensions provided, a minimum floorspace of 30" x 48" (76.2cm x 121.92cm) should be planned in front of every appliance. The orientation of the floor space provided will determine whether a parallel approach or perpendicular approach will be used. Whenever possible space for both approaches should be planned 48" x 48" (121.92.cm x 121.92cm). Just as with the turning circle, up to 19"

(48.26cm) of this clear floor space may extend into a knee space (under a sink/cooktop or adjacent to ovens/ranges).

The countertop height most practical for the wheelchair homemaker is 31" (78.74cm), with a 29" (73.66cm) distance from the floor to the bottom surface of the work top. The standard countertop depth of 24" (60.96cm) is impractical for the physically impaired homemaker. They will use only the front 16" (40.64cm) of the countertop's depth. The extra 8" (20.32cm) of depth should be used for storage, as their reach to above-counter storage will be limited. A bread board or chopping block is most functional when installed 27" (68.58cm) off the floor. If the homemaker has use of only one hand, the board can have a cut-out opening into which a mixing bowl can be placed for stability and safety.

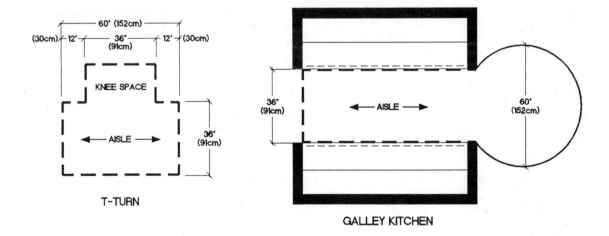

Figure 362 Wheelchair turning options with limited floor space.

Cabinetry Considerations

Cabinetry must be designed to allow items to be stored within the reach of the client, and as close to their first place of use as possible. All base cabinets must incorporate the best hardware for ease of drawer use. All base cabinets must also provide pull-out shelves, pull-out peg board storage and hanging door storage. Whenever possible, utilize shallow tall cabinets against unused walls. Lazy-susan revolving shelves also provide easy access.

Upper shelves are probably out of the homemaker's reach, yet some items may be kept there to be brought down by other family members or a friend when needed.

Below-the-counter storage is usable in all areas except the sink and food preparation center. These two spots should be left open for knee space.

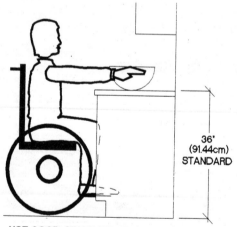

NOT GOOD. STANDARD 36" (91.44cm) HIGH WORK SURFACE IS A STRAIN ON WHEEL-CHAIR HOMEMAKER'S BACK AND ARMS, ESPECIALLY FOR A SMALLER WOMAN.

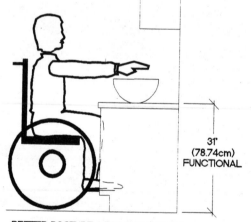

BETTER POSTURE, LESS TIRING WORK AT APPROXIMATELY 31" (78.74cm) HIGH SURFACE.

Figure 363   Barrier-free planning.

Cooking Center: The cooking appliances must be selected and installed carefully. The common freestanding range is least desirable. Separate appliances are much more functional. When selecting a cooking top, look for a staggered pattern of burners to make reaching over them safer. Or consider installing two two-burner cooktops, end-to-end, parallel to the countertop edge.

Controls must be on the front or side of the units. For a homemaker with limited reach or difficulty turning knobs, a cooktop with separate push button controls might be a wise recommendation. The wall oven should be installed so that the most used oven shelf is level with the countertops. Place electrical outlets near the front of the cabinets, on side walls, or directly on the cabinet face itself.

Clean-up Center: In the clean-up center, the sink should be shallow; 5" to 6 1/2" (12.7cm to 16.51cm) deep. This is the easiest to reach and the least likely to interfere with knee space. The drain should be at the rear, especially if a garbage disposal is used, for least intrusion into knee space.

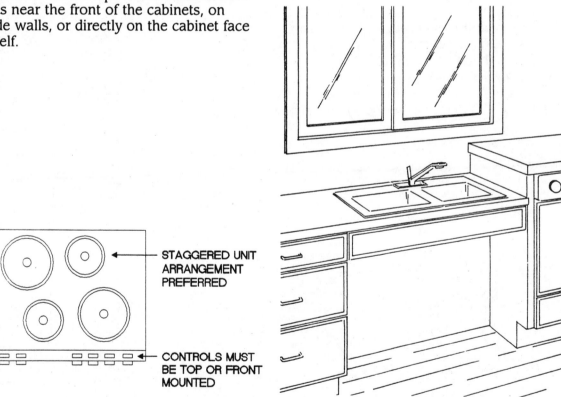

Figure 364 Barrier-free cooking surface.

STAGGERED UNIT ARRANGEMENT PREFERRED

CONTROLS MUST BE TOP OR FRONT MOUNTED

Figure 365 Barrier-free clean-up center.

Hot pipes should be to the rear and insulated to prevent serious injury caused by heat contact on legs which may be without sensation. The faucet should have a long swing spout. Single handle lever controls or separate blade-type controls should be used at the sink faucet. If the reaching ability of the client is limited, mount the sink sideways so that the faucet will be on the right or left, rather than to the back of the sink. A spray hose allows the homemaker greater freedom when working at the sink.

The installation of a dishwasher is important for convenience, but will interrupt the lowered counter height. If the unit is to be placed next to the sink, a 36" (91.44cm) high counter section will be needed. If it is installed a foot or so away, extra movement will be required. Discuss the alternatives with the client.

Mix Center: The mix center, which includes the refrigerator, is the last major area of concern. The refrigerator should be a model with full automatic defrost to eliminate the manual defrosting that is an almost impossible chore for the physically impaired homemaker. The refrigerator should have the freezer compartment on the bottom or be a side-by-side model for accessibility.

An automatic icemaker will eliminate the difficult task of carrying water-filled ice trays from the sink to the freezer. A refrigerator with slide-out shelves, deep door storage or revolving shelves will be most helpful.

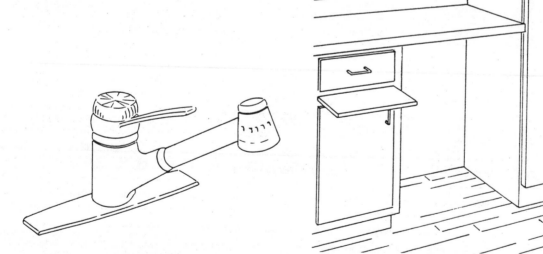

Figure 366 Barrier-free faucet.

Figure 367 Barrier-free mix center.

A properly planned kitchen can improve the physical and emotional well-being of a homemaker that uses a wheelchair. A well-designed kitchen will minimize their weaknesses and compensate for their disabilities. As professionals, we should be prepared to expend the special design services as necessary to plan and install a dream kitchen just right for the client's specific needs.

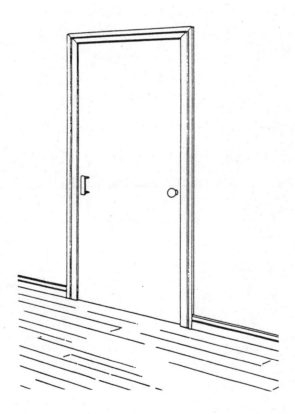

Figure 368 Barrier-free door hardware planning.

Figure 369 (Courtesy of Whirlpool Corporation) A kitchen planned for a client using a wheelchair.

Figure 370 The microwave oven is conveniently located.

Figure 372 Pull-out table area provides extra countertop at a lower height for the seated cook.

Figure 371 Pull-out chopping surfaces are at two heights to accommodate the seated cook as well as one standing.

Figure 373 An extension at the end of the standard 36" (91.44cm) island provides another work area for the seated cook.

Figure 374   Ironing board built into drawer makes ironing accessible from the wheelchair.

Figure 375   Planning the desk is somewhat limited because of apron panel hitting arms - wheelchair dimensions must be carefully considered.

CHAPTER **4**

Drawing and Presentation Standards for the Kitchen Professional

Successful kitchen designs rely on a complete and professional set of project documents. A complete drawing presentation includes a floor plan, mechanical plan, construction plan (if job requires) and interpretive sketches.

Such a presentation provides a clear and concise description of the project's scope for everyone involved. Errors caused

by misinterpreting information are minimized. And you, as the kitchen design specialist, present a professional image to the client and other tradespeople.

Examples of complete sets of project documents can be found in Appendix B.

For your convenience you will find metric equivalent representations within this manual.

Inspecting and Measuring the Design Space

PREPARING TO MEASURE

Before the project documents can be started, you must carefully measure and inspect the physical space. The measuring steps you take depend on whether the project involves remodeling or new construction.

To assist you, kitchen layout sheets and client survey forms are available from the **National Kitchen & Bath Association**. These forms include a 1/2" scale (1:24cm) layout grid and specifications list.

Other tools you'll need are:

- 25 ft. metal tape measure

- Pencils, pens of different colors

- Note pad or clipboard

MEASURING THE REMODELING JOB

When preparing for a remodeling job, it's wise to follow a few simple steps to insure concise and accurate planning.

- **1. Visually inspect the space** and draw a proportionally correct room outline. Include all windows

and doors: indicate north/south orientation and adjacent room or view information.

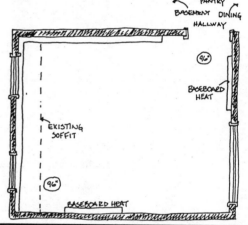

Figure 376 Draw the room with accurate proportions.

- **2. Measure the ceiling height.** Measuring floor to ceiling is difficult. Many designers prefer to mark a midpoint on the wall, measuring from the ceiling down to the mark and then from the mark to the floor. Others measure from the ceiling down, pushing the tape down with their knee while holding it flat against the wall, while still others prefer to push the tape up from the floor to the ceiling. The measurement should be repeated at several locations to determine levelness. Record the height in a circle at the center of the floor plan.

Figure 377 Measuring the ceiling.

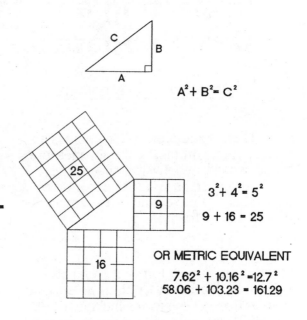

Figure 378 Functions of a Right Triangle.

- **3. Select a corner as a starting point.** If possible, clear a path approximately 3' (91.44cm) above the floor and measure the full length of the wall. Record the total dimension on the plan.

Check corners for squareness. The corner squareness is determined by marking a point 3' (91.44cm) out from the corner on one wall and 4' (121.92cm) out from the corner on the adjacent wall and measuring the distance between the two points. If the distance is 5' (152.4cm), the corner is square, but any other measurement indicates the corner is out of square. If this is the case, make a note on your plan.

> This formula is known as:
>   The Pythagorean Theorem
>
> $(A^2 + B^2 = C^2)$

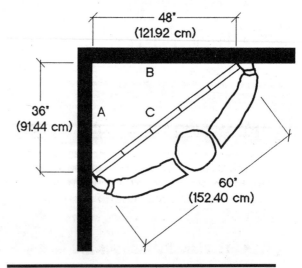

Figure 379 Determining corner squareness.

- **4. Return to the starting point** and measure from the corner to the nearest obstacle (door, window, pipe chase, etc.) and record results. Measure the obstacle from outside edge to outside edge and record the dimension. Continue the process until the opposite corner is reached.

- **5. Stop and confirm the accuracy of your measurements** by comparing the sum of all individual dimensions to the total wall measurement.

- **6. Repeat steps 3, 4 and 5** for each wall.

- **7. Complete the National Kitchen & Bath Association survey form** noting any important height dimensions; such as window heights from floor and ceiling, door heights, heating, ventilation and air conditioning units.

- **8. Identify plumbing and electrical/lighting centerlines** by returning to the starting point and measuring from corner to center of outlets, switches, fixtures, appliances, lighting, venting, and plumbing locations. Record center location with standard symbols found in the *NKBA Graphics and Presentations Standards* within this manual.

- **9. Make your final inspection.** Measure any free-standing furniture pieces, check electrical service panel conditions and check any areas such as basement or attic, which may be affected during the remodeling process. Take photos or videos of existing space to jog your memory during the design process.

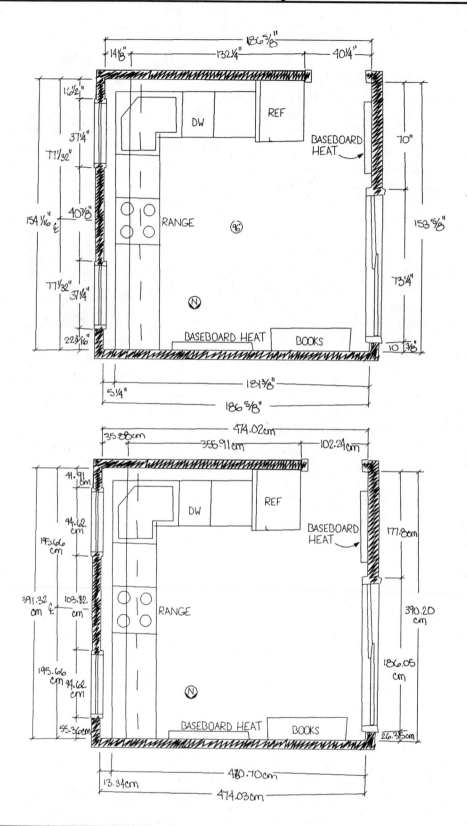

Figure 380 Jobsite floor plans with dimensions noted.

Figure 381 National Kitchen & Bath Association Survey Forms.

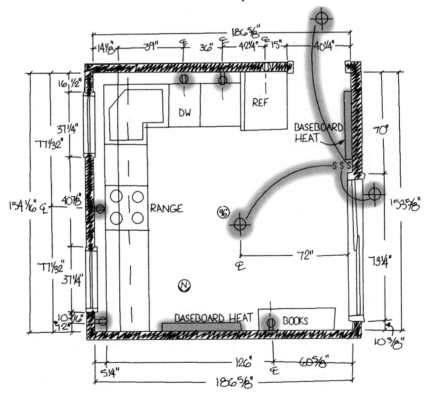

Figure 382 Indicate mechanical elements to clarify and eliminate possible errors later.

MEASURING NEW CONSTRUCTION

When measuring a new construction site during the framing stages the process is the same, however, it must be noted that all dimensions will be made from stud wall to stud wall during the jobsite visit.

Architectural elements will be located from stud wall to rough opening. Compare the measurements to the architect's blueprints. If there is any discrepancy, discuss the difference and any ramifications to the plan with the builder or homeowner.

Verify where doors and windows lead, their size, direction and trim size. Verify the type and thickness of the material for finishing the walls, ceilings, and floors.

After the jobsite has been measured, the draftsperson will adjust the rough dimensions; subtracting material and finish depths for each wall surface so that the plan reflects finished wall dimensions. Be sure to confirm what finished materials are to be used before placing any product orders. These finished dimensions can make a big difference in product specifications. Substituting 1/16" (.15cm) vinyl with a 1/2" (1.27cm) thick marble floor alters the finished floor to ceiling dimension, which in turn affects tall cabinet and soffit dimensions.

MEASURING UNUSUAL WALLS

Measuring unusual walls, such as angles and/or curves, requires more time and a different technique. The most accurate approach to measuring an un-usual angle is to first lay out a (90°) right triangle on the floor in the corner.

Trigonometric Formulas

Once the triangle is located on the floor, measure at least two of its legs and apply the appropriate trigonometric formula.

Begin by determining what angle needs to be found. Then identify the opposite, adjacent and hypotenuse sides of the triangle. The opposite side is the side which is directly opposite the angle. The hypotenuse is the longest side of the triangle and the remaining leg is termed the adjacent side. Use one of the following trigonometric formulas to determine the angle:

- **Sine** (SIN) equals the opposite side divided by the hypotenuse.

- **Cosine** (COS) equals the adjacent side divided by the hypotenuse.

- **Tangent** (TAN) equals the opposite side divided by the adjacent side.

In our example, the opposite side and hypotenuse are known, therefore the Sine Formula is appropriately selected. Your answer is a decimal number which should be rounded to the nearest ten thousandth. Then use the Table of Trigonometric Functions to find the correct angle. To use the table, look under the appropriate column (SIN, COS or TAN) and find the closest decimal number. Then find the corresponding angle which is shown at the far left of that row.

Table of Trigonometric Functions

Angle	Sin	Cos	Tan	Angle	Sin	Cos	Tan
1°	.0175	.9998	.0175	46°	.7193	.6947	1.0355
2°	.0349	.9994	.0349	47°	.7314	.6820	1.0724
3°	.0523	.9986	.0524	48°	.7431	.6691	1.1106
4°	.0698	.9976	.0699	49°	.7547	.6561	1.1504
5°	.0872	.9962	.0875	50°	.7660	.6428	1.1918
6°	.1045	.9945	.1051	51°	.7771	.6293	1.2349
7°	.1219	.9925	.1228	52°	.7880	.6157	1.2799
8°	.1392	.9903	.1405	53°	.7986	.6018	1.3279
9°	.1564	.9877	.1584	54°	.8090	.5878	1.3764
10°	.1736	.9848	.1763	55°	.8192	.5736	1.4281
11°	.1908	.9816	.1944	56°	.8290	.5592	1.4826
12°	.2079	.9781	.2126	57°	.8387	.5446	1.5399
13°	.2250	.9744	.2309	58°	.8480	.5299	1.6003
14°	.2419	.9703	.2493	59°	.8572	.5150	1.6643
15°	.2588	.9659	.2679	60°	.8660	.5000	1.7321
16°	.2756	.9613	.2867	61°	.8746	.4848	1.8040
17°	.2924	.9563	.3057	62°	.8829	.4695	1.8807
18°	.3090	.9511	.3249	63°	.8910	.4540	1.9626
19°	.3256	.9455	.3443	64°	.8988	.4384	2.0503
20°	.3420	.9397	.3640	65°	.9063	.4226	2.1445
21°	.3584	.9336	.3839	66°	.9135	.4067	2.2460
22°	.3746	.9272	.4040	67°	.9205	.3907	2.3559
23°	.3907	.9205	.4245	68°	.9272	.3746	2.4751
24°	.4067	.9135	.4452	69°	.9336	.3584	2.6051
25°	.4226	.9063	.4663	70°	.9397	.3420	2.7475
26°	.4384	.8988	.4877	71°	.9455	.3256	2.9042
27°	.4540	.8910	.5095	72°	.9511	.3090	3.0777
28°	.4695	.8829	.5317	73°	.9563	.2924	3.2709
29°	.4848	.8746	.5543	74°	.9613	.2756	3.4874
30°	.5000	.8660	.5774	75°	.9659	.2588	3.7321
31°	.5150	.8572	.6009	76°	.9703	.2419	4.0108
32°	.5299	.8480	.6249	77°	.9744	.2250	4.3315
33°	.5446	.8387	.6494	78°	.9781	.2079	4.7046
34°	.5592	.8290	.6745	79°	.9816	.1908	5.1446
35°	.5736	.8192	.7002	80°	.9848	.1736	5.6713
36°	.5878	.8090	.7265	81°	.9877	.1564	6.3138
37°	.6018	.7986	.7536	82°	.9903	.1392	7.1154
38°	.6157	.7880	.7813	83°	.9925	.1219	8.1443
39°	.6293	.7771	.8098	84°	.9945	.1045	9.5144
40°	.6428	.7660	.8391	85°	.9962	.0872	11.4301
41°	.6561	.7547	.8693	86°	.9976	.0698	14.3007
42°	.6691	.7431	.9004	87°	.9986	.0523	19.0811
43°	.6820	.7314	.9325	88°	.9994	.0349	28.6363
44°	.6947	.7193	.9657	89°	.9998	.0175	57.2900
45°	.7071	.7071	1.0000	90°	1.0000	.0000	

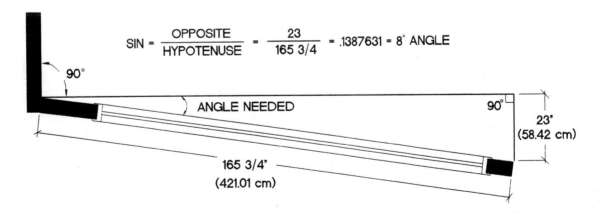

$$SIN = \frac{OPPOSITE}{HYPOTENUSE} = \frac{23}{165\ 3/4} = .1387631 = 8°\ ANGLE$$

Figure 383 Table of Trigonometric Functions - measuring an angled wall and determining its angle.

MEASURING A CURVED WALL

Measuring a curved wall requires that the radius of the curve be established. The radius is found by first locating a straight line which terminates at any two points along the curve. This line is referred to as a *Chord*. By determining the exact center of the chord and measuring the perpendicular length from this point to the wall, the *Rise* is established.

Use the following formulas to determine the radius:

- $\dfrac{(1/2 \text{ Chord})^2 + \text{Rise}^2}{\text{Rise}} = \text{Diameter}$

- $\dfrac{\text{Diameter}}{2} = \text{Radius}$

For kitchen planning purposes, a 36" (91.44cm) chord dimension is recommended because this measurement represents the widest cabinet you should place against a curved wall.

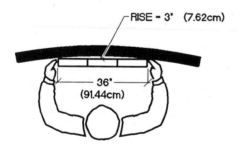

Figure 384 Measuring a curved wall.

For example, if you were to use a yardstick (36") (91.44cm) as a chord and found the rise to be 3" (7.62cm), the formula would be calculated as follows:

Imperial Formulation

- $\dfrac{(1/2 \ (36))^2 + 3^2}{3} =$

- $\dfrac{18^2 + 3^2}{3} =$

- $\dfrac{324 + 9}{3} =$

- $\dfrac{333}{3} =$

- $111 = \text{Diameter}$

- $\dfrac{111}{2} =$

- $55 \ 1/2" = \text{Radius}$

Metric Equivalent in Centimeters

- $\dfrac{1/2 \ (91.44 \ )^2 + 7.62^2}{7.62} =$

- $\dfrac{45.72^2 + 7.62^2}{7.62} =$

- $\dfrac{2090.3184 + 58.0644}{7.62} =$

- $\dfrac{2148.3828}{7.62} =$

- $281.94 = \text{Diameter}$

- $\dfrac{281.94}{2} =$

- $140.97 = \text{Radius}$

Now that the radius is established, the length of the curve (referred to as the arc below) can be determined with the following formula:

Formula: $A = \dfrac{\pi \times R \times <}{180}$

Legend: A = length of arc or curve
π = "pi" = 3.14
R = Radius
< = Angle
x = Multiply

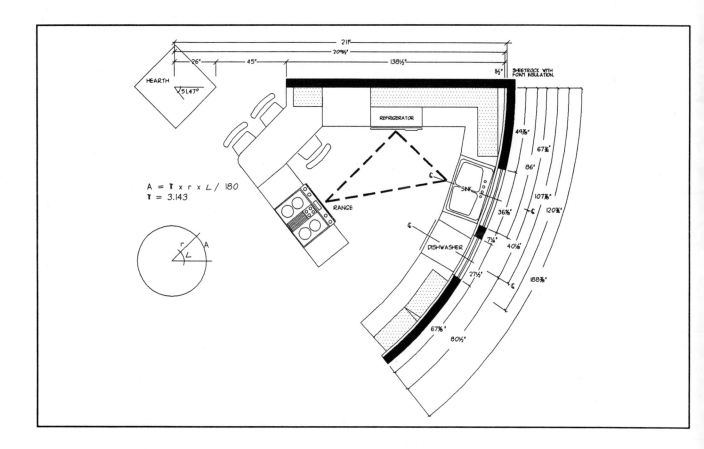

Figure 385 A kitchen which utilizes curves.

SECTION **2**

Preparation of the Plans

UNDERSTANDING BLUEPRINTS

Many kitchen specialists who are affiliated with decorative plumbing and hardware firms do not visit and measure the jobsite themselves. Much of their clientele consists of tradespeople or homeowners who are building a new home or planning a major renovation for which architectural plans have been prepared. Therefore, the kitchen specialist must have a clear understanding of how to read and understand blueprints.

CLARIFICATION OF TERMS

To begin our discussion, let's clarify some of the more common terms associated with plans preparation:

- **Blueprint:** This word is a holdover from early methods of reproducing builder's plans. In order to produce quantities of large sheets of paper, without using an expensive plate printing process, the "*blueprinting*" process was created and became the standard of the building industry.

  To make a real "*blueprint*", an original black and white drawing was reversed onto an ink negative, which made the black lines white on a blue background. This process is not frequently used today. Black line or blue line drawings are much more typical. However, while we still call these drawings "*a set of blueprints*", a better term would be "*plans*".

- **Plans:** This term represents a standardized set of drawings and diagrams which communicate the exact construction of a building. Plans may be on microfilm for bidding purposes or may be full-sized and stored rolled up in a tube or laid flat in shallow drawers.

  The industry has specified a standard language of symbols to represent construction materials in building plans. Additionally, *Architectural Graphics and Standards,* published by John Wiley & Sons, sets other drawing standards.

  A conscientious kitchen designer needs to learn this language of symbols and must be as proficient in understanding its meanings as in communicating in English.

  Sometimes communicating with symbols is complicated because of local dialects and accents that develop when a particular architect or company within one area develops specialized symbols for their own use. When this happens, a *"dictionary"* of these symbols is shown on the title sheet of the plans as a *"Key to Materials"*. Always check the key before attempting to read a set of plans.

- **Take-off:** This refers to a bidding firm reviewing the plans and developing an estimate for the specific part of the project they are responsible for. The kitchen specialist will *"take-off"* all of the kitchen fixtures and fittings, and perhaps the cabinetry and surfaces for his/her estimate. If the firm specializes in decorative hardware, the designer will do a *"take-off"* from the door schedule as well.

- **Specifications (Specs):** There are written documents accompanying the architect's plans, namely *"Specifications"* and *"Schedules"*. The specifications are descriptions, in words, of the materials to be used and the quality expected. *For example,* the *"specs"* would state the grade of wood that is to be installed in the flooring. Including specifications in plans would complicate the drawing beyond readability. Therefore, the specifications are generally a separate document.

Smaller projects might use a short form of specification based on a form developed by the **Federal Housing Administration** called *"Description of Materials"*. In the

mid 1960s, the **Construction Specification Institute** issued a standard designated, *"Format for Construction Specification"*, which is arranged as nearly as possible in the same order as the work will be performed. This form of specification is used on many projects in the industry.

The specifications are generally written by the architect or by a specification writer. In either case, the individual is expected to apply a knowledge of materials, building codes, and customer expectations to develop a detailed list. However, as a kitchen professional, it is highly recommended that you have your subcontractors verify that the specs and designs of the architect have met all codes, prior to bidding the job.

Because specifications give more detailed expectations of quality and quantity of materials than would be possible in illustrated plans, they need to be carefully reviewed during the **"take-off"**.

- **Schedule:** Within the plans there may be additional pages inserted which have lists of like items specified for the home. There will be a reference number circled on the plan which corresponds to a number on the schedule. *For example,* a schedule may list the exact size and construction of each door in the project.

Because the schedule is a tabulated list of materials needed for the job, it can be considered a short form of specifications for materials. Schedules are useful because they provide quick on-the-job information. *For example,* all the doors will be listed on the door schedule. Therefore, during the *"take-off"*, the schedule can be referenced, rather than painstakingly noting every single door on the plan.

A GUIDE TO PLANS

A complete set of Architectural plans contains:

- Title Page

- Site Plan

- Floor Plan

- Elevations

- Construction Details and Sections

- Footing and Foundation Details

- Structural Framing

- Mechanical Plans (Plumbing, Electrical, Ventilation, Air Conditioning, Heating, Etc.)

The plans may also include specific millwork drawings, interior design drawings and landscape plans.

Following this discussion you will find a series of graphics depicting the contents of a set of Architectural plans.

Title Page

This is the first page in a set of building plans. It may include any or all of the following:

- The name of the building or project

- The location

- The owner's name

- The architect and/or architectural firm's name

- The names of consulting engineers and/or Interior Designers.

- The set number (of the number of sets distributed)

- A key to the symbols for materials

- An index to the drawings

The title page may also contain a site plan if it is not on a separate sheet.

Site Plan

This is an overhead view of the property around the building. On most projects, it includes the entire property, showing the lot lines and the grades or layout of the land before construction begins. It is sometimes called a *"Plot Plan"*. When reviewing a site plan, make sure that you establish the property lines. Envision the property, as it will look upon completion. Pay particular attention to the orientation of the building on the site, and the affect of this orientation on the kitchen.

Floor Plan

The floor plan becomes the central reference point for all other construction drawings because it is the easiest to understand. Because it's an overhead *cut-away view* of the overall project, most people can imagine walking through the home by looking at a floor plan.

Generally, the floor plan shows the entire building. Building plans include separate sheets of floor plans for each story of the building, including the basement. It's possible to see the arrangement of the walls and partitions, stairs, doors and windows from these drawings.

On the floor plan there are numbers. These refer to detail drawings that follow or to a schedule of materials. Therefore, you can use the floor plan as a visual index to locate the specifics of each area shown. Sometimes numbers on the plan may also refer to exact sections of the specifications. If in doubt, go over the numbering code with the architect or client before beginning your "take-off".

The dimensions given on the plans are exact, whereas the drawings may not be perfectly to scale. Look for the note "*NTS*" *(Not to Scale).* Look for areas on the plan that are shaded or somehow differentiated from the balance of the plan. This plan notation generally indicates changes have been made. Always use the dimensions listed. Never scale a blueprint during the "take-off" stage.

Most architectural plans indicate dimensions from the center of partitions and support columns rather than from the finished wall surface. Architects follow this dimensioning process because

building materials (such as lumber) may vary in thickness, whereas the center point will always remain standard.

It is the standard of the kitchen industry to dimension finished walls only. This standard has been established because of the critical fit of the products specified for the kitchen. You will need to verify the finished wall dimensions of the project under consideration before you complete your "*take-off*".

Elevations

The elevation is a flat projection of one side of a building or space. In architectural plans, the elevations show the exterior views of the building and the sections show an interior cut view of the entire building. It is the standard in the kitchen industry to show interior wall views as individual elevations.

Construction Details and Sections

A section is a "*sliced*" open part of a building, showing inner construction. Sections can be implanted in other plans as a detail, or may be collected on pages of their own. Technically, there are several ways of representing the unseen details in a section. A good source of reference for you to further understand blueprint reading is, *Blueprint Reading for the Building Trades* by **John Traister**.

Standard sections of a kitchen plan will show a cut view of a wall illustrating cabinetry, molding, soffit and backsplash relationships.

A detail is a large scale blow-up of an important part of the building. *For example,* the installation of doors or kitchen framing might be shown in detail. Such details are small, but reveal important relationships of materials which cannot be communicated by a simple floor plan or elevation.

Several details may be located on their own detail sheet or they may be included on other drawing sheets.

Footings and Foundations

The foundation serves as an anchor for the building. The foundation plans show how the building is affixed to the concrete walls below.

Structural Framing

The structural framing is an illustration of what holds the building up. Before considering any design alternatives, find out if the walls surrounding the kitchen are load bearing walls or non-structural partitions.

Mechanicals

The mechanicals are a set of drawings, usually found at the back of the plans, which show the arrangement of the heating, ventilating, air conditioning, plumbing, electrical installation and specialized machinery.

Because many of these trades are specialized in themselves, it is not surprising that the mechanicals can be difficult to understand. Each trade has developed a sub-set of symbols and a specialized language to show the details.

It's critical for you to understand all of these mechanicals. You should ask: *"Is there any flexibility in the plumbing supply line, drain or vent locations?"*

You need to look for proper heating and air conditioning vents or ducts in the kitchen plans as well.

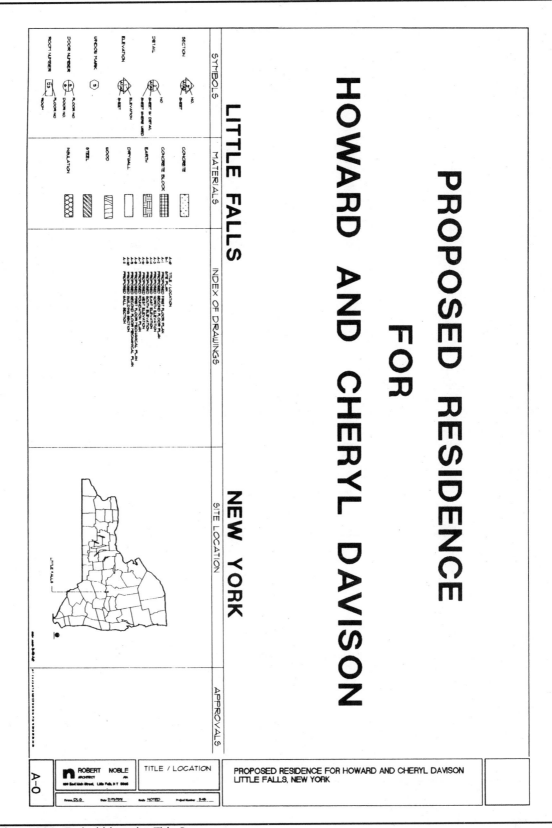

Figure 386 Typical blueprint Title Page

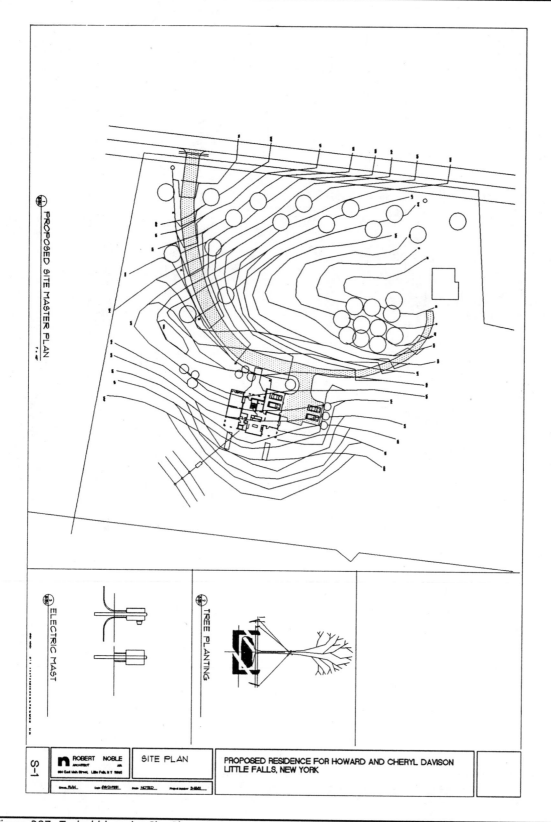

Figure 387 Typical blueprint Site Plan

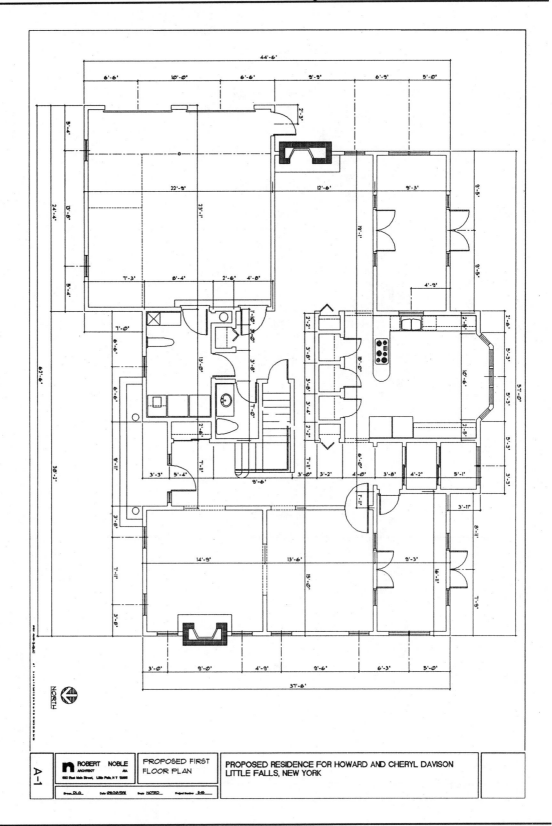

Figure 388 Typical blueprint Floor Plan

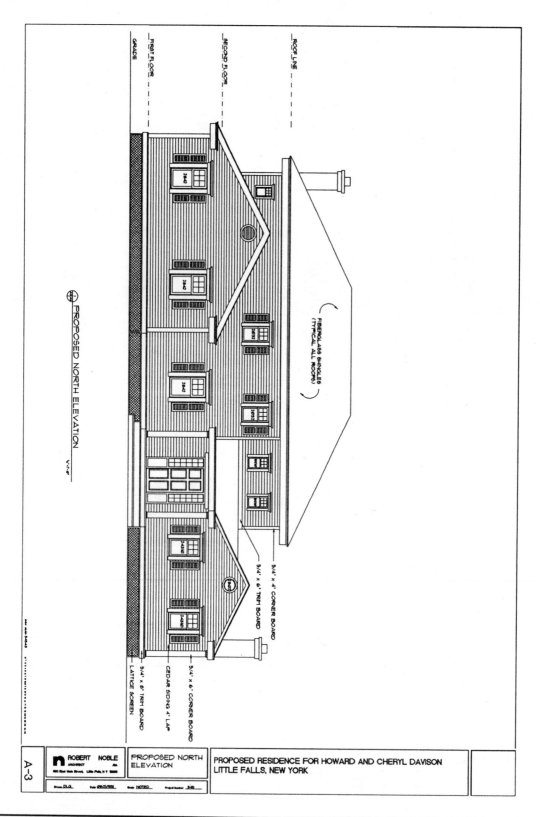

Figure 389 Typical blueprint Elevation

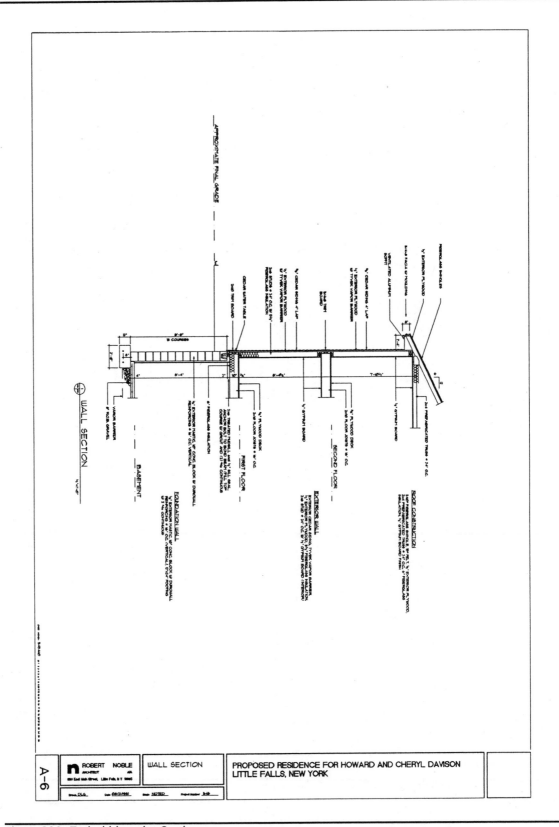

Figure 390 Typical blueprint Section

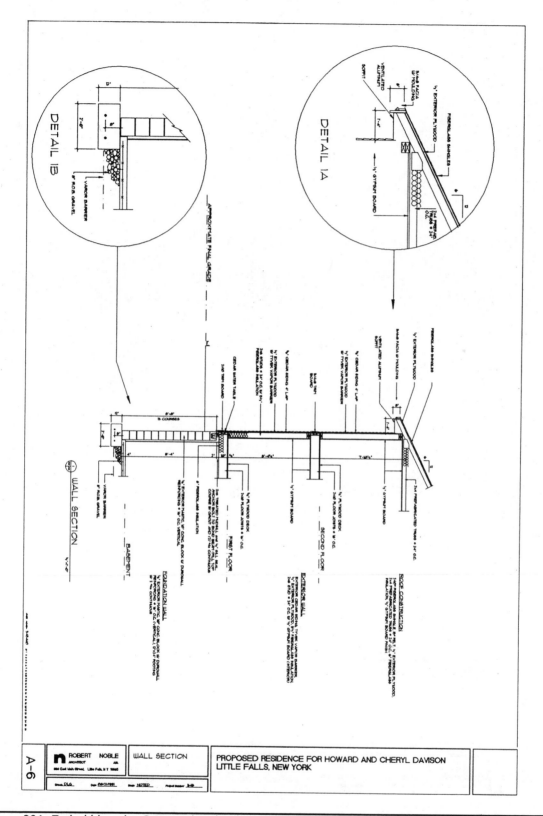

Figure 391   Typical blueprint Construction details

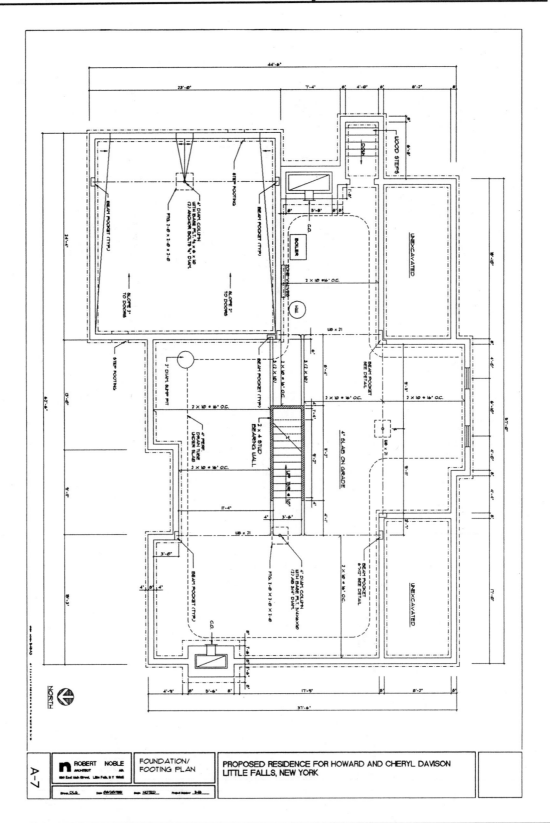

Figure 392 Typical blueprint Foundation Plan

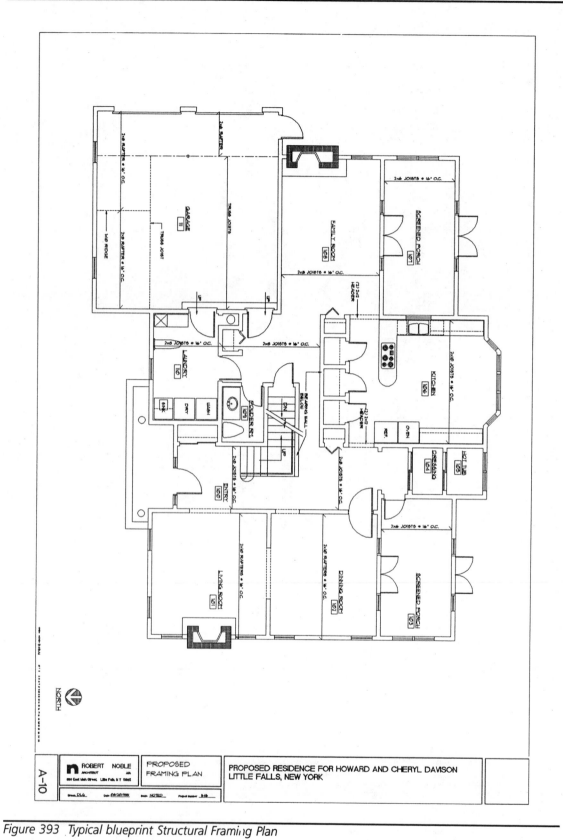

Figure 393 Typical blueprint Structural Framing Plan

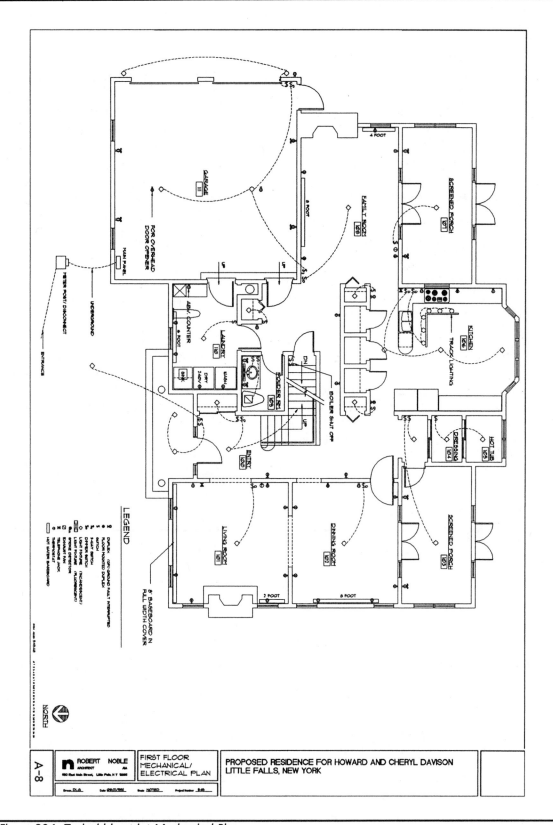

Figure 394 Typical blueprint Mechanical Plan

Miscellaneous Plans

You may find some additional drawings such as millwork drawings, which are provided by a supplier of equipment and materials, rather than by the architect. They are much more detailed drawings of a specific part of the project. Typically, locally-fabricated cabinet companies provide shop drawings.

There may also be a set of interior design plans showing the location of furniture, specifying the finish of walls and ceilings. Lastly, detail of final landscaping may be shown pictorially.

HINTS FROM THE SPECIALISTS

The showroom specialist, or any kitchen designer who is involved in new construction planning, needs to thoroughly understand a set of blueprints before the *"take-off"* begins.

Seasoned experts in the decorative plumbing and hardware industry share the following hints with you regarding how to read a blueprint:

- Make sure that you and your clients understand that rooms always look bigger in 1/2" (1.27cm) scale than in 1/4" (.63cm) or 1/8" (.31cm) scales. The same also applies for metric ratios.

- Don't ever plan a room that has furniture in it without knowing what size the furniture is and where it's going to be placed.

- When you're doing a hardware *"take-off"*, be methodical in your review. *For example,* when you are doing a *"take-off"* for doors, start by counting the number of doors in the entire plan or refer to the door schedule. Make sure you end up with that number of doors and corresponding hardware when you finish your *"take-off"*. Consider dividing the doors by groups: key lock, passage and privacy. You can then count the cabinet hardware by areas and total to check quantity.

Missing any item during the *"take-off"* is very costly: in terms of reordering, delay time, and customer frustration. **Check and double check!**

- If your clients add any items that are not on the schedule, consider whether they will change the plans. *For example,* if a client requests that you add a barbeque in an island, you have now changed the mechanical plans. You may need to add electrical and/or gas supply, along with duct work for ventilation. Any changes in framing, electrical, plumbing or construction that products require must be clearly communicated to the builder or architect so that the appropriate notes can be incorporated into the plans.

Drafting Basics

EQUIPMENT CONSIDERATIONS

Well-drafted plans start with the right equipment. Purchase the best quality equipment you can afford. **Drafting tools should be used for their intended purpose only and should always be kept clean.**

The following list of equipment is recommended:

- drafting paper (vellum)

- drafting board or portable draftpak

- T-Square, parallel bar or drafting machine

- pencils and leads

- pencil pointer (mechanical lead sharpener)

- architect's scale

- triangles

- erasers

- drafting tape

- templates

- compass

- curves

- dusting brush

- erasing shield

The following list of additional equipment may be useful, but is not required:

- plan enhancements (ie. stick-on ready artwork)

- pens and inks

- electric eraser

- lettering guide

- markers and colored pencils

- computer system with plotter and/or printer

Drafting Equipment

Drafting Paper: Special drafting paper is required for production of professional drawing presentations. The paper most often used is called "*Vellum 1000x*". This is translucent paper with high strength. Preprinted vellum paper is available for NKBA members through the **National Kitchen & Bath Association** in two sizes, 11" x 17" (27.94cm x 43.18cm) and 17" x 22" (43.18cm x 55.88cm).

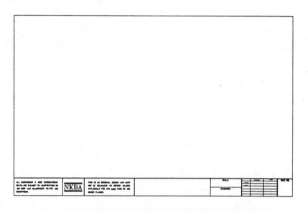

Figure 395 NKBA Vellum paper

Drafting Board: The drafting board should accommodate the largest size drawing paper you normally use.

The board's surface should be perfectly smooth and constructed so as not to warp or bend. If a T-Square is going to be used, the working edge (left or right-handedness) of the board must be straight and true. A 10° to 15° slope will provide a comfortable drawing surface, as well as a clear view of your work in progress. A portable draftpak includes the tilt option, storage and built-in parallel bar.

For used or worn surfaces, or to protect new surfaces, a vinyl covering can be mounted on the board surface. The common brand names for this material are **"Vyco"** and **"Borco"**.

T-Square/Parallel Bar: The T-Square is the most economical form of drafting straightedge equipment. It is used to draw horizontal lines and to keep the drawing square. To use a T-Square, hold it firmly against one edge

of the board and then slide it vertically along that edge to position your triangle or draw horizontal lines.

Figure 396 Portable draftpak station can be set up anywhere.

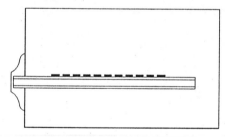

DRAW LINE ALONG TOP
OF T-SQUARE

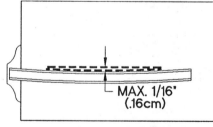

MAX. 1/16"
(.16cm)

TURN T-SQUARE OVER AND
DRAW A SECOND LINE

Figure 397 Determine whether the T-Square is square.

Use only the top edge of the T-Square for drawing lines. The bottom edge may not be parallel with the top edge which would result in an out-of-square drawing if both edges were used. To check the T-Square for straightness, draw a line from the T-Square's left edge to its right edge. Turn the T-Square over and draw another line beginning at the same location. If there is a difference of more than 1/16 of an inch (.15cm) at any location, the T-Square should not be used. For vertical lines, a triangle is required. A T-Square is not recommended for production of high quality drawing documents because it relys mostly on the user's skill.

Most kitchen designers prefer to use a parallel bar drafting system. The parallel bar works similarly to the T-Square, but is permanently attached to the drafting board. The parallel bar attaches to the board's corners with wires which glide on pulleys. Errors are limited with the use of a parallel bar because it is not hand-held and therefore, is less likely to slip out of squareness.

Drafting Machine: For the best quality drafting, a drafting machine or "*arm*" is recommended. These are expensive mechanical straight edges which enable the user to draw horizontal, vertical or any other angled line without additional equipment. There are various models available ranging from the compact, clip-on to larger V-track types. A drafting machine offers the highest level of linear accuracy possible. The straight edges are interchangeable allowing flexibility in working with different scales or changing from the imperial to the metric system.

Computers are fast becoming a replacement to standard drafting methods. Drawings are done with the aid of a computer system and then stored electronically onto a hard drive or floppy disks. Presentation drawings are either printed or plotted by mechanical means for easy and organized retrieval. A more detailed discussion on computers and computer aided design follows later in this publication.

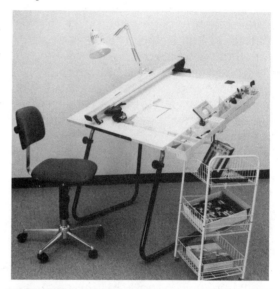

Figure 398 Drafting machine station.

Figure 399 Computer aided drafting station.

Pencils and Leads: The selection of pencils and drawing leads is next in importance. Most draftspeople avoid wooden cased drawing pencils, preferring a drafting lead holder. The holder acts as a shell for the lead and enables you to easily push the lead out for convenient sharpening. There are also mechanical pencils that hold very thin leads, which when pushed out do not require any sharpening. These save time and eliminate the extra tool, however the line quality is limited to the thickness of the lead and the thin leads break often until the user becomes accustomed to applying just the right amount of pressure.

There are 17 varieties of leads. They are classified by degrees of hardness and identified by a letter and/or number. The neutrals, such as B, HB, F and H are mid-range hardness. From B,2B to 6B the lead is consecutively softer. From 2H through 9H, the leads become consecutively harder. For most drafting purposes, the 3H, 2H, H and F are sufficient. You should experiment to discover which lead hardness works best for you. The softer leads, such as 2B and 3B, are recommended for pencil renderings with shades and shadows. The softer the lead is, the easier it flows and the more it will smear. The harder lead such as the 2H will produce a crisp line which will not smear as readily.

Practice is required to develop consistent pencil line work. As a line is drawn the pencil should be rotated between your fingers and the pressure exerted should remain constant. This insures consistent line width. **Do not press too hard because your paper may tear or have permanent indents.**

Pencil Pointer: A pencil pointer is used to sharpen the lead in a mechanical pencil. **Keeping a sharp point on the lead is one of the key elements in developing good line-work.** Leads can be sharpened on sandpaper, but to achieve the most efficient point, use a mechanical pencil pointer. These are available in many different brands and models ranging from portable and clip-on models to heavy, paper-weight types.

Architect's Scale: An architect's scale is used to measure and scale a drawing. The most common architect's scale is triangular in shape and offers eleven different scales in feet and inches:

IMPERIAL SCALE

FULL SCALE   1/16" Gradations

1/8"	=	1'0"
1/4"	=	1'0"
3/8"	=	1'0"
3/4"	=	1'0"
1/2"	=	1'0"
1"	=	1'0"
1 1/2"	=	1'0"
3"	=	1'0"
3/32"	=	1'0"
3/16"	=	1'0"

The most common metric scale offers six different scales (ratios):

METRIC SCALE

1cm = 10cm	(1:10 ratio)
1cm = 20cm	(1:20 ratio)
1cm = 30cm	(1:30 ratio)
1cm = 40cm	(1:40 ratio)
1cm = 50cm	(1:50 ratio)
1cm = 60cm	(1:60 ratio)

For your kitchen plans, all drawings will be prepared at the scale 1/2" =1'0", 1cm = 24cm or 1cm = 20cm. Flat scales are also available with four scales. These are sometimes preferred because they eliminate time spent hunting for the right scale.

MEASURING WITH A SCALE

To accurately measure with a scale, first select the proper edge and place it on the drawing parallel with the line to be measured. Start from the zero and count the number of full feet in the measurement and mark the exact point with a very sharp pencil. Then, start from the zero and going in the opposite direction, mark the number of inches.

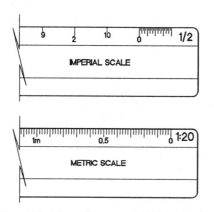

Figure 400 1/2" = 1' 0" or a 1:20cm ratio are the industry standards. (1:24 is used as a metric conversion)

Triangles: A handy drafting tool is a three-sided plastic piece called a triangle. It may list a different scale on each side and may also have kitchen appliance and equipment template outlines within the center spaces. The **National Kitchen & Bath Association** offers one of these to its members.

Triangles are used with both T-Squares and parallel bars to draw vertical and angular lines. The triangle rests on the horizontal straight edge to insure that vertical lines will be perpendicular

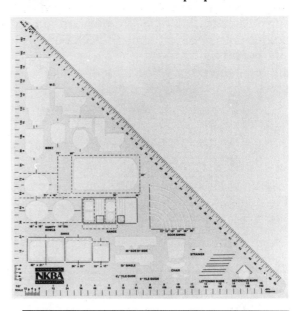

Figure 401 The NKBA Triangle.

to the horizontal lines. Two triangles are required; one with 45° angles and another with 30° and 60° angles. Both triangles should be made of clear or tinted plastic and have eased or beveled edges. The tinted plastic is easier to see and reduces shadows caused by overhead lighting. The beveled or eased edge makes the triangle easier to pick up and is absolutely necessary if any inking is to be done.

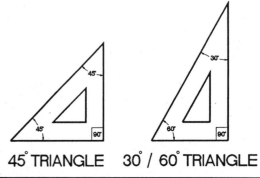

Figure 402 Two triangles are generally used for drafting.

Either triangle may be used to draw vertical lines. Begin by holding the T-Square or parallel bar firmly and placing the triangle horizontally along the upper edge. Slide the triangle into position and hold it with your left hand, pull the pencil upward along the vertical edge. If you are left-handed, reverse these instructions.

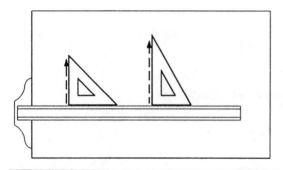

Figure 403 Draw vertical lines from the bottom of triangle upwards.

The same process is used to draw lines at angles. Locate the triangle and pull the pencil from the left to right always gradually rotating the pencil between your fingers. This will insure the most accurate and consistent line work. The most common angles, 75°, 60°, 45°, 30° and 15° can be easily drawn with the two triangles mentioned.

If odd angles are required, an adjustable triangle, which can be set at any desired angle, is available.

CHECKING FOR ACCURACY

To check the accuracy of a 90° angle of a triangle, draw a vertical line from its bottom to its top point. Turn the triangle over and draw another line beginning at the same location as the first line. If there is a difference of more than 1/32"

(.07cm) at the top of an eight inch line, the triangle should not be used.

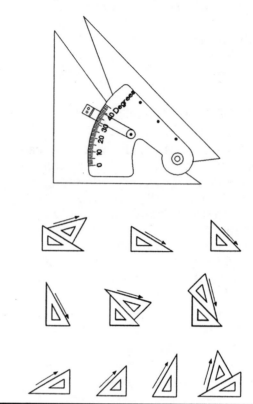

Figure 404 Triangles can be combined to achieve various other angles or an adjustable triangle may be used.

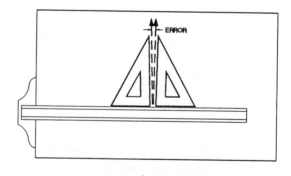

Figure 405 Determining whether the triangles are square.

Eraser: Erasing is a major part of the design and planning process. Choosing the appropriate eraser and proper technique is as important as drawing a line properly. The wrong eraser may stain or even tear the paper. Look for a soft eraser, such as the "*pink-pearl*" or "*white vinyl-lite*" brands which are most popular. These are available in convenient holders which can be refilled much like the lead holder. When erasing, be sure to hold the paper tightly in place and apply only as much pressure as is necessary. For hard to remove lines, place a smooth, hard surface under the area to be erased (a plastic triangle works well).

Drafting Tape: Drafting tape is necessary to hold your drawing in place throughout the drawing process. To easily remove the tape after completion of the drawing, drafting tape, not masking or scotch tape, should be used. Drafting tape can be purchased in a variety of widths and in packages with easy "*tear-off*" cutting edges. Also available are drafting tape "*dots*"; these are round pieces of tape which peel off a roll of paper. The dots are convenient to use and are less likely to roll up after the T-Square or parallel bar has passed over them a few times.

Templates: Templates for plan and elevational views are available for almost everything; kitchen appliances and equipment, door swings, circles and ellipses. Lettering templates are also available. Many of the templates for kitchen appliances and equipment available in drafting supply stores are designed for architects in 1/8"-1/4" scales. As a kitchen specialist you will require 1/2" or metric equivalent scaled templates. 1/2" scaled templates are available through the **National Kitchen & Bath Association** and the **American Society of Interior Designers**, as well as many manufacturers of cabinetry.

Using templates saves time and produces a consistent, professional-looking portfolio.

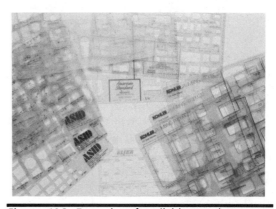

Figure 406 Examples of available templates.

Compass: A compass is used to draw circles or arcs which are not on your templates. Most compasses will produce circles with diameters ranging from 3/16" (.47cm) to 13" (33.02cm). The compass features one end with an adjustable needle point and another end with lead point. To keep the circle radius consistent, the pencil lead end must be sharpened in a beveled fashion with the beveled edge facing out. To sharpen the pencil lead point, rub the bevel side back and forth along sandpaper. The bevel point should be between 1/64"-1/32" shorter than the needle point.

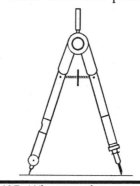

Figure 407 When templates are not available a compass can be used to draw any size circle.

DRAWING A COMPASS CURVE

While drawing the curve, hold the compass perpendicular to the paper with a light touch to avoid making a hole in the paper. Special attachments are also available for replacing the lead with an ink pen-point.

Curves: Irregular curves, commonly referred to as "*french*" curves, are used to draw curved lines other than circles or arcs. A clear or tinted plastic curve with several small curves and a few long slightly curved edges is recommended. To draw an irregular curve, plot several points through which the curve must pass, then select the curved edge which most closely matches.

For complex curved lines more points will be necessary and the curve may have to be drawn in sections, rotating and moving the irregular curve until the desired curvilinear line is completed. Flexible curves are also available. These are wires covered in a rubber-like material which can be manipulated to fit almost any large, curved shape.

Dusting Brush: A dusting brush typically has a handle with long, soft bristles made of nylon or horsehair. The brush is used for removing eraser shavings and graphite particles from the drawing without smudging. A brush is necessary to keep your drawing clean and clear of debris.

Figure 409 Use the dusting brush to keep drawings clear of debris.

Erasing Shield: An erasing shield is a thin, metal instrument with various shaped holes. This tool is used to isolate a specific area of the drawing to be erased, eliminating over erasing and redrawing.

Figure 408 The french curve can be used to draft accurate irregular curves.

Figure 410 Use an erasing shield to protect your drawing while erasing.

Additional Equipment

Plan Enhancements: Sheets of press or stick-on lettering, symbols and shading are an easy way to graphically enhance drawings. Lettering machines also enhance the plan by enabling you to type out letters or numbers onto clear sticky-back tape which is then applied to the drawing. These machines have become smaller and more economical in recent years.

The press-on lettering takes more time and precision to mount, although it looks more natural on the original drawing. However, if blueprints or photocopies are going to be used, the difference between the two isn't noticeable. Symbols such as electrical symbols, arrows, plants, trees and dot shading are also available in sheets of sticky-back or press-on format.

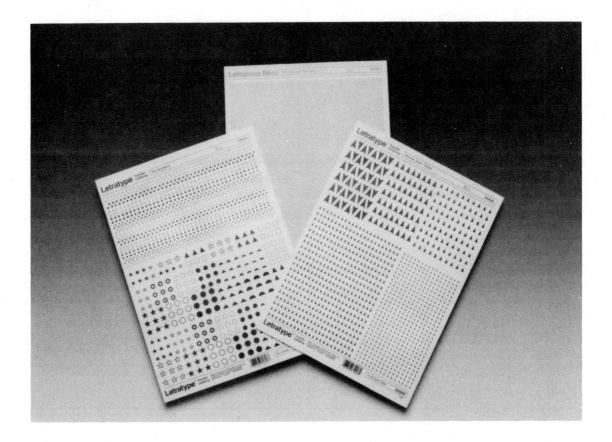

Figure 411 Various accessories and underlays can be used to enhance plans.

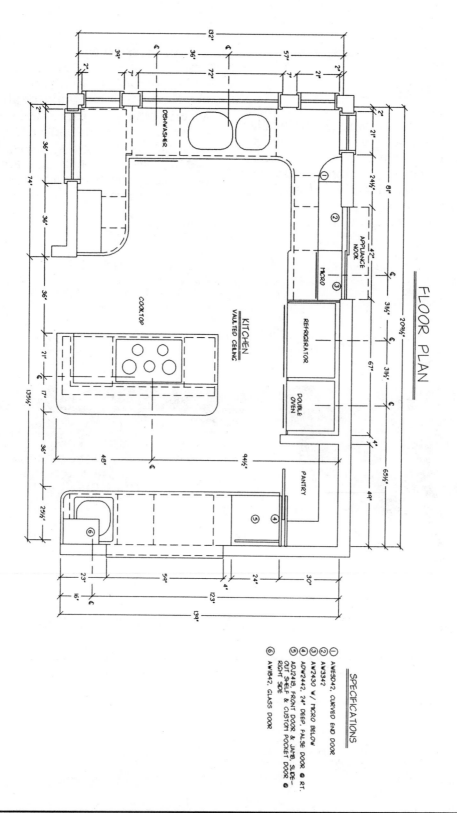

Figure 412 Floor plan before enhancements using imperial dimensions.

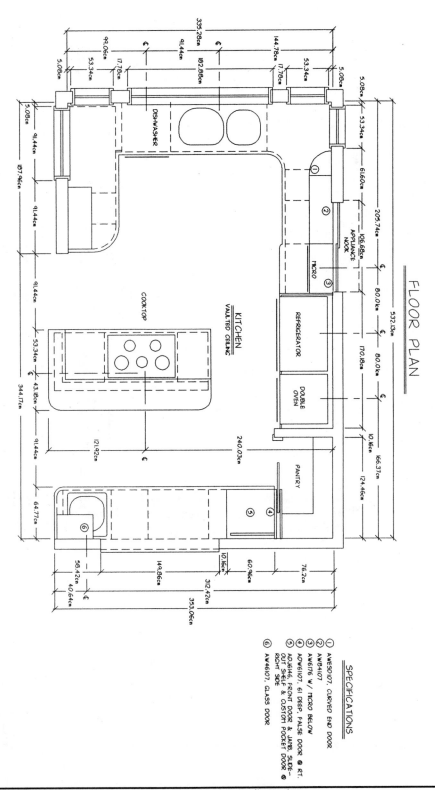

FLOOR PLAN

KITCHEN
VAULTED CEILING

DISHWASHER

COOKTOP

APPLIANCE NOOK

MICRO

REFRIGERATOR

DOUBLE OVEN

PANTRY

Figure 413 Floor plan before enhancements using metric dimensions.

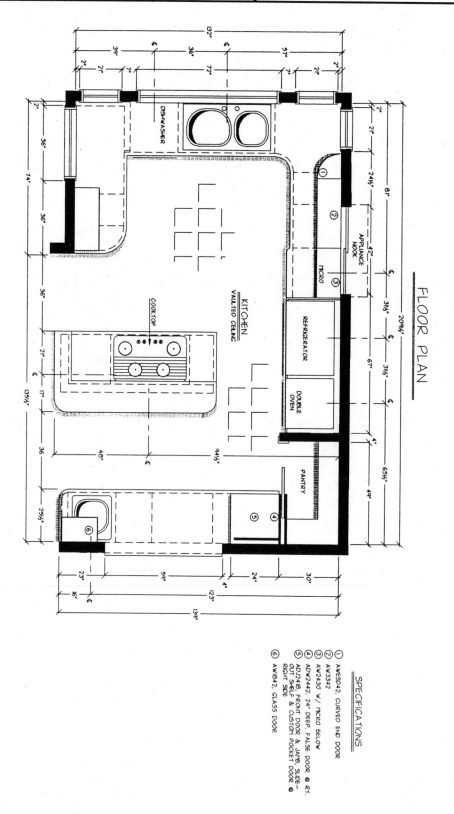

FLOOR PLAN

SPECIFICATIONS

1 AWES042, CURVED END DOOR
2 AW3342
3 AW2430 W/ MICRO BELOW
4 ADW2442, 24" DEEP, FALSE DOOR & JAMB, SLIDE-OUT SHELF & CUSTOM POCKET DOOR @ RT.
5 ADJ2418, FRONT DOOR & JAMB, SLIDE-OUT SHELF & CUSTOM POCKET DOOR @ RIGHT SIDE
6 AWIB42, GLASS DOOR

Figure 414 Floor plan after enhancements using imperial dimensions.

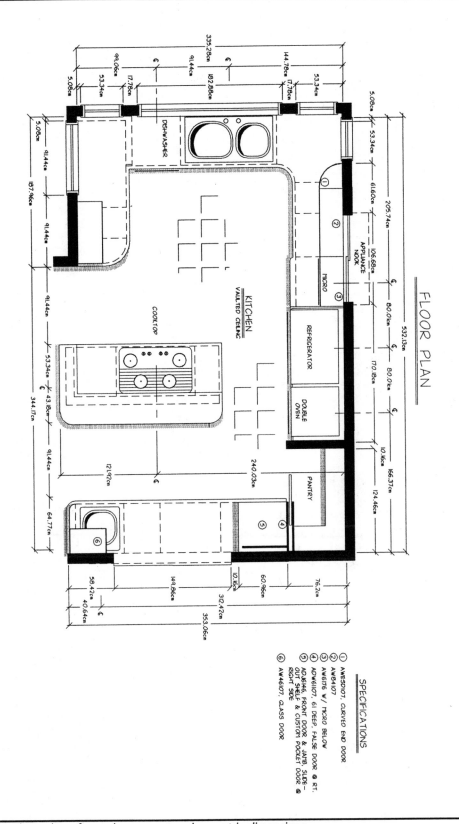

Figure 415 Floor plan after enhancements using metric dimensions.

Pens and Inks: An inking pen is one of the easiest and most economical ways to improve the quality of your drawings. In the past, inking a drawing was time-consuming and required skill because the only tool available was a ruling pen, which works like a fountain pen. They were hard to control because the ink was easily smeared and could unexpectedly drip onto the drawing. The technical pens available today eliminate these worries.

Although it still takes a bit of practice and the ink will smear if rubbed too soon, with a little patience, inking is easily learned. The technical pen is engineered to allow ink to flow out only when it is needed. Some pens are available with snap-on ink cartridge refills, virtually eliminating any handling of messy ink.

THE FIRST RULE OF INKING

The first rule of inking is to use a straight edge with a slightly raised or beveled edge to eliminate ink bleeding. You will find proper cleaning and maintenance of your pen vital. If the pen is not going to be used every few days, it should be emptied and cleaned after each use. There are cleaning solutions and machines available which are specially formulated to remove clogged ink.

Electric Eraser: An electric eraser will become one of your most used tools. It will save you time and improve the quality of your presentations. Today's electric erasers are light-weight and cordless. **Over erasing can wear a hole through the paper**, so use this tool carefully.

Lettering Guide: A lettering guide is used to draw guide lines for lettering.

By placing the pencil lead in the appropriate hole, the draftsperson can quickly

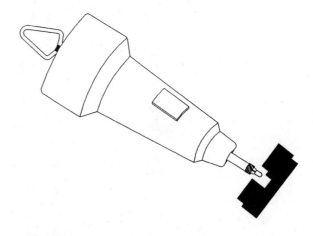

Figure 416 Electric eraser.

layout consistently even guide lines without measuring. This is recommended for areas such as the specifications on a floor plan.

Markers and Colored Pencils: To make your renderings beautiful, add color to your interpretive drawings. The mastering of color marker and pencil renderings is an art form all its own. Hinting at the color of cabinets and fixtures makes a presentation come to life.

There are a wide variety of colored pencils and markers from which to choose. When selecting colored pencils look for soft, heavily-pigmented leads which will give even tones and make blending easy. Markers should always be tested on the paper on which they are to be used to determine whether they will bleed or cause the line art ink to bleed.

The type of paper used with marker and pencil renderings will greatly affect the finished appearance. Transparent marker papers soften the colors; opaque white plotter or marker papers reveal the true brilliance of colors and blueprints or sepia prints mute colors. All of these papers are acceptable for marker and pencil renderings. Drafting vellum is not acceptable. The color will not adhere to vellum, it will puddle on top of the paper and run.

Computer Aided Drafting

Computer-Aided Drafting and Design programs (CADD) are a part of the design industry. Because of their speed and accuracy, computers are a powerful asset. If you currently own a computer, the investment in specialized design software is minimal. However, if you have nothing to build upon, expect to invest between $8,000 and $15,000 in combined software and hardware for a single drafting station.

There has recently been an influx of computer software packages for the kitchen and bathroom industry. The many software programs available can be categorized in one of two groups:

- The first category and most familiar to the industry is the pre-customized software program. The pre-customized program utilizes predetermined criteria to perform automatic placement of elements and fill-in of materials. *For example,* you type in dimensions of the room, select window and door placement, equipment placement and the computer completes the design, placing cabinets, fillers, tile, etc. These programs are easy to use, fast and offer three dimensional viewing in minutes. Some programs are available with a color and/or pricing option. These programs however are limited to kitchens and bathrooms only.

- Traditional drafting software programs act as a drafting tool, known as computer aided drafting (CAD). Using various commands, you draw the design on the computer screen with a mouse, digitizer or stylus, instead of on paper. A CAD program can be individually customized by the user and is limited only by the designer's imagination. These programs are broad in scope and are not limited to just kitchens and bathrooms. Complete homes and other building structures can be created.

Automated drafting encourages creative planning because it's easy to try a number of design options on the screen. Changes made by clients can also be made in the same manner. No more hours spent re-drawing and no more messy presentations caused by extensive erasing and white-outs!

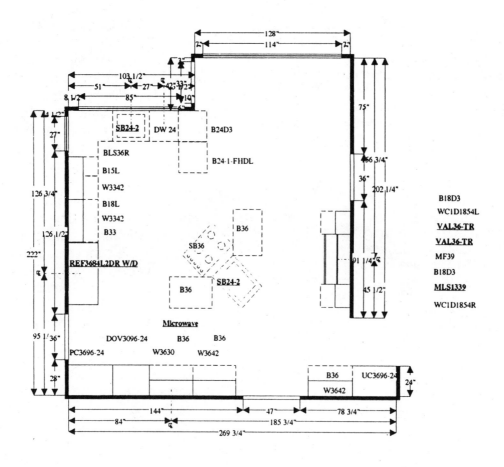

Figure 417 (Courtesy of Auto-Graph Designing Systems, Inc.) Drawing presentation completed by a computer.

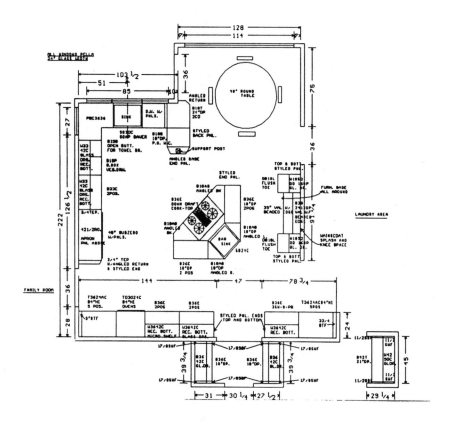

Figure 418 (Courtesy of Cabinetware) Drawing presentation completed by a computer.

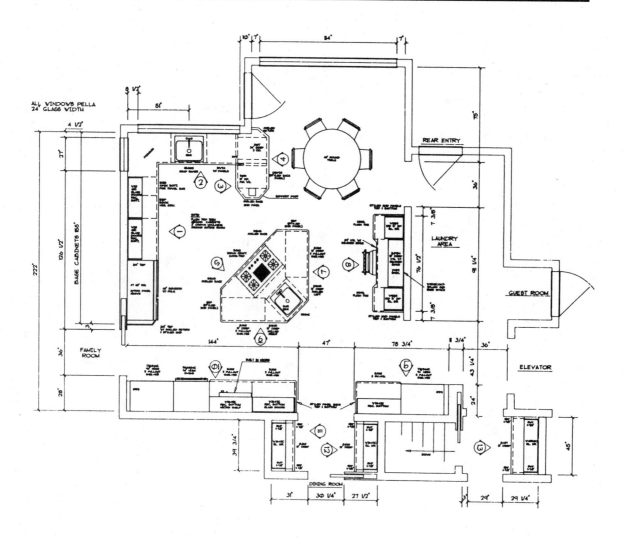

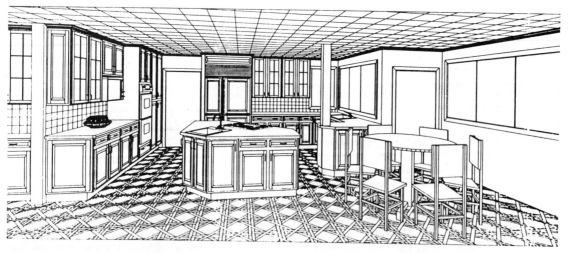

Figure 419 (Courtesy of CadKit) Drawing presentation completed by a computer.

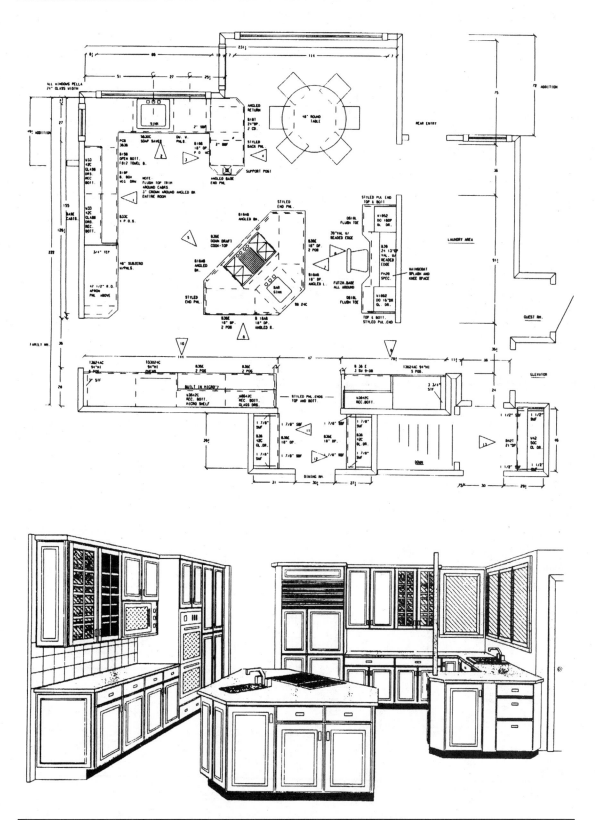

Figure 420 (Courtesy of Twenty-Twenty) Drawing presentation completed by a computer.

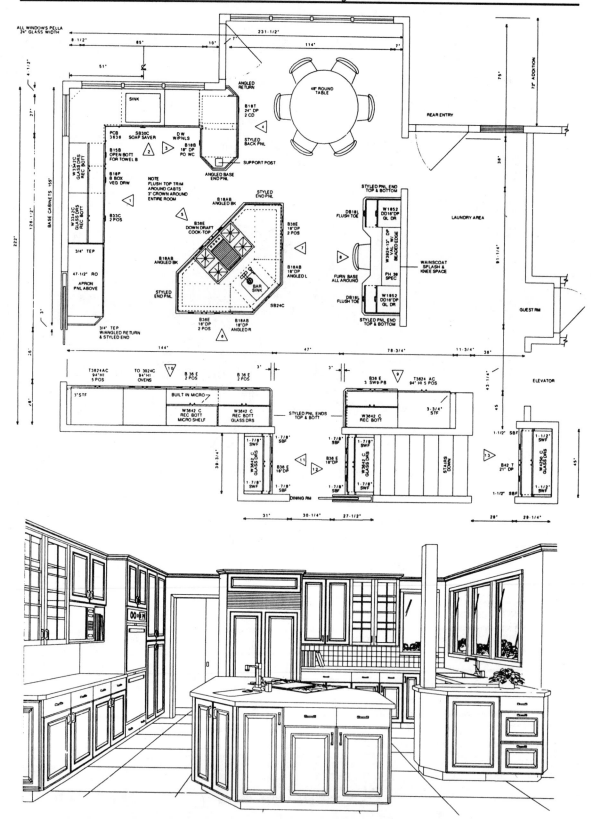

Figure 421 (Courtesy of Planit, USA) Drawing presentation completed by a computer.

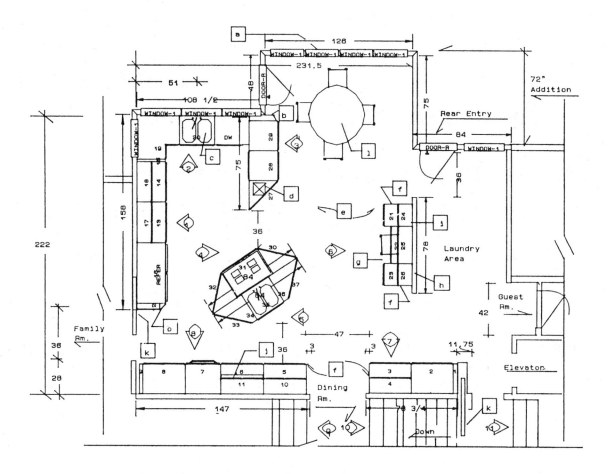

Figure 422 (Courtesy of Cabinet Vision) Drawing presentation completed by a computer.

SECTION **4**

The Importance of Lettering

ENHANCING DRAWING APPEARANCE

A drawing relies on lettering to convey information that is not graphically obvious. Skillful lettering enhances the appearance and more importantly, the clarity, of the drawing. By contrast, poor lettering is difficult to read and detracts from the drawing. Consistency is the most important element in performing skillful lettering.

Lettering Techniques

There are various techniques for lettering a drawing. Freehand lettering is generally preferred on design drawings. Freehand lettering is an acquired skill. After considerable experience, a draftsperson's freehand lettering takes on an individual style that frequently enhances the presentation. However, the beginning draftsperson should first master the single stroke gothic alphabet utilizing all capital letters. This technique has acquired universal acceptance from the Architectural community because it is easy to read and easily executed. Refer to *Figure 6.48* as a guide to develop your lettering skills.

Lettering Types

Mechanical sources may be used until you develop more skillful lettering. Notes can be typed on clear adhesive-backed film, then cut and applied directly to the drawing. Or use a lettering template. Templates (similar to stencils) are available for various lettering sizes and come with interchangeable scriber points. The template controls consistency in letter size and shape, but you are responsible for even spacing. The use of press or stick-on lettering, which was described previously under plan enhancements, is another option.

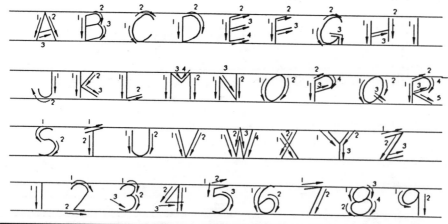

Figure 423 Follow this technique to develop skillful lettering.

CAD Lettering

With a CAD program, lettering is typed on the computer keyboard and printed in the standard Roman style typeface. Customizable drafting programs with additional software can produce an architectural styled lettering to replace the standard type.

A B C D E F G H I
J K L M N O P Q R
S T U V W X Y Z
1 2 3 4 5 6 7 8 9

STANDARD ROMAN LETTERING

A B C D E F G H I
J K L M N O P Q R
S T U V W X Y Z -
Ø 1 2 3 4 5 6 7 8 9

ARCHITECTURAL ROMAN LETTERING

Figure 424 Computers offer various lettering options.

Examples of Lettering Uses

Lettering completes a drawing by providing information such as identification, titles, dimensions, nomenclature, specifications or legends and notes. The most general information is shown in the largest lettering and the most detailed and specific information appears in the smallest size letters. Each sheet in a set of drawings must be identified with a title block.

Lettering Sizes

The title block pertains to the entire set of drawings and links each individual drawing sheet together as part of a total presentation. The title block should be the largest lettering on a drawing and will demand the most skill in composition and spacing. This can be automatically achieved by using preprinted vellum, such as the **National Kitchen & Bath Association** drafting sheets.

Titles within the drawing itself rank second in size hierarchy. *For example,* on a floor plan drawing, the title might be "*Kitchen*". On an elevation drawing, the title might be "*Elevation View A1*". If the drawing includes a list of specifications or legend symbols, then the title for the list would also appear in the second size category or approximately 1/4" (.63cm) high.

The third size of lettering is approximately 1/8" (.31cm) - 3/16" (.47cm) high and will include the list of specifications, symbol descriptions, nomenclature and dimensions.

The last and smallest lettering on a drawing is used for specific notes to explain drawing details. *For example,* on a floor plan, special areas of construction may be obscure without the addition of notes explaining the detailed design process. On an elevation, a note may be needed to indicate that a particular drawerhead is, "*not operable*". **Notes should be used only when needed to eliminate possible confusion.** For clarity, hand lettering should never be any smaller than 1/8" (.31cm). Therefore, the third lettering hierarchy will also include notes.

It's important to remain consistent in each lettering size category to ensure a professional, standardized drawing presentation.

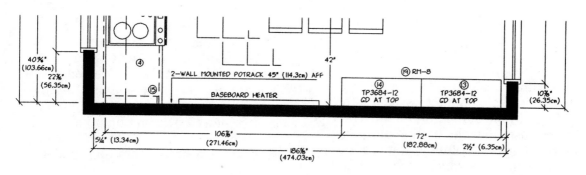

Figure 425 Typical lettering used on a kitchen plan.

Hand Lettering Training

Consistency is the key element in developing a skillful lettering technique.

There are five basic elements which aid in lettering consistency:

- height

- form

- direction

- weight

- spacing

Height: For consistent height of lettering and spacing between rows of lettering, guide lines are needed. It is nearly impossible to maintain straight horizontal lettering without the use of guide lines. On inked drawings, guide lines will be erased. On pencil drawings they will remain, therefore, **guide lines should be drawn with a sharp point and a light touch.**

A lettering guide helps to maintain consistency. Two guide lines should be used when all lettering will be upper case, which is the suggested standard. When upper and lower case lettering is used, three guide lines are required. The spacing of guide lines will vary according to the size of lettering required.

Typically, lettering ranges from 1/8" (.31cm) in height to 1/2" (1.27cm) in height. To determine the amount of space required between rows of lettering, the size of the lettering and the number of rows of lettering must be considered. Generally, the space is slightly smaller than the letter size. However, for small, lengthy notes, the space should be equal to the letter size to insure legibility.

Remember, consistency is the key, therefore make sure each letter terminates at the exact top and/or bottom of each guide line.

Lettering is used to communicate, therefore a simple and consistent form is vital. The gothic alphabet is the base from which the standard *"single stroke"* lettering technique has evolved. Slanted lettering should be avoided because it is directional and suggests movement which will detract from your plans.

Lettering should be kept vertical and maintain an oblong proportion. **Master the vertical, single stroke lettering technique illustrated before attempting to develop an individual style.**

Form: Form consistency refers to the vertical, horizontal, and curvilinear lines of each letter and how they relate to each other. Each straight line or curve should appear the same.

Direction: Directional consistency refers to the direction each stroke follows during the construction of each letter. Whenever possible, the strokes should be made by pulling, not pushing the pencil/pen across the paper. Generally a right-handed draftsperson will pull down and to the right. Practice develops consistency. If needed, a small triangle can be used as a quick and efficient way to maintain consistent vertical strokes.

Weight: Consistent line weight is also developed with practice. On pencil drawings, a *"2H"* or *"3H"* lead is recommended depending on the pressure you exert on the pencil. Rotate the pencil to keep a consistent point width and even line widths. Emphasize the start and end of each stroke by applying slightly more pressure.

When using a technical ink pen achieve the same effect by making slow and deliberate strokes and holding the pen point on the paper slightly longer at the start and end of each stroke. Keep in mind that the same technique for lettering should be used throughout the drawing presentation. **Do not mix styles or types of lettering.**

Spacing: The legibility of your lettering also depends on consistent spacing. Consistent letter spacing is not based on *"actual"* equal spaces, but rather *"perceived"* equal spaces. Each letter of the alphabet has a different profile, therefore, the letters must be visually spaced rather than measured. Letters with two vertical adjacent edges require more visual space than do angled or curved letters.

A helpful hint is to squint, if the letters appear as an even grey tone, then the spaces are even. However, if you squint and see gaps or varying gray tones, then the letters are perceived as unevenly spaced. The space between words should be larger than the space between individual letters.

For an attractive plan, try to leave twice as much space between words than between letters and leave slightly more space between sentences than between words.

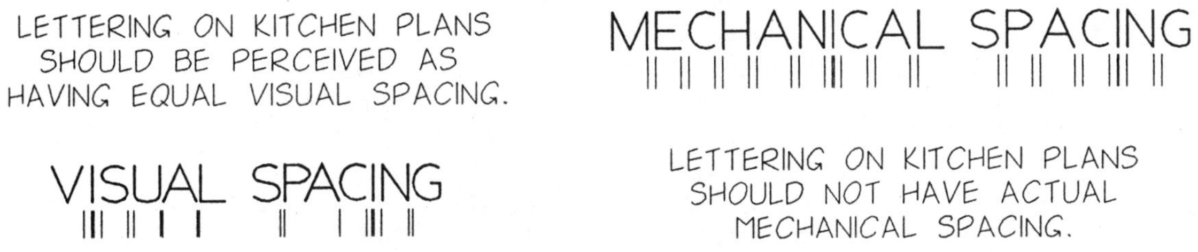

LETTERING ON KITCHEN PLANS SHOULD BE PERCEIVED AS HAVING EQUAL VISUAL SPACING.

VISUAL SPACING

MECHANICAL SPACING

LETTERING ON KITCHEN PLANS SHOULD NOT HAVE ACTUAL MECHANICAL SPACING.

Figure 426 Consistent spacing is based on appearance.

SECTION **5**

Lines and Techniques

LINE WORK

The major portion of a drawing consists of lines. Therefore, good line work is critical to the development of a professional drawing presentation. Just as skillful lettering develops through practice, so does good line work.

Layout Lines

To begin a drawing, layout lines should be kept as light as possible, similar to guide lines for lettering. We'll call these first lines *"layout lines"*. Whether the final drawing is to be ink or pencil, the initial layout lines should be drawn in a hard lead, such as a 3H or 4H. The pencil should be sharp at all times to insure accuracy.

The purpose of layout lines is to verify the drawing's limits and accuracy before any finished lines are drawn. If changes are required, layout lines can be easily erased, leaving no evidence of the change. As you acquire more experience, you'll spend less time drawing layout lines and move directly to drawing final lines.

Achieving Good Line Work

"Crisp", *"uniform"* and *"precise"* are words that characterize good line work. To achieve pencil lines with these qualities, remember to rotate the pencil between your fingers while drawing a line.

Whenever possible, a line should be drawn in a strong, single stroke. To maintain consistent line weight, apply equal pressure throughout the length of the line. Lines which fade or do not meet at corners will be exaggerated when reproduced and may result in misinterpretation.

The final goal of the drafting process is to produce an easily interpreted graphic presentation.

Types of Lines

Lines are used to indicate a variety of objects. **Visible object lines** are represented by a solid line. These include all edges which are in front of the cutplane and in clear view. In a floor plan visible object lines are used to show wall cabinets, tall cabinets and countertop surfaces.

Hidden object lines are represented by a series of short dashes. Any object edge which is under a visible object edge is indicated by the hidden object line. *For example,* base cabinets are under the countertop so they are drawn with a short dashed line. **Remember how important consistency is;** keep the dash length and the spacing between each dash the same. Using a 1/2" architects scale, alternate your dashes in 3" increments to provide a well proportioned hidden line.

Witness or extension lines are drawn as a solid line which is slightly lighter or thinner than visible object lines. These lines are used to terminate dimension lines. Witness lines begin approximately 1/16" (.16cm) to 1/8" (.32cm) outside of the object being dimensioned and extend approximately 1/16" (.16cm) to 1/8" (.32cm) beyond the dimension line.

Centerlines are drawn with alternating long and short dashes. Similar to witness lines, centerlines should appear slightly lighter and thinner than object lines. However, unlike witness lines, centerlines may extend into the object being located and begin with the proper centerline symbol.

Dimension lines are also thin lines, which terminate with arrows, dots or slashes. For our purposes, dimension lines are broken in the middle and the numerical dimension is centered in the opening. This technique used by mechanical draftspersons allows for all numbers to remain vertical and reduces errors caused by misreading the dimension. Equally acceptable is to maintain a solid dimension line and list the numerical dimension above the line. All dimensions and lettering should then be readable from the bottom edge and the right side of the plans. This is typically how architectural blueprints are dimensioned.

Cutting plane lines are represented by alternating one long dash with two short dashes. Such lines are used to indicate the origin of a section drawing when it is not obvious. The cutting plane line is typically darker and thicker than object lines and terminates with arrows indicating the direction of the section cut. Identification is required in both the plan and elevation views. Typical identification is by letters, such as A-A, B-B, etc.

More often kitchen design plans indicate elevations with a letter and an arrow pointing to the wall without the use of a cutting plane line.

Break lines are indicated by a continuous line interrupted by the break symbol. The line weight is the same as object lines. Break lines are used when the entire plan will not fit on the sheet of drafting paper. If the drawing is detailed on both sides of the break line, then two break symbols are required with blank space between the two symbols. This usage of break lines and symbols indicates a portion of the drawing has been cut out of the middle.

When the drawing is only detailed at one side of the line the indication is that the drawing continues and only one line is necessary. This will be common in kitchens that are part of a larger great room.

Overhead lines are indicated by a series of long dashes. Their line weight remains the same as object lines, they are used to indicate any object edges which are above the tall cabinets such as skylights, soffits, extensive moldings, etc. Using a 1/2" architects scale, alternate your dashes in 6" increments to provide a well proportioned overhead line.

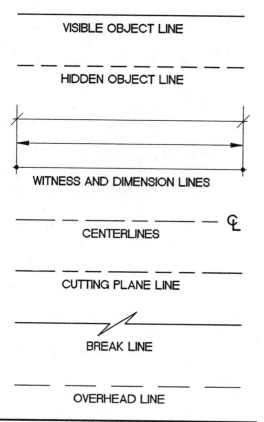

Figure 427 · Types of lines.

GEOMETRIC CONSTRUCTION

Geometric construction may be divided into two categories, simple and complex:

- the simple elements include points, lines and planes.

- the complex elements encompass the various solids.

All geometric construction begins with a point.

Simple Construction

Conceptually, a point is without shape, form or dimension. It simply represents a position in space. A point may serve to begin or end a line, mark the intersection of two or more lines, mark a corner when two lines or planes meet, or indicate the center of a field. When a point is extended, a line is formed.

A line may be:

- straight

- curved

- angular

A line expresses:

- direction

- movement and growth

- dimensional length

As a construction element a line can:

- join

- support

- surround

- describe an edge

- articulate a surface

A straight line may be:

- vertical

- horizontal ·

- diagonal

An Angle: When a line is manipulated by geometric construction it may bend, becoming an angle.

A Circle: When a line is formed that connects all the points that are an equal distance from one given point, a circle is formed.

An Arc: A section of a circle is called an arc.

Utilizing more complex mathematical formulas, lines can form an:

- ellipse

- parabola

- hyperbola

- various irregular curves

A Plane: When a line is given width, a plane is created. Conceptually, a plane has dimensional length and width, but no thickness. It may be visualized by comparing it to a piece of rigid paper. The shape of the plane is determined by its linear outline. The plane may take on any curved or angular shape the outline forms.

Complex Construction

The various solid forms which make up the complex elements consist of the:

- cube

- cylinder

- cone

- pyramid

- paraboloid

- sphere

A POINT

A LINE

A PLANE

Figure 428 The primary elements of drawing.

A solid form possesses length, width and depth, and occupies space in the environment. Solids are mostly comprised of various planes. It is important to understand how solids occupy space so that you can accurately depict them in your drawing.

The most common solids found in design are rectangular. The most simplistic rectangular form is the **cube**, which is comprised of six square planes of equal size enclosing space. A base cabinet is a rectangular form.

A **cylinder** is formed by two circular planes which are parallel and are connected creating an enclosed space. A cylindrical form might be a column or support leg for a countertop overhang.

A **cone** is generated by rotating a triangle about an axis and enclosing it with a circular plane at the bottom. This form may be found in a hanging pendant light fixture.

A **pyramid** is similar to a cone, except it is made entirely of triangular planes. The number of planes are dependent upon the shape of the base which is angular rather than circular. Many of today's kitchen faucets and accessories have pyramidal forms as hot and cold control handles.

A **paraboloid** is generated by rotating a parabola about an axis and enclosing it with an ellipse. The curvilinear shape of a contemporary island snack bar would be similar to the paraboloid form.

A **sphere** retains a circular shape from whatever angle it is viewed. A sphere is defined as an infinite number of points all equi-distant from one common point and radiating out in every direction. Perfect spheres are unusual in interiors, but portions of spheres are more commonly seen in faucet handles, lighting fixtures and kitchen appliances and equipment.

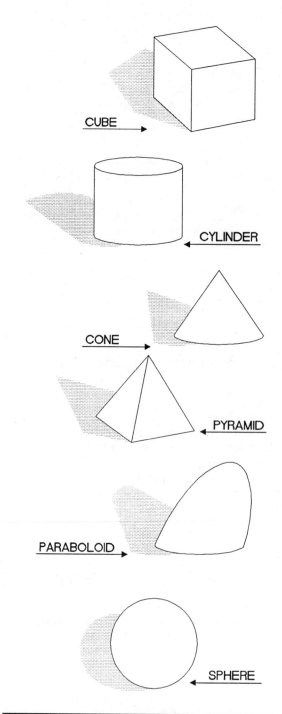

CUBE

CYLINDER

CONE

PYRAMID

PARABOLOID

SPHERE

Figure 429 Types of solid forms.

DRAWING TECHNIQUES

Drawing Parallel Lines

In instances when the floor plan contains an odd angled wall, you may want to repeat the angle elsewhere within the space. To draw this, place any side of your triangle along the given angled line. Move the straight edge in position along the bottom edge of your triangle. Holding the straight edge in place, slide the triangle into the new desired position being sure to keep the bottom edge against the straight edge. Draw your line.

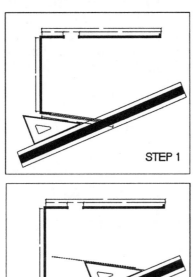

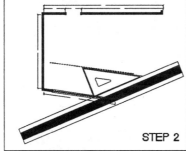

Figure 430 Constructing parallel lines.

Drawing Perpendicular Lines

Now that you've constructed the parallel line, you'll probably need to draw a perpendicular line through it. Place your straight edge in position with the 45° triangle (short side) aligned with the line. Hold the straight edge in place and slide the triangle until its at the desired place of intersection. Draw a line through the point.

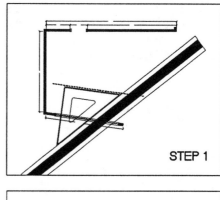

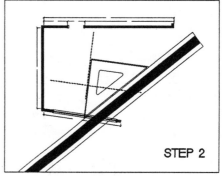

Figure 431 Constructing perpendicular lines.

Bisecting a Line

To produce symmetrical design drawings you will need to know how to bisect a line. For instance, given a length of wall on which you need to center a sink cabinet, you will first need to bisect the wall line in order to determine its midpoint.

One option is to bisect a line with a compass. Set the compass larger than half the length of the line and draw an arc from each end of the line so that the two arcs intersect each other. The line which passes through the two intersecting points of the arcs will bisect the line.

Another option is to use a straight edge and triangle to bisect a line. Hold the straight edge parallel to the line and draw an equal angle from each end with your triangle toward the center of the line. Then draw a vertical line through the intersection and bisect the line.

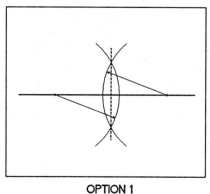

OPTION 1

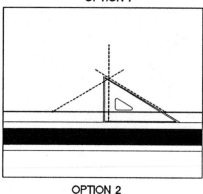

OPTION 2

Figure 432   Bisecting a line.

Dividing a Line into Equal Parts

Kitchen drawings often involve decorative tile patterns which need to be illustrated in both floor plan and elevation views. A common illustration might include a 3" x 3" (7.62cm x 7.62cm) tile accent stripe between two rows of 12" x 12" (30.48cm x 30.48cm) tiles. After the

12" (30.48cm) tile is drawn, the 3" (7.62cm) tile lines can be found by dividing the 12" (30.48cm) length into four equal parts. An easier method for dividing a line equally follows.

Draw a line from one end of the line to be divided at any angle. This line does not have to be the same length as the line to be divided, but rather should be of a length that can be easily divided by the required number of equal parts on the scale being used.

Mark the angled line into equal divisions using your scale. Draw a line from the last mark to the opposite end of the line to be divided. Parallel to that line, draw lines through the remaining marks and through the line to be divided.

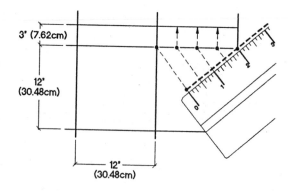

3" (7.62cm)

12" (30.48cm)

12" (30.48cm)

Figure 4.33   Dividing a line equally.

Dividing a Space into Equal Sections

A similar method is used when the space to be divided is between two parallel lines. Find the beginning and end of the number of sections required on your scale. Pivot the scale until it spans the space equally and mark the intermediate points. Draw parallel lines through the points.

This method can be used to draw windows with mullions, glass door cabinetry with mullions or locating light fixtures evenly within a given amount of space.

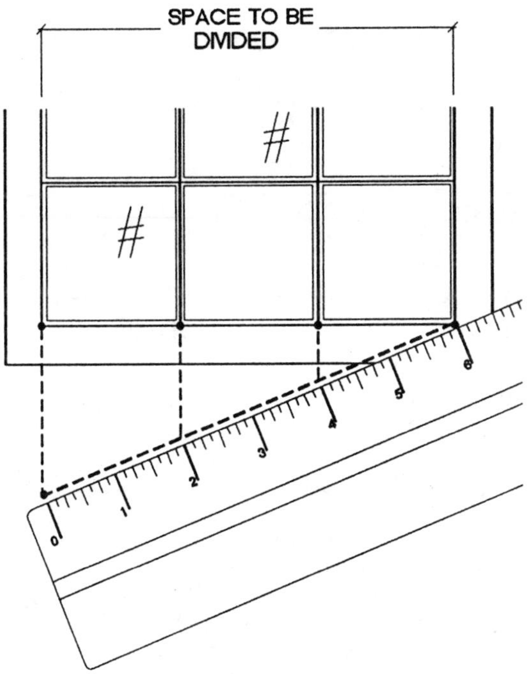

Definition of Angles

As a designer, you'll find yourself confronted with unusual angles. An angle is formed by the meeting of two lines. How the two lines meet will define the type of angle.

The three types of angles are:

- acute

- right

- obtuse

An *acute angle* is one that is less than 90°. An angle equal to 90° or with two perpendicular legs is a *right angle.* Any other angle more than 90° is called an *obtuse angle.*

SPACE TO BE DIVIDED

# #

Figure 434 Dividing a space equally.

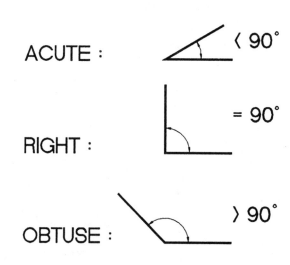

ACUTE : 〈 90°

RIGHT : = 90°

OBTUSE : 〉 90°

Figure 435 Types of angles.

Definition of Triangles

Angles are also used to define the types of triangles they create. An *acute triangle* has three angles each less than 90°. The *right triangle* has one angle equal to 90° and the *obtuse triangle* has one angle more than 90°.

You will encounter the right triangle in most angular design situations. To determine the dimensions of cabinetry to be installed on an angle, you'll need to identify the triangles it forms and their side dimensions.

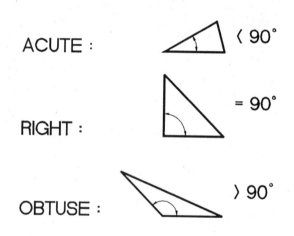

ACUTE :   ⟨ 90°

RIGHT :   = 90°

OBTUSE :   ⟩ 90°

Figure 436 *Types of triangles.*

First list the known geometric factors; one angle is 90°, one leg of the triangle is equal to the cabinet depth and the two other angles become known based on your choice for placement. The interior angles will add up to 180°. Therefore, if you are placing a cabinet at a 45° angle, the remaining angle will also be 45°. If your placing a cabinet at a 30° angle, the remaining angle will be 60°.

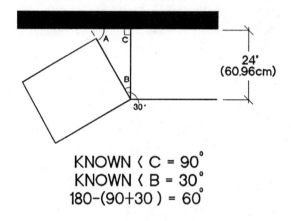

KNOWN ⟨ C = 90°
KNOWN ⟨ B = 30°
180−(90+30) = 60°

Figure 437 *Identifying geometric known factors.*

To compute the wall space required to place a 30" (76.2cm) wide desk drawer at a 45° angle in the corner, use the following formula.

Cw	=	Cabinet Width
Cd	=	Cabinet Depth
WSa	=	Wall space "a"
TW	=	Total Wall space
.7071	=	Formula constant

$$Cw \times .7071 = WSa$$
$$WSa + Cd = TW$$

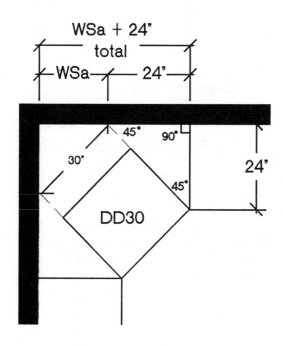

$$CW \times .7071 = WSa$$
$$30 \times .7071 = 21.21 \text{ OR } 21\ 1/4"$$
$$WSa + CD = WS \text{ total}$$
$$21\ 1/4 + 24 = 45\ 1/4$$

Figure 438 Determining the wall space required for an angled cabinet installation.

Constructing an Angle Equal to a Given Angle

In new construction, your drawings will often have to be taken from an architect's blueprint. To transfer an odd angle from a blueprint to your own drawing, follow these steps:

- Draw an arc of any radius from the intersection of the angle on the blueprint.

- Then draw an arc with the same radius on your drawing.

- Return to the blueprint. Determine the distance from intersection "x" to intersection "y" with your com-

pass. Draw an arc from intersection "y", through intersection "x".

- Repeat this process on your own working drawing. Draw the arc through the previous arc you just drew.

- The point of intersection of the two arcs will also intersect the angle's second leg.

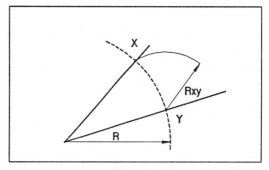

1 - BLUEPRINT

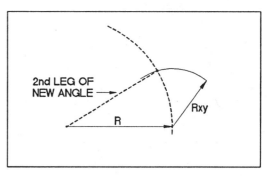

2 - NEW DRAWING

Figure 439 Constructing equal angles in plan view.

Constructing Curved Lines with Arcs

Drawing custom countertop plans will require constructing various curved lines.

- When the arc is tangent to a right angle, draw an arc with the given radius from the right angle intersection through the two legs.

- Where the arc intersects the legs, draw another arc inside the right angle from each point so they intersect.

- From their point of intersection, draw another arc, which will be tangent to the right angle legs.

- When the arc is tangent to two lines that are not perpendicular, the arc radius must be equal distance from each line.

Determine the radius center by constructing parallel lines equal distance from each line. Extend these lines until they cross. The point of intersection is the radius location.

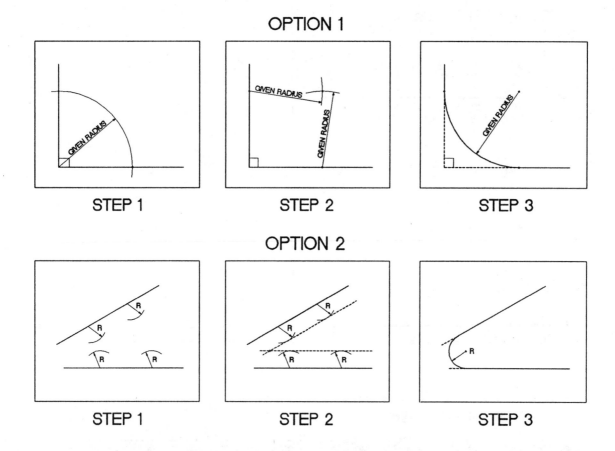

Figure 440 Constructing curved lines with arcs.

Constructing an Ellipse

You will need to construct an ellipse whenever you draw a perspective that has a circular element in it.

- First, determine where the widest point or *major axis* will fall and then where the thinnest point, called the *minor axis* will fall.

- On an edge of a sheet of paper, mark three points A, B and C so that AC equals half the major axis and BC equals half the minor axis.

- Slide point A up and down along the minor axis while pivoting from the same point and keeping point B on the major axis.

- Mark several points at C throughout the process and draw a smooth curve connecting these points.

An alternative is to sketch a rectangle which will contain the ellipse.

- Locate the major and minor axis.

- Then divide the rectangle by bisecting the line segments as illustrated in *step 1 of Figure 442*, bisecting a line.

Sketch the ellipse to align with the designated points.

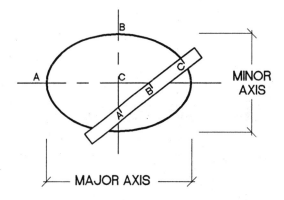

Figure 441 Constructing an ellipse in plan view.

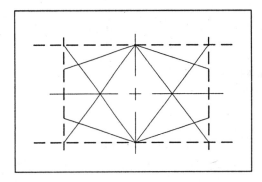

STEP 1

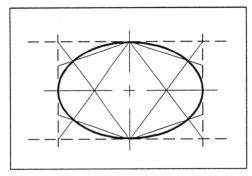

STEP 2

Figure 442 A second option for constructing an ellipse in plan view.

Drawing Symbols

FOLLOWING INDUSTRY STANDARDS

The use of graphic and presentation standards is necessary for universal industry communication. The following legends of symbols are those most frequently used in kitchen working drawings.

Wall and Partition Symbols

Typically, existing walls are shown as solid lines, approximately 1/4" (.64cm) thick with half walls shown as hollow lines. However, because drawing solid lines by hand is very time consuming, hollow lines are accepted in our industry. Be sure to note any walls that are not full height if you choose this method. Walls to be removed are shown with broken dashed lines. Existing openings that are to be enclosed are hatched with several parallel lines. Newly constructed walls should indicate the type of material used in construction, or use a symbol that is identified in the legend to distinguish them from existing partitions.

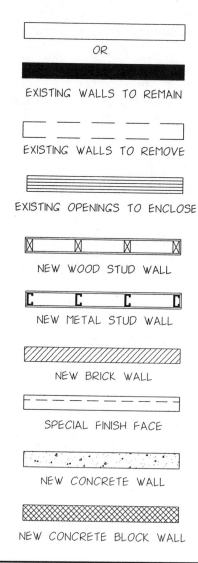

Figure 443   Wall and partition symbols.

Door Symbols

Doors should always indicate open or cased framing and the direction of swing. In most instances, a 45° swing is acceptable. If there are any questions as to clearance, a 90° swing should be shown. A door schedule reference is only required with new doors and is indicated by placing a letter within a circle inside each door opening. If there is only one new door, the schedule information can be indicated directly within the floor plan in note form.

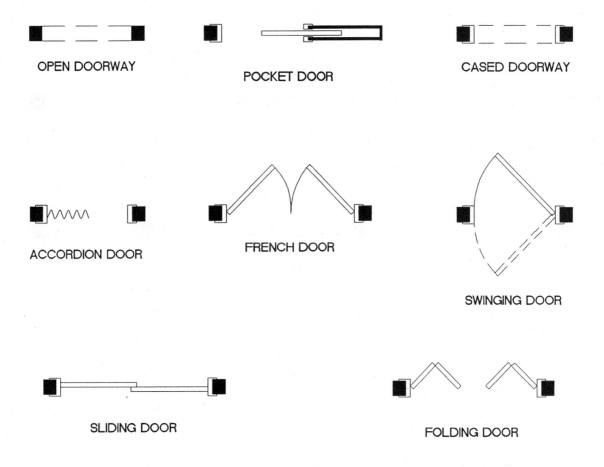

OPEN DOORWAY

POCKET DOOR

CASED DOORWAY

ACCORDION DOOR

FRENCH DOOR

SWINGING DOOR

SLIDING DOOR

FOLDING DOOR

Figure 444 Door symbols.

Window and Skylight Symbols

Open or cased framing should always be indicated on window symbols. Window sills are typically not shown unless a particular interior treatment is to be used. The indication of glass swings is optional and if shown, should be dotted lines. Skylights are shown in long dashed lines and are labeled inside. Pertinent information is referenced at the side.

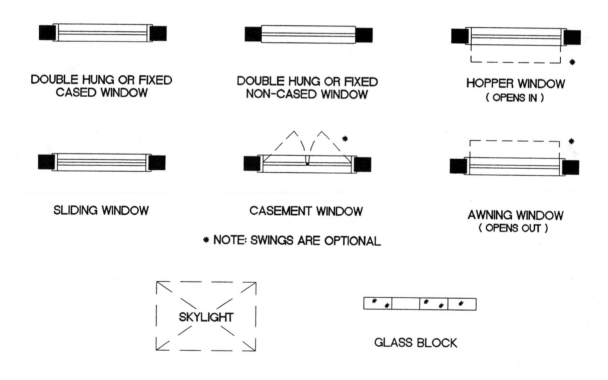

Figure 445 *Window, skylight and glass block symbols.*

Staircase Symbols

Stairs should be indicated with a directional arrow. The risers can be broken midway, unless the design incorporates the other floor, in which case the total number of risers should be indicated. Ramps are also shown with directional arrows and should always be shown full length. The slope should be indicated in new construction drawings. Be sure to indicate up or down with an arrow. The arrow should lead from the main floor area to the secondary area.

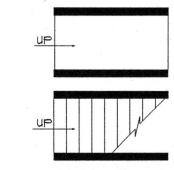

ACCEPTABLE TO BREAK STAIRS/RAMP
WHEN THE SECOND FLOOR DOES NOT
AFFECT THE DESIGN

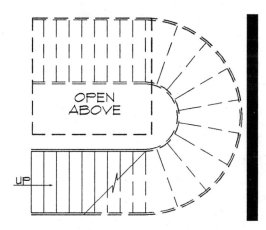

INDICATE THE ENTIRE STAIRWAY/RAMP
WHEN IT DOES AFFECT THE DESIGN

Figure 446 Staircase and ramp symbols.

Elevator Symbols

Elevators and hydraulic lifts are indicated with an outline of the interior size and an "x". The "x" is used to indicate that the unit runs through the entire space beyond floor and/or ceiling. Be sure to add appropriate door symbols to the elevator opening.

ADD APPROPRIATE
DOOR SYMBOL TO
ELEVATORS AND LIFTS

Figure 447 Elevator symbol.

Appliance Door Symbols

Kitchen appliance doors and handles are all shown with a thick solid line. They may be labeled within the floor plan. Many designers prefer to number them with an adjacent schedule to eliminate a cluttered drawing. It is optional to indicate door openings with a dotted line.

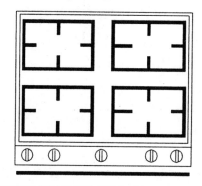

Figure 448 Appliance door symbols.

Finishing Materials Symbols

It is preferred to indicate decking and flooring materials in a blank area of the drawing. However, if the drawing does not allow for a clear indication, it is better not to show any, but be sure to include it in the specifications.

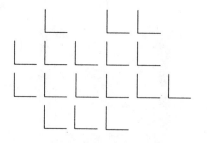

HINT AT FLOORING

Figure 449 Finishing materials symbol.

Cabinetry Symbols

Cabinetry in plan view should be indicated by an outline only. Do not indicate hidden features such as toekick or shelving.

The tall cabinets and wall cabinets will have a solid outline, previously described as a visible object line. The base cabinets will be indicated with a dotted line of the hidden line type.

When cabinets are stacked one above the other, the unit on top takes precedence. Use a note and arrow to indicate the cabinet at the bottom.

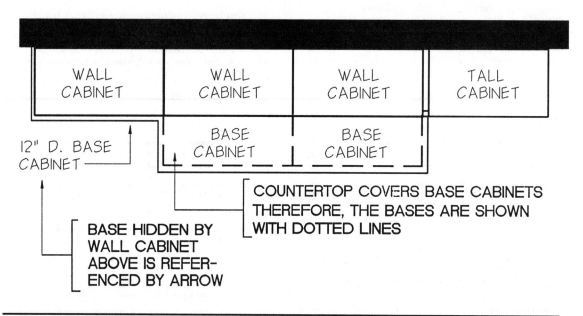

Figure 450 Cabinetry symbols.

Mechanical Symbols

For the purpose of kitchen plans, mechanical symbols include lighting, electrical and plumbing as well as heating and ventilation. The accuracy of illustrating these particular symbols is very important because the professional tradesperson must be able to interpret your drawing. These symbols are universal and will also be found on an architect's blueprint. Although symbols are universal, your mechanical plan should always include a legend to eliminate any questions.

S	SINGLE POLE SWITCH	OUTLET CONTROLLED BY LOW VOLTAGE SWITCHING WHEN RELAY IS INSTALLED IN OUTLET BOX	SURFACE MOUNTED FLUORESCENT LIGHT
S_2	DOUBLE POLE SWITCH	SINGLE RECEPTACLE OULET	WALL SCONCE
S_3	THREE WAY SWITCH	TRIPLEX RECEPTACLE OULET	DW DISHWASHER
S_4	FOUR WAY SWITCH	QUADRUPLEX RECEPTACLE OULET	GD FOOD WASTE DISPOSAL
S_{DM}	SINGLE POLE SWITCH w/ DIMMER	DUPLEX RECEPTACLE OUTLET-SPLIT WIRED	TC TRASH COMPACTOR
S_{3DM}	THREE WAY SWITCH w/ DIMMER	TRIPLEX RECEPTACLE OUTLET-SPLIT WIRED	R REFRIGERATOR OUTLET
S_{LM}	MASTER SWITCH FOR LOW VOLTAGE SWITCHING SYSTEM	CLOCK HANGER RECEPTACLE	H HOOD
S_L	SWITCH FOR LOW VOLTAGE SWITCHING SYSTEM	FAN HANGER RECEPTACLE	M MICROWAVE OVEN
S_{WP}	WEATHERPROOF SWITCH	INTERCOM	R ELECTRIC RANGE/COOKTOP
S_{RC}	REMOTE CONTROL SWITCH	TELEPHONE OUTLET	WO ELECTRIC SINGLE/DOUBLE OVEN
S_D	AUTOMATIC DOOR SWITCH	THERMOSTAT	G GAS SUPPLY
S_P	SWITCH AND PILOT LAMP	SMOKE DETECTOR	CT GAS COOKTOP
S_K	KEY OPERATED SWITCH	TELEVISION OUTLET	WO GAS SINGLE/DOUBLE OVEN
S_F	FUSED SWITCH	CABLE OUTLET	CW CLOTHES WASHER
S_T	TIME SWITCH	LOW VOLTAGE TRANSFORMER	CD CLOTHES DRYER
	CEILING PULL SWITCH	HANGING CEILING FIXTURE	HEAT REGISTER
	DUPLEX OUTLET	RECESSED CEILING DOWN LIGHTING	
	DUPLEX OUTLET WITH GROUND FAULT CIRCUIT INTERRUPTER	BUILT-IN LOW VOLTAGE TASK LIGHT	
	SWITCH AND SINGLE RECEPTACLE OUTLET	BUILT-IN FLUORESCENT LIGHT	
	SWITCH AND DUPLEX OUTLET	CONTINUOUS ROW FLUORESCENT LIGHTS	
	BLANKED OUTLET		
	JUNCTION BOX		

ANY STANDARD SYMBOL GIVEN ABOVE W/ THE ADDITION OF LOWERCASE SUBSCRIPT LETTERING MAY BE USED TO DESIGNATE A VARIATION OF STANDARD EQUIPMENT.

WHEN USED THEY MUST BE LISTED IN THE LEGEND OF THE MECHANICAL PLAN.

Figure 451 Mechanical symbols.

Typical Kitchen Appliance and Equipment Symbols

For the purpose of working drawings, kitchen appliance and equipment symbols should remain consistent throughout the set of drawings. The shapes of appliances and equipment such as cooktops and sinks may differ, but the illustrative details should remain consistent. Faucet and control locations should always be indicated on the floor plan and mechanical plan.

TYPICAL KITCHEN FIXTURES

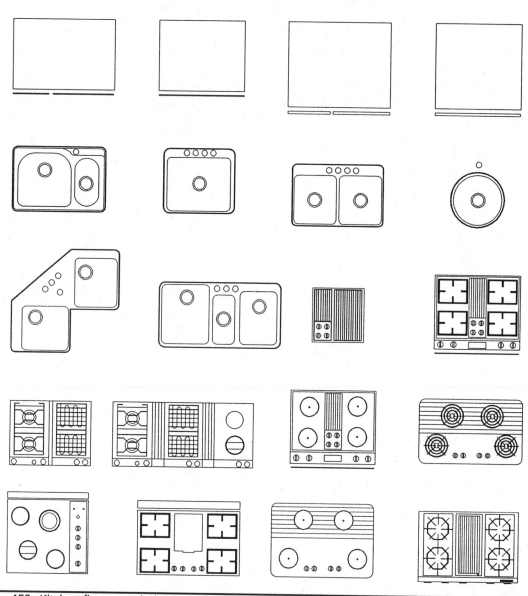

Figure 452 Kitchen fixture symbols.

SECTION **7**

Drawing a Floor Plan

10 STEPS IN DRAWING A FLOOR PLAN

To begin the drafting process, assemble your equipment within reach around your drawing board. Set your board at a comfortable incline (approximately 10° to 15°). The incline helps to insure accuracy by enabling you to see above the equipment, as well as reduces back strain caused by bending over your work.

Now you are ready to begin drawing your floor plan.

STEP 1

Tape your paper down to the board using drafting tape or dots. It is important to line it up with your straight edge to make sure the drawing will be square on the sheet of paper. If the paper has a preprinted border, align the border with your straight edge and then tape the paper in place. If there is no border, then the edge of the paper can be used to align with the straight edge.

STEP 2

Before you put pencil to paper, visualize the finished drawing. *Will you list specifications at the right side or at the bottom? Will there be a title?* Determine how much space your drawing will take up on the paper and don't forget to include space for the dimension lines. Use this information to determine where to locate the drawing on the paper. If more than one drawing will appear on the same sheet of paper, block out the spaces with light pencil outlines.

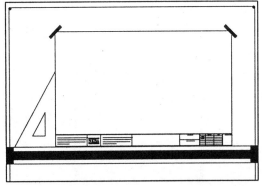

LINE PAPER EDGE OR BORDER LINE WITH STRAIGHT EDGES.

Figure 453 It is important to tape the paper down carefully.

STEP 3

Begin your drawing by lightly penciling in all of the walls. By drawing all of the walls in first, any mistakes caused by incorrect scaling or measuring will be caught before too much time is spent drawing in details.

STEP 4

When the walls are complete, locate the doors and windows. The openings should be located from at least two different reference points to insure accuracy. Make sure that you show the door or window casings so that the overall dimensions listed for these openings are clearly different from the actual pass-through opening.

Step 5

At this point, if there are any mistakes they should be apparent and easily altered because all your lines have been light layout lines so far. When all the measurements have been double checked, you can darken in the final wall, window and door lines.

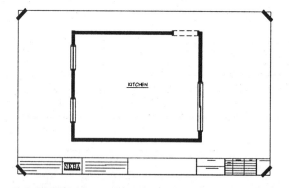

Figure 454 After the drawing is verified, darken in the walls.

STEP 6

Once the plan is on paper, draw in all your dimension lines, following a systematic method. Draw the line closest to the wall first, then the second and third set of lines. Locate the individual openings and sections of walls, then locate the centerlines of all appliances and lastly the total (overall) dimension for each wall. Don't forget your ceiling height in the center of the drawing.

STEP 7

The remaining major interior elements of the drawing should be drawn next (such as cabinets, equipment and furniture). These should be drawn in lightly at first and then darkened when everything is confirmed in final locations. Use the "*subtraction method*" to place all of the elements of the plan in the available space.

After the design has been finalized, darken all the solid object lines such as tall cabinets, wall cabinets and countertops. Then draw the final base cabinet lines with hidden lines (short dashes). Use a straight edge which has divided markings, such as those found on a drafting machine or triangle/template to keep the dashes consistent.

Make sure you lift your tools, as you move them across the paper to avoid smearing the pencil lead. Remember to erase carefully so that you don't tear the paper and use your drafting brush, not your hand, to remove eraser shavings and graphite.

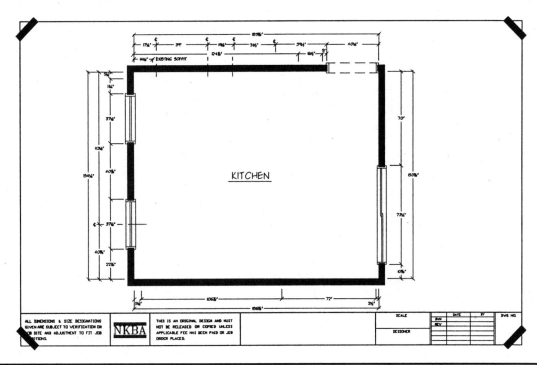

Figure 455 Indicate all required dimensions - imperial example.

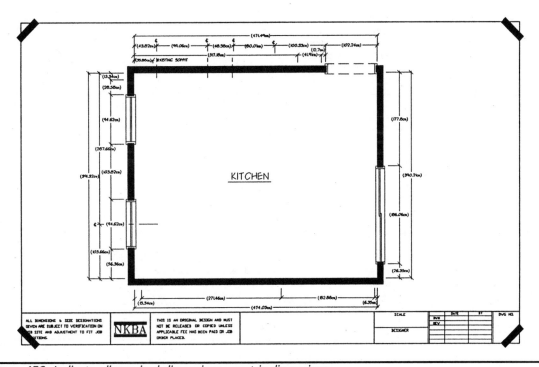

Figure 456 Indicate all required dimensions - metric dimensions.

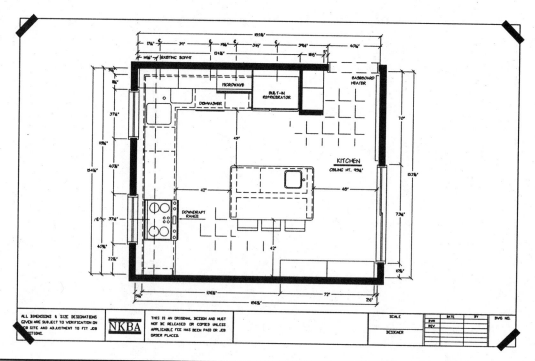

Figure 457 The interior details and notes are added to complete the floor plans - imperial example.

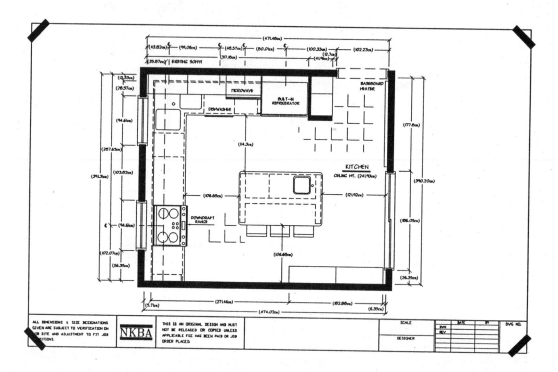

Figure 458 The interior details and notes are added to complete the floor plans - metric example.

STEP 8

Now you're ready to put in the details. Add any nomenclature, notes, accessories (such as plants, chairs and flooring) that are necessary.

STEP 9

Complete the list of specification details by corresponding numbers in the plan. (Refer to *Appendix B*, Graphic and Presentation Standards for more information).

STEP 10

Complete the title block. You should identify firm name, client information, job identification, drawing number, designer and draftsperson identification, drawing date and drawing scale. The title block may include additional information if desired.

CONSTRUCTION PLAN

The next drawing that may be required in a set of complete drawings for a kitchen design presentation, is the Construction Plan. This drawing is only required if walls or openings need to be altered from their original locations. A construction plan will show both the existing conditions of the structure or the Architect's blueprint and the changes required to the building in order to accomplish your design.

Note: Changes to the structure in any way must be approved by the builder/architect or licensed remodeler before proceeding with the project.

Special symbols are used to clearly illustrate the construction alterations necessary. For example, a wall is shown solid or hollow if it is to remain unchanged, new walls to be constructed are shown with the appropriate material symbol and existing openings to be closed are hatched with parallel lines. Universally accepted wall and partition symbols are indicated in *Figure 443*, however, whether you use these or other symbols, your construction plan should always include a legend with a sample of the symbol and its description.

The construction plan should include only the walls, their dimensions and the legend. The dimensions should be indicated to the interior finished surfaces and new windows and doors should be located by a centerline as well as from outside of casing to outside of casing. Additionally, new windows and doors should be noted by manufacturer brand and model numbers whenever possible.

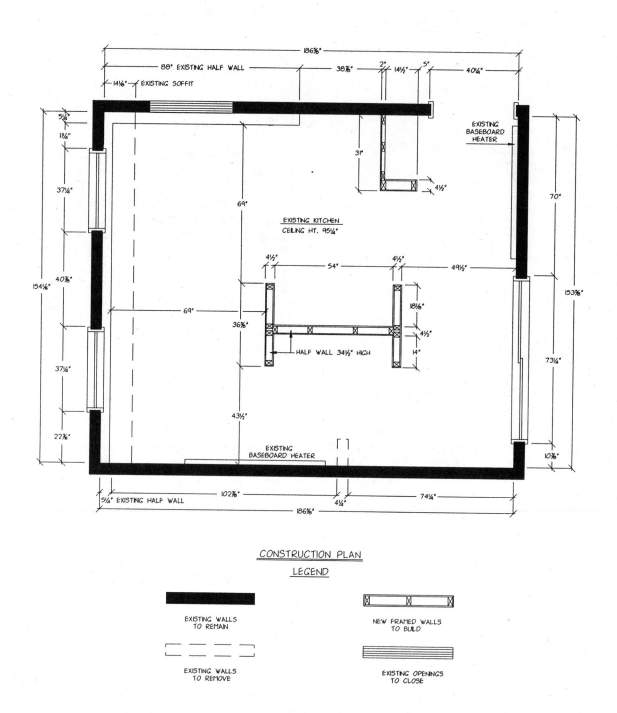

Figure 459 Construction plans illustrate existing and new construction - imperial example.

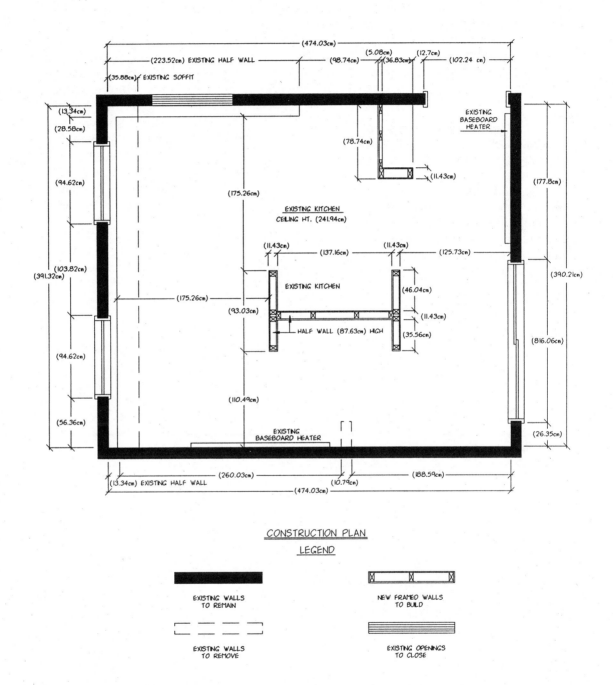

CONSTRUCTION PLAN

LEGEND

EXISTING WALLS
TO REMAIN

NEW FRAMED WALLS
TO BUILD

EXISTING WALLS
TO REMOVE

EXISTING OPENINGS
TO CLOSE

Figure 460 Construction plans illustrate existing and new construction - metric example.

MECHANICAL PLAN

For the purposes of kitchen design, a mechanical plan communicates to the allied trades, the exact location and specification of all plumbing, electrical, heating, ventilating fixtures and equipment and how they relate with the cabinetry.

A Mechanical Plan is required with every kitchen plan and will follow the construction plan or the floor plan if no construction is required. A mechanical plan should repeat the dimensions and cabinet layout of the floor plan, but will not include the nomenclature or specifications. Rather, the mechanical plan will show the appropriate mechanical symbols, as indicated in *Figure 451* and re-

peat the symbols in a legend with their description.

For example, all electrical appliances that require 120 volt electrical service will show a special purpose outlet symbol with initials corresponding to the appliance such as "dw" for dishwasher. Appliances requiring 240 volt services will use the circle with three parallel lines through it such as shown for an electric range. Ceiling fixtures such as lights, fans and vents are shown as if reflected in a mirror. This technique is commonly referred to as a reflected ceiling plan. All ceiling or floor mounted fixtures must be dimensioned with centerlines within the walls of the mechanical plan, additionally heights of switches, outlets, etc. should be indicated.

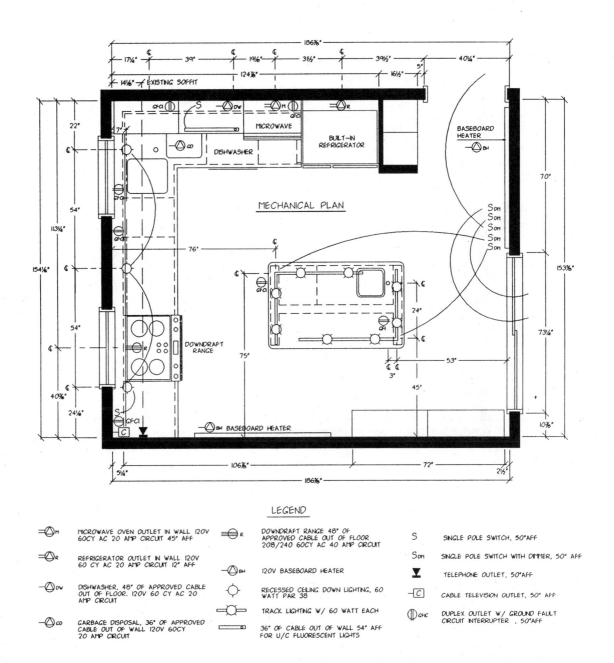

MECHANICAL PLAN

LEGEND

M	MICROWAVE OVEN OUTLET IN WALL 120V 60CY AC 20 AMP CIRCUIT 45" AFF
R	REFRIGERATOR OUTLET IN WALL 120V 60 CY AC 20 AMP CIRCUIT 12" AFF
DW	DISHWASHER, 48" OF APPROVED CABLE OUT OF FLOOR. 120V 60 CY AC 20 AMP CIRCUIT
GD	GARBAGE DISPOSAL, 36" OF APPROVED CABLE OUT OF WALL 120V 60CY 20 AMP CIRCUIT
R	DOWNDRAFT RANGE 48" OF APPROVED CABLE OUT OF FLOOR 208/240 60CY AC 40 AMP CIRCUIT
BH	120V BASEBOARD HEATER
	RECESSED CEILING DOWN LIGHTING, 60 WATT PAR 38
	TRACK LIGHTING W/ 60 WATT EACH
	36" OF CABLE OUT OF WALL 54" AFF FOR U/C FLUORESCENT LIGHTS
S	SINGLE POLE SWITCH, 50"AFF
S DM	SINGLE POLE SWITCH WITH DIMMER, 50" AFF
▼	TELEPHONE OUTLET, 50"AFF
C	CABLE TELEVISION OUTLET, 50" AFF
GFIC	DUPLEX OUTLET W/ GROUND FAULT CIRCUIT INTERRUPTER , 50"AFF

Figure 461 Mechanical plans indicate plumbing, electrical, heating and ventilation - imperial example.

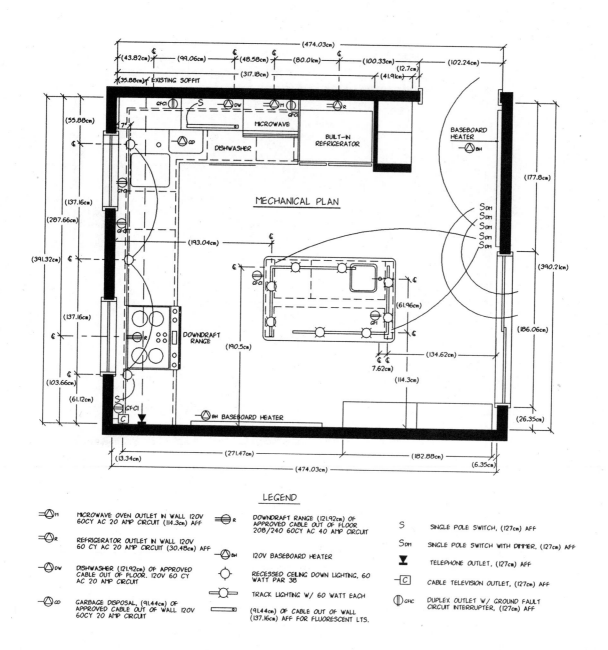

MECHANICAL PLAN

LEGEND

MICROWAVE OVEN OUTLET IN WALL 120V 60CY AC 20 AMP CIRCUIT (114.3cm) AFF

REFRIGERATOR OUTLET IN WALL 120V 60 CY AC 20 AMP CIRCUIT (30.48cm) AFF

DISHWASHER (121.92cm) OF APPROVED CABLE OUT OF FLOOR. 120V 60 CY AC 20 AMP CIRCUIT

GARBAGE DISPOSAL, (91.44cm) OF APPROVED CABLE OUT OF WALL 120V 60CY 20 AMP CIRCUIT

DOWNDRAFT RANGE (121.92cm) OF APPROVED CABLE OUT OF FLOOR 208/240 60CY AC 40 AMP CIRCUIT

120V BASEBOARD HEATER

RECESSED CEILING DOWN LIGHTING, 60 WATT PAR 38

TRACK LIGHTING W/ 60 WATT EACH

(91.44cm) OF CABLE OUT OF WALL (137.16cm) AFF FOR FLUORESCENT LTS.

S   SINGLE POLE SWITCH, (127cm) AFF

S_DM SINGLE POLE SWITCH WITH DIMMER, (127cm) AFF

▼   TELEPHONE OUTLET, (127cm) AFF

C   CABLE TELEVISION OUTLET, (127cm) AFF

GFIC DUPLEX OUTLET W/ GROUND FAULT CIRCUIT INTERRUPTER, (127cm) AFF

Figure 462 Mechanical plans indicate plumbing, electrical, heating and ventilation - metric example.

COUNTERTOP PLAN

A separate countertop plan is not required with your presentation to the client since the outline is indicated in the floor plan. However, you may find a countertop plan helpful in illustrating the installation or fabrication to the allied tradesperson particularly in complex projects, such as those that combine various counter materials or built-up edge treatments.

If you select to include a countertop plan it should show only the walls of the space and the outline of the cabinets, fxtures and equipment, applicable notes, details and dimensions. There may be up to three dimension lines for each counter section.

- The first dimension line should show the center of any cut-outs, such as those for sinks or cooktops.

- The second dimension line should indicate the overall counter length.

- The final dimension will indicate the overall available wall length.

Notes about cut-outs, corner treatments, depth changes, and such will need to be included with arrows pointing to the specific area. A detailed profile of the counter edge treatment is often provided at a blown-up scale to clearly illustrate the counter design and its overhang relative to the face of the cabinet.

Counters typically overhang the face of the door by 3/4" - 1". Therefore, it will be critical to know the exact thickness of the door. This level of detail will not only eliminate error by clearly communicating your ideas, but it will also help to establish you as the expert in the eyes of the consumer.

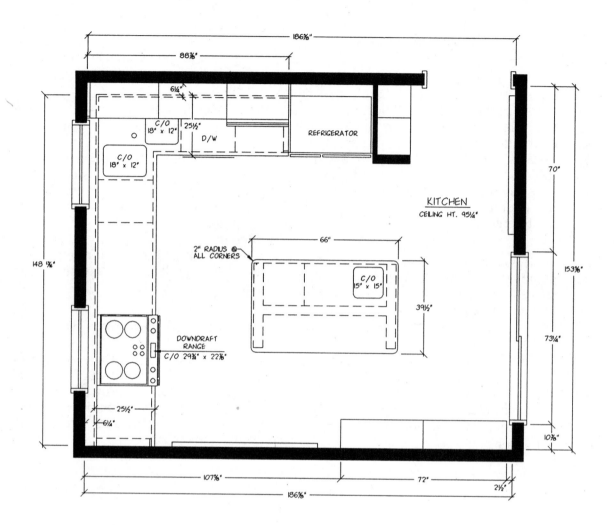

KITCHEN
CEILING HT. 95¼"

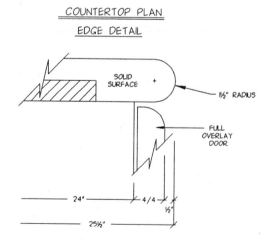

COUNTERTOP PLAN

EDGE DETAIL

SOLID SURFACE

1½" RADIUS

FULL OVERLAY DOOR

Figure 463 Countertop plans will help to convey details such as custom edge treatments - imperial dimensions.

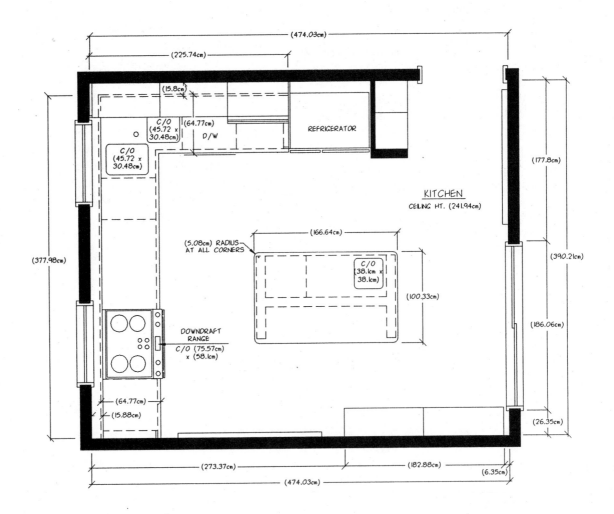

(474.03cm)

(225.74cm)

(15.8cm)

C/O
(45.72 x
30.48cm)

(64.77cm)

D/W

REFRIGERATOR

C/O
(45.72 x
30.48cm)

KITCHEN
CEILING HT. (241.94cm)

(177.8cm)

(377.98cm)

(5.08cm) RADIUS
AT ALL CORNERS

(166.64cm)

C/O
(38.1cm x
38.1cm)

(390.21cm)

(100.33cm)

(186.06cm)

DOWNDRAFT
RANGE
C/O (75.57cm)
x (58.1cm)

(64.77cm)

(15.88cm)

(26.35cm)

(273.37cm)

(182.88cm)

(6.35cm)

(474.03cm)

COUNTERTOP PLAN

EDGE DETAIL

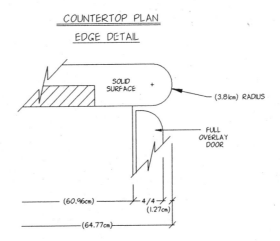

SOLID
SURFACE

(3.81cm) RADIUS

FULL
OVERLAY
DOOR

(60.96cm)

4/4
(1.27cm)

(64.77cm)

Figure 464 Countertop plans will help to convey details such as custom edge treatments - metric dimensions.

SOFFIT PLAN

A separate soffit plan is also not a requirement with your presentation to your client, but again, it may be helpful in conveying your design. Follow the same guidelines as provided for drawing a countertop plan.

However, if the soffit is a complex design such as one with multiple levels or steps, it is recommended to eliminate the outline of the cabinets. If you do not draw the cabinets on the soffit plan you must be careful to compare the soffit and cabinet dimensions in order to ensure consistent reveals.

Remember to include the thickness of doors when using full overlay styles and use the overhead line type to draw the soffit outline. Remember the overhead line type is a long dashed line.

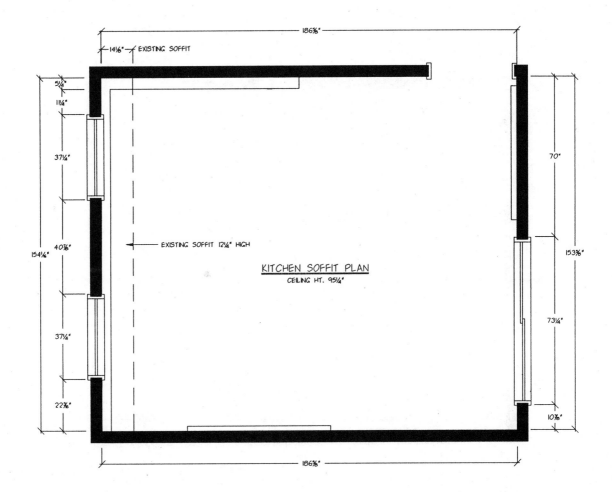

Figure 465 Soffit plans utilize the overhead line type.

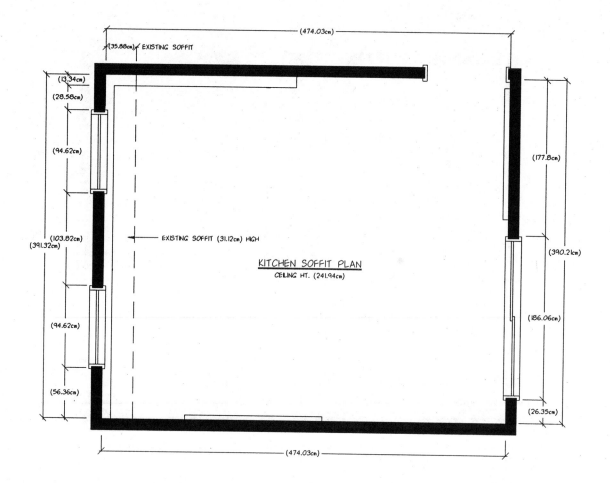

(474.03cm)

(35.88cm) EXISTING SOFFIT

(13.34cm)

(28.58cm)

(94.62cm)

(177.8cm)

(103.82cm)

EXISTING SOFFIT (31.12cm) HIGH

(391.32cm)

KITCHEN SOFFIT PLAN
CEILING HT. (241.94cm)

(390.2cm)

(94.62cm)

(186.06cm)

(56.36cm)

(26.35cm)

(474.03cm)

Figure 466 Soffit plans utilize the overhead line type.

INTERPRETIVE DRAWINGS

Elevations, paraline drawings and perspectives illustrate the vertical elements in a design that are not shown in a floor plan.

Elevations

An elevation is an orthographic drawing just like the floor plan, but drawn from another viewpoint. Elevations are true, scaled drawings in both height and width, however, elevations have no depth. If you choose to use elevations, several views will be required to illustrate the space. The various views should correspond with an elevation view symbol pointing to the view inside the floor plan.

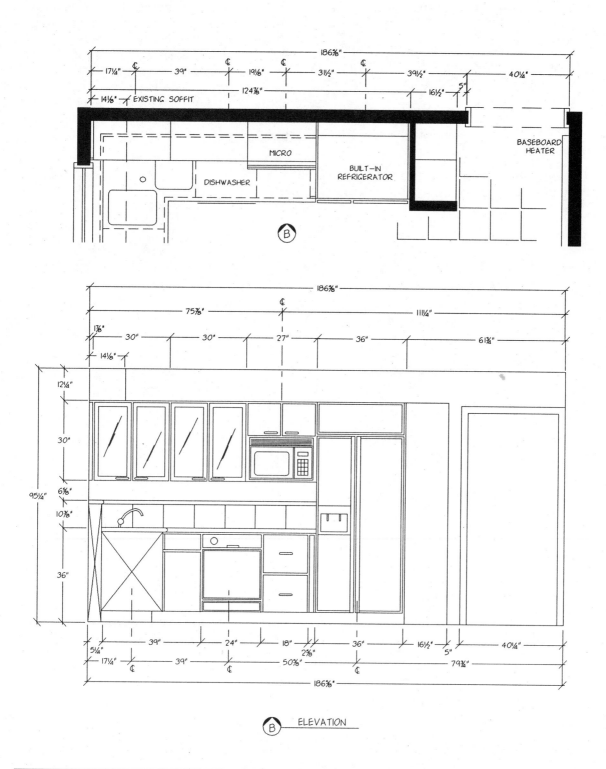

Figure 467 The elevations correspond directly to the plans - imperial dimensions.

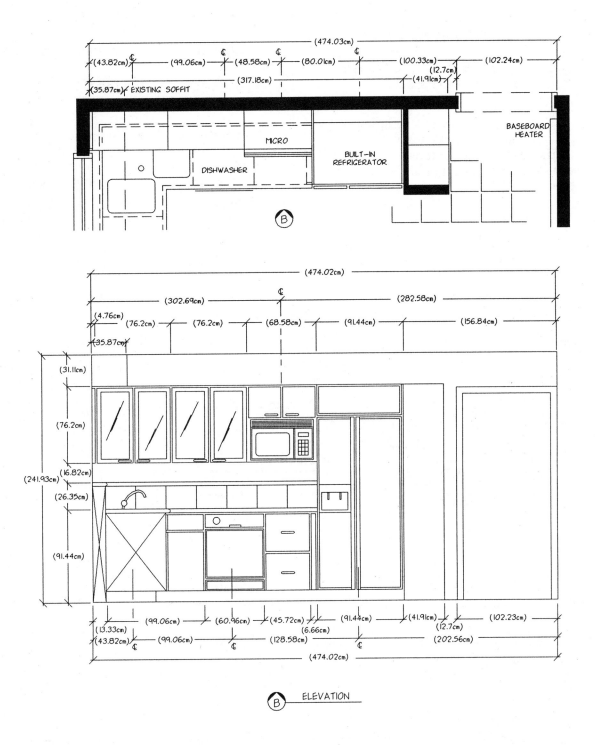

Figure 468 The elevations correspond directly to the plans - metric dimensions.

Paraline Drawings

Paraline drawings are similar to orthographic drawings and remain in a true scale format, yet offer a three dimensional view of the space.

All paraline drawings including oblique, diametric, isometric and trimetric, have three characteristics which separates them from other drawing types:

- all vertical lines remain parallel

- all horizontal lines remain parallel

- all lines parallel to the X,Y & Z axes are drawn to scale

The use of paraline drawings is not recommended for client presentations because the drawings tend to appear distorted. They are however, ideal for quick pictorial representation during the design idea process.

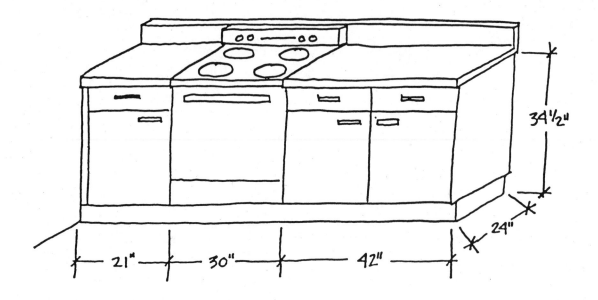

Figure 469 Paraline sketching can help the design idea process.

Perspective Sketch

The realistic appearance of a perspective sketch makes it the ideal type of interpretive drawing. The perspective relies on the appearance of the space, rather than on the true scale of the space.

There are three qualities inherent to perspectives that separate them from other drawing types:

- a diminishing size in relation to distance

- a vanishing or meeting of parallel lines as they recede

- a foreshortening of horizontal planes as they near the horizon line

There are various techniques used to develop perspective drawing presentations. Following are several examples which demonstrate both hand drawn and computer generated presentation techniques. As you view these drawings, notice how each different method of preparation takes on individual personality. In time, you too will develop your own personal style depending on your needs and preferences.

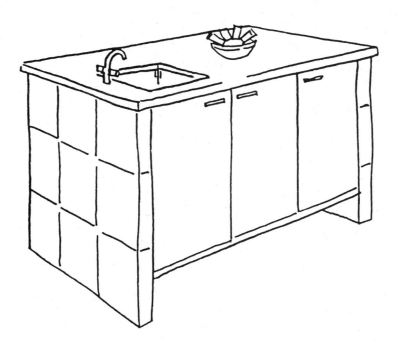

Figure 470 Perspective sketching can also be used to help the designer visualize how the surfaces selected will relate to one another.

Figure 471 *Perspectives take on individual style with the addition of shading and accessories.*

Figure 472 *Perspectives take on individual style with the addition of shading and accessories.*

Figure 473 Perspectives take on individual style with the addition of shading and accessories.

Figure 474 Perspectives take on individual style with the addition of shading and accessories.

Figure 475 Perspectives take on individual style with the addition of shading and accessories.

THE CONSTRUCTION METHOD

The original method used to construct perspectives involved complicated
and time-consuming identification of
points. Various points were plotted into
position by locating the plan on your
drawing and drawing lines from every
corner to a picture plane, transferring
the newly located points to yet another
location by connecting them with the
vanishing point.

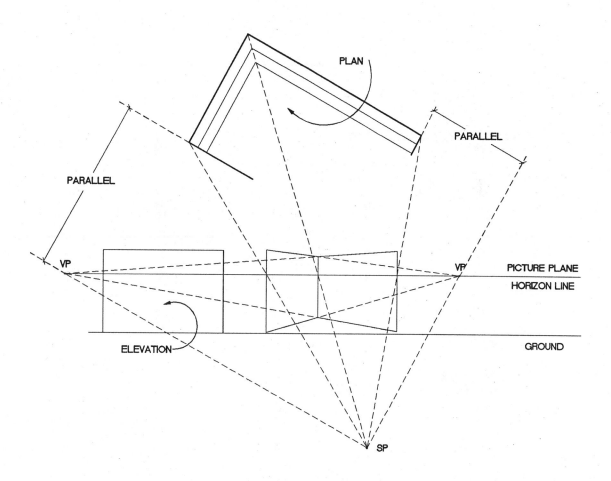

Figure 476 The construction method of perspective drawing.

THE GRID BASED METHOD

The grid method more commonly used today is based on the original construction method, but the confusing transformation of points has already been completed. The grids available from the **National Kitchen & Bath Association** have located points in one-foot increments, with additional, commonly used points, such as toekick and backsplash heights, also indicated. These are available in both one-point and two-point versions.

The following grid instructions are reprinted from the **National Kitchen & Bath Association Grid Instruction Manual**.

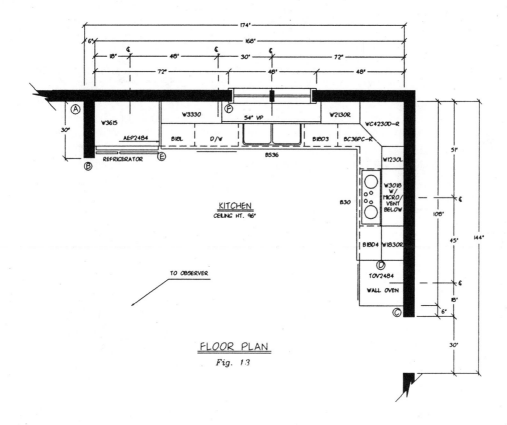

FLOOR PLAN
Fig. 13

Figure 477 A typical kitchen to be used to demonstrate the NKBA grid method of perspective drawing.

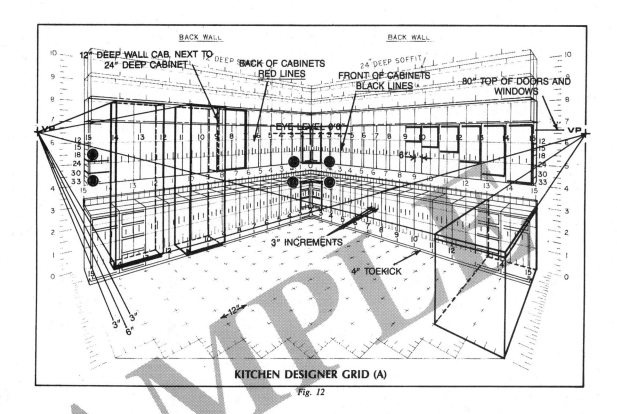

KITCHEN DESIGNER GRID (A)

Fig. 12

HELPFUL TWO POINT PERSPECTIVE TIPS

The eye level of the observer in the grid chart is the same height as the vanishing points (appx. 6′6″, 78″).

Heights of the wall cabinets are shown in six common sizes in figure 12. To find other sizes, simply "guesstimate" between the existing sizes shown (point Ⓐ- 21″ cabinet) and (point Ⓑ- 27″ cabinet).

The **80″ measurement** is the standard height of the tops of windows and doors. Use the measurements in red on the back wall to position windows and doors.

Use the base cabinet measurements for tall cabinets 24″ deep. Then carry the vertical lines up to the desired height.

Use the wall cabinet measurements for tall cabinets 12″ deep. Then carry the vertical lines down to the floor (construct toekick if necessary).

For diagonal corner base and wall cabinets, connect corresponding points on each wall with a horizontal line (points Ⓒ- Ⓒ: W2430 corner wall cabinet, and points Ⓓ- Ⓓ: B36 corner base cabinet). For a tall diagonal corner base cabinet (any size), carry the vertical lines up to the same height on each wall and connect with a horizontal line.

Figure 478 The NKBA kitchen grid method of perspective drawing.

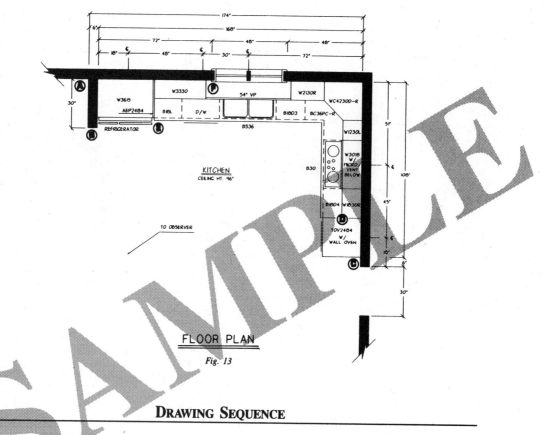

FLOOR PLAN

Fig. 13

DRAWING SEQUENCE

1 Find point Ⓐ 174″ (14′6″) on left back wall; draw 30″ deep wall, point Ⓑ, 96″ H and 6″ W (fig. #14).

2 Find point Ⓒ 108″ (9′0″) on right back wall; draw vertical line (fig. #14). Outline oven cabinet, point Ⓓ. Draw 24″ deep soffit lines above oven cabinet and then continue soffit lines around to the wall on the left side of the kitchen (fig. #14).

3 The W3615 is 24″ deep, point Ⓔ, and has a side panel right. Starting at 132″ (11′), draw a vertical line from the toekick to the 24″ deep wall cabinet line. Complete the remainder of the W3615 (fig. #14). Draw in the refrigerator.

4 Outline the remaining wall cabinets, drawing the valance, point Ⓕ **before** drawing the exposed side of the cabinet next to the window (fig. #14).

5 Finish toekick lines; draw countertop lines and divide base cabinets (fig. #15).

6 Find the right side of the window against the back wall. Measuring along the back wall and to the left, find the left side of the window. Draw window area not covered by wall cabinets (fig. #15).

Figure 478 The NKBA kitchen grid method of perspective drawing.

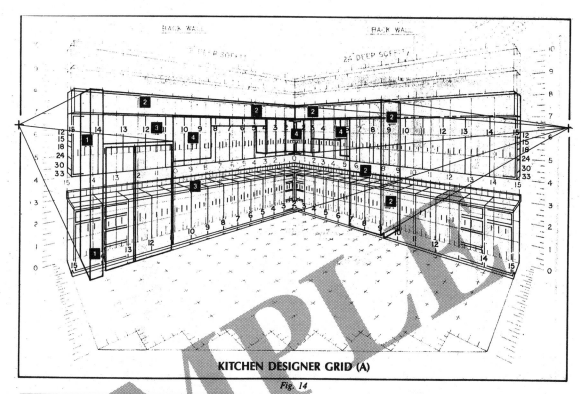

KITCHEN DESIGNER GRID (A)

Fig. 14

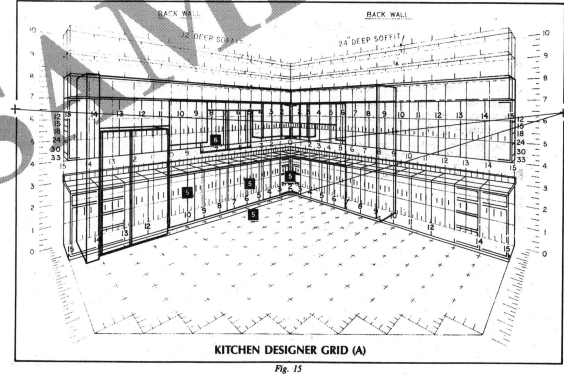

KITCHEN DESIGNER GRID (A)

Fig. 15

Figure 478 The NKBA kitchen grid method of perspective drawing.

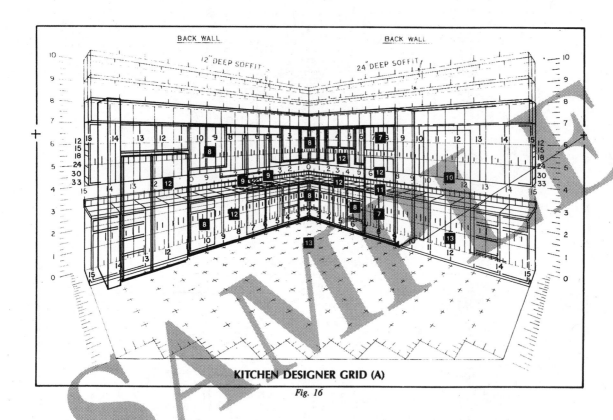

KITCHEN DESIGNER GRID (A)

Fig. 16

DRAWING SEQUENCE cont.

7 Draw oven cabinet doors. Bring forward the 18″ mark from the back wall for the upper doors and then use the left vanishing point for reference (fig. #16).

8 Draw wall cabinet doors and base cabinet doors and drawers. Shade doors and drawers while drawing! (The vertical sides of doors and drawers close to the observer and the tops of base doors and drawers). Shade toekick (fig. #16).

9 Draw sink and faucet; then draw the backsplash lines (fig. #16).

10 Find 114″ (9′6″) on the back right wall and draw 30″ door opening (fig. #16).

11 Outline single oven in wall oven cabinet (fig. #16).

12 Detail wall oven, cooktop, microwave and dishwasher to the left of the sink, and finish refrigerator (fig. #17).

13 Draw floor grid lines to add depth to drawing. Draw cabinet hardware on doors and drawers (fig. #17). Draw doorway and casement moldings to right of oven cabinet.

Figure 478 The NKBA kitchen grid method of perspective drawing.

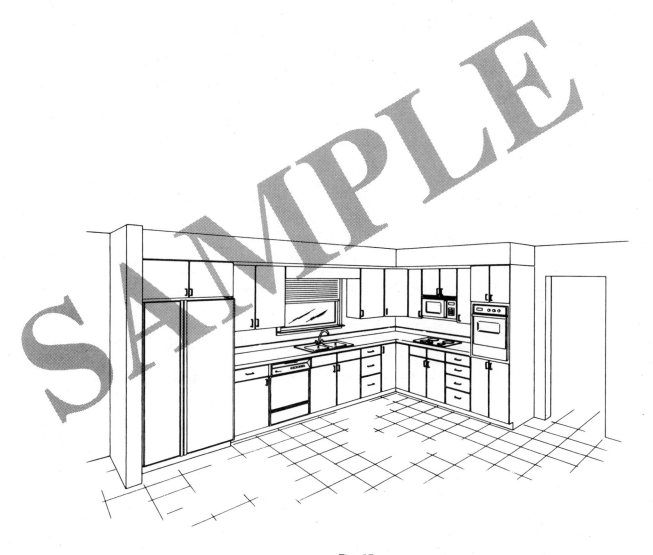

Fig. 17

Figure 478 The NKBA kitchen grid method of perspective drawing.

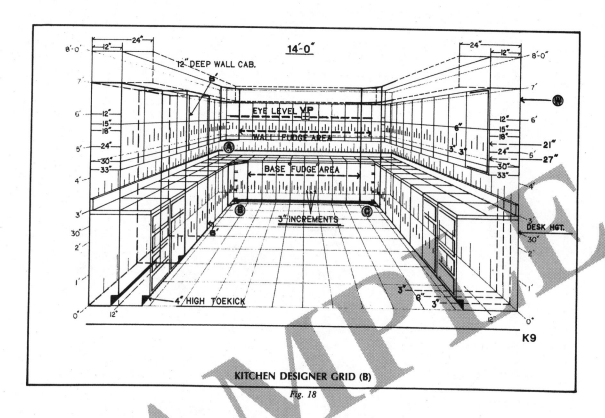

KITCHEN DESIGNER GRID (B)

Fig. 18

HELPFUL ONE POINT PERSPECTIVE TIPS

The eye level of the observer in the grid chart is the same height as the vanishing point (apprx. 78").

The window and door height measurement (point **W** fig. 18) can be transferred to the back wall by using the vanishing point. Use the **RED** wall measurements for positioning windows and doors.

Use the base cabinet measurements for tall cabinets 24" deep. Then carry the vertical lines up to the 24" soffit.

Use the wall cabinet measurements for tall cabinets 12" deep. Then carry the vertical lines down to the floor (construct toekick if necessary).

For diagonal corner base and wall cabinets, connect corresponding points on each wall. (Example **A** 12" corner wall with soffit); (Example **B** 36" corner base) and (Example **C** 36" tall corner cabinet with soffit above).

What if your kitchen is not the same size as the grid chart? FUDGE!!!

Example: Your kitchen back wall is between 105" and 108", use the 108" (9'-0") grid chart. You can easily "lose" 3" in the drawing. Remember, this is to be an artistic sketch and it will not be to scale.

Figure 478 The NKBA kitchen grid method of perspective drawing.

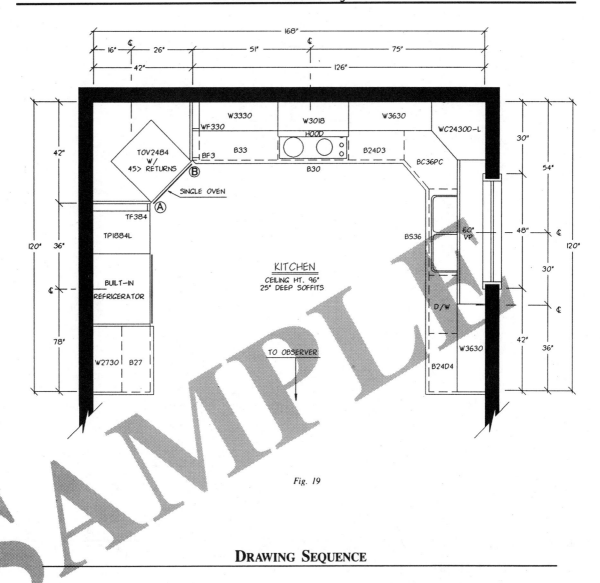

Fig. 19

DRAWING SEQUENCE

1 Draw vertical lines for each side of the diagonal oven cabinet (fig. 20 Ⓐ Ⓒ, Ⓑ Ⓓ), from the top of the toekick to the top of the 24″ deep soffit. Connect points Ⓐ Ⓑ , Ⓔ Ⓕ and Ⓒ Ⓓ .

2 Outline 36″ diagonal corner base. Align triangle with each side of the corner base cabinet and draw 24″ deep diagonal soffit above (fig. 20).

3 Draw the remainder of the 24″ deep soffit lines around the kitchen (fig. 20).

4 Draw the 24″ diagonal wall cabinet to the left of the window (fig. 20).

5 Draw vertical lines outlining refrigerator.

6 Outline wall cabinets to the right of the refrigerator.

7 Outline base cabinets and countertop to the right of the refrigerator (fig. 20).

8 Draw 36″ wall cabinet to the right of the window. Then draw valance (fig. 21).

9 Draw right side of diagonal wall cabinet to the left of the window (fig. 21).

10 Outline remaining wall and base cabinets, countertop and toekick. (Draw range hood before drawing vertical cabinet lines on each side of it) (fig. 21).

Figure 478 The NKBA kitchen grid method of perspective drawing.

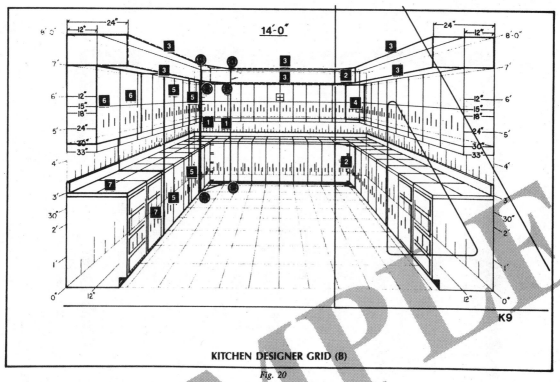

KITCHEN DESIGNER GRID (B)

Fig. 20

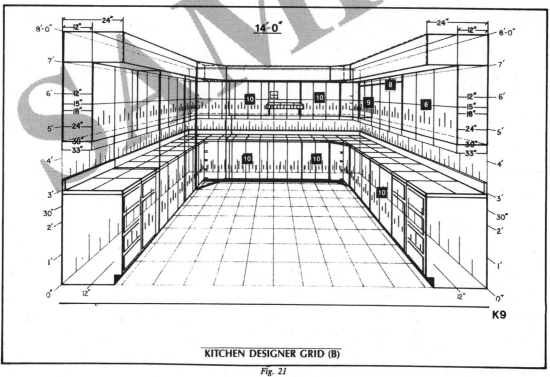

KITCHEN DESIGNER GRID (B)

Fig. 21

Figure 478 The NKBA kitchen grid method of perspective drawing.

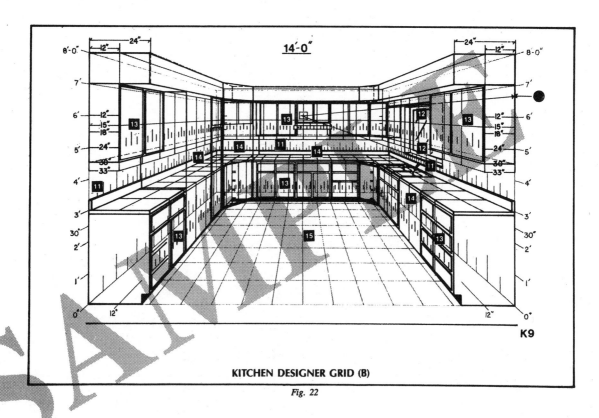

KITCHEN DESIGNER GRID (B)

Fig. 22

DRAWING SEQUENCE cont.

11 Draw sink and faucet, then the remaining backsplash lines (fig. 22).

12 Estimate 80″ (6′-8″, point ⑩- top of window), then use the **vanishing point** to draw the top and bottom of window. Note the hidden window lines on wall (fig. 22).

13 Draw wall cabinet doors and base cabinet doors and drawers. Shade the vertical sides of base and wall cabinet doors (left hand vertical lines on the left side of the grid and right hand vertical lines on the right side of the grid) as well as the tops of all drawers (fig. 22).

14 Draw oven, cooktop, refrigerator and dishwasher (fig. 22).

15 Draw cabinet hardware on doors and drawers. Shade toekick. Add a few floor and ceiling lines for added depth in the picture (fig. 22).

Figure 478 The NKBA kitchen grid method of perspective drawing.

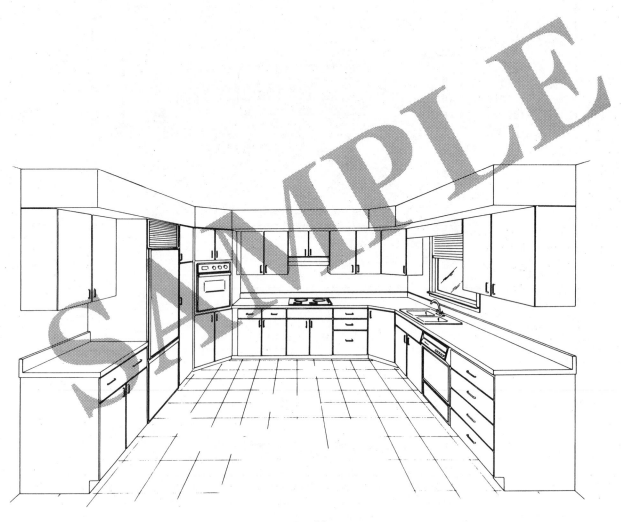

Fig. 23

Figure 478 The NKBA kitchen grid method of perspective drawing.

Choosing Perspective Types

Once you are familiar with the method used to construct a one and two-point perspective, your selection will be based on the type of project. Choosing the correct type of perspective (one-point or two-point) is important.

TWO-POINT

The two-point view is usually preferred because it is the most realistic. However, only two walls can be shown in a single view. Two views will be required to illustrate a complete space using two-point perspectives.

ONE-POINT

A one-point perspective illustrates three walls within a single view, elimi-nating the need for a second view. However, in very small and very large spaces, a one-point perspective view "crowds" the side walls and obscures details.

BIRDS-EYE

To illustrate small spaces without breaking them up or obscuring details, the one-point "birds-eye" perspective is recommended. A "birds-eye view" is taken from above the ceiling, looking down onto the floor. It encompasses all four walls. A "birds-eye view" is similar to looking down into a scale model. The "birds-eye view" is obviously not realistic. However, it does give a clear picture of the spatial relationship between the various elements of the room.

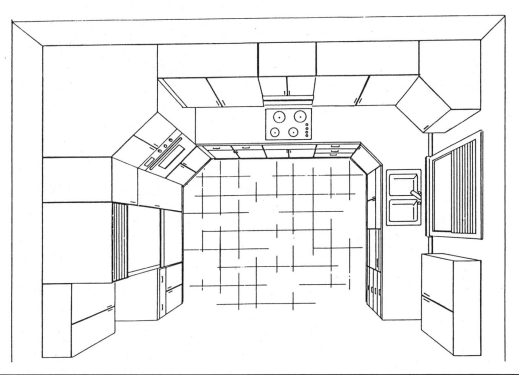

Figure 479 The birds-eye view perspective illustrates spatial relationships.

Enhancing the Perspective

Including shading, highlights, color, people and accessories to a perspective adds to the effect of realism. The lines of a drawing in perspective define the limits, but the drawing derives meaning through its figure-ground relationship. By thickening the profile line or lines of edges against space, a drawing becomes easier to interpret.

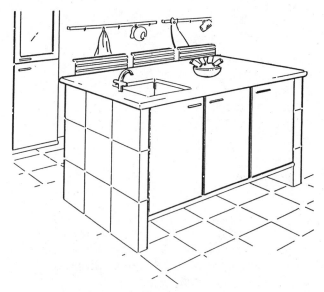

Figure 481 Darkening profile lines emphasize the 3D quality of a perspective drawing.

ADDING SHADING

Shading conveys even more information by defining dimension and direction. An otherwise flat object becomes three-dimensional by adding shadows. A light source is introduced which adds the degree of realism.

Because there are several light sources in an interior rather than one (the sun) in architectural drawings, it's difficult to calculate exact shadow delineation. Therefore, the standard practice is to consider two light sources coming from both upper left and upper right locations.

As you draw, think of the light shining over your left and right shoulders onto your drawing. The top and front surfaces of objects are in the most light and receive little or no shading. The sides of objects not in direct view, such as cabinet sides and the ceiling are in a light shade. The darkest shades are reserved for areas below overhangs. The

Figure 480 Lines define limits of objects.

principles behind these types of shadows are;

- parallel surfaces create parallel shadow edges

- perpendicular surfaces create sloping shadow edges.

By varying tonal values of shades, the perception of depth is enhanced. Two objects that appear equal in tone appear to be in the same spatial plane. If you vary the shade tones of each object, depth will be emphasized. There are several principles which may be applied to produce this affect. In black line artwork as illustrated here, the background is shaded and the foreground is left in pure, crisp line form. This technique will make two closer elements jump off the page at the viewer. If color is being used, the foreground will be bright, pure colors with dark outlines and the background should be lighter colors. When shading with pencil, the background can be blended by smudging the graphite and lightening it at the same time.

These shading techniques can be performed with pencil, pen or marker. Each medium has its own special look. The final presentation will vary depending, on your choice of medium and personal style.

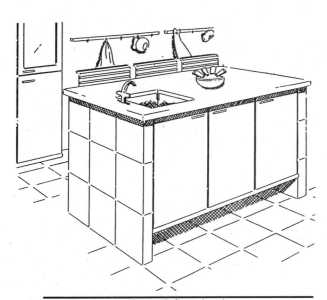

Figure 482 Shadows define depth.

Figure 483 Varying tone emphasizes depth.

ADDING PEOPLE AND ACCESSORIES

To add realism to a drawing, add people and accessories. There are several source books available with people and accessories that can be traced into your own drawing. Another good source is your local newspaper advertisement sections and department store cata-logues. These sources will give you models that are up-to-date.

If the size is not exactly right, reduce or enlarge it on a copy machine and then trace it into your drawing. Or incorporate it into your software package, making it available for use at a later time.

Figure 484 Trace people and accessories to add realism to drawings.

ENHANCING WITH COLOR

Color is the ultimate enhancement. Color evokes emotion and has a far reaching effect on the viewers perception of the design. To ignore color is to ignore one of the elements of design.

When selecting a coloring medium, be sure to also purchase black and several shades of cool grey. Begin your color collection with subtle, muted, neutral tones rather than the bright primary colors. The primary colors may look pretty, but will quickly overwhelm your drawing.

"Less is more," when applying color. Hint at color in different areas of the drawing. Use the markers and pencils together to enhance each other.

Markers give a smooth, solid appearance, ideal for base coats of solid color. They can stand on their own for such items as matte laminates and painted woods.

Use the colored pencils alone to add texture and highlights. Or go over the marker base with them.

With a little practice, your drawings will come to life.

STORING PROJECT DOCUMENTS

After you've completed your presentation drawings, you'll need a place to safely store them. The type of storage you choose depends on the type of presentation used. Use tubes or roll files for large, rolled drawings. Roll files may be vertical, horizontal or stepped. They may be made of cardboard, wood or wire.

Most professionals prefer to store drawings flat. For flat storage, there are vertical files where drawings hang on a pivoting clip that allows easy access. You may also choose flat files, which are stacks of shallow drawers sized to accommodate standard drawings. These are available in a variety of materials. Some feature drawers that can be pulled out and carried for transporting drawings.

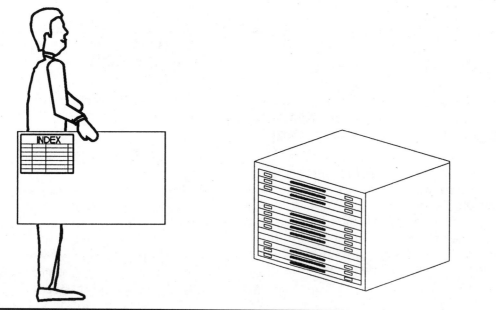

Figure 485 *Stacking horizontal storage converts to portfolio case.*

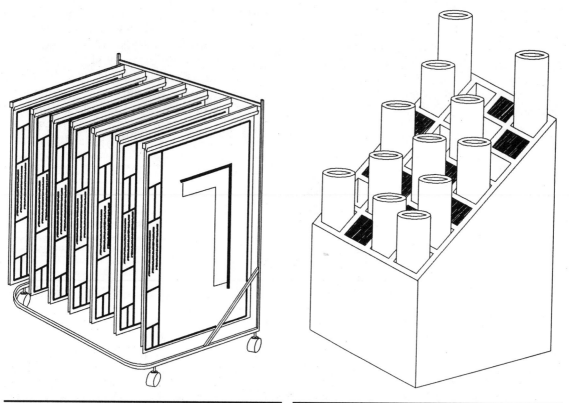

Figure 486 *Vertical hanging files are easily accessed.*

Figure 487 *Rolled drawings can be stored in a tiered storage unit for easy access.*

Plan Presentation

Traditional leather portfolios may also be used for transporting and presenting drawings. Zippered portfolios with open interiors for matted drawings or ring binders with acetate folders for loose drawings are available. Some smaller portfolios can be folded to resemble a table easel for convenient view-ing. Portfolios no larger than 18" x 24" (45.72cm x 60.96cm) are recommended so they can be easily viewed by clients.

Alternatively, selected drawings can be matted, framed and displayed on an easel. These can be in your showroom and then taken to trade shows or spec homes for marketing your services.

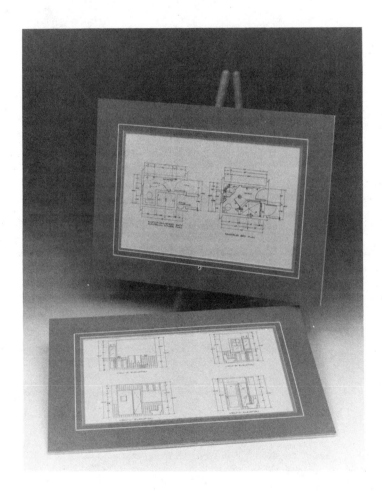

Figure 488 Table easels provide showroom display of drawings.

Figure 489 A portfolio case will allow presentation flexibility by traveling anywhere

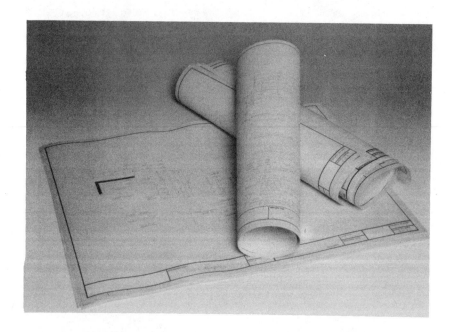

Figure 490 Rolled drawings are difficult to present.

Appendix A

NKBA KITCHEN PLANNING GUIDELINES

GUIDELINE   **CONTEMPORARY VARIABLE**   **OLD RULE**

Section I: Traffic and Workflow

Guideline #1

a. Doorways should be at least 32" (81cm) wide and not more than 24" (61cm) deep in the direction of travel.

Universal design criteria suggested increased minimum clearances.

Clearance between front of cabinet/appliance and blank face of assembly at right angle to be 30" (76cm).

b. Walkways (passages between vertical objects greater than 24" (61cm) deep in the direction of travel, where not more than one is a work counter or or appliance) should be at least 36" (91cm) wide.

Standards were needed for two-cook kitchens.

Clarification between working aisles and passageways was necessary.

Corner-to-corner clearance 28" (71cm).

Clearance between two cabinets opposite one another in working aisle to be 48" (121cm).

c. Work aisles (passages between vertical objects, both of which are work counters or appliances) should be at least 42" (106cm) wide in one-cook kitchens, at least 48" (122cm) wide in multiple-cook kitchens.

Guideline #2

The work triangle should total 26' (792cm) or less, with no single leg of the triangle shorter than 4' (122cm) nor longer than 9' (274cm). The work triangle should not intersect an island or peninsula by more than 12" (30cm). (The triangle is the shortest walking distance between the refrigerator, primary cooking surface and primary food preparation sink, measured from the center front of each appliance.)

Additional centers of activity and multiple cooks change the triangle into a rectangle or double triangle.

Various types of cooking activities during typical week place different demands on the kitchen, which affect the triangle criteria.

Work triangles must measure between 12' (366cm) and 26' (792cm).

GUIDELINE	CONTEMPORARY VARIABLE	OLD RULE

Section I: Traffic and Workflow (cont'd)

Guideline #3

No major traffic patterns should cross through the work triangle.	More interactive spaces have resulted in kitchens with multiple entrances and multiple cooks.	Household traffic must not cross the work triangle.

Guideline #4

No entry, appliance or cabinet doors should interfere with one another.	Increased number of appliances requires clearance rules for appliance doors as well as entry doors.	Doors not to interfere with work area.

Guideline #5

In a seating area, 36" (91cm) of clearance should be allowed from the counter/table edge to any wall/obstruction behind it if no traffic will pass behind a seated diner. If there is a walkway behind the seating area, 65" (165cm) of clearance, total, including the walkway, should be allowed between the seating area and any wall or obstruction.	Universal ergonomic consideration as well as safety call for adequate space allowance.	No mention in the past.

Section II: Cabinets and Storage

Guideline #6

Small Kitchens - = or < 150 sq. ft. - allow at least 144" of wall ca (14 sq.m) - allow at least 144" (366cm) of wall cabinet frontage, with cabinets at least 12" deep, and a minimum of 30" (76cm) high (or equivalent) which feature adjustable shelving. Difficult to reach cabinets above hood, oven or refrigerator do not count unless devices are installed within the case to improve accessibility.	New requirements were derived from findings of the Utensil Survey. Tall cabinets are now used in place of both wall and base cabinets. 12" (30cm) deep tall cabinet = 1 x base, 2 x wall 18" (46cm) deep tall cabinet = 1.5 x base, 3 x wall 21-24" (53cm - 61cm) deep tall cabinet = 2 x base, 4 x wall	96" (244cm) of wall cabinet frontage required.

GUIDELINE	CONTEMPORARY VARIABLE	OLD RULE

Section II: Cabinets and Storage (cont'd)

Guideline #6 (cont)

Large Kitchens - over 150 sq. ft. (14 sq.m) - allow at least 186" (472cm) of wall cabinet frontage, with cabinets at least 12" (30cm) deep, and a minimum of 30" (76cm) high (or equivalent) which feature adjustable shelving. Difficult to reach cabinets above the hood, oven or refrigerator do not count unless devices are installed within the case to improve accessibility.

Cabinet interior storage devices are commonly installed today.

Guideline #7

At least 60" (152cm) of wall cabinet frontage, with cabinets at least 12" (30cm) deep, a minimum of 30" (76cm) high (or equivalent), should be included within 72" (183cm) of the primary sink centerline.

Utensil Survey research indicated a need for significant storage near primary sink.

42" (107cm) of cabinet frontage must be within 72" (183cm) of the sink centerline.

Guideline #8

Small Kitchens - = or < 150 sq. ft. (14 sq.m) - allow at least 156" (393cm) of base cabinet frontage, with cabinets at least 21" (53cm) deep (or equivalent). The blind portion of a blind corner box does not count.

Large Kitchens - over 150 sq. ft. (14 sq.m) - require at least 192" (488cm) of base cabinet frontage, with cabinets at least 21" (53cm) deep (or equivalent). The blind portion of a blind corner box does not count.

Homes are bigger today.

Kitchen sizes vary regardless of house square footage. House size is not as big a factor as are family cooking and socializing preferences in determining kitchen square footage

Base cabinet frontage requires 96" (244cm).

Minimum acceptable base cabinet depth is 20" (51cm).

GUIDELINE	CONTEMPORARY VARIABLE	OLD RULE

Section II: Cabinets and Storage (cont'd)

Guideline #9

Small Kitchens - = or < 150 sq. ft. (14 sq.m) - allow at least 120" (305cm) of drawer or roll-out shelf frontage.	Roll-outs are used extensively in base cabinets in place of drawer units.	Minimum of nine drawers, equaling 120" (305cm) required.

Large Kitchens - over 150 sq. ft. (14 sq.m) - allow at least 165" (419cm) of drawer or roll-out shelf frontage.

Multiply cabinet width by number of drawers/roll-outs to determine frontage. Drawer/roll-out (38cm) cabinets must be at least 15" (38cm) wide and 21" (53cm) deep to be counted.

Guideline #10

At least five storage/organizing items, located between 15" - 48" (38cm - 122cm) above the finished floor (or extending into that area), should be included in the kitchen to improve functionality and accessibility. These items may include, but are not limited to: lowered wall cabinets, raised base cabinets, tall cabinets, appliance garages, bins/racks, swing-out pantries, interior vertical dividers, specialized drawers/shelves, etc. Full-extension drawers/roll-out shelves greater than the 120" (305cm) minimum for small kitchens or 165" (419cm) for larger kitchens, can be included.	Cabinet interior storage devices are common today.	No mention in the past.

GUIDELINE	CONTEMPORARY VARIABLE	OLD RULE

Section II: Cabinets and Storage (cont'd)

Guideline #11

For a kitchen with usable corner areas in the plan, at least one functional corner storage unit should be included.

Specialized corner cabinets are available today.

No mention in the past.

Section III: Appliance Placement and Use/Clearance Space

Guideline #12

At least two waste receptacles should be included in the plan; one for garbage and one for recyclables, or other recycling facilities should be planned.

Ecological concerns impact the space required around the clean-up sink.

No mention in the past

Guideline #13

Knee space (which may be open or adaptable) should be planned below or adjacent to sinks, cooktops, ranges, dishwashers, refrigerators and ovens whenever possible. Knee space should be a minimum of 30" (76cm) wide by 27" (69cm) high by 19" (48cm) deep. The 27" (69cm) height at the front of the knee space may decrease progressively as depth increases.

Address universal access, specifically needs of those who can not stand for long periods of time and/or wheelchair users.

No mention in the past.

Guideline #14

A clear floor space of 30" x 48" (76cm x 122cm) should be provided at the sink, dishwasher, cooktop, oven and refrigerator. (Measure from face of cabinet or appliance if toe kick is less than 9" (23cm) high.)

Address universal access, specifically to allow for wheelchair approach and clearance.

No mention in the past.

GUIDELINE	CONTEMPORARY VARIABLE	OLD RULE

Section III: Appliance Placement and Use/Clearance Space (cont'd)

Guideline #15

A minimum of 21" (53cm) clear floor space should be allowed between the edge of the dishwasher and counters, appliances and/or cabinets which are placed at a right angle to the dishwasher.

Presence of a potential clean-up helper should be considered when placing the dishwasher. Therefore, access to the appliance rather than the handedness of the cook is critical.

Recommended placement of the dishwasher is to the left of the sink.

Guideline #16

The edge of the primary dishwasher should be within 36" (91cm) of the edge of one sink.

Dishes are scraped and/or rinsed before loading a dishwasher.

No mention in the past.

Guideline #17

If the kitchen has only one sink, it should be located between or across from the cooking surface, preparation area or refrigerator.

The sink is the most frequently used center.

No mention in the past.

Guideline #18

There should be at least 24" (61cm) of clearance between the cooking surface and a protected surface above, or at least 30" (76cm) of clearance between the cooking surface and an unprotected surface above. (If the protected surface is a microwave hood combination, manufacturer's specifications may dictate a clearance less than 24" (61cm).)

Downdraft systems have led to more and more exposed and unprotected surfaces above the cooktop.

At least 24" (61cm) of clearance is needed between the cooking surface and the protective surface above. 30" (76cm) of clearance is necessary between the cooking surface and unprotected surface above.

GUIDELINE	CONTEMPORARY VARIABLE	OLD RULE

Section III: Appliance Placement and Use/Clearance Space (cont'd)

Guideline #19

All major appliances used for surface cooking should have a ventilation system, with a fan rated at 150 CFM minimum.	Ventilation systems are typical.	Ventilation systems required with at least 100 CFM. No requirement to exhaust to outside. Wall fans were okay.

Guideline #20

The cooking surface should not be placed below an operable window unless the window is 3" (8cm) or more behind the appliance and more than 24" (61cm) above it. Windows, operable or inoperable, above a cooking surface should not be dressed with flammable window treatments.	Some building and fire codes allow windows to be placed behind a cooking appliance.	Cooking surface cannot be placed under a window.

Section IV: Counter Surface and Landing Space

Guideline #21

Microwave ovens should be placed so that the bottom of the appliance is 24" - 48" (61cm - 122cm) above the floor.	Universal design requires lower placement of the microwave to insure accessibility.	Microwaves were not a consideration.

Guideline #22

At least two work-counter heights should be offered in the kitchen, with one 28" - 36" (71cm - 91cm) above the finished floor and the other 36" - 45" (36cm - 45cm) above the finished floor.	Assures universal accessibility.	No mention in the past.

GUIDELINE	CONTEMPORARY VARIABLE	OLD RULE

Section IV: Counter Surface and Landing Space (cont'd)

Guideline #23

Small Kitchens - = or < 150 sq. ft. (14 sq.m) - allow at least 132" (335cm) of usable countertop frontage.

Large Kitchens - over 150 sq. ft. (14 sq.m) - allow at least 198" (503cm) of usable countertop frontage.

Counters must be a minimum of 16" (41cm) deep, and wall cabinets must be at least 15" (38cm) above their surface for counter to be included in total frontage measurement. (Measure only countertop frontage, do not count corner space.)

Research indicates that 16" (41cm) is the minimum usable counter depth.

Certain cabinet configurations including appliance garages and cabinets that rest directly on the countertop are common today.

Industry standard in U.S. is 15" - 18" (38cm - 46cm). European standard is slightly higher.

108" (274cm) of countertop frontage is required. No counter depth is specified.

Corner space does not count.

Backsplash clearance of 15" (38cm) is required.

Guideline #24

There should be at least 24" (61cm) of countertop frontage to one side of the primary sink, and 18" (46cm) on the other side (including corner sink applications) with the 24" (61cm) counter frontage at the same counter height as the sink. The countertop frontage may be a continuous surface, or the total of two angled countertop sections. (Measure only countertop frontage, do not count corner space.)

Many kitchens have more than one sink.

Accessible planning has identified a more desirable clearance requirement to be 18" (46cm) if an obstacle blocks usable space on the return run of countertop. If there is no obstacle on the return run, the space is often used by the cook.

24" (61cm) of landing space is required to the right of the sink and 18" (46cm) on the left side of the sink.

Corner space does not count.

9" (23cm) of clearance is required from sink to corner.

GUIDELINE	CONTEMPORARY VARIABLE	OLD RULE

Section IV: Counter Surface and Landing Space (cont'd)

Guideline #25

At least 3" (8cm) of countertop frontage should be provided on one side of secondary sinks, and 18" (46cm) on the other side (including corner sink applications) with the 18" (46cm) counter frontage at the same counter height as the sink. The countertop frontage may be a continuous surface, or the total of two angled countertop sections. (Measure only countertop frontage, do not count corner space.)

Accommodate those with limited strength.

No mention in the past.

Guideline #26

At least 15" (38cm) of landing space, a minimum of 16" (41cm) deep, should be planned above, below or adjacent to a microwave.

Microwave ovens are standard equipment in contemporary kitchens.

Microwaves were not a consideration.

Guideline #27

In an open-ended kitchen configuration, at least 9" (23cm) of counter space should be allowed on one side of the cooking surface and 15" (38cm) on the other, at the same counter height as the appliance. For an enclosed configuration, at least 3" (8cm) of clearance space should be planned at an end wall protected by flame retardant surfacing material and 15" (38cm) should be allowed on the other side of the appliance, at the same counter height as the appliance.

Built-in appliances are very common.

Landing space of 15" (38cm) is required on either side of the cooktop.

GUIDELINE   **CONTEMPORARY VARIABLE**   **OLD RULE**

Section IV: Counter Surface and Landing Space (cont'd)

Guideline #28

The plan should allow at least 15" (38cm) of counter space on the handle side of the refrigerator or on either side of a side-by-side refrigerator or, at least 15" (38cm) of landing space which is no more than 48" (122cm) across from the refrigerator. (Measure the 48" (122cm) distance from the center front of the refrigerator to the countertop opposite it.)

Kitchen design preferences have led to plans including work islands and peninsulas, offering landing space across from, rather than next to, the refrigerator.

Side-by-side refrigerators don't allow landing space by the latch side of the appliance.

Landing space of 15" (38cm) or more required on the latch (handle) side of the refrigerator.

Guideline #29

There should be at least 15" (38cm) of landing space which is at least 16" (41cm) deep next to or above the oven if the appliance door opens into a primary traffic pattern. At least 15" x 16" (38cm x 41cm) of landing space which is no more than 48" (122cm) across from the oven is acceptable if the appliance does not open into a traffic area. (Measure the 48" (122cm) distance from the center front of the oven to the countertop opposite it.)

Safety must be considered in connection to family traffic through the kitchen.

15" (38cm) of landing space required next to or across from the oven.

No mention of traffic patterns.

GUIDELINE	CONTEMPORARY VARIABLE	OLD RULE

Section IV: Counter Surface and Landing Space (cont)

Guideline #30

At least 36" (91cm) of continuous countertop which is at least 16" (41cm) deep should be planned for the preparation center. The preparation center should be immediately adjacent to a water source.

If two or more people work in the kitchen simultaneously, each will need a minimum 36" (91cm) wide by 16" (41cm) deep preparation center of their own. If two people will stand adjacent to one another, a 72" (183cm) wide by 16" (41cm) deep space should be planned.

Foods and preparation techniques have changed. It is common today for more than one person to participate in meal preparation.

36" (91cm) or more of uninterrupted counter space is to be available for the mix center. Mix center is preferably located between sink and refrigerator.

Guideline #31

If two work centers are adjacent to one another, determine a new minimum counter frontage requirement for the two adjoining spaces by taking the longest of the two required counter lengths and adding 12" (30cm).

Clarification of integrated work centers was needed to accommodate contemporary design.

No mention in the past.

GUIDELINE	CONTEMPORARY VARIABLE	OLD RULE

Section IV: Counter Surface and Landing Space (cont'd)

Guideline #32

| No primary work centers (the primary sink, refrigerator, preparation or cooktop/range center) should be separated by a full-height, full-depth tall tower, such as an oven cabinet, pantry cabinet or refrigerator. | Because of multiple cooks and the increase in number of appliances, there is a need for primary and secondary work centers.

A microwave oven, as part of a double wall oven, or placed in a cabinet on a counter, creates a tall obstruction, yet must be considered a part of a primary center. | Work centers are not to be separated by tall appliances, cabinets or other obstructions. Continuous counter space between two or more centers is desirable. |

Guideline #33

| Kitchen seating areas require the following minimum clearances: | Eating space in the kitchen is a common request. | No mention in the past. |

30" (76cm) high tables/counters - allow a 30" (76cm) wide x 19" (48cm) deep counter/table space for each seated diner, and at least 19" (48cm) of clear knee space.

36" (91cm) high counters - allow a 24" (61cm) wide by 15" (38cm) deep counter space for each seated diner, and at least 15" (38cm) of clear knee space.

42" (107cm) high counters - allow a 24" (61cm) wide by 12" (30cm) deep counter space for each seated diner, and 12" (30cm) of clear knee space.

Guideline #34

| Open countertop corners should be clipped or radiused; counter edges should be eased to eliminate sharp corners. | Universal safety criteria. | No mention in the past. |

GUIDELINE	CONTEMPORARY VARIABLE	OLD RULE

Section V: Room, Appliance and Equipment Controls

Guideline #35

Controls, handles and door/drawer pulls should be operable with one hand, require only a minimal amount of strength for operation, and should not require tight grasping, pinching or twisting of the wrist. (Includes handles, knobs, pulls on entry and exit doors, appliances, cabinets, drawers and plumbing fixtures, as well as light and thermostat controls/switches, intercoms and other room controls.)

Universal use considerations; accommodates those with limited strength, dexterity and grasping abilities.

No mention in the past.

Guideline #36

Wall-mounted room controls (i.e; wall receptacles, switches, thermostats, telephones, intercoms etc.) should be 15" - 48" (38cm - 122cm) above the finished floor. The switch place can extend beyond that dimension, but the control itself should be within it.

Places controls within universal reach range.

No mention in the past.

Guideline #37

Ground fault circuit interrupters should be specified on all receptacles within the kitchen.

Universal design suggests an expansion of safety standards.

No mention in the past.

Guideline #38

A fire extinguisher should be visibly located in the kitchen, away from cooking equipment and 15" - 48" (38cm - 122cm) above the floor. Smoke alarms should be included near the kitchen.

Place devices within universal reach range. Emphasis on safety.

No mention in the past.

GUIDELINE	CONTEMPORARY VARIABLE	OLD RULE

Section V: Room, Appliance and Equipment Controls (cont'd)

Guideline #39

Window/skylight area should equal at least 10% of the total square footage of the separate kitchen, or a total living space which includes a kitchen.

Skylights are as popular as side windows today. Skylights provide more natural light per square foot of glazing.

Windows should equal 10% or more of the kitchen's square footage.

Guideline #40

Every work surface in the kitchen should be well-illuminated by appropriate task and/or general lighting.

Assures adequate lighting and promotes safety.

No mention in the past.

Appendix B

NKBA
Graphics and Presentation Standards

The following pages are reprinted from the National Kitchen & Bath Association Graphics and Presentations Standards for Kitchen Design.

They have been included so that you might gain a better and more clear insight into the concepts and requirements for good presentation techniques.

- This book is intended for professional use by residential kitchen designers. The procedures and advice herein have been shown to be appropriate for the applications described; however, no warranty (expressed or implied) is intended or given. Moreover, the user of this book is cautioned to be familiar with and to adhere to all manufacturers' planning, installation and use/care instructions. In addition, the user is urged to become familiar with and adhere to all applicable local, state and federal building codes, licensing and legislation requirements governing the user's ability to perform all tasks associated with design and installation standards, and to collaborate with licensed practitioners who offer professional services in the technical areas of mechanical, electrical and load bearing design as required for regulatory approval, as well as health and safety regulations.

- Information about this book and Certified Kitchen Designer programs may be obtained from the National Kitchen & Bath Association, 687 Willow Grove Street, Hackettstown, New Jersey 07840, Phone (908) 852-0033, Fax (908) 852-1695.

Table of Contents

Purpose

By standardizing floor plans and presentation drawings, Kitchen Designers will:

- Limit errors caused by misinterpreting the floor plans.

- Avoid misreading dimensions, which can result in costly errors.

- Prevent cluttering floor plans and drawings with secondary information, which often make the documents difficult to interpret.

- Create a clear understanding of the scope of the project for all persons involved in the job.

- Present a professional image to the client.

- Permit faster processing of orders.

- Simplify estimating and specification preparation.

- Help in the standardization of uniform nomenclature and symbols.

General Provisions Using Imperial Dimensions

I. Use of Standards

The use of these *National Kitchen & Bath Association Graphics and Presentation Standards* is strongly recommended. They contain a specific set of criteria which when applied by the Kitchen Specialist produce a series of project documents that include the following:

- The Floor Plan

- The Construction Plan

- The Mechanical Plan

- The Interpretive Drawings

     1) Elevations
     2) Perspective Drawings
     3) Oblique, Dimetric, Isometric and Trimetric
     4) Sketches

- Specifications

- Design Statement

- Contracts

Two sample sets of project documents for your review can be found in this publication, one uses imperial dimensions and the other is a metric conversion.

Paper: The acceptable paper for the original drawings of the floor plan, construction plan, mechanical plan, and interpretive drawings is set at a **minimum size of 11" x 17".** Translucent vellum tracing paper, imprinted with a black border and appropriate space available for the insertion of pertinent information is strongly recommended. Copies of original drawings should appear in blue or black ink only on white paper. Ozalid or photocopy prints are acceptable.

The use of lined yellow note paper, typing paper, scored graph paper or scored quadrille paper **is not acceptable.**

NKBA Drawing Aid #6002

II. The Floor Plan

1)   **Size and Scope of Floor Plan Drawings:** Kitchen floor plans should be drawn to a scale of 1/2 inch equals 1 foot (1/2 " = 1'0"). *** For metric dimensioning, see Use of Standards using Metric Dimensions beginning on page 677.**

* All base cabinetry should be depicted using a dashed line (----) while countertops are depicted using a solid line.

* The floor plan should depict the entire room when possible. When the entire room cannot be depicted, it must show the area where cabinetry and appliances are permanently installed.

* Floor plans must show all major structural elements such as walls, door swings, door openings, partitions, windows, archways and equipment.

* When the entire room cannot be depicted, the room must be divided by "*break lines*" (⟶⟋) and must show all major structural elements with adjoining areas indicated and labeled.

* Finished interior dimensions are used on all project documents to denote available space for cabinetry and/or other types of equipment. If the kitchen specialist is responsible for specifying the exact method of wall construction, finish and/or partition placement, the specialist should include partition center lines on the construction plan, as well as the finished interior dimensions.

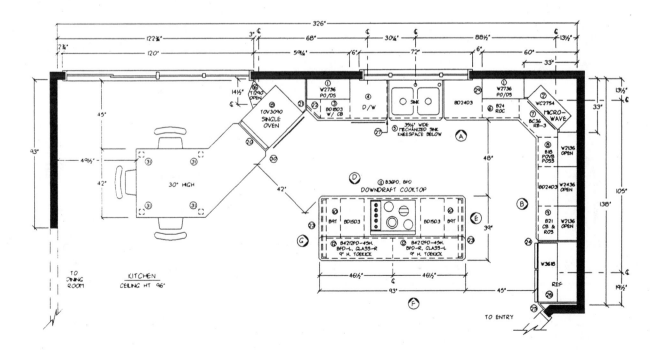

2) **Centerline (₵) dimensions:** must be given for equipment in two directions when possible.

- Mechanicals requiring centerlines include: cooktops, refrigerators, sinks, wall ovens, microwave ovens, fan units, light fixtures, heating and air conditioning ducts and radiators.

- Dimensions should be pulled from return walls or from the face of cabinets/equipment opposite the mechanical element.

- Centerlines on the mechanical plan will be indicated by the symbol (₵) followed by a **long-short-long broken line** that extends into the floor area.

- When the centerline dimension line is outside the floor area, it is typically shown as the second (and, if required, the third) line following the dimension line which identifies the individual wall segments.

₵ —— - —— - — - —— - —— - — - ——

3) **Dimensioning of Floor Plan:** All drawing dimensions used on kitchen floor plans must be given in **Inches and Fractions of Inches ONLY**, (ie. 124 1/4").

- Combining dimensions listed in feet and inches or the exclusive use of dimensions listed in feet and inches, **10' 4 1/4" is not acceptable** and should not be used under any circumstances. Again, this would also apply to the metric equivalent, do not combine meters and centimeters.

NOTE:
- Each set of dimensions should be at least 3/16" apart on separate dimension lines which are to intersect with witness lines. These intersecting points should be indicated by dimension arrows, dots, or slashes.

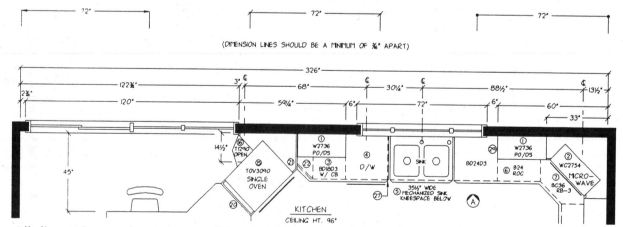

- All dimensions, whenever possible, should be shown **OUTSIDE** the wall lines.

- All lettering should be listed parallel to the title block at the bottom of the vellum paper and break the dimension line near its mid-point. This mechanical drafting technique eliminates errors in reading dimensions.

- An acceptable alternative is to draw all dimensions and lettering so that it is readable from the bottom edge or the right side of the plans with lettering on top of each dimension line.

The following dimensions **MUST** be shown on every floor plan as minimum requirements.

- Overall length of wall areas to receive cabinets, countertops, fixtures, or any equipment occupying floor and/or wall space. This dimension should always be the outside line.

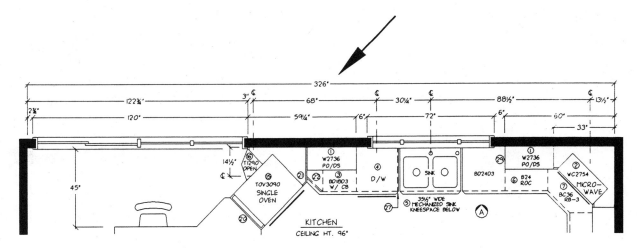

- Each wall opening, (windows, arches, doors and major appliances) and fixed structures (chimneys, wall protrusions and partitions) must be individually dimensioned. Dimensions are shown from outside trim. Trim size must be noted in the specification list. Fixtures such as radiators remaining in place must be outlined on the floor plan. These critical dimensions should be the first dimension line.

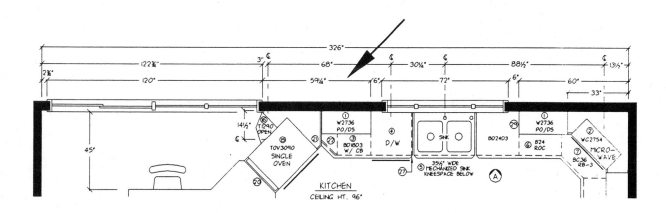

- Ceiling heights should appear on the floor plan. A separate plan for soffits is required when the soffit is a different depth than the wall or tall cabinet below. A separate soffit plan is recommended when the soffit is to be installed **PRIOR** to the wall or tall cabinet installation.

- Additional notes must be included for any deviation from standard height, width and depth. (cabinets, countertops, etc.)

- The exact opening must be given in height, width and depth for areas to be left open to receive equipment, cabinets and appliances at a future date.

- Items such as island and peninsula cabinets, must be shown with the overall dimensions given from countertop edge to opposite countertop edge, tall cabinet or wall. The exact location of the structure must be identified by dimensions which position it from two directions; from return walls or from the face of cabinets/equipment opposite the structure.

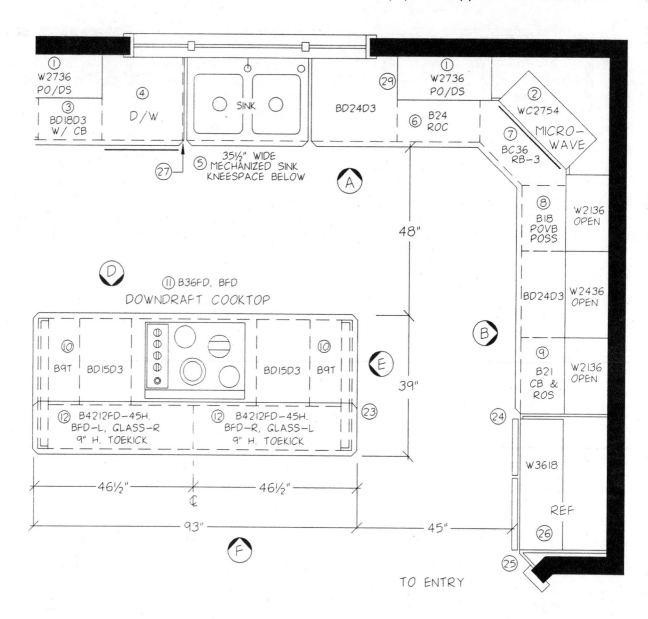

4) Cabinets/Appliances and Equipment Nomenclature and Designation on Floor Plans:

- Cabinets should be designated and identified by manufacturer nomenclature inside the area indicating their position. Cabinet system trim and finish items are designated outside their area, with an arrow clarifying exactly where the trim piece is located. ·

- To insure clarity, some design firms prefer to number and call out all the cabinet nomenclature in the Floor Plan specification listing.

- Equally acceptable is the use of a circled reference number to designate each cabinet on the Floor Plan and Elevations with the cabinet code listed within the individual unit width on the elevations or in a separate cross-reference list on the elevations.

- **Regardless of which cabinet designation system is selected from above, additional information for supplementary fixtures/equipment and special provisions pertaining to the cabinets must be indicated within the cabinet or equipment area by a reference number in a circle. This additional information should then be registered in a cross-referenced specifications listing on the same sheet.**

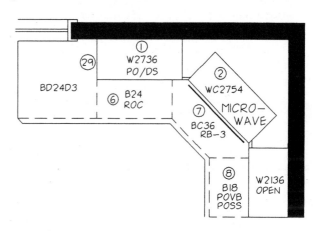

FLOOR PLAN SPECIFICATIONS

① SPECIAL PULL OUT & DOWN SHELVES

② WALL CORNER WITH MICROWAVE BELOW & 1⅞" ANGLED FILLER EACH SIDE

⑥ ROLL-OUT CART

⑦ BASE CORNER WITH 3 RECYCLING BINS

⑧ PULL-OUT VEGGIE BINS & STEP STOOL

㉙ LIGHT VALANCE CREATED ON ALL WALL CABS. WITH 1" RECESSED BOTTOMS

- Special order materials or custom design features, angled cabinets, unusual tops, molding, trim details, etc., should be shown in a section view, (sometimes referred to as a *"cut view"*), a plan view in a scale larger than (1/2 " = 1') (a metric equivalent is acceptable), or in elevation view.

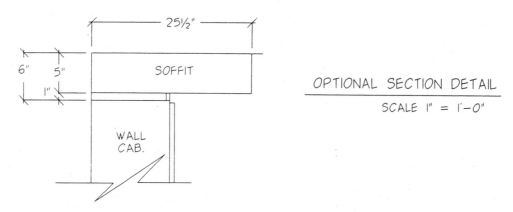

OPTIONAL SECTION DETAIL

SCALE 1" = 1'-0"

III. The Construction Plan

1)   The purpose of the construction plan is to show the relationship of the existing space with that of the new design. The construction plan is detailed separately so that it does not clutter the floor plan. However, if construction changes are minimal it is acceptable to combine the construction plan with either the floor plan or mechanical plan.

2)   **Construction Plan Symbols:**

- Existing walls are shown with solid lines or hollowed out lines at their full thickness.

- Wall sections to be removed are shown with an outline of broken lines.

- New walls show the material symbols applicable to the type of construction or use a symbol which is identified in the legend in order to distinguish them from existing partitions.

EXISTING WALLS TO REMOVE

OR

EXISTING WALLS TO REMAIN

EXISTING OPENINGS TO ENCLOSE

WOOD STUD   METAL STUD

CONCRETE   BRICK

CONCRETE BLOCK   SPECIAL FINISH FACE

NEW WALLS TO BE CONSTRUCTED

* Symbols adapted from Architectural Graphic Standards, 9th Edition

An Example of a Construction Plan:

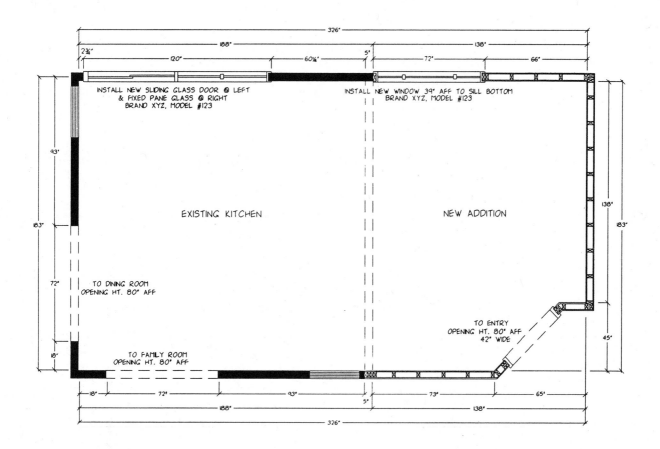

INSTALL NEW SLIDING GLASS DOOR @ LEFT
& FIXED PANE GLASS @ RIGHT
BRAND XYZ, MODEL #123

INSTALL NEW WINDOW 39" AFF TO SILL BOTTOM
BRAND XYZ, MODEL #123

EXISTING KITCHEN

NEW ADDITION

TO DINING ROOM
OPENING HT. 80" AFF

TO ENTRY
OPENING HT. 80" AFF
42" WIDE

TO FAMILY ROOM
OPENING HT. 80" AFF

CONSTRUCTION PLAN LEGEND

EXISTING WALLS TO REMAIN

NEW 16" O.C. WOOD STUD WALLS TO BUILD

EXISTING WALLS TO REMOVE

EXISTING OPENINGS TO ENCLOSE

IV. The Mechanical Plan

- By detailing separate plans for the mechanicals and/or construction, it will help to clearly identify such work without cluttering the kitchen floor plan.

- The mechanical plan should show an outline of the cabinets, countertops and fixtures without nomenclature.

- The mechanicals should be placed in the proper location with the proper symbols.

- All overall room dimensions should be listed.

1) The mechanical plan will consist of the Electrical/Lighting, Plumbing, Heating, Air Conditioning and Ventilation systems. If any minor wall/door construction changes are part of the plan, they should also be detailed on the mechanical plan.

2) A mechanical legend should be prepared on the plan. This legend will be used to describe what each symbol for special purpose outlets, fixtures or equipment means.

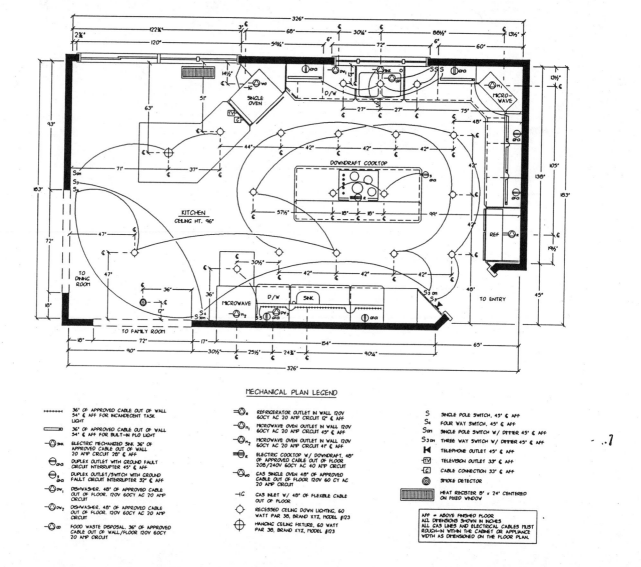

MECHANICAL PLAN LEGEND

3)   Centerline (℄) dimensions must be given for all equipment in two directions when possible.

- Mechanicals requiring centerlines include: cooktops, refrigerators, dishwashers, compactors, sinks, wall ovens, microwave ovens, fan units, light fixtures, heating and air conditioning ducts and radiators.

- Centerline dimensions should be pulled from return walls or from the face of cabinets/equipment opposite the mechanical element.

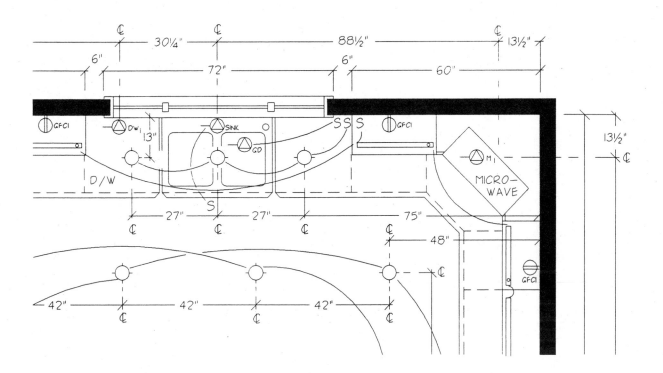

Centerlines on the mechanical plan will be indicated by the symbol (℄) followed by a **long-short-long broken line** that extends into the floor area.

4) Mechanical Plan Symbols:

S	SINGLE POLE SWITCH
S_2	DOUBLE POLE SWITCH
S_3	THREE WAY SWITCH
S_4	FOUR WAY SWITCH
S_{DM}	SINGLE POLE SWITCH w/ DIMMER
S_{3DM}	THREE WAY SWITCH w/ DIMMER
S_{LM}	MASTER SWITCH FOR LOW VOLTAGE SWITCHING SYSTEM
S_L	SWITCH FOR LOW VOLTAGE SWITCHING SYSTEM
S_{WP}	WEATHERPROOF SWITCH
S_{RC}	REMOTE CONTROL SWITCH
S_D	AUTOMATIC DOOR SWITCH
S_P	SWITCH AND PILOT LAMP
S_K	KEY OPERATED SWITCH
S_F	FUSED SWITCH
S_T	TIME SWITCH
(S)	CEILING PULL SWITCH
⊜	DUPLEX OUTLET
⊜GFCI	DUPLEX OUTLET WITH GROUND FAULT CIRCUIT INTERRUPTER
⊖s	SWITCH AND SINGLE RECEPTACLE OUTLET
⊜s	SWITCH AND DUPLEX OUTLET
(B)	BLANKED OUTLET
(J)	JUNCTION BOX
(L)	OUTLET CONTROLLED BY LOW VOLTAGE SWITCHING WHEN RELAY IS INSTALLED IN OUTLET BOX
⊖	SINGLE RECEPTACLE OULET
⊕	TRIPLEX RECEPTACLE OULET
⊕	QUADRUPLEX RECEPTACLE OULET
⊜	DUPLEX RECEPTACLE OUTLET–SPLIT WIRED
⊜	TRIPLEX RECEPTACLE OUTLET–SPLIT WIRED
(C)	CLOCK HANGER RECEPTACLE
(F)	FAN HANGER RECEPTACLE
◁|	INTERCOM
◀	TELEPHONE OUTLET
(T)	THERMOSTAT
◎	SMOKE DETECTOR

—[TV]	TELEVISION OUTLET
—[C]	CABLE OUTLET
[T]L	LOW VOLTAGE TRANSFORMER
⊗	HANGING CEILING FIXTURE
⊕	HEAT LAMP
▬	HEAT/LIGHT UNIT
▦	HEAT/FAN LIGHT UNIT
○	RECESSED CEILING DOWN LIGHTING
●	RECESSED CEILING VAPOR LIGHT
⊢⊢⊣	BUILT-IN LOW VOLTAGE TASK LIGHT
▭	BUILT-IN FLUORESCENT LIGHT
▭	CONTINUOUS ROW FLUORESCENT LIGHTS
▣	SURFACE MOUNTED FLUORESCENT LIGHT
▽	WALL SCONCE
⊖DW	DISHWASHER
⊖GD	FOOD WASTE DISPOSAL
⊖TC	TRASH COMPACTOR
⊜R	REFRIGERATOR OUTLET
⊖H	HOOD
⊖M	MICROWAVE OVEN
⊜R	ELECTRIC RANGE/COOKTOP
⊜WO	ELECTRIC SINGLE/DOUBLE OVEN
—|G	GAS SUPPLY
⊖CT	GAS COOKTOP
⊖WO	GAS SINGLE/DOUBLE OVEN
⊖CW	CLOTHES WASHER
⊜CD	CLOTHES DRYER
⊜SA	SAUNA
⊜ST	STEAM
⊜WP	WHIRLPOOL
⊖TW	TOWEL WARMER
▨	HEAT REGISTER

ANY STANDARD SYMBOL GIVEN ABOVE W/ THE ADDITION OF LOWERCASE SUBSCRIPT LETTERING MAY BE USED TO DESIGNATE A VARIATION OF STANDARD EQUIPMENT.

WHEN USED THEY MUST BE LISTED IN THE LEGEND OF THE MECHANICAL PLAN.

Symbols adapted from Architectural Graphic Standards, 9th Edition

V. Interpretive Drawings

Elevations and perspective renderings are considered interpretive drawings and are used as an explanatory means of understanding the floor plans.

- Under no circumstances should the interpretive drawings be used as a substitute for floor plans.

- In cases of dispute, the floor plans are the legally binding document.

- Because perspective drawings are not dimensioned to scale, many Kitchen Specialists include a disclaimer on their rendering such as this:

> This drawing is an artistic interpretation of the general appearance of the floor plan. It is not meant to be an exact rendition.

1) **Elevation:** Elevations must show a front view of all wall areas receiving cabinets and equipment as shown on the floor plan.

    Elevations should dimension all cabinets, counters, fixtures and equipment in the elevation as follows:

- Cabinets with toekick and finished height.

- A portion of the cabinet doors and drawer front should indicate style and, when applicable, placement of handles/pulls.

- Countertops indicate thickness and show back-splash

- All doors, windows or other openings in walls which will receive equipment. The window/door casing or trim will be listed within the overall opening dimensions.

- All permanent fixtures such as radiators, etc.

- All main structural elements and protrusions such as chimneys, partitions, etc.

- Centerlines for all mechanical equipment.

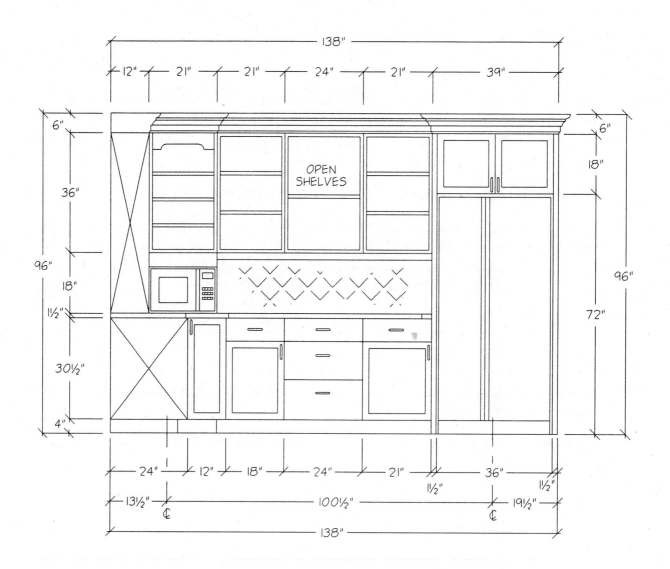

ELEVATION

NOTE:
DIMENSIONS MUST ACCURATELY
REPRESENT PRODUCTS USED.

2)   **Perspective Drawings:** Perspectives are **not drawn to scale.** Grids, which are avail-able through the **National Kitchen & Bath Association**, can be used as an underlay for tracing paper to accurately portray a perspective rendering. Two such grids are displayed on pages 660 and 661 for your reference.

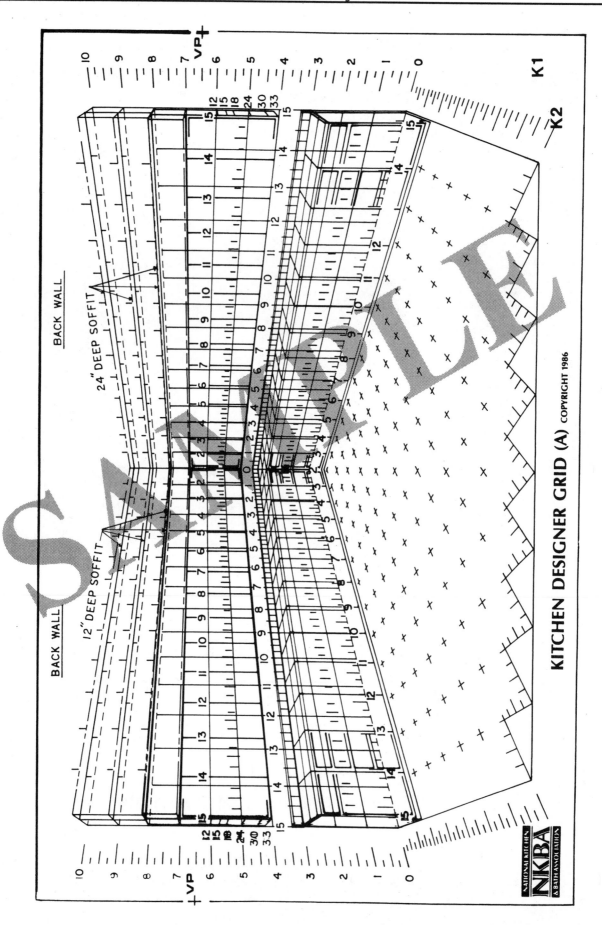

BACK WALL

24" DEEP SOFFIT

BACK WALL

12" DEEP SOFFIT

VP

K1

K2

KITCHEN DESIGNER GRID (A) COPYRIGHT 1986

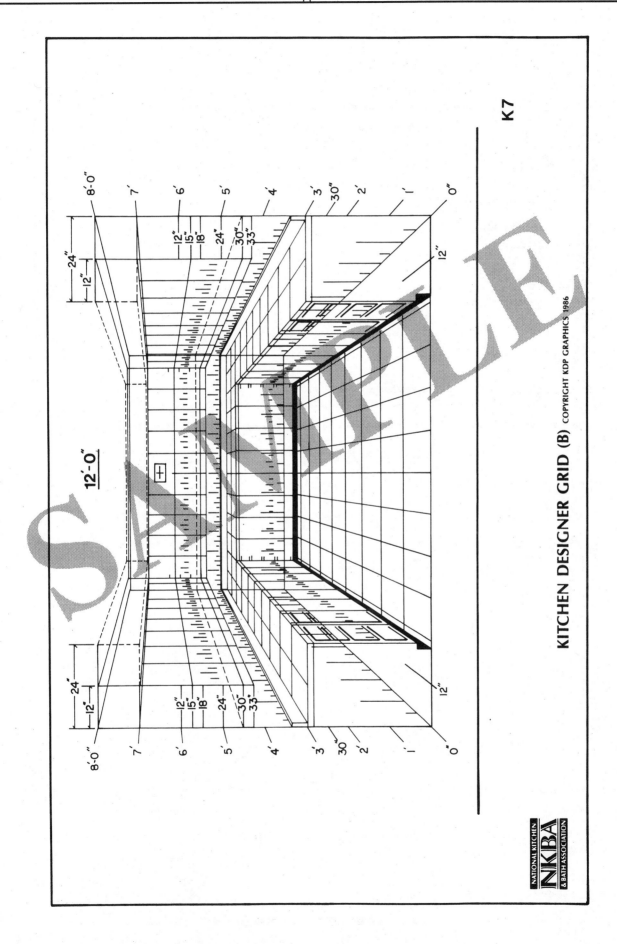

KITCHEN DESIGNER GRID (B) COPYRIGHT KDP GRAPHICS 1986

K7

Designers have the option of preparing a one-point or two-point perspective, with or without the use of a grid.

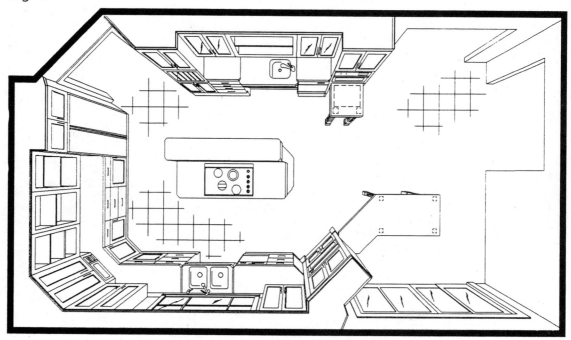

"Birds-Eye View" One Point Perspective

One Point Perspective

- The minimum requirement for perspectives shall be the reasonably correct representation of the longest cabinet or fixture run, or the most important area in terms of usage.

- Perspectives need not show the complete kitchen.

- Separate sectional views of significant areas or features are considered acceptable.

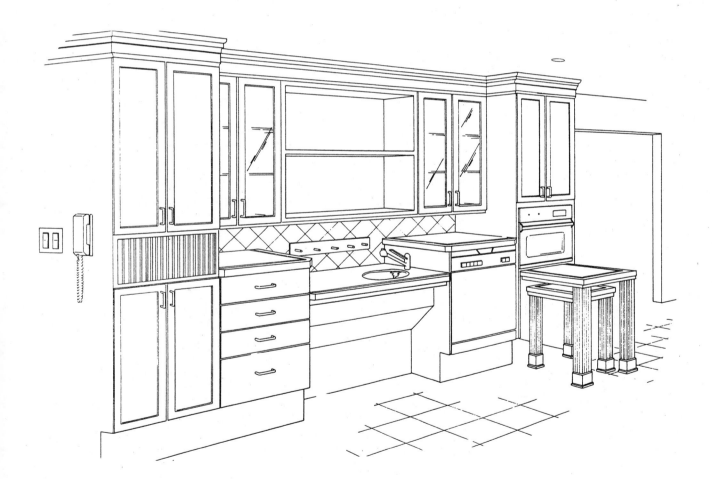

Two Point Perspective

3) **Oblique, Dimetric, Isometric and Trimetric:** Several types of interpretive drawings can be used to illustrate special cabinets and equipment, such as countertops or special order cabinets, where mechanical representation and dimensions are important. These drawings give a simple way to illustrate an object in three-dimensional views.

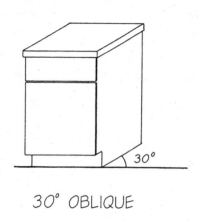

30° OBLIQUE

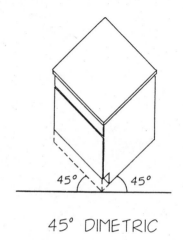

45° DIMETRIC

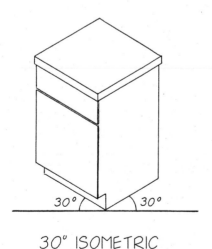

30° ISOMETRIC

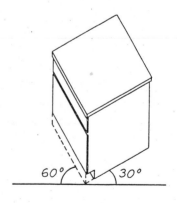

TRIMETRIC

4) **Sketches:** The use of sketches is a quick way to achieve a total picture of the kitchen without exact details in scaled dimensions. This quick freehand sketch can be studied, adjusted and sketched over, as the designer and client attempt to arrive at the most satisfactory layout for the kitchen. The quick sketch then can serve as a guide for drawing an exact plan of the kitchen.

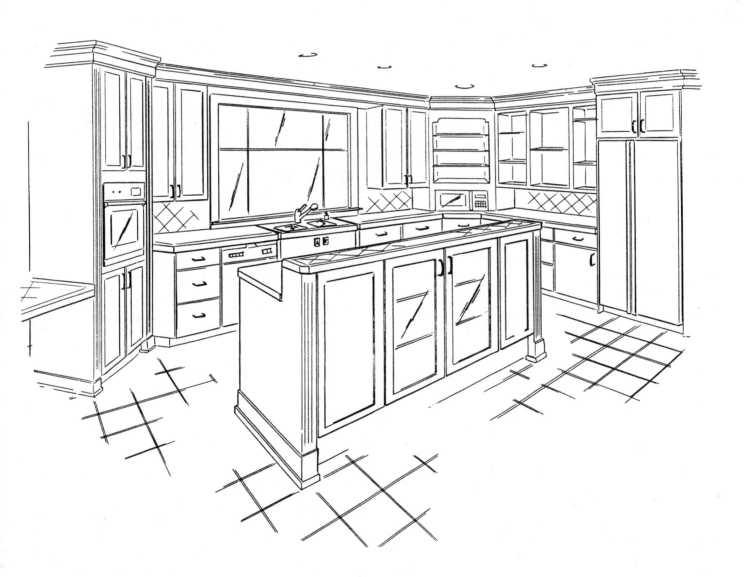

Perspective Sketch

VI. Sample Kitchen Project Drawings

The following set of sample project drawings have been prepared by a Certified Kitchen Designer under the direction of the **National Kitchen & Bath Association.** These sample drawings include:

- Floor Plan

- Construction Plan

- Mechanical Plan

- Countertop Plan *

- Soffit Plan *

- Elevations

- Perspectives

* It is recommended to prepare countertop and soffit plan drawings to further clarify project requirements.

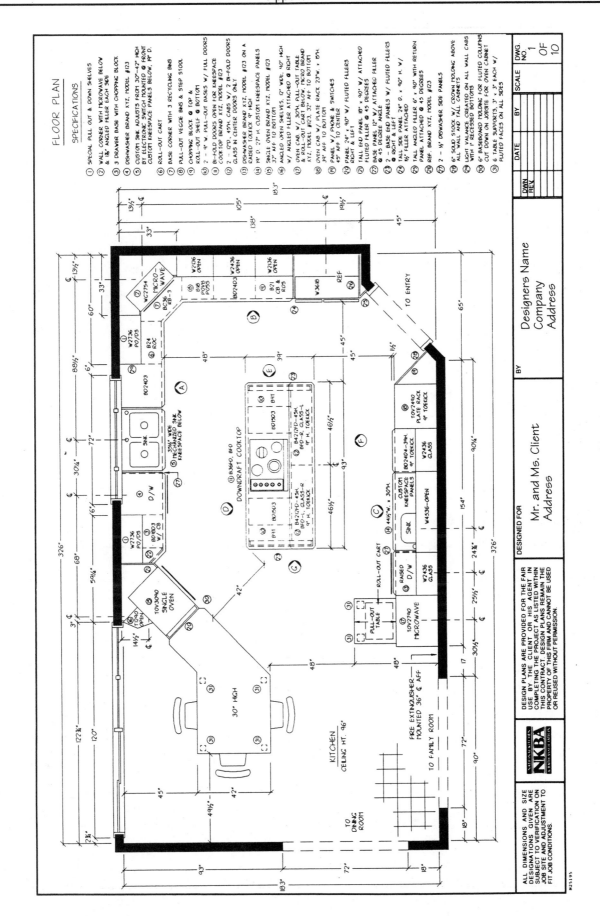

FLOOR PLAN

SPECIFICATIONS

① SPECIAL PULL-OUT & DOWN SHELVES
② WALL CORNER WITH MICROWAVE BELOW & 1¼" ANGLED FILLER EACH SIDE
③ 3 DRAWER BASE WITH CHOPPING BLOCK
④ DISHWASHER BRAND XYZ, MODEL #123
⑤ CUSTOM SINK ADJUSTS FROM 30"-42" HIGH BY ELECTRONIC SWITCH MOUNTED @ FRONT CUSTOM KNEESPACE PANELS BELOW, MY D.
⑥ ROLL-OUT CART
⑦ BASE CORNER WITH 3 RECYCLING BINS
⑧ PULL-OUT VEGGIE BINS & STEP STOOL
⑨ CHOPPING BLOCK @ TOP & ROLL-OUT SHELF @ BOTTOM
⑩ 2 - 9" W. PULL-OUT BASES W/ FULL DOORS
⑪ BI-FOLD DOORS OPEN FOR KNEESPACE COOKTOP BRAND XYZ, MODEL #123
⑫ 2 - 12"D, 45H, CABS W/ 2 BI-FOLD DOORS GLASS IN CENTER DOORS ONLY
⑬ DISHWASHER BRAND XYZ, MODEL #123 ON A RAISED TOEKICK 9" HIGH
⑭ 14" D. 27" H. CUSTOM KNEESPACE PANELS
⑮ SINGLE OVEN BRAND XYZ, MODEL #123 32" AFF TO BOTTOM
⑯ ANGLED OPEN SHELVES, 12" WIDE, 40" HIGH W/ ANGLED FILLER ATTACHED @ RIGHT
⑰ OVEN CAB. W/ 30"H. PULL-OUT TABLE & ROLL-OUT CART BELOW, MICRO BRAND XYZ, MODEL #123, 32" AFF TO BOTTOM
⑱ OVEN CAB W/ PLATE RACK 23"W. x 15¼ 34" AFF TO BOTTOM
⑲ PANEL W/ PHONE & SWITCHES 45" AFF TO CENTER
⑳ PANEL 24" x 90" W/ FLUTED FILLERS
㉑ TALL END PANEL 18" x 90" W/ ATTACHED FLUTED FILLER @ 45 DEGREES
㉒ BASE PANEL 12" W/ ATTACHED FILLER @ 45 DEGREE ANGLE
㉓ 2 - BASE END PANELS W/ FLUTED FILLERS @ RIGHT & LEFT
㉔ TALL SIDE PANEL 24" D. x 90" H. W/ 16" FILLER ATTACHED
㉕ TALL ANGLED FILLER 6" x 90" WITH RETURN PANEL ATTACHED @ 45 DEGREES
㉖ REF. BRAND XYZ, MODEL #123
㉗ 2 - 16" DISHWASHER SIDE PANELS
㉘ 6" SOLID STOCK W/ CROWN MOLDING ABOVE ALL WALL AND TALL CABINETS
㉙ LIGHT VALANCE CREATED ON ALL WALL CABS WITH 1" RECESSED BOTTOMS
㉚ 6" BASEBOARD MOLDING FOR FLUTED COLUMNS CUT DOWN ON JOBSITE FOR OVEN CABINET
㉛ 6 TABLE SUPPORTS, 3" x 3" EACH W/ FLUTED FACES ON ALL SIDES

DESIGNED FOR
Mr. and Ms. Client
Address

BY   Designers Name
                            Company
                            Address

DWN		DATE	BY	SCALE	DWG NO	1
REV						OF
						10

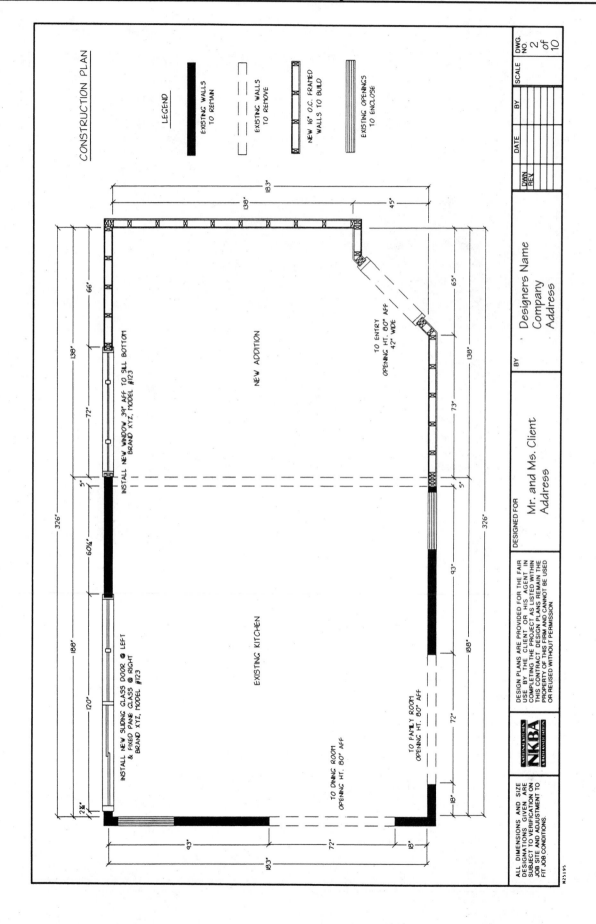

CONSTRUCTION PLAN

LEGEND

EXISTING WALLS TO REMAIN

EXISTING WALLS TO REMOVE

NEW 16" O.C. FRAMED WALLS TO BUILD

EXISTING OPENINGS TO ENCLOSE

INSTALL NEW WINDOW 34" AFF TO SILL BOTTOM BRAND XYZ, MODEL #123

INSTALL NEW SLIDING GLASS DOOR @ LEFT & FIXED PANE GLASS @ RIGHT BRAND XYZ, MODEL #123

NEW ADDITION

EXISTING KITCHEN

TO ENTRY
OPENING HT. 80" AFF
42" WIDE

TO DINING ROOM
OPENING HT. 80" AFF

TO FAMILY ROOM
OPENING HT. 80" AFF

ALL DIMENSIONS AND SIZE DESIGNATIONS GIVEN ARE SUBJECT TO VERIFICATION ON JOB SITE AND ADJUSTMENT TO FIT JOB CONDITIONS.

DESIGN PLANS ARE PROVIDED FOR THE FAIR USE BY THE CLIENT OR HIS AGENT IN COMPLETING THE PROJECT AS LISTED WITHIN THIS CONTRACT. DESIGN PLANS REMAIN THE PROPERTY OF THIS FIRM AND CANNOT BE USED OR REUSED WITHOUT PERMISSION

DESIGNED FOR

Mr. and Ms. Client
Address

BY

Designers Name
Company
Address

DWN
REV

DATE

BY

SCALE

DWG. NO. 2 of 10

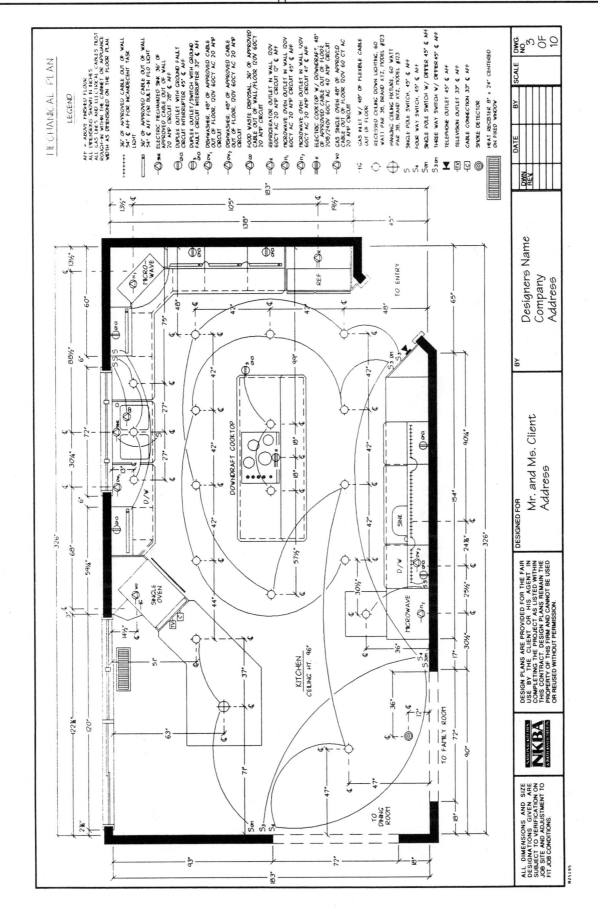

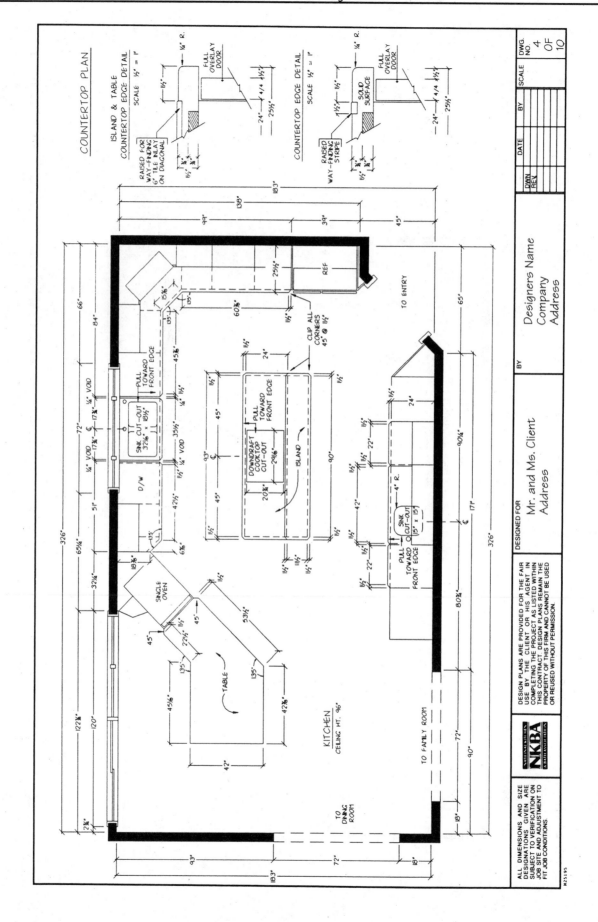

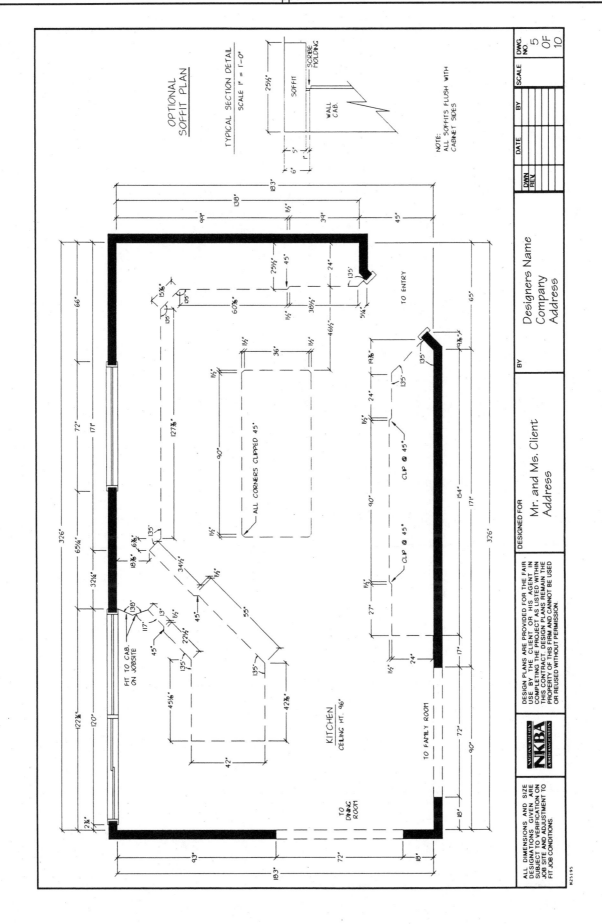

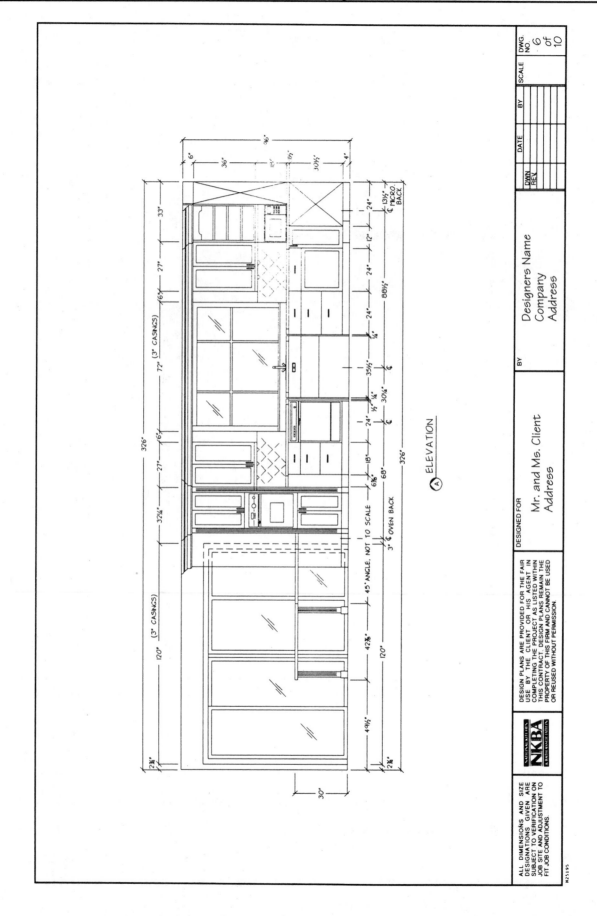

A ELEVATION

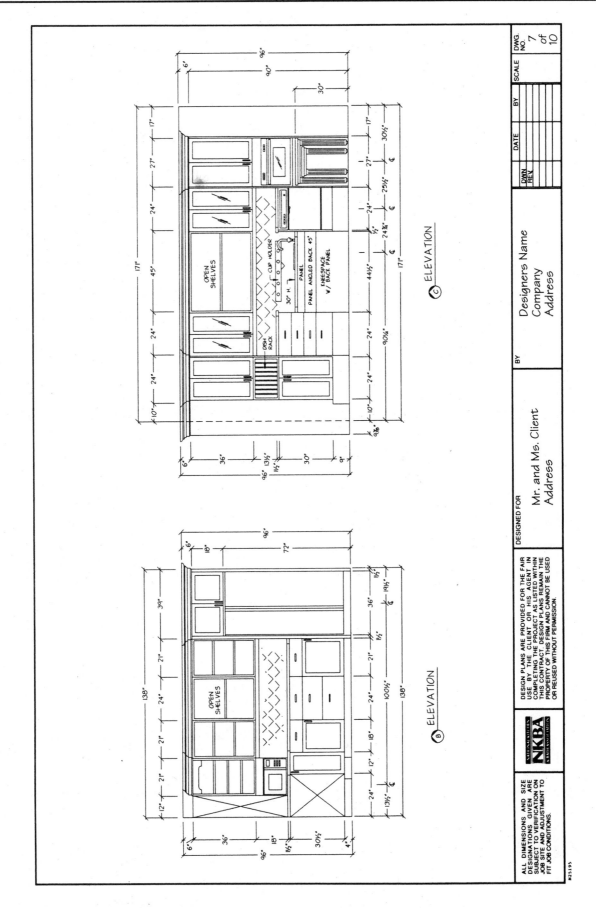

© ELEVATION

Ⓑ ELEVATION

OPEN SHELVES

CLIP HOLDER

DISH RACK

PANEL

PANEL ANGLED BACK 45°

KNEESPACE W/ BACK PANEL

30" H.

OPEN SHELVES

Designers Name
Company
Address

DESIGNED FOR

Mr. and Ms. Client
Address

DESIGN PLANS ARE PROVIDED FOR THE FAIR USE BY THE CLIENT OR HIS AGENT IN COMPLETING THE PROJECT AS LISTED WITHIN THIS CONTRACT. DESIGN PLANS REMAIN THE PROPERTY OF THIS FIRM AND CANNOT BE USED OR REUSED WITHOUT PERMISSION.

ALL DIMENSIONS AND SIZE DESIGNATIONS GIVEN ARE SUBJECT TO VERIFICATION ON JOB SITE AND ADJUSTMENT TO FIT JOB CONDITIONS.

NKBA

DWG. NO. 7 of 10

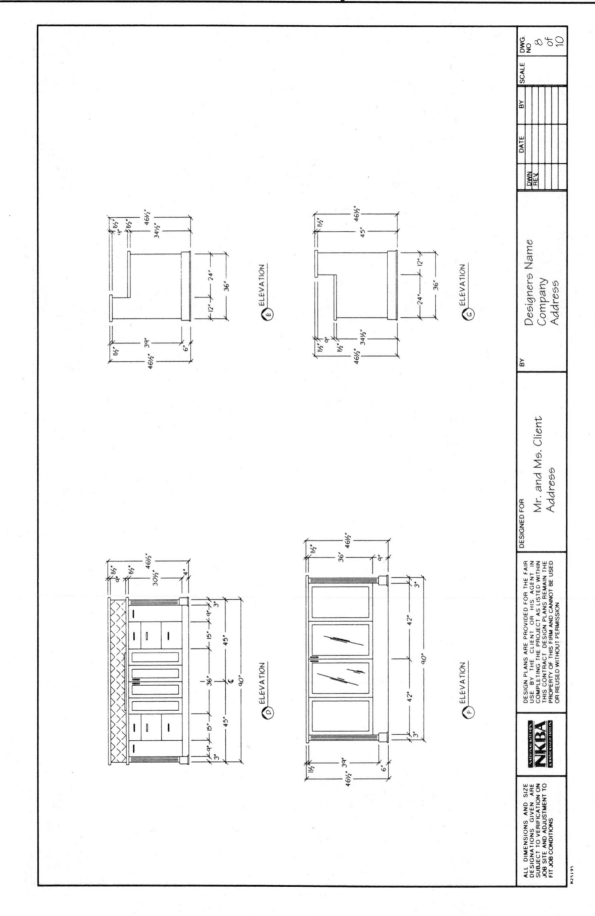

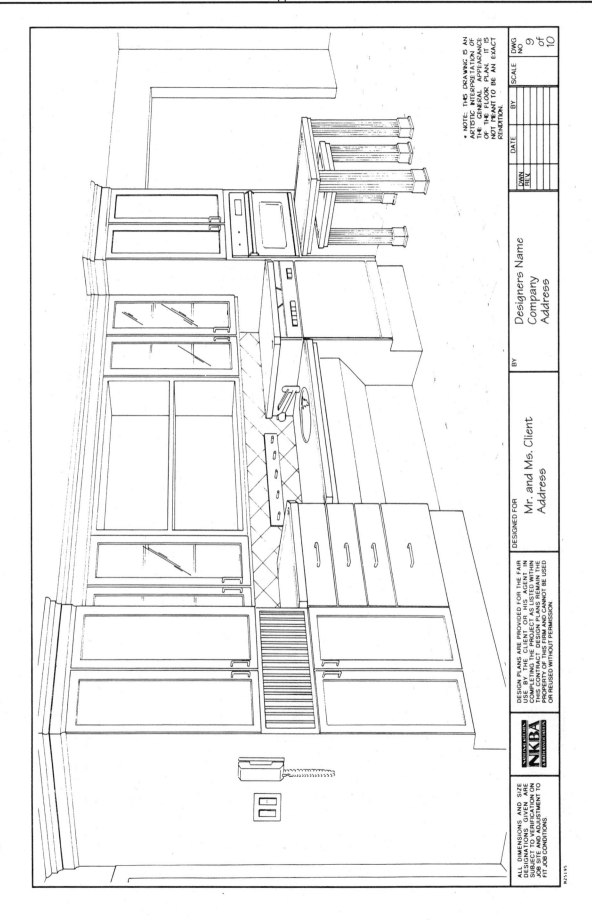

DWG NO 9 of 10

SCALE

BY

DATE

DWN
REV

BY

Designers Name
Company
Address

DESIGNED FOR

Mr. and Ms. Client
Address

NKBA
NATIONAL KITCHEN & BATH ASSOCIATION

DWG. NO. 10 of 10

SCALE

BY

DATE

DWN REV

Designers Name
Company
Address

BY

DESIGNED FOR

Mr. and Ms. Client
Address

NKBA
NATIONAL KITCHEN & BATH ASSOCIATION

General Provisions Using Metric Dimensions

I. Use of Standards

The use of these *National Kitchen & Bath Association Graphics and Presentation Standards* is strongly recommended. They contain a specific set of criteria which when applied by the Kitchen Specialist produce a series of project documents that include the following:

- The Floor Plan

- The Construction Plan

- The Mechanical Plan

- The Interpretive Drawings

    1) Elevations
    2) Perspective Drawings
    3) Oblique, Dimetric, Isometric and Trimetric
    4) Sketches

- Specifications

- Design Statement

- Contracts

Two sample sets of project documents for your review can be found in this publication, one uses imperial dimensions and the other is a metric conversion.

Paper: The acceptable paper for the original drawings of the floor plan, construction plan, mechanical plan, and interpretive drawings is set at a **minimum size of 28cm x 43cm.** Translucent vellum tracing paper, imprinted with a black border and appropriate space available for the insertion of pertinent information is strongly recommended. Copies of original drawings should appear in blue or black ink only on white paper. Ozalid or photocopy prints are acceptable.

The use of lined yellow note paper, typing paper, scored graph paper or scored quadrille paper <u>**is not acceptable.**</u>

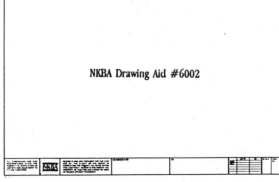

NKBA Drawing Aid #6002

II. The Floor Plan

1)   Size and Scope of Floor Plan Drawings: Kitchen floor plans should be drawn to a scale of 1 to 20 (ie. 1cm = 20cm). When the designer has a room dimensioned in imperial inches and wants to use a metric based cabinet brand, the industry norm is to use a 1:24 metric ratio as equal to a 1/2 inch scale. *** For imperial dimensions, see Use of Standards Using Imperial Dimensions beginning on page 646.**

- All base cabinetry should be depicted using a dashed line (– – – –) while countertops are depicted using a solid line.

- The floor plan should depict the entire room when possible. When the entire room cannot be depicted, it must show the area where cabinetry and appliances are permanently installed.

- Floor plans must show all major structural elements such as walls, door swings, door openings, partitions, windows, archways and equipment.

- When the entire room cannot be depicted, the room must be divided by *"break lines"* (⟋⟍) and must show all major structural elements with adjoining areas indicated and labeled.

Finished interior dimensions are used on all project documents to denote available space for cabinetry and/or other types of equipment. If the kitchen specialist is responsible for specifying the exact method of wall construction, finish and/or partition placement, the specialist should include partition center lines on the construction plan, as well as the finished interior dimensions.

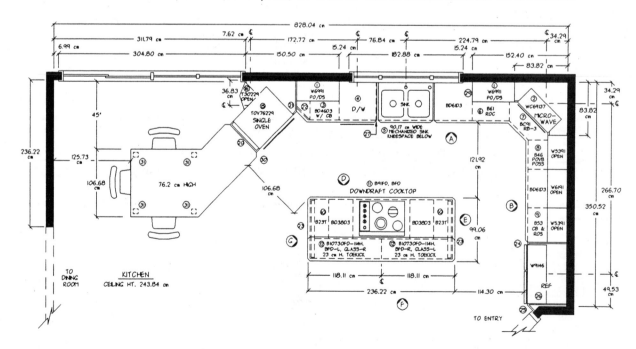

2) **Centerline (℄) dimensions:** must be given for equipment in two directions when possible.

- Mechanicals requiring centerlines include: cooktops, refrigerators, sinks, wall ovens, microwave ovens, fan units, light fixtures, heating and air conditioning ducts and radiators.

- Dimensions should be pulled from return walls or from the face of cabinets/equipment opposite the mechanical element.

- Centerlines on the mechanical plan will be indicated by the symbol (℄) followed by a **long-short-long broken line** that extends into the floor area.

- When the centerline dimension line is outside the floor area, it is typically shown as the second (and, if required, the third) line following the dimension line which identifies the individual wall segments.

℄ ——— · ——— · — · — · ——— · ——— · — · ———

3) **Dimensioning of Floor Plan:** When using metric dimensions, some designers also list all wall dimensions in inches. This double sizing helps all parties involved clearly understand the plans.

An example of Time Saving Formulas to convert between metrics would be as follows:

Inches to Centimeters, multiply the total number of inches by 2.54
Centimeters to Inches, multiply the total number of centimeters by .3937

NOTE:
- Each set of dimensions should be at least .5cm apart on separate dimension lines which are to intersect with witness lines. These intersecting points should be indicated by dimension arrows, dots, or slashes.

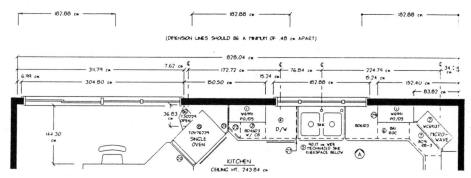

- All dimensions, whenever possible, should be shown **OUTSIDE** the wall lines.

- All lettering should be listed parallel to the title block at the bottom of the vellum paper and break the dimension line near its mid-point. This mechanical drafting technique eliminates errors in reading dimensions.

- An acceptable alternative is to draw all dimensions and lettering so that it is readable from the bottom edge or the right side of the plans with lettering on top of each dimension line.

The following dimensions **MUST** be shown on every floor plan as minimum requirements.

- Overall length of wall areas to receive cabinets, countertops, fixtures, or any equipment occupying floor and/or wall space. This dimension should always be the outside line.

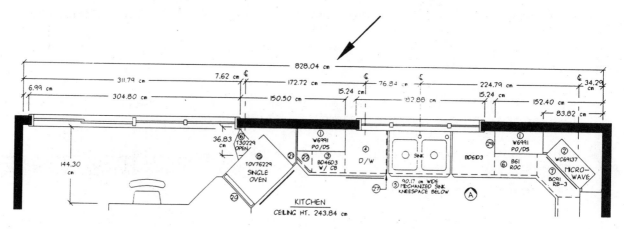

- Each wall opening, (windows, arches, doors and major appliances) and fixed structures (chimneys, wall protrusions and partitions) must be individually dimensioned. Dimensions are shown from outside trim. Trim size must be noted in the specification list. Fixtures such as radiators remaining in place must be outlined on the floor plan. These critical dimensions should be the first dimension line.

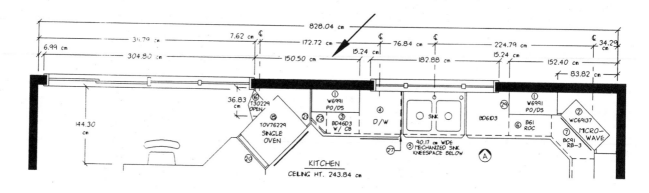

- Ceiling heights should appear on the floor plan. A separate plan for soffits is required when the soffit is a different depth than the wall or tall cabinet below. A separate soffit plan is recommended when the soffit is to be installed **PRIOR** to the wall or tall cabinet installation.

- Additional notes must be included for any deviation from standard height, width and depth. (cabinets, countertops, etc.)

- The exact opening must be given in height, width and depth for areas to be left open to receive cabinets and appliances at a future date.

- Items such as island and peninsula cabinets, must be shown with the overall dimensions given from countertop edge to opposite countertop edge, tall cabinet or wall. The exact location of the structure must be identified by dimensions which position it from two directions; from return walls or from the face of cabinets/equipment opposite the structure.

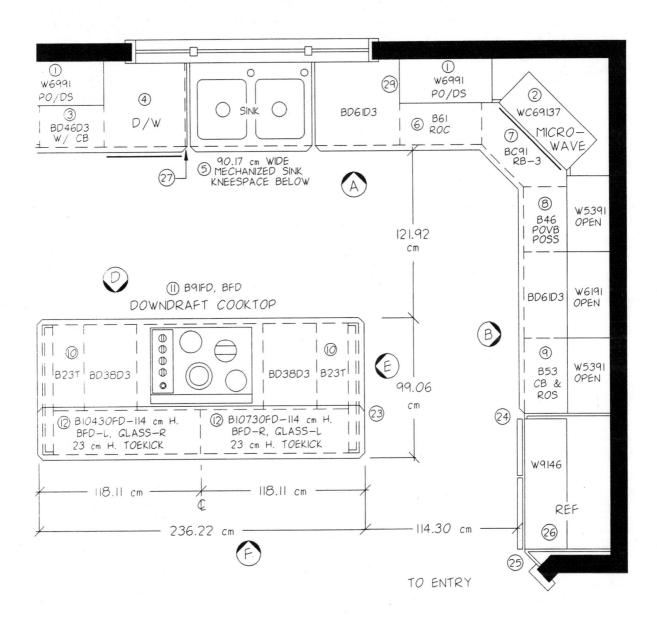

4) Cabinets/Appliances and Equipment Nomenclature and Designation on Floor Plans:

- Cabinets should be designated and identified by manufacturer nomenclature inside the area indicating their position. Cabinet system trim and finish items are designated outside their area, with an arrow clarifying exactly where the trim piece is located.

- To insure clarity, some design firms prefer to number and call out all the cabinet nomenclature in the Floor Plan specification listing.

- Equally acceptable is the use of a circled reference number to designate each cabinet on the Floor Plan and Elevations with the cabinet code listed within the individual unit width on the elevations or in a separate cross-reference list on the elevations.

- **Regardless of which cabinet designation system is selected from above, additional information for supplementary fixtures/equipment and special provisions pertaining to the cabinets must be indicated within the cabinet or equipment area by a reference number in a circle. This additional information should then be registered in a cross-referenced specifications listing on the same sheet.**

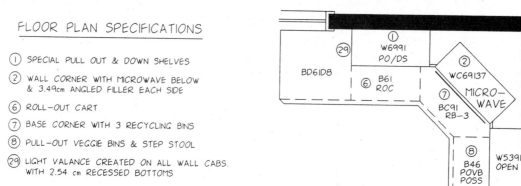

FLOOR PLAN SPECIFICATIONS

① SPECIAL PULL OUT & DOWN SHELVES
② WALL CORNER WITH MICROWAVE BELOW & 3.49cm ANGLED FILLER EACH SIDE
⑥ ROLL-OUT CART
⑦ BASE CORNER WITH 3 RECYCLING BINS
⑧ PULL-OUT VEGGIE BINS & STEP STOOL
㉙ LIGHT VALANCE CREATED ON ALL WALL CABS. WITH 2.54 cm RECESSED BOTTOMS

Special order materials or custom design features, angled cabinets, unusual tops, molding, trim details, etc., should be shown in a section view, (sometimes referred to as a "*cut view*"), a plan view in a scale larger than (1cm = 20cm), or in elevation view.

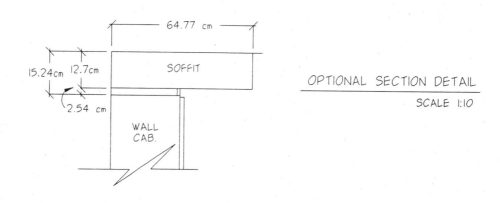

OPTIONAL SECTION DETAIL

SCALE 1:10

III. The Construction Plan

1)   The purpose of the construction plan is to show the relationship of the existing space with that of the new design. The construction plan is detailed separately so that it does not clutter the floor plan. However, if construction changes are minimal it is acceptable to combine the construction plan with either the floor plan or mechanical plan.

2)   **Construction Plan Symbols:**

- Existing walls are shown with solid lines or hollowed out lines at their full thickness.

- Wall sections to be removed are shown with an outline of broken lines.

- New walls show the material symbols applicable to the type of construction or use a symbol which is identified in the legend in order to distinguish them from existing partitions.

OR

EXISTING WALLS TO REMAIN

EXISTING WALLS TO REMOVE

EXISTING OPENINGS TO ENCLOSE

WOOD STUD   METAL STUD

CONCRETE   BRICK

CONCRETE BLOCK   SPECIAL FINISH FACE

NEW WALLS TO BE CONSTRUCTED

* Symbols adapted from Architectural Graphic Standards, 9th Edition

An Example of a Construction Plan:

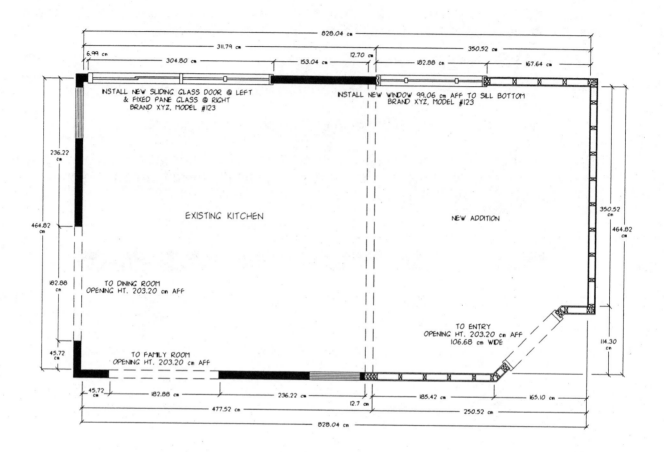

INSTALL NEW SLIDING GLASS DOOR @ LEFT
& FIXED PANE GLASS @ RIGHT
BRAND XYZ, MODEL #123

INSTALL NEW WINDOW 99.06 cm AFF TO SILL BOTTOM
BRAND XYZ, MODEL #123

EXISTING KITCHEN

NEW ADDITION

TO DINING ROOM
OPENING HT. 203.20 cm AFF

TO ENTRY
OPENING HT. 203.20 cm AFF
106.68 cm WIDE

TO FAMILY ROOM
OPENING HT. 203.20 cm AFF

CONSTRUCTION PLAN LEGEND

EXISTING WALLS TO REMAIN

NEW 40.64 cm O.C. FRAMED WALLS TO BUILD

EXISTING WALLS TO REMOVE

EXISTING WALLS TO ENCLOSE

IV. The Mechanical Plan

- By detailing separate plans for the mechanicals and/or construction, it will help to clearly identify such work without cluttering the kitchen floor plan.

- The mechanical plan should show an outline of the cabinets, countertops and fixtures without nomenclature.

- The mechanicals should be placed in the proper location with the proper symbols.

- All overall room dimensions should be listed.

1) The mechanical plan will consist of the Electrical/Lighting, Plumbing, Heating, Air Conditioning and Ventilation systems. If any minor wall/door construction changes are part of the plan, they should also be detailed on the mechanical plan.

2) A mechanical legend should be prepared on the plan. This legend will be used to describe what each symbol for special purpose outlets, fixtures or equipment means.

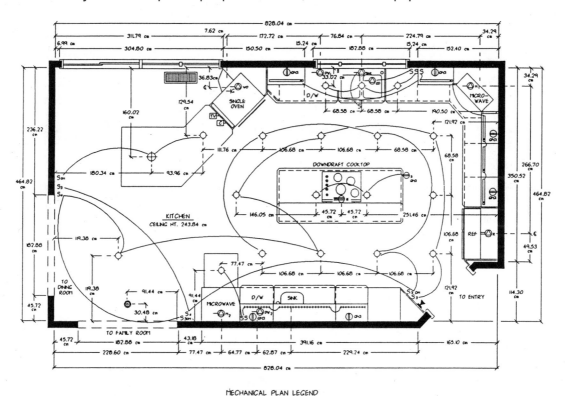

3)   Centerline (℄) dimensions must be given for all equipment in two directions when possible.

- Mechanicals requiring centerlines include: cooktops, refrigerators, dishwashers, compactors, sinks, wall ovens, microwave ovens, fan units, light fixtures, heating and air conditioning ducts and radiators.

- Centerline dimensions should be pulled from return walls or from the face of cabinets/equipment opposite the mechanical element.

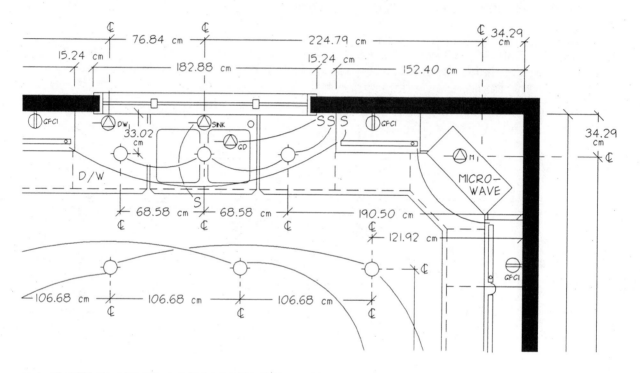

Centerlines on the mechanical plan will be indicated by the symbol (℄) followed by a **long-short-long broken line** that extends into the floor area.

4)   Mechanical Plan Symbols:

S	SINGLE POLE SWITCH
S_2	DOUBLE POLE SWITCH
S_3	THREE WAY SWITCH
S_4	FOUR WAY SWITCH
S_{DM}	SINGLE POLE SWITCH w/ DIMMER
S_{3DM}	THREE WAY SWITCH w/ DIMMER
S_{LM}	MASTER SWITCH FOR LOW VOLTAGE SWITCHING SYSTEM
S_L	SWITCH FOR LOW VOLTAGE SWITCHING SYSTEM
S_{WP}	WEATHERPROOF SWITCH
S_{RC}	REMOTE CONTROL SWITCH
S_D	AUTOMATIC DOOR SWITCH
S_P	SWITCH AND PILOT LAMP
S_K	KEY OPERATED SWITCH
S_F	FUSED SWITCH
S_T	TIME SWITCH
Ⓢ	CEILING PULL SWITCH
	DUPLEX OUTLET
$GFCI$	DUPLEX OUTLET WITH GROUND FAULT CIRCUIT INTERRUPTER
S	SWITCH AND SINGLE RECEPTACLE OUTLET
S	SWITCH AND DUPLEX OUTLET
B	BLANKED OUTLET
J	JUNCTION BOX
L	OUTLET CONTROLLED BY LOW VOLTAGE SWITCHING WHEN RELAY IS INSTALLED IN OUTLET BOX
	SINGLE RECEPTACLE OULET
	TRIPLEX RECEPTACLE OULET
	QUADRUPLEX RECEPTACLE OULET
	DUPLEX RECEPTACLE OUTLET—SPLIT WIRED
	TRIPLEX RECEPTACLE OUTLET—SPLIT WIRED
C	CLOCK HANGER RECEPTACLE
F	FAN HANGER RECEPTACLE
	INTERCOM
	TELEPHONE OUTLET
T	THERMOSTAT
	SMOKE DETECTOR

TV	TELEVISION OUTLET
C	CABLE OUTLET
T $_L$	LOW VOLTAGE TRANSFORMER
	HANGING CEILING FIXTURE
	HEAT LAMP
	HEAT/LIGHT UNIT
	HEAT/FAN LIGHT UNIT
	RECESSED CEILING DOWN LIGHTING
	RECESSED CEILING VAPOR LIGHT
	BUILT-IN LOW VOLTAGE TASK LIGHT
	BUILT-IN FLUORESCENT LIGHT
	CONTINUOUS ROW FLUORESCENT LIGHTS
	SURFACE MOUNTED FLUORESCENT LIGHT
	WALL SCONCE
DW	DISHWASHER
GD	FOOD WASTE DISPOSAL
TC	TRASH COMPACTOR
R	REFRIGERATOR OUTLET
H	HOOD
M	MICROWAVE OVEN
R	ELECTRIC RANGE/COOKTOP
WO	ELECTRIC SINGLE/DOUBLE OVEN
G	GAS SUPPLY
CT	GAS COOKTOP
WO	GAS SINGLE/DOUBLE OVEN
CW	CLOTHES WASHER
CD	CLOTHES DRYER
SA	SAUNA
ST	STEAM
WP	WHIRLPOOL
TW	TOWEL WARMER
	HEAT REGISTER

ANY STANDARD SYMBOL GIVEN ABOVE W/ THE ADDITION OF LOWERCASE SUBSCRIPT LETTERING MAY BE USED TO DESIGNATE A VARIATION OF STANDARD EQUIPMENT.

WHEN USED THEY MUST BE LISTED IN THE LEGEND OF THE MECHANICAL PLAN.

Symbols adapted from Architectural Graphic Standards, 9th Edition

V. Interpretive Drawings

Elevations and perspective renderings are considered interpretive drawings and are used as an explanatory means of understanding the floor plans.

- Under no circumstances should the interpretive drawings be used as a substitute for floor plans.

- In cases of dispute, the floor plans are the legally binding document.

- Because perspective drawings are not dimensioned to scale, many Kitchen Specialists include a disclaimer on their rendering such as this:

This drawing is an artistic interpretation of the general appearance of the floor plan. It is not meant to be an exact rendition.

---

1) **Elevation:** Elevations must show a front view of all wall areas receiving cabinets/equipment as shown on the floor plan.

Elevations should dimension all cabinets, counters, fixtures and equipment in the elevation as follows:

- Cabinets with toekick and finished height.

- A portion of the cabinet doors and drawer front should indicate style and, when applicable, placement of handles/pulls.

- Countertops indicate thickness and show back-splash.

- All doors, windows or other openings in walls which will receive equipment. The window/door casing or trim will be listed within the overall opening dimensions.

- All permanent fixtures such as radiators, etc.

- All main structural elements and protrusions such as chimneys, partitions, etc.

- Centerlines for all mechanical equipment.

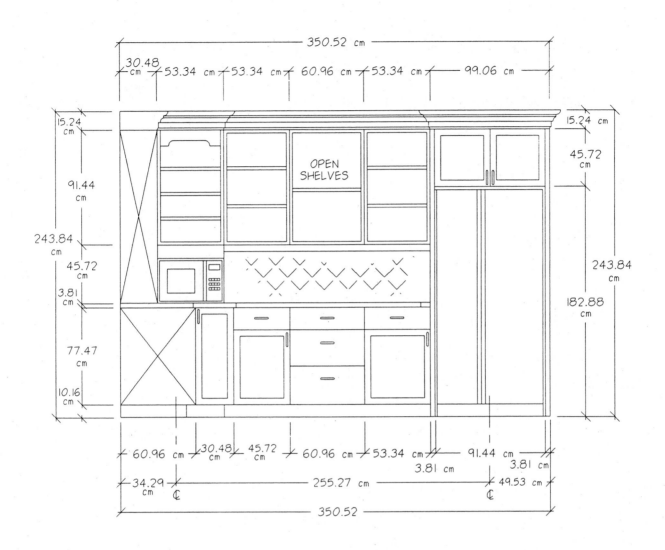

ELEVATION

Ⓑ

NOTE:
DIMENSIONS MUST ACCURATELY
REPRESENT PRODUCTS USED.

2) **Perspective Drawings:** Perspectives are **not drawn to scale.** Grids, which are available through the **National Kitchen & Bath Association**, can be used as an underlay for tracing paper to accurately portray a perspective rendering. Two such grids are displayed on pages 691 and 692 for your reference.

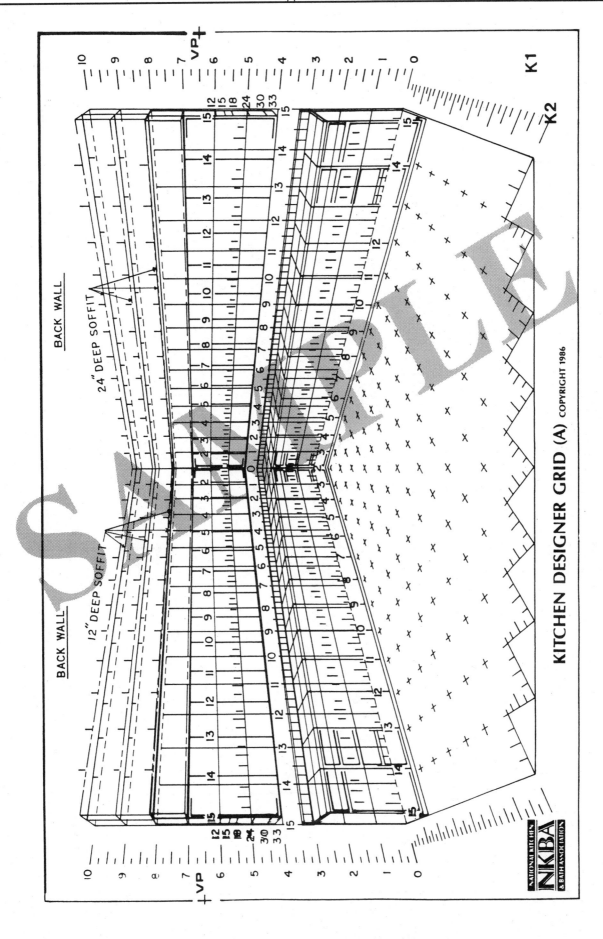

KITCHEN DESIGNER GRID (A) COPYRIGHT 1986

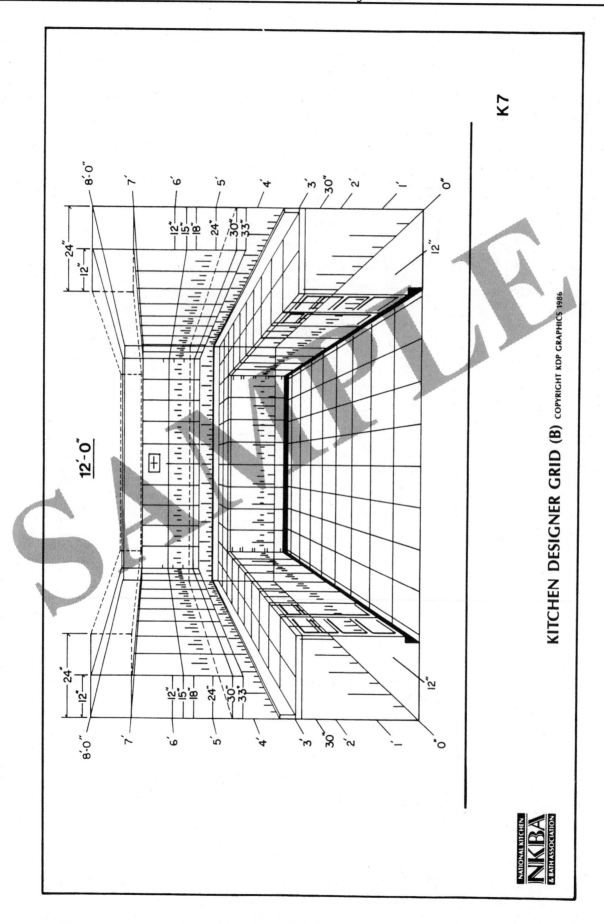

KITCHEN DESIGNER GRID (B) COPYRIGHT KDP GRAPHICS 1986

K7

Designers have the option of preparing a one-point or two-point perspective, with or without the use of a grid.

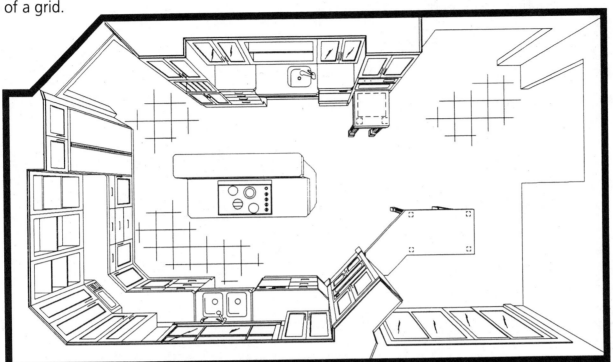

"Birds-Eye View" One Point Perspective

One Point Perspective

- The minimum requirement for perspectives shall be the reasonably correct representation of the longest cabinet or fixture run, or the most important area in terms of usage.

- Perspectives need not show the complete kitchen.

- Separate sectional views of significant areas or features are considered acceptable.

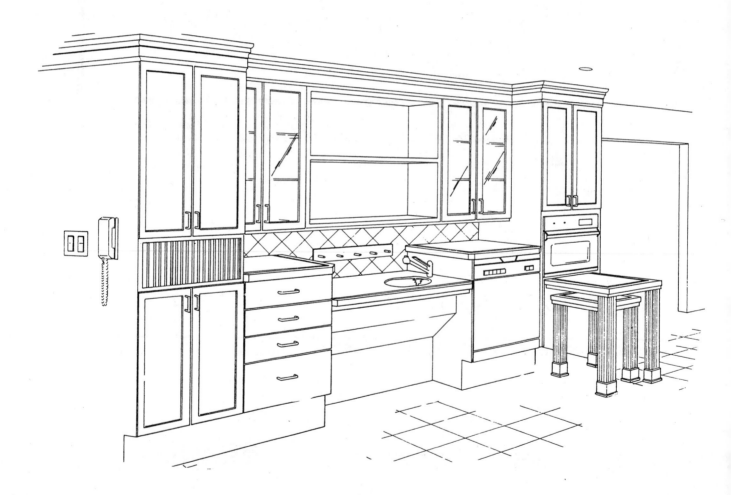

Two Point Perspective

3) **Oblique, Dimetric, Isometric and Trimetric:** Several types of interpretive drawings can be used to illustrate special cabinets and equipment, such as countertops or special order cabinets, where mechanical representation and dimensions are important. These drawings give a simple way to illustrate an object in three-dimensional views.

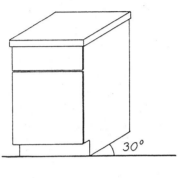

30° OBLIQUE

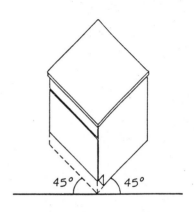

45° DIMETRIC

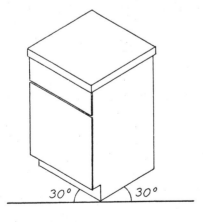

30° ISOMETRIC

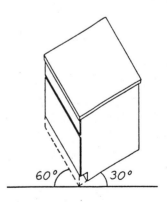

TRIMETRIC

4) **Sketches:** The use of sketches is a quick way to achieve a total picture of the kitchen without exact details in scaled dimensions. This quick freehand sketch can be studied, adjusted and sketched over, as the designer and client attempt to arrive at the most satisfactory layout for the kitchen. The quick sketch then can serve as a guide for drawing an exact plan of the kitchen.

Perspective Sketch

VI. Sample Kitchen Project Drawings

The following set of sample project drawings have been prepared by a Certified Kitchen Designer under the direction of the **National Kitchen & Bath Association.** These sample drawings include:

- Floor Plan

- Construction Plan

- Mechanical Plan

- Countertop Plan *

- Soffit Plan *

- Elevations

- Perspectives

* It is recommended to prepare countertop and soffit plan drawings to further clarify project requirements.

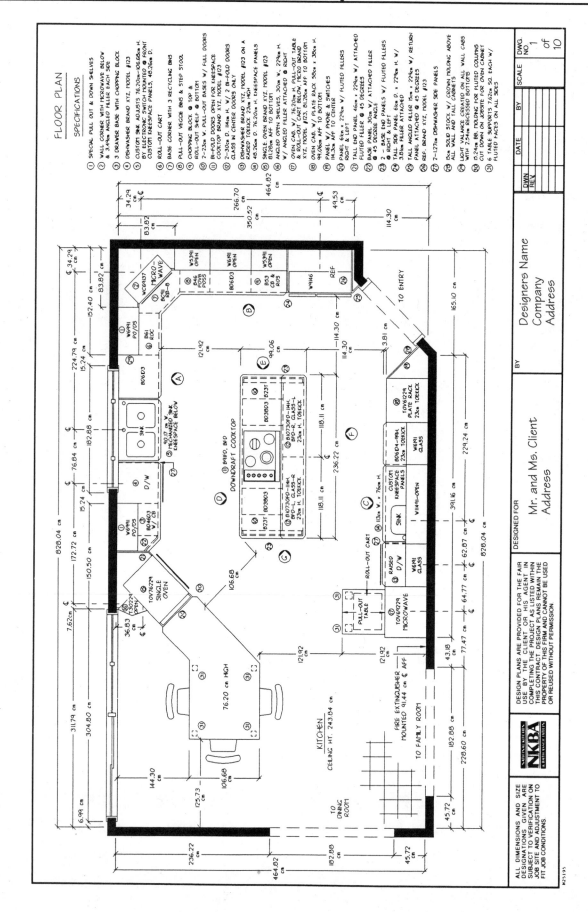

FLOOR PLAN

SPECIFICATIONS

1. SPECIAL PULL-OUT & DOWN SHELVES
2. WALL CORNER WITH MICROWAVE BELOW & 3.49cm ANGLED FILLER EACH SIDE
3. 3 DRAWER BASE WITH CHOPPING BLOCK
4. DISHWASHER BRAND XYZ, MODEL #123
5. CUSTOM SINK ADJUSTS 76.20cm-106.68cm H. BY ELECTRONIC SWITCH MOUNTED @ FRONT CUSTOM KNEESPACE PANELS, 48.26cm D.
6. ROLL-OUT CART
7. BASE CORNER WITH 3 RECYCLING BINS
8. PULL-OUT VEGGIE BINS & STEP STOOL
9. CHOPPING BLOCK @ TOP & ROLL-OUT SHELF @ BOTTOM
10. 2-23cm W. PULL-OUT BASES W/ FULL DOORS
11. BI-FOLD DOORS OPEN FOR KNEESPACE COOKTOP BRAND XYZ, MODEL #123
12. 2-30cm D. 14cm H. W/ 2 BI-FOLD DOORS GLASS N CENTER DOORS ONLY
13. DISHWASHER BRAND XYZ, MODEL #123 ON A RAISED TOEKICK 23cm HIGH
14. 48.26cm D. 76.20cm H. KNEESPACE PANELS
15. SINGLE OVEN BRAND XYZ, MODEL #123 81.28cm AFF TO BOTTOM
16. ANGLED OPEN SHELVES, 30cm W., 229cm H. W/ ANGLED FILLER ATTACHED @ RIGHT
17. OVEN CAB. W/ 76.20cm H. PULL-OUT TABLE & ROLL-OUT CART BELOW MICRO BRAND XYZ, MODEL #123, 81.28cm AFF TO BOTTOM
18. OVEN CAB. W/ PLATE RACK 58cm & 38cm H. 149.06cm AFF TO BOTTOM
19. PANEL W/ PHONE & SWITCHES 143.3cm AFF TO CENTER
20. TALL ANGLED FILLER 6cm & 229cm H. W/ FLUTED FILLERS RIGHT & LEFT
21. TALL END PANEL 46cm & 229cm W/ ATTACHED FLUTED FILLER @ 45 DEGREES
22. BASE PANEL 30cm W/ ATTACHED FILLER @ 45 DEGREE ANGLE
23. 2 - BASE END PANELS W/ FLUTED FILLERS @ RIGHT & LEFT
24. TALL SIDE PANEL 6cm D. x 229cm H. W/ 3.81cm FILLER ATTACHED
25. TALL ANGLED FILLER 15cm x 229cm W/ RETURN PANEL ATTACHED @ 45 DEGREES
26. REF. BRAND XYZ, MODEL #123
27. 2-127cm DISHWASHER SIDE PANELS
28. 8cm SOLID STOCK W/ CROWN MOLDING ABOVE ALL WALL AND TALL CABINETS
29. LIGHT VALANCE CREATED ON ALL WALL CABS WITH 2.54cm RECESSED BOTTOMS
30. 15.24cm BB. MOLDING FOR FLUTED COLUMNS G-11 DOWN ON JOBSITE FOR OVEN CABINET
31. 6 TABLE SUPPORTS 7.62cm SQ. EACH W/ FLUTED FACES ON ALL SIDES

NKBA

DESIGNED FOR

Mr. and Ms. Client
Address

BY

Designers Name
Company
Address

	DATE	BY	SCALE	DWG. NO. 1
DWN				of 10
REV				

M25195

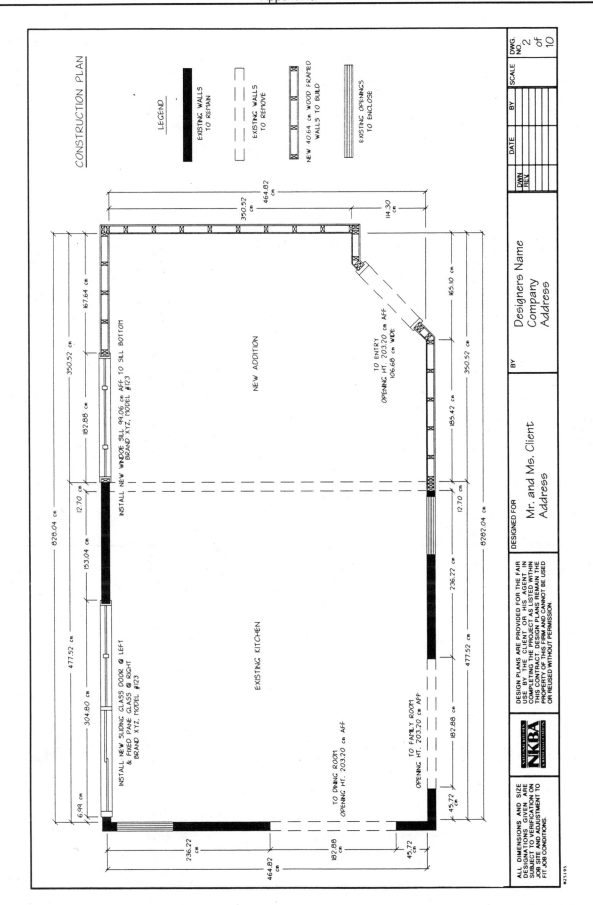

CONSTRUCTION PLAN

LEGEND

EXISTING WALLS TO REMAIN

EXISTING WALLS TO REMOVE

NEW 40.64 cm WOOD FRAMED WALLS TO BUILD

EXISTING OPENINGS TO ENCLOSE

NEW ADDITION

EXISTING KITCHEN

INSTALL NEW WINDOW SILL 94.06 cm AFF TO SILL BOTTOM BRAND XYZ, MODEL #123

INSTALL NEW SLIDING GLASS DOOR @ LEFT & FIXED PANE GLASS @ RIGHT BRAND XYZ, MODEL #123

TO ENTRY OPENING HT. 203.20 cm AFF 106.68 cm WIDE

TO DINING ROOM OPENING HT. 203.20 cm AFF

TO FAMILY ROOM OPENING HT. 203.20 cm AFF

464.82 cm
350.52 cm
114.30 cm
165.10 cm
167.64 cm
350.52 cm
182.88 cm
12.70 cm
153.04 cm
304.80 cm
477.52 cm
6.94 cm
828.04 cm
185.42 cm
12.70 cm
236.22 cm
477.52 cm
182.88 cm
45.72 cm
8282.04 cm
350.52 cm
236.22 cm
464.82 cm
182.88 cm
45.72 cm

DWG. NO. 2 of 10

SCALE

BY

DATE

DWN
REV

Designers Name
Company
Address

BY

DESIGNED FOR

Mr. and Ms. Client
Address

DESIGN PLANS ARE PROVIDED FOR THE FAIR USE BY THE CLIENT OR HIS AGENT IN COMPLETING THE PROJECT AS LISTED WITHIN THIS CONTRACT. DESIGN PLANS REMAIN THE PROPERTY OF THIS FIRM AND CANNOT BE USED OR REUSED WITHOUT PERMISSION

NKBA

ALL DIMENSIONS AND SIZE DESIGNATIONS GIVEN ARE SUBJECT TO VERIFICATION ON JOB SITE AND ADJUSTMENT TO FIT JOB CONDITIONS.

N25195

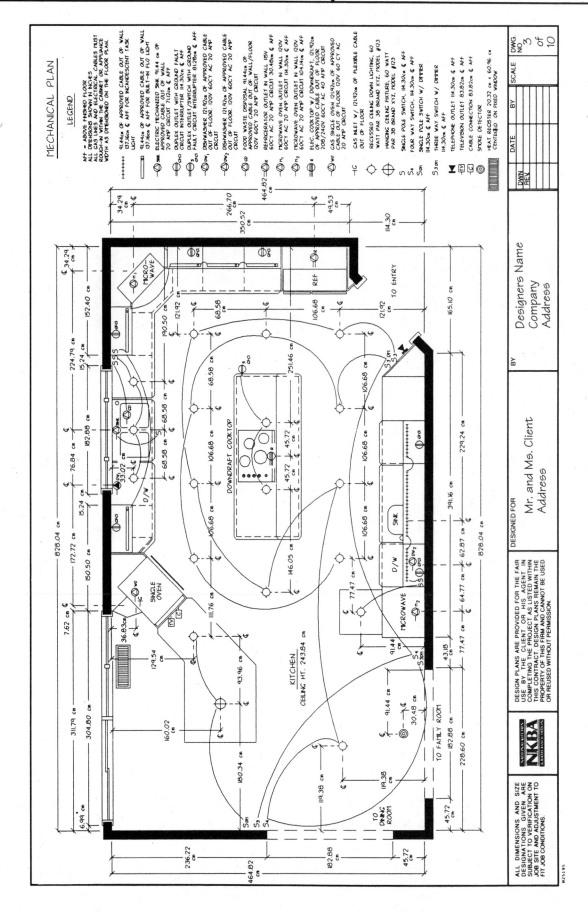

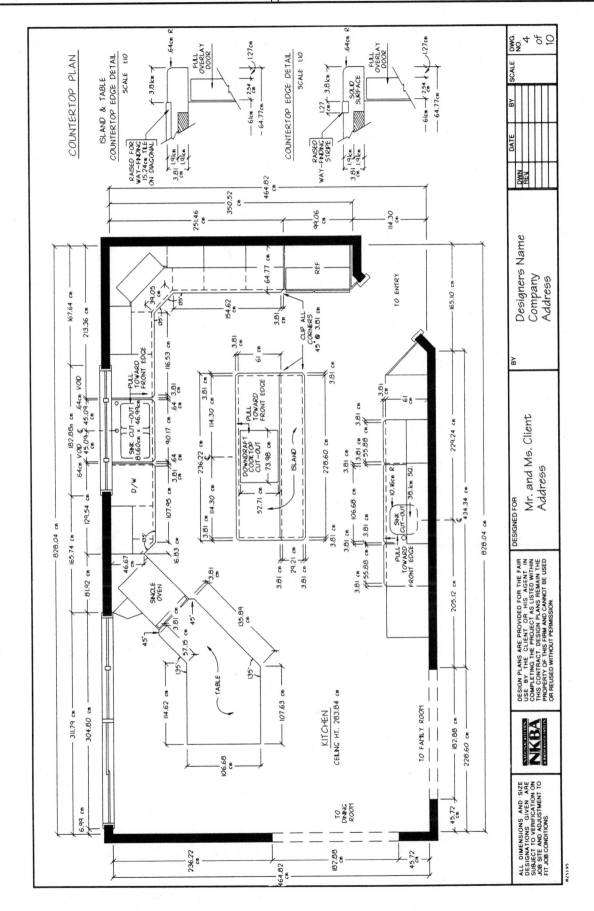

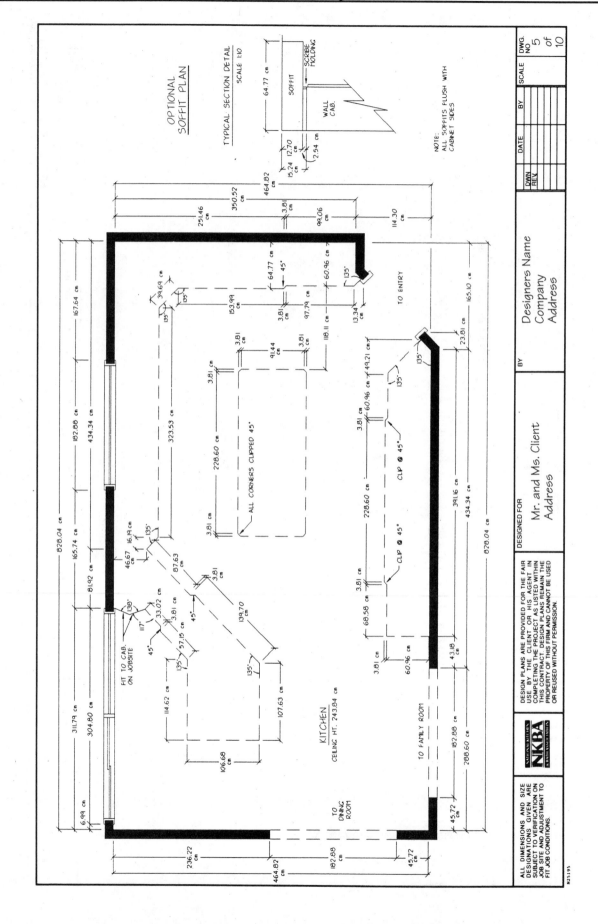

OPTIONAL
SOFFIT PLAN

TYPICAL SECTION DETAIL
SCALE 1:10

SOFFIT

SCRIBE
MOLDING

WALL
CAB.

64.77 cm

15.24 12.70 cm

2.54 cm

NOTE:
ALL SOFFITS FLUSH WITH
CABINET SIDES

KITCHEN
CEILING HT. 243.84 cm

ALL CORNERS CLIPPED 45°

FIT TO CAB.
ON JOBSITE

TO ENTRY

TO FAMILY ROOM

TO DINING ROOM

ALL DIMENSIONS AND SIZE
DESIGNATIONS GIVEN ARE
SUBJECT TO VERIFICATION ON
JOB SITE AND ADJUSTMENT TO
FIT JOB CONDITIONS.

N25195

DESIGN PLANS ARE PROVIDED FOR THE FAIR
USE BY THE CLIENT OR HIS AGENT IN
COMPLETING THE PROJECT AS LISTED WITHIN
THIS CONTRACT DESIGN PLANS REMAIN THE
PROPERTY OF THIS FIRM AND CANNOT BE USED
OR REUSED WITHOUT PERMISSION.

DESIGNED FOR

Mr. and Ms. Client
Address

BY

Designers Name
Company
Address

DWN
REV

DATE   BY   SCALE

DWG.
NO. 5
of
10

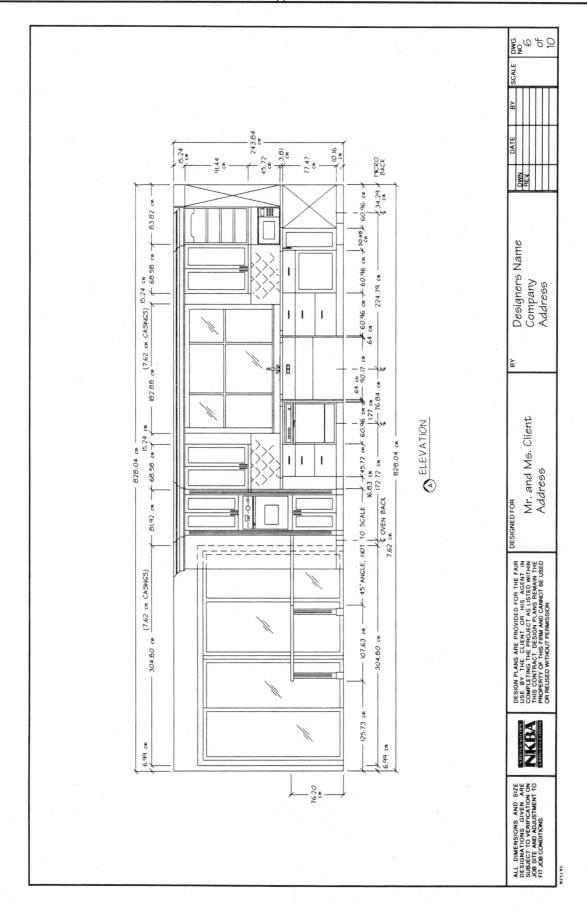

A ELEVATION

DESIGNED FOR

Mr. and Ms. Client
Address

BY

Designers Name
Company
Address

DATE | BY | SCALE | DWG. NO

DWN
REV

6 of 10

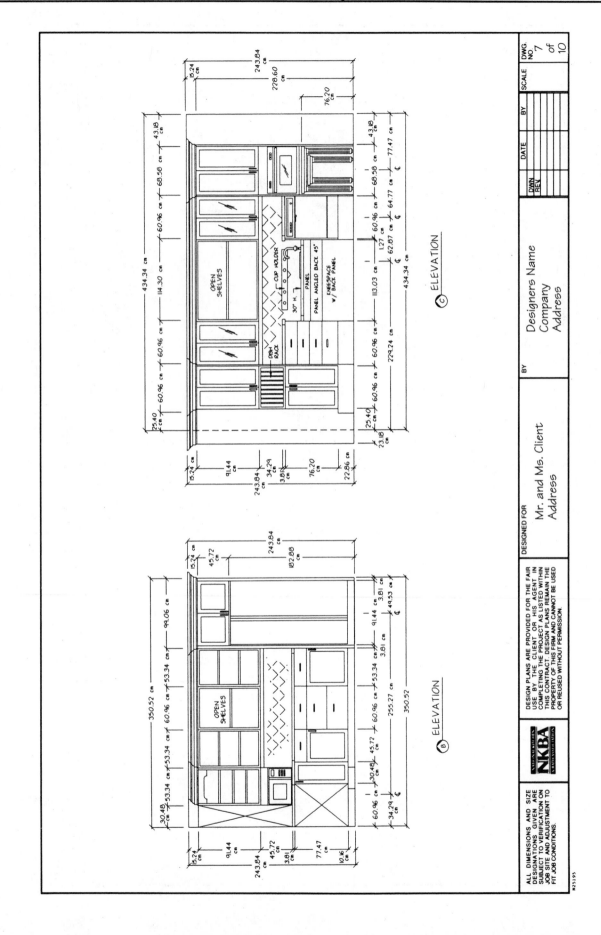

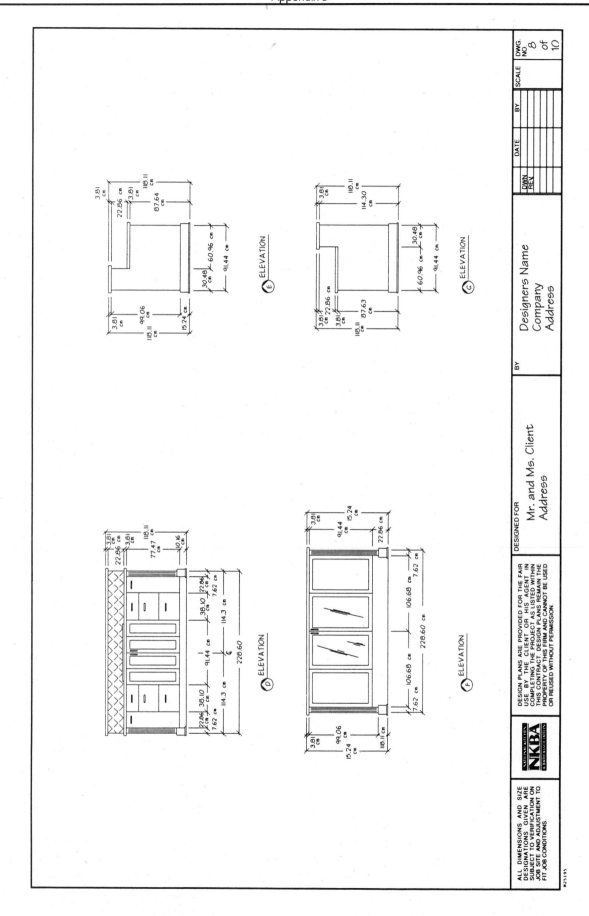

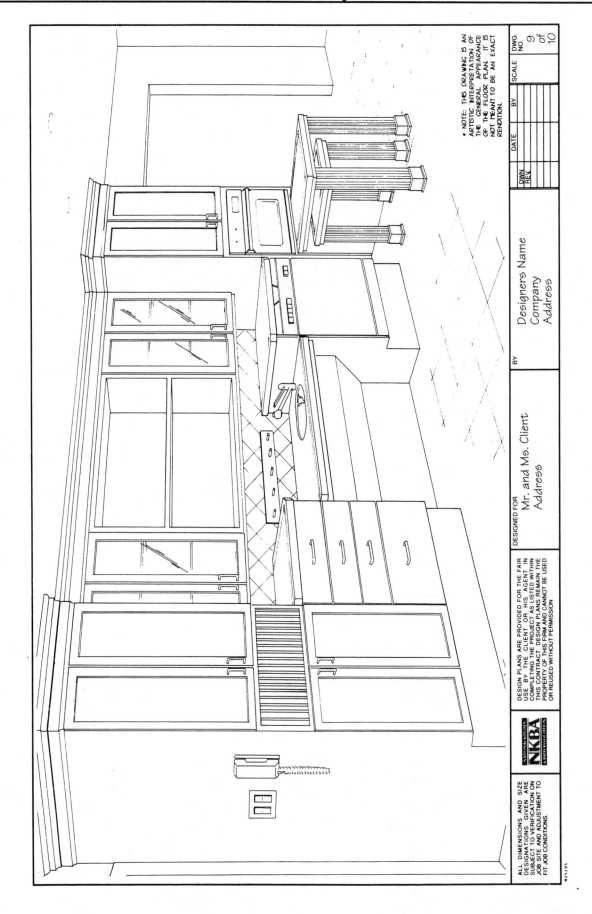

Specifications

The purpose of the project specifications is to clearly define the details of the products listed and the scope and limits of the job. Specifications may be listed on a separate form, may be part of the working drawings or a combination of both.

- Project specifications define the area of responsibility between the Kitchen Specialist and the purchaser.

- They should clearly define all material and work affected by the job, either directly or indirectly.

- They must clearly indicate which individual has the ultimate responsibility for all or part of the above.

The following Delegation of Responsibilities shall apply: Kitchen Specialists are responsible for the accuracy of the dimensioned floor plans and the selections and designations of all cabinets, appliances and equipment, if made or approved by them.

- Any equipment directly purchased by the Kitchen Specialist for resale, should be the responsibility of the Kitchen Specialist. Further, they must be responsible for supplying product installation instructions to the owner or the owner's agent.

- Any labor furnished by the Kitchen Specialist, whether by their own employees or through sub-contractors paid directly by them and working under their direction, should be the Kitchen Specialist's responsibility. **There should not be a Delegation of Total Responsibility to the Sub-Contractor Working Under these Conditions.**

- Any equipment purchased directly by the owner or the owner's agent from an outside source should be the responsibility of the owner or the owner's agent. The same applies to any sub-contractor, building contractor, or other labor directly hired and/or paid by the owner or the owner's agent.

- Specifications should contain descriptive references to all areas of work.

- All specification categories must be completed. If the job does not cover any given area, the words *"Not Applicable"*, *"N/A"*, or *"None"* should be inserted.

- In each area, the responsibility of either the Kitchen Specialist or the owner or the owner's agent must be assigned.

In all cases, the owner and the owner's agent must receive a completed copy of the project documents <u>PRIOR</u> to the commencement of any work.

STANDARD SPECIFICATIONS FOR KITCHEN DESIGN AND INSTALLATION

Name: Mr & Mrs Client

Home Address: Renovation Ave

City: _____ State _____ Phone (Home) (908) 813-6522

Mr. (Office) (908) 852-0033

Mrs. (Office) (212) 658-2585

(Jobsite) HOME *

Jobsite Address (HOME)

By Designer's Name

Hereafter called "Kitchen Specialist"

Kitchen Specialist will supply and deliver only such equipment and material as described in these specifications. Labor connected with this kitchen installation will be supplied by the Kitchen Specialist only as herein specified.

Any equipment, material and labor designated here as "Owner's responsibility" must be furnished and completed by the Owner, or the Owner's Agent in accordance with the work schedule established by the Kitchen Specialist.

Equipment, material and labor not included in these specifications can be supplied by the Kitchen Specialist at an additional cost for which authorization must be given in writing by the Owner, or the Owner's Agent.

All dimensions and cabinet designations shown on the floor plan, which are part of these specifications, are subject to adjustments dictated by job conditions.

All surfaces of walls, ceilings, windows and woodwork, except those of factory-made equipment, will be left unpainted or unfinished unless otherwise specified.

If specifications call for re-use of existing equipment, no responsibility on the part of the Kitchen Specialist for appearance, functioning or service shall be implied.

For factory-made equipment, the manufacturer's specifications for quality, design, dimensions, function and installation shall in any case take precedence over any others.

Cabinetry (as per approved drawing)

Manufacturer ABC

| Cabinet Exterior | ☒ Wood | ☐ Steel | ☐ Decorative Laminate | ☐ Other |

Cabinet Exterior Finish LIGHT OAK STAIN   Cabinet Interior Material MELAMINE Finish WHITE

Door Style FULL OVERLAY, RECESSED PANEL Hardware 4" D-PULL #458N

Special Cabinet Notes

| Furnished By | ☒ Kitchen Specialist | ☐ Owner | ☐ Owner's Agent |
| Installation By | ☒ Kitchen Specialist | ☐ Owner | ☐ Owner's Agent |

Countertops (as per approved drawing)

Manufacturer BRAND X/ BRANDY   Material SOLID SURFACE / TILE

Design Details Deck Thickness 3/4" Color WT/NAVY & WT. Edging Thickness 1½" Color WHITE / WOOD

Backsplash Thickness ——— Height ——— Color ———   End Splash Thickness ——— Height ——— Color ———

Special Countertop Notes SOLID SURFACE W/ ¼" radius top & ½" RAISED WAY-
FINDING STRIP 1½" FROM EDGE / TILE RAISED INLAY W/ WOOD EDGE 1½"

| Furnished By | ☒ Kitchen Specialist | ☐ Owner | ☐ Owner's Agent |
| Installation By | ☒ Kitchen Specialist | ☐ Owner | ☐ Owner's Agent |

Fascia & Soffit (as per approved drawing) OPTIONAL

| Construction | ☐ Flush | ☒ Extended | ☐ Recessed | ☐ N/A (Open) |

Finish Material DRYWALL - PAINTED

Special Fascia/Soffit Notes

5" HIGH, 25½" DEEP, 1" SCRIBE SPACE ABOVE CABINETS

| Furnished By | ☒ Kitchen Specialist | ☐ Owner | ☐ Owner's Agent |
| Installation By | ☒ Kitchen Specialist | ☐ Owner | ☐ Owner's Agent |

Lighting System

Description	Qty.	Model Number	Finish	Lamp Req.	Furnished By		Installed By	
					K.S.	O/OA	K.S.	O/OAS
RECESSED DOWN LIGHTS	18	1234	WHITE	60	X		X	
HANGING PENDANT	1	876	BLACK	60	X		X	
UNDER CAB. INCAND.	3	5647	WHITE	20	X		X	
UNDER CAB. FLUORS.	5	993	WHITE	13	X		X	

Special Lighting System Notes

UNDER CABINET LIGHTS 54" AFF TO ℄. INCANDESCENT
LOW VOLTAGE IS EQUIPPED WITH TRANSFORMER TO RECESS
IN CABINET BOTTOM.

BMF12

KEY

K.S. = Kitchen Specialist   O = Owner   OA = Owner's Agent

Appliances

Item	Brand Name	Model	Finish	Fuel	Furnished By K.S.	Furnished By O/OA	Installed By K.S.	Installed By O/OA	Hook Up By K.S.	Hook Up By O/OA
Range NA										
Cooktop	XYZ	123	BLACK	ELEC	X		X		X	
Oven	XYZ	123	BLACK	GAS	X		X		X	
Hood NA										
Warming Drawer NA										
Indoor Grill NA										
Microwave 1	XYZ	123	BLACK	ELEC	X		X		X	
Trim Kit	XYZ	89D	BLACK	—	X		X		X	
Refrigerator	XYZ	123	BLACK	ELEC	X		X		X	
Ice Maker	IN DOOR									
Trim Kit NA										
Freezer NA										
Trim Kit NA										
Dishwasher (2)	XYZ	123	BLACK	ELEC	X		X		X	
Trim Kit NA										
Conversion Kit NA										
Food Waste Disposal	XYZ	123	S.S.	ELEC	X		X		X	
Compactor NA										
Trim Kit NA										
Built-in Can Opener NA										
Built-in Toaster NA										
Built-in Mixing Ctr. NA										
Telephone/Intercom	PDQ	5128X	NAVY	—		X		X		X
Television	GENERICA	F87-Y	BLACK	ELEC		X		X		X
Radio NA										
VCR NA										
Washer NA										
Dryer NA										

Special Appliance Notes: TELEPHONE & CABLE OUTLET ROUGH-IN BY OTHERS FINAL PLACEMENT IN FINISH PANELS BY K.S.

Fixtures and Fittings

Item	Brand Name	Model	Finish	Fuel	Furnished By K.S.	Furnished By O/OA	Installed By K.S.	Installed By O/OA	Hook Up By K.S.	Hook Up By O/OA
Kitchen Sink #1	XYZ	123	SS	—	X		X		X	
No. of Holes	2									
Faucet	XYZ	123	BLACK	—	X		X		X	
Strainer	XYZ	123	SS	—	X		X		X	
Kitchen Sink #2	XYZ	456	SS	—	X		X		X	
No. of Holes	2									
Faucet	XYZ	123	BLACK	—	X		X		X	
Strainer	XYZ	123	SS	—	X		X		X	
Hot Water Dispenser (2)	XYZ	123	BLACK	—	X		X		X	
Chilled Water Dispenser NA										
Lotion Dispenser NA										
Water Purifier NA										

Special Fixtures and Fittings Notes: UNDERMOUNT SINK #1 & #2, INSTALL #2 WITH FAUCET AT RIGHT SIDE

Windows and Doors

Item	Brand Name	Model	Finish	Hardware	Furnished By K.S.	Furnished By O/OA	Installed By K.S.	Installed By O/OA
CASEMENT WINDOW	XYZ	123	WHITE	CHROME	X		X	
FIXED WINDOW	XYZ	345	WHITE	CHROME	X		X	
SLIDING GLASS DOOR	XYZ	789	WHITE	CHROME	X		X	

Special Window and Door Notes:

INSTALL FIXED WINDOW & SLIDING DOOR IN SINGLE CASING, PLACE FIXED AT RIGHT, SLIDER AT LEFT

Flooring

		Furnished By K.S.	Furnished By O/OA	Installed By K.S.	Installed By O/OA
Removal of Existing Floor Covering	REMOVE FLOOR & UNDERLAYMENT	X		X	
Preparation of Floor for New Surface	REPAIR & LEVEL AS REQUIRED	X		X	
Installation of Subfloor/Underlayment	NEW 5/8" PLYWOOD	X		X	
New Floor Covering Material Description:	VINYL				
Manufacturer ABC Pattern Name GEO-TILE					
Pattern Number 1234 Pattern Repeat 8" SQUARES					
Floor Covering Installation			X		X
Baseboard Material 4" COLONIAL BSBD. LIGHT OAK		X		X	
Transition Treatment			X		X
Remove and Repair Water Damaged Area AS REQUIRED		X		X	

Special Flooring Notes

FLOOR INSTALLATION BY OWNER'S AGENT WILL BE SCHEDULED WITH K.S. TO FACILITATE A TIMELY COMPLETION

Decorative Surfaces (wall, ceiling, window materials)

Removal Work: Wall _____ Ceiling X Window X   Preparation Work: Wall X Ceiling X Window X

Description	Brand Name	Model	Finish	Material Quantity	Furnished By K.S.	Furnished By O/OA	Installed By K.S.	Installed By O/OA
Remove existing ceiling	—	—	PLASTER	—	X		X	
REMOVE CURTAINS	—	—	—	—		X		X
& RODS/HARDWARE	—	—	—	—		X		X
INSTALL & PAINT CEILING	ABC	—	FLAT	1 GAL	X		X	
PAINT CASINGS	ABC	—	GLOSS	1 PT.	X		X	
PAINT WALLS	ABC	—	EGGSHELL	2 PT.	X		X	
TILE BACKSPLASH								

Special Decorative Surface Notes:

ALL PAINTED SURFACES IN "DESIGNER WHITE" COLOR, TILE BACK SPLASH INSTALLED ON A DIAGONAL, CENTER ROW WHITE, FIELD IN NAVY

BMF12

Electrical Work (except as described above in specific equipment sections)

	Furnished By		Installed By	
	K.S.	O/OA	K.S.	O/OA
Heating System Alteration RELOCATE EXISTING REGISTERS & ADD NEW	X		X	
New Service Panel existing 200 amps sufficient				
Code Update ALL DUPLEX OUTLETS WITH GFCI	X		X	
Details INSTALL ALL APPLIANCES ON DEDICATED	X		X	
CIRCUITS, VENT COOKTOP & OVEN	X		X	
THROUGH FLOOR TO OUTSIDE	X		X	

Plumbing (except as described above in specific equipment sections)

	Furnished By		Installed By	
	K.S.	O/OA	K.S.	O/OA
Heating System Alterations NA				
New Rough-in Requirements per mech. plan (2nd sink, d/w, ref.)	X		X	
Modifications to Existing Lines per Mech. plan (1st sink, d/w)	X		X	
Details				
- SPECIAL FLEXIBLE INSTALLATION REQUIRED	X		X	
FOR PRIMARY SINK THAT ADJUST FROM				
30"-42" AFF				
- 2ND D/W INSTALLED ON 9" HIGH DECK	X		X	
- SET SINK DRAIN BACK FOR KNEESPACE	X		X	

General Carpentry (except as described above in specific equipment sections)

	Furnished By		Installed By	
	K.S.	O/OA	K.S.	O/OA
Demolition Work EXISTING CEILING & WALL	X		X	
Existing Fixture and Equipment Removal DONATED TO CHARITY		X		X
Trash Removal ARRANGE FOR DUMPSTER RT. OF SITE	X		X	
Reconstruction Work (Except as Previously Stated)				
Windows PATCH SIDING, REHANG SHUTTERS	X		X	
Doors PATCH SIDING, REHANG SHUTTERS	X		X	
Interior Walls PATCH AS REQUIRED, NEW SURFACES	X		X	
1/2" DRYWALL PRIMED	X		X	
Exterior Walls ADDITION SIDING TO MATCH EXIST-	X		X	
ING AS CLOSE AS POSSIBLE				
Details				
CUSTOM KNEESPACE PANELS, ANGLED	X		X	
PANELS/FILLERS & MOLDING MITERS				
PERFORMED ON JOBSITE				

Miscellaneous Work		Responsibility	
		K.S.	O/OA
Trash Removal	EMPTY DUMPSTER ON DEMAND	X	
Jobsite/Room Cleanup	DAILY PICK-UP / SPECIAL POST PROJECT CLEAN	X	
Building Permit(s)	AS REQUIRED	X	
Structural Engineering/Architectural Fees	NA		
Inspection Fees	AS REQUIRED	X	
Jobsite Delivery	STORAGE BY K.S. UNTIL NEEDED	X	
Other			
	SUPERVISE INSTALLATION WORK & SCHEDULE	X	

I have read these specifications and approve:

Accepted: _Mrs. Client_

Accepted: _Mr. Client_

Date: 2/23/96

Authorized Company Representative

By: _Designer's Signature, CKD_

By: _____

Date: 2-23-96

Design Statement

The purpose of the design statement is to interpret the design problem and solution in order to substantiate the project to the client. Design statements may be verbal or written. Written statements maybe a separate document, may be part of the working drawings or a combination of both.

Design statements should clearly outline:

- design considerations and challenges of the project including, but not limited to: construction budget requirements, client needs and wants, special requests and lifestyle factors.

- how the designer arrived at their solution and addressed the design considerations and challenges for the project.

- aesthetic considerations such as use of principles and elements of design (ie. pattern repetition, finish/color/surface selections and other details).

It is important that a design statement be clear, concise and interesting to the reader. Written statements may be in either paragraph or bulleted/outline format. As a guideline, a design statement can be written in 250-500 words. Sample design statements follow, showing both acceptable formats.

Sample Design Statement - Paragraph Format

The primary design challenge in the kitchen design for Mr. and Ms. Client was to create a space that is safe and functional for the varying sizes and abilities of the family members. Mr. and Ms. Client are both in their 40's with family members including a 17 year old son, seven year old daughter and a 72 year old grandmother. The grandmother has arthritis, limited eyesight and sometimes uses a walker. Since both Mr. and Ms. Client work, the grandmother and the children frequent the kitchen during the day and all family members participate in meal preparation in the evenings and on weekends. The existing kitchen space was insufficient for the families request to work together in the space. The work aisles were narrow, counters had sharp edges and many fixtures and equipment were either out of reach or hard to use by the grandmother and child, posing safety hazards.

The solution began by building a room addition adjacent to the existing kitchen which increased the floor space by approximately 25%. This allowed us to plan generous walkways and work aisles that join multiple work stations within the kitchen. In order to accommodate all the users of the space, the work stations were designed at varied and adjustable heights. The primary sink adjusts from 30" - 42" high allowing flexibility from day to evening and weekends. The secondary work centers are at a stationary 30" height to accommodate the shorter/seated kitchen helpers. All cabinetry was planned with accessibility in mind. Cabinets are equipped with roll-out/pull-out accessories, reduced depths or open shelves. Solid surface counters are heat resistant and designed with special raised and color contrasted "way-finding" edges which aid the grandmother in maneuvering around the space. Additionally, sharp edges were virtually eliminated by clipping all counter corners at 45 degree angles.

A geometric pattern was created with navy blue and white ceramic tile on the floor and backsplash to compliment the light finish on the wood cabinets and achieve repetition/continuity throughout the space. Furthermore, the tile pattern provides contrast which also contributes to the functionality of the space. Finally, all appliances and fixtures were selected based on safety and ease of use, as well as aesthetics. All equipment and fixtures are accented with polished chrome. The faucets have lever handles, appliances have large graphics, high contrast indicators and touch-pad controls.

Sample Design Statement - Outline Format

The primary design challenge was to create a space that was safe and functional for all family members:

- Mr. and Mrs. Client (40's)

- 17 year old son

- Seven year old daughter

- 72 year old grandmother (arthritis, limited eyesight, sometimes uses walker)

The existing space was insufficient:

- work aisles were too narrow

- counters had sharp edges

- many fixtures/equipment out of reach or hard to use by child and grandmother

The solution:

- room addition increased floor space by 25%

- multiple workstations at various heights

- primary sink adjusts from 30"-42"

- cabinetry equipped with roll-out/pull-out accessories

- reduced depth storage and open shelves

- solid surface (heat-resistant) counters

- counter edges were clipped and designed with way-finding inlay stripe

- appliances were selected based on safety and ease of use

Aesthetics:

- tile pattern repeats geometric design

- white and navy color tiles match white counter with navy inlay stripe

- light finished wood cabinets compliment navy

- color contrasts provide safety factor for grandmother's limited eyesight

Contracts

All contract forms used **<u>must</u>** be in strict compliance with Federal, State and Municipal Laws and Ordinances. Reference local codes for compliance standards. Laws do vary, therefore, you should be sure your contracts meet all local requirements.

STANDARD FORM OF AGREEMENT FOR DESIGN AND INSTALLATION

Approved by the

National Kitchen & Bath Association

Between ....Purchaser

Home Address...

City ....State................................Zip.............................

Phone Number...

Delivery Address...

And Seller

1. The Seller agrees to furnish the materials and services set forth in the drawings (numbered...................................
and dated ....) and specifications annexed hereto.
The Purchaser agrees to make payment therefore in accordance with the schedule of payment.

Contract Price... $ ....

Sales Tax (if applicable) .... $ ....

.... $ ....

Total Purchase Price... $ ....

Schedule of Payment:

Upon signing of this agreement .... $ ....

Upon delivery of cabinets from manufacturer .... $ ....

Upon delivery of .... $ ....

Upon substantial installation of .... $ ....

This contract includes the terms and provisions as set forth herein. Please read and sign where indicated.

2. The standard form of warranty shall apply to the service and equipment furnished (except where other warranties of purchased products apply). The warranty shall become effective when signed by the Seller and delivered to the Purchaser. The warranty is for one year materials and labor.

3. The delivery date, when given, shall be deemed approximate and performance is subject to delays caused by strikes, fires, acts of God or other reasons not under the control of the Seller, as well as the availability of the product at the time of delivery.

4. The Purchaser agrees to accept delivery of the product or products when ready. The risk of loss, as to damage or destruction, shall be upon the Purchaser upon the delivery and receipt of the product.

5. The Purchaser understands that the products described are specially designed and custom built and that the Seller takes immediate steps upon execution of this Agreement to design, order and construct those items set forth herein; therefore, this Agreement is not subject to cancellation by the Purchaser for any reason.

6. No installation, plumbing, electrical, flooring, decorating or other construction work is to be provided unless specifically set forth herein. In the event the Seller is to perform the installation, it is understood that the price agreed upon herein does not include possible expense entailed in coping with hidden or unknown contingencies found at the job site. In the event such contingencies arise and the Seller is required to furnish labor or materials or otherwise perform work not provided for or contemplated by the Seller, the actual costs plus (   )% thereof will be paid for by the Purchaser. Contingencies include but are not limited to: inability to reuse existing water, vent, and waste pipes; air shafts, ducts, grilles, louvres and registers; the relocation of concealed pipes, risers, wiring or conduits, the presence of which cannot be determined until the work has started; or imperfections, rotting or decay in the structure or parts thereof necessitating replacement.

7. Title to the item sold pursuant to this Agreement shall not pass to the Purchaser until the full price as set forth in this Agreement is paid to the Seller.

8. Delays in payment shall be subject to interest charges of (   )% per annum, and in no event higher than the interest rate provided by law. If the Seller is required to engage the services of a collection agency or an attorney, the Purchaser agrees to reimburse the Seller for any reasonable amounts expended in order to collect the unpaid balance.

9. If any provision of this Agreement is declared invalid by any tribunal, the remaining provisions of the Agreement shall not be affected thereby.

10. This Agreement sets forth the entire transaction between the parties; any and all prior Agreements, warranties or representations made by either party are superseded by this Agreement. All changes in this Agreement shall be made by a separate document and executed with the same formalities. No agent of the Seller, unless authorized in writing by the Seller, has any authority to waive, alter, or enlarge this contract, or to make any new or substituted or different contracts, representations, or warranties.

11. The Seller retains the right upon breach of this Agreement by the Purchaser to sell those items in the Seller's possession. In effecting any resale on breach of this Agreement by the Purchaser, the Seller shall be deemed to act in the capacity of agent for the Purchaser. The purchaser shall be liable for any net deficiency on resale.

12. The Seller agrees that it will perform this contract in conformity with customary industry practices. The Purchaser agrees that any claim for adjustment shall not be reason or cause for failure to make payment of the purchase price in full. Any unresolved controversy or claim arising from or under this contract shall be settled by arbitration and judgment upon the award rendered may be entered in any court of competent jurisdiction. The arbitration shall be held under the rules of the American Arbitration Association.

Accepted: ....
                                        Purchaser

Accepted: ....   Accepted: ....
                                                                                        Purchaser

Date: ....   Date: ....

Titling Project Documents

Protecting Yourself

When you design a project for a client, you must protect yourself from liability when referring to the plans and drawings, and you must protect the plans themselves from being copied by your competitors.

When presenting the plans for a kitchen, **NKBA** recommends that you refer to the drawings as *"Kitchen Design Plans"* or *"Cabinet Plans"*. The design plans should have the following statement included on them in an obvious location in large or block letters.

DESIGN PLANS ARE NOT PROVIDED FOR ARCHITECTURAL OR ENGINEERING USE

The individual drawings incorporated in the overall kitchen design presentation must also be carefully labeled. It is suggested that you refer to these other drawings as ***"Floor Plans", "Elevations", "Artist Renderings", and "Mechanical Plans"***.

With respect to the *"Artist Rendering"* , **NKBA** suggests that you include a notation on the drawings which reads:

THIS RENDERING IS AN ARTIST'S INTERPRETATION OF THE GENERAL APPEARANCE OF THE ROOM, IT IS NOT INTENDED TO BE A PRECISE DEPICTION

The entire set of paperwork, which includes your design plans, specifications and contract, can be referred to as the **"Project Documents"**.

You should never refer to the design plan as an *"Architectural Drawing"*, or even as an "architectural-type drawing". **DO NOT USE THE WORDS** *"Architecture"*, *"Architectural Design"*, *"Architectural Phase"*, *"Architectural Background"*, or any other use of the word *"Architectural"* in any of the project documents that you prepare, or in any of your business stationary, promotional information or any presentation materials. Any such reference to the work that you do or documents that you prepare may result in a violation of various state laws. A court may determine that your use of the word *"Architecture/Architectural"*, could reasonably lead a client to believe that you possess a level of expertise that you do not. Worse yet, a court may find you liable for fraud and/or misrepresentation.

Laws do vary per state, therefore, it is important that you consult with your own legal counsel to be sure that you are acting within the applicable statutes in your area. You must clearly understand what drawings you are legally allowed to prepare, and what drawings must be prepared under the auspices of a licensed architect or engineer.

Protecting your "Kitchen Design Plans"

After drafting the design plans for your client, you should insure that they will not be copied or used by a competitor. This may be done by copyrighting the design plan that you prepare.

Copyright is an International form of protection/exclusivity provided by law to authors of original works, despite whether the work is published or not. Original works of authorship include any literary, pictorial, graphic, or sculptured works, such as your design plans, provided they are original works done by you.

Copyright protection exists from the moment the work is created in its final form and will endure fifty years after your death.

Naturally, if two or more persons are authors of an original work, they will be deemed *co-owners* of its copyright. For example; if you as the Kitchen Specialist collaborate with an Interior Designer, you will both be co-owners of the design copyright.

An original work generated by two or more authors is referred to as a *"joint work"*. Generally, a *"joint work"* results if the authors collaborated on the work or if each prepared a segment of it with the knowledge and intent that it would be incorporated with the contributions submitted by other authors. Accordingly, a *"joint work"* will only be found when each co-author intended his respective contribution to be combined into a larger, integrated piece. There is no requirement that each of the co-authors work together or even be acquainted with one another.

A work created by an employee within the scope of his employment is regarded as *"work made for hire"*, and is normally owned by the employer, unless the parties explicitly stipulate in a written agreement, signed by both, that the copyright will be owned by the employee. If you are an independent contractor, the *"works made for hire"* statutes do not include architectural drawings or other design plans, therefore, the copyright in any kitchen design created by you will remain vested with you until you contractually agree to relinquish ownership.

To secure copyright protection for your plans, you are required to give notice of copyright on all publicly distributed copies. The use of the copyright notice is your responsibility as the copyright owner and does not require advance permission from, or registration with, the Copyright Office in Washington, DC.

Copyright © Notice

A proper copyright notice must include the following three items:

- 1. The symbol ©, or the word "Copyright", or the abbreviation "Copy"; **(© is considered as the International symbol for copyright)**

- 2. The year of the first publication of the work; and

- 3. The name of the owner of the copyright in the work, or an abbreviation by which the name can be recognized, or a generally known alternative designation of the owner.

An example of a proper copyright notice would be:

Copyright © 1995 Joe Smith

The notice should be affixed to copies of your design plan in such a manner and location as to give reasonable notice of the claim of copyright.

As mentioned previously, you or your firm continue to retain copyright protection of your design plan even if the plan is given to the client after he has paid for it. Although the copyright ownership may be transferred, such transfer must be in writing and signed by you as the owner of the copyright conveyed. Normally, the transfer of a copyright is made by contract. In order to protect your exclusive rights, however, you should include a clause in your contract which reads:

> Design plans are provided for the fair use by the client or his agent in completing the project as listed within this contract. Design plans remain the property of (your name) and cannot be used or reused without permission of (your name).

This clause should also be in any agreement between you and a client who requests that you prepare a design plan for his review. Such a design plan usually serves as the basis for a subsequent contract between you and the client for the actual installation of the kitchen. This type of agreement will prevent the client from obtaining a design plan from you and then taking that plan to a competitor who may simply copy your plan.

So long as you retain the copyright in the design plan, you will be able to sue any party who has copied your design plan for infringement.

Glossary - Graphic Terms

Architects Scale: A measuring tool used to draw at a determined unit of measure ratio accurately; ie. 1/2" = 1', in which each half inch represents one foot.

3/32" = 1'	1/4" = 1'	1" = 1'
3/16" = 1'	3/8" = 1'	1 1/2" = 1'
1/8" = 1'	3/4" = 1'	3" = 1'

It is equally acceptable to use the metric equivalents. (inches x 2.54)

Break Symbol: Indicated by ($\longrightarrow\!\!\!\!\leftarrow$) and used to end wall lines on a drawing which actually continue or to break off parts of the drawing.

Color: A visual sensation which is a result of light reflecting off objects and creating various wavelengths which when reaching the retina produces the appearance of various hues.

Copyright: Is an International form of protection/exclusivity provided by law to authors of original works, despite whether the work is published or not. Original works of authorship include any literary, pictorial, graphic, or sculptured works such as design plans that are your own original works. The symbol (©) is considered as the International symbol for copyright exclusivity.

Dimension Lines: Solid lines terminating with arrows, dots or slashes which run parallel with the object it represents and includes the actual length of the line written in inches or centimeters inside or on top of the line. Whenever possible, dimension lines should be located outside of the actual walls of the floor plan or elevation.

Dimetric: A dimetric drawing is similar to oblique, with the exception that the object is rotated so that only one of its corners touches the picture plane. The most frequently used angle for the projecting line is an equal division of 45° on either side of the leading edge. A 15° angle is sometimes used when it is less important to show the *"roof view"* of the object.

Elevation: A drawing representing a vertical view of a space taken from a preselected reference plane. There is no depth indicated in an elevation, rather everything appears very flat and is drawn in scale.

Floor Plan: A drawing representing a horizontal view of a space taken from a preselected reference plane (often the ceiling). There is no depth indicated in a floor plan, rather everything appears very flat and is drawn in a reduced scale.

Isometric: The isometric, a special type of dimetric drawing, is the easiest and most popular paraline (three-dimensional) drawing. All axes of the object are simultaneously rotated away from the picture plane and kept at the same angle of projection (30° from the picture plane). All legs are equally distorted in length at a given scale and therefore maintain an exact proportion of 1:1:1.

Kroy Lettering Tape: Translucent sticky backed tape, which after running it through a special typing machine, creates a stick on lettering ideal for labeling drawing title blocks.

Lead: A graphite and clay mixture which is used for drawing and drafting in combination with a lead holder. Similar to a pencil without the wooden outer portion. Available in various degrees of hardness, providing various line weights.

Legend: An explanatory list of the symbols and their descriptions as used on a mechanical plan or other graphic representation.

Matte Board: A by product of wood pulp with a paper surface which has been chemically treated in order to be acid free and fade resistent. The use of matte board will protect drawings from fading, becoming brittle and bending or creasing.

Oblique: In an oblique drawing one face (either plan or elevation) of the object is drawn directly on the picture plane. Projected lines are drawn at a 30° or 45° angle to the picture plane.

Owners Agent: That person or persons responsible for mediating the clients requests with the designer and acting as the interpretor on any area the client is unsure of or in question on.

Ozalid Prints: More commonly referred to as *"Blueprints"*, are a method of duplicating drawings in which special paper coated with light sensitive diazo is used. This paper with drawing on transparent paper, is exposed to ultra violet light creating a negative, then the print is exposed again to the developer which produces the *"blackline"*, *"blueline"* or *"sepia print"* depending upon the paper used.

Perspective: The art of representing a space in a drawing form which appears to have depth by indicating the relationship of various objects as they appear to the human eye or through the lens of a camera.

Photocopy: A method of duplicating drawings in which light causes toner to adhere to paper of various sizes, typically *(8 1/2" x 11")*, *(11" x 14")* or *(11" x 17")*, producing prints in high contrast, which are similar to blackline ozalid prints.

Quadrille Paper: White ledger paper base with blue, non-reproducible ruling lines which all carry the same weight. * **NOTE: This is not an acceptable type of drafting paper for project documentation.**

Section:　Often referred to as a *"cut-view"*, these drawings are defined as an imaginary cut made through an object and used to show construction details and materials which are not obvious in standard plan or elevational views.

Technical Rapidograph Pens:　Provides for a smooth flow of ink with stainless steel points or *"Tungsten Carbide"* point of various sizes, again providing various line weights.

Tracing Paper:　Thin semi-transparent paper used for sketching. Also called *"bumwad"* paper.

Transfer Type:　Sometimes referred to as *"Press-Type"* or *"Rub-on-Type"*, is a translucent film with lettering or dot screen images which may be transferred to a drawing by rubbing the image after it is positioned on the drawing paper. When the film is lifted, the image remains on the drawing paper and the film is left blank.

Trimetric:　The trimetric drawing is similar to the dimetric, except that the plan of the object is rotated so that the two exposed sides of the object are not at equal angles to the picture plane. The plan is usually positioned at 30/60° angle to the ground plane. The height of the object is reduced proportionately as illustrated (similar to the 45° dimetric).

Vellum:　Rag stock which has been transparentized with synthetic resin resulting in medium weight transparent paper with a medium-fine grain or *"tooth"* which holds lead to the surface.

Witness Lines:　Solid lines which run perpendicular to the dimension line and cross the dimension line at the exact location of its termination. These lines should begin approximately 1/16" outside of the walls of the floor plan and end approximately 1/16" beyond the dimension line.

Appendix C

Imperial/Metric Comparison Chart

KITCHEN AND BATH FLOOR PLANS SHOULD BE DRAWN TO A
SCALE OF 1/2" EQUALS 1' FOOT (1/2" =1'- 0"). AN EQUALLY
ACCEPTABLE METRIC SCALE WOULD BE A RATIO OF 1 TO 20
(ie. 1 CM TO 20 CM)

	INCHES	MILLIMETERS	CENTIMETERS
◆ ACTUAL METRIC CONVERSION TO MILLIMETERS IS 1" = 25.4 MM . TO FACILITATE CONVERSIONS BETWEEN IMPERIAL + METRIC DIMENSIONING FOR CALCULATIONS UNDER 1", 24 MM IS USED.	1/8"	3 MM	.32 CM
	1/4"	6	.64
	1/2"	12	1.27
	3/4"	18	1.91
	1"	24	2.54
◆ TO FACILITATE CONVERSIONS BETWEEN IMPERIAL + METRIC FOR CALCULATIONS OVER 1", 25 MM IS TYPICALLY USED.			
	3"	75	7.62
	6"	150	15.24
◆ ACTUAL METRIC CONVERSION TO CENTIMETERS IS 1" = 2.54 CM.	9"	225	22.86
	12"	300	30.48
	15"	375	38.1
	18"	450	45.72
	21"	525	53.34
	24"	600	60.96
	27"	675	68.58
	30"	750	76.2
	33"	825	83.82
	36"	900	91.44
	39"	975	99.06
	42"	1050	106.68
	45"	1125	114.3
	48"	1200	121.92
	51"	1275	129.54
	54"	1350	137.16
	57"	1425	144.78
	60"	1500	152.4
	63"	1575	160.02
	66"	1650	167.64
	69"	1725	175.26
	72"	1800	182.88
	75"	1875	190.5
	78"	1950	198.12
	81"	2025	205.74
	84"	2100	213.36
	87"	2175	220.98
	90"	2250	228.6
	93"	2325	236.22
	96"	2400	243.84
	99"	2475	251.46
	102"	2475	259.08
	105"	2625	266.7
	108"	2700	274.32
	111"	2775	281.94
	114"	2850	289.56
	117"	2925	297.18
	120"	3000	304.8
	123"	3075	312.42
	126"	3150	320.04
	129"	3225	327.66
	132"	3300	335.28
	135"	3375	342.9
	138"	3450	350.52
	141"	3525	358.14
	144"	3600	365.76

Metric Conversion Chart

LENGTH

10 MILLIMETERS = 1 CENTIMETER (CM)
10 CENTIMETERS = 1 DECIMETER
10 DECIMETERS = 1 METER (M)
10 METERS = 1 DEKAMETER
100 METERS = 1 HECTOMETER
1,000 METERS = 1 KILOMETER

AREA

100 SQ. MILLIMETERS = 1 SQ. CENTIMETER
100 SQ. CENTIMETER = 1 SQ. DECIMETER
100 SQ. DECIMETERS = 1 SQ. METER
100 SQ. METERS = 1 ARE
10,000 SQ. METERS = 1 HECTARE
100 HECTARES = 1 SQ. KILOMETER

LINEAR DRAWING MEASUREMENTS

1 MILLIMETER (MM) = .03937"   1" = 25.4 MM   12" = 304.8 MM
1 CENTIMETER (CM) = .3937"   1" = 2.54 CM   12" = 30.48 CM
1 METER (M) = 39.37"   1" = .0254 M   12" = .3048 M

SQUARE MEASURE

1 SQ. INCH = 6.4516 SQ. CENTIMETERS
1 SQ. FOOT = 9.29034 SQ. DECIMETERS
1 SQ. YARD = .836131 SQ. METER
1 ACRE = .40469 HECTARE
1 SQ. MILE = 2.59 SQ. KILOMETERS

DRY MEASURE

1 PINT = .550599 LITER
1 QUART = 1.101197 LITER
1 PECK = 8.80958 LITER
1 BUSHEL = .35238 HECTOLITER

CUBIC MEASURE

1 CU. INCH = 16.3872 CU. CENTIMETERS
1 CU. FOOT = .028317 CU. METERS
1 CU. YARD = .76456 CU. METERS

LIQUID MEASURE

1 PINT = .473167 LITER
1 QUART = .946332 LITER
1 GALLON = 3.785329 LITER

LONG MEASURE

1 INCH = 25.4 MILLIMETERS
1 FOOT = .3 METER
1 YARD = .914401 METER
1 MILE = 1.609347 KILOMETERS

Glossary of Terms

Active Solar: In solar heating, active solar means that collectors and pumps that distribute heat are needed.

Aerator: A device used on the end of a faucet that mixes air with water so splashback is minimized.

Ampere (Amps): The measurement of the rate of flow of electricty.

Angle, Acute: An angle which is less that 90 degrees.

Angle, Obtuse: An angle which is more than 90 degrees.

Angle, Right: An angle equal to 90 degrees or two perpendicular legs.

Backsplash: A protective panel on the wall behind a sink or counter.

Ballast: A device that limits the electric current flowing into a fluorescent or high intensity discharge lamp.

Banquette: A built-in table with chairs in an alcove.

Barrier-free Design (Universal Design): A planning concept where safety is of paramount importance and no technological or physical barriers are placed in front of the user as they attempt to work in the space.

Base Cabinets: A cabinet which sits on the floor. Commonly has a single drawer over a single door.

Blind Cabinet: A cabinet that has shelf, pullout or swing-out apparatus to provide accessibility to a corner.

Brightness: Intensity of light from an object or surface that directly reaches the eye of the viewer.

Candela: The light produced from one candle in one direction.

Capillary Tube: A tube which connects to the condenser to the evaporator, metering the flow of liquid refrigerant to the evaporator.

Carbon Filter System: Removes contaminants from water as the water passes through a filter containing particles of carbon. The carbon absorbs the contaminants.

Cast Iron: A manufacturing process used to mold metal when it is so hot it is in a liquid state.

Cast Polymer: A fixture and surfacing material created by pouring a mixture of ground marble and polyester resin into a treated mold, where curing takes place at room temperature or in a curing oven.

Centerline (c/l): A line representing an axis of symmetry. Usually shown on plans as a broken line.

Centerlines: A designation noting a point equally distant from all points of a surface and/or object.

CFM: Cubic feet per minute.

CFM Rating: Cubic feet per minute a fan is capable of moving.

Circuit Breaker: Safety devices that keep the branch circuits and anything connected to them from overheating and catching fire.

Color Rendition Index (CRI): A scale which refers to the extent which a perceived color of an object under a light source matches the perceived color of that object under another source (such as daylight or incandescent lighting).

Color Temperature: Describes whether a light source has warm or cool tones.

Comfort Zone: The range of temperatures and humidities that humans are comfortable at.

Condenser: A long folded tube that receives hot, high-pressure refrigerant vapor pumped by a compressor.

Conduction Heat: A process by which heat is transferred through a substance, or from one substance to another that is in direct contact with it, by molecular activity.

Conduit: A hollow metal tube that contains electrical wiring.

Contrast: The brightness difference between surfaces in the field of view.

Convection Heat: Heat which is air heated by an element and then circulated. Involves the motion of heated matter itself from one place to another.

Corbel: Support bracket.

Corner Cabinet: A cabinet designed to fit specifically in a corner.

Corridor Kitchen: Close grouping of work centers on parallel walls.

Cross Lighting: Task lighting which provides even illumination from side to side and top to bottom.

Dado: A rectangular groove cut across the full width of an object to receive the end of another piece.

Dielectric Union: Union used to join two pipes of different materials in order to prevent the pipe materials from reacting chemically with each other and causing corrosion.

Diffuser: A device used to deflect air from an outlet in various directions. Also a device for distributing the light of a lamp evenly.

Dimmer Control (Rheostat Switch): A device which is used to vary the light output of an electric lamp.

Distiller: A heating element which boils water and as the steam condenses, impurities are removed.

Diverter: A knob, handle or button that is moved, pushed or turned to provide water output selections.

Drain/Waste/Vent (DWV) System: A system which carries water and waste out of the house.

Drawer Cabinet: A cabinet that features two, three, four or five drawers.

Drawings, Elevations: True, scaled drawings in both height and width, however they have no depth.

Drawings, Interpretive: Elevations, paraline drawings and perspectives which illustrate the vertical elements in a design that are not shown in a floor plan.

Drawings, Paraline: Drawings which are similar to orthographic drawings and remain in a true scale format, yet offer a three dimensional view of the space.

Efficacy: The term used to describe a light source's power to produce an effect.

Energy Efficiency Rating (EER): The efficiency of room air conditioners is measured by the ratio of the cooling output in BTUs divided by the power consumption.

Escutcheon Plate: A protective plate surrounding a hole in an object, used to enclose pipe or fitting at wall or floor covering..

Evaporator: A long tube which receives liquid refrigerant from the condenser.

Exhaust System: A system in which the air is captured by the ventilation unit and is exhausted outdoors.

Filler: Wood or veneer strips inserted merely to fill space.

Fitting: The term used for any device that controls water entering or leaving a fixture. Faucets, spouts, drain controls, water supply lines and diverter valves all come under this heading.

Flange: A projecting collar or edge designed to fit against the frame of a cabinet, etc.

Flat or Slab Doors: Doors which are made of flat pieces of lumber or plywood.

Flue Gas: A toxic gas produced during the combustion of fossil fuels.

Flush-mounted: A method of installation whereby a sink is installed completely even with the surrounding deck.

Focal Glow: A small area highlighted with a high brightness to provide sensory stimulation.

Food Flow Sequence: The path that food preparation activities take.

Footcandle: The unit of illumination when the foot is the unit of length; the illumination on a surface one square foot in area on which there is a uniformly distributed flux of one lumen.

Footlamberts: Measures the amount of light that is reflected.

Frame Construction: A method of construction where thin component parts form the sides, back, top and bottom of a cabinet.

Framed Doors: Doors made of laminate or wood which can be of a slab configuration, with a wood, thick PVC edging or metal frame around the doors and drawers.

Frameless Construction: A method of construction where the core material sides of a cabinet are connected with either a mechanical fastening or dowel system.

Functional Storage: Objects are stored to reduce unnecessary walking, searching and groping.

Fuse: Safety devides that keep the branch circuits and anything connected to them from overheating and catching fire.

Glitter (Sparkle): Small areas of high brightness which are desirable to provide sensory stimulation.

GPM: Gallons per minute. An abbreviation used to describe water flow ratings.

Granite: An igneous rock with visible coarse grains used as a surfacing material.

Ground Fault Circuit Interrupter (GFCI): A device that monitors the electrical circuit at all times and, upon detecting a ground fault (a leakage on the line to ground), removes power to the circuit.

Ground Wire: A bare copper wire or a coated green wire which does not carry current.

G-Shape Kitchen: Similar to U-shape kitchen, with an extra wall of cabinets and appliances as a peninsula leg or fourth wall.

Halogen Cooktop: Electricity passes through a tungsten filament inside a quartz-glass tube. Resistance causes the filament to heat up, and in the process, tungsten particles boil off.

Hammer, Water: A shock wave, sounding like a hammer being banged on the pipes, which is caused by the water supply being turned off quickly.

"Hard Water": Water that contains scale-forming minerals, such as calcium and magnesium.

Hardwood Lumber: Produced from deciduous trees that drop their broad leaves each year.

High-Intensity Discharge Light: Light emitted by a high-intensity electric lamp containing either mercury vapor, high-pressure sodium or metal halide. Generally used in outdoor lighting.

Home Run Supply Line: A supply line which goes all the way back to the main and the water heater.

Homogeneous: The term used when color goes all the way through an object.

Hydronic Heat: A form of central heat which carries its heat in water and circulates the hot water in pipes.

Induction Cooktop: Solid state power causes induction coils, located beneath a glass ceramic surface, to generate a magnetic field that induces current within ferro-magnetic cookware.

Integral: A method of installation whereby a fixture is fabricated from the same piece of material as the countertop material.

Junction Boxes: Rectangular, octagonal or circular boxes made of plastic or metal which house connections between wires.

Laminates: A surfacing material used on wall areas, countertops, cabinet interiors and cabinet doors.

Lamp: An artificial light source, such as an incandescent bulb or fluorescent tube.

Lamp, A: The common household bulb that has been used for years. Used in surface-mounted or suspended fixtures only because of its multi-directional distribution of light.

Lighting, Accent: A decorative form of lighting that spotlights objects.

Lighting, Ambient (General): Lighting that radiates a comfortable level of brightness.

Lamp, Parabolic Reflector: Projector type lamp with maximum light output for use in floodlighting and long light throws.

Lamp, R: A lamp which provides a beam of light that is directed outward and downward by a mirror-like reflective surface inside.

Lamp, Reflector: Lamp with built-in reflector that either floods or concentrates spotlight on a subject.

Lamp, Tungsten-Halogen: An incandescent lamp containing a halogen gas that burns bright white when ignited by a tungsten filament.

Lighting, Cove: Indirect lighting which flows upward and bounces off the ceiling.

Lighting, Fluorescent: A tubular lamp which produces heat by the absorption of radiation from another source.

Lighting, Incandescent: Produced when the filament is subjected to intense heat.

Lighting, Low-Voltage: Lighting system that utilizes 12-volt current instead of regular 120-volt household current.

Lighting, Task: Lighting which is focused on a specific task.

L-Shape Kitchen: Work centers are located on two adjacent walls, and cook surrounded by continuous counter space.

Lumens: The amount of light measured at the light source.

Luminaires: Term for lighting fixtures in the lighting industry.

Manifold: A horizontal pipe through which gas flows from the fuel line to the different orifices.

Marble: Recrystallized limestone, marble is brittle. A stone used for countertops and flooring.

Meter: Measures energy in watt-hours.

Molding: A decorative or construction strip designed to introduce outline or contour in edges or surfaces.

Mullion: A vertical piece which separates and supports windows, doors, or panels.

One-Wall Kitchen: Work centers are stretched along a single wall.

Paint Dragging: White or off-white paint is left in cabinet joints and within distressed sections for an "olde world" antique look.

Panel Doors: Doors which have a frame comprised of two horizontal rails and two vertical stiles, with a thinner panel floating in between.

Pantry Center: Tall storage cabinetry to store food stuff maintained near the preparation center. May also be used in the serving or dining area.

Passive Solar: In solar heating, passive solar means that the building itself is designed to capture the sun's heat.

Peninsula Cabinet: A wall cabinet that is accessible from two sides and is installed above a cabinet that juts out into the center of the room.

Pickled Finishes: A method where white pigment is rubbed into woods to enhance the grain, and which give wood cabinets the look of an antique scrubbed surface.

Pie-Cut Cabinet: A type of corner cabinet that requires 36" (91.44cm) on each wall, and features stationary shelving.

Pipe, Fixture Supply: The pipe bringing water from behind a wall to a fixture.

Pipe, Vent: The pipe installed to provide air flow to or from a drainage system or to provide air circulation within the system.

Pipe, Waste: The line that carries away the discharge from any fixture, except toilets, conveying it to building drain.

Plenum: A large, sheet-metal enclosure either above or below the furnace which distributes heated air.

Plugs: A "football" shaped plywood section that is used to replace knots in the veneer of plywood.

Primary Clean-up Sink Center: Houses recycling center, dishwasher and food waste disposer.

Preparation Center: Long, uninterrupted counter that may be placed between the sink and the cooking surface, or the sink and the refrigerator.

Pythagorean Theorem: In a right-angled triangle, the sum of the squares of the legs is equal to the square of the hypotenuse.

Radiant Heat: Heat which is transferred through invisible electromagnetic waves, at the speed of light (186,300 miles per second), from an infrared energy source.

Recovery Rate: The length of time required for the water heater to bring the temperature of the cold, stored water up to the temperature set on the dial.

Rheostat Switch (Dimmer Control): A device which is used to vary the light output of an electric lamp.

Rimmed: A mounting method whereby a sink sits slightly above the countertop with the joint between the sink and the countertop concealed by a metal rim.

Roll-out Shelf Cabinet: A base cabinet with roll-outs.

Rough-in: The installation of piping concealed in walls and floors to which supply lines and drain from a plumbing fixture are attached.

Secondary Sink Center: Generally associated with preparation center. May serve clean-up functions as well.

Self-rimming: A mounting method whereby a sink is designed to sit on top of the countertop.

Service Box: The control center for the home's electrical service.

Sink/Cooktop Cabinet: Base cabinet with shallow top drawers, or a tilt-down front which houses a plastic or stainless steel container.

Soffit (aka Bulkhead and Fascia): Identifies a boxed-in area above cabinets, etc. The underside of any overhead component.

Softwood Lumber: Produced from coniferous or evergreen trees that have needles or scale-like leaves and remain green throughout the year.

Sone Rating: A measurement of sound level.

Sparkle (Glitter): Small areas of high brightness which are desirable to provide sensory stimulation.

Stack: General term for the main vertical pipe of soil, waste or vent pipe system.

Stack, Vent: Vertical pipe providing circulation of air to and from any part of a drainage system.

Stamping: The term used to describe the cutting or forming of products from sheetmetal in a cold state.

Stile: An upright structural membrane of a frame. A vertical member in a frame or panel which secondary members are fitted into.

Subbase (aka Subbase and Plinth): The lowest point of an object with more than one horizontal subdivision.

Supply Branches: The two sets of pipes that run horizontally through the floor joists or concrete slab and deliver water from the supply main.

Supply Risers: Supply branches that run vertically in the wall to an upper story.

Subtraction Method: A method to lay out a kitchen plan which is generally known and accepted in the industry.

Swing-up Mix Shelf: A mechanical shelf which lifts up so that hand appliances can be easily stored.

Tee: A T-shaped pipe.

Terrazzo: A slurry mixture of stone chips consisting of marble and cement. Used as a flooring surface or wall treatment.

Traditional Storage: Similar objects are grouped in a given spot.

Transformer: A device which is used to reduce standard 120-volt household current to the 12-volts needed for low-voltage lighting systems.

Trap: Bent pipe section or device that holds a water deposit and forms a seal against the passage of sewer gases from the waste pipe into the room.

Underlayment: A form of particleboard that has a low density and low resin content.

Under-mounted: Installed from below the counter surfaces.

Universal Design (Barrier-free Design): A planning concept where safety is of paramount importance and no technological or physical barriers are placed in front of the user as they attempt to work in the space.

U-Shape Kitchen: Cook is surrounded on three sides with continuous countertop and storage system.

Vacuum Breaker: A device which prevents a vacuum in a water supply system to stop a backflow from occuring.

Valve, Diverter: A spring-loaded push or lift type used to divert or open secondary channels.

Vitreous China: A form of ceramics/porcelain that is "glass-like".

Volt: The measurement of electrical pressure.

Wainscoting: Decorative facing applied to the lower portion of an interior partition or wall.

Wall Units: Cabinets which are fixed to the walls with screws.

Water Supply System: Carries water from the municipal water system or well into the house and around to fixtures and appliances.

Watts (Wattage): The measurement of the amount of energy consumed by a light source.

Work Triangle: A method to develop the efficiency of a kitchen plan.

Zoned Heat: A division of the house into two or more parts with a separate heat source for each part.

Index